Lecture Notes in Computer Science　　12032

Xin Wang · Francesca Alessandra Lisi ·
Guohui Xiao · Elena Botoeva (Eds.)

Semantic Technology

9th Joint International Conference, JIST 2019
Hangzhou, China, November 25–27, 2019
Proceedings

 Springer

Editors
Xin Wang
Tianjin University
Tianjin, China

Guohui Xiao ⓘ
Free University of Bozen-Bolzano
Bozen-Bolzano, Italy

Francesca Alessandra Lisi ⓘ
University of Bari
Bari, Italy

Elena Botoeva ⓘ
Imperial College London
London, UK

ISSN 0302-9743 ISSN 1611-3349 (electronic)
Lecture Notes in Computer Science
ISBN 978-3-030-41406-1 ISBN 978-3-030-41407-8 (eBook)
https://doi.org/10.1007/978-3-030-41407-8

LNCS Sublibrary: SL3 – Information Systems and Applications, incl. Internet/Web, and HCI

This Springer imprint is published by the registered company Springer Nature Switzerland AG
The registered company address is: Gewerbestrasse 11, 6330 Cham, Switzerland

Preface

This is the first volume of the proceedings of the 9th Joint International Semantic Technology Conference (JIST 2019) held during November 25–27, 2019, in Hangzhou, China. JIST is a joint event for regional Semantic related conferences. Since its launched in Hangzhou in 2011, it has become the premium Asian forum on Semantic Web, Knowledge Graph, Linked Data, and AI on the Web. In 2019, JIST returned to Hangzhou, and the mission was to bring together researchers in the Knowledge Graph and Semantic Technology research community and other related areas to present their innovative research results and novel applications. This year's theme was "Open Web and Knowledge Graph."

The proceedings of JIST 2019 are presented in two volumes: the first one in LNCS and the second one in CCIS. The conference attracted high-quality submissions and participants from all over the world. There were 70 submissions from 8 countries. The Program Committee (PC) consisted of 52 members from 13 countries. Each PC has been assigned four papers on average and each submission was reviewed by at least three PC members. The committee decided to accept 24 full papers (34.3%) in volume 1 (LNCS) and 22 other papers (31.4%) in volume 2 (CCIS). In addition to the paper presentations, the program of JIST 2019 also featured three tutorials, three keynotes, one special forum on Open Knowledge Graph, and poster presentations.

We are indebted to many people who made this event possible. As the organizers of JIST 2019, we would like to express our sincere thanks to the PC members and additional reviewers for their hard work in reviewing the papers. We would also like to thank the sponsors, support organizations, all the speakers, authors, and participants for their great contributions. Last but not least, we would like to thank Springer for their support in producing these proceedings.

December 2019

Xin Wang
Francesca A. Lisi
Guohui Xiao
Elena Botoeva

Organization

General Chairs

Huajun Chen   Zhejiang University, China
Diego Calvanese   Free University of Bozen-Bolzano, Italy

Program Chairs

Xin Wang   Tianjin University, China
Francesca A. Lisi   Università degli Studi di Bari, Italy

Special Session Track Chairs

Kewen Wang   Griffith University, Australia
HakLae Kim   Jungang University, South Korea

Local Organizing Chairs

Qingpin Zhang   Zhejiang University, China
Wen Zhang   Zhejiang University, China

Industrial Forum Chair

Haofen Wang   Leyan Tech., China

Poster and Demo Chairs

Kang Liu   CASIA, China
Chutiporn Anutariya   Asian Institute of Technology, Thailand

Workshop Chairs

Yuan-Fang Li   Monash University, Australia
Xianpei Han   ISCAS, China

Tutorial Chairs

Xiaowang Zhang   Tianjin University, China
Jiaoyan Chen   Oxford University, UK

Sponsorship Chair

Jinguang Gu   Wuhan Science and Technology University, China

Proceeding Chairs

Guohui Xiao   Free University of Bozen-Bolzano, Italy
Elena Botoeva   Imperial College of London, UK

Publicity Chairs

Meng Wang   Southeast University, China
Naoki Fukuta   Shizuoka University, Japan

Program Committee

Carlos Bobed   everis and NTT Data, Spain
Fernando Bobillo   University of Zaragoza, Spain
Huajun Chen   Zhejiang University, China
Wenliang Chen   Soochow University, China
Gong Cheng   Nanjing University, China
Dejing Dou   University of Oregon, USA
Jianfeng Du   Guangdong University of Foreign Studies, China
Alessandro Faraotti   IBM, Italy
Naoki Fukuta   Academic Institute Shizuoka University, Japan
Jinguang Gu   Wuhan University of Science and Technology, China
Xianpei Han   ISCAS, China
Wei Hu   Nanjing University, China
Ryutaro Ichise   National Institute of Informatics, Japan
Takahiro Kawamura   National Agriculture and Food Research Organization,
                            Japan
Evgeny Kharlamov   Bosch Center for Artificial Intelligence and University
                            of Oslo, Norway
Martin Kollingbaum   University of Aberdeen, UK
Kouji Kozaki   Osaka Electro-Communication University, Japan
Weizhuo Li   Academy of Mathematics and Systems Science, CAS,
                            China
Yuan-Fang Li   Monash University, Australia
Juanzi Li   Tsinghua University, China
Francesca A. Lisi   Università degli Studi di Bari, Italy
Kang Liu   Institute of Automation, CAS, China
Yinglong Ma   NCEPU, China
Theofilos Mailis   National and Kapodistrian University of Athens,
                            Greece
Riichiro Mizoguchi   Japan Advanced Institute of Science and Technology,
                            Japan

Trina Myers	James Cook University, Australia
Jeff Z. Pan	University of Aberdeen, UK
Guilin Qi	Southeast University, China
Guozheng Rao	Tianjin University, China
Edelweis Rohrer	Universidad de la Republica, Uruguay
Tong Ruan	ECUST, China
Floriano Scioscia	Politecnico di Bari, Italy
Wei Shen	Nankai University, China
Jun Shen	University of Wollongong, Australia
Umberto Straccia	ISTI-CNR, Italy
Thepchai Supnithi	NECTEC, Thailand
Hideaki Takeda	National Institute of Informatics, Japan
Kerry Taylor	The Australian National University, Australia, and University of Surrey, UK
Xin Wang	Tianjin University, China
Meng Wang	Southeast University, China
Zhe Wang	Griffith University, Australia
Haofen Wang	Shanghai Leyan Technologies Co., Ltd., China
Shenghui Wang	OCLC Research, USA
Zhichun Wang	Beijing Normal University, China
Tianxing Wu	Nanyang Technological University, Singapore
Gang Wu	Northeastern University, China
Guohui Xiao	Free University of Bozen-Bolzano, Italy
Bin Xu	DCST, Tsinghua University, China
Xiang Zhang	Southeast University, China
Xiaowang Zhang	Tianjin University, China
Amal Zouaq	University of Ottawa, Canada

Additional Reviewers

Tonglee Chung	Yulin Shen
Shumin Deng	Sylvia Wang
Michel Gagnon	Kemas Wiharja
Yuhao He	Kang Xu
Zixian Huang	Lingling Zhang
Natthawut Kertkeidkachorn	Wen Zhang
Bao Zhu Liu	Leyuan Zhao
Juan Li	Qianru Zhou
Shutian Ma	Xiaoduo Zhou
Shirong Shen	

Contents

Incorporating Term Definitions for Taxonomic Relation Identification

Yongpan Sheng[1], Tianxing Wu[2], and Xin Wang[3(✉)]

[1] School of Computer Science and Engineering,
University of Electronic Science and Technology of China, Chengdu, China
shengyp2011@gmail.com
[2] School of Computer Science and Engineering, Nanyang Technological University,
Singapore, Singapore
wutianxing@ntu.edu.sg
[3] College of Intelligence and Computing,Tianjin University, Tianjin, China
wangx@tju.edu.cn

Abstract. Taxonomic relations (also called "is-A" relations) are key components in taxonomies, semantic hierarchies and knowledge graphs. Previous works on identifying taxonomic relations are mostly based on linguistic and distributional approaches. However, these approaches are limited by the availability of a large enough corpus that can cover all terms of interest and provide sufficient contextual information to represent their meanings. Therefore, the generalization abilities of the approaches are far from satisfactory. In this paper, we propose a novel neural network model to enhance the semantic representations of term pairs by encoding their respective definitions for the purpose of taxonomic relation identification. This has two main benefits: (i) Definitional sentences represent specified corpus-independent meanings of terms, hence definition-driven approaches have a great generalization capability to identify unseen terms and taxonomic relations which are not expressed in domain specificity of the training data; (ii) Global contextual information from a large corpus and definitions in the sense level can provide richer interpretation of terms from a broader knowledge base perspective, and benefit the accurate prediction for the taxonomic relations of term pairs. The experimental results show that our model outperforms several competitive baseline methods in terms of F-score on both specific and open domain datasets.

Keywords: Taxonomic relation identification · Definition-driven approach

1 Introduction

Taxonomic relation (also called "is-A" relation) identification is a task to determine whether a specific pair of terms[1] holds the taxonomic relation or not. Concretely, given a pair of terms (x, y), if y holds a semantically border category that includes x, we call y a hypernym of x and x a hyponym of y [26]. For instance, *"scientist"* is a hypernym of *"Einstein"*, *"actor"* is a hypernym of *"Mel Gibson"*, *"Paris"* is a hyponym of *"exciting city"*. The accurate prediction of these taxonomic relations benefits for a variety of downstream applications, such as serving as building blocks for semantic structure

---

[1] This paper uses "terms" to refer to any words or phrases.

© Springer Nature Switzerland AG 2020
X. Wang et al. (Eds.): JIST 2019, LNCS 12032, pp. 1–17, 2020.
https://doi.org/10.1007/978-3-030-41407-8_1

construction including taxonomies, semantic hierarchies and knowledge graphs, and facilitating question answering systems [7].

Previous approaches for this task can be generally classified into two categories: linguistic and distributional approaches. Linguistic approaches rely on lexical-syntactic patterns (e.g., A typical pattern is *"A such as B"*) to capture textual expressions associated with taxonomic relations, and match them with given documents or multiple Web sources to identify taxonomic relations between terms [20, 28]. These patterns can be created manually [28] or learnt automatically [20, 26]. Despite their higher precision in several applications, such identified patterns are too specific to cover the wide range of complex linguistic circumstances, and the ambiguity of natural language compounded by data sparsity makes linguistic matching methods less robust. In contrast, distributional methods focus on embedding the two terms of interest into context-aware vector representations, and then predict their taxonomic relation based on these representations. The usage of term embeddings [16] allows machines to make predictions from the entire corpus.

These approaches, however, make use of linguistic features as well as contextual information of terms alone acquiring in a large corpus, often with unsatisfactory results. In many real-word settings, we can also explore the value of external evidence, primarily textual definition evidence related to terms, which can be extracted from structured knowledge resources, to express corpus-independent meanings of terms for the purpose of enhancing the generalization ability of the system to unseen terms, and even to the scenario of low-resource languages. Humans, too, often benefit from richer information deriving from the definitions of terms when trying to determine the taxonomic relation between the terms even for terms they have not been exposed in the training data.

Based on the above considerations, we propose a neural network model[2], which can enhance the representations of term pairs by encoding their separative definitions, instead of just focusing on the meaning of each term. Moreover, we formulate the taxonomic relation detection problem as $(x_{hypo}, d_x, y_{hyper}, d_y, 1/0)$, where x_{hypo} and d_x denote hyponym and its definition, respectively. While y_{hyper} and d_y denote hypernym and its definition, respectively. The binary value "1/0" indicates y_{hyper} is x_{hypo}'s hypernym or not. Technically, we first model the representation for each pair in $\{(x_{hypo}, y_{hyper}), (x_{hypo}, d_y), (d_x, y_{hyper}), (d_x, d_y)\}$ and given as the input to a top-performing baseline system (Sect. 3.1) to obtain four separate representations, which are concatenated by heuristic matching strategies in the form of a joint vector representation. The overall representation is fed into a softmax classifier to determine whether the taxonomic relation holds or not (Sect. 3.2).

The experimental results show that our approach achieves the state-of-the-art performance on both general and specific domain datasets. In addition, another advantage of our proposed model is that it has the capacity to generalize the taxonomic relation properties of pairs that even are not being expressed in domain specificity of the training data. The key contributions of our work are highlighted as follows:

– We propose a novel neural network model which accounts for the taxonomic relation detection problem primarily by the knowledge of the term definitions. Definitions

---

[2] The dataset and the code for our model are available at https://github.com/shengyp/Taxonomic-relation/.

can provide complementary knowledge to the context from corpus, so that our proposed model enables better tolerance for unseen terms, rare terms, and terms with biased sense distribution.

- Our model enables combine distributional model with definition encoding, rather than a simple concatenation of the two subsystems. This benefits to generate more indicative features across distributional contexts and definitions for the accurate prediction of taxonomic relations of term pairs.
- The experiment results on both general and domain-specific datasets corroborate the effectiveness and robustness of our model over several competitive models in F-score metrics.

2   Related Work

Taxonomic relation identification is one of the most topics in NLP research. Many approaches have been explored for this task can be divided into two branches, including linguistic and distributional approaches.

In linguistic approaches, the range of pre-defined rules or lexical-syntactic patterns are leveraged to extract taxonomic relations from text corpus. Patterns are either chosen manually [9] or learnt automatically via bootstrapping [26]. While such approaches can result in taxonomic relations with relatively high accuracies. Unfortunately, using patterns as features may result in the sparsity of the feature space [19]. More approaches require the co-occurrence of the two terms in the same sentence, which strongly hinders the recall of these methods. Higher recall can be achieved contributes to distributional methods.

In distributional approaches, by studying the relations of distributional representations (word embeddings) derived from contexts, between hypernyms and their respective hypernyms, the taxonomic relations can be identified by learning semantic prediction models, especially for several unsupervised measures [10,22]. Such approaches draw primarily on the distributional hypothesis [8], which states that terms appear in similar context may share semantic relationship. The main advantage of distributional approaches is that they can discover relations not directly expressed in the text. However, such approaches depend on the choice of feature from domain specificity of the training data, e.g., an IT corpus hardly mentions "apple" as a fruit. Furthermore, rare terms are poorly expressed by their sparse global context and, more generally, these methods would not generalize to the low-resource language setting.

Our proposed model shares the same inspiration with distributional methods. More importantly, it is beyond the framework of distributional models acquiring context-aware term meaning in a large corpus, and instead explore a novel information resources - definitive sentences, to enhance the robustness of the system.

3   The Proposed Method

In this section, we first briefly describe a top-performing neural network architecture. This could be viewed as a baseline system to encode a pair of texts. Then, we elaborate on the adaptation we make towards the architecture so that the resulting system can better serve the taxonomic relation identification problem.

3.1 The Baseline System

For the design of the baseline system, we follow the idea of Siamese Network [21], as shown in Fig. 1. Concretely, the two identical sentence encoders share the same set of weights during training, and generate two neural representations. We observe from the figure that the system mainly consists of three layers from bottom to top: (i) Sentence input layer; (ii) Sentence encoding layer; (iii) Sentence output layer. We will explain the last two layers in detail in the following subsection. And the sentence input layer will be introduced in Sect. 3.2.

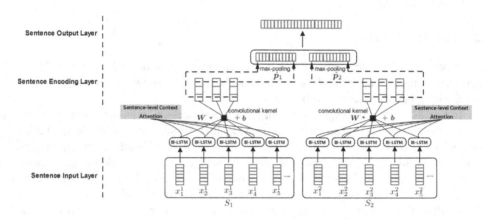

Fig. 1. Architecture of the baseline system

Sentence Encoding Layer. Take the sentence encoder on any one side as an example. Given a sentence S_i ($i = 1$ or 2) with length L, our goal is to find a neural representation of S_i. We first map L words of S_i to a sequence of word embedding vectors $\{x_j^i\}$ ($j = 1, ..., L$, and the dimension of word embedding denotes as d_m), based on the pre-trained embeddings that will be described in the following Sect. 4.1. Then we employ a Bi-LSTM which is composed of a forward LSTM and backward LSTM component, to process $\{x_j^i\}$ in the forward left-to-right and the backward right-to-left directions, respectively. In each direction, the reading of $\{x_j^i\}$ is modelled as a recurrent process with a single hidden state. Given an initial value, the state changes its value recurrently, and each time-step consumes an incoming word.

Take the forward LSTM component as an example. Denoting the initial hidden state as $\overrightarrow{h}_0$, the recurrent state transition values can be calculated by $\{\overrightarrow{h}_1, \overrightarrow{h}_2, ..., \overrightarrow{h}_L\}$ when it reads the input $\{x_1, x_2, ..., x_L\}$. At time t, the current hidden state vector $\overrightarrow{h}_t$ is computed based on the previous hidden $\overrightarrow{h}_{t-1}$, the previous cell c_{t-1} and the current input word embedding x_t. The detail computations of the forward LSTM are defined as follows [6]:

$$\hat{i}_t = \delta(W_{xi}x_t + W_{hi}\overrightarrow{h}_{t-1} + b_i),$$

$$\hat{f}_t = \delta(W_{xf}x_t + W_{hf}\overrightarrow{h}_{t-1} + b_f),$$

$$o_t = \delta(\boldsymbol{W}_{xo}\boldsymbol{x}_t + \boldsymbol{W}_{ho}\overrightarrow{\boldsymbol{h}}_{t-1} + \boldsymbol{b}_o),$$

$$u_t = \delta(\boldsymbol{W}_{xu}\boldsymbol{x}_t + \boldsymbol{W}_{hu}\overrightarrow{\boldsymbol{h}}_{t-1} + \boldsymbol{b}_u),$$

$$i_t, \boldsymbol{f}_t = softmax(\hat{\boldsymbol{i}}_t, \hat{\boldsymbol{f}}_t),$$

$$c_t = \boldsymbol{f}_t \odot c_{t-1} + i_t \odot u_t,$$

$$\overrightarrow{\boldsymbol{h}}_t = o_t \odot tanh(c_t), \tag{1}$$

where i_t, $\boldsymbol{f}_t$, o_t and u_t are an input gate, a forget gate, an output gate and an actual input at t time, respectively. The activation function of the LSTM δ is set to $tanh$. $\boldsymbol{W}_{(.)}$ represent trained weight matrices, c_t is a vector representation of state in recurrent cell at time step t, and $\boldsymbol{b}_x(x \in \{i, o, f, u\})$ is a bias vector. $\odot$ denotes the Hadamard product.

The backward LSTM component follows the same recurrent state transition process as described in Eq. (1). Starting from an initial state h_{n+1}, which is a model parameter, it reads the input $\{\boldsymbol{x}_n, \boldsymbol{x}_{n-1}, ..., \boldsymbol{x}_0\}$, changing its value to $\{\overleftarrow{\boldsymbol{h}}_n, \overleftarrow{\boldsymbol{h}}_{n-1}, ..., \overleftarrow{\boldsymbol{h}}_0\}$, respectively. A separate set of parameters $\boldsymbol{W}_{(.)}$ and $\boldsymbol{b}_x$ are used for the backward component.

Finally, the Bi-LSTM concatenates the vector value of $\overrightarrow{\boldsymbol{h}}_t$ and $\overleftarrow{\boldsymbol{h}}_t$ to represent the encoding information of $\boldsymbol{x}_t$ at t time, which is denoted as $h_t = [\overrightarrow{\boldsymbol{h}}_t; \overleftarrow{\boldsymbol{h}}_t]$.

An additive attention mechanism [2] is exploited to the resulting hidden states corresponding to $\{h_t\}$ ($t = 1, ..., L$). That is a weighted calculation for learning more accurate and focused sentence representations, based on the following formulas:

$$g_t = \sum_i \alpha_i^t h_i, \tag{2}$$

where h_i is the column vector denoting the hidden state of x_i, ϵ_i can be regarded as the intermediate attention representation of x_i in the sentence and can be obtained from a linear transformation of h_i. α_i denotes the attention weight of x_i (i.e., namely *attention vector* α) and is computed by the combination of weighted values in ϵ_i.

$$\alpha_i^t = \frac{e^{u^T \epsilon_i}}{\Sigma_j e^{u^T \epsilon_j}}, \tag{3}$$

$$\epsilon_i = tanh(\boldsymbol{W}_a h_i + \boldsymbol{b}_a), \tag{4}$$

where $\boldsymbol{W}_a$ is a trained weight matrices, u^T denotes transpose of a trained parameter u. $\boldsymbol{b}_a$ is a bias vector.

We concatenate contextual information vector for each time step as follows:

$$g = [g_1, g_2, ..., g_L], \tag{5}$$

In our task, the indicative features related to the taxonomic relation are likely to appear in any area of the sentence under different contexts. Hence, we should encode the sentence further by utilizing all local features and form better neural representations globally. When using a neural network, the convolution approach is a natural means of extracting local features with a sliding window of length l over the sentence [4].

Here, typically the size of the sliding window l is 3. Then, it combines all fine-grained features via a max-pooling operation to obtain a fixed-sized vector for the output of the convolution operation.

Here, convolution is defined as a matrix multiplication between a sequence of vectors $\mathbf{g}$ which is formed by Eq. (5), a convolution matrix $\mathbf{W} \in \mathbb{R}^{d_m \times (d_m \times l)}$ and a bias vector $\mathbf{b}$ with a sliding window [30]. Let us define the vector $\mathbf{q}_i \in \mathbb{R}^{d_m \times l}$ as the concatenation of a sequence of input representations g in the i-th window, we have:

$$q_i = g_{i:i+l-1}; (1 \leq i \leq L - l + 1). \tag{6}$$

Hence, the output of a single convolutional kernel $\mathbf{p}_i$ (i.e., i-th window) can be expressed as follows:

$$p_i = f(\mathbf{W}q_i + b), \tag{7}$$

where f is the activation function. A convolutional layer can comprise d_c convolutional kernels which could result in a output matrix $P = [p_1, p_2, ..., p_{d_c}] \in \mathbb{R}^{d_c \times (d_m - l + 1)}$. Then, a max-pooling operation is applied to this matrix to obtain maximum valued features as follows:

$$\hat{p} = max(P) = \sum_i max(p_i). \tag{8}$$

Sentence Output Layer. In our settings, the neural representation of each sentence S_i ($i = 1, 2$) (term can be treated as short sentence) is generated using Eq. (8), and can be shortly denoted as $\hat{p}_i$ ($i = 1, 2$). Finally, we obtain the overall representation for the sentence pair by concatenating $\hat{p}_1$ and $\hat{p}_2$.

3.2 Our Proposed Model

Based on the baseline system, we make the adaptation of this architecture for taxonomic relation identification problem and the overall architecture of our proposed model is shown in Fig. 2.

The Sentence Input Strategy. For a distributional method such as Shwartz *et al.* [23] directly concatenates the term path representation vector and term embedding vector as the input of an off-the-shelf classifier. However, to the best of our knowledge, a simple combination of term distributional representation and definition encoding could not integrate with the advantages of these two subsystems. Moreover, the analysis on our datasets hints that our model can obtain more indicative features by modeling the term pair such as (term, definition), which may cross the distributional models and definition encoding. For instance, the definition of term "*dolphin*" in WordNet is "*large slender food and game fish widely distributed in warm seas*". Intuitively, when the system meets the term pair ("*dolphin tuna*", "*percoid fish*"), it should be easy to make the decision on the taxonomic relation since "*fish*" appears in the definitive sentence.

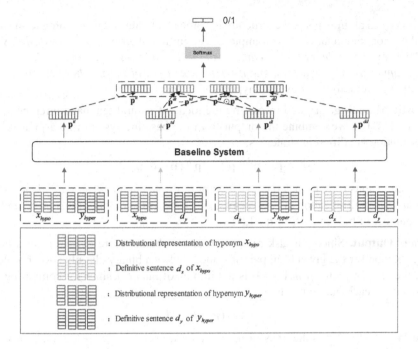

Fig. 2. Architecture of our proposed model.

Inspired by the above observations, we investigate four strategies to define the input representations on the baseline system as described in the baseline system, including: (x_{hypo}, y_{hyper}), (x_{hypo}, d_y), (d_x, y_{hyper}) and (d_x, d_y). Moreover, we obtain four separate representations based on the above combinations as the output: $\mathbf{p}^{tt}$ from (x_{hypo}, y_{hyper}), $\mathbf{p}^{td}$ from (x_{hypo}, d_y), $\mathbf{p}^{dt}$ from (d_x, y_{hyper}), and $\mathbf{p}^{dd}$ from (d_x, d_y). In the following, we further give the explanations of these combinations with more details:

The baseline system over (x_{hypo}, y_{hyper}), which considers two vector representations as the input, and outputs a joint vector representation. This combination intends to model embeddings from a hyponym to its hypernym via a network with weights. It actually is common with a pioneer work in this field [5], which employs uniform linear projection and piecewise linear projection to map the embeddings of a hyponym to its hypernym.

The baseline system over (x_{hypo}, d_y) and (d_x, y_{hyper}) also outputs a joint vector representation. These combinations benefit to generate indicative features across distributional context and definition for discriminating taxonomic relations from other semantic relations, e.g., as we described in the beginning of this subsection, the hyponym or prominent context words of the hyponym are expected to appear in its hypernym's definition, and vice versa. Based on our high-quality training data, this can provide direct clues for inferring taxonomic relation between the terms.

The baseline system over (d_x, d_y) may provide an alternative evidence for interpreting the terms. Inherent structure information in definitive sentences is often important to understand term meanings for the purpose of accurately detecting taxonomic relations. The assumption in the background is that: if two sentences represent the features of fine-grained alignments in the structure in some level, their corresponding terms may hold the taxonomic relation. For example, the definition of term *"apple"* and *"Malus"* in WordNet are *"An apple is a sweet, edible fruit produced by an apple tree (Malus domestica)"*, *"apple trees; found throughout temperate zones of the northern hemisphere."* respectively. Actually, *"Malus"* is a hypernym of *"apple"*.

Heuristic Matching. Inspired in part by the ideas of natural language inference provided by [14, 18], we combine the output from the baseline system into a joint vector representation via different strategies:

$$p = [\mathbf{p}^{tt}; \mathbf{p}^{dd}; \mathbf{p}^{td} - \mathbf{p}^{dt}; \mathbf{p}^{td} \odot \mathbf{p}^{dt}], \tag{9}$$

where semicolons refer to the concatenation of multiple column vectors, $\odot$ denotes the element-wise multiplication of two vectors, $p \in \mathbb{R}^{4d_h}$ is the output of this layer, and d_h is the number of hidden units of the LSTMs.

Softmax Output. Since our task refers to predict whether there exists or not a taxonomic relation for the given term pair, it is modeled as a binary classification problem. Thus, the feature vector p in Eq. (9) is fed into a softmax classifier for computing the confidence of each output result:

$$o = W_1(p \circ r) + b. \tag{10}$$

where $W_1 \in \mathbb{R}^{n_1 \times 4d_h}$ is the transformation matrix, and $o \in \mathbb{R}^{n_1}$ is the final output of the network. n_1 is equal to 2.

Loss Function and Training. Given an input instance $x_i = (x_{hypo}, d_x, y_{hyper}, d_y, 1/0)$, our model with parameter θ outputs the vector o computed in Eq. (10), which is a 2-dimensional vector, where the i-th value o_i of o is the probability score for determining the taxonomic relation of term pair (x_{hypo}, y_{hyper}) is holds or not, and the sum of values in o is to 1. To obtain the conditional probability $p(i|x_i, \theta)$, we apply a softmax operation as:

$$p(i|x_i, \theta) = \frac{e^{o_i}}{\Sigma_k e^{o_k}}, \tag{11}$$

Given all of our training instances $T = \{x_i \mid i = 1, 2, ..., N\}$, we can then define the negative log-likelihood loss function:

$$J(\theta) = -\sum_{i=1}^{N} log \, p(y_i|x_i, \theta), \tag{12}$$

where θ denotes the parameters in our model. We train the model through a simple optimization technique called stochastic gradient descent (SGD) over shuffled mini-batches with the Adadelta rule. Regularization is implemented by a dropout [11] and L_2 norm.

4   Experiments and Analysis

In this section, we first provide an overview of datasets and the pre-trained method for word embeddings in Sect. 4.1. We then describe the experimental settings in Sect. 4.2 and investigate the performance results of different methods on both specific and open domain datasets in Sect. 4.3. Finally, the error analysis is discussed in Sect. 4.4.

Table 1. Dataset used in the experiments

Dataset	#Train		#Test		#Validation	
Splits	Random splits	Lexical splits	Random splits	Lexical splits	Random splits	Lexical splits
BLESS [3]	12459	757	2376	675	404	103
Conceptual Graph (See footnote 4)	58484	29475	19610	7808	4079	2095
WebIsA-Animal (See footnote 5)	5614	3784	1942	1021	407	249
WebIsA-Plant (See footnote 5)	5534	2933	1610	861	305	169

4.1 Dataset

Random and Lexical Dataset Splits. As pointed out by Levy *et al.* [13], mostly supervised distributional lexical inference methods tend to learn a dependent semantics of a single term, instead of learning the relation between two terms, this can be expressed as "lexical memorization" phenomenon. To address this, Levy *et al.* [13] made a suggestion of splitting the train and test sets such that each of them will contain distinct term pairs for presenting the model from overfitting during training.

To investigate such behaviors, we also follow the solution for a lexical split of our dataset. In this case, we maintain roughly a ratio of 14:5:1 for training set, test set and validation set partitioned randomly. Moreover, we maintain roughly a ratio of 8:1 for positive instances and negative instances in random or lexical splits in our datasets. The overall statistics of the datasets used in the experiments are summarized in Table 1. We present briefly the summary of each dataset below.

- **BLESS** dataset [3][3]. It consists of 200 distinct, unambiguous concepts. Each of which is involved with other terms, called *relata*, in some relations. We extract from BLESS 12,994 pairs of terms for the following four types of relations: taxonomic relation, "meronymy" (a.k.a. part-of relation), "coordinate" (i.e., two terms having the same hypernym), and random relations. From these term pairs, we set taxonomic relations as positive instances, while other relations form the negative instances.
- **Conceptual Graph**. This is a popular taxonomic benchmark dataset derived from Microsoft Concept Graph project[4]. It contains more than 5 million unique concepts, 12 unique million entities and 85 million taxonomic relations. We randomly pick the term pairs with possible (direct and indirect) taxonomic relation, along with high frequencies as the positive instances, while the term pairs are as negative instances when their relation frequencies are relatively lower.
- **WebIsA-Animal, Plant** dataset. WebIsA[5] is a publicly large-scale database containing more than 400 million taxonomic relation pairs. In this work, we select

---

[3] https://sites.google.com/site/geometricalmodels/shared-evaluation.

[4] https://concept.research.microsoft.com/Home/Download.

[5] http://webdatacommons.org/isadb/.

1.1M subset pertaining to two specified domains (i.e., the classes like "Animal" and "Plant"). The positive instances are created by extracting all possible (direct and indirect) taxonomic relation from the taxonomies. The negative instances are generated by randomly pairing two terms do not have any taxonomic relation.

Term Definition Collection. In this work, we pick two types of structured knowledge sources, including WordNet and the complete English Wikipedia, for extracting definitive descriptions for term pairs. We chose WordNet as the source of textual definitions partly because WordNet has been used for related tasks before, e.g., Snow *et al.* [26] constructed a larger taxonomic relation dataset based on WordNet, and partly because a number of accurate definitions of terms in sense level are available in WordNet. However, some literatures, e.g., Shwartz *et al.* [24], claimed that only limited coverage for almost all knowledge resources particularly to several rare or recently pairs, e.g., ("*Bullet tuna*", "*fish*"), ("*lead acid battery*", "*automobile*"). As the English Wikipedia can be viewed as the complementary data source to WordNet. Concretely, for each term pair in the training set, we first try to extract their respective definition from WordNet based on the term in strings[6]. For a few pairs which contain terms not covered by WordNet. We then switch to Wikipedia in which the term can be involved, and select the top-2 sentences in the first subgraph in the introductory sections, as its definitive description. If we are failed in two knowledge resources, we set definitions the same as the term in strings. As a result, we obtain the training instances in the form of (x_{hypo}, d_x, y_{hyper}, d_y, 1/0) for our experiments, where each term is accompanied by its definition.

Pre-trained Word Embeddings. To cover abundant words in the terms and definitions and provide the better support for initial input of our model. We use two large-scale textual corpus to train word embeddings. The first contains 570M entity content pages consisting of approximately 40 million sentences extracted from the English wikipedia[7]. The second is larger in size and derived from extended abstracts of DBpedia[8], then we employ the NLPIR system[9] for segmentation and Skip-gram method [15] for training. Note that the out-of-vocabulary words in the training set are randomly initialized with sampling values that meet the uniformly distributional representation in the range of $(-0.05, 0.05)$. As to the word or phrase with more than one word, we treat it as a whole to learning word embedding, instead of using character-level embeddings.

Pre-trained embeddings as preliminary inputs used in our model are not being updated in training, mainly for two reasons: (i) Reduce the number of needed parameters in the training stage; (ii) Improve the generalization capability of the model as it ensures that the words in training and the new words in the test set lie in the same space.

---

[6] As WordNet sorts sense definitions by sense frequency [17], we only choose the top-1 sense definition to denote a term.

[7] https://dumps.wikimedia.org/wikidatawiki/20180320/.

[8] http://tagesnetzwerk.de.

[9] https://github.com/NLPIR-team/NLPIR.

4.2   Experimental Settings

Compared Methods. In a series of previous works [12,26,27], several pattern-based, text-based inference methods have been applied for taxonomic relation identification. Their experiments showed that these methods achieve the F-score lower than 65% in most cases, which are not suggested to be strong baselines to compare with our approach. To make the convincing conclusion, in the experiments, we use the following competitive baseline methods for comparison:

- **Word2Vec + SVM.** This model first obtain the two term embeddings by applying the Skip-gram method [15] on the same corpus used for training pre-trained word embeddings as ours, and then combine their vectors to train an off-the-shelf SVM classifier for the taxonomic relation identification. Note that, in the Skip-gram model, if a term with more than one word, its embedding is calculated as the average of all words in the term.
- **DDM + SVM** [29]. This learns term embeddings via a dynamic distance-margin model, and then a SVM classifier is trained on concatenation of term pair vectors for the taxonomic relation detection.
- **DWNN + SVM** [1]. This is a extended copy of **DDM** [29], it not only utilizes the information of hypernyms and hyponyms, but also considers the contextual information between them via a dynamic weighting neural network when learning term embeddings.
- **Best unsupervised (dependency-based context)** [25]. This is the best unsupervised method, which implements similarity measurement over weighted dependency based context vectors.
- **Ours**$_{SubInput}$. This is the variant of our method. The collection $\{(x_{hypo}, y_{hyper}),$ $(x_{hypo}, d_y), (d_x, y_{hyper}), (d_x, d_y)\}$ provided for each input vector pair is changed to its sub-collection $\{(x_{hypo}, y_{hyper}), (d_x, d_y)\}$. We use the sub-script *SubInput* to denote this setting.
- **Ours**$_{Concat}$. This is the variant of our method. To form the joint representation to distributional features, we directly concatenate the output of the four separate representations from term pairs as follows: $\mathbf{p}^{tt}$ from (x_{hypo}, y_{hyper}), $\mathbf{p}^{td}$ from (x_{hypo}, d_y), $\mathbf{p}^{dt}$ from (d_x, y_{hyper}), and $\mathbf{p}^{dd}$ from (d_x, d_y), rather than relying on the heuristic matching. We use the sub-script *Concat* to denote this setting.

Evaluation Metrics. We observed that diverse relatively straightforward, generic domain terms and entities especially in the open domain datasets, are usually used for hyponyms, may correspond to the same hypernyms, e.g., (*"volleyball"*, *"sport"*), (*"hockey"*, *"sport"*), (*"fishing"*, *"sport"*), (*"overfishing"*, *"sport"*). We therefore ranked these term pairs by the frequency of hypernym, and report Precision at rank 200 (P@200), Recall at rank 200 (R@200), and F-score at rank 200 (F@200). On the one hand, it benefits to further evaluate the effectiveness of our approach by encoding term definitions, because they are usually near-hyponyms in these term pairs, but the respective corresponding taxonomic relation may not be true. On the other hand, it is well-suited for validating the capability of discriminating coordinate relations from other relations in the datasets for different methods. As for the Lexical Splits, we report the Mean Average Precision (P), Mean Average Recall (R), and Mean Average F-score (F).

Parameter Tuning. We conducted extensive experiments to determine the optimal configuration of parameters for our model. There are two types of parameters in the model: the first type includes weights and biases in the model layers, which can be initiated randomly and learned afterwards from each iteration; the second type includes the parameters that should be configured manually. In particular, we select six most common hyper-parameters for our model, namely the dimension of word embedding d_m in the input representation layer, the number of hidden units of all the LSTMs d_h, convolutional filters length Fl, number of filters Nr in the CNN component of the baseline system, the learning rate lr, and the ratio of dropout ρ. Since the weight $\mathbf{W}$ and bias $\mathbf{b}$ in each neural layer can be learned automatically via the evolution of model network, we focus on turning the hyper-parameters d_m, d_h, Fl, Nr, lr, and ρ. In practice, we train our models with a batch size of 128 for at most 100 epochs for each experiment and performed parameter selection strategy[10] on the validation set to tune parameters of the model for better convergence. Finally, we set $d_m = 300$, $d_h = 300$, $Fl = 3$, $Nr = 2$, $lr = 10^{-4}$, $\rho = 0.1$, and early-stopping on validation accuracy. Our model is implemented using the TensorFlow[11] machine learning framework.

4.3   Performance on Specific and Open Domain Datasets

For domain-specific datasets (i.e., WebIsA-Animal (See footnote 5) and WebIsA-Plant (See footnote 5)), the experimental results are given in Table 2. On a random split, we can see that **Ours** method achieves significantly improvements on the average of F-score by 8.1% and 14.8% compared to the **Word2Vec** and **DDM** methods. This indicates that **Ours** method is effective to further improving the performance of our task. Moreover, although **DWNN** is similar to **DDM**, the average F-measure is improved by 10.2% compared to **DDM** as it considers both the meanings of hypernym and hyponym as well as the contextual information between them in the process of the term embedding learning, while **DDM** ignores the effects of contextual information for taxonomic relation identification. **Best unsupervised** method achieves the average F-score 73.3% and is not effective for our task due to the heavily depending on the availability of a large enough corpus that can provide dependency-based context (i.e., considering a syntactic distributional space for terms by computing their neighbors in the dependency parse tree).

Similarity, for open domain datasets (BLESS [3] and Conceptual Graph (See footnote 4)), the experimental results are given in Table 3. On a random split, our method improves the average F-score by 11.6% compared to **Word2Vec**, by 3.5% compared to **DDM**, and by 2.3% compared to **DWNN** methods. The **Word2Vec** embeddings are mainly depend on co-occurrence based similarity, which is not effective for the classifier to accurately identify the whole of the taxonomic relations. **DDM** only learns term embeddings from the distributional contexts from the corpus, **DWNN** takes more

---

[10] We employ grid search for a range of hyper-parameters, and picked the combination of ones that yield the highest F-score on the validation set.

[11] https://www.tensorflow.org/.

Table 2. Performance comparison of different methods on domain-specific datasets (including WebIsA-Animal and WebIsA-Plant). We report Precision at rank 200 (P@200), Recall at rank 200 (R@200), F-score at rank 200 (F@200) for Random Splits, and Mean Average Precision (P), Mean Average Recall (R), Mean Average F-score (F) for Lexical Splits. The best performance in the F-score column is boldfaced (the higher, the better).

Datasets	WebIsA-Animal						WebIsA-Plant					
	Random splits (@200)			Lexical splits			Random splits (@200)			Lexical splits		
Method	P	R	F	P	R	F	P	R	F	P	R	F
Previous methods												
Word2Vec + SVM	0.796	0.706	0.748	0.785	0.674	0.725	0.817	0.730	0.771	0.708	0.623	0.663
DDM + SVM	0.706	0.620	0.660	0.655	0.521	0.580	0.759	0.695	0.726	0.712	0.517	0.599
DWNN + SVM	0.893	0.714	0.794	0.820	0.550	0.658	0.916	0.705	0.797	0.875	0.689	0.771
Best unsupervised	0.897	0.625	0.737	0.730	0.510	0.600	0.827	0.650	0.728	0.702	0.609	0.652
Our method and its variants												
Ours$_{SubInput}$	0.693	0.747	0.719	0.617	0.404	0.488	0.677	0.722	0.699	0.618	0.689	0.652
Ours$_{Concat}$	0.877	0.707	0.783	0.734	0.637	0.682	0.895	0.699	0.785	0.752	0.645	0.694
Ours	0.914	0.755	**0.827**	0.892	0.697	**0.783**	0.920	0.799	**0.855**	0.881	0.692	**0.775**

consideration on the contextual information between the hypernym and its hyponym, rather than their respective meanings. While our method can learn more indicative features related to the taxonomic relations under the guidance of both the distributional contexts and encoded definitions. Besides, we observe an interesting scenario is that the Precision of **DDM** improves significantly in the open domain datasets compared to the specific domain datasets. One possible explanation is that the method learns term embeddings using pre-extracted taxonomic relations from Probase, and if a relation dose not in Probase, there is high possibility that it becomes a negative instance and be recognized as a non-taxonomic relation by the classifier. Therefore, the training data extracted from Probase plays an import role in this method. For open domain datasets (BLESS [3] and Conceptual Graph (See footnote 4)), there are approximately 75%–85% of taxonomic relations in these datasets found in Probase, while only approximately 25%–45% of relations in domain-specific datasets (WebIsA-Animal (See footnote 5) and WebIsA-Plant (See footnote 5)) can be found in Probase. Therefore, **DDM** achieves better performance in the open domain datasets than the specific ones. Our approach, in contrast, mainly depends on the valuable evidence - corpus-independent textual definitions, thus, it has better generalization capability and could achieve higher F-score in domain-specific datasets.

4.4 Error Analysis

We analyse two categories of error cases in the experiments, including inaccurate definitions and other relations[12].

---

[12] In our settings, meronymy, coordinate relations, and term pairs with reversed positions of the hypernym and hyponym (shortly denoted as reversed error), are considered as other relations.

Table 3. Performance comparison of different methods on open domain datasets (including BLESS and Conceptual Graph). We report Precision at rank 200 (P@200), Recall at rank 200 (R@200), F-score at rank 200 (F@200) for Random Splits, and Mean Average Precision (P), Mean Average Recall (R), Mean Average F-score (F) for Lexical Splits. The best performance in the F-score column is boldfaced (the higher, the better).

Datasets	BLESS						Conceptual Graph					
	Random splits (@200)			Lexical splits			Random splits (@200)			Lexical splits		
Method	P	R	F	P	R	F	P	R	F	P	R	F
Previous methods												
Word2Vec + SVM	0.719	0.693	0.706	0.702	0.648	0.674	0.750	0.629	0.684	0.699	0.608	0.650
DDM + SVM	0.839	0.744	0.789	0.785	0.684	0.731	0.889	0.669	0.763	0.764	0.675	0.717
DWNN + SVM	0.914	0.677	0.778	0.792	0.545	0.646	0.930	0.697	0.797	0.885	0.640	0.743
Best unsupervised	0.654	0.590	0.620	0.675	0.541	0.601	0.731	0.557	0.632	0.702	0.607	0.651
Our method and its variants												
Ours$_{SubInput}$	0.675	0.659	0.670	0.621	0.600	0.610	0.683	0.623	0.652	0.608	0.572	0.589
Ours$_{Concat}$	0.864	0.719	0.785	0.803	0.677	0.735	0.874	0.760	0.813	0.760	0.679	0.717
Ours	0.871	0.723	**0.790**	0.811	0.694	**0.748**	0.899	0.775	**0.832**	0.854	0.728	**0.786**

Inaccurate Definition. The error statistics show that this kind of error account for approximately 78%, 83% and 86% total errors in BLESS [3], Conceptual Graph (See footnote 4), and WebIsA (See footnote 5), respectively. For example, our model obtains the definition "*fruit with red or yellow or green skin and sweet to tart crisp whitish flesh*" for the term "*Apple*" in the pair ("*Apple*", "*IT company*"), however, a correct detection may require another definition "*Apple Inc. is an American multinational technology company headquartered in Cupertino*", which comes from the article's abstract of the English Wikipedia[13]. This is a common issue due to the ambiguity of entity mentions. To alleviate this problem, we will explore more advanced entity liking techniques, or extract more accurately one from all highly related definitions by combining current context, along with the efficient ranking algorithm.

As to the roughly expression or misleading information errors appearing in definitions. We shall illustrate two term pairs for further analysis. The definition of "*volleyball*" in the first term pair ("*volleyball*", "*game*") is: "*a game in which two teams hit an inflated ball over a high net using their hands*", and the initial prediction result of our model is the value of 1. If we removed the phrase "*a game*" in the definition, and then the model outputs the value of 0 as the prediction result. Similarly, in the second term pair ("*mexico*", "*latin american country*"), the initial prediction result of our model is the value of 1, and the definition of "*mexico*" is: "*a republic country in the southern of latin America*". If we removed the phrase "*of latin America*" in the definition, and then our model outputs the value of 0 as the prediction result. These demonstrate that our model is more sensitive for the prominent context words which depict the taxonomic relation in the definitions. Meanwhile, the definitions indeed provide more rich

---

[13] https://en.wikipedia.org/wiki/Apple_Inc.

knowledge for understanding the term pairs. But when we cannot obtain the enough information in the definitions of the terms, our model is not enough intelligent to avoid either inaccurate or misleading errors without human-crafted knowledge.

Apart from the above situation, due to parts of term and entities pairs are rare ones, e.g., ("*coma*", "*knowledge*"), ("*bacterium*", "*microorganism*"), ("*chromium*", "*metal*"). As a consequence, it is difficult for the model to make a correct decision alone when only encoding their term meanings as the definitions in our model.

Other Relations. In this case, the majority of errors stem from confusing meronymy and taxonomic relations. For example, in fact, the term pair ("*paws*", "*cat*") is of the meronymy relation, rather than the taxonomic relation. We found that such a problem has been also reported in [23], and one possible solution for reducing this error is: adding more negative instances of this kind to the datasets.

The remained errors in the case are with respect to the type of the reversed error. In order to reduce most errors of this type, based on the previous literature study [29], one possible solution is: integrating the learning of term embeddings with the distance measure as the feature (e.g., 1-norm distance) into the model.

5   Conclusion

In this paper, we presented a neural network model, which can enhance the representations of term pairs by incorporating their separative accurately textual definitions, for identifying the taxonomic relation of pairs. In our experiments, we showed that our model outperforms several competitive baseline methods and achieves more than 82% F-score on two domain-specific datasets. Moreover, our model, once trained, performs competitively in various open domain datasets. This demonstrates the good generalization capacity of our model. Apart from this, we also conducted detailed analysis to give more insights on the error distribution.

In the future, our work can be extended by addressing the following issues: one is to consider how to integrate multiple types of knowledge (e.g., word meanings, definitions, knowledge graph paths, and images) to enhance the representations of term pairs and further improve the performance of this work. Since our model seems straightforwardly applicable for multi-class classification problem via some tuning, hence, the other work is to investigate whether this model would be used to the task of multiple semantic relations classification.

Acknowledgments. This work is supported by the National Natural Science Foundation of China (61572353, 61402323), the National High-tech R&D Program of China (863 Program) (2013AA013204), and the Natural Science Foundation of Tianjin (17JCYBJC15400).

References

1. Anh, T.L., Tay, Y., Hui, S.C., Ng, S.K.: Learning term embeddings for taxonomic relation identification using dynamic weighting neural network. In: EMNLP, pp. 403–413 (2016)
2. Bahdanau, D., Cho, K., Bengio, Y.: Neural machine translation by jointly learning to align and translate. In: ICLR (2015)

3. Baroni, M., Lenci, A.: How we blessed distributional semantic evaluation. In: Proceedings of the GEMS 2011 Workshop on GEometrical Models of Natural Language Semantics, pp. 1–10 (2011)
4. Collobert, R., Weston, J., Bottou, L., Karlen, M., Kavukcuoglu, K., Kuksa, P.: Natural language processing (almost) from scratch. J. Mach. Learn. Res. **12**, 2493–2537 (2011)
5. Fu, R., Guo, J., Qin, B., Che, W., Wang, H., Liu, T.: Learning semantic hierarchies via word embeddings. In: ACL (Volume 1: Long Papers), pp. 1199–1209 (2014)
6. Graves, A., Schmidhuber, J.: Framewise phoneme classification with bidirectional LSTM and other neural network architectures. Neural Netw. **18**(5–6), 602–610 (2005)
7. Harabagiu, S.M., Maiorano, S.J., Paşca, M.A.: Open-domain textual question answering techniques. Nat. Lang. Eng. **9**(3), 231–267 (2003)
8. Harris, Z.S.: Distributional structure. Word **10**(2–3), 146–162 (1954)
9. Hearst, M.A.: Automatic acquisition of hyponyms from large text corpora. In: COLING, pp. 539–545. Association for Computational Linguistics (1992)
10. Kiela, D., Rimell, L., Vulić, I., Clark, S.: Exploiting image generality for lexical entailment detection. In: ACL-IJCNLP (Volume 2: Short Papers), pp. 119–124 (2015)
11. Kingma, D.P., Ba, J.: Adam: a method for stochastic optimization. In: ICLR (2015)
12. Kotlerman, L., Dagan, I., Szpektor, I., Zhitomirsky-Geffet, M.: Directional distributional similarity for lexical inference. Nat. Lang. Eng. **16**(4), 359–389 (2010)
13. Levy, O., Remus, S., Biemann, C., Dagan, I.: Do supervised distributional methods really learn lexical inference relations? In: NAACL, pp. 970–976 (2015)
14. Liu, Y., Sun, C., Lin, L., Wang, X.: Learning natural language inference using bidirectional LSTM model and inner-attention (2016). https://arxiv.org/abs/1605.09090
15. Mikolov, T., Chen, K., Corrado, G., Dean, J.: Efficient estimation of word representations in vector space. In: ICLR (Workshop Poster) (2013)
16. Mikolov, T., Sutskever, I., Chen, K., Corrado, G.S., Dean, J.: Distributed representations of words and phrases and their compositionality. In: NIPS, pp. 3111–3119 (2013)
17. Miller, G.A.: WordNet: An Electronic Lexical Database. MIT Press, Cambridge (1998)
18. Mou, L., et al.: Natural language inference by tree-based convolution and heuristic matching. In: ACL (2014)
19. Nakashole, N., Weikum, G., Suchanek, F.: Patty: a taxonomy of relational patterns with semantic types. In: EMNLP-CoNLL, pp. 1135–1145 (2012)
20. Navigli, R., Velardi, P., Faralli, S.: A graph-based algorithm for inducing lexical taxonomies from scratch. In: IJCAI, pp. 1872–1877 (2011)
21. Neculoiu, P., Versteegh, M., Rotaru, M.: Learning text similarity with Siamese recurrent networks. In: Proceedings of the 1st Workshop on Representation Learning for NLP, pp. 148–157 (2016)
22. Santus, E., Lenci, A., Lu, Q., Schulte im Walde, S.: Chasing hypernyms in vector spaces with entropy. In: EACL, pp. 38–42 (2014)
23. Shwartz, V., Goldberg, Y., Dagan, I.: Improving hypernymy detection with an integrated path-based and distributional method. In: ACL, pp. 2389–2398 (2016)
24. Shwartz, V., Levy, O., Dagan, I., Goldberger, J.: Learning to exploit structured resources for lexical inference. In: CoNLL, pp. 175–184 (2015)
25. Shwartz, V., Santus, E., Schlechtweg, D.: Hypernyms under Siege: linguistically-motivated artillery for hypernymy detection. In: EACL, pp. 65–75 (2017)
26. Snow, R., Jurafsky, D., Ng, A.Y.: Learning syntactic patterns for automatic hypernym discovery. In: NIPS, pp. 1297–1304 (2004)
27. Wong, M.K., Abidi, S.S.R., Jonsen, I.D.: A multi-phase correlation search framework for mining non-taxonomic relations from unstructured text. Knowl. Inf. Syst. **38**(3), 641–667 (2014)

28. Wu, W., Li, H., Wang, H., Zhu, K.Q.: Probase: a probabilistic taxonomy for text understanding. In: SIGMOD, pp. 481–492 (2012)
29. Yu, Z., Wang, H., Lin, X., Wang, M.: Learning term embeddings for hypernymy identification. In: IJCAI, pp. 1390–1397 (2015)
30. Zeng, D., Liu, K., Lai, S., Zhou, G., Zhao, J., et al.: Relation classification via convolutional deep neural network. In: COLING, pp. 2335–2344 (2014)

Report on the First Knowledge Graph Reasoning Challenge 2018
Toward the eXplainable AI System

Takahiro Kawamura[1]([⊠])[iD], Shusaku Egami[2], Koutarou Tamura[3,4],
Yasunori Hokazono[4], Takanori Ugai[5], Yusuke Koyanagi[5], Fumihito Nishino[5],
Seiji Okajima[5], Katsuhiko Murakami[5], Kunihiko Takamatsu[6], Aoi Sugiura[7],
Shun Shiramatsu[8], Xiangyu Zhang[8], and Kouji Kozaki[9]

[1] National Agriculture and Food Research Organization, Tokyo, Japan
takahiro.kawamura@affrc.go.jp
[2] National Institute of Maritime, Port and Aviation Technology, Tokyo, Japan
[3] NRI Digital, Ltd., Yokohama, Japan
[4] Nomura Research Institute, Ltd., Tokyo, Japan
[5] Fujitsu Laboratories Ltd., Kanagawa, Japan
[6] Kobe Tokiwa University, Kobe, Japan
[7] Kobe City Nishi-Kobe Medical Center, Kobe, Japan
[8] Nagoya Institute of Technology, Nagoya, Japan
[9] Osaka Electro-Communication University, Osaka, Japan

Abstract. A new challenge for knowledge graph reasoning started in 2018. Deep learning has promoted the application of artificial intelligence (AI) techniques to a wide variety of social problems. Accordingly, being able to explain the reason for an AI decision is becoming important to ensure the secure and safe use of AI techniques. Thus, we, the Special Interest Group on Semantic Web and Ontology of the Japanese Society for AI, organized a challenge calling for techniques that reason and/or estimate which characters are criminals while providing a reasonable explanation based on an open knowledge graph of a well-known Sherlock Holmes mystery story. This paper presents a summary report of the first challenge held in 2018, including the knowledge graph construction, the techniques proposed for reasoning and/or estimation, the evaluation metrics, and the results. The first prize went to an approach that formalized the problem as a constraint satisfaction problem and solved it using a lightweight formal method; the second prize went to an approach that used SPARQL and rules; the best resource prize went to a submission that constructed word embedding of characters from all sentences of Sherlock Holmes novels; and the best idea prize went to a discussion multi-agents model. We conclude this paper with the plans and issues for the next challenge in 2019.

Keywords: Knowledge graph · Open data · Reasoning · Machine learning

© Springer Nature Switzerland AG 2020
X. Wang et al. (Eds.): JIST 2019, LNCS 12032, pp. 18–34, 2020.
https://doi.org/10.1007/978-3-030-41407-8_2

1   Background and Goal of the Challenge

In the near future, social systems regarding transportation and the economy are expected to incorporate artificial intelligence (AI)-related techniques. These systems will make critical decisions without human intervention. To safely and securely use AI techniques in society, we need to confirm whether the AI system is working appropriately. However, recent machine learning techniques, such as deep learning, hide the internal process of their decisions and predictions, and humans do not understand the reason for their conclusions. Therefore, there is increasing consideration of AI techniques that have explainability or interpretability, which means the AI system can explain the reason for the conclusion.

Moreover, although machine learning is attracting attention, we believe that the combination of inductive learning techniques and deductive knowledge reasoning techniques will be necessary in the near future. For example, considering the autonomous vehicle, in which the system inevitably has accountability when an incident or accident occurs, there is a strong demand for learning and estimating techniques for situation recognition around the vehicle based on a front camera and radar sensors. However, traffic rules and vehicle operation are predefined knowledge; thus, both must be integrated into the final system to realize the autopilot.

To the best of our knowledge, however, there is no dataset that can be used to evaluate the inductive learning techniques and the deductive knowledge reasoning techniques. Most datasets frequently used for relation estimation, such as FB15k and WN18, only include simple facts, such as hasSpouse and is-a. Such datasets cannot be used for tasks like the autopilot, in which several sub-tasks must be combined to achieve the overall goal. However, most knowledge bases depend on certain domains like factories [1] and few knowledge bases can be applied as large-scale general datasets for machine learning. The datasets for evaluating explainable AI using estimation and reasoning must include not only the basic relationships of data fragments, but also the temporal, causal, and statistical relationships in real society.

Therefore, we decided to establish a challenge to promote the development of explainable AI, with particular emphasis on combining estimation and reasoning. The goals of this challenge are to (**1**) construct large-scale knowledge graphs including structural and/or sequential relations, such as social problems and human relationships, as common datasets to evaluate reasoning and estimation techniques, (**2**) aggregate such techniques from a wide variety of researchers and information technology (IT) engineers as a means of open science by opening the knowledge graphs to the public, and (**3**) conduct objective evaluation and classification after designing appropriate metrics for explainability. In the challenge, we also used the knowledge graph in a Resource Description Framework (RDF) to provide a dataset and relationships of the data fragments in a unified machine-readable form for estimation and reasoning.

The remainder of this paper is organized as follows. Section 2 introduces the knowledge graph constructed for the 2018 challenge, and Sect. 3 presents the winning proposed approaches. Section 4 describes the evaluation methods and results, and Sect. 5 introduces related works. Finally, Sect. 6 considers the 2019 challenge.

2   Knowledge Graph Construction

The subject of the first challenge in 2018 was *The Speckled Band*, a short Sherlock Holmes story[1]. The challenge task was to correctly identify the criminals and to explain the reason, such as the evidence and methods, based on a knowledge graph, which represented the case, background, and characters of the novel. The reasons for using a mystery story as the subject are as follows:

- The story includes complicated relationships in real society, but is a virtually closed world; thus, we can set an answer and control several conditions to get this answer.
- Some stories would require statistical processes and machine learning to handle uncertain information and evidence photographs, and some stories would need to complement common sense knowledge not written in the novel; thus, we can promote the integration of estimation and reasoning.
- The story intrinsically has explainability for humans since, if the readers are not convinced, it does not hold as a mystery story.
- Using a famous story could attract attention to the challenge.

2.1   Process of Holding the Challenge

We first held five open workshops from November 2017 to April 2018, where we discussed the schema design of the graph and methodology of the knowledge construction, and we then worked towards the actual construction. The total number of participants in the workshops was 110.

In the schema design, we first discussed the contents to be included in the knowledge for estimation and reasoning, and their expression through the trial construction of the knowledge graph. Following feedback and opinions from the participants, we decided on the basic policy to focus on scenes in a novel and the relationship of those scenes, including the characters, objects, places, etc., with related scenes. In the schema, a scene ID (IRI) has subjects, verbs, objects, etc. as edges to mainly represent five Ws (When, Where, Who, What, and Why). Thus, by tracing the scene IDs, we can query the temporal transition and causal relationship of events and the characters' actions in conjunction with the static information of the characters, objects, and places. Moreover, common-sense knowledge can be added as axioms and rules. Tables such as timetables and pictures, such as evidence photographs, can also be linked to the graph. In addition, sentences in the novel are included as literal values for natural language processing.

In the knowledge graph construction, we first extracted sentences to be represented in the graph (approximately 500 sentences in *The Speckled Band*). Participants manually modified the original sentences to the simple sentences and

---

[1] https://en.wikipedia.org/wiki/Canon_of_Sherlock_Holmes.

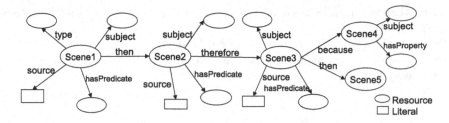

Fig. 1. Architecture of the knowledge graph

annotated the semantic roles (five Ws in this case) to each clause in the schema defined files in Google Sheets. We then normalized the notations of the subject, verb, object, etc. and added the relationships of the scenes, such as temporal transitions. Finally, we transformed the sheet into a Resource Description Framework (RDF) file. Thus, the knowledge graph includes facts written in the story, testimonies of characters, and the contents introduced by Holmes' s reasoning, which are all types of information used to identify criminals. Notably, indirect information not useful for criminal identification, such as emotional landscapes, should also be incorporated in the knowledge graph. However, we leave this as an issue for after the first year.

We then opened the knowledge graph to the public and collected the methods to identify criminals and the results. Application guidelines were published at the official website[2] (in Japanese). After opening the knowledge graph to the public, we held three orientation meetings in August, September, and October 2018, and more than 200 participants, including engineers in tech ventures and researchers at universities and companies, conducted the active discussion. The application deadline was the end of October 2018, and presentations of all applications and an awards ceremony were held at an event collocated with the 8th Joint International Semantic Technology Conference (JIST 2018).

2.2   Details of the Schema

Figure 1 presents the overall architecture of the knowledge graph.

Several properties are used to describe each scene. To summarize the information related to each scene, the properties share a scene ID as the *subject*; noting that the *subject* is not the subject of each scene or sentence. These properties are as follows:

- subject: person or object that is a subject in a scene
- hasPredicate: verb to the above subject in the scene
- hasProperty: property to the above subject (a scene has either hasPredicate or hasProperty)
- whom, what, where, how, why: persons, objects, or place that are details of the scene

---

[2] http://challenge.knowledge-graph.jp/.

- when, then, after, if, because, etc.: the relationship between scenes (the values are scene IDs)
- time: absolute time the scene occurs (xsd:DateTime)
- source: original sentences that describe the scene (Literal in English and Japanese)

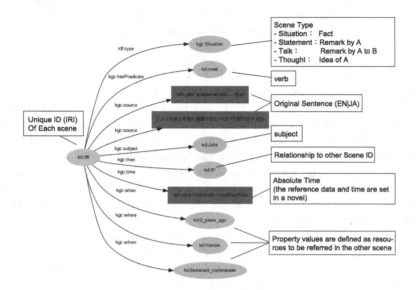

Fig. 2. Example of a scene graph

Figure 2 presents an example of a scene description. If a scene describes a remark from X (rdf:Type of the scene ID is Statement) or a thought of X (rdf:Type of the scene ID is Thought), the kgcc:infoSource property has X as an information source. In addition, there is the case where one or some of subject, whom, what, place, etc. has more than one value in a scene. In the case that the relationship of the values is AND, the scene has more than one triple with the same property and different values. In the case of OR, the value is an instance (resource) of a type ORobj that represents an OR combination, and the resource has several values through the kgcc:orTarget property. To handle the negation form of verbs, the negative verbs are linked to the corresponding positive verbs with the kgcc:Not or kgcc:canNot property. Figure 3 shows a list of classes and properties, and the knowledge graph that was opened to the public can be accessed at our Linked Data visualization tool[3].

---

[3] http://knowledge-graph.jp/visualization/.

3 Approach for Estimation and Reasoning Techniques

Estimation and reasoning techniques include several existing information retrieval, relation extraction, and knowledge management techniques; however, since this challenge focuses on explainability for human use in social problems, we note the following unique difficulties. In real social problems, every single issue is an individual case, and it is hard to collect problems with the same pattern. Thus, data and/or knowledge of the problems cannot necessarily be "big data." One single relation estimation, i.e., a reasoning step that can be explained with similarity in embedded vector spaces is insufficient. Aggregating them to lead to the overall goal is essential.

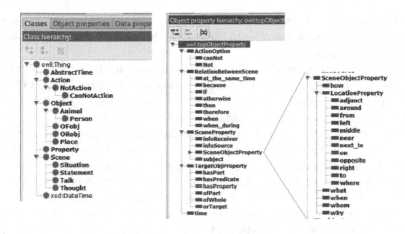

Fig. 3. Class and property list

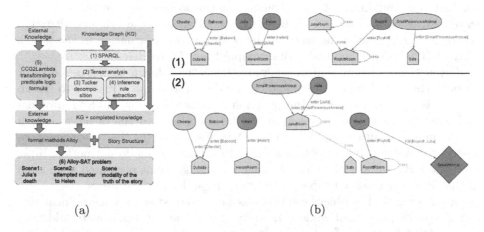

(a)   (b)

Fig. 4. (a) NRI team's approach, (b) One of the solution corresponding to the day of Julia's death: night (1) and mid-night (2). Due to lack of the facts it cannot identify whether the small poisonous animal stays in the safe or Roylott's room in the night.

With respect to the above difficulties, we had eight original submissions (5 submissions with implementation, 3 submissions of ideas only). The following subsections briefly introduce the four approaches that respectively obtained the first prize, the second prize, the best resource prize, and the best idea prize. More details can be found in the results announcement page on the official website.

3.1   Submission of NRI

In describing the crime situation mathematically from the knowledge graph in the text, and complementing the missing knowledge, we analyzed the knowledge graph as relational data and considered treating them as satisfiability (SAT) problems while searching for possible situations. An overview of our method is shown in Fig. 4(a).

In the following, we explain the contributed methods. For detailed scripts and condition settings, please refer to the materials listed on the official website's results announcement page.

First, we try to complement the knowledge lacking in the information in the text by Tucker decomposition. One scene is described by three axis, SVO forms (subject, predicate, object) to shorten the calculation time. Although some of the complemented knowledge is difficult to interpret, there are a large number of knowledge items suggesting that Animal has done something to Julia, although the accuracy is not high. Among the information on the deceased Julia, the few items on the activities aimed at her were judged to be strong.

Second, we rewrite a given sentence as a predicate logic expression. We analyzed the SAT problem using the Analyzer with the converted predicate logic equation and facts (situation in the scene). Also, we introduced external knowledge such as the list of killing methods for the closed-room murder, structure of the house, and list of animals living in India [3]. Information on actors, killing methods, and buildings/locations common to the scene is represented as a predicate logical expression, and we listed the possibility of the criminal situation shown in Fig. 4(b) with the facts on the person and the situation in the scenes "day of Julia's death" and "day of attempted murder to Helen."

Given the testimony and information, Roylott is shown as the perpetrator on both the day of Julia's death and on the day of attempted murder to Helen.

In this experiment, we set the situation in tensor analysis and SAT problem and used the former to complement the information and the latter to search for the matching situation. Only the SVO axis was used for the tensor analysis, whereby it was possible to obtain a suggestion that people do not notice. However, the large number of complementary knowledge items presented is an issue in that it was necessary for people to interpret and select the items.

And, using SAT problem solution has been suggested that mechanical reasoning can be performed while persuasive explanation is retained. In addition, Our method has room for the development to solve with contradict facts by weighted-SAT, which solves a problem by weighting formulas and facts, and to narrow the solution space using evolutionary computation by proposing hypothesis. Upgrading the algorithm of by these approach within the framework of

SAT problem is a subject for future works. By using the SAT problem solution method here, we hope that we will help explore basic artificial intelligence and machine learning technology with a high interpretability in the future.

CCG2lambda [4] and AlloyAnalyzer greatly contributed to this analysis.

3.2 Submission of Team Kamikotanaka 411, Fujitsu

Overall Structure and Created Ontology

Overall Structure: Team Kamikotanaka 411 tried to find the criminal by inferring who had the motive, the opportunity, and the method.

An ontology representing motives and methods of murder like Fig. 5 was made, and it was added to the provided knowledge graph of "The Adventure of the Speckled Band". We applied programs to judge the motive, opportunity, and method to the extended knowledge graph. The final overall judgment was made manually based on the judgment result of the characters.

Created Ontology: In order to infer the criminal, various kinds of evidence and various analyses are conducted by comparing them with various knowledge related to the crime. This time, the knowledge for the three analyses from (a) analysis of motives, (b) analysis of opportunities, (c) analysis of means. The Criminal White Paper contains statistics on motives for crimes, and we listed the possible motives for the crime mainly from the statistics. Human relations are described based on "An Agent Relationship Ontology" from the viewpoint of describing inheritance. As for the means, since there are various Japanese words which indicate the means of murder, various ways of killing were enumerated on the basis of the backward coincidence of "killing" in the Japanese dictionary. These can be described in detail as structured data with attributes (service, action, place, object) and values.

Finding Crimes from Motives, Opportunities, and Means

Motives: We set a basic policy that one will have a motive for murder if the target of murder is clear under circumstances where it is not unnatural to have a motive for murder. Then we established a rule to infer the characters concerned through creating an ontology of motives for murder to describe situations in which a motive for murder occurs.

As a result of inference using the processing system of SHACL, the following three results were obtained. (1) *Roylott* may kill *Julia* and *Helen* for *money*, (2) *Villagers* may kill *Roylott* for *self-defense*, (3) *Helen* may kill *Roylott* for *self-defense*.

Opportunities: We set a basic policy that any person who could get into the room of Julia on the night of the murder can be the criminal. And the inferring process was divided into a part which infers the relation of time by inferring each whereabouts at the time of the incident and a part which infers the relation of space.

The locations of the characters at the time of the incident were deduced by obtaining the information of the scenes with the same time as the time of the incident, and excluding the scenes which were inferred to be after the occurrence of the incident by the property "then". It is inferred that the five characters who were near the crime scene were as follows: Julia, Helen and Roylott were in their own bedrooms and Roma was in the garden.

Next, we infer whether Helen, Roylott and Roma, other than the murdered Julia, could move to the bedroom where Julia was in. Enumerating the connections that are made by the hole, and describing the connections that people cannot pass through.

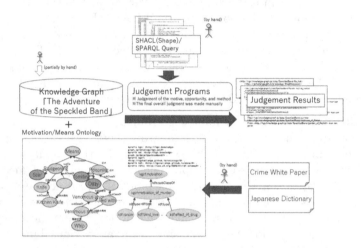

Fig. 5. Overall structure

Means: A part which narrows down the killing method based on the condition of the victim and the scene on the night of the incident and a part which deduces the person who satisfies the necessary condition for carrying out the narrowed killing method were implemented. It was inferred from this query that the method of killing was poisoning, and the symptoms were "dizziness", "pale" and "no scar". "Murder with venomous snake" or "Venom killing" is inferred as a feasible measure for Roylott. The reason was the whip which was in his room.

Total Judgement

From the above, it is inferred that Roylott killed Julia by the use of a venomous snake for money.

3.3   Submission of Team FLL-ML, Fujitsu

The FLL-ML team applied machine learning based methods to predicting the criminal of "The Adventure of the Speckled Band" (TSB) and explaining the reason for the prediction.

In order to predict the criminal of TSB, we trained a classifier for classifying TSB characters into 3 classes (Criminal, Victim, Other) by using the word vectors corresponding to characters appearing in the short stories of Sherlock Holmes (SH) series other than TSB. We automatically extracted 14,619 word segmented sentences and the list of SH characters from 22 short stories of SH in the Aozora Bunko as training data for the criminal prediction model. We also manually annotated each character in the list with the 3-class classification.

As the reason for judging as the criminal, we presented the sentences which indicated the motive/means to cause the crime from the sentences which were semantically close to the criminal. We trained another classifier for classifying sentences into 3 classes (Motive, Means, Other) with 2,930 annotated sentences from the short stories of SH other than TSB and then the average word vectors in the sentences (sentence vectors) were used for the sentence features. Semantic distances between the criminal and sentences are calculated by the Euclidean distances between the word vector corresponding to the criminal and sentence vectors. As for the output of the actual sentence indicating motives/means, top 30 sentences that have high motives/means scores were presented from sentences close to criminals as candidates, and sentences which indicate motives/means were manually selected from the candidates.

As the result of criminal prediction, the character with the highest criminal score was Roylott, and the next was Helen. The victim was expected to be Julia, if Roylott was the criminal. Roylott's motive for the crime was presumed to be a tantrum or money problem, but the means of the crime could not be identified. Table 1 shows an example of sentences presumed to indicate the motives for the crime.

Table 1. Example of sentences presumed to indicate the motives

Motive	Basis
Tantrum	In a fit of anger, however, caused by some robberies which had been perpetrated in the house, he beat his native butler to death and narrowly escaped a capital sentence
Money	Nothing was left save a few acres of ground, and the two-hundred-year-old house, which is itself crushed under a heavy mortgage

The result of the criminal prediction was not different from the general interpretation of TSB. As for the motives of Roylott's crime, tantrums and money problems were extracted, but because Roylott's crime was premeditated, a tantrum was inappropriate as a motive. However, since there are no other teams that consider tantrums as a motive in this Knowledge Graph Reasoning Challenge, we have found that machine learning can be used to roughly grasp matters that are difficult to cover by knowledge. On the other hand, our explanation method is too simple for explaining complicated procedure such as the means of the crime in TSB. As the future, we have to consider the construction of the knowledge which can explain complicated procedure and how to associate the knowledge with the prediction results.

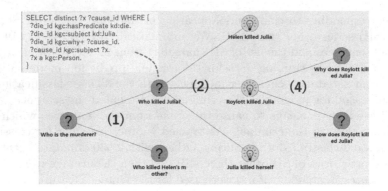

Fig. 6. An instance of IBIS structure

3.4 Submission of Nagoya Institute of Technology

In this section, we describe an approach to the explainability using agent-based discussion on "who is the criminal", which was conceived in Nagoya Institute of Technology. This unimplemented idea is based on the assumption that structured discussion as questions and answers can improve the explainability.

In mystery novels, sidekick characters accompanying detectives have an important role. The sidekicks often ask questions to the detectives and try to make naive inferences or hypotheses. Such scenes with discussion enable readers to grasp the background of the incident and the process of the inference. From this viewpoint, the explainability can be ensured by generating questions and multiple hypotheses for each question and by evaluating each hypothesis. This idea is inspired by a research project [5,6] to develop autonomous facilitator agents for online discussion based on generating facilitators' questions using the issue-based information system (IBIS) [7].

The procedure of the automated agent-based discussion is designed as follows, where G is the knowledge graph representing the content of the novel.

1. As shown in (1) of Fig. 6, issue nodes for asking who is the murderer for each victim v appearing in G are appended to the IBIS structure.
2. A hypothesis isKilledBy(v, x), i.e., v is killed by x, is generated for each pair of a victim v and a murderer x. As shown in (2) of Fig. 6, the hypothesis isKilledBy(v, x) is appended to the IBIS structure as an idea node.
3. A discussion agent $d(v, x)$ is assigned to each hypothesis isKilledBy(v, x) to try generate detail explanation of the hypothesis. The agent $d(v, x)$ firstly has a knowledge graph $G_{v,x}$, a duplication of G. The agent $d(v, x)$ appends isKilledBy(v, x) to $G_{v,x}$ and the IBIS node.
4. A facilitator agent generate questions such as "How does x killed v?" and "Why does x killed v?" and append them to the IBIS structure as issue nodes as shown in (4) of Fig. 6.
5. A discussion agent $d(v, x)$ respectively try to generate hypotheses to answer the questions from the facilitator agent, e.g., a hypothesis $how(v, x)$ about

how x killed v and a hypothesis $why(v, x)$ about why x killed v. These explanations are appended to $G_{v,x}$ and the IBIS structure.

6. A discussion agent $d(v, x)$ respectively try to disprove a hypothesis isKilledBy(v, x') for each $x' \neq x$. $d(v, x)$ tries to generate counterargument against $how(v, x')$ and $why(v, x')$. If the counterargument is successfully generated, $d(v, x)$ appends it to $G_{v,x'}$, the knowledge of $d(v, x')$, and to the IBIS structure.

7. The facilitator agent evaluates each cnsstcy(v, x), scores representing the consistency of $G_{v,x}$ including the hypothesis isKilledBy(v, x), and selects a candidate of murderer $x_v = \arg\max_x \{\text{cnsstcy}(v, x)\}$ for each victim v. The selected discussion agent $d(v, x_v)$ outputs the hypothesis isKilledBy(v, x_v) and its explanation $how(v, x_v)$ and $why(v, x_v)$.

In this procedure, there are some remaining issues on developing a generation method of questions and hypotheses and on defining the consistency metric cnsstcy(v, x). As a future work, the procedure should be improved in respect of these remaining issue and it should be implemented for verification.

4 Evaluation

Designing appropriate metrics is necessary for evaluating estimation and reasoning techniques that have explainability. In addition to leading to the correct answer, several metrics, such as explainability, utility, novelty, and performance, should be designed. Then, the proposed approaches are evaluated for their advantages and disadvantages based on the metrics, and classified into categories that correspond to practical use cases. The evaluation is based not only on numerical metrics, but also on a qualitative comparison of the approaches and the common recognition of problems through discussion and peer reviews of evaluators and applicants. The Defense Advanced Research Projects Agency eXplainable AI (DARPA XAI) described in Sect. 5 states that the current AI techniques have a trade-off between accuracy and explainability, so both properties should be measured. In particular, to measure the effectiveness of the explainability, DARPA XAI rates user satisfaction regarding its clarity and utility. Referring to such activities, we designed the following metrics for this challenge and will further improve them for future challenges. We first share the basic information of the proposed approaches, and then discuss the evaluation of experts and of the general public.

4.1 Basic Information

First, the following information was investigated and shared with experts in advance. The experts were seven board members of the Special Interest Group on Semantic Web and Ontology (SIGSWO) in the Japan Society of Artificial Intelligence.

Correctness of the Answer: Check if the resulting criminal was correct or not, regardless of the approach. The criminal, in this case, is the one designated in the novel or story. In the case that several criminals are presented, if the criminal in the novel is included among them, we decided the approach as correct but made a note.

Feasibility of the Program: Check if the submitted program correctly worked and the results were reproduced (excluding idea-only submissions).

Performance of the Program: Referential information on the system environment and performance of the submitted program, except for the idea only.

Amount of Data/Knowledge to Be Used: How much did the approach use the knowledge graph (the total number of scene IDs used)? If the approach used external knowledge and data, we noted information about them.

4.2 Expert Evaluation

Over more than a week, the experts evaluated the following aspects according to five grades (1–5). For estimation and/or reasoning methods, they considered:

Significance: Novelty and technical improvement of the method.

Applicability: Is the approach applicable to the other problems? As a guide, 3 means applicable to the other novels and stories and 5 means applicable to other domains.

Extensibility: Is the approach expected to have a further technical extension? For example, if a problem is solved, can the process or result be further improved?
    For use of knowledge and data, they considered the following:

Originality of Knowledge/Data Construction: Originality of knowledge/data construction (amount × quality × process). For example, how much external knowledge and data were prepared?

Originality of Knowledge/Data Use: How efficiently were the provided knowledge and self-constructed knowledge used? For example, was a small set of knowledge used efficiently, or was a large set of knowledge used to simplify the process.
    They also considered the following:

Feasibility of Idea (for Idea Only): Feasibility of idea including algorithms and data/knowledge construction.

Logical Explainability: Is an explanation logically persuadable? As a guide, 1 indicates no explanation and evidence, 3 indicates that some evidence in any form is provided, and 5 indicates that there is an explanation that is consistent with the estimation and reasoning process.

Effort: Amount of effort required for the submission (knowledge/data/system).

Table 2. Results per metrics by experts (ave.)

Application #	A	B	C	D	E	F	G	H
Significance	3.43	3.29	4.14	3.00	4.71	2.29	3.43	3.43
Applicability	2.86	3.50	3.00	2.00	3.71	2.33	3.86	3.86
Extensibility	3.14	3.67	4.00	2.14	4.14	3.17	3.29	3.00
Originality of knowledge/data construction	3.14	4.00	4.14	2.71	4.14	2.33	3.29	2.57
Originality of knowledge/data use	3.43	3.17	4.14	2.86	4.14	1.83	3.14	2.57
Feasibility of idea (for idea only)						2.17	3.57	2.86
Logical explainability	3.57	2.33	**4.71**	3.43	4.00	2.50	3.43	3.00
Effort	3.57	4.17	4.57	3.00	4.71	3.17	4.00	3.00
Average	3.31	3.45	4.10	2.73	**4.22**	2.52	3.49	3.06

Table 3. Results by experts and the public

Metrics	Tot. score		Explain.	
	1st	2nd	1st	2nd
Ave. (pub)	4.26	4.04	4.11	3.97
Med. (pub)	4.50	4.00	4.00	4.00
S.D. (pub)	0.67	0.65	0.78	0.69
Ave. (exp)	4.22	4.10	4.00	4.71
Med. (exp)	–	–	4.00	5.00

4.3   General Examination

Although the experts had a long time to determine whether a logical explanation could be held, the general examination that has a time constraint focused on the psychological aspect of the explanations, that is, the satisfaction with the explanation. In the presentation before the examination, the applicants had 15 min to present their submissions (10 min for idea-only submissions). In November 2018, the 45 participants of the SIGSWO meeting answered to the total score and explainability according to five grades (1–5). The forms were distributed in advance, and explained. After all the presentations, the forms were collected.

We added the total score to include psychological impressions other than explainability, such as presentation quality and entertainment aspects. If we only had a score for explainability, such aspects could be mixed in the explainability score.

4.4   Evaluation Results

Tables 2 and 3 present part of the evaluation results. In terms of the results of the general examination, we compared averages, medians, and standard deviations of the total scores and the scores for the explainability. Comparing the first and second prizes, we found that the averages of both the total score and the score for the explainability were higher for this first prize. The median of the total score in the first prize was higher than that of the second prize, but the median of the score for the explainability in the first prize was the same as the that of the second prize. Moreover, the standard deviations of both the total score and the score for the explainability were bigger for the first prize than for the second prize. The paired t-test ($\alpha = 0.05$) indicated that difference in total score had a statistically significant difference between the first and second prizes, but the score for the explainability was not significantly different.

In terms of the results of the experts, the averages of each metric in the first prize were higher than those of the second prize, except for the explainability score, which was statistically significantly higher for the second prize according to the t-test. We should note that the standard deviations of the averages for each metric were less than 0.1; thus, there were no big differences among their evaluations. Among the metrics, explainability had the least variance, and the effort required had the biggest variance.

Therefore, the final decision was left to the expert peer review. As a result, we decided this prize order, since the metrics other than the explainability of the first prize were higher than or equal to the second prize. At the same time, the evaluation of the estimation and reasoning techniques including explainability, which was a key goal of this challenge, was left to the future challenge. In addition to the first and second prize, we gave a best resource and a best idea prize based on the comments of the experts.

5   Related Work

In terms of AI development with explainability, the Defense Advanced Research Projects Agency (DARPA) started the eXplainable AI (XAI) project in 2017. DARPA XAI is a research and development project to help soldiers understand, trust, and manage future AI partners[4], and it is developing machine learning techniques to generate more explainable models while retaining the high-level learning function. At the same time, the model should be able to translate an explanation that is more understandable and useful to human users using the latest human-computer interaction (HI) techniques. The integration of the eXplainable AI model and human interaction was intended from the beginning of the project. Specifically, two tasks corresponding to the DARPA missions, data analytics, and autonomy were set as problems to be solved. The data analytics task is technically a classification problem of multimedia data and indicates the basis for the decision to the human analyst when automatically identifying targets from images. The autonomy task is a reinforcement learning problem of an autonomous system, such as the type used in drones and robots, and presents why the next action was selected in a given situation to human operators using the autopilot mode. To indicate the reason, three methods are discussed. Deep explanation shows which features are important for identification in deep learning [2]. Interpretable models mainly use random forests, Bayesian networks, and probabilistic logics, and they show the meanings and correlations of nodes in the constructed network. Model induction handles a model as a black box and creates a simpler and more analytical model with the same input and output.

The explainability of AI also has a social need. The Japanese Ministry of Internal Affairs and Communications prepared ten general principles for AI promotion and its risk reduction in 2018. Although these are not rules, they are

---

[4] https://www.darpa.mil/program/explainable-artificial-intelligence.

expected to evoke public opinion by discussion in and outside Japan. The principle of transparency (#9) defines that service providers and business users of AI must pay attention to the verification possibilities of input and output, and the explainability of AI system/service results. The principle of accountability (#10) defines that service providers and business users of AI should have accountability to stakeholders including consumers and end-users. In the European Union (EU), article 22 in the General Data Protection Regulation (GD-PR) enforced May 2018 defines that service providers of data-based decision-making must have the responsibility to safeguard users rights, at least the right to obtain human intervention.

Accordingly, in top conferences of AI and neural networks, such as IJCAI, AAAI, NIPS, and ICML, papers and workshops that have "expandability" as a keyword and that analyze the properties of AI models have significantly increased since 2016. However, there is no research activity like this challenge, which uses knowledge graphs including social problems as common test-sets and tries to solve the problems with explainability, aiming to integrate inductive estimation and deductive reasoning.

Although knowledge graphs and schema constructed for this challenge are our original work, related works include EventKG [8], ECG [9], and Drammer [10]. Knowledge graphs such as Wikidata and DBpedia focus on entities of persons and objects, but EventKG is a Knowles graph that describes 690,000 historic and modern events to generate question answering and history (timeline) from specific aspects. It uses a schema that extends temporal relation expressions based on the Simple Event Model [11]. Although there are similarities to our schema, e.g., definitions of event relationships, the granularity of their events is much bigger than one of our scenes; thus, it is difficult to describe who, whom, and what for each scene using the EventKG schema[5]. ECG provides a schema to annotate extracted information when directly constructing a knowledge graph from a news event that is described in natural languages. However, since it is for automatic extraction, the schema is simple and only includes who, what, where, and when. Drammer focuses on fictional contents and aims not only to sequentially express the content, but also to dramatically present the narrative contents, and it define a schema (or, ontology) including conflict of characters, story segmentation, emotional expression, and belief. That is an intensive work constructed after analysis of several dramas, but is different from our schema for expressing facts and relations in real society.

6   Conclusion and Future Work

This paper reports on the first knowledge graph reasoning challenge, held in 2018, which aimed to promote AI techniques with explainability. In particular, for the development of AI techniques integrating inductive machine learning

---

[5] More precisely, it is possible in the EventKG schema, but the graph becomes complicated and is hard to construct such that specific information is difficult to find in the graph.

(estimation) and deductive knowledge reasoning, this challenge constructed and published a knowledge graph based on a short mystery story as an evaluation test-set, collected proposals of methods for estimating and/or reasoning about a criminal with the explanation, and evaluated the proposed approaches based on several metrics.

In the second challenge that started in June 2019, five knowledge graphs were constructed from five different mystery novels. In the third or fourth challenge, we plan to have knowledge graphs of real social problems, e.g., books listing best practices of social problem solving, instead of mystery novels. Moreover, we will make this challenge an international event and promote it as a common academic problem setting. The results of these challenges will be annually reported and open to the public.

Acknowledgments. We would like to express our gratitude to all the participants in the workshops, technical meetings, and other events that have been held so far. This work was supported by JSPS KAKENHI Grant Number 19H04168.

References

1. Mehdi, G., et al.: Semantic rule-based equipment diagnostics. In: d'Amato, C., et al. (eds.) ISWC 2017. LNCS, vol. 10588, pp. 314–333. Springer, Cham (2017). https://doi.org/10.1007/978-3-319-68204-4_29
2. Brina, O., Cotton, C.: Explanation and justification in machine learning: a survey. In: Proceedings of IJCAI 2017 Workshop on Explainable AI (2017)
3. Fauna_of_India Wiki. https://en.wikipedia.org/wiki/Fauna_of_India. Accessed 18 Jan 2019
4. Mineshima, K., Tanaka, R., Gomez, P.M., Miyao, Y., Bekki, D.: Building compositional semantics and higher-order inference system for a wide-coverage Japanese CCG parser. In: Proceedings of the 2016 Conference on Empirical Methods in Natural Language Processing, pp. 2236–2242 (2016)
5. Kitagawa, K., Shiramatsu, S., Kamiya, A.: Developing a method for quantifying degree of discussion progress towards automatic facilitation of web-based discussion. In: Lujak, M. (ed.) AT 2018. LNCS (LNAI), vol. 11327, pp. 162–169. Springer, Cham (2019). https://doi.org/10.1007/978-3-030-17294-7_12
6. Ikeda, Y., Shiramatsu, S.: Generating questions asked by facilitator agents using preceding context in web-based discussion. In: Proceedings of the 2nd IEEE International Conference on Agents, pp. 127–132 (2017)
7. Noble, D., Rittel, H.W.: Issue-based information systems for design. In: Proceedings of the Computing in Design Education, pp. 275–286 (1988)
8. Gottschalk, S., Demidova, E.: EventKG: a multilingual event-centric temporal knowledge graph. In: Gangemi, A., et al. (eds.) ESWC 2018. LNCS, vol. 10843, pp. 272–287. Springer, Cham (2018). https://doi.org/10.1007/978-3-319-93417-4_18
9. Rospocher, M., et al.: Building event-centric knowledge graphs from news. J. Web Semant. **37–38**, 132–151 (2016)
10. Lombardo, V., Damiano, R., Pizzo, A.: Drammar: a comprehensive ontological resource on drama. In: Vrandečić, D., et al. (eds.) ISWC 2018. LNCS, vol. 11137, pp. 103–118. Springer, Cham (2018). https://doi.org/10.1007/978-3-030-00668-6_7
11. van Hage, W.R., Malaise, V., Segers, R., Hollink, L., Schreiber, G.: Design and use of the simple event model (SEM). J. Web Semant. **9**(2), 128–136 (2011)

Violence Identification in Social Media

Julio Vizcarra[1(✉)], Ken Fukuda[1], and Kouji Kozaki[2]

[1] Human Augmentation Research Center, National Institute of Advanced Industrial
Science and Technology, Tokyo 135-0064, Japan
{julio.vizcarra,ken.fukuda}@aist.go.jp
[2] Department of Engineering Informatics, Faculty of Information
and Communication Engineering, Osaka Electro-Communication University,
Osaka 572-0837, Japan
kozaki@osakac.ac.jp

Abstract. A knowledge-based methodology is proposed for the identification of type and level of violence presented implicitly in shared comments on social media. The work was focused on the semantic processing
taking into account the content and handling comments as excerpts of
knowledge. Our approach implements similarity measures, conceptual
distances, graph theory algorithms, knowledge graphs and disambiguation processes.

The methodology is composed for four stages. In the (1) "knowledge
base construction" the types and levels of violence are described as well
as the knowledge graphs' administration. Mechanisms of inclusion and
extraction were developed for the knowledge base's handling and content
understanding. The (2) "social media data collection" retrieves comments and maps the social graph's structure. In the (3) "knowledge processing stage" the comments are transformed to formal representations
as extracts of knowledge (graphs). Finally in the (4) "violence domain
identification" the comments are classified by their type and level of
violence. The evaluation was carried out comparing our methodology
with the baselines: (1) a dataset with comments labeled by crowdFlower
users, (2) news from social network Twitter, (3) a similar research and
(4) typical lexical matching.

Keywords: Knowledge engineering · Conceptual similarity ·
DBpedia · Topic identification · Violence · Social media

1 Introduction

During the recent years the rapid growth and popularity of the social media
through social networks and channels, blogs, forums or any public resource on
the Internet for inter-personal communication have motivated the people to share
opinions, thoughts and concerns in the world around them. The users usually
transmit implicitly emotions and present patterns of conduct as response to
people or specific topics which can describe social phenomenons. One important
social issue in the social media is the violence; it may include blaming, verbal

© Springer Nature Switzerland AG 2020
X. Wang et al. (Eds.): JIST 2019, LNCS 12032, pp. 35–49, 2020.
https://doi.org/10.1007/978-3-030-41407-8_3

assault, humiliation, intimidation, etc. Some types of violence are for instance gender, elder or relationship abuse, threat, intentionally frightening, excessively criticizing, etc., which can lead in physical aggression. Hence the importance of an in-depth analysis and identification of violent patterns on the user-generated data in order to classify endangered groups and potential aggressors. Once the identification is performed prevention mechanisms can be applied on the people through social plans.

Current efforts in violence identification that motivated our proposal are carried out by international organizations. These initiatives are for instance: (1) the World Health Organization (WHO) published in March 2017 the estimation of mortality caused by interpersonal violence (global health estimates 2015: deaths by cause, age, sex, by country and by region, 2000–2015) [16]. In this study, many countries were listed such as Mexico, Brazil, Colombia, India, Pakistan, Nigeria as countries with high number of deaths caused by interpersonal violence. Furthermore, on january 2016 in an historic summit the (2) United Nations (UN) established the sustainable development goals (SDGs) (17 goals to transform the world) [2] to accomplished by 2030. The goal 16 encourages to the countries that compose the UN to promote just, peaceful and inclusive societies where all forms of violence and related death rates have to be significantly reduced everywhere Moreover, the goal 5 mentioned that importance of "gender equality where women and girls continue to suffer discrimination and violence in every part of the world". Gender equality is not only a fundamental human right, but a necessary foundation for a peaceful, prosperous and sustainable world.

Based on the previous motivations the present work aims in the identification of violence in comments on social media. In this gap the methodology focuses in a better understanding of content, context and sense with a semantic approach. The main contributions are: (1) the identification of violent comments based on well-defined knowledge graphs. (2) The methodology computes similarities measures and conceptual distances in order to discover semantically violent content on social media.

2   Background

Describing briefly the current state-of-the-art in relation with our proposal some of research lines and works are listed. Regarding the topic analysis in social media, the work of Garimella et al. [11] constructed a conversation graph about a topic measuring the amount of controversy from characteristics of the graph. Analyzing the relation between opinion and topic, the work of Xiong et al. [18] proposed an opinion model on topic interactions, individual opinions and topic features which are represented by a multidimensional vector in order to measure an user's action towards a specific topic. Discovering topics, the work of Davis et al. [9] proposed an unsupervised methodology which identifies new topics prevalent in both social media and news. The work was able to rank topics by relevance, media focus, user's attention and level of interaction. Georgiou et al. [12] proposed a topic and community detection algorithm utilizing social characteristics and geographic locations. The community's discovery was computed by a defined subset of social attributes. These attributes can include user's demographics like location, age, gender, race, or characteristics like political affiliation, supporting soccer team, hobbies, etc. Filtering comments by their topics, the work of Nguyen et al. [15] implemented machine learning techniques that discriminate online conversations in depression communities from other subgroups using linguistic and topic analysis.

In the behavior recognition area on social networks, Cheng et al. [7] implemented a support vector machine (SVM). This supervised machine learning model was employed to build algorithms for automatically classifying comment in weibo (a Chinese social network) and users in suicide risk or emotional distress. Considering the relation between topic and location, Dokuz et al. [10] proposed a method of interest measures in order to discover important locations socially. The approach computes historical user's data and preferences by a important locations mining algorithm. The interest measures are location density, visit lifetime and user prevalence to quantify socially important locations. Implementing an hybrid data mining model, Yao et al. [19] combined data mining, location and behavior analysis on social networks in order to find out the spatial temporal path. They proposed an individual mobility pattern approach which was able to generate multiple spatial temporal paths from social media data and reflecting the diverse patterns existing in an individual trajectory.

Regarding the sentiment analysis, the work of Birjali et al. [4] tackled the suicide by a machine learning and semantic approach. They processed semantically the comments on twitter and classified them into suspects with risk. In the evaluation, the concepts considered suitable for suicide were used for training in the classification model, this training was processed manually.

Reviewing the state-of-the-art, most of the works were focused in identifying a topic exploring social attributes by means of linguistic-lexical processing that dismisses the semantic level and the implicit content. There was a variety of machine learning techniques that are focused on specific cases of studies, limited number of topics and require large high quality labeled datasets. Comparing our proposal with the related work the main advantage is the effort of understanding the content on the semantic level, discover the word's sense based on the context. Our methodology covers a wide number of types of violence using large knowledge graphs which during the recent years have become rich and robust for the human understanding. Our contribution creates a bridge between lexical and semantic levels for processing the implicit information in the violence identification.

3   Methodology

This section describes our contribution in four main stages that compose the methodology. In first stage "knowledge base construction" the knowledge is described and the types of violence are defined. The second stage "social media data collection" retrieves and stores comments as well as maps the social graph structure. The "knowledge processing stage" produces formal representations as graphs for each comment. Finally the "violence domain identification" estimates the type and level of violence of each comment applying graph theory algorithms and semantic processing.

3.1 Knowledge Base Construction Stage

In this section the knowledge base (KB) is constructed by integrating the general knowledge graphs such as Wordnet (WN) and DBpedia. The concepts are defined as well as their relation with violence. The conceptual distances are calculated (distance from one node to other in the knowledge graph) and shortest paths among concepts are estimated.

General Knowledge Graphs. The graphs that describe the knowledge through concepts and semantic relations are listed as follows:

- WordNet (WN) [1] (version 3.1). WordNet is a large lexical database of English nouns, verbs, adjectives and adverbs which are grouped into sets of cognitive synonyms (synsets) expressing a distinct concept. Synsets are interlinked by means of conceptual-semantic and lexical relations.
- The Japanese WordNet [5,13]. It was originally developed at the National Institute of Information and Communications Technology (NICT) to support natural language processing research in Japan.
- Open Multilingual WordNet [5,6]. It provides access to 34 Open WordNets merged and linked to the Princeton English WordNet.

Violence Description. In this process the violence is described by consulting DBpedia [3]. The methodology is able to describe any domain. However, for our case of study we focused on "violence". The knowledge graph DBpedia is composed by the following elements Tv_x that can describe types of violence through DBpedia hierarchy: resources (wikipedia articles) linked to subjects, subjects linked to categories and categories. All DBpedia elements are connected through DBpedia relations Rdb. Let us define as expansion on the violence domain $DBEx_{vd}$ (Eq. 1) as the iterative process of getting elements Tv_x (types of violence) starting from the root node Tv_0 (category: violence) until reaching a maximum number of iterations α (Fig. 1).

$$DBEx_{vd} = \{Tv_x \mid \rho(Tv_x, Tv_y), \rho \in Rdb, Tv_x \in DBpedia\} \tag{1}$$

After expanding on DBpedia the next step is to calculate the level of violence for each resource $DBlvR_x$. This calculation takes into account the total number of subjects linked to a resource that belong to the domain violence c_t (subjects that were discovered in the expansion) and the distance δ between resource and the root violence Tv_0 (Eq. 2).

$$DBlvR_x = \frac{1}{c_t}\left[\sum_1^n = \frac{1}{d_i}\right], d_i = \delta(Tv_0, Tv_x) \tag{2}$$

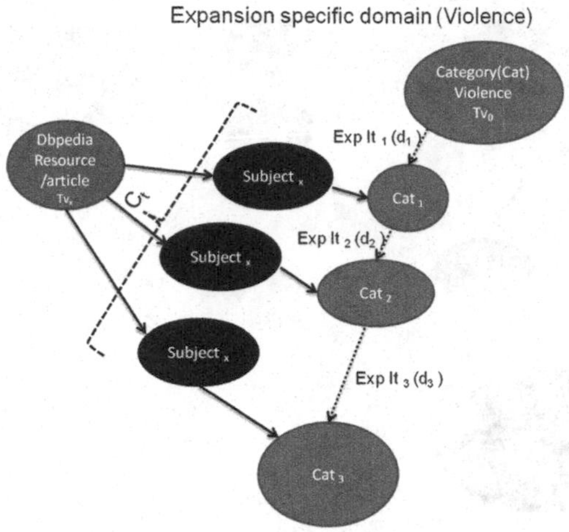

Expansion specific domain (Violence)

Fig. 1. Expansion on DBpedia from the root violence

During the violence description the subjects that belong to only one category related with violence are discarded in further processing due the low level of violence. This exclusion aims in the reduction of misclassification for comments with violence.

Disambiguation and Mapping of Violence Domain. Once the violence description was computed the next step is to execute disambiguation and mapping between DBpedia resources (violence domain) and the knowledge graph WordNet (general knowledge). This processing is executed in two steps:

- Disambiguation. In this process the DBpedia resource's title is disambiguated in order to associate each concept to only one sense in the knowledge base Wordnet. In this processing the following cases are presented:
  - Resource's title with single word. In this case the unique word is disambiguated by adding to the disambiguation process the category's title that belongs. The next step is to disambiguate the set of words.
  - Resource's title with multiple words. In this case the disambiguation process computes all the words that compose the resource's title.
  The disambiguation process between DBpedia and Wordnet is depicted in the Fig. 2). This process associates a Wordnet's sense to each concept that composes the resource's title.
- Mapping DBpedia. After the disambiguation process the resource's title is mapped into the knowledge graph by linking the DBpedia resource's concept(s) to their sense(s) in Wordnet (Fig. 3)).

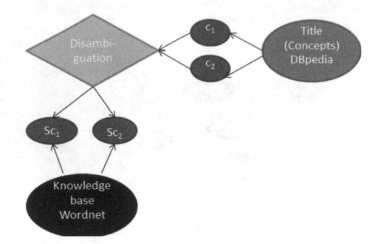

Fig. 2. Disambiguation between DBpedia and Wordnet

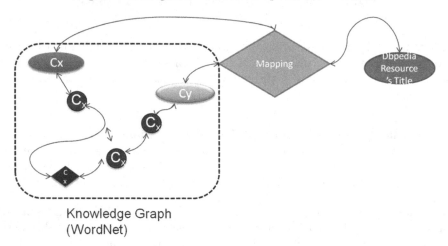

Knowledge Graph
(WordNet)

Fig. 3. Mapping between DBpedia and Wordnet

3.2 Social Media Data Collection

In this stage the social media's information is retrieved collecting users, comments and the structure of the social graph for a public event or user's profile. Considering the current popularity the social networks (SN), Twitter and Facebook were selected for the discovery and data extraction. In case of Facebook for a given user's name a scanning process retrieves the comments and their replies exploring public posts, photos, videos. Similarly for the SN Twitter the posts and their replies are retrieved for a maximum lapse of seven days due to the policies.

3.3   Knowledge Processing Stage

In this stage each comment from the social media is transform to a formal representation as a graph. The concepts are expanded, disambiguated and connected through semantic relationships. The process computes the concepts as first step with (1) natural language processing and negation handling. The next step executes (2) automatic graph construction. As result of this stage a graph is associated to a comment which represents the content, sense and context.

Natural Language Processing. In this step for each concept in the comment a natural language pre-processing is computed in order to provide to the next stages of the methodology adequate terms that match with the knowledge base. The processes related are listed as follows:

– Tokenizer. In this process a sequence of strings is divided into individual words called tokens.
– Removal of stop words. If a concept belongs to a stop word list (words with little meaning) it is removed. The words related with negation (no. not, etc.) are first identified in order to compute the negation processing. After they are removed.
– Lemmatization. The purpose of this processing is to reduce words (inflected or derived) to their word lemma (dictionary form). Each concept is reduced to its lemma by using Stanford CoreNLP [14] .
– Removal of unknown concepts in the knowledge graph. This process is executed in order to reduce number of words and discard concepts that cannot be located into the knowledge graph. This step also reduces extra processing.
– Part-of-speech. This process identifies the part-of-speech of each sentence in order to identify the concepts negated as well as reduce disambiguation by limiting the number of senses for a word.
– Negation. In this process the concepts affected by negation are identified and handled.

Negation Handling. Once the negated concepts were processed by natural language processing the next step is to compute the negation. In order to identify negation, the Standford corenlp [14] was implemented. Once the concept negated is identified the following actions are applied:

– Concept negated has inverse relations. If the concept negated has an inverse semantic relation in the knowledge graph then the concept is exchange to the inverse concept. Specifically, we used the WordNet's relation "Antonym". This scenario is mainly presented with adjectives, e.g. "The person is not aggressive may imply the person is gentle". In the example the word aggressive is exchange by gentle.
– Concept negated has no inverse relations. This scenario is mainly presented in nouns. In this case this concept is discarded because the negation implies the absence of this concept in the context (e.g. "there is not issue", the word "issue" is removed).

Automatic Graph Construction. The methodology is based on the idea of expansion in the knowledge graph. This process constructs graphs by graph theory algorithms and semantic processing. The concepts obtained from the natural language processing are transform to a graph. The construction is based on the large knowledge graphs implementing expansion, semantic similarities, disambiguation and graph theory algorithms (Vizcarra et al. [17]).

3.4   Violence Domain Identification

This section describes the process for identifying the type and level of violence presented in a comment. The first step "violence domain expansion" expands the formal representation of the comment (graph) on the knowledge graph Wordnet in order to find concepts related with violence (DBpedia resources). The next step "violence identification" estimates type and level of violence of each comment based on similarity metrics and conceptual distances.

Violence Domain Expansion. In this process $WnEx_{vd}$ each concept (sense) of a comment is expanded in the knowledge graph (Wordnet) in order to retrieve a set of concepts $c_v x \in KB$ associated with a DBpedia resource. Each concept $c_x \in Comment$ with sense s_y is expanded until finding a concept $c_v x$ linked to a resource in domain of violence Tv_x (type of violence) (Eq. 3). A number of iterations α is pre-established obtaining a set of concepts $cv_x \in KB$ with relation to a set of resources in the domain of violence Tv_x. In this stage the level of violence $DBlvR_x$ (distance from a topic to the root violence), the shortest distance δ from c_x to cv_x and type of violence Tv_x are retrived (Fig. 4).

$$WnEx_{vd} = \{Tv_x \mid cv_x \rightarrow Tv_x, \delta(c_x, cv_x), [c_x, cv_x] \in WN\} \qquad (3)$$

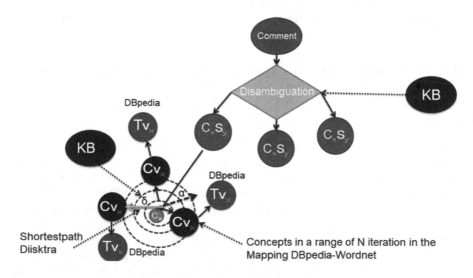

Fig. 4. Expansion on the domain violence

Violence Identification. In this identification the first step is to estimate the distance $WNlvR_x$ between a concept c_x and the resource Tv_x by retriving the previous expansion $WnEx_{vd}$. The estimation considers the total of distances from the concepts $c_x \in Comment$ to the resources Tv_x (Eq. 4) in a pre-established range of iterations α.

$$WNlvR_x = \left\{ \sum_1^n = \frac{1}{1+d_i} \mid d_i = \delta(c_x, c_{vdx}), c_x \in Comment, c_{vdx} \to Tv_x \right\} \tag{4}$$

Once the value $WNlvR_x$ was calculated in a radius of iterations α, the next step is to measure the level of violence for the comment $lvRcomment_x$ (Eq. 5).

$$lvRcomment_x = (WNlvR_x)(DBlvR_x) \tag{5}$$

The final step is to select the main type(s) of violence Tv_x for a comment $SCcomment_x$ by either (1) selecting all the resources Tv_x linked to a comment where the value of $lvRcomment_x$ is higher than a pre-established threshold value or (2) select the resource Tv_x with highest $lvRcomment_x$ value (Eqs. 6 and 7).

$$SCcomment_x = \{Tv_x \mid Tv_x \to lvRcomment_x, lvRcomment_x > Threshold\} \tag{6}$$

$$SCcomment_x = Tv_x, Tv_x \to lvRcomment_x, Max(lvRcomment_x) \tag{7}$$

4 Evaluation

The evaluation was carried out using the dataset "hate-speech-and-offensive-language" [8] where a set of comments were manually labeled by a group of CrowdFlower users. These users classified the comments into three classes: 0 as hate speech, 1 as offensive language and 2 as neither. Additionally, we compared our methodology with hashtags on Twitter. We consider as violent comments those that include hashtags such as "gender based violence, violence, domestic violence". Conversely comments with lack of violence included hashtags "happiness, assertive, trust". Our methodology explored the expansion on the violence domain until 3(L3) and 4 (L4) levels (iterations) on the knowledge graph Wordnet. This limitation reduces the number of concepts-resources from DBpedia in the calculation. The evaluation on the dataset "hate-speech-and-offensive-language" was carried out for the total number of comments (25 000 comments approximately) for the levels L3 and L4. As baseline a lexical matching (Base-lineLM) between the comment and DBpedia resources was performed using for the identification a threshold higher than 0.1 (methodology Eq. 6). Moreover, as complementary baseline our approach was compared with the research of Davidson et al. [8] (BaselineATD) which implemented machine learning techniques in the classification on the same dataset "hate-speech-and-offensive-language."

Evaluation with Hate-Speech-and-Offensive-Language Dataset. In this section some relevant examples from the dataset "hate-speech-and-offensive-language" were processed by our methodology and presented in Table 1.

Considering the "type of violence" that corresponds to the comment, we manually evaluated the accuracy of each estimation (limited to 500 comments). The results are presented in the Fig. 5 for the expansion levels L4 and L3.

Table 1. Examples processed on dataset hate-speech-and-offensive-language

Subject estimated (Methodology)	Violence level	Comment
Parental abuse by children	0.333	Baby monkey bathtime
Academic abuse	0.25	When ur teacher tells u that u have homework this bit** need to go!!!
Call bombing	0.1666	U see the da** phone ringing?" when you married bit**** makes demands!!!! you haven't called me
peer abuse	0.25	I heard you was looking for candy man, bit**
Human branding	0.208	My grandma used to call me a porch monkey all the time... come to think of it she did refer to a broken bottle as a nig*** knife

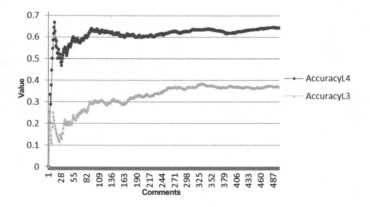

Fig. 5. Evaluation type of violence

The evaluation that considers "level of violence" related to comments for L4, L3 and baselines is shown in Fig. 6.

Table 2 presents the confusion matrix considering the processing "level L3 and L4".

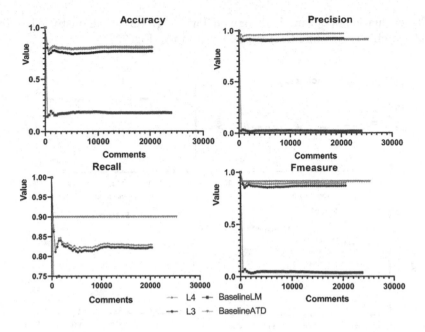

Fig. 6. Evaluation level of violence

Table 2. Confusion Matrix L3 and L4

(a) L3   (b) L4

		Actual Values				Actual Values	
		Pos	Neg			Pos	Neg
Predicted Values	Pos	15886 (TP)	1341 (FP)	Predicted Values	Pos	16705 (TP)	522 (FP)
	Neg	1 (FN)	3428 (TN)		Neg	1 (FN)	3428 (TN)

Evaluation with Twitter CNN's Account. In this section the results and evaluation on Twitter for the account: "CNN news" are introduced. Some relevant examples processed by our methodology are presented in the Table 3.

Table 3. Examples processed on twitter

Subject estimated (Methodology)	Violence percentage	Comment
Police abuse	0.250	Macron authorizes military to shoottokill yellow vest protooters as legitimacy collaps
Gay bashing	0.571	g** nig*** couldn't wait to act like bit****
Regime change	0.020	Cant you see these ho** wont change

The evaluation of our methodology on Twitter (level L4) against the baseline lexical matching (Baseline LM) is presented in the Fig. 7.

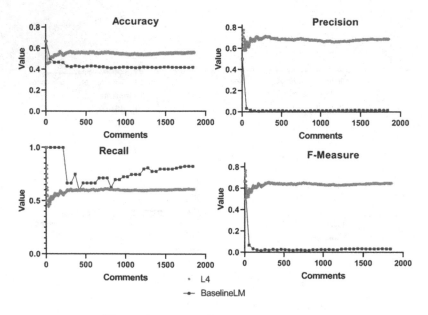

Fig. 7. Twitter evaluation using hashtags

The individual evaluation of each hashtag (level L4) on Twitter is presented in the Fig. 8.

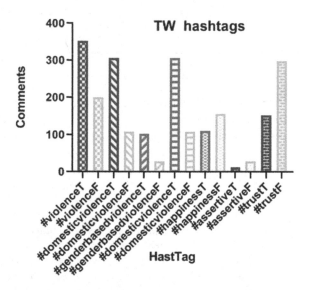

Fig. 8. Twitter evaluation L4 for each hashtag

The confusion matrix for the identification of violent and nonviolent hashtags is presented in Table 4. It is important to notice that the identification of violent hashtags performed better than nonviolent using a threshold >0.1 (methodology Eq. 6).

Table 4. Confusion matrix hashtags on Twitter

		Actual Values	
		Positive	Negative
Predicted Values	Positive	759 (TP)	337 (FP)
	Negative	273 (FN)	484 (TN)

4.1 Discussion of the Evaluation

In this section a discussion is introduced based on the previous experiments. We compared our methodology against the baselines of labeled data from the dataset "hate-speech-and-offensive-language" and comments on Twitter. In the evaluation on the dataset, we obtained similar performance (precision, recall, F-Measure) compared to the best performing model of Davidson et al. [8] but also defining type and level of violence in the classification. Similarly, we presented considerably better identification than lexical matching. On the other hand, in the evaluation on Twitter the identification was moderately better compared to the lexical matching.

Regarding the implementation's performance, we noticed that the increment of levels of expansion in Wordnet increments the number of DBpedia's resources in the calculations as well as improves slightly the identification. Despite of the precision is higher, the increment of level of expansion has the incovenient that consumes more resources (memory and time). The handling of negation improves the performance of our estimations because this scenario is frequently presented in violent comments. In the evaluation on Twitter, the classification performed better for comments with violent hashtags compared to the nonviolent.

5 Conclusions

In this paper a content-based methodology was proposed for the identification of level and type of violence. The novelty of the presented work is the capability of handling the comments as excerpts of knowledge. We provided a mechanism of semantic processing using knowledge graphs, graph theory algorithms, semantic similarities and disambiguation.

We performed several experiments in order to compare our contribution with the baselines. For instance, we compared our approach with the dataset "hate-speech-and-offensive-language" and hashtags in Twitter. We proposed as baselines the lexical matching between comments and DBpedia resources, a similar research which its evaluation was performed on same dataset. In addition, during the identification we explored the increment of levels of expansion in the discovery of concepts with violence through the levels (iterations) 3 and 4. The expansion until level 4 performed the best precision but limiting the number of comments processed due the high consumption of resources such as memory and processing time.

Regarding influence of negation, this processing was included due the high number of comments that presented this scenario. The negation handling improved the performance of our methodology because we noticed that the negation is frequently used in violent comments.

Some of the main advantages of our proposal are: (1) the effort of understanding the content on the semantic level. The (2) violence identification executes a disambiguation processes in order to discover the context and words' sense in the estimations. As (3) the methodology is based on a well-structured knowledge base, the definition of concepts related with violence is more accurate and covers a wider number of types of violence. (4) Regarding the adaptability our system is flexible which implies it might be focused on other domains not limited to violence by just modifying the knowledge base.

The results obtained in the present work can be consulted at the github site: https://github.com/samscarlet/SBA/tree/master/ViolenceAnalysis.

Acknowledgments. This work was supported in part by Council for Science, Technology and Innovation, "Cross-ministerial Strategic Innovation Promotion Program (SIP), Big-data and AI-enabled Cyberspace Technologies". (funding agency: NEDO), JSPS KAKENHI Grant Number JP17H01789 and CONACYT.

References

1. Princeton university "about wordnet." wordnet. Princeton university (2010). http://wordnet.princeton.edu
2. Assembly, G.: Sustainable development goals. SDGs), Transforming our world: the 2030 (2015)
3. Auer, S., Bizer, C., Kobilarov, G., Lehmann, J., Cyganiak, R., Ives, Z.: DBpedia: a nucleus for a web of open data. In: Aberer, K., et al. (eds.) ASWC/ISWC -2007. LNCS, vol. 4825, pp. 722–735. Springer, Heidelberg (2007). https://doi.org/10.1007/978-3-540-76298-0_52
4. Birjali, M., Beni-Hssane, A., Erritali, M.: Machine learning and semantic sentiment analysis based algorithms for suicide sentiment prediction in social networks. Procedia Comput. Sci. **113**, 65–72 (2017)
5. Bond, F., Baldwin, T., Fothergill, R., Uchimoto, K.: Japanese SemCor: a sense-tagged corpus of Japanese. In: Proceedings of the 6th Global WordNet Conference (GWC 2012), pp. 56–63 (2012)
6. Bond, F., Foster, R.: Linking and extending an open multilingual wordnet. In: Proceedings of the 51st Annual Meeting of the Association for Computational Linguistics (Volume 1: Long Papers), vol. 1, pp. 1352–1362 (2013)
7. Cheng, Q., Li, T.M., Kwok, C.L., Zhu, T., Yip, P.S.: Assessing suicide risk and emotional distress in chinese social media: a text mining and machine learning study. J. Med. Internet Res. **19**(7), e243 (2017)

8. Davidson, T., Warmsley, D., Macy, M., Weber, I.: Automated hate speech detection and the problem of offensive language. In: Proceedings of the 11th International AAAI Conference on Web and Social Media, ICWSM 2017, pp. 512–515 (2017)
9. Davis, D., Figueroa, G., Chen, Y.S.: SociRank: identifying and ranking prevalent news topics using social media factors. IEEE Trans. Syst. Man Cybern. Syst. **47**(6), 979–994 (2016)
10. Dokuz, A.S., Celik, M.: Discovering socially important locations of social media users. Expert Syst. Appl. **86**, 113–124 (2017)
11. Garimella, K., Morales, G.D.F., Gionis, A., Mathioudakis, M.: Quantifying controversy on social media. ACM Trans. Soc. Comput. **1**(1), 3 (2018)
12. Georgiou, T., El Abbadi, A., Yan, X.: Extracting topics with focused communities for social content recommendation. In: Proceedings of the 2017 ACM Conference on Computer Supported Cooperative Work and Social Computing, pp. 1432–1443. ACM (2017)
13. Isahara, H., Bond, F., Uchimoto, K., Utiyama, M., Kanzaki, K.: Development of the Japanese wordnet (2008)
14. Manning, C.D., Surdeanu, M., Bauer, J., Finkel, J., Bethard, S.J., McClosky, D.: The stanford CoreNLP natural language processing toolkit. In: Association for Computational Linguistics (ACL) System Demonstrations, pp. 55–60 (2014). http://www.aclweb.org/anthology/P/P14/P14-5010
15. Nguyen, T., ODea, B., Larsen, M., Phung, D., Venkatesh, S., Christensen, H.: Using linguistic and topic analysis to classify sub-groups of online depression communities. Multimed. Tools Appl. **76**(8), 10653–106762 (2017)
16. World Health Organization: World health statistics 2015. World Health Organization (2015)
17. Vizcarra, J., Kozaki, K., Ruiz, M.T., Quintero, R.: Content-based visualization system for sentiment analysis on social networks. In: JIST (2018)
18. Xiong, F., Liu, Y., Wang, L., Wang, X.: Analysis and application of opinion model with multiple topic interactions. Chaos Interdisc. J. Nonlinear Sci. **27**(8), 083113 (2017)
19. Yao, H., Xiong, M., Zeng, D., Gong, J.: Mining multiple spatial-temporal paths from social media data. Future Gener. Comput. Syst. **87**, 782–791 (2018)

Event-Oriented Wiki Document Generation

Fangwei Zhu[1,2,3], Zhengguo Wang[4], Juanzi Li[1,2,3(✉)], Lei Hou[1,2,3],
Jiaxin Shi[1,2,3], Shining Lv[4], Ran Shen[4], and Junjun Jiang[5]

[1] DCST, Tsinghua University, Beijing 100084, China
solitaryzero@foxmail.com, {lijuanzi,houlei}@tsinghua.edu.cn,
shijx12@163.com
[2] KIRC, Institute for Artificial Intelligence, Tsinghua University, Beijing, China
[3] Beijing National Research Center for Information Science and Technology,
Beijing, China
[4] State Grid Zhejiang Electric Power Research Institute, Hangzhou 310014, China
[5] State Grid Zhejiang Yuhuan Power Supply Company, Yuhuan 317600, China

Abstract. We aim to automatically generate event-oriented Wikipedia
articles by viewing it as a multi-document summarization problem. In
this paper, we propose a new model named WikiGen, which consists
of two parts: the first one induces a general topic template from existing Wikipedia articles, and the second one generates a summary for
each topic by collecting, filtering, and integrating relevant web news,
which will be assembled into the full document. Our evaluation results
show that WikiGen is capable of generating fluent and comprehensive
Wikipedia documents and outperforms previous work, achieving state-
of-the-art ROUGE scores.

Keywords: Wikipedia · Text summarization · Topic template

1 Introduction

An event means a particular thing happening at a specific time and place [1].
An event is usually described by multiple related news, which describe it from
different aspects in an unorganized way. Human-constructed Wikipedia articles for events compress these related news into a more organized way, which
is more comprehensive and detailed, helping readers to learn about the event
more efficiently. However, writing a Wikipedia document manually can be time-
consuming and difficult, so automating the writing process is a valuable research
topic.

There have been various methods aiming to automatically generate
Wikipedia documents, which generally employ a two-step structure: first induce
some topics from existing related Wikipedia articles as the content table, then

---

F. Zhu and Z. Wang—Equal contribution.

© Springer Nature Switzerland AG 2020
X. Wang et al. (Eds.): JIST 2019, LNCS 12032, pp. 50–66, 2020.
https://doi.org/10.1007/978-3-030-41407-8_4

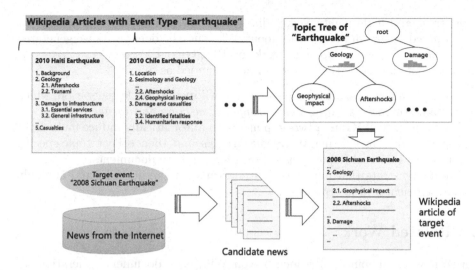

Fig. 1. The data flow of our model. A multi-layer topic template called topic tree, along with word distributions of topics will be induced from existing Wikipedia documents of certain event type. Then we will collect candidate news excerpts related to target event from the Internet, and generate summaries for each topic to get Wikipedia article for the target event.

collect a summary for each topic from web news. However, there exists several flaws in these methods. First, they usually use a single-layer content table, neglecting the widespread use of multi-layer content tables as shown in Fig. 1, which is able to depict the whole event with different granularity. Second, they fail to explicitly utilize the word distribution of topics. Third, they do not filter out noises that are inevitable in web news, posing a potential threat to the quality of generated documents.

In this paper, we propose a new model named **WikiGen** to automatically generate corresponding Wikipedia document for a new event. This model consists of two parts: topic tree induction and a two-step summary generation. Given a certain event type (e.g., *earthquake*), we first combine structural and textual relation to induce a topic tree from existing Wikipedia documents belong to the given type (e.g., *2010 Haiti Earthquake*, *2010 Chile Earthquake*, etc.), then utilize word distribution of different topics to generate unique summaries for each topic in the previous generated topic tree: we will coarsely identify related snippets from web data at first, and afterwards further select sentences with an extractive neural network model, thus forming final results.

As there is no standard benchmark for event-oriented Wikipedia article generation, we constructed a dataset on three event types: *earthquake*, *election* and *tornado*, which contains about 2000 documents and has 190 candidate excerpts per document on average. We conducted extensive experiments on our dataset to evaluate the performance of both topic tree induction and summary generation. Experimental results show that WikiGen is capable of generating fine-grained topic trees and high-quality Wikipedia documents. Specifically, the topic trees we inducted retain an accuracy of about 95%, and the documents we generated significantly outperform previous works on ROUGE-1 F1 score.

The contribution of this paper can be concluded as follows:

- We build a new dataset for event-oriented wikipedia article generation, which contains three event categories: *earthquake*, *election* and *tornado*;
- We propose **WikiGen**, a two-step model to automatically induce multi-layer topic trees from existing Wikipedia articles and then collect topic-specific summaries for each topic, thus forming high-quality documents;
- We demonstrate that our model outperforms existing models, and is highly data-efficient and interpretable.

2   Related Work

There have been some works focusing on Wikipedia document generation. In general, these works share a common two-step structure: first determine a topic template for the new document, then generate a topic-specific summary for each topic in the template.

Topic Template Induction. Notice that human written articles have different subtitles due to personal preference, a general topic template should be inducted to ensure consistency. Previous works tend towards generating single-layer templates: Google's WikiSum [10] generates only abstracts; Sauper and Barzilay [12] clusters the titles of existing Wikipedia articles and chooses the most common titles of each cluster as the template. WikiWrite [3] discovers similar existing articles and copys their content table as new templates. However, compared with multi-layer content tables used in real Wikipedia articles, single-layer templates fail to reflect the hierarchical structure of points of interest in real-world events, and lack details in different aspects. To address this problem, Hu [7] tries to build multi-layer topic templates by combining structural dependency and textual correlation to judge subtopic relations between topics.

Topic-Specific Summary Generation. After determining the topic template, generating topic-specific summary can be viewed as a document summarization problem. Sauper and Barzilay [12] made the first attempt in 2009, which uses integer linear programming (ILP) to rank excerpts retrieved from the Internet, and then finds optimal excerpts with rank scores for each topic. WikiWrite [3] took one step further, adding new features like sentence importance, intra-sentence similarity and linguistic quality and generated more fluent documents. With the rise of deep learning, attempts of utilizing neural networks have also been made. There have been extractive models like SummaRunner [11] and DeepChannel [14] aiming to choose core sentences from raw documents, and abstractive methods like PointerGenerator [13] trying to capture important information to generate the summary. In the Wikipedia document generation field, WikiSum [10] uses a decoder-only transformer based on attention mechanism [15] instead of ILP to summarize long sequences and achieves a state-of-the-art performance. Lebret [8] notices the existence of infobox, a Wikipedia exclusive structure, and merges those structured data into biography generation.

We gain inspiration mostly from Google's work [10], however, we induct multi-layer topic trees to achieve more comprehensive and detailed results. In addition, out model has an extra filtering step with modified topic model to tackle with the noise in web articles.

3   Method

We aim to generate a Wikipedia document for a given new event name based on existing human-authored Wikipedia articles. We assume that relevant information can be found in a wide range of websites across the internet, however, noise like irrelevant pages and advertisements needs to be dealt with.

Formally, we have three parts of inputs:

- The target event name t;
- An existing Wikipedia article set $WK = \{a_i\}_{i=1}^{n_{WK}}$ of the same event type as the target;
- A set of probably relevant documents collected from the Internet $NW = \{d_j\}_{j=1}^{n_{NW}}$.

Each Wikipedia document $a_i = \{T_i, R_i\}$ contains a text set $T_i = \{(g, s_g)\}$ and a relation set $R_i = \{(g_x, g_y)\}$. The text set contains some sections, each having a name g and a corresponding text description s_g; The relation set consists of some subtopic relations (g_x, g_y), which means that section g_x appears as a subsection of section g_y in this document.

Our goal is to integrate these information into a Wikipedia article for the target event. To achieve this, we propose **WikiGen**, which consists of two parts: topic template induction and topic summary generation. The overall data flow can be viewed in Fig. 1.

3.1   Topic Template Induction

Provided with the Wikipedia document set WK, topic template induction aims to find latent topics $T_c = \{t\}$ from existing sections g, and then identify subtopic relations $R_c = \{(t_i, t_j)\}$ on the base of subsection relations $R_i = \{(g_x, g_y)\}$. Topics and subtopic relations will form a topic tree $H_c = \{T_c, R_c\}$ as the final multi-layer topic template.

Topic Discovery. There exist similar sections in Wikipedia documents, for example, "Tectonics" and "Tectonic background", and merging these similar sections into one topic could greatly reduce the redundancy in our generated document. The topic discovery process can be viewed as an unsupervised clustering problem whose expected cluster number is unknown.

We use an double-pass incremental clustering algorithm to tackle with this problem. This algorithm is based on the work of Hammouda [6], which combines histogram with single-pass incremental clustering. However, there exist sections like "Overview" which have high similarities with most of other sections, and when they become the core of a new cluster, the cluster would contain dissimilar sections and lead to unexpected results.

To deal with the problem, we add an extra clustering pass. Our method uses a high threshold in the first pass to form small core clusters with high confidence, then lowers the threshold in the second pass to distribute the remaining sections into existing clusters. This algorithm avoids the influence of "Overview" sections and renders more credible results. See Algorithm 1 for the full algorithm, where

$$
\begin{aligned}
HR_{new1} &= \frac{count(sim(d_i, d_j) > \sigma_1)}{count(d_i, d_j)} \\
HR_{new2} &= \frac{count(sim(d_i, d_j) > \sigma_2)}{count(d_i, d_j)}
\end{aligned}
\tag{1}
$$

Algorithm 1. Two-pass incremental clustering

Require: Document set D
Ensure: Section cluster set L.
1: $L = []$, second pass candidates $P = []$
2: **for** document $d \in D$ **do**
3:     **for** cluster $C \in L$ **do**
4:         Simulate adding d to C and calculate HR_{new1}
5:         **if** $(HR_{new1} \geq \lambda_1)$ **then**
6:             Add d to C, remove d from P
7:             **break**
8:         **end if**
9:         **if** $(HR_{new} \geq \lambda_2)$ **then**
10:             Add d to P
11:         **end if**
12:     **end for**
13:     **if** (d not in any cluster) **AND** (d not in P) **then**
14:         Create new cluster C, add d to C, add C to L
15:     **end if**
16: **end for**
17: **for** document $d \in D$ **do**
18:     **for** cluster $C \in L$ **do**
19:         Simulate adding d to C and calculate HR_{new2}
20:         **if** $(HR_{new2} \geq \lambda_2)$ **then**
21:             Add d to C
22:             **break**
23:         **end if**
24:     **end for**
25:     **if** d not in any cluster **then**
26:         Create new cluster C, add d to C, add C to L
27:     **end if**
28: **end for**

In practice, we use the TF-IDF similarity of all texts under two sections as the similarity between sections. Titles that occur only once and clusters whose numbers of occurrence are less than 3 are discarded. We use the cluster list after the second pass as the topic list T_c, where every topic is denoted by the most frequently appeared title.

Subtopic Relation Discovery. After acquiring the topic list T_c, we need to further identify the subtopic relation set $R_c = \{(t_i, t_j)\}$ and combine them to get the complete topic tree H_c.

Previous work use a probabilistic model to build the whole tree from the top. That model aims to maximize the occurrence probability of every topic in the tree under its father topic, and its goal can be described as Eq. 2.

$$
\begin{aligned}
H^* &= argmax_H P(N|H) \\
&= argmax_H P(root) \prod_{n \in N \backslash root} P(n|par_H(n)) \\
&= argmax_H \sum_{n \in N} log P(n|par_H(n))
\end{aligned}
\tag{2}
$$

However, there exists a circumstance where previous method fails to identify the correct relations: a common topic x frequently appears as a subtopic of another common topic y, x occurs 51 times and y occurs 50 times in total. But in one document with poor quality, x is the subtopic of a rare topic z which appears only once. Under this circumstance, $P(x|y) = 0.5 P(x|z) = 1$, the previous method will tend to mark x as a subtopic of z rather than y, which is obviously wrong.

The root cause of this problem is that father topics don't have to co-occur with their child topics. For example, "Nuclear Plant Damage" is a subtopic of "Damage" in earthquake events, but not every earthquake will cause damage to nuclear plants. It is acceptable that child topic is absent from their father topics' occurrence.

In our model, we also use the probabilistic model. However, we build the topic tree from bottom to top, aiming to maximize the co-occurrence probability of every topic in the tree with its child topics. In other words, we will find the best father topic of every topic instead of finding its best child topics. If we view the whole hierarchical structure of the topic tree as a Bayesian network, we can represent the joint probability of all nodes N as Eq. 3. Given that we already know the occurrence probability of every topic n, the goal to maximize become Eq. 4. We can get the most reasonable topic tree when H^* gets its max value.

$$
P(N|H) = \prod_{n \in N \backslash root} P(par_H(n)|n) \cdot \prod_{n \in N \backslash root} P(n)
\tag{3}
$$

$$H^* = argmax_H P(N|H)$$

$$= argmax_H \prod_{n \in N \backslash root} P(par_H(n)|n) \cdot \prod_{n \in N \backslash root} P(n) \tag{4}$$

$$= argmax_H \sum_{n \in N \backslash root} log P(par_H(n)|n)$$

We combine two features to evaluate the probability of subtopic relations:

- **Structural Information:** A subtopic relation is more convincible if it appears frequently. Assume that t_j as a subtopic of t_i, the weight of their structural information can be represented as Eq. 5, where $n(t_i, t_j)$ means the number of t_i being a father topic of t_j, $n(t_j)$ means the total occurrence number of t_j, T_c means the possible number of subtopics of t_i. α is a Laplacian smooth factor to avoid the disturbance of zero value.[1]

$$P_{struc}(t_i|t_j) = \frac{n(t_i, t_j) + \alpha}{n(t_j) + \alpha \cdot |T_c - 1|} \tag{5}$$

- **Textual Correlation:** For topic t_j and its father topic t_j, it can be expected that the word distribution of t_j resembles that of t_j, which corresponds with hierarchical Dirichlet model. If we use the normalized bag of words model to measure word distribution, the weight of textual correlation can be represented as Eq. 6, where $Z = \frac{\prod_{w \in V} \Gamma(\alpha \phi_{t_i, w})}{\Gamma(\prod_{w \in V} \alpha \phi_{t_i, w})}$ is the normalize factor $\Gamma(\cdot)$ is standard Gamma distribution. Specially, when t_j is the root topic, if root topic doesn't have any text description, we set $log(P_{text}(t_i|t_j)) = 0$.

$$P_{text}(t_i|t_j) = \frac{1}{Z} \prod_{w \in V} \phi_{t_j, w}^{\beta \phi_{t_i, w} - 1} \tag{6}$$

After normalizing P_{struc} and P_{text}, we calculate a weighted average as the final weight of certain relation:

$$w(t_i, t_j) = \lambda \cdot log(P_{struc}(t_i|t_j)) + (1 - \lambda) \cdot log(P_{text}(t_i|t_j)) \tag{7}$$

If we view every topic as a node and every relation as a directed edge, building the topic tree can be converted into finding a maximum spanning tree in a directed graph. We utilize the classic Chu-Liu/Edmonds [4,5] algorithm to extract a maximum spanning tree as the final topic tree $H = (T, R)$.

3.2   Topic Summary Generation

In this step, we need to generate a corresponding summary for each topic t from corpus NW. Note that the total length of the corpus could be exceeding long, using bare neural network could face serious lack of memory and low training efficiency. We use two steps to acquire a comprehensive and detailed summary:

---

[1] $\alpha = 1.0$ in experiments.

first coarsely filter the corpus with an augmented topic model to identify related excerpts and reduce the input scale, then utilize neural networks to further filter those excerpts, generating the text s_g for each topic g.

Coarse Filtration. Provided excerpts $e_1, e_2, \ldots, e_n$ and topic g, this step aims to discard excerpts with low relativity to g and reduce the corpus to a reasonable scale.

A reasonable approach is ranking these excerpts with relativity and pick some top excerpts as the new input of next step. Google used the TF-IDF similarity between excerpts and topic name to measure relativity, but TF-IDF is not capable of identifying synonyms. Assume that we are looking for excerpts belonging to "Damage" topic, TF-IDF will neglect excerpts containing "injury" or "death", which often appear to be the correct choice.

We use an augmented topic model to better weigh the contribution of synonyms. In the previous step, we can acquire topic set $T = t$ and Wikipedia text WK_t of each topic t. According to the topic model, every topic has its specific word distribution, and words closely related to the topic will appear more frequently. If the contribution of certain word to given topic could be measured, we could better sort excerpts according to the sum of all words' distribution in the excerpts.

For each topic t, we use the bag of words model to process its Wikipedia text WK_t. Its word probability distribution $F_t = \{(w, p_{w,t})\}$ can be acquired through tokenizing and normalizing. It is obvious that if a word w appears frequently under topic t, w should have a closer connection to t; However, if w simultaneously appears in many other topics, its contribution should be lowered in accordance. Taking these rules into consideration, we use Eq. 8 to quantify the contribution of word w to topic t.

$$W(w,t) = \frac{p_{w,t}}{\sum_{tt \in T} \frac{p_{w,tt}}{p_{w,t}}} = \frac{p_{w,t}^2}{\sum_{tt \in T} p_{w,tt}} \tag{8}$$

Specially, if w only occurs under one topic t, $\sum_{tt \in T} \frac{p_{w,tt}}{p_{w,t}} = 1$, $W(w,t) = p_{w,t}$, which corresponds with our expectation. If w doesn't appear under t, we set $W(w,t) = 0$.

$$Score(e,t) = \frac{\sum_{w \in e} W(w,t)}{|e|} \tag{9}$$

Considering the features of documents about events, four additional optimizing steps have been conducted:

- **Remove Stopwords:** Stopwords appear frequently but contain little information. We use NLTK, a Python library, to identify stopwords and remove them.
- **Discard Low-frequency Words:** Rare words usually have high contributions $W(w,t)$, but words with abnormally low frequency may appear in noise like links or comments rather than meaningful text. We remove words appearing only once to ensure the confidence of contribution values.

- **Stemming:** The same word may appear in different tenses (for example "damage" and "damaged"). We use snowball stemmer to stem words, reducing the disturbance of tenses.
- **Requiring High-contribution Words:** Name of places and people appear fairly frequent in Wikipedia documents and thus have considerable contribution, but they have no direct connection with topics. We record k words $w_1, w_2, \ldots, w_k$[2] with highest contribution for each topic t, and if an excerpt doesn't contain any of these k words, its contribution $Score(e, t)$ is set to 0.

For every candidate excerpt e of topic t, we calculate the arithmetic mean of all words in e as its contribution (See Eq. 9). After sorting excerpts by contribution, we choose top excerpts with total length no longer than $L = 1000$ and concatenate them to generate new text D as the input of fine-grained filtration.

Fine-Grained Filtration. After the coarse filtration step, the scale of new input corpus D becomes suitable for neural networks. Due to limited training data, we have high requirement on data efficiency of the model. We choose DeepChannel [14] (see Fig. 2) after comparison, which utilizes channel model to select most significant sentences from the input document and represents well in small datasets.

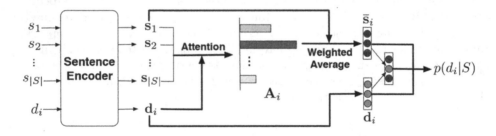

Fig. 2. The structure of DeepChannel.

In practice, we use D as the raw document and its corresponding Wikipedia text S as the golden summary. The model has been pretrained on the CNN/Dailymail dataset. 7 most significant sentences will be selected from each raw document as the final summary.

4 Dataset Construction

Among previous work, [12] and [3] didn't provide dataset, meanwhile the dataset of [10] isn't event-oriented and contains only abstracts rather than full Wikipedia articles, leading to the fact that we don't have an available existing dataset. Considering that Wikipedia itself changes over time, it is also nearly impossible to reconstruct previous datasets. We constructed a new dataset for our task.

---

[2] $k = 20$ in experiment.

For every existing Wikipedia article a_i, We build a web corpus D_j for each section g in it to simulate documents collected for the new event. Given that Wikipedia articles can be viewed as human-authored summaries, we build the web corpus D_j on two sources:

- **Cited references:** A well-written Wikipedia document should cite the source of its important information in the *Reference* section. For each Wikipedia article a_i, we extract undecorated text snippets from websites listed in the *Reference* section as cited corpus C_g.
- **Search results:** We found that a portion of cited websites are no longer available, so additional data needs to be collected. Search engines can efficiently find relevant information about certain entity, however, appropriate search queries have to be provided. We employ query [2], combining document title t and section name g to build a appropriate search query for each section. For example, *"2008 Sichuan earthquake" Geology* for section *Geology* in article *2008 Sichuan earthquake*. We use the first 20 result pages of Bing search engine for each query. After removing results of Wikipedia websites, we extract text from remaining pages as searched corpus S_g.

We use *BeautifulSoup*, a Python library, to remove useless information like scripts and styles in web pages. Moreover, we discarded text snippets whose length is greater than 400 or less than 5 to reduce noises like comments and advertisements. The full web corpus D_j can be achieved by combining filtered C_g and S_g.

5   Experiments

In this section, we will build a new dataset to evaluate the performance of Wiki-Gen. We conducted experiments on topic template induction and topic summary generation, results show that WikiGen outperforms previous work on both fields.

5.1   Dataset

We choose three event categories, *earthquake*, *election* and *tornado*, from English Wikipedia to build our dataset. The data source is XML dump of English Wikipedia from *WikiMedia*. See Table 1 for detailed parameters of our dataset.

Table 1. WikiGen dataset parameters

Category	Earthquake	Election	Tornado
Document number	322	1544	201
Average section number	6.59	3.20	7.55
Average section text length	113.4	25.7	100.6
Maximum section text length	2230	1910	2077
Average candidate excerpt number	193.3	177.5	644.7
Average candidate excerpt length	78.9	78.0	55.1

5.2 Topic Template Induction

We compare our method with Hu's work [7] to evaluate it both quantitatively and qualitatively. To compare more precisely, we don't discard low-frequency topics according to Hu's experiment.

Evaluation Method. We use F1-score to evaluate the performance of different methods. Assume that R is the generated subtopic relation set and R_{gt} is the ground-truth subsection relation set, we can calculate precision with Eq. 10 and recall with Eq. 11, where g_i, g_j are sections and t_k, t_l are topics.

$$precision = \frac{|\{(g_i, g_j)|(g_i \in t_k)\&(g_j \in t_l)\&((t_k, t_l) \in R)\}|}{|\{(g_i, g_j)|(g_i \in t_k)\&(g_j \in t_l)\&(t_k! = t_l)\}|} \tag{10}$$

$$recall = \frac{|\{(g_i, g_j)|(g_i \in t_k)\&(g_j \in t_l)\&((t_k, t_l) \in R)\}|}{|\{(g_i, g_j)|(g_i \in t_k)\&(g_j \in t_l)\}|} \tag{11}$$

$F1 - score = 2 \cdot \frac{precision \cdot recall}{precision + recall}$ acts as the final measurement. In experiment, we set $\sigma_1 = 0.5$, $\lambda_1 = 0.8$, $\sigma_2 = 0.3$, $\lambda_2 = 0.6$.

Quantitative Analysis Results show that our method far outperforms Hu's method, increasing F1-score by over 30%. Meanwhile, our double-pass method achieved better performance on two out of three event categories, and its overall performance is also better. Even in the category "earthquake" where single-pass method gets a better result, our double-pass method can avoid the mistake of putting "Geology" and "Damage" into the same cluster which occurs in single-pass method. These results prove that finding small "cores" first do does help (Table 2).

Table 2. F1-score of topic template induction methods

	Earthquake	Election	Tornado	Overall
Hu	0.434	0.780	0.586	0.586
WikiGen (Single-pass)	**0.854**	0.937	0.949	0.914
WikiGen (Textual correlation only)	0.816	0.727	0.674	0.740
WikiGen (Structural dependency only)	0.844	0.953	0.957	0.918
WikiGen (Full model)	0.844	**0.953**	**0.957**	**0.918**

We note that adding textual correlation does not improve the F1-score obviously, it may happen as a result of the fact that text of different topics after clustering already differ greatly from each other.

Qualitative Analysis. We take the topic tree of category "election" as example (See Fig. 3). There are first-level topics like "Results", "Preliminaries" and "Campaign" under the root topic, followed by more detailed topics, for example

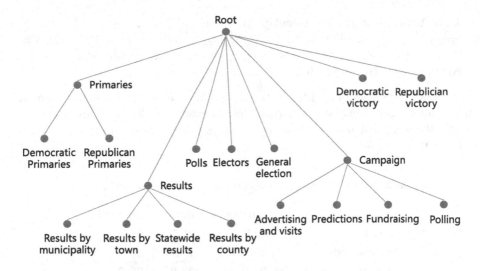

Fig. 3. Topic tree of category "election".

"Democratic Preliminaries" and "Republican Preliminaries" under "Preliminaries". Compared with single-layer topic templates, our result has a hierarchical structure to help readers better learn about different aspects of the whole event. This type of structure also matches the way we recognize events in the real world.

5.3 Topic Summary Generation

There exist three major factors which would greatly affect the result of topic summary generation:

- **Method of Coarse Filtration:** *TF-IDF, text embedding, augmented topic model*;
- **Corpus of Coarse Filtration:** *citation only, search result only, combined*;
- **Corpus of Fine-grained Filtration:** *DeepChannel (from scratch), DeepChannel (pretrained), lead-7, random*.

Evaluation Method. We use the classic ROUGE [9] score to measure our model. Due to the fact that the length of section text varies greatly in our dataset (there exists text longer than 2000 words while the average length is 100), considering only precision (which prefers short text) or recall (which prefers long text) both produce bias. We use the ROUGE-1 F1 score, which combines precision and recall, to evaluate the results.

Method of Coarse Filtration. We use three different methods to calculate the similarity between excerpt e and topic t:

- **TF-IDF:** We combine document title ti_d and topic name t as $q = (ti_d + t)$, then calculate the TF-IDF cosine similarity between e and q as the final result

- **Text Embedding:** We calculate these embedding: v_w of word w, $v_t = \frac{1}{|WK_t|} \sum_{w \in WK_t} v_w$ of topic t, $v_e = \frac{1}{|e|} \sum_{w \in e} v_w$ of excerpt e with GLOVE, then use the cosine similarity between v_t and v_e as the result;
- **Augmented Topic Model:** See Sect. 3.3.1 for $Score(e, t)$.

Table 3 shows results of different methods. We can see that our augmented topic model significantly outperforms other methods by 2–4%. This is due to the specific word distribution under certain topic, like "plate" in topic *Tectonics* and "death" in topic *Damage*.

Table 3. ROUGE-1 F1 scores about Methods of Coarse Filtration

	Earthquake	Election	Tornado
TF-IDF	22.5	21.7	22.9
Text embedding	20.2	18.2	20.3
Augmented topic model	**26.0**	**23.9**	**26.2**

Corpus of Coarse Filtration. The quality of corpus is a key factor to the quality of generated document. We compared the F1-score of coarse filtration under different corpus in Table 4. Meanwhile, given that the result of coarse filtration acts as the input of fine-grained filtration, its recall, which indicates the integrity of results, is also important. See Table 5 for recall results.

Table 4. ROUGE-1 F1-score of different corpus

	Earthquake	Election	Tornado
Citation only	22.7	16.5	19.5
Search result only	**28.2**	**28.1**	**28.7**
Combined	26.0	23.9	26.2

Table 5. ROUGE-1 recall of different corpus

	Earthquake	Election	Tornado
Citation only	48.9	28.9	32.3
Search result only	**63.9**	**62.5**	**48.2**
Combined	62.3	59.6	46.8

Results show that using search results greatly improved the performance compared with using only citations. Two reasons may contribute to this phenomena: first, some cited pages of old events have been outdated and no longer available; second, a percentage of cited pages are written in languages other than English, but search engine can provide us with English results only.

Although only using search results can achieve better scores on both F1-score and recall, we decided to use combined corpus as the model input. The reason is twofold: first, cited sources are chosen by human authors and mainly consists of first-time news and information from authoritative websites, which matches what we except to gather when new event happens; second, some websites in search results copy sentences from Wikipedia articles, making their ROUGE scores higher than normal. To make the experimental environment more close to real scenarios, we didn't discard cited sources.

Corpus of Fine-Grained Filtration. Considering that we have limited training data, we merge all three event categories, and divide all data into training set, verification set and test set by the ratio of 80%/10%/10%. We use four different methods to generate the final document: random, lead-7, DeepChannel from scratch and pretrained DeepChannel. Moreover, we choose sentences with highest ROUGE-1 F1 scores as the theoretically optimal result. See Table 6 for results.

If we merge the result two steps in topic summary generation (See Fig. 4 for results), we can find that WikiGen using pretrained DeepChannel gets the best

Table 6. ROUGE-1 F1 scores about methods of fine-grained filtration

	Precision	Recall	F1
Random	40.5	43.7	36.4
Lead-7	42.1	**46.9**	38.8
WikiGen (from scratch)	45.4	39.4	39.5
WikiGen (pretrained)	**52.3**	39.2	**42.8**
Theoretically optimal	68.1	56.7	59.5

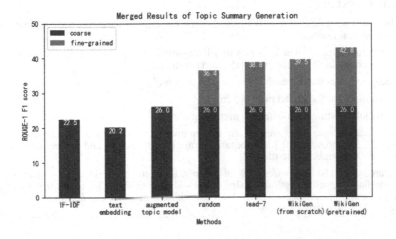

Fig. 4. Merged results

result. Lead-7 gets higher recall scores but its F1 score is far lower than our model, proving that WikiGen is capable of selecting key sentences. Meanwhile, fine-grained filtration can greatly improve the quality of generated documents, which matches the way how human writers write articles – first coarsely select relevant materials then rewrite them, and proves the correctness of our model.

Comparison with Previous Work. It is quite difficult to directly compare our method with previous work for the following reasons: (1) Our method focuses on events rather than general entities, direct comparing with methods orient towards entities would cause bias; (2) No available datasets have been provided by previous work, and it is impossible to rebuild former datasets due to the constantly changing Internet and Wikipedia; (3) No executable model code has been provided by previous work, making it even harder to compare with them. However, we tried our best to conduct some comparision with those works. We choose the "Disease" category in previous work, which has a maximum recall of 59 that resembles our dataset, to compare with the results of our model. Table 7 demonstrates the results. We can see that our model far outperforms previous work on F1 score. There is some lack in recall score, partly because our model tends to choose sentences that relate closely to the topic, which reduces the breadth of coverage.

Table 7. ROUGE-1 scores compared with previous works.

	Precision	Recall	F1
Sauper	36	39	37
WikiSum	25	**48**	29
WikiGen (from scratch)	45.4	39.4	39.5
WikiGen (pretrained)	**52.3**	39.2	**42.8**

Tectonic setting:

- The longmen shan fault system is situated in the eastern border of the tibetan plateau and contains several faults .
- This earthquake ruptured at least two imbricate structures in longmen shan fault system , i.e. the beichuan fault and the guanxian – anxian fault .
- The tectonic plates that hit each other was the indian plate against eurasia .
- The movement for the indian plate is 50mm.
- The two plates hitting each other is a pretty big clue .
- in the epicentral area , the average slip in beichuan fault was about 3.5 metres (11 ft) vertical , 3.5 metres (11 ft) horizontal - parallel to the fault , and 4.8 metres (16 ft) horizontal - perpendicular to the fault .
- In the area about 30 kilometres (19 mi) northeast of the epicenter , the surface slip on beichuan fault was almost purely dextral strike - slip up to about 3 metres (9.8 ft) , while the average slip in guanxian – anxian fault was about 2 metres (6 ft 7 in) vertical and 2.3 metres (7 ft 7 in) horizontal .

Fig. 5. Results of topic "Tectonics"

Case Analysis. To comprehensively judge the effect of our model, we use the title "2008 Sichuan Earthquake" as input to generate a full Wikipedia document with multiple topics. See Fig. 5 for part of the results.

Results show that although the documents we generated is not as fluent as those written by human, our model captured the most important information under different topics, for example the number of people injured in *Damage* and the Longmenshan Fault in *Tectonics*. The results have great value in the form of both first-time summary and reference for human writing.

6   Conclusion

In this paper, we propose a new model named WikiGen to automatically generate Wikipedia documents for new events. This model will induce a multi-layer topic tree for each event category and generate a summary from gathered news for each topic. For topic tree generation, we use a double-pass incremental clustering algorithm to convert this step into finding a maximum spanning tree in a directed graph. For topic summary generation, we imitate the way human write articles, designing a two-step procedure to generate the full document: first coarsely filter useful information with an augmented topic model, then generate a reasonable summary with the DeepChannel model pretrained on CNN/Dailymail dataset.

Our method outperforms comparable methods on both topic tree generation and topic summary generation. Results show that our model is capable of generating comprehensive and detailed Wikipedia documents, and can be easily expanded to other fields. Our model also shows high data efficiency, being able to produce high-quality result with litter training data. In the future, we will try to rearrange selected sentences to acquire more fluent documents.

Acknowledgement. The work is supported by NSFC key projects (U1736204, 61533018, 61661146007), research fund from State Grid Zhejiang Electric Power Research Institute and THUNUS NExT Co-Lab.

References

1. Allan, J., Carbonell, J., Doddington, G., Yamron, J., Yang, Y.: Topic detection and tracking pilot study final report. In: Proceedings of the Darpa Broadcast News Transcription & Understanding Workshop (1998)
2. Aula, A.: Query formulation in web information search. In: ICWI (2003)
3. Banerjee, S., Mitra, P.: WikiWrite: generating Wikipedia articles automatically. In: IJCAI (2016)
4. Chu, Y.J., Liu, T.H.: On shortest arborescence of a directed graph. Sci. Sinica **14**(10), 1396 (1965)
5. Edmonds, J.: Optimum branchings. J. Res. Nat. Bureau Standard B **71**(4), 233–240 (1967)
6. Hammouda, K.M., Kamel, M.S.: Incremental document clustering using cluster similarity histograms. In: Proceedings of the IEEE/WIC International Conference on Web Intelligence (WI 2003). IEEE (2003)

7. Hu, L., et al.: Learning topic hierarchies for Wikipedia categories. In: ACL (2015)
8. Lebret, R., Grangier, D., Auli, M.: Neural text generation from structured data with application to the biography domain. In: EMNLP (2016)
9. Lin, C.Y.: Rouge: a package for automatic evaluation of summaries. In: ACL (2004)
10. Liu, P.J., et al.: Generating Wikipedia by summarizing long sequences. arXiv preprint arXiv:1801.10198 (2018)
11. Nallapati, R., Zhai, F., Zhou, B.: SummaRuNNer: a recurrent neural network based sequence model for extractive summarization of documents. In: AAAI (2017)
12. Sauper, C., Barzilay, R.: Automatically generating Wikipedia articles: a structure-aware approach. In: ACL (2009)
13. See, A., Liu, P.J., Manning, C.D.: Get to the point: summarization with pointer-generator networks. In: ACL (2017)
14. Shi, J., Liang, C., Hou, L., Li, J., Liu, Z., Zhang, H.: DeepChannel: salience estimation by contrastive learning for extractive document summarization. In: AAAI (2019)
15. Vaswani, A., et al.: Attention is all you need. In: NIPS (2017)

A Linked Data Model-View-* Approach for Decoupled Client-Server Applications

Torsten Spieldenner$^{(\boxtimes)}$ and René Schubotz

Saarbrücken Graduate School of Computer Science, German Research Center
for Artifical Intelligence (DFKI), 66123 Saarbrücken, Germany
{torsten.spieldenner,rene.schubotz}@dfki.de

Abstract. *Separation of concern* is found to be a crucial design requirement for maintainable, extendable and understandable software. Research has been done on software design patterns that ensure strict separation of concerns and by this avoid cross cutting concerns in modules of large-scale software projects. In particular, *Model-View-** design patterns attempt to decouple local data and business logic from user interfaces, keeping both extendable and exchangeable. Targeting Web-applications, technologies from the domain of Linked Data and Semantic Web have been found suitable to decouple clients from servers. While the potential of both Model-View-Patterns and Linked Data interfaces is often convincingly outlined, there exists to this point little to no work that shows how the findings in said fields can be successfully employed to design large-scale decoupled client-server Web applications. In this paper, we show how lifting a suitable data representation of a Web server application run-time to Linked Data allows to build client-server applications following a decoupled Model-View-Presenter-ViewModel design pattern. This removes the need for fixed server-side APIs, detaches clients from server specifics, and allows clients to implement their business logic entirely on expected semantics of the server data.

Keywords: Linked Data · Semantic Web · Web of Things · Model-View-Presenter · View model · Software design

1 Introduction

Separation of concern, the separation of parts of programs with distinct purpose in both architecture and code, is found to be a crucial design requirement for maintainable, extendable and understandable software [1–5].

For a clean separation within runtime applications, the paradigm of Aspect oriented Programming [2] motivates to decouple application modules to avoid *cross-cutting concerns*, in particular *code tangling* (logic of a module directly depends on code implemented in other modules), and *code scattering* (code that implements a certain aspect of an application is distributed over several modules).

© Springer Nature Switzerland AG 2020
X. Wang et al. (Eds.): JIST 2019, LNCS 12032, pp. 67–81, 2020.
https://doi.org/10.1007/978-3-030-41407-8_5

In this respect, *Model-View (MV*)* design patterns separate application data from user interfaces and user interaction [1,3,6,7]. The respective findings were also transferred to the development of Web applications [8].

However, separation of concern on architecture level is a not strong enough requirement for Web applications. In fact, introducing the Web layer for client-server communication bears the danger of introducing undesired close couplings between server and client applications.

This problem becomes obvious in architectures that employ current middleware solutions like Apache Thrift[1] [9] or Google Protobuf[2]. These were designed to make client-server communication easier and more straight-forward. However, they model interaction as Remote-Procedure-Call [10] or similar message-based interaction methods. Respective message formats, RPC APIs, as well as datatypes used for communication are described in domain specific Interface Definition Languages (IDL). The respective descriptions are obviously closely coupled to the server data model, and in turn, clients are closely coupled to a specific interface definition as offered by the server. How crucial a well defined and consistently maintained IDL is, is after all also prominently emphasized in the Protobuf specification, taking as example that *"(the keyword) 'Required' is forever"*[3].

A proposed remedy to decouple clients from servers on network level comes from the world of the Semantic Web [11]. Among others, Verborgh [12] and Mayer [13] emphasize the importance of a sufficiently semantically described server API, such that client applications may learn about provided data and means of interaction without previous knowledge of the server's interfaces. Meeting these requirements can be ensured by fulfilling Fielding's Hypermedia Constraints [14] on server-data, respectively ensure Level 3 Richardson Maturity on server data and interfaces [15].

In this paper, we present a client-server Web architecture that achieves complete separation of concerns by the following steps:

1. Based on a suitable *ViewModel*, we provide a machine-processable and understandable Semantic Web (Linked Data) representation as *View* on the server data.
2. Clients build a local *Data Access Layer* to the server data from the semantic information provided by the *View*. The Linked Data representation of the server data enables this step to be done without any previous knowledge about specific server data and interfaces on client-side.
3. We connect server and client in a *Model-View-Presenter-View-Model* pattern[4].

As result, clients are completely decoupled from any server data model and interfaces, but implement their local logic based entirely on expected server-side data semantics.

---

[1] https://thrift.apache.org/.
[2] https://developers.google.com/protocol-buffers/9.
[3] https://developers.google.com/protocol-buffers/docs/proto.
[4] https://msdn.microsoft.com/en-us/en-en/magazine/hh580734.aspx.

Having presented a lifting of a suitable runtime data model to a Linked Data integration layer before in [5], the work in this paper shows how actual software design profits from the so gained concise, machine-readable Linked Data integration layer.

The remainder of the paper is structured as followed: We provide an overview over relevant related work and background on employed technologies in Sects. 2 and 3. Section 4 describes the generation of the server-side Linked Data API. Interaction with the API on client-side is described in Sect. 5. We analyze the resulting architecture w.r.t the MVPVM pattern, and resulting decoupling of application modules, in Sect. 6. We close with Conclusion and a brief outlook on Future Work in Sect. 7.

2   Related Work

Enriching Web services an applications with Linked Data APIs and lifting them to a Linked Data architecture [16] has faced much attention in research in recent years.

Especially in the domain of Internet of Things (IoT), work has been carried out to find suitable expressive Linked Data representations of devices and interfaces [13,17,18], up to using the W3C recommendation of the Linked Data Platform[5] as integration layer for heterogeneous IoT devices [19] with the goal to overcome a lack of sufficiently described Web APIs [20,21]. Also for existing Enterprise applications, the Linked Data Platform has been found to be a suitable integration layer [22].

An often considered case for Linked Data application development is the simplification of creating User Interfaces (UI) for existing datasets. The Information Workbench by Haase et al. [23] supports widget-based Linked Data application development, mainly for data integration, providing users with a rich UI that can be customized by an SDK. LD-R by Khalili et al. [24,25] are Linked Data driven Web components[6] for quick bootstrapping of Linked Data based Web UIs, along with an approach to map SPARQL queries to interactive UI components [26]. LD Viewer by Lukovnikov et al. [27] is a framework, based on the DBPedia viewer, for customizable Linked Data UI presentations.

When it comes to connecting clients to servers, research has been evolving around simpler and more versatile usage of the SPARQL query language[7]. This includes work to wrap stored SPARQL queries into HTTP Web APIs in *BASIL* by Daga et al. [28], and vice versa, JSON-based Web APIs into SPARQL queryable endpoints, as for example in *SPARQL Micro Services* by Michel et al. [29,30].

Fafalios et al. present *SPARQL-LD* [31,32], which generalizes the semantics of the SPARQL1.1 SERVICE keyword to dynamically fetch RDF datasets from Web resources, also during evaluation of the query. Vogelgesang et al. present

---

[5] https://www.w3.org/TR/ldp/.

[6] https://developer.mozilla.org/en-US/docs/Web/Web_Components.

[7] https://www.w3.org/TR/sparql11-overview/.

$SPARQ\lambda$ [33], which modifies parts of the query semantics of the SPARQL GRAPH keyword to dynamically specify target datasets during query execution, and by this use pre-stored SPARQL queries as lambda function like micro-services.

While existing work mostly considers static datasets, as for example legacy databases [34] or existing RDF datasets [24,25,27], we explicitly provide an approach that uses a Linked Data Platform representation of *run-time application data* as API towards Web clients. Unlike existing approaches that focus on UI development as View on the Linked Data representations [23–27], our approach targets general Web application development and does not limit client business logic to UI rendering and interaction. The semantically enriched Linked Data representation on server-side of our approach highly supports SPARQL-based client queries, and by this profits from findings in respective research [31–33]. The respective architecture is not tied towards a specific framework, but we provide a thorough analysis how any client-server based application benefits from the advantages of the Linked Data Platform by implementing a Model-View-based design pattern.

3   Preliminaries

The proposed architecture in this paper is based mainly on three core technologies resp. design choices: We build the architecture around a *Model-View-** like design pattern, precisely, a *Model-View-Presenter-ViewModel* pattern[8]. We employ an *Entity-Component-Attribute* data model [5,35] as *ViewModel* on server-side, and base the server-side *View* on the server data on the W3C *Linked Data Platform* recommendation (see Footnote 5). In the following, we outline the core concepts as to be understood for the remainder of the paper.

3.1   Model-View-* Patterns

Model-View-* patterns, a class of software design patterns introduced in the 1980's with the *Model-View-Controller* pattern [6], aim at improving the development of User Interfaces (UI) on application data. The pattern decouples a suitable representation of application data (*Model*) from the respective User Interface (*View*), introducing the role of a *Controller* to build the UI, and adapt both Model and View based on user input. The pattern was extended continuously to achieve a more flexible decoupling of application modules, resulting in patterns of *Model-View-Presenter* [1], *Model-View-ViewModel* [7], and finally, the *Model-View-Presenter-ViewModel* pattern (see Footnote 8) (see also Fig. 1). The latter employs a *ViewModel* as optimized representation of the application's underlying domain objects for the presenter to render the *View*. The *Business Logic* requests data within the *ViewModel* from the *Presenter*, using the *Data Access Layer* to transparently retrieve data from persistence spaces. *View* and *ViewModel* are kept consistent using suitable data bindings between both representations.

---

[8] https://msdn.microsoft.com/en-us/magazine/hh580734.aspx.

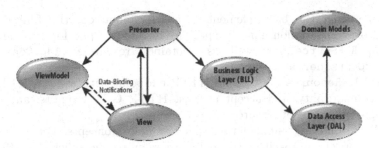

Fig. 1. The Model-View-Presenter-ViewModel pattern as by Bill Kratochvil (see Foot-note 8). Diagram source: (see Footnote 8)

3.2   Entity-Component-Attribute Data Model

The Entity-Component-Attribute data model has been found a suitable choice for loosely coupled extendable server implementations in various systems [4, 35–38].

Its strength lies in the concept of *inheritance by composition*: specialization of run-time objects is not determined by classic inheritance as in object oriented programming languages. Rather, various aspects of a run-time object are modeled in independent *Components* that can be dynamically attached to and detached from run-time objects, *Entities*, also during application run-time.

We employ the Entity-Component-Attribute model as understood and formalized by Spieldenner et al. [5]. They define concepts of Entities, Components, and Attributes as follows:

$\mathbf{E} = \{(n_\mathbf{e}, \mathbf{C_e}) \parallel n_\mathbf{e} \in \Sigma^+\}$ set of Entity instances $\mathbf{e} = (n_\mathbf{e}, \mathbf{C_e})$, n_e the unique identifier for $\mathbf{e}$ over alphabet Σ, and $\mathbf{C_e}$ the set of component instances attached to $\mathbf{e}$.

$\mathbf{C_e} = \{(n_\mathbf{c}, p_\mathbf{c}, \mathbf{A_{c,e}}) \mid n_\mathbf{c} \in \Sigma^+, p_\mathbf{c} \in \mathcal{P_C}\})$ the set of all Component instances $\mathbf{c} = (n_\mathbf{c}, p_\mathbf{c}, \mathbf{A_{c,e}})$ attached to an entity instance $\mathbf{e}$, $n_\mathbf{c}$ the unique identifier for $\mathbf{c}$, $\mathcal{P_C}$ set of Component prototypes, $p_\mathbf{c}$ the prototype that $\mathbf{c}$ is an instance of, and $\mathbf{A_{c,e}}$ the set of all attribute instances attached to $\mathbf{c}$.

$\mathbf{A_{c,e}}$ the set of all Attribute instances $\mathbf{a} = (n_\mathbf{a}, v, t)$ attached to a Component instance $\mathbf{c}$, with $n_\mathbf{a} \in \Sigma^+$ unique identifier for $\mathbf{a}$, v the Attribute instance's current *value*, and t the runtime type of $\mathbf{a}$.

For more details on the aforementioned concepts, we refer to the original paper [5].

3.3   Linked Data Platform

The W3C *Linked Data Platform* recommendation (see Footnote 5) provides best practices for read-write Linked Data applications on the Web, based on a minimal model in terms RDF[9] resources. Moreover access patterns to these different resources are specified for Linked Data clients.

---

[9] https://www.w3.org/TR/rdf-concepts/.

Deriving from the basic element of a `ldp:Resource`, the Linked Data Platform recommendation further specifies resource types for general RDF data (`ldp:RDFSource`), as well as container resources (`ldp:Container`, `ldp:BasicContainer`, and others).

Every `ldp:Resource` must be an HTTP endpoint with at least HTTP/1.1 protocol compatibility, and accept at least HTTP GET requests, and others depending on the type of resource.

The W3C LDP recommendation specifies more concepts. For a complete documentation of all specified concepts, we refer to the official specification document.

3.4 Richardson Maturity Model

The Richardson Maturity Model [15] sets requirements to Web applications towards their maturity as suitable hypermedia endpoints. For applications to fulfill the principle of "Hypermedia As The Engine Of Application State" (HATEOAS) [39], they need to reach in particular Level 3 of Richardson Maturity Model (3-RMM).

In short, a 3-RMM compliant application provides its data as Web Resources, unambiguously identified by resolvable URIs, over which the application state is read and changed using HTTP operations GET, PUT, POST, DELETE. Clients can follow links from resources to others to explore data self-driven. Using HTTP operations HEAD or OPTIONS, clients can learn all necessary information about the state of the resource, and the provided methods to interact with it.

3-RMM compliance is considered a crucial requirement for the design of decoupled Linked Data applications [12].

4 Server-Side Linked Data Generation

We base our server-implementation on an Entity-Component-Attribute (ECA) based model (cf. Sect. 3.2). The choice of an Entity based model is justified, as it is not only applied widely for example in large scale IoT applications [4,37] where it was shown to be a suitable choice for maintainable and extendable software architectures [4,5]. It is moreover basis for data models in the major 3D game engines, as for example Unreal Engine[10] or Unity 3D[11]. The findings in this paper are thus transferable to a wide range of nowadays' applications, and not limited to very specific, hand tailored use-cases.

By employing the methods described in this section, we achieve the following:

The entity hierarchy structure of the application runtime is indexed by Web resources from top (collection of objects maintained by application) to bottom (single attribute values that contain actual runtime data). The resulting structure is compliant to the W3C Linked Data Platform specification.

---

[10] https://www.unrealengine.com/.
[11] https://www.unity.com/.

With relations between all types of resources explicitly modeled in terms of Linked Data Platform terms, clients can infer additional relations based on application domain specific semantics.

Thus, clients are able to identify sub-graphs of the entire application graph, as well as subscription endpoints for runtime data, by overlaying their own, domain-semantic influenced view on the structural representation of the server data.

In the following, we outline how we achieve to lift the ECA based server application to a Linked Data representation. By ensuring Level 3 Richardson Maturity Model compliance, we ensure moreover that data can be autonomously explored and interpreted by clients.

A detailed discussion of how the chosen architecture supports our claim of a separation of concern between server data, server API, and client applications, will follow in Sect. 6.

4.1 Linked Data Representation of Runtime Data

We are referring to [5] as foundation for the mapping from ECA model based application runtimes to a Linked Data representation. In brief, we perform the following steps to describe the concepts of Entities, Components, and Attributes in terms of Linked Data Platform containers and resources:

We follow the formalization of the ECA model as defined in [5] and summarized in Sect. 3.2. Based on this definition, we generate for each Entity ①, Component ②, and Attribute ③, the following respective sets of RDF triples:

We employ functions $\nu : \Sigma^+ \rightarrow$ IRI and $\rho : \mathcal{P}_\mathbf{C} \rightarrow$ IRI as minting functions for fresh IRIs, following the approach of ECA2LD by Spieldenner et al. [5].

$$\frac{(n_\mathbf{e}, \mathbf{C_e}) \in \mathbf{E} \quad \forall (n_\mathbf{c}, p_\mathbf{c}, \mathbf{A_{c,e}}) \in \mathbf{C_e}}{}$$

①
$\nu(n_\mathbf{e})$ rdf:type ldp:BasicContainer .
$\nu(n_\mathbf{e})$ dct:identifier "$n_\mathbf{e}$"^^xsd:String .
$\nu(n_\mathbf{e})$ ldp:hasMemberRelation dct:hasPart .
$\nu(n_\mathbf{e})$ dct:hasPart $\nu(n_\mathbf{c})$.

$$\frac{(n_\mathbf{c}, p_\mathbf{c}, \mathbf{A_{c,e}}) \in \mathbf{C_e} \quad \forall (n_\mathbf{a}, v, t) \in \mathbf{A_{c,e}}}{}$$

②
$\nu(n_\mathbf{c})$ rdf:type ldp:BasicContainer .
$\nu(n_\mathbf{c})$ dct:identifier "$n_\mathbf{c}$"^^xsd:String .
$\nu(n_\mathbf{c})$ dct:isPartOf $\nu(n_\mathbf{e})$.
$\nu(n_\mathbf{c})$ ldp:hasMemberRelation dct:hasPart .
$\nu(n_\mathbf{c})$ dct:hasPart $\nu(n_\mathbf{a})$.
$\nu(n_\mathbf{c})$ rdfs:isDefinedBy $\rho(p_\mathbf{c})$.

$$\frac{(n_\mathbf{a}, v, t) \in \mathbf{A_{c,e}}}{}$$

③
$\nu(n_\mathbf{a})$ rdf:type ldp:RDFResource .
$\nu(n_\mathbf{a})$ dct:identifier "$n_\mathbf{a}$"^^xsd:String .
$\nu(n_\mathbf{a})$ dct:isPartOf $\nu(n_\mathbf{c})$.
$\nu(n_\mathbf{a})$ rdf:value $\nu(n_a^v)$.

We changed the way how ECA2LD renders Attribute values directly as suitable RDF representation in step ③. We instead provide Attribute values as separate resource with resolvable URI $\nu(n_a^v)$. This allows the server to specify further interaction methods on Attribute values, as described in Sects. 4.2 and 4.3.

We moreover extend above representations by generating triple sets to describe collections of Entities. We for this assume an entity collection $\mathbf{E}$ to be assigned a unique name $n_{\mathbf{E}}$.

$$④ \quad \frac{\forall(n_{\mathbf{e}}, \mathbf{C_e}) \in \mathbf{E}}{\begin{array}{l}\nu(n_{\mathbf{E}}) \ \texttt{rdf:type ldp:BasicContainer} \ . \\ \nu(n_{\mathbf{E}}) \ \texttt{ldp:contains} \ \nu(n_{\mathbf{n_e}}) \ .\end{array}}$$

The respective Entity collection resource then serves as entry point for client applications to explore the server data.

The resulting RDF modeled Linked Data Platform representation allows to further augment the resources with domain semantic information. For this, the RDF description of the data structure serves as input for RDF mapping vocabularies like SPIN SPARQL[12], RIF in RDF[13], the LDIF framework[14] or the R2R framework[15]. For a detailed explanation of domain semantic augmentation, we refer to the original paper [5]. In the context of our approach, additional domain semantic information on top of the structural description allows clients to identify relevant resources based on domain semantic information.

4.2   RESTful Operations on Runtime Data:

Each of the resources generated according to the rules in the previous section provide an HTTP REST compliant endpoint that is maintained within the ECA2LD library. The route to the resource is determined by the minting functions $\nu : \Sigma^+ \to$ IRI and $\rho : \mathcal{P}_{\mathbf{C}} \to$ IRI.

HTTP operations GET, POST, PUT, DELETE allow to retrieve, (re)place, amend, or delete the triple sets as produced by ①–④ respectively, and also to read and update Attribute values on the respective Attribute value endpoints. Information about further interaction possibilities with the resource can be obtained by using the HTTP OPTIONS operation.

Respective functionality is already implemented in the ECA2LD library on Entity, Component, and Attribute level. We extended the implementation to support respective operations on Entity Collection and Attribute value level.

4.3   Realtime Subscription Pub/Sub:

The mapped structure from steps ①–④ remains mostly static during execution of an application. Realtime run-time runtime data is aggregated in Attribute

---

[12] https://www.w3.org/Submission/2011/SUBM-spin-sparql-20110222/.
[13] https://www.w3.org/TR/rif-in-rdf/.
[14] http://ldif.wbsg.de/.
[15] http://wifo5-03.informatik.uni-mannheim.de/bizer/r2r/.

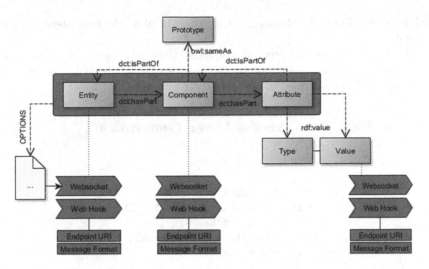

Fig. 2. Web resources and respective endpoints that are generated for each of the elements of the runtime application.

resources as provided by ③, and can be retrieved using the respective resource indicated by the Attribute's `rdf:value`.

We extend the modes of interaction beyond the HTTP operations as described in Sect. 4.2 by providing as part of the returned RDF datagram a description of provided real-time subscription endpoints according to the following rule:

$$\forall \text{Attribute Values } v_a, \texttt{Protocol p}$$

⑤ $$\frac{\nu(n_v^a) \; \texttt{sub:endpoint} \; \sigma_s(v_a) \, .}{\sigma_s(v_a) \; \texttt{sub:protocol} \; p.}$$
$$\sigma_s(v_a) \; \texttt{rdf:format} \; f.$$

⑤: For each `AttributeValue` v_a of `Attribute` a, a resource with resolvable URI $\nu(n_v^a)$ is created that contains a forward link to a resolvable resource $\sigma_s(v_a)$. The predicate `sub:endpoint` describes the resource with URI $\sigma_s(v_a)$ as endpoint for clients to open a subscription channel with protocol **p**, p a suitable RDF predicate to refer to **p**, for realtime updates of attribute value v_a of attribute a. `rdf:format` points to a description f of the message serialization format emitted by subscription resource $\sigma_s(v_a)$. Defining suitable representations f of the message format beyond xsd compatible atomic types is subject to future work.

We extended the ECA2LD library such that the respective subscription endpoint is wired to the respective Attribute value in the ECA model by an observer pattern. In our specific implementation, we use the Event mechanisms in C#[16]. By this, subscribing to a subscription resource $\sigma_s(v_a)$ by its URI as offered by

---

[16] https://docs.microsoft.com/en-us/dotnet/standard/events/.

the RDF description in ⑤, clients can keep their local model consistent with the server data.

Figure 2 shows the set of created resources, their relation to each other, and examples of further interaction methods that can be retrieved by clients after performing the steps outlined in Sects. 4.1, 4.2 and 4.3.

5   Client-Side Data Access Layer Generation

```
SELECT ?value WHERE {
   ?entity dct:identifier [$entityID] ,
      dct:hasPart/dct:hasPart [
         dct:identifier [$fieldName],
         rdf:value ?value
      ] .
}
```

Fig. 3. Example of a parameterized SPARQL query for clients to retrieve routes to HTTP resources based on field names.

We aim to keep the *Business Logic* of the client independent of the server's data model, and will for this use the Linked Data *View* onto the server data from Sect. 4 to build a *Data Access Layer* between client business logic and server data.

Based on both structural and domain semantic information provided on each of the HTTP resources on server-side, clients identify relevant resources that provide access to specific pieces of data. For this, clients may either explore the server-data autonomously by following links between the resources, or by performing queries against a RDF query processor provided by the server. Figure 3 shows a respective (parameterized) SPARQL query to retrieve `Attribute Value` endpoints based on field names used for components. The parameters `[$entityID]` and `[$fieldName]` may be resolved and set by the client business logic before performing the query.

The returned result of such queries (or of the autonomous exploration) is a set of URIs that point to Linked Data resources. Once the relevant Linked Data resources are identified, clients retrieve relevant modes of interaction directly on these URIs via `HTTP OPTIONS` requests (cf. Sects. 4.2 and 4.3). Requests to these URIs are handled by the ECA2LD *Presenter* on server-side, applied to the *ViewModel*, and ultimatively on the local server-side domain models.

The so generated Data Access Layer reduces interaction between client and server to basic HTTP request dispatch and handling. All relevant information for client-server interaction is gathered by clients dynamically from information provided by the server during run-time. By this, clients do not require previous knowledge about server data or APIs or build the Data Access Layer.

6 Discussion

In the following we discuss how the proposed architecture provides a valid implementation of the Model-View-Presenter-ViewModel pattern (Sect. 6.1), and show 3-RMM compliance of the data-centric server interface (Sect. 6.2).

6.1 MVPVM Pattern in Resulting Architecture

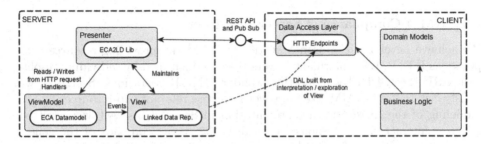

Fig. 4. The manifestation of the MVPVM pattern in our proposed client-server architecture.

In this section, we show that by the design choices presented in Sects. 4 and 5, we implement a Model-View-Presenter-ViewModel pattern as shown in Fig. 4. For this, we first discuss the realization of *ViewModel*, *View*, and *Presenter* on server-side. Following, we discuss realization of *Data Access Layer*, and how *Business Logic* accesses it, on client-side.

Presenter: The ECA2LD Library. ECA2LD creates the Linked Data Platform resources along with a respective RDF graph that describes the resources on every level of the ECA model. The *Presenter* handles HTTP requests and provides subscription channels. Via those, it adapts data in the *ViewModel* and the *View* accordingly.

ViewModel: The domain objects modeled in terms of Entities, Components, and Attributes. The *ViewModel* provides an intermediate layer between the native data *Model* of the server, and any attached *View*.

View: The RDF Graph describing the Linked Data Platform resources, relations between them, and modes of interaction as created by ECA2LD. Changes in the *(View)Model* are reflected in the *View* by the Event system implemented in ECA2LD.

Data Access Layer: Wrapper around HTTP and subscription endpoints as provided by steps in Sects. 4.2 and 4.3. The client builds the Data Access Layer dynamically by exploring the server-side Linked Data *View* on the data according to Sect. 5.

Business Logic: Implemented on Client-side in client-domain specific implementations. The *Business Logic* uses the *Data Access Layer* to connect to the respective endpoints on server side, and by this, ultimately, to the server-side *View-Model*.

The client keeps its local data consistent to the server-data by using the Data Access Layer to either poll via HTTP or listen to incoming messages on the subscription channels. By the chosen Architecture, the client-side business logic is thus completely decoupled from any domain model specifics on server side.

6.2 RMM-Compliance of Server Interfaces

We achieve Level 1 Richardson Maturity (1-RMM) by providing resource endpoints as HTTP/1.1 conformant servers that are identified by individual resolvable URIs (Sect. 4.1). By supporting standard HTTP operations (Sect. 4.2), we satisfy criteria for 2-RMM. We moreover advertise relevant sub-resources by the modeling of the Linked Data representation in Sect. 4.1, as well as permitted resource interactions as response to an OPTIONS request on each of the generated resources (Sect. 4.3). By this, we in the whole establish 3-RMM maturity level.

Consequently, the Linked Data representation on server-side allows clients to interpret the data without previous knowledge, thus building the local Data Access Layer without the need of initial knowledge about the server's data structures. This decouples client and server on the network layer.

In conclusion, with conformance to the MVPVM pattern as discussed in Sect. 6.1, and 3-RMM maturity level as discussed in Sect. 6.2, we have achieved:

– **Decoupling of server and client on architecture level** by implementing the client-server application following a *Model-View-Presenter-ViewModel* approach
– **Decoupling of server and clients on network layer** by a self-describing Linked Data server API with Level 3 Richardson Maturity Model compliance
– Consequently, clients build a local *Data Access Layer* based on expected server-side data semantics and **decouple client Business Logic from the server domain model**.

7 Conclusion and Future Work

In this paper, we presented how by lifting a server-application to a Linked Data representation, client-server interaction can be realized with a Model-View-Presenter-ViewModel (MVPVM) pattern. This results in a complete separation of concern between server run-time and data model, server network API, and client and server, allowing for scalable, maintainable and extendable Web applications.

While separation of concern on architecture level has always been the purpose of Model-View patterns, lifting the pattern to Linked Data finally allows to abstract from local domain models, and build the pattern around an explorable and understandable data and interface representation. By this, we brought the often proclaimed benefit of Linked Data interfaces to actual application in a widely applied design pattern.

We considered the automatically generated Linked Data representation of server run-time data as *View* on the server data for client applications, the respective mapping routine as *Presenter*, and links to the respective data resources from client to server as *Data Access Layer* on client-side. The Data Access Layer can be build by clients autonomously by exploiting knowledge derived from the provided Linked Data representation in the *View*. The resulting architecture removes the need for fixed server-side API, and instead provides direct access to server-data via HTTP and publish-subscribe mechanisms.

The current architecture does not yet consider secure communication between client and server. We plan to extend the capabilities of extendable subscription channels by secured and encrypted communication protocols. The current implementation does so far only support XSD compliant datatypes for Attribute values. We are working on proper semantic description of complex structured data and binary IoT device streams as serialization/de-serialization instructions for client on Attribute value endpoints.

Acknowledgements. The work described in this paper has been partially funded by the German Federal Ministry of Education and Research (BMBF) through the project Hybr-iT under the grant 01IS16026A, and by the German Federal Ministry for Economic Affairs and Energy (BMWi) through the project SENSE under the grant 01MT18007A.

References

1. Bower, A., McGlashan, B.: Twisting the triad. Tutorial Paper for European Smalltalk User Group (ESUP) (2000)
2. Kiczales, G., et al.: Aspect-oriented programming. In: Akşit, M., Matsuoka, S. (eds.) ECOOP 1997. LNCS, vol. 1241, pp. 220–242. Springer, Heidelberg (1997). https://doi.org/10.1007/BFb0053381
3. Syromiatnikov, A., Weyns, D.: A journey through the land of model-view-design patterns. In: 2014 IEEE/IFIP Conference on Software Architecture, pp. 21–30. IEEE (2014)
4. Spieldenner, T., Byelozyorov, S., Guldner, M., Slusallek, P.: FiVES: an aspect-oriented approach for shared virtual environments in the web. Vis. Comput. **34**(9), 1269–1282 (2018)
5. Spieldenner, T., Schubotz, R., Guldner, M.: ECA2LD: from entity-component-attribute runtimes to linked data applications. In: Proceedings of the International Workshop on Semantic Web of Things for Industry 4.0. Extended Semantic Web Conference (ESWC 2018), International Workshop on Semantic Web of Things for Industry 4.0, Located at 15th ESWC Conference, Heraklion, Crete, Greece, 3–7 June 2018. Springer (2018)
6. Krasner, G.E., Pope, S.T., et al.: A description of the model-view-controller user interface paradigm in the smalltalk-80 system. J. Object Oriented Program. **1**(3), 26–49 (1988)

7. Sorensen, E., Mikailesc, M.: Model-view-viewmodel (MVVM) design pattern using windows presentation foundation (WPF) technology. MegaByte J. **9**(4), 1–19 (2010)
8. Leff, A., Rayfield, J.T.: Web-application development using the model/ view/controller design pattern. In: Proceedings Fifth IEEE International Enterprise Distributed Object Computing Conference, pp. 118–127. IEEE (2001)
9. Slee, M., Agarwal, A., Kwiatkowski, M.: Thrift: scalable cross-language services implementation. Facebook White Paper, vol. 5, no. 8 (2007)
10. Birrell, A.D., Nelson, B.J.: Implementing remote procedure calls. ACM Trans. Comput. Syst. (TOCS) **2**(1), 39–59 (1984)
11. Berners-Lee, T., Hendler, J., Lassila, O., et al.: The semantic web. Sci. Am. **284**(5), 28–37 (2001)
12. Verborgh, R., Steiner, T., Van Deursen, D., Van de Walle, R., Vallés, J.G.: Efficient runtime service discovery and consumption with hyperlinked RESTdesc. In: 2011 7th International Conference on Next Generation Web Services Practices, pp. 373–379. IEEE (2011)
13. Mayer, S., Verborgh, R., Kovatsch, M., Mattern, F.: Smart configuration of smart environments. IEEE Trans. Autom. Sci. Eng. **13**(3), 1247–1255 (2016)
14. Fielding, R.T., Taylor, R.N.: Principled design of the modern web architecture. ACM Trans. Internet Technol. (TOIT) **2**(2), 115–150 (2002)
15. Fowler, M.: Richardson Maturity Model: steps toward the glory of REST (2010). http://martinfowler.com/articles/richardsonMaturityModel.html
16. Heath, T., Bizer, C.: Linked data: evolving the web into a global data space. Synth. Lect. Semant. Web Theory Technol. **1**(1), 1–136 (2011)
17. Keppmann, F.L., Maleshkova, M.: Smart components for enabling intelligent web of things applications. In: INTELLI 2016, p. 128 (2016)
18. Schubotz, R., Vogelgesang, C., Antakli, A., Rubinstein, D., Spieldenner, T.: Requirements and specifications for robots, linked data and all the REST. In: Proceedings of Workshop on Linked Data in Robotics and Industry 4.0. Workshop on Linked Data in Robotics and Industry 4.0 (LIDARI-2017), 2nd Workshop on Linked Data in Robotics and Industry 4.0, Located at Semantics 2017, Amsterdam, Netherlands. CEUR (2017)
19. Bader, S.R., Maleshkova, M.: Virtual representations for an iterative IoT deployment. In: Companion of the The Web Conference 2018, pp. 1887–1892. International World Wide Web Conferences Steering Committee (2018)
20. Maleshkova, M., Pedrinaci, C., Domingue, J.: Investigating web APIs on the world wide web. In: 2010 Eighth IEEE European Conference on Web Services, pp. 107–114. IEEE (2010)
21. Bülthoff, F., Maleshkova, M.: RESTful or RESTless – current state of today's top web APIs. In: Presutti, V., Blomqvist, E., Troncy, R., Sack, H., Papadakis, I., Tordai, A. (eds.) ESWC 2014. LNCS, vol. 8798, pp. 64–74. Springer, Cham (2014). https://doi.org/10.1007/978-3-319-11955-7_6
22. Mihindukulasooriya, N., García-Castro, R., Esteban-Gutiérrez, M.: Linked data platform as a novel approach for enterprise application integration. In: COLD (2013)
23. Haase, P., Hütter, C., Schmidt, M., Schwarte, A.: The information workbench as a self-service platform for developing linked data applications. In: WWW 2012 Developer Track, pp. 18–20 (2012)

24. Khalili, A., Loizou, A., van Harmelen, F.: Adaptive linked data-driven web components: building flexible and reusable semantic web interfaces. In: Sack, H., Blomqvist, E., d'Aquin, M., Ghidini, C., Ponzetto, S.P., Lange, C. (eds.) ESWC 2016. LNCS, vol. 9678, pp. 677–692. Springer, Cham (2016). https://doi.org/10.1007/978-3-319-34129-3_41
25. Khalili, A., de Graaf, K.A.: Linked data reactor: towards data-aware user interfaces. In: Proceedings of the 13th International Conference on Semantic Systems, pp. 168–172. ACM (2017)
26. Khalili, A., Merono-Penuela, A.: WYSIWYQ - what you see is what you query. In: VOILA@ ISWC, pp. 123–130 (2017)
27. Lukovnikov, D., Stadler, C., Lehmann, J.: LD viewer-linked data presentation framework. In: Proceedings of the 10th International Conference on Semantic Systems, pp. 124–131. ACM (2014)
28. Daga, E., Panziera, L., Pedrinaci, C.: A BASILar approach for building web APIs on top of SPARQL endpoints. In: CEUR Workshop Proceedings, vol. 1359, pp. 22–32 (2015)
29. Michel, F., Zucker, C.F., Gandon, F.: SPARQL micro-services: lightweight integration of web APIs and linked data. In: LDOW 2018-Linked Data on the Web, pp. 1–10 (2018)
30. Michel, F., Faron-Zucker, C., Gandon, F.: Bridging web APIs and linked data with SPARQL micro-services. In: Gangemi, A., et al. (eds.) ESWC 2018. LNCS, vol. 11155, pp. 187–191. Springer, Cham (2018). https://doi.org/10.1007/978-3-319-98192-5_35
31. Fafalios, P., Tzitzikas, Y.: SPARQL-LD: a SPARQL extension for fetching and querying linked data. In: International Semantic Web Conference (Posters & Demos) (2015)
32. Fafalios, P., Yannakis, T., Tzitzikas, Y.: Querying the web of data with SPARQL-LD. In: Fuhr, N., Kovács, L., Risse, T., Nejdl, W. (eds.) TPDL 2016. LNCS, vol. 9819, pp. 175–187. Springer, Cham (2016). https://doi.org/10.1007/978-3-319-43997-6_14
33. Vogelgesang, C., Spieldenner, T., Schubotz, R.: SPARQλ: a functional perspective on linked data services. In: Ichise, R., Lecue, F., Kawamura, T., Zhao, D., Muggleton, S., Kozaki, K. (eds.) JIST 2018. LNCS, vol. 11341, pp. 136–152. Springer, Cham (2018). https://doi.org/10.1007/978-3-030-04284-4_10
34. Groth, P., Loizou, A., Gray, A.J.G., Goble, C., Harland, L., Pettifer, S.: API-centric linked data integration: the open PHACTS discovery platform case study. Web Semant. Sci. Serv. Agents World Wide Web 29, 12–18 (2014)
35. Alatalo, T.: An entity-component model for extensible virtual worlds. IEEE Internet Comput. 15(5), 30–37 (2011)
36. Dahl, T., Koskela, T., Hickey, S., Vatjus-Anttila, J.: A virtual world web client utilizing an entity-component model. In: NGMAST, pp. 7–12. IEEE (2013)
37. Moltchanov, B., Rocha, O.R.: A context broker to enable future IoT applications and services. In: 2014 6th International Congress on Ultra Modern Telecommunications and Control Systems and Workshops (ICUMT), pp. 263–268. IEEE (2014)
38. Wiebusch, D., Latoschik, M.E.: Decoupling the entity-component-system pattern using semantic traits for reusable realtime interactive systems. In: 2015 IEEE 8th Workshop on Software Engineering and Architectures for Realtime Interactive Systems (SEARIS), pp. 25–32. IEEE (2015)
39. Parastatidis, S., Webber, J., Silveira, G., Robinson, I.S.: The role of hypermedia in distributed system development. In: Proceedings of the First International Workshop on RESTful Design, pp. 16–22. ACM (2010)

JECI: A Joint Knowledge Graph Embedding Model for Concepts and Instances

Jing Zhou[1], Peng Wang[1,2]($\boxtimes$), Zhe Pan[1], and Zhongkai Xu[1,2]

[1] School of Computer Science and Engineering, Southeast University, Nanjing, China
pwang@seu.edu.cn
[2] School of Cyber Science and Engineering, Southeast University, Nanjing, China

Abstract. Concepts and instances are important parts in knowledge graphs, but most knowledge graph embedding models treat them as entities equally, that leads to inaccurate embeddings of concepts and instances. Aiming to address this problem, we propose a novel knowledge graph embedding model called JECI to **jointly embed concepts and instances**. First, JECI organizes concepts in the knowledge graph as a hierarchical tree, which maps concepts to a tree. Meanwhile, for an instance, JECI generates a context vector to represent the neighbor context in the knowledge graph. Then, based on the context vector and supervision information generated from the hierarchical tree, an embedding learner is designed to precisely locate an instance in embedding space from the coarse-grained to the fine-grained. A prediction function, as the form of convolution, is designed to predict concepts of different granularities that an instance belongs to. In this way, concepts and instances are jointly embedded, and hierarchical structure is preserved in embedds. Especially, JECI can handle the complex relation by incorporating neighbor information of instances. JECI is evaluated by link prediction and triple classification on real world data. Experimental results demonstrate that it outperforms state-of-the-art models in most cases.

Keywords: Knowledge graph · Embedding · Hierarchical tree · Context vector

1 Introduction

Knowledge graphs organize the human knowledge in the form of triple facts (*head entity, relation, tail entity*), abridged as (h, r, t), which are also usually recorded as (*subject, predicate, object*). The goal of knowledge graph embedding is to embed entities and relations to a continuous low-dimensional vector space. It can encode both topology structure and semantic information of knowledge graph

---

Supported by National Key R&D Program of China (2018YFD1100302).

X. Wang et al. (Eds.): JIST 2019, LNCS 12032, pp. 82–98, 2020.
https://doi.org/10.1007/978-3-030-41407-8_6

into the embeddings of entities and relations. It enables the knowledge graph more computable, which benefits tasks such as knowledge graph completion and relation extraction.

Recent years have witnessed the rapid development of knowledge graph embedding [1]. Network-based one-hot representation is simple and interpretable [2], but it often suffers from computational efficiency and data sparsity due to the complicated network structure and the long tail distribution of the knowledge graphs. To tackle this issue, distributed knowledge graph embedding models are proposed to learn low dimensional embeddings by machine learning and deep learning. Some of the them utilize triple facts observed in the knowledge graph to learn embeddings. Among which, translation-based models view the relation as translation from the head entity to the tail entity. In TransE [3], the embedded entity h and t can be linked in lower error by embedded relation r, i.e., $h + r \approx t$ when (h, r, t) actually exists in the knowledge graph. TransH [4], TransR/CTransR [5] and TransD [6] are proposed to improve TransE in dealing with complex relations. DistMult [7], HolE [8] and ComplEx [9] model the multi-relational data in knowledge graph as matrices or tensors to capture the inherent semantics between entities and relations. SLM [10], SME [11] and ConvE [12] apply neural networks to model connections between entities and relations. Though the matrices, the tensors and the networks can better capture the semantics, they also cause expensive computation due to the large amount of parameters. In addition, there are many models taking advantage of multi-source information besides triple facts, such as the entity types [13,14], the relation paths [15], the textual descriptions [10,16], the logical rules [17,18] and so on.

Although these knowledge graph embedding models achieve promising experimental results, most of them ignore differences between instances and concepts, and treat them as entities equally, which causes following drawbacks:

- Unique features of concepts and instances are not captured in embeddings. Concepts are abstract and can be seen as categories, which contain sub-concepts and similar instances. However, instances are specific and each of them refers to a unique physical object, which may belong to more than one concept [19].
- Hierarchical structure of concepts is ignored. Concepts are hierarchical naturally. As shown in Fig. 1(a), (*Scientist, subClassOf, Person*) and (*Writer, subClassOf, Person*) form the hierarchical structure, in which concepts of different granularities are in different layers.
- Transitivity of isA relation is not preserved. *InstanceOf* and *subClassOf* are special relations in knowledge graphs, called *isA*[20]. They have the property of transitivity, which is useful for knowledge graph completion. As shown in Fig. 1(b), if (*Coco, instanceOf, Dog*) and (*Dog, subClassOf, Animal*) are facts in knowledge graph, then we can infer that *Coco* is also an instance of *Animal*, which is represented by the dotted line.

These problems have been discussed in few works. In SSE [13], instances belonging to the same concept are supposed to lie close to each other in the embedding space. TKRL [14] incorporates entity types (i.e., concepts) as

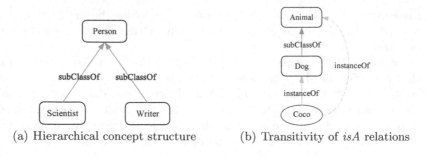

(a) Hierarchical concept structure   (b) Transitivity of *isA* relations

Fig. 1. Examples of features of *isA* relations.

assistant information for learning embeddings. TransC [21] models each concept as a sphere and each instance as a point in a same semantic space. The relative position between the point and the sphere is used to model the relation between the instance and the concept. However, the sphere is unable to capture the complex semantics of the concepts, since the sphere is a highly symmetrical spatial geometry. Moreover, although the instances are constrained inside the spheres, TransC still has limitations in dealing with complex relations existing in most knowledge graph embedding models.

In order to reduce the impact caused by differences between concepts and instances, we propose a novel knowledge graph embedding model to jointly embed concepts and instances, named JECI. For each instance, we generate a context vector from its neighbors and design a prediction function based on the context vector, which is formalized as a circular convolution. The prediction function is utilized to progressively predict which hierarchical concepts the instance belongs to in the order of coarse to fine granularity, based on the *subClassOf* relation and *instanceOf* relation. Then JECI locates the instance in embedding space using the most fine-grained concept it belongs to. We minimize the gap between the prediction and the reality, and iteratively learn the embeddings. In this way, concepts and instances are jointly embedded. For relational triples, we select triple-based models such as TransE and TransD to learn the embeddings. Take TransE, TransH, TransR, TransD, HolE, DistMult, ComplEx and TransC as baselines, experiments on YAGO39K and M-YAGO39K [21] show that JECI achieves outer performance in most cases. The main contributions of this paper can be summarized as follows:

- We propose a novel knowledge graph embedding model, which can distinguish concepts and instances.
- Hierarchical structure of concepts is preserved in our embedding model due to the progressive predictions for instances.
- Transitivity of *isA* relations (i.e., *subClassOf* and *instanceOf*) is captured.
- Problem of complex relations is also addressed in our model by incorporating neighbor information of instances.

The rest of this paper is organized as follows. In Sect. 2, significant symbols and definitions used throughout this paper are listed. In Sect. 3, we introduce

JECI model in detail. The performance of our model is shown in Sect. 4 with experiments. Finally, Sect. 5 draws the conclusion and the future work.

2 Preliminaries

For clear illustration, the symbols used throughout the paper are summarized in Table 1. Bold italic $\boldsymbol{x}$ denotes the embedding of x.

Given a knowledge graph $\mathcal{KG}$ with instances, concepts and relations, it can be formalized as $\mathcal{KG} = \{\mathcal{I}, \mathcal{C}, \mathcal{R}, \mathcal{S}\}$. There are three kinds of relations in this knowledge graph: (1) *InstanceOf* relation, which indicates that an instance is an instantiation of a concept, denoted as r_e. For example, (*Shakespeare, instanceOf, writer*) indicates that Shakespeare is an instance of writer. (2) *SubClassOf* relation, which indicates that a concept is a subconcept of the other concept, denoted as r_c. For example, (*writer, subClassOf, Person*) indicates that a writer is also a person. (3) *General* relation, which indicates the relation between two instances. For example, (*Shakespeare, write, Hamlet*) indicates that Shakespeare wrote Hamlet. Relations set $\mathcal{R}$ is formalized as $\{r_e, r_c\} \cup \mathcal{R}_l$, where $\mathcal{R}_l$ is a set of general relations. Then three kinds of triple sets are denoted as follows: (1) *InstanceOf* triples set $\mathcal{S}_e = \{(i, r_e, c) | i \in \mathcal{I} \land c \in \mathcal{C}\}$. (2) *SubClassOf* triples set $\mathcal{S}_c = \{(c_i, r_c, c_j) | c_i \in \mathcal{C} \land c_j \in \mathcal{C}\}$. (3) Relational triples set $\mathcal{S}_l = \{(h, r, t) | h \in \mathcal{I} \land t \in \mathcal{I} \land r \in \mathcal{R}_l\}$. Thus, triples set $\mathcal{S}$ is composed of these three disjoint triple sets corresponding to three kinds of relations respectively, formalized as $\mathcal{S}_e \cup \mathcal{S}_c \cup \mathcal{S}_l$.

Definition 1 (Neighbor context). *Neighbor context for an instance x is defined as a set of its neighbors in the knowledge graph, denoted as $N(x) = \{i | (x, r, i) \in \mathcal{S}_l \lor (i, r, x) \in \mathcal{S}_l\}$.*

Table 1. Symbols and descriptions.

Symbols	Descriptions
$\mathcal{KG}$	knowledge graph
$\mathcal{I}$	instances set
$\mathcal{C}$	concepts set
r_e	*instanceOf* relation
r_c	*subClassOf* relation
$\mathcal{R}_l$	general relations set
$\mathcal{R}$	relations set
$\mathcal{S}_l$	relational triples set
$\mathcal{S}_e$	*instanceOf* relation triples set
$\mathcal{S}_c$	*subClassOf* relation triples set
$\mathcal{S}$	triples set
$\mathcal{HT}$	hierarchical tree
N	neighbor context

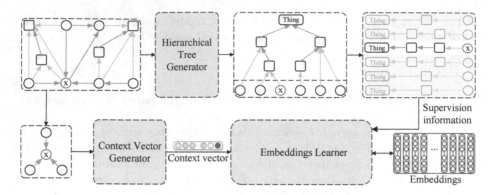

Fig. 2. Overview of JECI model.

Definition 2 (Problem of Complex relations). *Complex relations refer to 1-to-N, N-to-1 and N-to-N relations. Problem of complex relations is that, in translation-based models, if $(h_i, r, t) \in S_l$ $(i = 1, \cdots, m)$ exist in the knowledge graph, i.e., r is a N-to-1 relation, then $h_1 \approx \cdots \approx h_m$. Similarly, 1-to-N and N-to-N relations can also cause this problem.*

For example, *cityOf* is a typical N-to-N relation. (*Boston, cityOf, America*), (*NewYork, cityOf, America*) and (*Chicago, cityOf, America*) are correct triples. After learning by translation-based models such as TransE, the embeddings of *Boston, NewYork* and *Chicago* might be similar to each other.

3   JECI Model

This paper emphasizes the differences between concepts and instances in knowledge graphs, and proposes a novel knowledge graph embedding model, named **JECI**, to **jointly embed concepts and instances** to low dimensional vectors. As shown in Fig. 2, JECI has three functional parts: hierarchical tree generator, context vector generator and embeddings learner. Hierarchical tree generator maps hierarchical concepts in a knowledge graph to a tree. Context vector generator extracts neighbors of a target instance from the original knowledge graph and utilizes them to generate a context vector. Embeddings learner first links instances to the leaf nodes of the tree, and obtains supervision information from the tree. Then it learns embeddings based on the context vector and the supervision information. The details of these three parts will be illustrated below.

3.1   Hierarchical Tree Generator

Concepts are naturally hierarchical, which provide a way to classify or locate instances. Tree is suitable for representing hierarchical structure. Thus, this part aims to organize concepts in knowledge graph with the form of tree. The tree with *Thing* as the root is composed of hierarchical concepts, named hierarchical tree, denoted as $\mathcal{HT}$. $\mathcal{HT}$ is built as following steps:

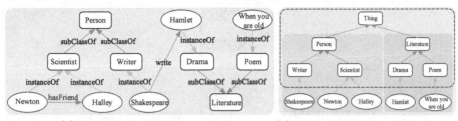

(a) Part of a knowledge graph   (b) Hierarchical tree with instances

Fig. 3. Example of mapping a knowledge graph to a hierarchical tree and linking instances to the tree. (Color figure online)

- All concepts in $\mathcal{C}$ are mapped to independent trees with single nodes respectively.
- For each triple $(c_i, r_c, c_j) \in \mathcal{S}_c$, the tree with c_i as the root is mapped to a sub-tree of c_j, r_c is mapped to the branch between c_i and c_j. Many independent trees are constructed when this step is finished.
- JECI introduces an assistant concept *Thing* satisfying $(c, r_c, Thing)$ for all concepts in $\mathcal{C}$ and maps *Thing* to a tree with single node. Then All independent trees are mapped to sub-trees of *Thing*.

In this way, all concepts are organized as $\mathcal{HT}$ and the hierarchical structure is preserved in the tree. We can infer that all nodes in $\mathcal{HT}$ are corresponding to concepts in $\mathcal{C}$ and all branches in $\mathcal{HT}$ are corresponding to *subClassOf* relations.

$(c_i, subClassOf, c_j)$ indicates that the concept c_j is more coarse-grained than the concept c_i, that is c_j is more general than c_i. If $(c_i, r_c, c_k) \in \mathcal{S}_c \wedge (c_j, r_c, c_k) \in \mathcal{S}_c \wedge (c_i, r_c, c_j) \in \mathcal{S}_c$, the sorted order by the granularity is $c_i < c_j < c_k$. JECI ensures that the more coarse-grained concepts lie closer to *Thing* in $\mathcal{HT}$, i.e., the tree with c_i as the root is mapped to a sub-tree of c_j, then the tree with c_j as the root is mapped to a sub-tree of c_k.

For example, Fig. 3(a) shows a part of a knowledge graph, with concepts represented by squares, instances represented by circles, *subClassOf* relations represented by green arrows, *instanceOf* relations represented by yellow arrows and general relations represented by blue arrows. The concepts in the knowledge graph are mapped to a hierarchical tree inside the dotted square (shown in Fig. 3(b)).

3.2 Context Vector Generator

In context vector generator, a target instance is used as the input, and it will generate a context vector for the target instance, which is one of the inputs of embeddings learner. A context of the target instance is a set of instances, from which we can obtain some features of the target instance. JECI randomly select N neighbors defined in Definition 1 of the target instance as its context. As shown in Fig. 4, the context generator conducts following steps to generate a context vector for a given instance x.

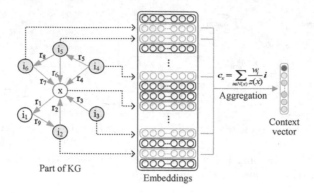

Fig. 4. Illustration of the context vector generator.

- Generating neighbor context $N(x)$ for x based on the knowledge graph, and picking up their embeddings.
- Aggregating the embeddings of the instances in $N(x)$ as context vector of x, denoted as $\boldsymbol{c}_x$.

We have tried several aggregating methods for constructing the context vector, including addition, multiplication and simple concatenation. The experiments show that addition is more effective than others. We assume that not all neighbors make same contributions to the target instance. Intuitively, if i_1 and i_2 are both neighbors of x, and i_1 is linked to more instances than i_2, i.e., $|N(i_1)| > |N(i_2)|$, it is reasonable to suppose that i_2 makes more contribution to x than i_1. Based on this point of view, we define the addition operation for generating context vector as:

$$\boldsymbol{c}_x = \sum_{i \in N(x)} \frac{w_i}{z(x)} \boldsymbol{i} \tag{1}$$

where $w_i \in (0,1)$ is the weight of neighbor i's contribution to x, defined as $w_i = e^{-|N(i)|}$. $z(x)$ is a normalized factor, formalized as follows.

$$z(x) = \sum_{i \in N(x)} w_i \tag{2}$$

Since we incorporate neighbor information of instances into model, JECI is able to address the problem of complex relations, because neighbors provide more information for precisely locating the target instance. For example, *hasFriend* is a N-to-N relation in Fig. 5, *Era*, *Matt* and *Alice* are the candidates for ? to hold (*Bob, hasFriend, ?*). If we know *Mary* is the common neighbor of ? and *Bob*, then the ? is constrained to *Alice*.

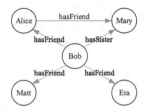

Fig. 5. Example of complex relation.

3.3   Embeddings Learner

The function of embeddings learner is to locate an instance x in embedding space based on its context vector $\boldsymbol{c}_x$. In real world, if we want to find a man who meets some conditions, it is difficult to find out a man directly from all people around the world, because the population is quite large. But it is efficient to find out the most suitable man by narrowing down the searching area step by step based on the conditions, and finally checking everyone in a small area. Inspired by this, we design a progressive way to locate an instance in embedding space. That is, based on the context vector containing neighbor information, we want to find out a most suitable instance. We progressively predict which concepts the instance belongs to from the most coarse-grained to the most fine-grained, finally we use the most fine-grained concept to locate the instance.

We design a prediction function $G_{\boldsymbol{c}_x}$ for locating an instance in embedding space, based on a context vector $\boldsymbol{c}_x$. If we know the target instance belongs to a concept $c^{(k)}$, then we can use $G_{\boldsymbol{c}_x}$ to predict a sub-concept of $c^{(k)}$ that the target instance is most likely to belong to, denoted as $G_{\boldsymbol{c}_x}(\boldsymbol{c}^{(k)})$. When $c^{(k)}$ is the most fine-grained concept that the target instance belongs to, then $G_{\boldsymbol{c}_x}(\boldsymbol{c}^{(k)})$ is the predicting location in embedding space of the target instance. To predict more precisely, information contained in $\boldsymbol{c}_x$ and $\boldsymbol{c}^{(k)}$ are supposed to be exchanged as sufficiently as possible. So, we adopt the circular convolution of $\boldsymbol{c}_x$ and $\boldsymbol{c}^{(k)}$ as the prediction function. As shown in Fig. 6, in the t-th calculation, the circular convolution first rotates the elements of $\boldsymbol{c}_x$ to the left for t times, which then is conducted an element-wise product with $\boldsymbol{c}^{(k)}$, resulting in the t-th element of $G_{\boldsymbol{c}_x}(\boldsymbol{c}^{(k)})$, denoted as $[G_{\boldsymbol{c}_x}(\boldsymbol{c}^{(k)})]_t$, formalized as follows, where d denotes the dimension of embeddings.

$$[G_{\boldsymbol{c}_x}(\boldsymbol{c}^{(k)})]_t = [\boldsymbol{c}_x \circledast \boldsymbol{c}^{(k)}]_t = \sum_{i=0}^{d-1}[\boldsymbol{c}_x]_{(i+t)mod\ d} \cdot [\boldsymbol{c}^{(k)}]_i, t = 0, 1, \cdots, d-1 \quad (3)$$

In order to obtain the hierarchical concepts an instance belongs to, JECI links instances to $\mathcal{HT}$ as shown in Fig. 3(b): For $x \in \mathcal{I}$, if x belongs to a set of concepts and there is a *subClassOf* relation between any two concepts in the set, then JECI links x to the concept which is the most fine-grained. For example, if $(x, r_e, c_i) \in \mathcal{S}_e \wedge (x, r_e, c_j) \in \mathcal{S}_e \wedge (c_i, r_c, c_j) \in \mathcal{S}_c$, JECI links x to

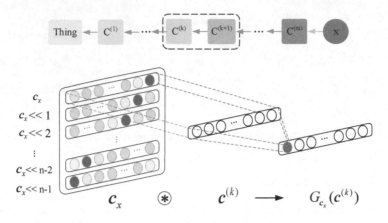

Fig. 6. Circular convolution for prediction. Concepts are represented by squares and instances are represented by circles. The deeper the red is, the more fine-grained the concept is. ⊛ representes circular convolution. (Color figure online)

c_i by r_e. If x is the instance of multiple concepts (leaf nodes of $\mathcal{HT}$), JECI preserves all these links. Thus, as shown in Fig. 6, the hierarchical concepts that an instance x belongs to are on the path from *Thing* to the leaf node that the instance is linked to, denoted as $p = \{Thing, c^{(1)}, \cdots, c^{(k)}, c^{(k+1)}, \cdots, c^{(m)}\}$. For simplification, concept *Thing* is denoted as $c^{(0)}$. Such path has following features: for $k = 0, \cdots, m-1$, $(c^{(k)}, subClassOf, c^{(k+1)}) \in \mathcal{S}_c$ and for $k = m$, $(x, instanceOf, c^{(m)}) \in \mathcal{S}_e$. Thus, the sorted order by granularity of these hierarchical concepts is $c^{(0)} > c^{(1)} > \cdots > c^{(k)} > c^{(k+1)} > \cdots > c^{(m)}$. If an instance belongs to multiple concepts (leaf nodes of $\mathcal{HT}$), the set of multiple p is denoted as $P(x)$.

The prediction function G_{c_x} is utilized to locate the target instance step by step. Specifically, in the k-th step ($k = 0, \cdots, m-1$), we predict a sub-concept of $c^{(k)}$ that the target instance is most likely to belong to, denoted as $G_{c_x}(c^{(k)})$, which is more fine-grained than $c^{(k)}$. Then $G_{c_x}(c^{(k)})$ is supposed to be close to $c^{(k+1)}$ in embedding space. In the last step, JECI predict the location of the target instance in embedding space, denoted as $G_{c_x}(c^{(m)})$, which is supposed to be close to x. The distances between the predicting results and the real embeddings are formalized in Eq. 4, called scoring function.

$$f_1(c^{(k)}, c^{(k+1)}, c_x) = ||G_{c_x}(c^{(k)}) - c^{(k+1)}||_{L_1/L_2}, \ k = 0, \cdots, m-1$$
$$f_1(c^{(m)}, x, c_x) = ||G_{c_x}(c^{(m)}) - x||_{L_1/L_2}, k = m \tag{4}$$

A lower score indicates that the results of the prediction function are more precise. Then we adopt the margin-based loss function in Eq. 5 as the optimized objective.

$$L_1 = \sum_{x \in \mathcal{I}} \sum_{p \in P(x)} \sum_{k=0}^{m} [\gamma_1 + f_1(\xi_k) - f_1(\xi'_k)]_+ \tag{5}$$

Algorithm 1. Embeddings Learner (CBOW): jointly learning concepts and instances

Input: Embeddings of concepts and instances, target instance x, neighbor context $N(x)$, context vector c_x, supervision path $p = \{c^0, c^1, \cdots, c^{(k)}, c^{(k+1)}, \cdots, c^m\}$, margin γ_1, learning rate η

1: Initialize: $loss \leftarrow 0$
2: **for all** $c^{(k)} \in p, k = 0, \cdots, m - 1$ **do**
3:    $c^{(k+1)'} \leftarrow sample(M(c^{(k+1)}))$
4:    Score of positive $subClassOf$ triple $(c^{(k)}, r_c, c^{(k+1)})$:
     $f_1(c^{(k)}, c^{(k+1)}, c_x) = ||c_x \circledast c^{(k)} - c^{(k+1)}||_{L1/L2}$
5:    Score of negative $subClassOf$ triple $(c^{(k)}, r_c, c^{(k+1)'})$:
     $f_1(c^{(k)}, c^{(k+1)'}, c_x) = ||c_x \circledast c^{(k)} - c^{(k+1)'}||_{L1/L2}$
6:    $loss \leftarrow loss + [\gamma_1 + f_1(c^{(k)}, c^{(k+1)}, c_x) - f_1(c^{(k)}, c^{(k+1)'}, c_x)]_+$
7: **end for**
8: $x' \leftarrow sample(M(x))$
9: Score of positive $instanceOf$ triple $(c^{(m)}, r_e, x)$:
   $f_1(c^{(m)}, x, c_x) = ||c_x \circledast c^{(m)} - x||_{L1/L2}$
10: Score of negative $instanceOf$ triple $(c^{(m)}, r_e, x')$:
    $f_1(c^{(m)}, x', c_x) = ||c_x \circledast c^{(m)} - x'||_{L1/L2}$
11: $loss \leftarrow loss + [\gamma_1 + f_1(c^{(m)}, x, c_x) - f_1(c^{(k)}, x', c_x)]_+$
12: **for all** $e \in N(x) \bigcup p \bigcup \{c^{(k)'}|k = 1, \cdots, m\} \bigcup \{x, x'\}$ **do**
13:    Update: $e \leftarrow e - \eta \frac{\partial loss}{\partial e}$
14: **end for**

where $m + 1$ denotes the number of concepts in path p. ξ_k denotes a positive triple $(c^{(k+1)}, subClassOf, c^{(k)})$, ξ_k' is a negative triple by corrupting ξ_k. For $k = 0, \cdots, m - 1$, we generate the negative triple $(c^{(k+1)'}, subClassOf, c^{(k)})$ by replacing $c^{(k+1)}$. To improve the quality of negative sampling, we get $c^{(k+1)'}$ by sampling from the set of sibling nodes of $c^{(k+1)}$ in $\mathcal{HT}$, i.e., the set $M(c^{(k+1)}) = \{a|a \in \mathcal{C} \wedge (a, r_c, c^{(k)}) \in \mathcal{S}_c \wedge (c^{(k+1)}, r_c, c^{(k)}) \in \mathcal{S}_c \wedge a \neq c^{(k+1)}\}$. Similarly, when $k = m$, we generate the negative triple $(x', instanceOf, c^{(m)})$ by sampling x' from the set $M(x) = \{a|a \in \mathcal{I} \wedge (a, r_e, c^{(m)}) \in \mathcal{S}_e \wedge (x, r_e, c^{(m)}) \in \mathcal{S}_e \wedge a \neq x\}$.

We can find that p actually takes the role of supervision information, so we call it supervision path. Note that, during locating the target instances, hierarchical concepts and neighbor instances are involved in learning jointly, i.e., $subClassOf$ triples and $instanceOf$ triples are jointly learned. This is the core of JECI. The algorithm for locating an instance based one of its supervision paths is shown in Algorithm 1.

There are two strategies can be chosen for learning $subClassOf$ triples and $instanceOf$ triples: CBOW and Skip-Gram [22]. The above model adopts the CBOW, using the context vector to locate the target instance in embedding space, while Skip-Gram uses the embedding of target instance to locate each instance in the neighbor context. So the instances not linked to $\mathcal{HT}$ can also be trained in the form of neighbors of other instances linked to $\mathcal{HT}$.

For relational triples, we adopt triple-based knowledge graph embedding models to encode the semantic connections between the instances, including translation-based models and semantic matching models, etc. These models differ from each other mainly in the scoring functions for a given relational triple. Take the basic translation-based model TransE as an example, it considers the general relations as translation operations between the head instances and the tail instances. Its scoring function for (h, r, t) is formalized in Eq. 6. It adopts the margin-based loss function as the objective function, formalized in Eq. 7.

$$f_2(h, r, t) = ||\boldsymbol{h} + \boldsymbol{r} - \boldsymbol{t}||_{L_1/L_2} \qquad (6)$$

$$L_2 = \sum_{\tau \in \mathcal{S}_l} \sum_{\tau' \in \mathcal{S}'_l} [\gamma_2 + f_2(\tau) - f_2(\tau')]_+ \qquad (7)$$

where τ represents a positive relational triple (h, r, t), τ' is a negative sample (h', r, t) or (h, r, t'). The more misleading, the more valid a negative sample is. For example, we get h' from instances linked to concepts which t belongs to. The candidates set is formalized as $M(t) = M_1 \bigcup M_2 \bigcup \cdots \bigcup M_n$, where n is the number of concepts t belongs to and $M_i = \{x | x \in \mathcal{I} \wedge (x, r_e, c_i) \in \mathcal{S}_e \wedge (t, r_e, c_i) \in \mathcal{S}_e \wedge x \neq t\}$.

TransE suffers the problem of complex relations defined in Definition 2. In JECI, the neighbor information of instances and the hierarchical concepts they belong to are incorporated into learning, so JECI enables the embeddings of ? in $(?, r, t)$ differ from each other and the problem of complex relations is addressed when TransE is combined with JECI.

Finally, we define the overall loss function in Eq. 8 by adding two loss functions in Eqs. 5 and 7, and adopt SGD algorithm to minimize the loss value and iteratively update the embeddings of concepts, instances and general relations.

$$L = L_1 + L_2 \qquad (8)$$

4   Experiments

4.1   Datasets

Since most datasets used in previous works mainly consist of instances or concepts such as FB15K [3] and WN18 [11], they are not suitable for evaluating our model. We adopt the datasets YAGO39K and M-YAGO39K proposed in TransC [21] and move the *subClassOf* triples in the valid sets and the test sets to the training set. Compared to YAGO39K, the valid and the test datasets of M-YAGO39K include new triples inferred based on the transitivity of *isA* relations from the existing triples in the training. The detailed statistics of new YAGO39K and M-YAGO39K are shown in Table 2.

Table 2. Statistics of YAGO39K and M-YAGO39K.

Datasets	YAGO39K	M-YAGO39K
#Instance	39, 374	39, 374
#Concept	46, 100	46, 110
#Relation	39	39
#Relational Triple	354, 997	354, 997
#*InstanceOf* Triple	442, 836	442, 836
#*SubClassOf* Triple	32, 067	32, 311
#Valid(Relational Triple)	9, 341	9, 341
#Valid(*InstanceOf* Triple)	5, 000	8, 650
#Test(Relational Triple)	9, 364	9, 364
#Test(*InstanceOf* Triple)	5, 000	8, 650

4.2 Link Prediction

Link prediction is to predict the missing head instance or tail instance for an incomplete relational triple based on the trained embeddings on condition of our work. For each testing relational triple (h, r, t), we adopt the method proposed in [23] to replace h and t respectively with all instances in $\mathcal{I}$ and use the scoring function in Eq. 6 to calculate the scores for each restructured triple. After ranking these restructured triples in ascending order based on the scores, we can get the rank of (h, r, t).

Following most previous works, we adopt the mean reciprocal rank (MRR) of all the correct instances and the proportion of correct instances that rank no larger than N(Hits@N) as the evaluation metrics. Note that, a restructured triple may have already existed in relational triples set $\mathcal{S}_l$. In order to eliminate the negative impact on evaluation caused by such false negative triples, we adopt a filtering method proposed in TransE, that is filtering the false negative triples from candidates triples before ranking, then we get filtered results, called Filter to compare with the previous results called Raw. Hits@N adopts the results of Filter in evaluation.

We use YAGO39K for training the model for 1000 rounds and evaluation. The valid dataset is utilized to select the learning rate η for SGD among $\{0.1, 0.01, 0.001\}$, the dimension of embeddings d among $\{20, 50, 100\}$, the number of neighbors N among $\{3, 5, 7\}$, margin γ_1 and γ_2 among $\{0.1, 0.3, 0.5, 1, 2\}$. The optimal hyperparameters are $\eta = 0.001$, $d = 100$, $N = 5$, $\gamma_1 = 1$ and $\gamma_2 = 1$. We choose L2 distance to evaluate the difference between the prediction and the reality in Eq. 4.

Table 3 shows the results, parts of which are referred from [21]. The cbow and sg denote strategies of learning *instanceOf* triples and the *subClassOf* triples. JECI outperforms the baselines in most cases, since embeddings of instances are learned by incorporating the hierarchical concepts they belong to. Neighbor information is also incorporated to help address the problem of complex relations.

Table 3. Experimental results of relational triples link prediction.

Models	MRR		Hits@N		
	Raw	Filter	Hits@1	Hits@3	Hits@10
TransE	0.114	0.248	12.3	28.7	51.1
TransH	0.102	0.215	10.4	24.0	45.1
TransR	0.112	0.289	15.8	33.8	56.7
TransD	0.113	0.176	8.9	19.0	35.4
HolE	0.063	0.198	11.0	23.0	38.4
DistMult	**0.156**	0.362	22.1	43.6	66.0
ComplEx	0.058	0.362	29.2	40.7	48.1
TransC (unif)	0.087	0.421	28.3	50.0	69.2
TransC (bern)	0.112	0.420	29.8	50.2	69.8
JECI (cbow)	0.088	0.418	28.6	49.7	69.8
JECI (sg)	0.122	**0.441**	**30.0**	**51.1**	**70.1**

Table 4. Experimental results of relational triples classification.

Models	Accuracy	Precision	Recall	F1-score
TransE	92.1	92.8	91.2	92.0
TransH	90.8	91.2	90.3	90.8
TransR	91.7	91.6	91.9	91.7
TransD	89.3	88.1	91.0	89.5
HolE	92.3	92.6	91.9	92.3
DistMult	93.5	93.9	93.0	93.5
ComplEx	92.8	92.6	**93.1**	92.9
TransC (unif)	93.5	94.3	92.6	93.4
TransC (bern)	93.8	94.8	92.7	93.7
JECI (cbow)	93.4	94.8	92.6	93.7
JECI (sg)	**93.9**	**95.2**	**93.1**	**94.1**

Especially, the sg strategy performs better than the cbow strategy, since the Skip-Gram takes turns to use the target instance to locate each instance in the neighbor context, enabling the target instance to be encoded with more precise semantic information from the neighbors.

4.3   Triple Classification

Triple classification is to judge whether a given triple is correct or not. In this task, we use the YAGO39K and M-YAGO39K for evaluation. Besides the hyper-parameters mentioned in link prediction, we set a threshold δ_r for each relation r, including general relations, *instanceOf* and *subClassOf*. We obtain these by maximizing the classification accuracy on valid set. For a relational triple (h, r, t), if the score calculated by the Eq. 6 is lower than δ_r, the triple will be classified as a positive one, otherwise negative. For an *instanceOf* triple (x, r_e, c), we first generate c_x, and then utilize it to progressively predict which concepts x belongs to. If there exists a path containing c and each score calculated by the Eq. 4 is lower than δ_{r_c} or δ_{r_e}, the triple will be classified as a positive one, otherwise negative.

We use same method in link prediction to select hyperparameters. The optimal hyperparameters for YAGO39K are $\eta = 0.001$, $d = 100$, $N = 5$, $\gamma_1 = 0.1$ and $\gamma_2 = 1$. The optimal hyperparameters for M-YAGO39K are $\eta = 0.001$, $d = 100$, $N = 5$, $\gamma_1 = 0.3$ and $\gamma_2 = 1$. Tables 4, 5 are the results of relational triples and *instanceOf* triples, respectively.

Table 5. Experimental results of *instanceOf* triples classification.

Datasets	YAGO39K				M-YAGO39K			
Models	Accuracy	Precision	Recall	F1-score	Accuracy	Precision	Recall	F1-score
TransE	82.6	83.6	81.0	82.3	71.0↓	81.4↓	54.4↓	65.2↓
TransH	82.9	83.7	81.7	82.7	70.1↓	80.4↓	53.2↓	64.0↓
TransR	80.6	79.4	82.5	80.9	70.9↓	73.0↓	66.3↓	69.5↓
TransD	83.2	84.4	81.5	82.9	72.5↓	73.1↓	71.4↓	72.2↓
HolE	82.3	86.3	76.7	81.2	74.2↓	81.4↓	62.7↓	70.9↓
DistMult	**83.9**	**86.8**	80.1	83.3	70.5↓	86.1↓	49.0↓	62.4↓
ComplEx	83.3	84.8	81.1	82.9	70.2↓	84.4↓	49.5↓	62.4↓
TransC (unif)	80.2	81.6	80.0	79.7	85.5↑	88.3↑	81.8↑	85.0↑
TransC (bern)	79.7	83.2	74.4	78.6	85.3↑	86.1↑	**84.2↑**	85.2↑
JECI (cbow)	82.7	84.1	81.0	82.8	86.0↑	88.2↑	81.2↑	84.6↑
JECI (sg)	**83.9**	86.6	**83.0**	**84.8**	**86.1↑**	**88.7↑**	84.1↑	**86.3↑**

As shown in Table 4, JECI outperforms all previous models in classifying relational triples on YAGO39K, since it incorporates the neighbor information. Besides, the information of hierarchical concepts also works for more precise classification.

From Table 5, we can find significant drops of previous works except TransC in most cases. TransC and JECI perform much better in M-YAGO39K. Since previous works do not differentiate concepts and instances, and the transitivity of *isA* relations is not encoded. Especially, compared to TransC, JECI gets an improvement. Because JECI learns the *subClassOf* triples and the *instanceOf* triples jointly, which works for encoding more information of the transitivity of *isA* relations into embeddings.

4.4 Limitations

Experimental results demonstrate that JECI outperforms state-of-the-art models in most cases. However, there exist some limitations.

- Neighbor information is incorporated into JECI, which helps solve the problem of complex relations. But it is just part of information in knowledge graphs. And when we extract the neighbors of an instance, we treat different relations equally.
- In fact, most knowledge graphs dynamically change mainly among instances. In other words, the concepts and the connections between the concepts are almost constant over time. We construct the hierarchical tree before training and assume that such structure will not change. Thus, JECI is not suitable for a few part of knowledge graphs with concepts changing.

5 Conclusion

In this paper, we propose a novel knowledge graph embedding model called JECI. JECI differentiates the concepts and the instances in the knowledge graph and jointly embeds them in a low-dimensional space. It encodes the transitivity of *isA* relations by progressively predicting hierarchical concepts which an instances belongs to, and using the circular convolution as the prediction function. Furthermore, JECI takes advantage of the neighbor information of the instances in the knowledge graph to address the problem of complex relations existing in some knowledge graph embedding models, e.g., TransE and TransC. The experimental results show that JECI improves the performance of link prediction and triple classification in most cases, especially outperforms the major baselines in handling the transitivity of *isA* relations.

In the future, we will explore the following researches to improve the limitations mentioned above: (1) Taking the differences of kinds of relations into consideration when extracting the neighbors of an instance. (2) Incorporating more information into our model to better solve the problem of complex relations, such as multimodal information of the instances. (3) Designing an incremental learning method based on our model to learn the embeddings of unregistered instances and concepts. (4) Learning the structure of the hierarchical tree dynamically, rather than constructing it directly. (5) Constructing a new dataset such as a products knowledge graph and evaluating our model by fine-grained entity typing [24], i.e., identifying types in different granularities of a giving instance.

References

1. Wang, Q., Mao, Z., Wang, B., Guo, L.: Knowledge graph embedding: a survey of approaches and applications. IEEE Trans. Knowl. Data Eng. **29**(12), 2724–2743 (2017)
2. Turian, J., Ratinov, L., Bengio, Y.: Word representations: a simple and general method for semi-supervised learning. In: Proceedings of the 48th Annual Meeting of the Association for Computational Linguistics, pp. 384–394 (2010)
3. Bordes, A., Usunier, N., Garcia-Duran, A., Weston, J., Yakhnenko, O.: Translating embeddings for modeling multi-relational data. In: Advances in Neural Information Processing Systems, pp. 2787–2795 (2013)

4. Wang, Z., Zhang, J., Feng, J., Chen, Z.: Knowledge graph embedding by translating on hyperplanes. In: Proceedings of the 28th AAAI Conference on Artificial Intelligence, pp. 1112–1119 (2014)
5. Lin, Y., Liu, Z., Sun, M., Liu, Y., Zhu, X.: Learning entity and relation embeddings for knowledge graph completion. In: Proceedings of the 29th AAAI Conference on Artificial Intelligence, pp. 2181–2187 (2015)
6. Ji, G., He, S., Xu, L., Liu, K., Zhao, J.: Knowledge graph embedding via dynamic mapping matrix. In: Proceedings of the 53rd Annual Meeting of the Association for Computational Linguistics, vol. 1, pp. 687–696 (2015)
7. Yang, B., Yih, W., He, X., Gao, J., Deng, L.: Embedding entities and relations for learning and inference in knowledge bases. In: 3rd International Conference on Learning Representations (2015)
8. Nickel, M., Rosasco, L., Poggio, T.A., et al.: Holographic embeddings of knowledge graphs. In: Proceedings of the 30th AAAI Conference on Artificial Intelligence, pp. 1955–1961 (2016)
9. Trouillon, T., Welbl, J., Riedel, S., Gaussier, É., Bouchard, G.: Complex embeddings for simple link prediction. In: International Conference on Machine Learning, pp. 2071–2080 (2016)
10. Socher, R., Chen, D., Manning, C.D., Ng, A.: Reasoning with neural tensor networks for knowledge base completion. In: Advances in Neural Information Processing Systems, pp. 926–934 (2013)
11. Bordes, A., Glorot, X., Weston, J., Bengio, Y.: A semantic matching energy function for learning with multi-relational data. Mach. Learn. **94**(2), 233–259 (2014)
12. Dettmers, T., Minervini, P., Stenetorp, P., Riedel, S.: Convolutional 2D knowledge graph embeddings. In: Proceedings of the 32nd AAAI Conference on Artificial Intelligence, pp. 1811–1818 (2018)
13. Guo, S., Wang, Q., Wang, B., Wang, L., Guo, L.: Semantically smooth knowledge graph embedding. In: Proceedings of the 53rd Annual Meeting of the Association for Computational Linguistics, pp. 84–94 (2015)
14. Xie, R., Liu, Z., Sun, M.: Representation learning of knowledge graphs with hierarchical types. In: Proceedings of the 25th International Joint Conference on Artificial Intelligence, pp. 2965–2971 (2016)
15. Lin, Y., Liu, Z., Luan, H., Sun, M., Rao, S., Liu, S.: Modeling relation paths for representation learning of knowledge bases. In: Proceedings of the 2015 Conference on Empirical Methods in Natural Language Processing, pp. 705–714 (2015)
16. Zhong, H., Zhang, J., Wang, Z., Wan, H., Chen, Z.: Aligning knowledge and text embeddings by entity descriptions. In: Proceedings of the 2015 Conference on Empirical Methods in Natural Language Processing, pp. 267–272 (2015)
17. Guo, S., Wang, Q., Wang, L., Wang, B., Guo, L.: Jointly embedding knowledge graphs and logical rules. In: Proceedings of the 2016 Conference on Empirical Methods in Natural Language Processing, pp. 192–202 (2016)
18. Ding, B., Wang, Q., Wang, B., Guo, L.: Improving knowledge graph embedding using simple constraints. In: Proceedings of the 56th Annual Meeting of the Association for Computational Linguistics, pp. 110–121 (2018)
19. Asprino, L., Basile, V., Ciancarini, P., Presutti, V.: Empirical analysis of foundational distinctions in linked open data. In: Proceedings of the 27th International Joint Conference on Artificial Intelligence, pp. 3962–3969 (2018)
20. Miller, G.: WordNet: an on-line lexical database. special issue of the international. J. Lexicogr. **3**(4) (1990)

21. Lv, X., Hou, L., Li, J., Liu, Z.: Differentiating concepts and instances for knowledge graph embedding. In: Proceedings of the 2018 Conference on Empirical Methods in Natural Language Processing, pp. 1971–1979 (2018)
22. Mikolov, T., Chen, K., Corrado, G., Dean, J.: Efficient estimation of word representations in vector space. In: 1st International Conference on Learning Representations (2013)
23. Bordes, A., Weston, J., Collobert, R., Bengio, Y.: Learning structured embeddings of knowledge bases. In: Proceedings of the 25th AAAI Conference on Artificial Intelligence, pp. 301–306 (2011)
24. Ling, X., Weld, D.S.: Fine-grained entity recognition. In: Proceedings of the 26th AAAI Conference on Artificial Intelligence, pp. 94–100 (2012)

Enhanced Entity Mention Recognition and Disambiguation Technologies for Chinese Knowledge Base Q&A

Gang Wu[1,2](✉), Wenfang Wu[1], Hangxu Ji[1], Xianxian Hou[1], and Li Xia[1]

[1] School of Computer Science and Engineering, Northeastern University,
Shenyang 110004, China
wugang@mail.neu.edu.cn

[2] State Key Laboratory for Novel Software Technology, Nanjing University,
Nanjing 210023, China

Abstract. Entity linking, which usually involves mention recognition and entity disambiguation, is an important task in knowledge base question and answer (KBQA). However, due to the diversity of Chinese grammatical structure, the complexity of Chinese natural language expressions and the lack of contextual information, there are still many challenges in the task of the Chinese KBQA. We discussed two subtasks of the entity linking separately. For the mention recognition part, in order to get the only topic entity mention of the question, we proposed a topic entity mention recognition algorithm based on sequence annotation. The algorithm combines a variety of feature vectors based on word embedding, and uses model BiGRU-CRF model to perform sequence labeling modeling. We also proposed an entity disambiguation algorithm based on a similarity calculation with extended information. The algorithm not only realized the information expansion by crawling the candidate entity for related problems, but also made full use of contextual information by combining lexical level similarity and sentence semantic similarity. In addition, the experimental results show that the proposed entity linking solution possesses huge advantages compared to several baseline systems.

Keywords: Entity linking · Mention recognition · Entity disambiguation · Chinese knowledge base Q&A

1 Introduction

Entity linking (EL) [4], which serve as the underlying technology of the Chinese KBQA, is the process of chaining the fragments of the entities in the text to the entities in the knowledge base. It still faces many challenges. The first important challenge facing Chinese EL is the complexity of Chinese expression and the lack of contextual information due to short text. The substantial existing large number of EL work mainly focuses on long text in English, for example, the traditional naming recognition method BiLSTM-CRF [9] has achieved creditable results in English named entity recognition. However, in the case of short

© Springer Nature Switzerland AG 2020
X. Wang et al. (Eds.): JIST 2019, LNCS 12032, pp. 99–115, 2020.
https://doi.org/10.1007/978-3-030-41407-8_7

text which lacks context, the effective use of contextual information is of vital importance. Another challenge is that there are usually multiple references to an entity in the KB. Entity disambiguation is required to address the above issue. Entity disambiguation is often seen as a sorting problem. For example, Zheng et al. [16] realized entity disambiguation based on Pairwise and Listwise Learning to Rank (L2R) methods respectively. However, the pre-existent methods often focuses on the information at the lexical level or at shallow semantic level. In response to the above problems, the following will be presented from two aspects, namely mention recognition and entity disambiguation.

Topic Entity Mention Recognition Module Based on Sequence Annotation. In view of the above mentioned challenge presented in short text, this paper combines various features to construct a feature vector based on word embedding. We also propose an improved dedicated sequence labeling model, which can obtain the exclusive topic entity mention of the question. When the BiGRU model is used for sequence labeling, the labeling is not performed on each and every word comprised of the topic entity mention, instead the words before and after the mention are specially labeled to mark the beginning and end of the mention. Through experimental verification, the proposed algorithm can overcome the influence of the sparse feature of the entity's mention formation in the existing model, and makes the model focus on the learning of the contextual information of the topic entity.

Entity Disambiguation Based on Extended Information Similarity Calculation. For another challenges, entity disambiguation is dedicated to calculating information similarity from multiple perspectives. In this paper, the similarity calculation is embodied as the calculation of the similarity between the user's question and the questions related to the candidate entity. In order to make full use of the contextual information of the short text, the similarity is calculated at the lexical and semantic levels respectively, then is combined with the popularity of the entity. To obtain deep semantic information, the convolutional neural networks (CNN) are applied. The superiority of the proposed method is proved by experimental comparison with the classical similarity calculation method based on average vector.

The main contributions of this study are: (i) The training speed is improved by replacing the traditional LSTM model with a simpler GRU model. (ii) In order to describe the possibility that the words are included in the topic entity mention from different perspectives, we extract a series of features, such as part of speech, and then combine these features with the word embedding to construct the feature vector. (iii) In the aspect of entity disambiguation, we not only expand the information of the candidate entities, but also take the lexical level similarity, the semantic level similarity, and the entity popularity into consideration to make the most out of the contextual information. (iv) This paper applies CNN to obtain deep semantic information.

2   Related Work

In this section, some work related to our study are discussed, including mention recognition research and Entity disambiguation research.

2.1   Mention Recognition Research

The mention recognition process is similar to the named entity recognition. Named entity recognition [7] is to identify and include the proper nouns such as the names of people, organizations or places, etc., and date and time with specific meaning in the text. The difference between mention recognition and named entity recognition lies in their goal. The goal of named entity recognition is to identify and classify the entities in the text, and the target of the mention recognition is to identify the reference to the knowledge base entity in the text at a high recall rate.

The two original methods for entity recognition, were based on Wikipedia [1, 13] and statistics. Since the 1990s, statistical-based methods have been the mainstream method for entity recognition. For example, Lafferty [10] proposed to use the conditional random field (CRF) to convert the named entity recognition problem into sequence labeling problem. With the rise of deep learning, researchers turned their focus to neural network-based named entity recognition. For example, the LSTM-CRF model [9], in which the vector representation of each word in the input text is first learned, and then based on the vector representation, the best label for each word is decoded by LSTM-CRF. Compared with these methods, the main advantage of our methods is that our algorithm is more suitable for Chinese short text topic entity mention recognition task by extracting different features and optimizing the training model.

2.2   Entity Disambiguation Research

Entity disambiguation, which is based on a given entity reference, context, and corresponding set of candidate entities, is the process of determining the reference to an exact entity. Most EL systems perform entity disambiguation in a supervised way, such as classification [11,14], Learning to Rank, and graph-based [5,8] methods. The L2R method automatically constructs a sorting model by extracting features, combining them, and then training. Ratinov [12] constructed local features and global features, and then used the ranking SVM training to get the sorting model. Compared with these methods the main advantages of our methods is that we have considered different aspects, including lexical similarity and deep semantic similarity, to achieve full use of limited short text context.

3   Topic Entity Mention Recognition

In order to find the proper facts from the KB to answer the input question, it is necessary to identify the fragments of the topic entities in the corresponding fact triad in the question. This process is called the recognition of the topic entity. In this paper, we consider the topic entity mention recognition as a sequence labeling problem, and ensure a high recall rate of entity mention recognition by considering all the n-grams in the question.

To describe the possibility that the words are included in the topic entity from different perspectives, this paper extracts a series of features and splices them with the word embedding to form the feature vector. These vectors are used as the input of the BiGRU-CRF model, and the topic entity mention of the question is obtained by labeling. The details of the model are presented in Sect. 3.1.

3.1 Algorithm Description

The process of the topic entity mention recognition algorithm based on the sequence annotation model is shown in Fig. 1. The annotation set of the model is defined as: **B**, the previous position of the topic entity's mention and marks the beginning of the mention; **E**, the latter position of the topic entity's mention and marks the end of the mention; **O**, other locations. The pre-processing of the question is performed before the task begins, which includes the segmentation, the part-of-speech tagging of each word, the named entity recognition, dependency parsing analysis and semantic role labeling.

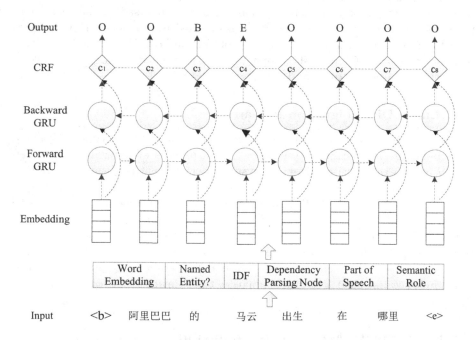

Fig. 1. Process of topic entity mention recognition algorithm

Firstly, the input of the model is constructed. Considering that there may be multiple candidate entity mentions in the sentence, such as in the question "阿里巴巴的马云出生在哪里 (Where was Yun Ma of Alibaba born)", both "阿里巴巴[1]" and "马云[2]" may be referred to as the topic entity. Therefore, this paper extracts some features by preprocessing and splices them with the word embedding to eliminate these interferences. These selected features will be detailed in Sect. 3.2. Secondly, the feature vector is input into the BiGRU model. In this paper, BiGRU model is used to construct sequence annotation model. GRU model has a strong learning ability for the long-term dependence between word sequences. Compared with LSTM [2], GRU has a simpler structure, fewer parameters, and a faster training speed. The model uses two opposite GRU layers, starting from the front-end and the back-end respectively, thus learns the forward and backward contextual features. The output of the hidden state of the two GRU layers are spliced as the output of the BiGRU network.

Thirdly, since the topic entity of the question is composed of consecutive text fragments, and there is a strong dependence between adjacent words in the sentence, this paper adds a CRF [3] layer after the BiGRU. The CRF layer can automatically learn some constraint rules from the training data and use these rules to ensure that the labels output by the BiGRU are legal. Consequently, the CRF layer predicts the global optimal labeling sequence. As shown in Fig. 1, enter "<b> 阿里巴巴的马云出生在哪里 <e>", where "<b>", "<e>" are the beginning and end of the sentence, respectively, and the output label sequence is "OOBEOOOO".

Finally, the combination of the annotation sequence is used to get the topic entity mention of the sentence.

The parametric description of the algorithm is as follows:

Take W as a set of all n-grams constructed from the result of the question segmentation, defining $p(w|q)$ as the probability that one of the n-grams (w) is the topic entity of the question (q). The objective function can be defined as:

$$\hat{w} = \arg\max p(w|q) \tag{1}$$

The representation of the input sentence is defined as the word sequence form $q = (w_1, w_2, ..., w_n)$, and the predicted label sequence of the word is $y = (y_1, y_2, ..., y_n)$. Then the score of the predicted labeling sequence is:

$$S(q, y) = \sum_{t=1}^{n} H(q)_{t,y_t} + \sum_{t=1}^{n} T_{y_t, y_{t+1}} \tag{2}$$

Where $H(q)$ is the output score matrix of BiGRU, $H(q)_{i,j}$ represents the score of the jth mark of the ith word in the question; T represents the transition matrix

---

[1] Alibaba Co.
[2] Yun Ma is the creator of Alibaba Co.

of the CRF, and $T_{i,j}$ represents the transition score from the label i to the label j. Softmax is used to normalize all possible annotation sequences for the input:

$$p(y|q) = \frac{S(q,y)}{\sum_{\bar{y} \in Y_q} e^{S(q,\bar{y})}} \tag{3}$$

Y_q represents the collection of all possible labeling sequences of the word sequence q of the input sentence. In this process, the objective function can be transformed into a probability p(y|q) that maximizes the correct labeling sequence. And in the training process, the maximum likelihood estimation (MLE) is used to maximize the logarithmic probability of the annotation sequence.

$$\log(p(y|q)) = S(q,y) - \log\left(\sum_{\bar{y} \in Y_q} e^{S(q,\bar{y})}\right) \tag{4}$$

Finally, the model generates the highest-ranked sequence of the labels as output:

$$\hat{y} = \arg\max_{\bar{y} \in Y_q} S(q,\bar{y}) \tag{5}$$

3.2   Feature Extraction

Whether the Word Is a Named Entity. According to the analysis, under the traditional named entity recognition label system, words representing names of people, places or institutions are more likely to be referred to as topic entities. Therefore, according to the result of the named entity recognition in the preprocessing, "Whether the Word is a Named Entity" is spliced with the word embedding as a binary feature.

IDF. The IDF indicates the importance of a word in a sentence, and the word with a smaller IDF value is less likely to be part of the topic entity mention. In this paper, the IDF of the word is counted in the Wikipedia corpus, and the IDF value is mapped to a real value vector of dimension d_{IDF}. The IDF calculation is as follows.

$$IDF_w = \log\frac{D}{I_W + 1} \tag{6}$$

Where D is the total number of documents in the corpus and I_w is the number of documents containing the word w.

The Dependency Parsing Node of the Word. According to the results of dependency parsing in preprocessing, this paper maps the parent node in the dependency parse tree as a feature, and maps it into a real value vector of dimension d_{par}. For example, the question "阿里巴巴的马云出生在哪里", in which the words "阿里巴巴" and "马云" are the candidate topic entity mentions of the question. According to the analysis of the dependency syntax, "阿里巴巴" depends on "马云", and there is a relation "attribute" between the two, "马云" as the parent node is more likely to be referred to as the topic entity.

Part of Speech. Considering that the topic entity of the question is all nominal, it can be added to the model as an important feature to avoid interference from other words or phrases. In this paper, the part-of-speech tagging results of each word are mapped into a real-valued vector of dimension d_{pos}.

The Semantic Role of the Word. In most instances, the topic entity mentions in the question often only correspond to a single semantic role or part of a semantic role. By mapping the semantic role labels of the words in the preprocessing results to a real value vector of dimension d_{srl}.

4   Entity Disambiguation

Entity disambiguation refers to the process of generating a set of candidate entities that may be chained by a given entity, and by using valid information, finding the entity item that is most likely to be chained in the current context. In this paper, the entity disambiguation is regarded as a sorting problem. According to the characteristics of Chinese question, an entity disambiguation algorithm based on extended information similarity calculation is proposed, which transforms the similarity calculation problem between topic entity and candidate entity into the similarity calculation of their extension information.

4.1   Entity Disambiguation Framework

The input to the model is the set of candidate entities and the topic entity mention for the question, and the output is the score for each candidate entity in the candidate entity set. The set of candidate entities is obtained according to the referential-entity mapping file. The candidate entity with a higher score, it is more likely to be the correct entity that the topic entity refers to. The similarity calculation of the entity disambiguation module based on the extended information is divided into the following steps (see in Fig. 2).

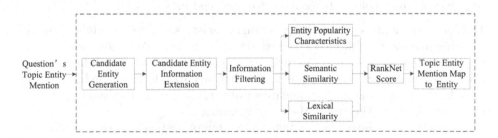

Fig. 2. Entity disambiguation framework

Candidate Entity Information Extension. For each candidate entity in the set of candidate entities, the candidate question set is composed of Baidu Knows[3]

---

[3] https://zhidao.baidu.com.

first three relevant pages with the candidate entity's name as the searching keyword. This set of questions can be seen as extended information for the candidate entity. For instance, for the candidate entity "锤子 (锤子公司)[4]" in the candidate entity set, searching on Baidu Knows with its name as a key can obtain several problems such as "锤子公司的经营理念是什么? (What is the business philosophy of the Smartisan?)". A certain number of questions are selected to form a problem set, which is regarded as the extended information of the candidate entity.

Information Filtering. Firstly, the user's question and the questions in the candidate question set are segmented, and the stop words are filtered out. The Jaccard Distance [6] is then used to calculate the literal similarity between the user's question and each question in the candidate question set. Finally, by setting a threshold, the candidate question whose similarity is lower than or equal to the threshold is filtered out.

The Similarity Calculation at the Lexical Level. For the topic entity mention and a candidate entity, when calculating the similarity between the two, the first consideration is the lexical feature. The closer the two words literarily are, the more synomyms they share, that is, the higher the similarity between the topic entity and the candidate entity will be (detailed in Sect. 4.2).

The Similarity Calculation at the Semantic Level. In Chinese natural language, some subtle linguistic differences often lead to huge semantic differences. Therefore, in addition to the similarity calculation at the lexical level, it is necessary to pay attention to the deep semantic feature of the text. For example, the question "红辣椒中女主角是谁饰演的? (Who is the actress in the leading role of Paprika?)" and the question "女主角红辣椒是谁饰演的? (Who plays the leading role Paprika?)" have a high degree of similarity in the lexical level, but their semantics are very different, and there is no correlation between the topic entities. In the process of semantic similarity calculation, this paper uses CNN to represent the whole sentence in vector (detailed in Sect. 4.2).

Extract the Entity Popularity Characteristics. In the candidate entity ordering process, in addition to context similarity feature, the priori information of the candidate entity is also crucial to the ordering of the candidate entity. Entity popularity refers to the possibility that an entity is mentioned in a question. In this paper, the entity popularity feature is defined as the ranking of each candidate entity in the "referral-entity" mapping.

For example, if the entity mention "饺子 (Dumplings)", the corresponding set of candidate entities can be obtained through the "referential-entity" mapping file as shown in the Fig. 3, and the ranking is obtained by corpus statistics. Under the condition that there is no other available information, it can be known

---

[4] Smartisan Technology Co., Ltd., commonly known as Smartisan, is a Chinese multinational technology company headquartered in Beijing and Chengdu.

that, according to the popularity, the probability that the entity mention "饺子" chain to "饺子 (中国传统食物) (Dumplings (Chinese traditional food))" is greater than the probability of the chain to entities such as "饺子 (《七龙 珠》中的人物) (Dumplings (characters in "Dragon Ball"))" or "饺子 (李碧华作 品) (Dumplings (Li Bihua's short story collection))".

Candidate Score Calculation. Using the RankNet L2R method, the lexical similarity, the semantic similarity and the entity popularity feature are integrated to output the score of the candidate entity.

饺子	饺子_(中国传统食物)	1
饺子	饺子_(《七龙珠》中的人物)	2
饺子	饺子_(李碧华作品)	3
饺子	三更2之饺子	4
饺子	饺子_(《怪物大师》人物)	5
饺子	海猴子_(盗墓笔记小说中虚拟怪物)	6

Fig. 3. Entity candidates with ranking corresponding to mention "dumpling"

4.2 Question Similarity Calculation

A detailed description of the question similarity calculation mentioned above will be demonstrated in this section. This paper calculates the similarity at two different levels, namely the lexical and semantic levels.

Similarity Based on Lexical Level. This paper uses the space vector model to calculate the lexical similarity between the user's question and the candidate question corresponding to the candidate entity. Firstly, according to the word segmentation result in the sentence preprocess, the stop words are filtered out, and the topic entity mention is also regarded as a stop word. Then, only a few words are kept in each sentence, and each word represents a dimension. The word dimension is 0 or 1, indicating whether the word appears in the current question. For example, after the word segmentation process, the stop words are filtered, and the word set obtained by the question "小罗伯特. 唐尼饰演过什 么角色? (What roles have Robert Downey Jr. played?)" is {饰演 (play), 角色 (roles)}, and the word set corresponding to the question "小罗伯特. 唐尼在《钢 铁侠》饰演什么角色? (What role does Robert Downey play in Iron Man?)" is {《钢铁侠》(Iron Man), 饰演, 角色}. The two vectors represented by {饰演, 角 色, 《钢铁侠》} are denoted by 1, 1, 0 and 1, 1, 1, respectively.

Let s denote the user's question, m denote the topic entity mention in the question, V_s denote the space vector representation of the question s, and c denote a candidate entity in the candidate entity set. c_i represents the ith

candidate question corresponding to the candidate entity, and the space vector is V_{ci}, and the similarity between the V_s and the V_{ci} can be represented by the cosine distance (Eq. 7).

$$\cos\left(m, c\right) = \frac{V_s \cdot V_{c_i}}{|V_s||v_{c_i}|} \tag{7}$$

Then, the similarity between the topic entity mention (m) and the candidate entity (c) can be calculated by the average of the similarity between the user's question and the K candidate questions (Eq. 8).

$$sim(m, c) = \frac{1}{k} \sum_{i=1}^{k} \cos(v_s, v_{c_i}) \tag{8}$$

Similarity Based on Semantic Level. Two parallel CNN [15] models are used to learn the semantic vector representations of the user's questions and candidate entity related questions, respectively, and the similarity between the two is calculated (see in Fig. 4).

The convolutional layer obtains the feature map vector by performing a convolution operation and an activation function on the word embedding matrix. Two convolution kernels of different window sizes, 1 and 2, are used in the convolutional layer to extract local features of different granularities to maximize information utilization. The activation function after the convolutional layer in this paper uses ReLU.

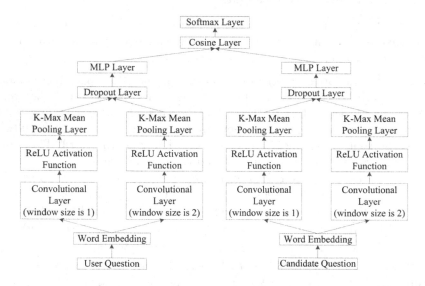

Fig. 4. Similarity computation based on Convolution Neural Network

The pooling layer is used to select a variety of semantic combinations, to extract the main features, and to transform the variable length input into a fixed length output. This paper uses an improved pooling technique called K-Max mean pooling technology, which combines the max-pooling and the mean-pooling method to reduce the influence of noise while retaining the word order information and more important features in the sentence. By selecting the largest top K values in each feature mapping vector input, the average value is taken as the sampling result, and finally a fixed-length one-dimensional vector is output.

The output after the pooling operation passes through a Dropout layer. Each feature that Dropout extracts from the pooling layer is set to 0 according to a certain probability, which can avoid the over-fitting phenomenon caused by the excessive dependence of the model on certain features. For the main features extracted, nonlinear recombination is performed by multi-layer perceptron to obtain semantic vector representations of two input questions of the same length, and then the semantic similarity is represented by cosine distance. Finally, the semantic similarity is normalized by the Softmax layer.

5 Experiments

5.1 Data Sets

This paper uses the knowledge base files, training data and test data provided by the Chinese Q&A evaluation task in the open field of CCKS 2018. The task in the CCKS uses PKU BASE as the specified knowledge graph. The file "pkubase-mention2ent.txt" in PKU BASE assists in the entity link, and the file describes the mapping relationship of the entity in the knowledge base in the format of "mention\t candidate entity\t ranking of candidate entities".

The training set and verification set include 1200 and 400 labeled data respectively. The test set consists of about 400 questions that do not contain the results of the annotation. The problems in the data set are all single-factual type, that is, the question can be answered simply through a triple in the KB, and the answer to the question is the entity or attribute in the KB.

5.2 Evaluation Metric

The evaluation indicators used in this paper include recall rate, precision and comprehensive evaluation indicators.

- R = number of correctly regcognized entities/number of entities in the sample
- P = number of correctly regcognized entities/number of regcognized entities
- F1: weighted harmonic mean of recall rate and precision (Eq. 9)

$$F1 = \frac{(\alpha^2 + 1)P * R}{\alpha^2(P + R)} \tag{9}$$

Where R is the recall rate and P is the accuracy rate. Both values are between 0 and 1. Generally speaking, the two are correlated, but sometimes there will be contradictory situations. In this case, the F1 value needs to be considered. When the F1 value is high, it indicates that the experimental results are better. α, as a balance factor, usually has a value of 1, in the absence of other conditions or assumptions, indicating that recall is as important as accuracy.

5.3 Topic Entity Mention Recognition

Experimental Description. Firstly, the method of this paper is compared with the N-Gram and N-Gram+ entity recognition methods for the mention recognition recall rate. Then, this paper also compares the Named Entity Recognition Tool of Harbin Institute of Technology's Language Technology Platform (LTP), and the open source LSTM-CRF named entity recognition model which is currently the best in English datasets as the baseline systems. In addition, the effects of each of the several types of features proposed in this paper on the topic entity mention recognition algorithm are compared.

Parameter Settings. In the experiment based on the BiGRU-CRF model, the word embedding is initialized by the pre-trained Skip-Gram model in the open source tool word2vec. The dimension of the set word embedding is 300, and the hidden layer dimension of the forward and reverse GRUs is set to 256. The parameters are randomly initialized in the interval $[-0.08, 0.08]$, and the mini-batch size is set to 10. In the training process, the Stochastic Gradient Descent (SGD) algorithm is used to update the parameters. The learning rate is set to 0.015 and the momentum is set to 0.9. In addition, in order to reduce the influence of over-fitting, a layer of Dropout is added to both ends of the BiGRU model in the experiment, and the value is set to 0.3.

Experimental Results. Firstly, the two N-Gram and N-Gram+ mention recognition (MR) methods and the BiGRU-CRF model-based topic entity mention recognition algorithm were tested by the test set and their recall were compared. Both N-Gram and N-Gram+ methods are set their target for identifying as many entities as possible. According to the experimental results in Table 1, it can be seen that compared with the above two methods, the topic entity mention recognition algorithm has no loss in recall. Then, the named entity recognition (NER) tool of the language technology platform of Harbin Institute of Technology (HIT) and the open source LSTM-CRF NER model were used as the baseline system and the topic entity recognition algorithm of this paper was verified by the test set (see in Table 2).

Table 1. Comparison of MR recall

MR method	R
N-Gram	94.8
N-Gram+	92.9
Topic Entity MR	**94.9**

Table 2. Experimental result of topic MR

MR method	R	P	F1
HIT NER	80.9	77.3	79.1
LSTM-CRF	85.2	83.8	84.5
Topic Entity MR	**94.9**	**94.9**	**94.9**

As shown in the above experimental results: (i) HIT's tools contain a limited number of entity categories. When it comes to open-field KBQA, it does not cover all entity categories, resulting in poor results. (ii) due to the complexity and diversity of Chinese natural language expression, traditional LSTM-CRF model fails to achieve the expected results. (iii) Unlike the above two baseline systems, the topic entity mention recognition algorithm only produces one mention for each question on the basis of ensuring a high recall rate, so the recall, precision and F1 are equal, the following experiments are as the same. The algorithm proposed in this paper showed great advantage compared with the two baseline.

This paper also incorporates a variety of features to describe the possibility of words as the topic entity from different dimensions. In addition, we compare the effects of various proposed features on the algorithm (see in Table 3).

After analysis, it can be found that the semantic role is based on the part-of-speech tagging and dependency syntax analysis, and it is the most obvious improvement of the mention recognition effect of the topic entity.

Table 3. Influence of different features on topic mention recognition

Features	R/P/F1
None	89.7
Whether the Word is a Named Entity	91.8
IDF	90.3
The Dependency Parsing Node of the Word	92.1
Part of Speech	91.6
The Semantic Role of the Word	**93.7**

5.4 Entity Disambiguation

Experimental Description. The mainstream disambiguation methods mostly sort candidate entities according to the similarity between the candidate entities and the mentions. The key to this similarity calculation is how to represent the calculation method of features and similarities. In the experiment of entity disambiguation, we implement two similarity calculation methods based on average word embedding as the baseline system: (i) Based on the traditional contextual co-occurrence entity, the average word embedding of the context entity is used to represent the candidate entity and the topic entity mention. (ii) Using the information extension method proposed in this paper, the average word embedding of the related questions of the user's input question and the candidate entity are calculated separately.

In addition, the lexical level similarity, the semantic similarity based on CNN and the popularity characteristics of candidate entities are compared respectively to the entity disambiguation algorithm. We also perform a two-two combined experimental comparison of the above three characteristics. In the evaluation of the experimental results, in order to eliminate the influence of the topic entity mention recognition module on the entity disambiguation, this paper only performs entity disambiguation on the identified correct topic entity. Therefore, the experimental results of the recall rate, accuracy rate and F1 are equal.

Parameter Settings. In the semantic similarity calculation model based on CNN, the word embedding is pre-trained on the Wikipedia Chinese corpus through the Skip-gram model in the open source word2vec tool. When information filtering is performed on the candidate entity related to the problem obtained by the crawl, the similarity threshold is set to 0.5. In this paper, the word vector dimension is set to 256, the convolution layer uses two sizes of convolution kernels, which are 1 and 2 respectively, and the pooling layer uses K-Max mean pooling operation, and the value of K is set to 2. The number of nodes in the fully connected layer is also 256 in the experiment. The mini-batch gradient is used during the training process. The size of the batch is set to 10, the initial learning rate is 0.05, and the attenuation is 0.4 for every three rounds after the 35th round. The nulling probability of Dropout is 0.3.

Experimental Results. According to statistics, the dataset used by the Chinese Q&A evaluation task in the open field of CCKS 2018 contains 3094,108 groups of mappings that refer to entities. As shown in Table 4, there are 791,910 mentions to two or more KB entities. The entity ambiguity reaches a ratio of 29.4%. The two baseline systems and the entity disambiguation algorithm proposed in this paper were respectively verified by the test set. The experimental results are shown in Table 5.

Table 4. Statistics of mapping results between mention and entities

Number of corresponding entities	Mention quantity
1	1900038
>1	791910

Table 5. Experimental result of entity disambiguation

Entity disambiguation method	R/P/F1
Similarity based on average word embedding of context entities	72.6
Similarity based on question average word embedding	75.3
Similarity based on lexical level	80.2
Similarity based on semantic level	84.5
Entity popularity	73.4
Lexical and semantic similarity	86.1
Lexical similarity and Entity popularity	81.5
Semantic similarity and Entity popularity	85.3
Combining three feature algorithms (our)	**87.2**

Analysis of the experimental results indicates the following conclusions.

1. Due to the short text of the user's input question and the neglect of semantic similarity factors such as word order, the two traditional methods show in the table are less effective in entity disambiguation.
2. Regardless of the context similarity, entity disambiguation can still be achieved to a certain extent by only sorting the candidate entities by the popularity characteristics of the candidate entities, but the effect is relatively poor.
3. The CNN is used to learn and express the deep semantics of the questions and calculate their similarity, which better represents the semantic similarity between the topic entity and the candidate entity.It is the most important feature in the entity disambiguation algorithm.
4. Combining the semantic similarity with the lexical similarity, and the popularity of candidate entities, inputing the three characteristics into the L2R model, the best entity disambiguation effect is obtained.

5.5   Knowledge Base Q&A Overall Experiment

In order to study the impact of EL technology on the precision of the KBQA, this paper uses the baseline system provided by the NLPCC 2017 open domain KBQA evaluation task. The baseline system utilizes a semantic analysis method based on CNN to recognize and map question-named entities and relationships. The question topic entity link method proposed in this paper is integrated into the baseline system, and the named entity recognition part is replaced by our algorithm. The above-mentioned baseline system and the KBQA system integrated with the topic EL method are respectively verified by the test set. We also evaluated the accuracy of our system when using lexical-based similarity and semantic-based similarity separately, and the experimental results are shown in Table 6.

Table 6. Experimental result of KBQA

KBQA system	Recall	Precision	F1
Base line (semantic analysis)	53.6	52.3	51.5
Lexical-based similarity	54.8	56.1	53.5
Semantic-based similarity	59.3	68.2	69.7
Topic entity link (our)	**74.8**	**71.6**	**73.2**

Based on the analysis of the experimental results, it can be noticed that the effect of the EL directly affects the performance of the final KBQA system. The semantic-based similarity method uses CNN to obtain more contextual semantic information, thus it is better than lexical-based similarity measure. Compared with the baseline, the topic entity linking method proposed in this paper takes full consideration of the characteristics of Chinese question sentences, and makes full use of limited context information to perform entity disambiguation, so that the recall and precision of the KBQA system are greatly improved. It can be concluded that the topic entity link method in this paper is more suitable for the Chinese KBQA task.

6   Conclusion

Entity linking are the key step in the KBQA. The current entity linking mainly include two parts: mention recognition and entity disambiguation. For the topic entity recognition part, this paper uses BiGRU-CRF model to carry out sequence labeling modeling, and extracts a series of features and word embedding stitching to construct feature vectors to ensure a high recall rate. For the entity disambiguation part, this paper proposed an entity disambiguation algorithm based on a similarity calculation with extended information. The algorithm not only considers the literal similarity feature, but also calculates the deep semantic similarity based on the CNN, making full use of the contextual semantic information in the short text question.

Although the method based on entity link proposed in this paper has achieved satisfying results in the knowledge Q&A system, there are still some shortcomings. In practice, in many cases, to answer a question, you may need to use more than two triples in the knowledge base. It needs to infer the indirect relationship between different triplet entities through reasoning, and call such problems a complex problem. The topic entity linking technology proposed in this paper can theoretically be extended to the topic entity link of complex questions, and then work can be carried out.

Acknowledgements. Gang Wu is supported by the NSFC (Grant No. 61872072), the State Key Laboratory of Computer Software New Technology Open Project Fund (Grant No. KFKT2018B05), and the National Key R&D Program of China (Grant No. 2016YFC1401900).

References

1. Basile, P., Caputo, A.: Entity linking for tweets. Encycl. Seman. Comput. Rob. Intell. **01**(01), 1630020 (2017)
2. Graves, A.: Supervised Sequence Labelling with Recurrent Neural Networks. Studies in Computational Intelligence, vol. 385. Springer, Heidelberg (2008). https://doi.org/10.1007/978-3-642-24797-2
3. Gutmann, B., Kersting, K.: TildeCRF: conditional random fields for logical sequences. In: European Conference on Machine Learning (2006)
4. Hachey, B., Radford, W., Nothman, J., Honnibal, M., Curran, J.R.: Evaluating entity linking with wikipedia. Artif. Intell. **194**(3), 130–150 (2013)
5. Han, X., Le, S., Zhao, J.: Collective entity linking in web text: a graph-based method (2011)

6. Hancock, J.M.: Jaccard Distance (Jaccard Index, Jaccard Similarity Coefficient) (2014)
7. Hkiri, A.O.E., Mallat, S., Zrigui, M.: Improving coverage of rule based NER systems. In: International Conference on Information & Communication Technology & Accessibility (2016)
8. Hoffart, J., et al.: Robust disambiguation of named entities in text. In: Conference on Empirical Methods in Natural Language Processing (2015)
9. Huang, Z., Xu, W., Yu, K.: Bidirectional LSTM-CRF models for sequence tagging. arXiv preprint arXiv:1508.01991 (2015)
10. Lafferty, J., McCallum, A., Pereira, F.C.: Conditional random fields: probabilistic models for segmenting and labeling sequence data (2001)
11. Pilz, A., Paaß, G.: From names to entities using thematic context distance (2011)
12. Ratinov, L.A., Dan, R., Downey, D., Anderson, M.: Local and global algorithms for disambiguation to wikipedia. In: Meeting of the Association for Computational Linguistics: Human Language Technologies (2011)
13. Shen, W., Wang, J., Han, J.: Entity linking with a knowledge base: issues, techniques, and solutions. IEEE Trans. Knowl. Data Eng. 27(2), 443–460 (2015)
14. Wei, Z., Yan, C.S., Jian, S., Tan, C.L.: Entity linking with effective acronym expansion, instance selection and topic modeling. In: International Joint Conference on Artificial Intelligence (2011)
15. Yao, H., Liu, H., Zhang, P.: A novel sentence similarity model with word embedding based on convolutional neural network: sentence similarity model with word embedding based on convolutional neural network. Concurrency Comput. Pract. Experience 30, e4415 (2018)
16. Zheng, Z., Li, F., Huang, M., Zhu, X.: Learning to link entities with knowledge base. In: Human Language Technologies: The Conference of the North American Chapter of the Association for Computational Linguistics (2010)

Dispute Generation in Law Documents via Joint Context and Topic Attention

Sheng Bi[1] , Xiya Cheng[1] , Jiamin Chen[1] , Guilin Qi[1(✉)] , Meng Wang[1] ,
Youyong Zhou[2] , and Lusheng Wang[2]

[1] School of Computer Science and Engineering, Southeast University, Nanjing, China
{bisheng,chengxiya,cjm,gqi,meng.wang}@seu.edu.cn
[2] School of Law, Southeast University, Nanjing, China
yyzhlaw@163.com, lusheng.wang@gmail.com

Abstract. In this paper, we study the Dispute Generation (DG) problem from the plaintiff allegation (PA) and the defendant argument (DA) in a law document. We are the first to formulate DG as a text-to-text natural language generation (NLG) problem. Since the logical relationships between a PA and a DA are rather difficult to identify, existing models cannot generate accurate disputes, let alone find all disputes. To solve this problem, we propose a novel Seq2Seq model with two dispute detection modules, which captures relationships among the PA and the DA in two ways. First, in the context-level detection module, we employ hierarchical attention mechanism to learn sentence representation and joint attention mechanism to match right disputes. Second, in the topic-level detection module, topic information is taken into account to find indirect disputes. We conduct extensive experiments on the real-world dataset. The results demonstrate the effectiveness of our method. Also the results show that the context-level and the topic-level detection modules can improve the accuracy and coverage of generated disputes.

Keywords: Dispute generation · Seq2Seq model · Topic information · Context-level · Topic-level

1 Introduction

Dispute Generation (DG) deals with the problem of generating dispute automatically from materials of a legal case, and plays an important role in judicial decision. There is no formal definition of a dispute in law, but we can consider DG as the task of generating a problem which is disputed in a case, as shown in Fig. 1. DG plays a vital role in the judicial decision. Valid DG not only improves the efficiency of the court hearing but also provides convenience for mediation between the parties. What's more, since the dispute is one component of the law document, DG makes contributions to law documents writing.

As far as we know, at present time no explicit attempts have been made to automatically generating disputes from a case document. However, DG is part

X. Wang et al. (Eds.): JIST 2019, LNCS 12032, pp. 116–129, 2020.
https://doi.org/10.1007/978-3-030-41407-8_8

of a legal assistant system, so we introduce some work on legal assistant systems. Existing work on legal assistant system mostly focuses on charge prediction. [8] employs text mining methods to extract features from precedents and applies a classifier to automatically classify judgments. [10] proposes an attention-based neural network method to jointly model the charge prediction task and the relevant article extraction task. Besides, there are also works on identifying the relevant domain which a specific legal text belongs to [2] and answering legal questions as a consulting problem [6].

Recently, text generation models are widely used and achieve a great success, which provide a novel way for DG. Text generation models can handle multiple inputs and generate novel words. The neural attention Seq2Seq model can set attention to the input words and pay more attention to the useful part, which improves the accuracy of output generation [15]. What's more, [21] proposes a topic aware Seq2Seq (TA-Seq2Seq) model to incorporate topic information into response generation, which can generate informative and interesting responses.

It is well recognized that the dispute stands where the parties cannot agree and detecting disputes only from context-level is not enough, which brings about one challenge when applying text generation models to the DG task. The challenge is how to get the overlapping topic distribution of what the disputed parties said and help generate disputes. For example in Fig. 1, according to "divide the defendant bank deposit" and "I don't have any deposits and have always been living in areas", our model should have the ability to compute the topic contribution of these two sentences and conclude that they argue over the same topic about defendant bank deposit. Moreover we can infer a dispute about the couple jointly owned property division. As a consequence, for DG task, our model should not only ensure the naturalness and consistency of generation like existing models do, but also focus on the topic distribution to better generate accurate disputes.

In order to tackle the challenge, we propose a novel Seq2Seq architecture consisting of context-level and topic-level dispute detection modules. The context-level detection module employs a neural network with hierarchical attention mechanism [12] to learn sentence vector representation. With joint context mechanism, the correct disputes can be obtained in literal level. The topic-level detection module obtains the overlapping topic distribution of sentences in the two input documents through the Latent Dirichlet Allocation (LDA) model and leverages topic attention. We joint the two topic attentions to detect those indirect disputes in semantic level.

Our contributions in this paper are listed as follows:

(1) We are the first to formulate DG task as text generation problem and release a real-world dataset for this task.

(2) We propose a Seq2Seq model with two dispute detection modules. The context-level detection module is applied to improving generation accuracy. Moreover the topic-level detection module is used to get the overlapping topic distribution and generate all the disputes.

Plaintiff Allegation

被告婚后无故与原告发生争吵，甚至对原告进行打骂，还在大年初一晚上将原告推出家门。夫妻感情已彻底破裂。现请求法院判决：1、准予与被告离婚。2、分割被告银行存款。# After the marriage, the defendant had quarrels with the plaintiff for no reason, even beat and scolded the plaintiff, and threw him out of the house on Spring Festival. Thus, the alienation of mutual affection occurred. Now the plaintiff requests the court to order: 1. Allow the plaintiff and the defendant to divorce. 2. Divide the defendant bank deposit.

Defendant Argument

我不同意离婚，我们夫妻感情没有破裂。大年初一晚上将原告推出家门属实，但并未对原告进行殴打。另外，我没有存款，一直都是欠款生活。# I disagree with the divorce. Our mutual affection has not broken down. I did throw the plaintiff out of the house on Spring Festival, but I did not beat him. Besides, I do not have any deposits and have always been living in arrears.

Disputes

夫妻感情是否破裂。原被告婚姻期间的夫妻共同财产分割。# Whether the mutual affection is broken; the couple jointly owned property division during the marriage.

Fig. 1. An example of a plaintiff allegation, a defendant argument and disputes from a legal document in a case. Disputes are generated from the plaintiff allegation and the defendant argument. Each dispute and its corresponding content in a plaintiff allegation and a defendant argument are showed in the same color. (Color figure online)

(3) We conduct extensive experiments on the dataset. The results show that our model significantly outperforms the state-of-art models on the same dataset. Also, our model does improve the accuracy and coverage of the generated disputes.

2   Related Work

Our work is mainly relevant to previous legal-related work and recent studies on Seq2Seq text generation.

2.1   Legal-Related Work

Legal-related work coverages many aspects and significantly contributes to legal assistant systems. Earlier work is mainly related to text classification with machine learning. [2] identify the relevant domain which a specific legal text belongs to based on the association between a legal text and its domain label. [8] employ text mining methods to extract features from precedents and apply a text classifier to automatically classify judgments.

Recent advances in Natural Language Processing and Deep Learning provide experts with the tools to build models, which can satisfy more complex requirement with more complicated structures. [10] propose an attention-based neural network framework that can jointly model the charge prediction task and the relevant article extraction task. However, this work only focuses on high-frequency charges, without paying attention to few-shot and confusing ones. To address these issues, [5] introduce discriminative legal attributes into consideration and propose a novel attribute-based multi-task learning model for charge prediction. Specifically, their model learns attribute-free and attribute-aware fact representation jointly by utilizing attribute-based attention mechanism. [9] formalize judgment prediction task as Legal Reading Comprehension and present a novel neural LRC model, AutoJudge, to incorporate law articles for judgment prediction. [22] propose a novel task of court view generation and formulate it as a text-to-text generation problem. They propose a label-conditioned Seq2Seq model with attention to decode court views conditioned on encoded charge labels.

2.2 Text Generation

Owing to the development of neural networks [1,17] first apply modern neural networks and propose sequence-to-sequence model for text generation. However, this method cannot set the focus on the crucial sentence, keyword. Thus [15] propose a neural attention Seq2Seq model (S2SA) to abstractive text summarization and achieve state-of-the-art on the two sentence-level summarization dataset, DUC-2004, and Gigaword. Since S2SA ignores the hierarchical structure of a document, [12] extend this model by trying a hierarchical attention architecture to capture the hierarchy of sequence-to-word structure.

There are still some problems in neural generation, such as repetitions and omitting information. To avoid repetitions and help cover all and only the input, [11,19] adopt coverage as an extra input to attention mechanism and use a GRU to update the coverage vector each step, which penalizes attending to input that has already been covered. To handle rare or unknown words and copy from the input, [4] incorporate copying mechanism into neural network-based Seq2Seq learning and propose a new model called CopyNet with encoder-decoder structure. At each time step, the model decides whether to copy from the input or to generate from the target vocabulary. Both coverage and copy mechanism are adopted by [16], who present a hybrid pointer-generator architecture [20] with coverage.

Since the complexity of legal documents, we need to learn the relevance of context and semantic between the plaintiff allegation and the defendant argument. We apply hierarchical attention architecture and incorporate topic information, borrowing ideas from TA-Seq2Seq [21].

3 Problem Formulation

The dispute generation is formulated as follows: given a PA X_p and a DA X_d, our goal is to output a dispute context Y. Here, the PA $X_p = (x_{p,1}, x_{p,2}, \cdots, x_{p,r})$, the DA $X_d = (x_{d,1}, x_{d,2}, \cdots, x_{d,s})$ and generated disputes $Y = (y_1, y_2, \cdots, y_l)$ are word sequences. By taking advantage of hierarchical attention network, we obtain sentence vectors S_p and S_d from the PA and the DA respectively. To make our model much succincter, we omit how to get sentence vectors in Fig. 3 and use sentence vectors S_p and S_d as inputs directly. We additionally use the topic distribution of sentences in a PA $T_p = (t_{p,1}, t_{p,2}, \cdots, t_{p,m})$, and the topic distribution of sentences in a DA $T_d = (t_{d,1}, t_{d,2}, \cdots, t_{d,n})$ as extra inputs for better detecting disputes. The model maximizes the generation probability of Y conditioned on X_p, X_q, T_p, T_q.

4 Model

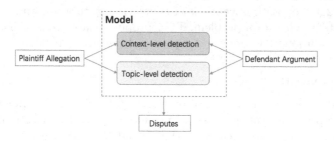

Fig. 2. The overall framework of our model with two dispute detection modules, a context-level detection module, and a topic-level detection module. Solid arrows present the generation process.

In this section, we present our model. The overall architecture of our model is shown in Fig. 2. Drawing inspiration from recent work on neural machine translation, we modify the successful seq2seq attentional model [15] by adding context-level and topic-level dispute detection modules. As is shown in Fig. 3, our model consists of three parts: context-level detection, topic-level detection, and a word sequence decoder. In context-level detection, we use hierarchical attention network to detect sentences in the PA and the DA. Then we use joint context attention by combining the two sentence attentions to match right disputes. The topic-level detection is used to obtain the overlapping topic distribution between sentences in the PA and the DA and help detect correct disputes. We calculate joint topic attention by combining the two topic attentions from the topic distributions of a PA and a DA, which are obtained from a pre-trained LDA model[1]. Finally, we concatenate the joint context attention and topic attention to affect the generation of words in the word sequence decoder.

Our proposed model is novel in the following ways. First, for capturing disputes we design context-level detection module and topic-level detection module to handle the challenge in literal and semantic level given in the Introduction section. Second, a novel joint attention mechanism is designed for disputes decoding.

We describe the details of different components in the following sections.

Context-Level Detection. As is shown in Fig. 3, for context-level detection, the input $S_p = (g_{p,1}, g_{p,2}, ..., g_{p,m})$ are sentence vectors calculated from hierarchical attention network as well as another input $S_d = (g_{d,1}, g_{d,2}, ..., g_{d,m})$. All things considered, in an attempt to clarify and simplify the computation process, S_p and S_d are limited to having the same length with each other. Given a source sequence X of a PA, we use a bidirectional GRU to get annotations of

---

[1] https://radimrehurek.com/gensim/models/ldamodel.html.

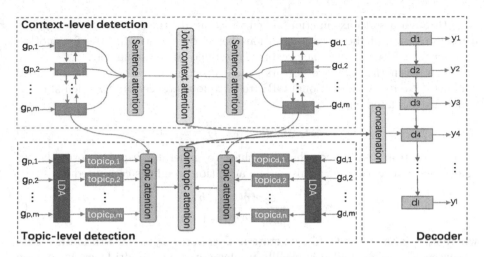

Fig. 3. Our novel Seq2Seq model with two dispute detection modules, a context-level detection module, and a topic-level detection module. Given the input of a plaintiff allegation and a defendant argument, joint context attention and joint topic attention are used to guide the generation of disputes.

words by summarizing information from both directions for words, and therefore incorporate the contextual information in the annotation.

The encoder RNN calculates the hidden state at time t by

$$h_{p,it} = GRU(x_{p,it}, h_{p,it-1}), t \in [1, r], i \in [1, m] \tag{1}$$

However, not all words contribute equally to the representation of the sentence meaning. To tackle this issue, we introduce an attention mechanism to extract such words that are important to the meaning of the sentence and aggregate the representation of those informative words to form a sentence vector. The attention weight is computed as follows:

$$u_{p,it} = tanh(W_\omega h_{p,it} + b_\omega) \tag{2}$$

$$\alpha_{p,it} = \frac{exp(u_{p,it}^T u_{p,\omega})}{\sum_t exp(u_{p,it}^T u_{p,\omega})} \tag{3}$$

$$g_{p,i} = \sum_t \alpha_{p,it} h_{p,it} \tag{4}$$

where $u_{p,it}$ is a hidden representation of the word annotation $h_{p,it}$, which is obtained through a one-layer MLP (multi-layer perceptron). $u_{p,\omega}$ is the context vector which is regarded as a high level representation of a fixed query "what is the informative word" over input words. $u_{p,\omega}$ is randomly initialized and jointly learned during the training process. Moreover W_ω and b_ω are parameters. In order to measure the importance of the word, we compute the similarity of $u_{p,it}$ with a word level context vector $u_{p,\omega}$ and get a normalized importance weight

$\alpha_{p,it}$ through a softmax function. Then we compute the sentence vector $g_{p,i}$ as a weighted sum of the word annotations based on the weights. As for another encoder for a DA, the sentence vector is obtained in the same way.

Then given the sentence vectors $g_{p,i}$, a document vector can be obtained similarly. We use a bidirectional GRU to encode sentences, and hidden state at time t is calculated as:

$$h_{p,i} = GRU(g_{p,i}, h_{p,i-1}), i \in [1, m] \tag{5}$$

For rewarding sentences that are clues to generate disputes correctly, we again use an attention mechanism. The attention weight is computed as

$$\alpha_{p,jb} = \frac{exp(\eta(s_{j-1}, h_{p,b}))}{\sum_i exp(\eta(s_{j-1}, h_{p,i}))} \tag{6}$$

where s_{j-1} is the $j-1$-th hidden state in decoder, $h_{p,b}$ is the b-th hidden state in sentence encoder, and η is usually implemented as a multi-layer perceptron (MLP) with tanh as an activation function. To get the joint context attention, we combine the sentence attention of PA $\alpha_{p,jb}$ and DA $\alpha_{d,jb}$ to get a overall context attention β_{jb}.

$$\beta_{jb} = \alpha_{p,jb} \cdot W_b \cdot \alpha_{d,jb} \tag{7}$$

where W_b is a matrix.

Topic-Level Detection. Inspired by topic aware Seq2Seq model [21], we use topic attention from the topic distribution $T_p = (t_{p,1}, t_{p,2}, \cdots, t_{p,m})$ in a PA, which is obtained from LDA model given the input of sentences. The attention weight of $t_{p,q}$ is computed by

$$m_{p,jq} = \frac{exp(\eta_o(s_{j-1}, t_{p,q}, h_{p,m}))}{\sum_{l=1}^m exp(\eta_o(s_{j-1}, t_{p,l}, h_{p,m}))} \tag{8}$$

where $h_{p,m}$ is the final hidden state of the input message, which is used to weaken the effect of topics that are irrelevant to the input message in generation and highlight the importance of relevant topics. η_o is a multilayer perceptron. The topic attention of a DA $m_{d,jq}$ can be obtained in the same way.

Different from topic aware Seq2Seq model, we combine the topic attention of PA $m_{p,jq}$ and the topic attention of DA $m_{d,jq}$ to get overall topic attention α_{jq}. This method is particularly useful in finding similar topics between a PA and a DA and helping generate disputes more accurately. The overall topic attention can be computed by

$$\alpha_{jq} = m_{p,jq} \cdot W_q \cdot m_{d,jq} \tag{9}$$

where W_q is a matrix.

Then we concatenate the joint context attention β_{jb} and the joint topic attention α_{jq} to obtain the context vector c_j.

$$c_j = \sum_{j=1}^m (\beta_{jb} h_{p,j} + \alpha_{jq} t_{p,j}) + \sum_{j=1}^n (\beta_{jb} h_{d,j} + \alpha_{jq} t_{d,j}) \tag{10}$$

where $t_{p,j}$ is one of the embeddings of topics in T_p, and $t_{d,j}$ is one of the embeddings of topics in T_d.

The joint context attention and the joint topic attention form a joint attention mechanism which allows the input message and the topics to affect the generation probability jointly. The primary advantage of the joint attention is that it makes words in disputes not only relevant to the message but also related to the topics of the message.

Word Generation. We define the generation probability $p(y_j)$ by

$$p(y_j = \omega) = \begin{cases} \frac{1}{Z} e^{\Psi_{V(s_j, y_{j-1}, \omega)}} & \text{if } \omega \in V, \\ 0 & \text{if } \omega \notin V. \end{cases} \tag{11}$$

$$s_j = GRU(y_{j-1}, s_{j-1}, c_j) \tag{12}$$

where V is a vocabulary of disputes. $\Psi_{V(s_j, y_{j-1})}$ is defined by

$$\Psi_{V(s_j, y_{j-1}, \omega)} = \sigma(w^T(W_V^d \cdot s_j + W_V^y \cdot y_{j-1} + b_V)) \tag{13}$$

where $\sigma(\cdot)$ is tanh, w is a one-hot indicator vector of word ω, and W_V^d, W_V^y, and b_V are learning parameters. $Z = \sum_{v \in V} e^{\Psi_{V(s_j, y_{j-1}, v)}}$ is a normalizer.

5 Experiments

In this section, we describe the dataset used for training and evaluation, give implementation details, introduce baseline models, explain how model output is evaluated and report evaluation results.

5.1 Dataset

We create a dataset semi-automatically where each piece of data is a tuple consisted of a PA, a DA, and corresponding disputes. To improve data diversity, we crawl 14,2394 legal judgments about all kinds of matrimonial disputes from China Judgments Online[2], and extract PA, DA and disputes from these legal judgments. Then we preprocess these data and limit length like filtering those data whose PA or DA is too short or too long to make a more standard dataset and for better training. Since some legal judgments don't have explicit disputes to extract, we hire four students who major in law to label the judgments and conclude disputes. Finally, there are 96437 data tuples left to be our dataset. We break down the dataset into a training set, a validation set, and a testing set in a ratio of 8:1:1. If readers are interested in our dataset, please contact the author by sending your personal information to *bisheng@seu.edu.cn*.

---

[2] http://wenshu.court.gov.cn.

5.2   Implementation Details

We employ jieba[3] for Chinese word segmentation. The word embedding size is set to 300, the value of embedding is randomly initialized with uniform distribution in $[-0.1, 0.1]$. In the context-level detection, the hidden size of GRU is set to 300 for each direction in Bi-GRU. In the topic-level detection, the hidden size of GRU is set to 300 for each direction in Bi-GRU. We choose ROUGE as the update metric. Adam [7] is adopted to optimize the model with initial learning rate $= 0.0001$, gradient clipping $= 0.1$, and dropout rate $= 0.5$. Model performance will be checked on the validation set after every 1000 batches training and keep the parameters with the lowest ROUGE. Training process will be terminated if model performance is not improved for successive eight times. We repeat all the experiments for ten times, and report the average results.

5.3   Baseline Models

We compare our models with the following state-of-the-art baselines:

S2SA. $S2SA$ is a standard sequence-to-sequence model with attention mechanism, which has proven to be successful in text generation tasks [15].

HRED. $HRED$ is a hierarchical recurrent encoder-decoder model. It decomposes the context as two-level hierarchy using Recurrent Neural Networks (RNN). The lower RNN encodes sequence of words which is then fed into the higher level RNN to get a hierarchical context representation [12].

Ours$_{context}$. $Ours_{context}$ is our model with only context-level module, which is used to verify the effectiveness of joint context attention of our model.

Ours$_{topic}$. $Ours_{topic}$ is our model with only topic-level module, which is used to verify the effectiveness of joint topic attention of our model.

In all models, we set the dimensions of word embeddings as 512, and the dimensions of the hidden states of both the encoder and decoder as 512. All models are initialized with Gaussian distributions $\mathcal{X} \sim \mathcal{N}(0, 0.01)$ and trained with Adam algorithm. The batch size is 64 and the initial learning rate is 0.001. To handle rare or unknown words and improve the generation quality, we incorporate copy mechanism in our models, $Ours_{context}$ and $Ours_{topic}$. Therefore, we don't compare our models with more advanced models such as CopyNet.

5.4   Evaluation Metrics

Both automatic and human evaluation metrics are used to analyze the model's performance.

---

[3] https://github.com/fxsjy/jieba.

Automatic Evaluation. We adopt BLEU-1 [13] and ROUGE [3] to evaluate the generation performance. BLEU-1 is a 1-gram precision-based metric. ROUGE reports the F1 scores for ROUGE-1, ROUGE-2, and ROUGE-L which respectively measure the word-overlap, bigram-overlap, and longest common sequence between a generated dispute and a reference dispute. ROUGE-1 and ROUGE-2 are used as a means of assessing informativeness and ROUGE-L is used as a means of assessing fluency.

Human Annotation. In addition to automatic evaluation, we evaluate the generated disputes by eliciting human judgments for 300 randomly sampled legal judgments. Three annotators who have expertise in law are invited to do an evaluation. The evaluation metrics are listed as follows: (1) **Naturalness.** Naturalness is used to rate the fluency of the generated disputes, and whether it is consistent in context. We adopt five scales for naturalness evaluation (five is for the best, and one for the worst). (2) **Accuracy, Recall and F1 Measure.** It's challenging for a machine to judge whether a generated dispute is correct or not. For example, a generated dispute is "Whether the plaintiff should restore the bride price", but the reference dispute is "Whether the DA should restore the bride price". They are so similar that the machine will put correct label on the generated dispute which is wrong from the point of human being. Thus, we need human judgments to judge whether the disputes are correct. Score one for disputes that are correct, zero for disputes that are wrong. With the annotation results, we can calculate the accuracy, recall and F1 measure of our model, aiming to evaluate how many disputes have been accurately expressed in the generation results.

5.5   Evaluation Results

In an automatic evaluation from Table 1, our model is considerably better than all the baselines. $Ours_{context}$ and $Ours_{topic}$ are both have better performances than $S2SA$, which verifies the effectiveness of hierarchical attention mechanism. However, the results of $Ours_{context}$, $Ours_{topic}$ and $HRED$ are about the same, obviously worse than the results of $Ours$, which proves that the combination of context-level module and topic-level module is pretty effective.

Table 2 shows the human annotation results, and it is clear that our model gets the best performance and generate much more informative and accurate disputes. Our model is observed to have the highest naturalness, accuracy, recall and F1-measure scores among these text generation models. Similar to the results of automatic evaluation, $Ours_{context}$ and $Ours_{topic}$ both perform better than $S2SA$, but are inferior to our complete model. This result further verifies our claim that it is not enough to detect only from context-level. Topic-level detection is helpful for detecting indirect disputes and enriching the content of generated disputes.

Overall, our model substantially outperforms all other baselines in all metrics. Especially for thematic consistency and disputes accuracy, our model illustrates an extraordinary balance between them, with observable improvements on both sides. This balance is mainly contributed from the proposed framework consisted of context-level and topic-level detection modules.

Table 1. Results of automatic evaluation.

Model	B-1	R-1	R-2	R-L
$S2SA$	34.4	48.3	23.3	39.4
$HRED$	37.2	51.2	28.4	42.3
$Ours_{context}$	36.9	51.7	27.2	41.1
$Ours_{topic}$	35.3	49.2	25.1	38.4
$Ours$	**40.5**	**53.1**	**32.4**	**44.5**

Table 2. Results of human annotation.

Model	Nat.	Acc.	Recall	F1
$S2SA$	2.5	26.5	13.6	18.3
$HRED$	3.1	37.5	22.5	23.7
$Ours_{context}$	3.0	36.5	21.6	24.8
$Ours_{topic}$	2.8	33.8	20.8	21.3
$Ours$	**3.8**	**40.7**	**33.3**	**36.9**

5.6 Case Study

We conduct case studies for better understanding the model performances. Figure 4 compares our model with baselines using examples. From the comparison, it is clear that our model has higher accuracy on generating disputes than baselines, and all disputes are generated which are similar to the reference disputes.

PA	被告婚后无故和原告发生争吵，甚至对原告进行打骂，还在大年初一晚上将原告推出家门。夫妻感情已彻底破裂。现请求法院判决：1、准予与被告离婚。2、分割被告银行存款。3、原告带走陪嫁物（电冰箱一台，电视机一台）。# After the marriage, the defendant had quarrels with the plaintiff for no reason, even beat and scolded the plaintiff, and threw him out of the house on Spring Festival. Thus the alienation of mutual affection occurred. Now the plaintiff requests the court to order: 1. Allow the plaintiff and the defendant to divorce. 2. Divide the defendant bank deposit. 3. The plaintiff takes away the dowry (one refrigerator and one TV set)
DA	我不同意离婚，我们夫妻感情没有破裂。大年初一晚将原告推出家门属实，但并未对原告进行殴打。另外我没有存款，一直都是欠款生活。而且原告所述的陪嫁物都是用我的钱购买，只是结婚时从我家拉来做陪嫁物。# I disagree with the divorce. Our mutual affection has not broken down. I did throw the plaintiff out of the house on Spring Festival, but I didn't beat him. Besides, I don't have any deposits and has always been living in arrears. The dowry mentioned by the plaintiff was purchased with my money but only married from my house to make a dowry.
Gold	夫妻感情是否破裂。原被告婚姻存续期间的夫妻共同财产分割。陪嫁物的归属权。# Whether the mutual affection is broken ; the couple jointly owned property division during the marriage ;the dowry's ownership.
S2SA	无故与原告争吵。夫妻感情破裂。与被告离婚。# Quarrelling with the plaintiff for no reason; the mutual affection is broken; divorcing from the defendant.
HRED	打骂原告。夫妻感情破裂。没有银行存款。# Beating and scolding the plaintiff; the mutual affection is broken; no bank deposit .
Ours	夫妻双方感情是否破裂。夫妻婚后共同财产分割问题。陪嫁物的归属权问题。# Whether the mutual affection is broken ; the couple jointly owned property division problem after marriage ; the dowry's ownership problem.
$Ours_{context}$	夫妻感情是否破裂。# Whether the mutual affection is broken .
$Ours_{topic}$	银行存款问题。陪嫁物归属问题。# The bank deposit problem ; the dowry's ownership problem.

Fig. 4. Case study. We mark three correct disputes and their corresponding content in the plaintiff allegation and the defendant argument in yellow, green and purple. From this case, it is clear that our model generates all correct disputes and other methods only generate one right dispute and even several wrong disputes compared with the gold. (Color figure online)

The context-level detection is used to solve this condition where the PA and the DA have distinct disputes in the context. As is shown in Fig. 4, without context-level detection, some baselines generate wrong disputes. For example, the wrong dispute "Beating and scolding the plaintiff", generated by *HRED*, is not important enough to be a dispute although it is described similarly in both PA and DA. Moreover, $Ours_{context}$ only generates correct dispute, which verifies the effectiveness of context-level detection.

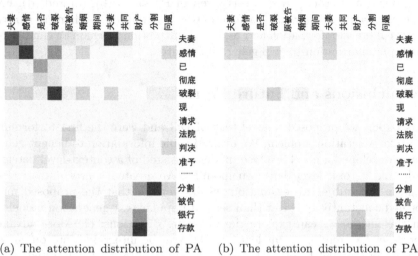

(a) The attention distribution of PA on the context level.

(b) The attention distribution of PA on the topic level.

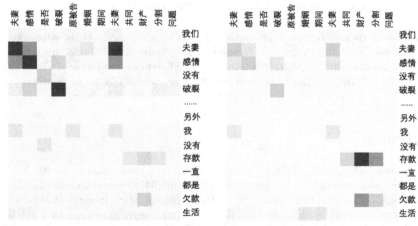

(c) The attention distribution of DA on the context level.

(d) The attention distribution of DA on the topic level.

Fig. 5. The heatmap represents a soft alignment between the input (right) and the generated dispute (top). The columns represent the attention distribution over the input after generating each word. For topic level, these key words are paid attention to because they are topic words by the means of LDA model.

In addition, some baselines omit several disputes in the generation. In this example, the plaintiff also argues with the DA about the topic of the ownership of the dowry problem. $Ours_{topic}$ correctly generates this dispute. In contrary, $S2SA$, $HRED$ don't detect the dispute and generate nothing, which verifies the importance and efficiency of topic-level detection in helping improve the coverage and generate all disputes. As a result, our model yields a substantial improvement over previous state-of-the-art models.

With the purpose of presenting the procedure how our model operates in detail, four examples of generation is given in Fig. 5(a), (b), (c) and (d). From these four pictures, it is clear that context-level attention mechanism can capture critical literal information and topic-level attention mechanism can discover latent topic information to help generate disputes.

6   Conclusions and Future Work

In this paper, we proposed a novel task of DG and were the first to formulate it as a text generation problem. We utilized topic information to benefit generation and developed a novel Seq2Seq model consisted of a context-level detection module and a topic-level detection module. We created a new dataset. Both automatic and subjective evaluation results verified that the proposed model performed substantively better than several popular text generation models.

In the future, we can explore the following directions: (1) More advanced technologies like reinforcement learning [18] can be integrated into our model. (2) Apply our model to other language generation tasks. (3) Limited by the dataset, we can only verify our proposed model on matrimonial disputes. A more general and larger dataset will benefit the research on DG.

Acknowledgement. Research presented in this paper was partially supported by the National Key Research and Development Program of China under grants (2018YFC0830200, 2017YFB1002801), the Natural Science Foundation of China grants (U1736204), the Judicial Big Data Research Centre, School of Law at Southeast University.

References

1. Bahdanau, D., Cho, K., Bengio, Y.: Neural machine translation by jointly learning to align and translate. arXiv preprint arXiv:1409.0473, September 2014
2. Boella, G., Caro, L.D., Humphreys, L.: Using classification to support legal knowledge engineers in the Eunomos legal document management system. In: Fifth International Workshop on Juris-Informatics (JURISIN) (2011)
3. Chin-Yew, L.: ROUGE: a package for automatic evaluation of summaries. In: Proceedings of the ACL-04 Workshop, pp. 74–81. Association for Computational Linguistics (2004)
4. Gu, J., Lu, Z., Li, H., Li, V.O.: Incorporating copying mechanism in sequence-to-sequence learning. In: Association for Computational Linguistics (2016)

5. Hu, Z., Li, X., Tu, C., Liu, Z., Sun, M.: Few-shot charge prediction with discriminative legal attributes. In: Proceedings of COLING (2018)
6. Kim, M.-Y., Xu, Y., Goebel, R.: Legal question answering using ranking SVM and syntactic/semantic similarity. In: Murata, T., Mineshima, K., Bekki, D. (eds.) JSAI-isAI 2014. LNCS (LNAI), vol. 9067, pp. 244–258. Springer, Heidelberg (2015). https://doi.org/10.1007/978-3-662-48119-6_18
7. Kingma, D.P., Ba, J.: Adam: a method for stochastic optimization. In: ICLR (2015)
8. Liu, Y.H., Chen, Y.L.: A two-phase sentiment analysis approach for judgement prediction. J. Inf. Sci. **44**, 594–607 (2017)
9. Long, S., Tu, C., Liu, Z., Sun, M.: Automatic judgment prediction via legal reading comprehension. In: Proceedings of EMNLP (2017)
10. Luo, B., Feng, Y., Xu, J., Zhang, X., Zhao, D.: Learning to predict charges for criminal cases with legal basis. In: Proceedings of EMNLP (2017)
11. Mi, H., Sankaran, B., Wang, Z., Ittycheriah., A.: Coverage embedding models for neural machine translation. In: Empirical Methods in Natural Language Processing (2016)
12. Nallapati, R., Zhou, B., dos santos, C.N., Gulcehre, C., Xiang, B.: Abstractive text summarization using sequence-to-sequence RNNs and beyond. In: Computational Natural Language Learning (2016)
13. Papineni, K., Roukos, S., Ward, T., Zhu, W.: BLEU: a method for automatic evaluation of machine translation. In: the 40th Annual Meeting of the Association for Computational Linguistics, pp. 311–318 (2002)
14. Raghav, K., Reddy, P.K., Reddy, V.B.: Analyzing the extraction of relevant legal judgments using paragraph-level and citation information. AI4J Artif. Intell. Justice (2016)
15. Rush, A.M., Chopra, S., Weston., J.: A neural attention model for abstractive sentence summarization. In: Empirical Methods in Natural Language Processing (2015)
16. See, A., Liu, P.J., Manning, C.D.: Get to the point: summarization with pointer-generator networks. In: Proceedings of the 55th Annual Meeting of the Association for Computational Linguistics (Volume 1: Long Papers), pp. 1073–1083, July 2017
17. Sutskever, I., Vinyals, O., Le, Q.V.: Sequence to sequence learning with neural networks. In: Advances in Neural Information Processing Systems 27: Annual Conference on Neural Information Processing Systems 2014, pp. 3104–3112 (2014)
18. Sutton, R.S., Barto, A.G.: Reinforcement learning: an introduction. J. Artif. Intell. Res. **47**, 253–279 (1998)
19. Tu, Z., Lu, Z., Liu, Y., Liu, X., Li, H.: Modeling coverage for neural machine translation. In: Association for Computational Linguistics (2016)
20. Vinyals, O., Fortunato, M., Jaitly, N.: Pointer networks. In: Neural Information Processing Systems (2002)
21. Xing, C., et al.: Topic aware neural response generation. In: Proceedings of AAAI, pp. 3351–3357 (2017)
22. Ye, H., Jiang, X., Luo, Z., Chao, W.: Interpretable charge predictions for criminal cases: learning to generate court views from fact descriptions. In: Proceedings of NAACL-HIT, pp. 1854–1864 (2018)

Richpedia: A Comprehensive Multi-modal Knowledge Graph

Meng Wang[1,2(✉)], Guilin Qi[1,2], HaoFen Wang[3], and Qiushuo Zheng[4]

[1] School of Computer Science and Engineering, Southeast University, Nanjing, China
[2] Key Laboratory of Computer Network and Information Integration
(Southeast University), Ministry of Education, Nanjing, China
{meng.wang,gqi}@seu.edu.cn
[3] Intelligent Big Data Visualization Lab, Tongji University, Shanghai, China
carter.whfcartet@gmail.com
[4] School of Cyber Science and Engineering, Southeast University, Nanjing, China
qs_zheng@seu.edu.cn

Abstract. Large-scale knowledge graphs such as Wikidata and DBpedia have become a powerful asset for semantic search and question answering. However, most of the knowledge graph construction works focus on organizing and discovering textual knowledge in a structured representation while paying little attention to the proliferation of visual resources on the Web. To improve the situation, in this paper, we present Richpedia, aim to provide a comprehensive multi-modal knowledge graph by distributing sufficient and diverse images to textual entities in Wikidata. We also set RDF links (visual semantic relations) between image entities based on the hyperlinks and descriptions in Wikipedia. The Richpedia resource is accessible on the Web via a faceted query endpoint and provides a pathway for knowledge graph and computer vision tasks, such as link prediction and visual relation detection.

Keywords: Knowledge graph · Multi-modal · Wikidata

Resource type: Dataset
Permanent URL: http://rich.wangmengsd.com
Github Repository: https://github.com/wangmengsd/richpedia

1 Introduction

With the rapid development of Semantic Web technologies, various knowledge graphs are published on the Web using Resource Description Framework (RDF), such as Wikidata [18] and DBpedia [2]. Knowledge graphs provide for setting RDF links among different entities, thereby forming a large heterogeneous graph, supporting semantic search [19], question answering [16] and other intelligent services. Meanwhile, public availability of visual resource collections has attracted much attention for different Computer Vision [6,10] (CV) research purposes,

© Springer Nature Switzerland AG 2020
X. Wang et al. (Eds.): JIST 2019, LNCS 12032, pp. 130–145, 2020.
https://doi.org/10.1007/978-3-030-41407-8_9

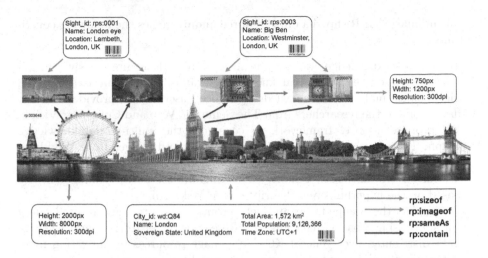

Fig. 1. Graphical illustration of multi-modal knowledge graph.

including visual question answering [20], image classification [15], object and relationship detection [11], etc. And we have witnessed promising results by encoding entity and relation information of textual knowledge graphs for CV tasks. Whereas most knowledge graph construction work in the Semantic Web and Natural Language Processing (NLP) [3,13,14] communities still focus on organizing and discovering only textual knowledge in a structured representation. There is a relatively small amount of attention in utilizing visual resources for KG research. A visual database is normally a rich source of image or video data and provides sufficient visual information about entities in KGs. Obviously, making link prediction and entity alignment in wider scope can empower models to make better performance when considering textual and visual features together.

In order to bring the advantages of Semantic Web to the academic and industry community, a number of KGs have been constructed over the last years, such as Wikidata [18] and DBpedia [2]. These datasets make the semantic relationships and exploration of different entities possible. However, there are few visual sources within these textual KGs. In order to improve visual question answering and image classification performance, several methods [5,7,12,20] have been developed for connecting textual facts and visual resources, but the RDF links [4] from different entities and images to objects in the same image are still very limited. Hence, little of the existing data resources is bridging the gap between visual resources and textual knowledge graphs.

As mentioned above, general knowledge graphs focus on the textual facts. There is still no comprehensive multi-modal knowledge graph dataset prohibiting further exploring textual and visual facts on either side. To fill this gap, we provide a comprehensive multi-modal dataset (called Richpedia) in this paper, as shown in Fig. 1.

In summary, our Richpedia data resource mainly makes the following contributions:

- To our best knowledge, we are the first to provide comprehensive visual-relational resources to general knowledge graphs. The result is a big and high-quality multi-modal knowledge graph dataset, which provides a wider data scope to the researchers from The Semantic Web and Computer Vision.
- We propose a novel framework to construct the multi-modal knowledge graph. The process starts by collecting entities and images from Wikidata, Wikipedia, and Search Engine respectively. Images are then filtered by a diversity retrieval model. Finally, RDF links are set between image entities based on the hyperlinks and descriptions in Wikipedia.
- We publish the Richpedia as an open resource, and provide a faceted query endpoint using Apache Jena Fuseki[1]. Researchers can retrieve and leverage data distributed over general KGs and image resources to answering more richer visual queries and make multi-relational link predictions.

The rest of this paper is organized as follows. Section 2 describes the construction details of proposed dataset. Section 3 describes the overview of Richpedia ontology. The statistics and evaluation are reported in Sect. 4. Section 5 describes related work and finally, Sect. 6 concludes the paper and identifies topics for further work.

2   Richpedia Construction

A knowledge graph (KG) can often be viewed as a large-scale multi-relational graph consisting of different entities and their relations. We follow the RDF model [4] and introduce the definition of the proposed multi-modal knowledge graph, Richpedia, as follows:

Richpedia Definition: Let $\mathcal{E} = \mathcal{E}_{\mathcal{KG}} \cup \mathcal{E}_{\mathcal{IM}}$ be a set of general KG entities $\mathcal{E}_{\mathcal{KG}}$ and image entities $\mathcal{E}_{\mathcal{IM}}$, $\mathcal{R}$ be a set of relations between entities. $\mathcal{E}$ and $\mathcal{R}$ will be denoted by IRIs (Internationalized Resource Identifiers)[2]. $\mathcal{L}$ be the set of literals (denoted by quoted strings, e.g. "London", "750px"), and $\mathcal{B}$ be the set of blank nodes. A Richpedia triple $t = \langle subject, predicate, object \rangle$ is a member of set $(\mathcal{E} \cup \mathcal{B}) \times \mathcal{R} \times (\mathcal{E} \cup \mathcal{L} \cup \mathcal{B})$. Richpedia, i.e., multi-modal KG, is a finite set of Richpedia triples.

Figure 2 illustrates the overview of Richpedia construction pipeline, which mainly includes three phases: **data collection** (described in Sect. 2.1), **image processing** (described in Sect. 2.2) and **relation discovery** (described in Sect. 2.3).

---

[1] https://jena.apache.org/documentation/fuseki2/index.html.
[2] https://www.w3.org/TR/rdf11-concepts/#dfn-iri.

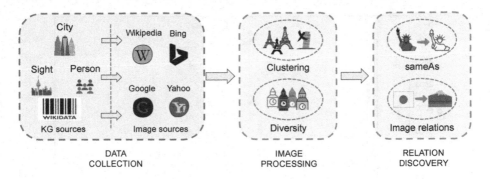

Fig. 2. Overview of Richpedia construction pipeline.

2.1 Data Collection for Richpedia

Differing from general KGs, our focus is to construct a multi-modal dataset which contains comprehensive image entities and their relations. Therefore, we consider following sources to populate Richpedia.

- Wikidata[3] is becoming an increasingly important knowledge graph in the research community. We collect the KG entities from Wikidata as $\mathcal{E}_{\mathcal{KG}}$ in Richpedia.
- Wikipedia[4]: Wikipedia contains images for KG entities in Wikidata and a number of related hyperlinks among these entities. We will collect part of the image entities from Wikipedia and relations between collected KG entities and image entities. We will also discover relations between image entities based on the hyperlinks and related descriptions in Wikipedia.
- Google[5], Yahoo[6], and Bing[7] image sources: To obtain sufficient image entities related to each KG entity, we implemented a web crawler taking input as KG entities to image search engines Google Images, Bing Images, and Yahoo Image Search, and parse query results.

According to the Richpedia definition, we need to extract two types of entities (KG entities $\mathcal{E}_{\mathcal{KG}}$ and image entities $\mathcal{E}_{\mathcal{IM}}$), and generate Richpedia triples.

Entity IRI Creation: Wikidata already contains unique IRI for each KG entity, we add these IRIs to Richpedia as the KG entities. In current version, we mainly collected 30,638 entities about cities, sights, and famous people. With these IRIs, the attribute information, i.e., knowledge facts, of these KG entities can be directly queried on Wikidata.

For image entities, intuitively we can collect images from Wikipedia and create corresponding IRIs in Richpedia. However, as shown in Fig. 3, a large

---

[3] https://www.wikidata.org/wiki/Wikidata:Main_Page.
[4] https://www.wikipedia.org/.
[5] https://www.google.com/.
[6] https://search.yahoo.com/.
[7] https://www.bing.com/.

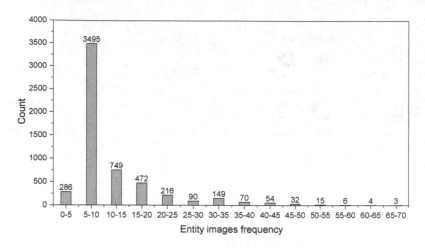

Fig. 3. The entity image frequencies in Wikipedia. There are a large portion of entities that only have a few images.

portion of images for KG entities are actually long-tail. In other words, each KG entity will have very few visual information in Wikipedia. Therefore, as mentioned above, we obtained sufficient images from open sources and processed to filter out final image entities (details will be given in Sect. 2.2). After that, we will create IRIs for each image entity. In current version, we have collected 2,883,162 images entities and kept 99.2 images per entity on average.

Triple Generation: In Richpedia, we focus on constructing three types of triples as follows:

$\langle e_i, rp\text{:imageof}, e_k \rangle$ indicates that an image entity e_i is an image of a KG entity e_k. An example is

$$\langle rp\text{:001564}, rp\text{:imageof}, wd\text{:Q3130} \rangle,$$

where rp:001564 is an image entity, i.e., a picture of *Sydney*, and wd:Q3130 is the KG entity in Wikidata.

$\langle e_i, rp\text{:attribute}, l \rangle$ indicates the visual feature (rp:attribute and numerical values l) of an image entity e_i. An example is

$$\langle rp\text{:001564}, rp\text{:size}, 700 * 1600 \rangle.$$

where rp:001564 is a picture of *Sydney* and its pixel information $700 * 1600$.
$\langle e_i, rp\text{:relation}, e_k \rangle$ establishes the semantic visual relations (rp:relation) between two image entities. An example is

$$\langle rp\text{:000001}, rp\text{:contain}, rp\text{:000002} \rangle.$$

where rp:000001 is a picture of *London* and it contains another image entity *London Eye* rp:000002.

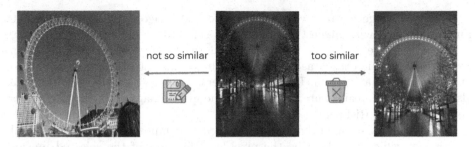

Fig. 4. Example of image entity diversity.

Since the each IRI is unique, we can directly generate the triple link the $\langle e_i, rp\text{:imageof}, e_k \rangle$ and $\langle e_i, rp\text{:attribute}, l \rangle$ during data collection. For the triple $\langle e_i, rp\text{:relation}, e_k \rangle$, we will leverage related hyperlinks and text in Wikipedia to discover the relations (details will be given in Sect. 2.3).

2.2 Richpedia Images Processing

After collecting image entities, we need to process and screen high-quality images. Because our data comes from open sources, they will be ranked by search engines with the high relevance score to the query. From the multi-modal knowledge graph perspective, the ideal image entities to a KG entity are not only relevant but ideally also diverse. For instance, Fig. 4 shows the image diversity, the left and middle image entity should be saved in Richpedia whereas the right should be filtered. It is intuitive to utilize clustering based methods to achieve the image diversity screening. In this paper, we employ a simple but pragmatic below method.

Diversity Image Retrieval: Given image entities crawled from search engines for a KG entity, we first apply clustering algorithm K-means on visual features to obtain clusters of images. The similarity between two images during the clustering is measured based on histogram-intersection in colour spaces. Specifically, we first converted RGB values of two image entities e_i and e_j into the hue (H), saturation (S), and value (V) coordinates of the HSV color space using methods in [9]. Then, the similarity between two image entities can be defined as the histogram intersection of the normalized histogram as follows:

$$sim(e_i, e_j) = \sum_{k=1}^{n} \min \left(H_k(e_i) - H_k(e_j) \right), \tag{1}$$

where e_i, e_j are image entities. A color histogram of image entity e is an n-dimensional vector, $H_k(e)$, where each element represents the frequency of color k in image e.

For each image cluster, we will collect top-20 images in following process. First, the image with highest visual score is selected as the top ranked image. The second image is the one which has the largest distance to the first image. The third image is chosen as the image with the largest distance to both two previous images, and so on. During the diversity image detection retrieval, we also generate $\langle e_i, rp:$attribute$, l \rangle$ triples for the given image entity to provide its visual features in Richpedia.

After the acquisition of the images, we need to compute some different visual descriptors, which can describe the pixel-level features of the selected images (for instance, gray distribution and texture information for images). We then use these descriptors to calculate the similarity between the images, where the similarity can be calculated by integrating the distance between different descriptors. There are the descriptors we compute are the following:

- **Gradation Histogram Descriptor:** Gradation histogram is a statistic of gradation distribution. Gradation histogram refers to the frequency of the gray size of all pixels in the image. Gradation histogram is a function of gray level, which represents the number of pixels with a certain gray level in the image and reflects the frequency of a certain gray level in the image. We transform the image from color to grayscale and use the OpenCV lib to calculate the *Gradation Histogram Descriptor*. Finally, each image entity generates a description vector with 256 dimensions.
- **Color Layout Descriptor:** *Color Layout Descriptor* reflects the composition distribution of colors in the image, which colors appear and the probability of various colors, color histogram is the representation of the image color feature. Color histograms are insensitive to geometric transformations such as rotation of the observation axis, translation and scaling with little amplitude, and are not sensitive to changes in image quality (such as blurring). Therefore, the differences in the global color distribution of the two images can be measured by comparing the differences in color histograms. We respectively calculate the three channels (R, G, B) of the color histograms.
- **Color Moment Descriptor:** *Color Moment* is a simple and effective method to represent color features. There are first moment (mean), second moment (variance) and third moment (skewness). Since the color information is mainly distributed in the low order moment, the first-order moment, second-order moment and third-order moment are sufficient to express the color distribution of the image, and the color moment has been proved to be effective to represent the color distribution in the image. We calculate three moments of the *Color Moment*.
- **GLCM Descriptor:** Gray-level co-occurrence matrix is a common method to describe texture by studying the spatial correlation of gray. As the texture is formed by the grayscale distribution appearing repeatedly in the spatial position, there will be a certain grayscale relationship between the two pixels separated by a certain distance in the image space, that is, the spatial correlation characteristics of the grayscale in the image. We compute the *GLCM Descriptor* of the images.

Fig. 5. Example of Richpedia relations discovery.

- **Histogram of Oriented Gradient Descriptor:** Histogram of Oriented Gradient (HOG) is a feature descriptor that is used in the field of computer vision and image processing for target detection. This technique is used to calculate the statistics of the direction information of local image gradients. We extract the edges of the grayscale image by computing its gradient (using Sobel and Laplacian kernels).

2.3 Richpedia Relation Discovery

In this section, we mainly introduce the process of triple $\langle e_i, rp{:}\text{relation}, e_k \rangle$ generation. It is hard to directly detect these semantic relations based on pixel features of different images. The collected images from open sources are naturally linked to the input crawling seeds, i.e, KG entities, and image entities from Wikipedia and Wikidata. Therefore, we can leverage related hyperlinks and text in Wikipedia to discover the semantic relations (rp:relation) between image entities. Next we take rp:contain and rp:nearBy as examples to illustrate how to discover semantic relations among image entity *Place de la Concorde*, *Obelisk of Luxor*, and *Fountain of River Commerce and Navigation*.

As shown in Fig. 5, images of *Place de la Concorde*, *Obelisk of Luxor*, and *Fountain of River Commerce and Navigation* are extracted from the *Place de la Concorde* Wikipedia article. From the semantic visual perspective, we could find that *Place de la Concorde* contains *Obelisk of Luxor* and *Fountain of River Commerce and Navigation*, and *Obelisk of Luxor* is near by *Fountain of River Commerce and Navigation*. To discover these relations, we collect textual descriptions around these images and propose three effective rules to extract final relations:

*Rule*1 : If there is one hyperlink in the description, its pointing Wikipedia entity corresponds to the image entity with a high probability. We detect the keywords from the description by Stanford CoreNLP. Then, relation will be discovered by a string mapping algorithm between keywords and predefined relation ontology. For instance, if we get the word 'left' in the textual descriptions between the two entities, we will get the 'nearBy' relation.

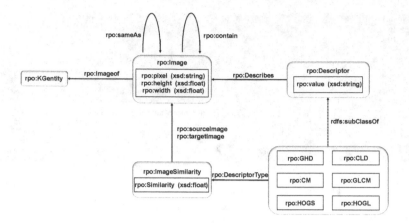

Fig. 6. Richpedia ontology overview.

*Rule*2 : If there are multiple hyperlinks in the description, we detect the core KG entity based on the syntactic parser and syntactic tree. Then, we take input as the core KG entity and reduce this case to *Rule*1.

*Rule*3 : If there is no hyperlink pointing to other articles in the description, we employ the Stanford CoreNLP to find the corresponding KG entities which have Wikipedia articles and reduce this case to *Rule*1 and *Rule*2. Because *Rule*3 relies on the NER results which have low quality than annotated hyperlinks, its priority is lower than the first two rules.

3   Ontology

In this section, we describe the ontology we built for Richpedia, which consists of comprehensive image entities, multiple descriptors of image entities, and relationships among image entities. We create a custom lightweight Richpedia ontology to represent the data as RDF format, all the files formatted following the N-Triples guidelines (https://www.w3.org/TR/n-triples/). All Richpedia resources are identified under the http://rich.wangmengsd.com/resource/ namespace. The ontology is described at http://rich.wangmengsd.com/ontology/.

As shown in Fig. 6, the overview of Richpedia ontology is as followed. The classes are displayed in the box. The solid edges represent the relation between instances of two classes, the dotted lines represent the relation between the classes themselves; for conciseness, the data type properties are listed in the class boxes.

A **rpo:KGentity** is an existing text knowledge graph entity that contains a lot of existing attribute information. A **rpo:Image** is an abstract resource representing an image entity of Richpedia dataset, describing the height and width of the image and the url of the image in the display website. The data types of **rpo:Height** and **rpo:Width** are both *xsd:float*. A **rpo:KGentity** links

```
@prefix    rpo:      <http://rich.wangmengsd.com/ontology/>
@prefix    rp:       <http://rich.wangmengsd.com/resource/>
rp:16.jpg    a       rpo:Image;
    rpo:Imageof      rps:0001;
    rpo:Height       600;      rpo:Width      900;
```

Fig. 7. RDF example of an image entity.

```
rp:16.jpg.GHD     a     rpo:GHD;
    rpo:Describes     rp:16.jpg;
    rpo:value      "[2823.0 ,  218.0 ,  256.0 ,  205.0 ,  ...]";
rp:16.jpg.CLD     a     rpo:CLD;
    rpo:Describes     rp:16.jpg;
    rpo:value      "[189.0 ,  62.0 ,  66.0 ,  49.0 ,   ...]";
rp:16.jpg.CM     a     rpo:CM;
    rpo:Describes     rp:16.jpg;
    rpo:value      "[64.8369 ,  92.1214 ,  195.548 ,  ...]";
rp:16.jpg.GLCM     a     rpo:GLCM;
    rpo:Describes     rp:16.jpg;
    rpo:value      "[0.0123 ,  0.0035 ,  0.0011 ,  ...]";
rp:16.jpg.HOGL     a     rpo:HOGL;
    rpo:Describes     rp:16.jpg;
    rpo:value      "[0.0666 ,  0.0120 ,  0.0033 ,  0.0012 ,  ...]";
```

Fig. 8. RDF example of the descriptors.

to many **rpo:Image**s by the relation of **rpo:imageof**. Between the images, there maybe some semantic relations, such as **rpo:sameAs**, **rpo:contain** and so on. In Fig. 7, we show the example of the RDF for the **rpo:Image** representation of London eye.

A **rpo:Descriptor** is a visual descriptor of the image, it link to the **rpo:Image** by the relation **rpo:visual-describe**. A **rpo:Descriptor** has five subclasses, such as **rpo:GHD**, **rpo:CLD**, **rpo:CM**, **rpo:GLCM** and **rpo:HOG**. They describe the image in terms of grayscale, color, texture, edge and etc. For instance, in Fig. 8, there is the descriptor of the above image about London eye.

A **rpo:ImageSimilarity** is used to express the degree of similarity between images, it includes the **rpo:Similarity** which calculates between **rpo:sourceImage** and **rpo:targetImage** by the specified descriptor. **rpo:Similarity** represents the similarity of two images on the pixel level. Following, we show the example of it in Fig. 9.

```
rp:gray_sim1     a      rpo:ImageSimilarity;
    rpo:sourceImage     rp:0.jpg;
    rpo:targetImage     rp:3997.jpg;
    rpo:Similarity      0.7750442028045654;
    rpo:DescriptorType     rpo:GHD;

rp:0.jpg     rpo:similar     rp:3997.jpg
```

Fig. 9. RDF example of a visual similarity relation.

Table 1. Statistics of Entities

	#KG entities	#Image entities
City	507	46,864
Sight	8,494	827,492
Person	20,984	2,040,414

Table 2. Statistics of Richpedia triples

	#Overall
$\langle e_i, rp\text{:imageof}, e_k \rangle$	2,708,511
$\langle e_i, rp\text{:attribute}, l \rangle$	2,491,283
$\langle e_i, rp\text{:relation}, e_k \rangle$	114,469,776

4   Statistics and Evaluation

In this section, we report the statistical data of Richpedia and a preliminary evaluation of its accuracy. At present Richpedia includes 2.8 million entities and 172 million Richpedia triples.

Statistics of KG entities and image entities are depicted in Table 1. The numbers of the city entities, sight entities, and person entities in Richpedia are 507, 8,494, and 20,984. For image entities, there are 46,864 images of cities, 827,492 images of sights, and 2,040,414 images of famous people. The number of the Richpedia triples of three different types are depicted in Table 2. As shown in Table 2, there are 2,708,511 relations between KG entities and image entities, 114,469,776 relations among image entities, and 2,491,283 relations between image entities and values such as pixel information.

To evaluate the accuracy of image entities distribution to the given KG entities, we manually construct 10,000 image distributions as ground-truths and compared it with the result of our diversity image retrieval model. The precision is 94% and the recall is 86%. For the images wrongly or have not been distributed to entities, the reason is that we choose the image which has the largest distance to the collected image in the same cluster during the diversity image retrieval. Therefore, some noisy points may mix in our final results and decrease the precision, and some images may not be ranked within the top-20 and decrease the recall.

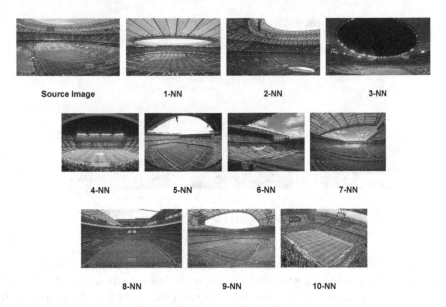

Fig. 10. 10 nearest neighbors of an image of *Russian Luzhniki Stadium* using HOG.

As for the accessibility of data, due to the capacity limitation of our website server, we set up an online access platform that only displays some of the Richpedia data, but we provide Google Cloud Driver download link for all data. In the Google Driver download link, you can find the download link of the full data and the link of nt files about the data description, including the visual relations between the images, the image feature descriptors and so on. With respect to sustainability, because of the large size of the dump, we have not yet found a mirror host to replicate the data. Because we have a long-term plan for Richpedia, hence the dataset will be inactive maintenance and development. As for updating the dataset, although it is expensive to build the original dataset, we plan to implement incremental updates. The descriptors for these images can then be computed, while only the k-nn similarity relations involving new images (potentially pruning old relations) need to be computed.

Using the visual descriptors of image entities generated in Sect. 2.2, we design an experiment to calculate the similarity between image entities. First, we use the OpenCV library to calculate the visual descriptors for each image entity. Next, we use visual descriptors to calculate the similarity between images. For each image entity, we calculate ten nearest neighbors for image entities according to each visual descriptor, for calculating the nearest neighbor image entities, we have the classical algorithm and fast approximate NN matching algorithm.

The problem of nearest neighbor search is a major problem in many applications, such as image recognition, data compression, pattern recognition and classification, machine learning, document retrieval system, statistics and data analysis. However, solving this problem in high-dimensional space seems to be a very difficult task, and no algorithm is obviously superior to the standard brute force search. As a result, more and more people turn their interest to a

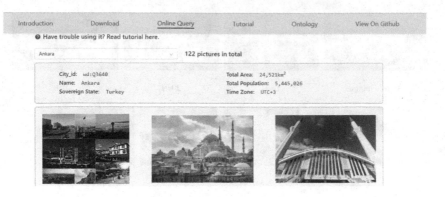

Fig. 11. Results of querying entity about *Ankara*.

class of algorithms that perform the approximate nearest neighbor search. These methods have proved to be good enough approximation in many practical applications and most cases, which is much faster than the exact search algorithm. In computer vision and machine learning, finding the nearest neighbor in training data is expensive for a high-dimensional feature. For high-dimensional features, the randomized k-d forest is the most effective method at present.

For the image entities of online access platform, because the amount of image entities is small, which is about tens of thousands, we use the classical nearest neighbor algorithm to calculate the similarity between image entities. The advantage of this algorithm is that it traverses all data sets, so it has relatively high accuracy and can perfectly reflect the similarity between image entities. However, its shortcomings are obvious. The classical nearest neighbor algorithm, for each image entity, we need to traverse all other image entities, it belongs to brute force search, so it has high time complexity and will consume a lot of time and computing costs. But for the complete Richpedia dataset, if we want to calculate the similarity between image entities, we can only choose Fast Library for Approximated Nearest Neighbors (FLANN) since it has been proven to scale for large datasets. Although it will decrease inaccuracy, it is an optimal choice for large data sets in terms of integration accuracy and time complexity.

We design an experiment which contains 30,000 images. We configured FLANN with a goal precision of 95% and tested it on a brute-forced gold standard. First, we use the classical nearest neighbor algorithm to calculate, however, while it took 18 days to compute with 8 threads, when we test on the FLANN, it finished in 15 hours with 1 thread. Finally, FLANN achieved the precision of 76%. In Fig. 10, we show an example of similarity search results based on HOG descriptor, which captures information about edges in an image.

5   Use-Cases

We first provide some examples of queries on the online access platform.

Fig. 12. Results of querying relations about Beijing Zoo entity.

First, we can query the entity information in Richpedia, including image entities and KG entities. The first step is to select the entity category of the query, and then select the entity we want to query specifically. For example, in Fig. 11, if we want to query the KG entity information and image entity information of the city of *Ankara*, we can select the corresponding *Ankara* label in the drop-down selector. The above half of the page that appears after that is the KG entity information of *Ankara*, and the below half is the image entities of *Ankara*.

Second, we can query the visual semantic relation between image entities through Richpedia's online access platform. After we select the entity for querying, we can view the visual semantic relation of the image entity by clicking on the corresponding image entity. For example, when we want to query an image entity who has a **rpo:sameAs** relation with the *Beijing Zoo* image entity, we can click on the image entity and get the result as shown in the Fig. 12.

6 Related Work

Amongst the available datasets describing multimedia, the emphasis has been on capturing the high-level metadata of the multimedia files (e.g., author, date created, file size, width, duration) rather than audio or visual features of the multimedia content itself [1,8]. Recently, several methods [5,7,12,17,20] have been developed for connecting textual facts and visual resources. IMGpedia [5] is a linked dataset that provides visual descriptors and similarity relationships for Wikimedia Commons. This dataset is also linked with DBpedia and DBpedia Commons to provide semantic context and further metadata. Zhu et al. [20] exploited knowledge graphs for visual question answering, but it was created specifically for the purpose, and consequently contains a small amount of very specific images, and also proposed a knowledge base framework to handle all kinds of visual queries without training new classifiers for new tasks, these annotations represent the densest and largest dataset of image descriptions, objects, attributes, relationships, and question answers. Visual Genome dataset [7] aims

at collecting dense image annotations of objects, attributes, and their relationships. Unfortunately, the visual relationship between IMGpeida [5] is limited to
pixel level similarity, not for the relations between semantic, visual-relational
facts in [7] still limit to provide relational information within the same image.
For instance, a relation "nextTo" between *London Eye* and *River Thames* may
be discovered due to they appeared in a same image, but there is no further
information about the relations between *London Eye* and *London*. MMKG [12]
intended to perform relational reasoning across different entities and images in
different knowledge graphs. However, it was constructed specifically for textual
knowledge graph completion and focused on small datasets (FB15K, DBPE-
DIA15K and YAGO15K). MMKG also did not consider the diversity of images
when distributing images to related textual entities.

7   Conclusion and Future Work

This paper presents the process of constructing a multimodal knowledge graph
(Richpedia). Our work is to collect images from the Internet for entities in textual
knowledge graphs. Then, images are filtered by a diversity retrieval model and
RDF links are set between image entities based on the hyperlinks and descriptions in Wikipedia. The result is a big and high-quality multimodal knowledge
graph dataset, which provides a wider data scope to the researchers from The
Semantic Web and Computer Vision. We publish the Richpedia as an open
resource and provide a facet query endpoint. As future work, our plan is to
broaden the type and scope of entities, so that Richpedia becomes more comprehensive and covers more topics.

Acknowledgment. This work was supported by National Science Foundation of
China with Grant Nos. 61906037 and U1736204; National Key Research and Development Program of China with Grant Nos. 2018YFC0830201 and 2017YFB1002801;
the Judicial Big Data Research Centre, School of Law at Southeast University with
Grant No.4313059291; the Fundamental Research Funds for the Central Universities
with Grant No.4009009106.

References

1. Addis, M., Allasia, W., Bailer, W., Boch, L., Gallo, F., Wright, R.: 100 million
   hours of audiovisual content: digital preservation and access in the prestoprime
   project. In: Proceedings of the 1st International Digital Preservation Interoperability Framework Symposium, p. 3. ACM (2010)
2. Bizer, C., et al.: DBpedia-a crystallization point for the web of data. Web Semant.
   Sci. Serv. Agents World Wide Web **7**(3), 154–165 (2009)
3. Collobert, R., Weston, J., Bottou, L., Karlen, M., Kavukcuoglu, K., Kuksa, P.:
   Natural language processing (almost) from scratch. J. Mach. Learn. Res. **12**, 2493–
   2537 (2011)
4. World Wide Web Consortium, et al.: Rdf 1.1 concepts and abstract syntax (2014)

5. Ferrada, S., Bustos, B., Hogan, A.: IMGpedia: a linked dataset with content-based analysis of wikimedia images. In: d'Amato, C., et al. (eds.) ISWC 2017. LNCS, vol. 10588, pp. 84–93. Springer, Cham (2017). https://doi.org/10.1007/978-3-319-68204-4_8

6. Heaton, R.K., Staff, P.: Wisconsin card sorting test: computer version 2. Odessa Psychol. Assess. Resour. **4**, 1–4 (1993)

7. Krishna, R., et al.: Visual genome: connecting language and vision using crowdsourced dense image annotations. Int. J. Comput. Vision **123**(1), 32–73 (2017)

8. Kurz, T., Kosch, H.: Lifting media fragment URIs to the next level. In: LIME/SemDev@ ESWC (2016)

9. Lee, S., Xin, J., Westland, S.: Evaluation of image similarity by histogram intersection. In: Color Research & Application: Endorsed by Inter-Society Color Council, The Colour Group (Great Britain), Canadian Society for Color, Color Science Association of Japan, Dutch Society for the Study of Color, The Swedish Colour Centre Foundation, Colour Society of Australia, Centre Français de la Couleur, vol. 30, no. 4, pp. 265–274 (2005)

10. Lejuez, C., Kahler, C.W., Brown, R.A.: A modified computer version of the paced auditory serial addition task (PASAT) as a laboratory-based stressor. Behav. Therapist (2003)

11. Liang, X., Lee, L., Xing, E.P.: Deep variation-structured reinforcement learning for visual relationship and attribute detection. In: Proceedings of the IEEE Conference on Computer Vision and Pattern Recognition, pp. 848–857 (2017)

12. Liu, Y., Li, H., Garcia-Duran, A., Niepert, M., Onoro-Rubio, D., Rosenblum, D.S.: MMKG: multi-modal knowledge graphs. arXiv preprint arXiv:1903.05485 (2019)

13. Manning, C., Surdeanu, M., Bauer, J., Finkel, J., Bethard, S., McClosky, D.: The Stanford CoreNLP natural language processing toolkit. In: Proceedings of 52nd Annual Meeting of the Association for Computational Linguistics: System Demonstrations, pp. 55–60 (2014)

14. Manning, C.D., Manning, C.D., Schütze, H.: Foundations of Statistical Natural Language Processing. MIT Press, Cambridge (1999)

15. Marino, K., Salakhutdinov, R., Gupta, A.: The more you know: using knowledge graphs for image classification. In: Proceedings of the IEEE Conference on Computer Vision and Pattern Recognition, pp. 2673–2681 (2017)

16. Trivedi, P., Maheshwari, G., Dubey, M., Lehmann, J.: LC-QuAD: a corpus for complex question answering over knowledge graphs. In: d'Amato, C., et al. (eds.) ISWC 2017. LNCS, vol. 10588, pp. 210–218. Springer, Cham (2017). https://doi.org/10.1007/978-3-319-68204-4_22

17. Vaidya, G., Kontokostas, D., Knuth, M., Lehmann, J., Hellmann, S.: DBpedia commons: structured multimedia metadata from the wikimedia commons. In: Arenas, M., et al. (eds.) ISWC 2015. LNCS, vol. 9367, pp. 281–289. Springer, Cham (2015). https://doi.org/10.1007/978-3-319-25010-6_17

18. Vrandečić, D., Krötzsch, M.: Wikidata: a free collaborative knowledgebase. Commun. ACM **57**(10), 78–85 (2014)

19. Yih, W.t., Chang, M.W., He, X., Gao, J.: Semantic parsing via staged query graph generation: question answering with knowledge base. In: Proceedings of the 53rd Annual Meeting of the Association for Computational Linguistics and the 7th International Joint Conference on Natural Language Processing (Volume 1: Long Papers), vol. 1, pp. 1321–1331 (2015)

20. Zhu, Y., Zhang, C., Ré, C., Fei-Fei, L.: Building a large-scale multimodal knowledge base system for answering visual queries. arXiv preprint arXiv:1507.05670 (2015)

DSEL: A Domain-Specific Entity Linking System

Xinru Zhang[1], Huifang Xu[2], Yixin Cao[3], Yuanpeng Tan[2], Lei Hou[1(✉)],
Juanzi Li[1], and Jiaxin Shi[1]

[1] Tsinghua University, Beijing, China
zhangxr1221@gmail.com, {houlei,lijuanzi}@tsinghua.edu.cn,
shijx12@gmail.com
[2] Artificial Intelligence Application Department,
China Electric Power Research Institute, Beijing, China
{xuhuifang,tanyuanpeng}@epri.sgcc.com.cn
[3] National University of Singapore, Singapore, Singapore
caoyixin2011@gmail.com

Abstract. Entity linking refers to the task of resolving multiple named entity mentions in a document to their correct references in a knowledge base (KB). It can bridge the gap between unstructured nature language documents that computers hardly understand and a structured semantic Knowledge Base which can be easily processed by computers. Existing studies and systems about entity linking mainly focus on the open domain, which may cause three problems: 1. linking to unconcerned entities; 2. time and space consuming; 3. less precision. In this paper, we address the problem by restricting entity linking into specific domains and leveraging domain information to enhance the linking performance. We propose an unsupervised method to generate domain data from Wikipedia and provide a domain-specific neural collective entity linking model for each domain. Based on domain data and domain models, we build a system that can provide domain entity linking for users. Our system, Domain-Specific neural collective Entity Linking system (DSEL), supporting entity linking in 12 domains, is published as an online website, https://dsel.xlore.org.

Keywords: Entity Linking · Domain Generation · Graph convolution network

1 Introduction

Entity linking (EL) aims to link the textual named entity mentions in the unstructured document to proper KB entities. It is a fundamental task for many NLP problems such as question answering, relation extraction. The task has been extensively studied [1,6,11] in recent years, and many EL systems [9,10,16] have been built.

The main challenge of the entity linking task is the ambiguity of named entity mentions. A named entity mention may refer to many KB entities, and an entity

© Springer Nature Switzerland AG 2020
X. Wang et al. (Eds.): JIST 2019, LNCS 12032, pp. 146–161, 2020.
https://doi.org/10.1007/978-3-030-41407-8_10

often has multiple surface names, such as its full name, partial names, aliases, abbreviations, and alternate spellings. For example, the entity "Air Jordan" can be identified by the plain text "Jordan" or "AJ" while the mention "Jordan" can refer to 43 entities in Wikipedia. For a given document, an entity linking system should detect the concerned mentions and link them to correct entities in the knowledge base. Another challenge of the entity linking task is filtering through all recognized named entity mentions finding more meaningful, user-concerned ones. Existing entity linking systems try to link named entities as many as possible, however, many linkages are unnecessary. As it shows in Fig. 1, for the given document, Babelfy and TagMe detect as many entity mentions (Babelfy also detects concept mentions) as possible and link them to corresponding entities (concepts), however, many linkages of them are futile, such as "brand" and "style".

Air Jordan is a brand of basketball shoes, athletic, casual, and style clothing produced by Nike. It was created for former NBA player and 5 time NBA MVP Michael Jordan.	Air Jordan is a brand of basketball shoes, athletic, casual, and style clothing produced by Nike. It was created for former NBA player and 5 time NBA MVP Michael Jordan.
Babelfy	TagMe

Fig. 1. Linking results of two entity linking systems. The left side shows the results from Babelfy, where named mentions in orange are concept links, while the blues are entity links. The right side is the result of TagMe who doesn't consider the difference between concept and entity. (Color figure online)

Extensive research papers are focusing on the challenge of named entity ambiguity. Currently, DNN shows its ability to solve the problem, existing NN models for entity disambiguation have two paradigms: local models, which disambiguate mentions independently relying on textual context information [2,3,7], and global (collective) models, which resolve multiple mentions in a document simultaneously by encouraging their target entities to be coherent [4]. Although current models seem very effective in the experimental test sets, it is still difficult to get satisfactory performance in practical scenarios, especially when target entities come from specific domains. We argue that one critical bottleneck is that current EL models are mostly designed and deployed for the open domain, which contains millions of entities from totally different domains of real-world and thus is too difficult for a single model to handle. For example, as we mentioned before, *Jordan* can refer to 43 entities in Wikipedia, it will cost lots of time and space for disambiguation. The second challenge, meaningful linkages, is rarely been considered, but quite important in practice. To solve the two challenges, we propose to move entity linking systems towards specific domains. By doing so, we can not only reduce the searching space and problem complexity but also leverage domain information (e.g., domain priors) to boost the performance. Besides, the linking results are about the specified domain, which is more meaningful than open domain results.

To provide domain-specific entity linking, we propose an unsupervised approach to generate domain data from Wikipedia. We generated and published 12 domain datasets. As for the model, inspired by [1], we build a candidate graph for multiple mentions in a document, and then utilize graph convolution networks for information aggregation. Our models share the same framework but are trained on different domain-specific datasets. Compared with the model trained on the open domain, our domain-specific systems are demonstrated to perform significantly better. Our key contributions in this work are as follows:

1. Provide an unsupervised approach to generate domain data from Wikipedia utilizing its category system and trained category embeddings. Currently, we have published 12 domain datasets.
2. Build an entity linking system, including dictionary-based mention parsing & candidate generation and domain-specific neural collective entity linking model, and publish the system as an online service.

2   Definition and Framework

2.1   Problem Definition

We introduce some concept definitions and problem formulation in this section.

Definition 1. *A knowledge base KB contains a set of entities $E = \{e_j\}$. Each entity corresponds a page containing title, textual description, hyperlinks pointing to other entities, infobox, etc.*

Definition 2. *A text corpus D contains a set of words $D = \{w_1, w_2, ..., w_{|D|}\}$. A mention m is a word or phrase in D which may refer to an entity e in KB. In this paper, we pre-train word and entity representations, and use low-dimensional vectors vw and ve to denote the embedding of word w and entity e in KB.*

Definition 3. *An anchor $a \in A$ is a hyperlink in KB articles, which links its surface text mention m to an entity e. Ae, m denotes the set of anchors of mention m pointing to entity e. Anchor Dictionary is the dictionary that we build through utilizing all the anchors in KB. Each a in the anchor dictionary may refer to a set of entities Em = ej.*

Definition 4. *Problem Definition. Given a document $D = \{w_1, w_2, ..., w_{|D|}\}$ and a knowledge base KB. The task is to find out the mentions $M = \{m_1, ..., m_k\}$ in D and link them to their referent KB entities. We resolve the problem into two phases. In Mention Parsing, we detect mentions M and generate a candidate entity set $C = \{e_1, e_2, ..., e_{|C|}\}$ for each mention m_j. In Entity Disambiguation, we select the most probable entity e_j in the candidate set C for each mention m_j. The disambiguation process can be described as an optimization problem:*

$$\arg\max_{\Gamma} \Phi(c, \Gamma)$$

where c represents global context and $\Gamma = \{e_1, ..., e_k\}$, e_i is one of the candidate KB entities of m_i.

2.2   The Classical Pipeline of an Entity Linking System

As we mentioned above, entity linking is a task about linking textual mentions in a given document to the corresponding entities in a large scale structured KG. The classical process pipeline of an entity linking system is contains three main processes: 1. mention detection, 2. candidate generation, 3. entity disambiguation.

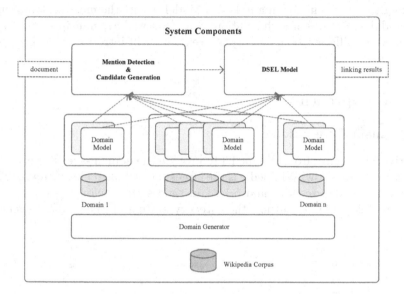

Fig. 2. System framework. Our system contains three parts: Domain Generation, Mention Detection & Candidates Generation, and Domain-specific Entity Linking Model. When the user inputs a document and a domain, our system detects mentions in the document and maps them to their corresponding KB entities.

Mention Detection aims to find out entity mentions M in the textual document D, challenges of this stage lay on the various expression forms of an entity.

Candidate Generation tries to filter out irrelevant entities in the knowledge base and retrieve a candidate entity set E_m which contains possible entities that entity mention $m \in M$ may refer to. After the previous two stages, given a document D, we have already got a mention set M and a corresponding candidate entity set E.

Entity Disambiguation ranks candidate entities E_m for each entity mention m and then links the mention to the KG entity e_m^* that has the highest ranking score. Many EL researchers only focus on this stage. The input of this process is mentions M in the given document and the corresponding candidate entities $C = \{C_1, ...\}$.

2.3 Our System

As it shows in Fig. 2, our system consists of three components: Domain Generator, Mention Detection & Candidates Generation, and Domain-Specific Entity Linking (DSEL) Model. Domain Generator extracts training data and mention-candidate pairs for specific domains from the whole Wikipedia corpus. Mention Detection & Candidates Generation identifies mentions and candidate entities according to the specified domain. DSEL Model selects the most probable entity from candidate entities of each mention. Note that we have multiple DSEL models trained on different domain corpus. Next, we will introduce the three parts respectively.

3 Our Approach

3.1 Domain Generation

We derive 12 domains from Wikipedia to provide the domain-specific entity linking system. As we know, Wikipedia is the largest encyclopedia in existence. There are around 1.3 M categories and 5.1 M instances that belong to the category system in Wikipedia. We utilize the category system of Wikipedia to generate

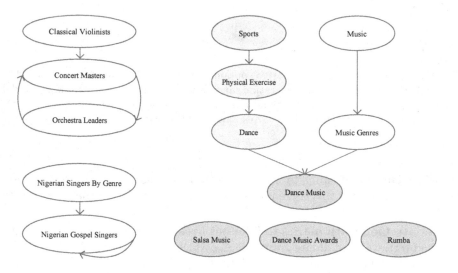

Fig. 3. Two traits of category system in Wikipedia. As it shows in the left graph, there exist circle paths in the category system of Wikipedia. The right graph shows that some categories may cause domain overlap because their parent categories come from different domains.

domain data for further use. The key idea behind domain data generation is traversing the category tree of Wikipedia from seed categories of a domain to generate domain categories, then obtaining articles under those categories to construct domain data. Ideally, given a set of seed categories of a domain, we can derive domain categories from the category tree by traversing it. However, Wikipedia is an online encyclopedia that everyone can edit. Inevitably, there are three impediments may lead to unexpected results (Fig. 3):

1. There are categories for administration such as "Mathematics-related lists" and "Sports administration" who have no contribution to the domain and will introduce semantic bias.
2. The category tree is, in fact, a graph but a tree. There exist circle paths between two category nodes.
3. A category may belong to more than one domain, which will cause severe domain overlaps and will blur the boundary between two domains.

Algorithm. Considering the listed impediments above, we bring forward an algorithm that can efficiently obtain categories of a domain. Algorithm 1 describes how we derive domain categories and instances.

1. Given a top category for a domain, retrieve its first-layer sub-categories and then filter irrelevant categories such as administration categories.
2. Get the top-k layer categories as seed categories of the domain, calculate the average embedding of category for further use.
3. Traverse the i-th layer, $i > k$, calculate the cosine similarity with the average category embedding for each category in the layer, then sort those categories by the similarity score, drop last $droprate_i\%$ categories of this layer.
4. Stop traverse when $i > max\_depth$.

Category Embedding. Category embedding is used to capture the domain semantic vectorial representation of a category. To capture the semantic of a category for the domain, we borrow the idea behind skip-gram: predicting the related domain categories of a given category.

As far as we know, there isn't a proper dataset that can help use to train such models, so we propose an unsupervised method to build such dataset. Our approach assumes that in most cases, categories in one entity belong to the same domain. We first retrieve categories of an entity and then arrange them m times by random order to obtain m different category lists. After that, we can generate a category sequence for an entity by catenating those category lists. Randomly arranging the categories m times can alleviate order effect of categories. We obtain category sequences of all instances in Wikipedia as the input of skip-gram model and get vectorial embedding for each category.

Result: domain_categories
category_queue = top_layer_categories;
level_len = category_queue.size();
curr_depth = 1;
seed_depth = k;
domain_categories = list([]);
while *category_queue is not empty* **do**
    head_category = category_queue.pop();
    level_len-=1;
    push all sub categories of head_category into category_queue;
    domain_categories.append(head_category);
    if *level_len == 0* **then**
        if *curr_depth == seed_depth* **then**
            calculate average category embedding of current
            domain_categories.;
        end
        if *curr_depth > seed_depth* **then**
            sort categories in category_queue by the cosine similarity with
            average category embedding.;
            drop last $droprate_{curr\_depth}\%$ categories in the queue;
        end
        curr_depth ++;
        if *curr_depth > max_depth* **then**
            break ;
        end
        level_len = category_queue.size();
    end
end

Algorithm 1: Domain categories generation

3.2   Mention Parsing and Candidate Generation

Mention parsing detects the possible entity mentions in the input document D by searching a pre-built anchor dictionary. Therefore, dictionary building and parsing algorithm are the major concerns.

Dictionary Building. In Wikipedia, the anchor text of a hyperlink pointing to an entity page provides useful name variations of the pointed entity. An anchor can be a synonym, abbreviation or title of an entity. For example, anchor text "Apple" may point to the page of Apple Inc., Apple Corps. or Apple (fruit) in different documents. Inversely, the entity Apple Inc. also has other anchor texts, such as "Apple Computer Inc." By extracting anchor texts and their corresponding hyperlinks from KB articles, we can construct an anchor dictionary, where the keys are mentions and values are candidate entities, as shown in Table 1. A mention may refer to several entities and an entity may have several mentions.

Thus, we can generate the candidate entities referred by a mention easily by querying the dictionary.

Parsing Algorithm. To accelerate parsing process, we use a fast string searching algorithm to parse mentions in anchor dictionaries, Aho1Corasick Algorithm. It is a kind of dictionary-matching algorithm that locates elements of a finite set of strings (the "dictionary") within an input text and it matches all strings simultaneously. Informally, the algorithm constructs a finite state ma- chine that resembles a trie with additional links between the various internal nodes. With the pre-built anchor dictionary, we could construct the automaton o-line. In particular, the complexity of the algorithm is linear in the length of the strings plus the length of the searched text plus the number of output matches, which is efficient for online process.

However, because the automaton find all matches simultaneously, there could be a quadratic number of conflicts (substrings and overlaps). To solve the problem, we design an algorithm to choose a match which could be most probable to be an entity mention. For two conflicting mentions m_1 and m_2, if m_1 is much longer, we regard m_1 to be more specific than m_2. For example, the mention "Jordan air" is more specific than "Jordan". Besides, if m_1 has the same length with m_2, we choose the one with greater link probability. We assume a mention name with greater link probability is more likely to be linked in text and has less ambiguity intuitively. Furthermore, the parsing algorithm detects mentions iteratively until there is no conflicting mentions in the text. Finally, we could generate candidate entity set $C = \{e_1, e_2, ..., e_{|C|}\}$ for mention m_j.

3.3   Domain NCEL Model

Embedding. We train word and entity embedding into the same vector space, inspired by [15]. This model consists of the following three models based on the skip-gram model: (1) the conventional skip-gram model that learns to predict neighboring words given the target word in text corpora, (2) the KB graph model that learns to estimate neighboring entities given the target entity in the link graph of the KB, and (3) the anchor context model that learns to predict neighboring words given the target entity using anchors and their context words in the KB. By jointly optimizing these models, the method simultaneously learns the embedding of words and entities. We trained embeddings on both open domain dataset and domain-specific dataset to feed the domain specific disambiguation model.

Input Features. The input of our model contains local features and global features. Local features represent how compatible that the entity is with the context text of its corresponding mention. There are two typos of local features for each candidate entity: string similarity by calculating the edit distance and entity-context similarity by computing the similarity between the entity and the average sum of context words weighted by attentions.

Global features represent the topic coherence among entities, mentions and plain text of a given document. We extract two types of global features to capture the global semantic, neighbor mention compatibility and subgraph structure. We compute the similarities between the candidate entity and all neighbor mentions to represent the neighbor mention compatibility. As for the subgraph structure feature, we firstly build an entity graph where nodes are candidate entities of all mentions and edges are their similarity, then for each candidate entity, extract candidate entities of neighbor mentions to build a subgraph as another global feature.

Disambiguation Model. Following [1], we implement a domain-specific entity linking model. The inputs of our model include domain-specific and open-domain vectorial features of entities and words, and relatedness sub-graphs of candidates. We use a multilayer perceptron to integrate these different features, and then convey information between each candidate and its context candidates via a sub-graph convolution network layer. After sub-graph convolution, a fully connected layer maps abstract hidden states to probabilities of candidates being mention's corresponding KB entities.

4   Experiments

4.1   Dataset

The dataset we used in our work is the Wikipedia corpus dumped in March 2018. To the best of our knowledge, there isn't a proper domain dataset that can both provide sufficient plain text and mention-entity relations for the task of entity linking, so we built 12 domain dataset from Wikipedia for domain model training and system usage. Wikipedia is the largest online encyclopedia that everybody can edit, we extracted 5,133,361 instances and 1,376,896 categories for our work. Table 1 shows the detailed statistics of the 12 domains.

Table 1. Dataset statistics.

Domain	ID	Instances	Categories	Mentions
Mathematics	0	28,182	1,021	16,129
Music	1	244,193	21,108	96,732
Politics	2	84,640	5,396	70,347
Law	3	679,932	61,367	318,372
Computing	4	4383,392	18,329	193,821
Military	5	64,619	6737	53,430
Sports	6	448,341	51,804	129,898
Health	7	161,417	11,750	93,717
Philosophy	8	69,660	3,156	47,655
Energy	9	23,534	3,860	17,561
Geography	10	637,295	63,076	287,656
Education	11	246,229	14,282	129,274

4.2   Domain Generate

Settings. For the generation Algorithm 1, we set $k = 4$, which means we assume that top-four-layer categories are credible domain categories. $droprate_{depth}$ is set as 0.5 for the 5_{th} layer and will increase 0.1 each time along with traverse depth until 0.8. The max_depth is set as 20 (Fig. 4).

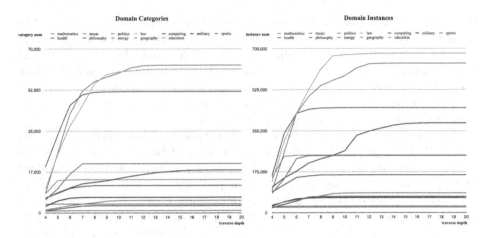

Fig. 4. Domain categories and instances amount increases along with traverse depth.

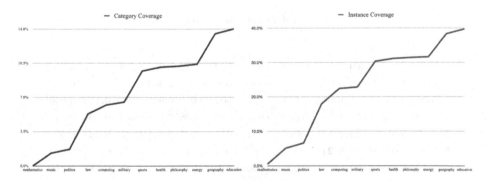

Fig. 5. The coverage of total domain instances and categories. The vertical coordinate is the category/instance coverage ratio of extended domains, while the horizontal coordinate represents the new-added domain. For example, the instance coverage value at 'politics' is the instance coverage of mathematics, music, and politics.

Domain Coverage. We calculate the coverage of the 12 domains and the ratio of entities that cross domains. The amount of total instances of the 12 domains is 2,104,760, while the total instances of the whole dataset are 5,300,338.

Some instances not contained in our pre-defined domains because the domains are manually set, as it shows in Fig. 5, the coverage increases after introducing new domain.

As the Fig. 5 shows, there are three ratio jumps when adding **music**, **law** and **sports**, that means the three domains are more independent to other domains and have more content. The experiment below also reveals this phenomenon.

Domain Overlap Ratio. The domain overlap ratio explains the proportion of category/instances that appears in other domains. This can give us an insight into the rationality of the domain. Tables 2 and 3 reveal the overlap ratio of domain categories and instances respectively, IDs are domain IDs and the mapping relations from ID to Domain Name can be found in Table 1. The value at the i-th row and the j-th column means the proportion of categories/instances in the i-th domain appearing in the j-th domain.

The maximum value of category overlap ratio is 0.655 where $i = 2$ and $j = 3$, that means 65.5% categories in domain **politics** also belongs domain **law**, and there are 5.7% categories in law belongs to **politics**. We also noticed that the total category amount is 5,396 for **politics** comparing 61,367 for **law**. The instance overlap ratio of three pairs of domains is over 0.5, they are 83.1% instances of **politics** also belong to **law**, 52.3% **military** instances belong to **law**, and 50.6% health instances belong to **law**. Intuitively, the results above mean that there are more law-related content in Wikipedia than politics, military and health, and politics may be a sub-domain of law.

Table 2. Category overlap ratio

ID	0	1	2	3	4	5	6	7	8	9	10	11
0	1.000	0.062	0.000	0.025	**0.289**	0.001	0.012	0.024	0.050	0.000	0.015	**0.114**
1	0.003	1.000	0.000	0.007	0.015	0.000	0.005	0.003	0.000	0.000	0.009	0.005
2	0.000	0.003	1.000	**0.655**	0.083	0.088	0.004	0.065	0.035	0.002	**0.112**	0.040
3	0.000	0.002	0.057	1.000	0.047	0.024	0.005	0.056	0.014	0.005	**0.140**	0.045
4	0.016	0.018	0.024	**0.160**	1.000	0.004	0.032	0.077	0.024	0.003	**0.141**	0.092
5	0.000	0.002	0.070	**0.219**	0.012	1.000	0.004	0.023	0.000	0.000	0.098	0.022
6	0.000	0.002	0.000	0.006	0.011	0.000	1.000	0.027	0.001	0.000	0.035	0.017
7	0.002	0.006	0.029	**0.296**	**0.120**	0.013	**0.122**	1.000	0.008	0.009	0.073	0.067
8	0.016	0.005	0.061	**0.289**	**0.141**	0.001	0.024	0.030	1.000	0.000	**0.109**	**0.136**
9	0.000	0.000	0.003	0.091	0.016	0.000	0.001	0.029	0.000	1.000	0.051	0.004
10	0.000	0.003	0.009	**0.136**	0.041	0.010	0.029	0.013	0.005	0.003	1.000	0.015
11	0.008	0.008	0.015	**0.193**	**0.118**	0.010	0.063	0.055	0.030	0.001	0.068	1.000

Table 3. Instance overlap ratio

ID	0	1	2	3	4	5	6	7	8	9	10	11
0	1.000	0.019	0.012	**0.114**	**0.458**	0.005	0.023	0.063	0.091	0.006	0.074	**0.250**
1	0.002	1.000	0.007	0.052	0.053	0.003	0.021	0.017	0.006	0.000	0.062	0.024
2	0.004	0.020	1.000	**0.831**	**0.271**	**0.183**	0.024	**0.184**	**0.123**	0.008	**0.337**	**0.174**
3	0.004	0.018	**0.103**	1.000	**0.179**	0.049	0.030	**0.120**	0.047	0.011	**0.264**	**0.137**
4	0.033	0.034	0.059	**0.318**	1.000	0.017	0.089	**0.141**	0.065	0.011	**0.203**	**0.185**
5	0.002	0.012	**0.239**	**0.523**	**0.106**	1.000	0.024	**0.104**	0.016	0.005	**0.325**	0.064
6	0.001	0.011	0.004	0.046	0.076	0.003	1.000	0.045	0.019	0.000	0.083	0.041
7	0.011	0.026	0.096	**0.506**	**0.335**	0.041	**0.126**	1.000	0.048	0.023	**0.200**	**0.200**
8	0.037	0.021	**0.149**	**0.468**	**0.362**	0.015	**0.128**	**0.112**	1.000	0.003	**0.232**	**0.319**
9	0.008	0.003	0.029	**0.320**	**0.181**	0.015	0.015	**0.164**	0.011	1.000	**0.191**	0.077
10	0.003	0.023	0.044	**0.282**	**0.122**	0.033	0.058	0.050	0.025	0.007	1.000	0.080
11	0.028	0.024	0.059	**0.379**	**0.288**	0.017	0.076	**0.131**	0.090	0.007	**0.208**	1.000

4.3   Model Validation

To demonstrate the superiority of our domain-specific models against open-domain models, we randomly selected 400k open-domain Wikipedia articles as control data and trained our DSEL model on domain training data and control data respectively, and then evaluated both on domain validation data. Experimental results are listed in Table 4. We can see those domain-specific models perform stably and significantly better than general ones.

Table 4. Model validation results. The left side lists results of domain-specific models, while the right side shows results of open-domain models.

Domain	Precision*	Recall*	F1*	Precision	Recall	F1
Computing	**0.921**	**0.783**	**0.846**	0.586	0.498	0.538
Education	**0.932**	**0.796**	**0.859**	0.673	0.575	0.620
Energy	**0.947**	**0.810**	**0.873**	0.544	0.462	0.500
Geography	**0.907**	**0.762**	**0.828**	0.528	0.441	0.481
Health	**0.931**	**0.801**	**0.861**	0.551	0.473	0.509
Law	**0.936**	**0.750**	**0.832**	0.574	0.484	0.525
Mathematics	**0.942**	**0.811**	**0.872**	0.622	0.533	0.574
Military	**0.930**	**0.772**	**0.844**	0.603	0.501	0.547
Music	**0.937**	**0.775**	**0.848**	0.629	0.516	0.567
Philosophy	**0.941**	**0.808**	**0.869**	0.615	0.525	0.567
Politics	**0.930**	**0.770**	**0.842**	0.584	0.482	0.528
Sports	**0.904**	**0.783**	**0.839**	0.522	0.448	0.482

4.4   Category Embedding

We propose category embedding to generate more semantic-related domain data. To verify the validity of category embedding, we compute the distance between domain categories. We randomly select m categories from each domain and compute the average distance between each two domains n times.

$$distance(i,j) = \frac{1}{n} \sum_{k=1,\ldots,n} \frac{1}{m*m} \sum_{c_{ki} \in DC_{ki}} \sum_{c_{kj} \in DC_{kj}} cos(c_{ki}, c_{kj})$$

DC_{ki} represents the randomly selected categories in the k-th time for domain i, n is the time of randomly selecting m domain categories. In this experiment, we set $n = 10$ and $m = 100$. The results are listed in Table 5.

Table 5. Average domain category distance.

ID	0	1	2	3	4	5	6	7	8	9	10	11
0	**0.151**	0.021	0.062	0.056	0.069	0.063	0.008	0.072	0.072	0.084	0.044	0.069
1	0.026	**0.221**	0.019	0.00	0.040	0.00	0.03	0.008	0.021	0.006	0.001	0.00
2	0.042	0.00	**0.172**	0.149	0.074	0.176	0.033	0.108	0.082	0.110	0.103	0.097
3	0.066	0.003	0.141	**0.165**	0.075	0.164	0.041	0.086	0.073	0.134	0.125	0.130
4	0.060	0.023	0.078	0.060	**0.116**	0.075	0.031	0.073	0.031	0.062	0.056	0.075
5	0.070	−0.01	0.201	0.170	0.094	**0.201**	0.303	0.141	0.073	0.160	0.161	0.127
6	0.013	−0.01	0.015	0.040	0.029	0.054	**0.133**	0.045	−0.00	0.101	0.057	0.063
7	0.056	0.015	0.097	0.103	0.081	0.109	0.042	**0.165**	0.038	0.100	0.091	0.114
8	0.063	0.001	0.076	0.065	0.042	0.074	0.003	0.026	**0.112**	0.038	0.089	0.077
9	0.079	0.025	0.146	0.153	0.094	0.172	0.075	0.172	0.032	**0.365**	0.142	0.125
10	0.062	0.002	0.115	0.140	0.065	0.147	0.055	0.095	0.051	0.118	**0.163**	0.121
11	0.079	0.008	0.114	0.106	0.065	0.147	0.074	0.109	0.061	0.124	0.105	**0.167**

5   System Implementation

We develop a website, https://dsel.xlore.org. When receiving a text and specified domain, our system will choose a domain dictionary to parse mentions and generate corresponding candidates, and then feed identified mentions and candidates to our pre-trained domain model to predict target KB entity for each mention. Once getting prediction results, the system will render them to the web page for users or return JSON data for developers.

6   Related Work

Wikipedia is the largest meaningful, half-structured online crowd-sourced, openly-investigable encyclopedia. Numerous knowledge bases have been built

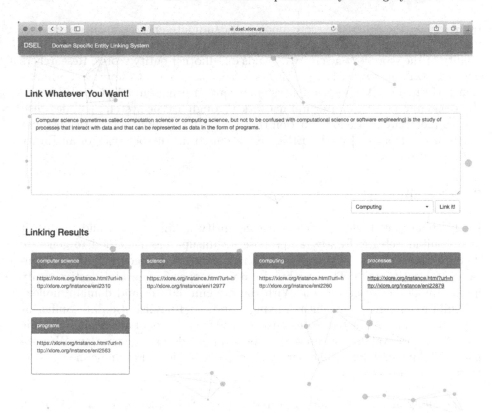

Fig. 6. System screenshot. Users input the plain text document, select a domain, click the button 'Link it!', and then our system will return the linking results of the document.

based on it. The category system of Wikipedia consists of two parts: entity-category and category hierarchy. The former refers to adding tags, called categories, to a Wikipedia article, and the latter is the way to organize all categories in Wikipedia, both parts are user-generated. The category system has been well studied [5,12,13] and proved valuable for introducing semantic information. The category hierarchy is far away from perfection since the definition of subcategory relation is not clear enough for a knowledge base, and there are many categories are added for the administration of the category system itself. As we want to capture the domain semantics from category system, it's okay for us that the subcategory relation is not clear. As for the administration categories, we directly remove them since they will introduce semantic bias (Fig. 6).

Entity linking models can be classified into two types: local models and global models. Local models [2,3,15] resolve mention ambiguity by computing the similarity between candidate entities and mention contexts, to make semantic of target entity aligns with local context. Global models [1,4,6] solve the problem by modeling the coherence score among all candidate entities in the given document. Definition 4 reveals it is difficult to optimize the problem because the quality of the score for one entity depends on all other entity scores. Researchers explored various approaches limiting the searching space to improve optimization performance. [11] proposed a system for integrating symbolic knowledge into the reasoning process of a neural network through a type system, [14] designed a label hierarchy aware loss function that relies on the ultrametric tree distance between labels and [8] used NER types to constrain the behavior of an Entity Linking system.

7   Conclusion

In this paper, we build a domain-specific entity linking system and publish it as an online website. Firstly, we propose an unsupervised method to generate domain dataset from Wikipedia, including instances, categories, and mention-candidate entity pairs. Then we build a domain-specific neural collective entity linking model for each domain. With the domain dataset and domain models, we build a domain-specific entity linking system and publish it online. Sufficient experiments are conducted to demonstrate the superiority of our domain-specific models and the validity of category embedding for domain generation. We published 12 domain datasets and our DSEL system is released as an online website, http://dsel.xlore.org.

Acknowledgments. The work is supported by NSFC key projects (U1736204, 61533018, 61661146007), Key Technology Develop and Research Project of SGCC (5400-201953257A-0-0-00), Ministry of Education and China Mobile Joint Fund (MCM20170301), and THUNUS NExT Co-Lab.

References

1. Cao, Y., Hou, L., Li, J., Liu, Z.: Neural collective entity linking. arXiv preprint arXiv:1811.08603 (2018)
2. Chen, Z., Ji, H.: Collaborative ranking: a case study on entity linking. In: Proceedings of the Conference on Empirical Methods in Natural Language Processing, pp. 771–781. Association for Computational Linguistics (2011)
3. Chisholm, A., Hachey, B.: Entity disambiguation with web links. Trans. Assoc. Comput. Linguist. **3**, 145–156 (2015)
4. Durrett, G., Klein, D.: A joint model for entity analysis: coreference, typing, and linking. Trans. Assoc. Comput. Linguist. **2**, 477–490 (2014)
5. Faralli, S., Stilo, G., Velardi, P.: What women like: a gendered analysis of Twitter users' interests based on a twixonomy. In: Ninth International AAAI Conference on Web and Social Media (2015)
6. Han, X., Sun, L., Zhao, J.: Collective entity linking in web text: a graph-based method. In: Proceedings of the 34th International ACM SIGIR Conference on Research and Development in Information Retrieval, pp. 765–774. ACM (2011)
7. Lazic, N., Subramanya, A., Ringgaard, M., Pereira, F.: Plato: a selective context model for entity resolution. Trans. Assoc. Comput. Linguist. **3**, 503–515 (2015)

8. Ling, X., Singh, S., Weld, D.S.: Design challenges for entity linking. Trans. Assoc. Comput. Linguist. **3**, 315–328 (2015)
9. Mihalcea, R., Csomai, A.: Wikify!: linking documents to encyclopedic knowledge. In: Proceedings of the Sixteenth ACM Conference on Conference on Information and Knowledge Management, pp. 233–242. ACM (2007)
10. Moro, A., Raganato, A., Navigli, R.: Entity linking meets word sense disambiguation: a unified approach. Trans. Assoc. Comput. Linguist. **2**, 231–244 (2014)
11. Raiman, J.R., Raiman, O.M.: Deeptype: multilingual entity linking by neural type system evolution. In: Thirty-Second AAAI Conference on Artificial Intelligence (2018)
12. Schönhofen, P.: Identifying document topics using the wikipedia category network. Web Intell. Agent Syst. Int. J. **7**(2), 195–207 (2009)
13. Strube, M., Ponzetto, S.P.: Wikirelate! computing semantic relatedness using Wikipedia. In: AAAI, vol. 6, pp. 1419–1424 (2006)
14. Wu, C., Tygert, M., LeCun, Y.: Hierarchical loss for classification. arXiv preprint arXiv:1709.01062 (2017)
15. Yamada, I., Shindo, H., Takeda, H., Takefuji, Y.: Joint learning of the embedding of words and entities for named entity disambiguation. arXiv preprint arXiv:1601.01343 (2016)
16. Zhang, J., Cao, Y., Hou, L., Li, J., Zheng, H.-T.: XLink: an unsupervised bilingual entity linking system. In: Sun, M., Wang, X., Chang, B., Xiong, D. (eds.) CCL/NLP-NABD -2017. LNCS (LNAI), vol. 10565, pp. 172–183. Springer, Cham (2017). https://doi.org/10.1007/978-3-319-69005-6_15

Exploring the Generalization
of Knowledge Graph Embedding

Liang Zhang[1], Huan Gao[1(✉)], Xianda Zheng[2], Guilin Qi[1,2], and Jiming Liu[3]

[1] School of Computer Science and Engineering, Southeast University, Nanjing, China
{230169435,gh,gqi}@seu.edu.cn
[2] School of Cyber Science and Engineering, Southeast University, Nanjing, China
zhengxianda@seu.edu.cn
[3] Itibia Technologies, Suzhou, China
jiming@itibia.com

Abstract. Knowledge graph embedding aims to represent structured entities and relations as continuous and dense low-dimensional vectors. With more and more embedding models being proposed, it has been widely used in many tasks such as semantic search, knowledge graph completion and intelligent question and answer. Most knowledge graph embedding models focus on how to get information about different entities and relations. However, the generalization of knowledge graph embedding or the link prediction ability is not well-studied empirically and theoretically. The study of generalization ability is conducive to further improving the performance of the model. In this paper, we propose two measures to quantify the generalization ability of knowledge graph embedding and use them to analyze the performance of translation-based models. Extensive experimental results show that our measures can well evaluate the generalization ability of a knowledge graph embedding model.

1 Introduction

Knowledge graph contains abundant structured information. It represents the real world things in the form of a directed graph, in which nodes represent entities and the edges of nodes represent relations. Generally speaking, a knowledge graph contains enormous triple facts, also denoted as (h, r, t) which consists of head entity, relation and tail entity. Due to the difficulties in dealing with structured information, special graph algorithms need to be designed for knowledge graph. However, this measure leads to inefficiency. Therefore, knowledge representation learning has been proposed to alleviate this problem. Knowledge representation learning or knowledge graph embedding aims at mapping entities and relations to continuous and low-dimensional vector spaces for easy computation and analysis. Knowledge graph embedding has been widely applied in various fields, such as knowledge graph completion [1], intelligent question answering and semantic search [2]. Especially in the task of knowledge graph completion, some models have achieved quite well performance [3,4].

© Springer Nature Switzerland AG 2020
X. Wang et al. (Eds.): JIST 2019, LNCS 12032, pp. 162–176, 2020.
https://doi.org/10.1007/978-3-030-41407-8_11

However, many knowledge graph embedding models focus on how to build the model rather than the ability of generalization. Even though there are some studies on the generalization ability of models, researchers only care about the size of parameters. In fact, many knowledge graph embedding models could be regarded as a linear neural network model [5]. The learning process of these models is also a process of deep learning. Generalization is an important aspect to reflect the complexity of a model in the problems of deep learning. However, in deep learning, the generalization ability of the model can not be well described according to the scale of parameters. For example, even though there are more parameters than training data, good results can still be obtained [6]. Besides, different optimization approaches may obtain different optimal results leading to varieties of generalization results [7,8]. And sometimes the gradient descent will also reduce the complexity of the model in the field of deep learning [9,10]. Numerous factors affect the generalization ability of the model while people pay little attention to the generalization of knowledge graph embedding models. Intuitively, the better the generalization ability of a model, the more effective the model will be. The lack of research on model generalization ability will probably hinder the progress of model effects. As the number of knowledge graph embedding models increase, it is difficult to assess the model with good generalization ability from so many models. Therefore, it is necessary to evaluate the generalization ability of knowledge graph embedding. Because link prediction is the main task of response generalization ability, we use the link prediction ability as the generalization ability of the knowledge graph embedding model. There are many factors affecting the generalization ability of the model, in addition to the parameters, other measures are needed to be proposed. This paper intend to quantify the generalization ability or the link prediction ability by generalization error and empirical error.

As far as we know, this is the first work on studying the generalization ability of a knowledge graph embedding model. However, some work on analyzing knowledge graph embedding models is related to our work. For example, Chandrahas et al. [11] studied the geometric characteristics of the knowledge graph embedding model. But they did not analyze the generalization ability.

Our contributions mainly include the following three points:

First, we give a formal definition of the generalization ability of the knowledge graph embedding model, which is the sum of the generalization error and the empirical error.

Second, we define a set of analytical methods and propose two measures to quantify the generalization ability of an embedding model. We use the L_p norm to measure the generalization error and use the upper bound to measure the empirical error.

Third, we conduct extensive experiments to analyze translation-based knowledge graph embedding models. The experimental results show that our method can evaluate the generalization ability of a translation based knowledge graph embedding model effectively.

2   Related Work

2.1   Analysis of Translation-Based Knowledge Graph Embedding Models

In recent years, more and more knowledge graph embedding models have been proposed. The most representative models are translation-based models, such as TransE [12], TransH [13], TransR [14] and so on. TransE interprets the relations as translating operations between head and tail entities on the low-dimensional vector space. The TransE model is relatively simple, thus, it performs well in 1-to-1 relations while has issues in modeling 1-to-N, N-to-1, and N-to-N relations. To improve the situation, many improved models of TransE have been proposed. TransH attempts to solve the problem of TransE by modeling relations as hyperplanes and projecting h and t to the relational-specific hyperplane, allowing entities to play different roles in different relations. TransR models entities and relations in distinct semantic space and projects entities from entity space to relation space when learning embeddings. Other translation models such as TransA [15] and TransD [16] are also representative models.

2.2   Analysis of Generalization in Deep Learning

Although research on the generalization of models in the field of knowledge graph embedding is currently insufficient, many researchers have shown a strong interest in evaluating generalization ability in deep learning. Neyshabur et al. [17] considered several suggested explanations, including norm, sharpness, and robustness and study how these measures can ensure generalization. Through these measurements, they tried to explain different experimental phenomena. Kawaguchi et al. [18] studied why deep learning can show good generalization results from a more theoretical perspective, thus a non-empty, numerical rigorous generalization guarantee is provided for deep learning. Different from the theoretical research of the former, Zhang et al. [19] re-examined the generalization of deep learning from the perspective of image classification experiment. These studies show that the factors affecting the generalization ability of deep learning models are not only parameters or network depth or training algorithms. These studies has inspired and guided our work.

Although the knowledge graph embedding models sometimes have good results in knowledge graph completion or in other tasks, the overall performance of the model is not satisfying. TransE model is underfitting in many cases. For example, in the task of link prediction, TransE's Hits@10 on FB15K is only 47.1%, less than 50%. The other TransH and TransR are not very high. This lower accuracy may be constrained by the generalization ability of the model. Therefore, clarifying the mechanism of the generalization ability of the knowledge graph embedding model is helpful for researchers to quickly identify models with good generalization ability from many models. Besides, it is also helpful for further research and development in this field.

3   Problem Definition

Our goal is to analyze the generalization ability of the knowledge graph embedding model. By researching on generalization, we hope to find some criterions or conclusions that affect the performance of the model. Because there are many models of knowledge graph embedding, but we are only focused on translation-based models in this paper. Translation-based models can be regarded as a linear neural network model. Most of the models are improved on this, essentially an embedding matrix is transformed into a zero matrix after elementary transformation of the matrix. As shown in Fig. 1, the learning process of entities and relations in the model is a deep learning process.

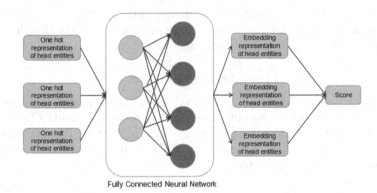

Fully Connected Neural Network

Fig. 1. Knowledge graph embedding framework based on neural network representation

Regarding the training process of the models, when the training loss of a model is equal, the higher the complexity of a model is, the worse its generalization ability will be. Therefore, we hope to find the knowledge graph embedding model with the lowest complexity. We propose the generalization ability F of the model consists of empirical error and generalization error:

$$F = \sigma_{emp} + \sigma_{gen}. \tag{1}$$

We hope that the empirical error and the generalization error of the model will be as small as possible. In order to measure these two indicators effectively, this paper try to find some measures to quantify the generalization ability.

4   Analytical Methods

According to the generalization ability of the model, which is measured by the empirical error and the generalization error, we propose two measures. In order to measure the generalization error, we use the L_p norm of relation. For the measurement of empirical error, we adopt the method of inspecting the upper bound of empirical error. For the knowledge graph embedding model, its parameters are the weights of the fully connected neural network, so we can transform the capacity of the neural network model into a norm to measure the parameters in the model. The remaining question becomes how to measure the capacity of the model.

4.1   Measurement of Generalization Error

Consider a model whose input is x, output is y, and model parameters are w:

$$y = f_w(x). \tag{2}$$

In many cases, we want to get a robust model which is less sensitive to input, so that the generalization ability of the model appropriately can be improved. Square multiplication of all parameters in the embedded matrix. The formula is applied on the basis of Lipshitz constraints:

$$\|f_w(x_1) - f_w(x_2)\| \leq C(w) \cdot \|x_1 - x_2\|. \tag{3}$$

The implication of this constraint is that when the change of x is sufficiently small, we also want the change of model to be sufficiently small. $C(w)$, as the upper bound of the change, is a constant only related to the parameters of the model. If x_1 and x_2 are approximated sufficiently, then the left side can be approximated by a first-order term:

$$\left\| \frac{\partial(f)}{\partial(x)} W(x_1 - x_2) \right\| \leq C(W, b) \cdot \|x_1 - x_2\|. \tag{4}$$

For a specific model, we hope to estimate the expression of $C(w)$, and the smaller the $C(w)$ is, the better its generalization will be. Obviously, to ensure that the left side does not exceed the right side, the absolute value of the f/x term (each element) must not exceed a constant. This requires us to use activation functions with upper and lower bounds of derivatives, and the commonly used activation functions, such as sigmoid, tanh, ReLU, satisfy this condition. It is assumed that the gradient of the activation function is bounded, especially for commonly used ReLU activation function, which is still 1. So the $\partial(f)/\partial(x)$ term has only one constant. For now only $\|W(x_1 - x_2)\|$ is to be considered. After transformation, it is found that C is only related to the norm of weight:

$$\|W(x_1 - x_2)\| \leq C \|x_1 - x_2\|. \tag{5}$$

This problem is now transformed into a matrix norm problem. After numerous experiments, the L_p norm was used as the first measure. The L_p norm can be expressed as:

$$\|x\|_p = (|x_1|^p + |x_2|^p + \cdots + |x_n|^p)^{\frac{1}{p}}. \tag{6}$$

The Euclidean norm from above falls into this class and is the 2-norm, and the 1-norm is the norm that corresponds to the Manhattan Distance.

For an embedding model of knowledge graph based on translation, the whole training process of the model is actually to train two matrices, one is an entity matrix and the other is relation matrix. The score function of TransE is:

$$f(h, r, t) = \|h + r - t\|. \tag{7}$$

We use $\mathbf{M}_e$ to express the embedding matrix of entities and use $\mathbf{M}_r$ to express the embedding matrix of relations. Matrix of entity includes head entity matrix $\mathbf{M}_h$ and tail entity matrix $\mathbf{M}_t$. According to the formula 7, the embedding matrix of head entities and the embedding matrix of tail entities cancel each other, because there is a minus sign in front of the tail entity, and finally only the embedding matrix of relation remains:

$$
\mathbf{M}_h + \mathbf{M}_r - \mathbf{M}_t =
\begin{bmatrix} e_{1,1} & \cdots & e_{1,m} \\ \vdots & \ddots & \vdots \\ e_{n,1} & \cdots & e_{n,m} \end{bmatrix}
+
\begin{bmatrix} r_{1,1} & \cdots & r_{1,m} \\ \vdots & \ddots & \vdots \\ r_{n,1} & \cdots & r_{n.m} \end{bmatrix}
-
\begin{bmatrix} e_{1,1} & \cdots & e_{1,m} \\ \vdots & \ddots & \vdots \\ e_{n,1} & \cdots & e_{n,m} \end{bmatrix}
$$
$$
=
\begin{bmatrix} r_{1,1} & \cdots & r_{1,m} \\ \vdots & \ddots & \vdots \\ r_{n,1} & \cdots & r_{n,m} \end{bmatrix}
= \mathbf{M}_r. \tag{8}
$$

Therefore, the generalized error σ_{gen} can be measured by the L_p norm of the relation matrix $\mathbf{M}_r$. Since a matrix can be viewed as a two-dimensional array, it can be directly converted into a vector form:

$$
\mathbf{M}_r =
\begin{bmatrix} r_{1,1} \\ \vdots \\ r_{n,m} \end{bmatrix}. \tag{9}
$$

Then we can use the formula 6 to obtain the L_p norm of relation:

$$\sigma_{gen} = \|\mathbf{M}_r\|_p = (|r_{1,1}|^p + |r_{2,1}|^p + \cdots + |r_{n,m}|^p)^{\frac{1}{p}}. \tag{10}$$

It can also be found that the L_p norm of the head entity and the L_p norm of the tail entity cancel each other, and only the L_p norm of the relation is left at last. So we consider the L_p norm of the relation as a criterion to measure the generalization error. The generalization error of the model is only related to the norm of the relation parameter matrix, namely the L_p norm of the relation.

4.2   Measurement of Empirical Error

Except for the L_p norm of relation, the second measure of the generalization ability is the upper bound of model empirical error. If the upper bound is smaller, the convergence will be faster and the performance of the model will be better. For a translation-based knowledge graph embedding model, we define the scoring function as f, the head entity as h, the relation as r, and the tail entity as t.

The h', r' and t' correspond to the replaced head entity, relation and tail entity respectively. We use $f(h,r,t)$ to express positive triples and use $f(h',r',t')$ to express negative triples. Margin is a hyperparameter used to measure the interval between positive and negative triples. The error function of the model is as follows:

$$\sigma_{emp} = \left| margin - f(h,r,t) + f(h',r',t') \right|. \tag{11}$$

According to the error function which represents the learning model, we use cauchy inequality [20] to transform and get the result:

$$\sigma_{emp} = \left| margin - f(h,r,t) + f(h',r',t') \right| < |margin| + |-f(h,r,t)|$$
$$+ \left| f(h',r',t') \right|. \tag{12}$$

Because neither the $|-f(h,r,t)|$ and the $\left| f(h',r',t') \right|$ are will exceed the maximum of the scoring function $maxf(h,r,t)$, so we can draw the following conclusions:

$$\sigma_{emp} = \left| margin - f(h,r,t) + f(h',r',t') \right| < |margin| + |-f(h,r,t)|$$
$$+ \left| f(h',r',t') \right| \tag{13}$$
$$< margin + 2 * maxf(h,r,t).$$

Through the formula 13, we find the upper bound of the empirical error. The upper bound of the empirical error is twice of the triple with the highest score. Through the above methods, it can be quickly found out where the upper bound of the error is. Finally, we hope to find a model with less upper bound of empirical risk.

5   Experiment

In this section, we present the experimental design and results of our methods. We have quantified the generalization error and the empirical error by two measures, and further analyzed them.

5.1   Experimental Design

Our goal is to verify the two measures proposed by us. According to the Sect. 3, we also put forward two hypotheses. One is that the smaller the relation L_p norm of the model is, the stronger its generalization ability will be. Another is that the smaller the upper bound empirical error of the model is, the faster its convergence will be. Since our method only validates translation-based models, so we selected TransE, TransH, and TransR to test our method.

For the generalization error, according to the proof in Sect. 3, the generalization error is only related to the L_p norm of the relation. And the smaller the L_p norm of the relation is, the smaller the generalization error of the model will be. So we could see from the experimental results that the generalized results of the model and the relation L_p norm show the opposite trend. That is to say, when the L_p norm is small, the generalization ability of the corresponding model should be better. To reflect the generalization result more intuitively, we use MRR to evaluate the generalization ability. The higher the value of MRR is, the better of the model effect will be.

For the empirical error, according to the upper bound of empirical error and the convergence rate of the model, we can obtain the corresponding results. That is, as the convergence of the model becomes faster and faster, the upper bound of empirical error should be smaller and smaller when the optimal objective is reached. And to correspond to the upper bound of the empirical error with the convergence rate of the model, we choose different embedding sizes to carry out experiments. In Fig. 2, we limit the loss of the TransE model to roughly the same situation which facilitates comparison. We also adopt the same strategy for TransH and TransR. The experimental design is that the size of embedding is 50, 100, 150, 200, 250, 300 under the same loss. And the larger the embedding size of the model, the less time it takes to complete the training is, and the smaller the upper bound of the corresponding empirical error will be. That is to say, according to the experimental results, we should see that the upper bound of the empirical error decreases with the increase of embedding size. In training set, the upper bound is $max(\|h\| + \|r\| + \|t\|)$. We first load the embedding matrix of the model and the data of the training set. Then the corresponding L_p norm values are calculated and recorded by the algorithm, and finally, the L_p norm curve is formed. In order to find the upper bound of the empirical error, we traverse the case of the training set and record the relevant data.

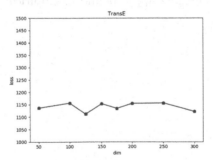

Fig. 2. Control the loss of the model in approximately the same situation.

5.2 Datasets and Experimental Settings

The dataset in this experiment is FB15K. FB15K is a subset of Freebase [21], the freebase is made up of factual triples. For example, the triple (*Bill Gates, founded, Microsoft Corporation.*) builds a relation of *founded* between the name entity *Bill Gates* and the organization entity *Microsoft Corporation.* FB15K contains part of it, it contains 592,213 triples, which consists of 14,951 entities and 1,345 relations. The statistics of datasets are listed in Table 1.

Table 1. Statistics of data sets

Dataset	Rel	Ent	Train	Valid	Test
FB15K	1345	14951	483142	50000	59071

We use OpenKE [22] framework to train-related models. Some of the main parameter settings are changed according to the actual situation. For a fairer comparison, the parameters of all models are set as follows: the learning rate is 0.001, the margin is (1.0), the optimization method is stochastic gradient descent (SGD) [23].

5.3 Experimental Results

For each model, we get the experimental results and show them with three graphs. These three pictures respectively reflect the relation L_p norm, the MRR result and the upper bound of the empirical error. For the generalization error, we use a L_p norm to measure it and We get a reverse concave curve. About TransE model, the MRR result is in Fig. 3(a) and the relation L_p norm is in Fig. 3(b) are examined respectively. The upper bound of empirical error corresponds to Fig. 3(c).

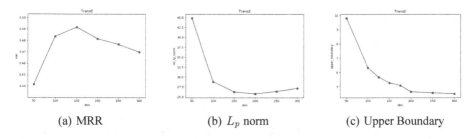

| (a) MRR | (b) L_p norm | (c) Upper Boundary |

Fig. 3. Experimental results of the TransE model. According to the dimensions set by the experiment, we record the training of the model in different dimensions, and calculate the MRR value, the relation L_p norm and the upper bound of empirical error.

Similarly, we experimented with the TransH and TransR model. The results of the TransH model are as follows: the MRR results of TransH are shown in Fig. 4(a). The relation L_p norm of TransH corresponds to Fig. 4(b). The upper boundary is Fig. 4(c). We also get the results of the TransR model from Fig. 5(a) to Fig. 5(c). Under the different embedding sizes, we record the time overhead of three models on different sizes and get some results. For convenience, we use epoch to measure the training time required under different embedding size settings when the model achieves approximately the same loss. The results correspond to Tables 2, 3 and 4, respectively. Generally speaking, the complexity of the TransH model itself is higher than that of TransE, so its convergence is relatively slow. The complexity of the TransH model itself refers to the model construction. For example, TransE only assumes that the tail entity is translated from the head entity through the relation. TransH adds operations such as projection of head and tail entities. This is different from the complexity discussed in this article. Since the TransR model uses TransE as its training, its convergence will be faster.

5.4   Discussion

Through a large number of experiments, we can draw some important conclusions and enlightenment for translation-based knowledge graph embedding.

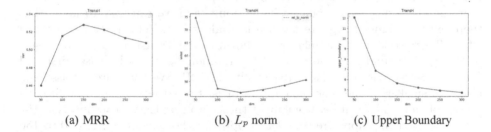

(a) MRR   (b) L_p norm   (c) Upper Boundary

Fig. 4. Experimental results of the TransH model. Like TransE model, MRR results, L_p norms and upper bounds of empirical errors are obtained respectively.

Firstly, we can use the relation L_p norm to approximate its generalization error of the model. For the TransE model, we first look at its MRR result in Fig. 3(a). The abscissa are different embedding dimensions, and the ordinate is the relative value, which is convenient for comparison and drawing. MRR is the mean reciprocal ranking of model training results. It corresponds to the generalization ability. The higher its value is, the better the generalization result of the model will be. Here we use the link prediction to illustrate the MRR. For a scoring function of knowledge graph embedding model based on translation, take TransE as an example, we hope that the smaller of the $\|h + r - t\|$ after the model training is, and then the better of the result will be. For a triple (h, r, t),

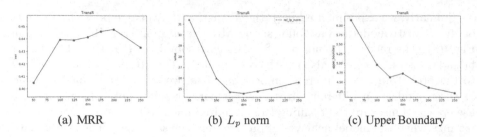

(a) MRR   (b) L_p norm   (c) Upper Boundary

Fig. 5. Experimental results of the TransR model. It can be seen that the experimental results of TransE and TransH are almost the same. TransR is slightly different from the former two. It may be that the structure of the model itself has an effect on the experiment. But on the whole, it is quite in line with our goal. Due to the relatively fast convergence of TransR model, we have selected 50, 75, 100, 125, 150, 175, 200, 225 and 250 values as the abscissa dimensions in the (a), (b) and (c).

we first predict the tail entity and input $(h, r, ?)$. Then bring all the entities in? and calculate it get a value according to the scoring function, and then sort it according to the score. Find the tail entity t according to the sorting table, and record the rank value at this time. Predict the header entity in the same way, then process all the cases in the test set in this way, and finally make the rank values according to the mean reciprocal, finally get the MRR. We can see that the MRR curve increases first and then decreases in Fig. 3(a). This shows that the curve has a maximum at some point, and we can easy to know that there exists an embedding size interval to make the model achieve the optimal effect. Then we look at the relation L_p norm of the TransE model. As a result in Fig. 3(b), we find that the curve of the relation L_p norm decreases first and then increases, it is contrary to the result of MRR. We have already assumed that the smaller of the relational L_p norm is, the stronger the generalization ability of the model will be. Combining these two graphs, we can find that the trends of the two graphs are completely opposite. For example, from 50 to 150 dimensions, the value of MRR is getting larger and larger. On the contrary, the value of relation L_p norm is getting smaller and smaller. After 200 or so dimensions, the value of MRR is getting smaller and smaller, while the value of the relational norm is getting larger and larger. We can see from the graph that in the range of 150 to 200, the MRR and the relation L_p norm of the TransE reach the maximum and minimum respectively, that is to say, this interval is the dimension interval in which the generalization ability of reaches the maximum. This confirms our previous assumptions in the experimental design section. The lower the relation L_p norm of TransE is, the higher of the generalization ability will be. Since MRR corresponds to the generalization result of, we can conclude that the smaller of the relation L_p norm is, the better its generalization ability of the model will be. In this way we can find the best experimental dimension. Since TransH is an improvement based on TransE, its corresponding experimental results will be better and better reflect our hypotheses. As can be seen from

Fig. 4(a) and (b), the MRR and the relation L_p norm of TransH model are almost opposite in about 150 dimensions. Since the TransH model is designed to solve the problem that the TransE model can not deal with the modeling of complex relations, its experimental results can better confirm our hypotheses. As can be seen from Fig. 4(b), and its minimum value can be seen more clearly. From Fig. 4(a) and (b), we can see that the MRR and relation L_p norm of TransH reach their maximum and minimum values almost simultaneously in the 150 dimensions. The relation L_p norm curve of TransH has a more obvious turning point. Although the experimental results of TransR are not as perfect as TransH, they are also very consistent with our hypotheses. As can be seen from Fig. 5(a) and (b), the MRR and relation L_p norm of TransR also reach maximum and minimum values in the dimensions range of 150 to 200 respectively. We can see from the Fig. 5(a) that it is not as smooth as TransE or TransH, but fluctuate slightly, which may be related to the nature of the model itself, because the complexity of TransR model is higher than the former two, and this is not the content of this paper. Even so, the experimental results of TransR are very consistent with our hypotheses. Through these experiments, we measured the generalization error σ_{gen} of the model.

Secondly, we measured the upper bound of empirical error. According to our hypotheses, the upper bound of the empirical error should become smaller and smaller with the training of the model, that is, the model is closer to the minimum error and achieves the optimization. From the Figs. 3(c), 4(c) and 5(c), we can see that with the increase of dimensions, the upper boundary of empirical error is smaller and smaller, which indicates that the convergence of the model is faster and faster, and finally the optimal result is obtained. Combining with Tables 2, 3 and 4 we also prove that the time required to achieve similar loss under different embedding sizes decreases with the increase of dimensions, which coincides with the trend of empirical error upper bound curve, that is the higher of the dimensions are, the smaller the error upper bound of the model will be. For example, we first look at the upper boundary of the TransE model in Fig. 3(c). As the dimensions increase, the upper boundary of the model becomes smaller and smaller, the higher the dimensions are, the faster the decline will be. According to the inference in Sect. 3, the upper bound of the empirical error is twice that of the corresponding value when the score of the model scoring function is maximized by a triple. The smaller the upper bound of the model is, the faster its convergence will be. Referring to the training time when the TransE model achieves the same loss in different dimensions, we can see from Table 2 that the higher the dimensions are, the shorter of the training time will be and the convergence rate of the model will also be accelerated. The upper boundary in Fig. 3(c) also decreases with the increase of dimensions, which shows that the smaller the upper bound is, the faster the convergence of the model will be. So we prove that $max(\|h\| + \|r\| + \|t\|)$ can be used to reflect the empirical error through experiments. TransR and TransH have similar results. Generally speaking, the upper bound of their empirical error decreases with the increase of dimensions, which is consistent with our previous assumptions and experimental design. Through these experimental analyses, we measure the upper bound of empirical error σ_{emp}.

Table 2. Convergence time of the TransE model under different embedding sizes

Embedding size	50	100	150	200	250	300
Epoch	4000	800	450	310	260	230

Table 3. Convergence time of the TransH model under different embedding sizes

Embedding size	50	100	150	200	250	300
Epoch	11000	1500	850	620	480	420

Table 4. Convergence time of the TransR model under different embedding sizes

Embedding size	50	100	125	150	175	200	250
Epoch	10000	600	290	255	235	220	173

According to the previous definition, the generalization ability consists of generalization error σ_{gen} and empirical error σ_{emp}. Through experiments, we test these two errors and verify our hypotheses. Whether the empirical error or the generalization error of, the smaller the two errors are, the better its generalization ability will be. Finally, through experiments, we have certain guiding significance for the training of the model about knowledge graph embedding. For example, we can quickly estimate the upper bound of the empirical error of the knowledge graph embedding model based on translation and select the corresponding parameter dimensions of the model with a good generalization effect by measuring the generalization error.

6   Conclusion and Future Work

In this paper, we proposed a set of methods to measure the generalization of knowledge graph embedding models by analyzing the empirical error and the generalization error. We propose two measures to quantify the generalization ability using the relation L_p norm and the upper bound of empirical error. Through our methods, the generalization ability of the model can be measured effectively, which is beneficial to the further study of the model construction. We will explore the following research directions in future: (1) in this paper we mainly verify the influence of dimension on the training results, but there are many factors that can affect the generalization, therefore we will further study the other factors on the training, such as using different optimization methods. (2) Since our method is only focused on translation-based models, it is necessary to explore other types of models, such as the neural network model for knowledge graph embedding. (3) According to the guidance of model generalization research, we will attempt to construct a new and effective knowledge graph embedding model.

Acknowledgment. Research presented in this paper was partially supported by the National Key Research and Development Program of China under grants (2018YFC0830200, 2017YFB1002801), the Natural Science Foundation of China grants (U1736204), the Judicial Big Data Research Centre, School of Law at Southeast University.

References

1. Trouillon, T., Welbl, J., Riedel, S., Gaussier, É., Bouchard, G.: Complex embeddings for simple link prediction. In: International Conference on Machine Learning, pp. 2071–2080 (2016)
2. Szumlanski, S., Gomez, F.: Automatically acquiring a semantic network of related concepts. In: Proceedings of the 19th ACM International Conference on Information and Knowledge Management, pp. 19–28. ACM (2010)
3. Xiao, H., Huang, M., Meng, L., Zhu, X.: SSP: semantic space projection for knowledge graph embedding with text descriptions. In: Thirty-First AAAI Conference on Artificial Intelligence (2017)
4. Shi, B., Weninger, T.: ProjE: embedding projection for knowledge graph completion. In: Thirty-First AAAI Conference on Artificial Intelligence (2017)
5. Guan, S., Jin, X., Wang, Y., Cheng, X.: Shared embedding based neural networks for knowledge graph completion. In: Proceedings of the 27th ACM International Conference on Information and Knowledge Management, pp. 247–256. ACM (2018)
6. Neyshabur, B., Tomioka, R., Srebro, N.: In search of the real inductive bias: on the role of implicit regularization in deep learning. arXiv preprint arXiv:1412.6614 (2014)
7. Keskar, N.S., Mudigere, D., Nocedal, J., Smelyanskiy, M., Tang, P.T.P.: On large-batch training for deep learning: generalization gap and sharp minima. arXiv preprint arXiv:1609.04836 (2016)
8. Neyshabur, B., Salakhutdinov, R.R., Srebro, N.: Path-SGD: path-normalized optimization in deep neural networks. In: Advances in Neural Information Processing Systems, pp. 2422–2430 (2015)
9. Hoffer, E., Hubara, I., Soudry, D.: Train longer, generalize better: closing the generalization gap in large batch training of neural networks. In: Advances in Neural Information Processing Systems, pp. 1731–1741 (2017)
10. Neyshabur, B., Tomioka, R., Srebro, N.: Norm-based capacity control in neural networks. In: Conference on Learning Theory, pp. 1376–1401 (2015)
11. Sharma, A., Talukdar, P., et al.: Towards understanding the geometry of knowledge graph embeddings. In: Proceedings of the 56th Annual Meeting of the Association for Computational Linguistics (Volume 1: Long Papers), pp. 122–131 (2018)
12. Bordes, A., Usunier, N., Garcia-Duran, A., Weston, J., Yakhnenko, O.: Translating embeddings for modeling multi-relational data. In: Advances in Neural Information Processing Systems, pp. 2787–2795 (2013)

13. Wang, Z., Zhang, J., Feng, J., Chen, Z.: Knowledge graph embedding by translating on hyperplanes. In: Twenty-Eighth AAAI Conference on Artificial Intelligence (2014)
14. Lin, Y., Liu, Z., Sun, M., Liu, Y., Zhu, X.: Learning entity and relation embeddings for knowledge graph completion. In: Twenty-Ninth AAAI Conference on Artificial Intelligence (2015)
15. Xiao, H., Huang, M., Hao, Y., Zhu, X.: TransA: an adaptive approach for knowledge graph embedding. arXiv preprint arXiv:1509.05490 (2015)
16. Ji, G., He, S., Xu, L., Liu, K., Zhao, J.: Knowledge graph embedding via dynamic mapping matrix. In: Proceedings of the 53rd Annual Meeting of the Association for Computational Linguistics and the 7th International Joint Conference on Natural Language Processing (Volume 1: Long Papers), pp. 687–696 (2015)
17. Neyshabur, B., Bhojanapalli, S., McAllester, D., Srebro, N.: Exploring generalization in deep learning. In: Advances in Neural Information Processing Systems, pp. 5947–5956 (2017)
18. Kawaguchi, K., Kaelbling, L.P., Bengio, Y.: Generalization in deep learning. arXiv preprint arXiv:1710.05468 (2017)
19. Zhang, C., Bengio, S., Hardt, M., Recht, B., Vinyals, O.: Understanding deep learning requires rethinking generalization. arXiv preprint arXiv:1611.03530 (2016)
20. Dragomir, S.S.: A survey on Cauchy-Bunyakovsky-Schwarz type discrete inequalities. J. Inequal. Pure Appl. Math. 4(3), 1–142 (2003)
21. Bollacker, K., Evans, C., Paritosh, P., Sturge, T., Taylor, J.: Freebase: a collaboratively created graph database for structuring human knowledge. In: Proceedings of the 2008 ACM SIGMOD International Conference on Management of Data, pp. 1247–1250. ACM (2008)
22. Han, X., et al.: OpenKE: an open toolkit for knowledge embedding. In: Proceedings of the 2018 Conference on Empirical Methods in Natural Language Processing: System Demonstrations, pp. 139–144 (2018)
23. Bottou, L.: Large-scale machine learning with stochastic gradient descent. In: Lechevallier, Y., Saporta, G. (eds) Proceedings of COMPSTAT 2010. Physica-Verlag HD, Heidelberg (2010). https://doi.org/10.1007/978-3-7908-2604-3_16

Incorporating Instance Correlations in Distantly Supervised Relation Extraction

Luhao Zhang, Linmei Hu, and Chuan Shi[✉]

Beijing University of Posts and Telecommunications, Beijing, China
{zhangluhao,hulinmei,shichuan}@bupt.edu.cn

Abstract. Distantly-supervised relation extraction has proven to be effective to find relational facts from texts. However, the existing approaches treat the instances in the same bag independently and ignore the semantic structural information. In this paper, we propose a graph convolution network (GCN) model with an attention mechanism to improve relation extraction. For each bag, the model first builds a graph through the dependency tree of each instance in this bag. In this way, the correlations between instances are built through their common words. The learned node (word) embeddings which encode the bag information are then fed into the sentence encoder, i.e., text CNN to obtain better representations of sentences. Besides, an instance-level attention mechanism is introduced to select valid instances and learn the textual relation embedding. Finally, the learned embedding is used to train our relation classifier. Experiments on two benchmark datasets demonstrate that our model significantly outperforms the compared baselines.

Keywords: Relation extraction · Graph convolution network · Knowledge graph

1 Introduction

Relation extraction aims to extract semantic relations between pairs of entities from plain texts. Due to the significant power and large incompletion of knowledge graphs (KGs), this task has become an important task in KG construction and completion. It can be modeled as a supervised classification task after the entity pair is identified by named entity recognizer. Formally, given the entity pair (e_1, e_2) and the instances (sentences) containing the entity pair, it aims to predict the relation label r between e_1 and e_2 from a predefined relation set. As shown in Fig. 1 a, given a bag of instances $(S_1, S_2, \cdots, S_m)$ that all contain entity pair $(Barack\_Obama, United\_States)$, the task is to classify the relation label $president$ to them.

Supervised relation extraction methods demand large-scale labeled data, while manual labeling is time-consuming. Therefore, [14] proposes distant supervision to address the challenge. It assumes that if two entities have a relation

© Springer Nature Switzerland AG 2020
X. Wang et al. (Eds.): JIST 2019, LNCS 12032, pp. 177–191, 2020.
https://doi.org/10.1007/978-3-030-41407-8_12

Examples for triplet (*Barack_Obama, United_States, president*):

S_1: *Barack_Obama* lifted the ban on travel to the *United_States* by those infected with HIV.

S_2: *Barack_Obama* was the first African American to be the president to *United_States*.

...

S_m: *Barack_Obama* is an American attorney and politician who served as the 44th president of the *United_States*.

Fig. 1. An example of entity pair $(Barack\_Obama, United\_States)$, their relation label *president*, and corresponding training instances

in a KG, then all instances mentioning the two entities express this relation. Thus, a large number of labeled data can be generated automatically by distant supervision. However, since not all sentences containing the target entities exactly express their relations in KGs, it often suffers from the noisy data that are labeled by mistake [16,21].

Recently, significant progress has been made in the use of deep neural networks for relation extraction [21,22]. To alleviate the noise in distant supervised datasets, attention has been utilized by [4,13]. Some efforts have also been made on leveraging relevant side information to improve relation extraction. [17] uses entity type and relation alias information from KGs. [11] incorporates entity descriptions to provide background knowledge. Due to the usage of more relevant information imposing soft constraints while prediction, they achieve better performance.

However, these models treat the instances within a bag independently and ignore the semantic correlations among the instances. For example, in Fig. 1, the instance S_1 does not express the relation label *president* directly. However, the existing S_2 can provide significant background knowledge without other side information. Therefore, it is significant to build the correlation among multiple instances. Besides, the graph convolution network has shown its superiority in learning the structural correlation in social networks.

Therefore, in this paper, we propose a novel GCN based model **ICRE** to incorporate the instance correlations for improving relation extraction. Inspired by recent work on GCNs, we note that the semantic structure can be built through the dependency tree, which is shown in Fig. 2(a). Therefore to model the correlation among instances within a bag, we construct the graph for each bag based on dependency trees after pruning by removing stop words, shown in Fig. 2(b). After the graph construction, we utilize a graph convolution network that maps every node into an embedding vector, which explores the correlation among instances. Through feeding the learned node (word) embeddings into the instance encoder, we capture the context information of each instance. Besides, an attention mechanism is introduced to attend over the bag of instances for relation classification.

Finally, the learned graph embeddings are used for our relation classification. The contributions of this paper can be summarized as follows:

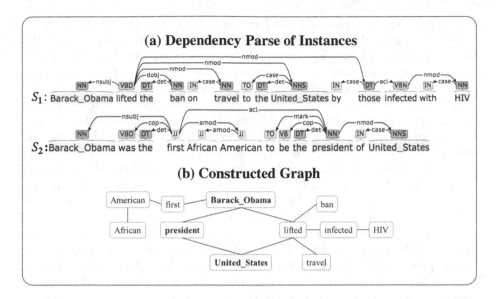

Fig. 2. The dependency parse tree of two instances and the constructed graph.

(1) We propose a novel GCN based model **ICRE** to incorporate the instance correlations for improving relation extraction.
(2) The learned node embeddings through GCNs are viewed as our new word embeddings, which may contain the implied background knowledge in other instances.
(3) Extensive experiments on a benchmark dataset demonstrate that our model significantly outperforms compared baselines.

2   Related Work

2.1   Distantly Supervised Relation Extraction

Most supervised relation extraction methods require large-scale labeled training data while manual labeling is expensive. Distant Supervision (DS) proposed by [14] is an effective method for automatically labeling large-scale training data under the assumption that if two entities have a relation in a KG, then all sentences mentioning those entities express this relation. However, the DS assumption does not work in all cases and causes the mislabeling problem. Therefore, plenty of research works have been proposed to mitigate the issue of noisy labeling. [9,15,16] introduce multi-instance learning where the sentences mentioning the same entity pair are processed at a bag level. Nevertheless, these methods rely on the features extracted by NLP tools, such as POS tagging.

With the development of deep learning, neural networks have proved to be an efficient way to extract valid features from sentences in recent years. [21,22] adopt

Convolution Neural Networks (CNN) to learn instance representations automatically. [4,13] employ an attention mechanism to alleviate noise in distantly supervised datasets by learning a weight distribution over multiple instances. [23] proposes a path-based neural relation extraction model to encode the relational semantics from both direct sentences and inference chains.

On the one hand, these RE systems rely on noisy instances from distant supervision. To make up for that deficiency, [17] utilizes available side information from knowledge bases, including entity type and relation alias information. [6] incorporates the hierarchical information of relations to make full use of rich semantic correlations among relations. [5] proposes a joint representation learning framework of KGs and text corpus for relation extraction for knowledge graph completion. Besides, [11] introduces a sentence-level attention model and entity descriptions to extract relations under distant supervised.

On the other hand, the training data from distant supervision have not been made use of. Recently, considerable research effort has been made to probe the intrinsic potential of datasets. [19] proposes a non-independent and identically distributed (non-IID) relevance embedding to capture the relevance of sentences in the bag. [20] employs the sentence-level selective attention to reduce the effect of noisy or mismatched sentences while capturing the correlation among relations to improve the quality of attention weights. However, these existing methods learn the representation of instances dependently and ignores the propagation of the valid information contained in the instances.

2.2   Graph Convolution Networks

Recently, as the development of deep learning, graph neural networks have attracted wide attention. To generalize neural networks, such as CNN, to work on arbitrary graphs, many efforts have been made [2,3,8]. [12] presented graph convolution networks (GCN) that achieved state-of-the-art classification performance on some graph datasets. Then, GCNs have been widely explored in many NLP tasks and outperformed traditional deep learning models. Specifically, TextGCN [18] employs GCN for text classification, which builds the graph by modeling the documents and words as nodes. Additionally, [1] constructs graphs through the syntactic dependency trees of sentences and uses GCN to encode them and improve machine translation.

Prior works [7,14] have exploited features from syntactic dependency trees for improving relation extraction. Therefore, to model the semantic correlations among the instances in a bag, we utilize their dependency trees and common words to build the graph after pruning by removing the stop words. Then we propose our model **ICRE** that designs an attention-based relation classifier with graph convolution network to extract the textual relation representation from a bag.

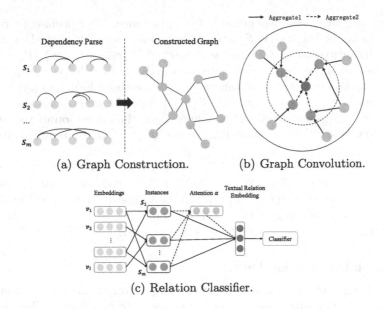

(a) Graph Construction.   (b) Graph Convolution.

(c) Relation Classifier.

Fig. 3. Illustration of our model **ICRE**.

3   Our Proposed Model

In this section, we will detail our proposed GCN-based model with an attention mechanism for relation extraction. As shown in Fig. 2, our model ICRE consists of four steps:

(1) **Graph Construction.** As shown in Fig. 3(a), we first get the dependency parse tree for all instances in both the training set and testing set through NLP tools. Then we build a graph with the dependency tree of each instance in the same bag.

(2) **Graph Convolution Layer.** For the constructed graph, we exploit the graph convolution network to learn the node embeddings, shown as Fig. 3(b).

(3) **Relation Classifier.** As observed from Fig. 3(c), the learned embeddings are taken as the new representations of words and be employed to initialize each instance embedding with them. Then CNN is used as another encoder to capture the semantic information of each instance. Besides, an attention mechanism is introduced to attend over the bag of instances for relation classification. Finally, the learned graph representation is used to train the relation classifier and get its corresponding relation label.

3.1   Graph Construction

Given a bag of instances $B = \{s_1, s_2, \cdots, s_m\}$, in which each instance $s_i = \{w_1, w_2, \cdots, w_n\}$ contains the same entity pair (h, t), we first utilize Stanford

NLP tools to get the base dependency of each instance. After pruning by removing stop words, the graph $G(V, E)$ of this bag is constructed through the common words or the entity pair (h, t), where vertex set $V = \{v_1, v_2, \cdots, v_l\}, |V| = l$ consists of words and the dependency between words are modeled as edges. In this way, the correlations between instances are built without losing semantic information. Let $\mathbf{X} = \{\mathbf{x}_1, \mathbf{x}_2, \cdots, \mathbf{x}_l\} \in \mathbb{R}^{l \times d_f}$ denote the graph's feature matrix with each row representing a vertex, where d_f is the dimension of the feature vectors. Specifically, We initialize feature vector $\mathbf{x}_i$ with the pre-trained word vectors.

For convenience, we introduce the adjacency matrix $\mathbf{A} \in \mathbb{R}^{l \times l}$ of G and its degree matrix $\mathbf{D}$, where $\mathbf{D}_{ii} = \sum_j \mathbf{A}_{ij}$. Note that, a word never connects to itself in dependency trees, which results in that the information in the word self is lost in the convolution operation. Thus, every node is assumed to be connected to itself, so that the diagonal elements of $\mathbf{A}$ are set to 1.

3.2   Graph Convolution Layer

The graph convolution network [12] is an adaptation of the convolution neural network for encoding graphs, which has proven to be reliable. Therefore, to learn the representation of nodes, we employ graph convolution network as our encoder. Generally, GCN can capture information about immediate neighbors with one layer of convolution. And as multiple GCN layers are stacked, information about high-order neighborhoods are integrated. For a one-layer GCN, we first normalize the adjacency matrix as $\tilde{A}$:

$$\tilde{\mathbf{A}} = \mathbf{D}^{-\frac{1}{2}} \mathbf{A} \mathbf{D}^{-\frac{1}{2}}. \tag{1}$$

Then the new d_k-dimensional node representation matrix $\mathbf{H}^{(1)} \in \mathbb{R}^{l \times d_k}$ is computed as:

$$\mathbf{H}^{(1)} = f(\tilde{\mathbf{A}} \mathbf{X} \mathbf{W}_0), \tag{2}$$

where $W_0 \in \mathbb{R}^{l \times d_k}$ is the weight matrix and f is an activation function.

To extract the higher-order substructure features, we stack multiple graph convolution layers as follows:

$$\mathbf{H}^{(t+1)} = f(\tilde{\mathbf{A}} \mathbf{H}^{(t)} \mathbf{W}_t) \tag{3}$$

where t denotes the layer number and $\mathbf{H}^{(0)} = \mathbf{X}$. Generally, we utilize the result $\mathbf{H}^{(t)}$ of the final layer as our node embeddings $\mathbf{V}$.

In this way, we build the correlation between instances while not lose the semantic information through the dependency tree. Through higher-order convolution operation, the background knowledge implied in other instances is propagated.

3.3   Relation Classifier

For each instance $s_i = \{w_1, w_2, \cdots, w_n\}$ in the bag B, taking the learned embeddings $\mathbf{V}$ as the representations of words, we initialize each word as:

$$\mathbf{w}_i = \mathbf{v}_i \oplus \mathbf{p}_{i1} \oplus \mathbf{p}_{i2}, \tag{4}$$

where $\mathbf{v}_i$ is the corresponding node embedding of w_i, and $\mathbf{p}_{i1}$ and $\mathbf{p}_{i2}$ are its position representations to encode relative distances to the target entities (h, t) into d_p-dimensional vectors. For example, in the instance "Barack_Obama is the president of United_States", the relative distance from the word "president" to the head entity *Barack_Obama* is 3 and tail entity *United_States* is 2.

Then, we use CNN with window size c as another encoder to capture the semantic information of each instance s_i.

$$\mathbf{z}_i = \text{CNN}(\mathbf{w}_{i-\frac{c-1}{2}}, \cdots, \mathbf{w}_{i+\frac{c-1}{2}}), \tag{5}$$

$$[\mathbf{s}]_j = \max\{[\mathbf{z}_1]_j, \cdots, [\mathbf{z}_n]_j\}, \tag{6}$$

where $\mathbf{s} \in \mathbb{R}^h$ is the sentence (instance) embedding, $[\cdot]_j$ is the j-th value of a vector and function max denotes max-pooling.

Afterwards, we use an instance-level attention mechanism to learn the textual relation embedding from a bag. Formally, for each bag of instances $B = \{s_1, s_2, \cdots, s_m\}$, there are their corresponding representation $\mathbf{s}_i, i \in m$. The attention weights α_i is calculated as:

$$\alpha_i = \frac{\exp(\mathbf{e}_i)}{\sum_{i=1}^{l} \exp(\mathbf{e}_i)}, \tag{7}$$

where $\mathbf{e}_i$ is a query-based function which scores how well the vertex v_i and the predict relation label r matches. Specifically, $\mathbf{e}_i$ is calculated as follows:

$$\mathbf{e}_i = \mathbf{s}_i \mathbf{W}_e \mathbf{r}, \tag{8}$$

where $\mathbf{W}_e$ is a weighted diagonal matrix, and $\mathbf{r}$ is the corresponding query vector of relation label r which indicates the representation of relation r.

Then, we leverage the calculated attention vector over instances to reduce the weights of noisy instances. Therefore, we learn the representation $\hat{\mathbf{s}}$ of bag B as the weighted average of the instance embeddings $\mathbf{s}_i$:

$$\mathbf{s} = \sum_{i=1}^{l} \alpha_i \mathbf{s}_i. \tag{9}$$

Finally, to compute the confidence of each relation class, we feed the representation of graph G into a softmax classifier after being processed by a linear transformation. Formally,

$$\mathbf{P}(r|G, B) = Softmax(\mathbf{W}_s \hat{\mathbf{s}} + \mathbf{b}_s), \tag{10}$$

where $\mathbf{W}_s$ is the parameter matrix and $\mathbf{b}_s$ is the bias.

3.4 Model Training

Given N bags in training set $\{B_1, B_2, \cdots, B_z\}$ and their corresponding labels $\{r_1, r_2, \cdots, r_z\}$, we build the graph sets $\{G_1, G_2, \cdots, G_z\}$ to learn word embeddings as the input of our model. Additionally, we employ cross entropy as our loss function:

$$L = -\sum_{i=1}^{z} \log \mathbf{P}(r_i|G_i, B_i), \tag{11}$$

Finally, we minimize the loss function with L_2 normalization:

$$\min J = L + \eta \|\Theta\|^2, \tag{12}$$

where η is the regularization coefficient and Θ denotes the parameter in our model. Stochastic gradient descent (SGD) is used to optimize the loss function.

Table 1. Details of Riedel dataset

DataSet	Data split	Sentences	Entities	Entity pairs
Riedel	Train	570,088	63,696	281,270
	Test	172,448	16,706	96,678
GIDS	Train	11,297	9,874	6,498
	Test	5,663	5,226	3,247

4   Experiments

4.1   Dataset

In our experiments, we evaluate our model over two benchmark datasets as following:

Riedel. The dataset is developed by [15] by aligning Freebase with New York Times (NYT) corpus, which has been widely used for distantly supervised relation extraction [5,13]. Specifically, the training set consists of the sentences from the year 2005–2006 and the test set includes those from the year 2007. Stanford NER[1] is used to annotate the entity mentions. Consequently, there are 53 relation labels containing a special relation NA that indicates there is no relation between the target entity pair.

GIDS. Google Distant Supervision (GIDS) dataset is created by extending the Google relation extraction corpus with additional instances for each entity pair and assures that the at-least-one assumption of multi-instance learning [10]. The details of two datasets are summarized in Table 1.

---

[1] https://stanfordnlp.github.io/CoreNLP/.

4.2   Baselines

We compare our model with the following baselines:

- **Mintz** [14]. A multi-class logistic regression model which exploits manual textual features of instances to train a relation classifier.
- **MultiR** [9]. A probabilistic graphical model for multi-instance learning with overlapping relations that combines an instance-level extraction model with a simple and corpus-level component for aggregating the individual facts.
- **MIMLRE** [16]. A graphical model with latent variables to multi-instance multi-label learning for relation extraction.
- **CNN+ATT** [13]. A deep learning model that encodes the instance by convolution neural network (CNN) and designs an instance-level attention to reduce the noise.
- **ICRE**. Our proposed model.

Noting that, Mintz, MultiR and MIMILRE are based on human-designed features. The results on Riedel dataset are obtained from their corresponding paper. Therefore, we just select CNN+ATT as the baseline compared with our method in terms of GIDS dataset.

4.3   Evaluation Metrics

Following previous works [11,13], the model is evaluated held out with comparing the relations discovered from test corpus with those in Freebase. We report the Precision-Recall curve and top-N precision (P@N) metric on the Riedel dataset. To further evaluate the performance of our model, we use average mean precision (MAP) and F1 value as metrics over GIDS dataset.

Table 2. Parameter settings.

Parameter	Value
Word Dimension d_w	50
Position Dimension d_p	5
Hidden Layer Dimension d_h	230
Learning Rate α	0.5
Regularization Coefficient η	0.0001
Dropout Probability p	0.5
Layer Number t	2

4.4   Experiment Settings

For all models, we employ the word embeddings pre-trained by word2vec tool[2] on NYT corpus. We select the learning rate α between $\{0.1, 0.01, 0.005, 0.0001\}$ for minimizing the loss. We set other parameters by following the settings used in [5,11]. Dropout strategy is employed on the output layer to prevent overfitting. All parameters used in our experiments are detailed in Table 2. All experiments are conducted on a machine with four GPUs (NVIDIA GTX-1080*4).

4.5   Precision-Recall Curve on both Datasets

Figure 4 shows the compared results in terms of Precision-Recall Curves on both datasets. Especially, on the GIDS dataset, we just select CNN+ATT as the baseline which is based on the neural network. Overall, we observe that: (1) Both the neural network-based approaches CNN+ATT and ICRE have more obvious advantages than Mintz, MultiR and MIMLRE, which are based on human-designed features. And when the recall is greater than 0.1, the performance of feature-based methods drops out quickly. These demonstrate that the limitation of human-designed features and the advancement of deep learning models in relation extraction. (2) Our method ICRE shows better performance than CNN+ATT, illustrating that ICRE learns more high-quality textual relation representation from instances than CNN+ATT. The reason is that ICRE utilizes GCN to encode the correlation between instances, resulting in the implied background knowledge is propagated in the constructed graph.

4.6   P@N Evaluation

As shown in Table 3, we report Precision@N of different approaches on the Riedel dataset. The evaluation results are consistent with the Precision-Recall curves. CNN+ATT and our method ICRE both outperform Mintz, MultiR and MIMLRE. These further demonstrate that the human-designed feature cannot concisely express the semantic meaning of the sentences, and the inevitable error brought by NLP tools will hurt the performance of relation extraction. In contrast, neural network-based methods that learn the representation of each sentence automatically can express the sentence well. Simultaneously, ICRE significantly outperforms all baselines. Compared with CNN+ATT, in terms of metric P@100, P@200 and P@300, our model improves the performance by 2.8%, 2.8%, and 1.6% respectively. The reason is that ICRE explores the correlation between instances and uses a better encoder GCN to capture this structure. In this way, the background knowledge implied in the instances is propagated in the constructed graph.

---

[2] https://code.google.com/p/word2vec/.

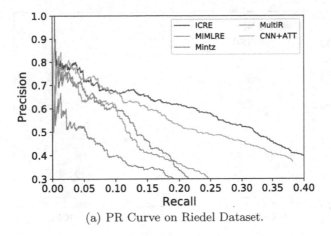

(a) PR Curve on Riedel Dataset.

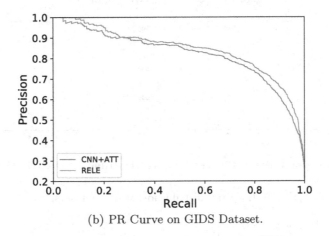

(b) PR Curve on GIDS Dataset.

Fig. 4. Precision-recall curves of different methods on both dataset. ICRE achieves higher precision over the entire range of recall compared to all baselines.

Table 3. Evaluation results P@N of different models.

P@N(%)	100	200	300	Mean
Mintz	54.0	50.5	45.3	49.9
MultiR	75.0	65.0	62.0	67.3
MIMLRE	70.0	64.5	60.3	64.9
CNN+ATT	76.2	73.1	67.4	72.2
ICRE	78.4	75.2	68.5	74.0

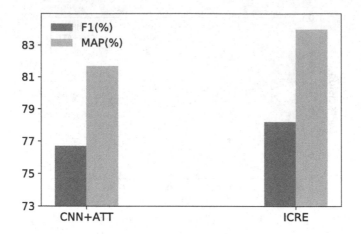

Fig. 5. Comparison on GIDS dataset.

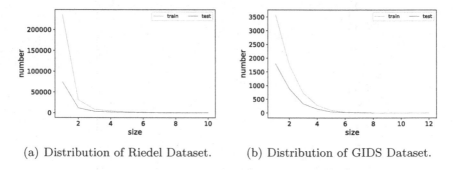

(a) Distribution of Riedel Dataset.   (b) Distribution of GIDS Dataset.

Fig. 6. Long tail distribution of two datasets.

4.7   Results on GIDS Dataset

Based on the results on the Riedel dataset, we compare our method ICRE with
CNN+ATT on the GIDS dataset in terms of F1 and MAP. As shown in Fig. 5, our
model consistently achieves better performance, which verifies the effectiveness
of our model on exploring the correlation among instances. In detail, in terms
of F1 and MAP, ICRE increases about 2% and 7.5% respectively.

4.8   Effect of Instance Number

As shown in Fig. 6, most of relations are long-tail in both Riedel and GIDS
datasets. We can observe the fact that about half of the data is in single instance.
Therefore, existing distantly supervised relation extraction methods may only
rely on limited information, resulting in the poor performance of the multi-
instance mechanism. To further verify the effectiveness of our model with limited
numbers of instances, we change the test settings following previous studies. We
randomly select one instance and two instances respectively for each entity pair

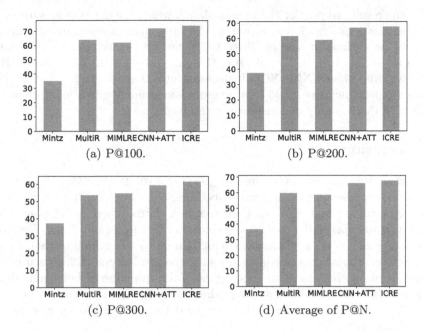

(a) P@100.
(b) P@200.
(c) P@300.
(d) Average of P@N.

Fig. 7. P@N evaluation on the dataset which contains one instance for each entity pair from Riedel.

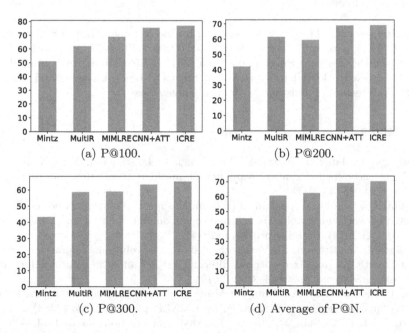

(a) P@100.
(b) P@200.
(c) P@300.
(d) Average of P@N.

Fig. 8. P@N evaluation on the dataset which contains two instances for each entity pair from Riedel.

and use the results to predict the relation label, which are denoted as **One** and **Two**. As shown in Figs. 7 and 8, our model still maintains advantages in all situations. Note that, in case of **Two**, GCN can propagate the valid features between them. However, in case of **One**, there are no other instances and ICRE also outperforms than CNN+ATT. It demonstrates that our graph convolution layer over dependency tree could capture more fine-grained semantic information even though there is only one instance in the bag.

5   Conclusion

In this work, we consider leveraging the graph convolution network to encode the dependency tree and learn word embeddings. In this way, the correlations among instances are built through their common words. Then, another encoder CNN is used to capture the context information of each instance itself. Besides, an instance-level attention mechanism is introduced to select valid instances and learn the textual relation embedding. Finally, the learned embedding is used to train our relation classifier. Our model takes full advantage of both structural and context information, while avoiding the imposed noise. Experiments on two benchmark datasets demonstrate that our model significantly outperforms the compared baselines.

In the future, we will explore more advanced encoder, such as graph attention networks. Besides, we expire to discover more complex correlations and utilize the advanced encoders.

Acknowledgement. This work is supported by the National Natural Science Foundation of China (No. 61772082, 61806020, 61702296, 61972047), the National Key Research and Development Program of China (2017YFB0803304), the Beijing Municipal Natural Science Foundation (4182043), the CCF-Tencent Open Fund, and the Fundamental Research Funds for the Central Universities.

References

1. Bastings, J., Titov, I., Aziz, W., Marcheggiani, D., Simaan, K.: Graph convolutional encoders for syntax-aware neural machine translation. arXiv preprint arXiv:1704.04675 (2017)
2. Bruna, J., Zaremba, W., Szlam, A., Lecun, Y.: Spectral networks and locally connected networks on graphs. In: International Conference on Learning Representations (ICLR2014), CBLS, April 2014 (2014)
3. Defferrard, M., Bresson, X., Vandergheynst, P.: Convolutional neural networks on graphs with fast localized spectral filtering. In: Advances in Neural Information Processing Systems, pp. 3844–3852 (2016)
4. Du, J., Han, J., Way, A., Wan, D.: Multi-level structured self-attentions for distantly supervised relation extraction. In: EMNLP, pp. 2216–2225 (2018)
5. Han, X., Liu, Z., Sun, M.: Neural knowledge acquisition via mutual attention between knowledge graph and text. In: AAAI, pp. 4832–4839 (2018)
6. Han, X., Yu, P., Liu, Z., Sun, M., Li, P.: Hierarchical relation extraction with coarse-to-fine grained attention. In: EMNLP, pp. 2236–2245 (2018)

7. He, Z., Chen, W., Li, Z., Zhang, M., Zhang, W., Zhang, M.: See: syntax-aware entity embedding for neural relation extraction. In: Thirty-Second AAAI Conference on Artificial Intelligence (2018)

8. Henaff, M., Bruna, J., LeCun, Y.: Deep convolutional networks on graph-structured data. arXiv preprint arXiv:1506.05163 (2015)

9. Hoffmann, R., Zhang, C., Ling, X., Zettlemoyer, L., Weld, D.S.: Knowledge-based weak supervision for information extraction of overlapping relations. In: ACL, pp. 541–550 (2011)

10. Jat, S., Khandelwal, S., Talukdar, P.: Improving distantly supervised relation extraction using word and entity based attention. arXiv preprint arXiv:1804.06987 (2018)

11. Ji, G., Liu, K., He, S., Zhao, J., et al.: Distant supervision for relation extraction with sentence-level attention and entity descriptions. In: AAAI, pp. 3060–3066 (2017)

12. Kipf, T.N., Welling, M.: Semi-supervised classification with graph convolutional networks. arXiv preprint arXiv:1609.02907 (2016)

13. Lin, Y., Shen, S., Liu, Z., Luan, H., Sun, M.: Neural relation extraction with selective attention over instances. In: ACL, vol. 1, pp. 2124–2133 (2016)

14. Mintz, M., Bills, S., Snow, R., Jurafsky, D.: Distant supervision for relation extraction without labeled data. In: ACL/IJCNLP, pp. 1003–1011 (2009)

15. Riedel, S., Yao, L., McCallum, A.: Modeling relations and their mentions without labeled text. In: ECML/PKDD, pp. 148–163 (2010)

16. Surdeanu, M., Tibshirani, J., Nallapati, R., Manning, C.D.: Multi-instance multi-label learning for relation extraction. In: EMNLP-CoNLL, pp. 455–465 (2012)

17. Vashishth, S., Joshi, R., Prayaga, S.S., Bhattacharyya, C., Talukdar, P.: Reside: improving distantly-supervised neural relation extraction using side information. In: EMNLP, pp. 1257–1266 (2018)

18. Yao, L., Mao, C., Luo, Y.: Graph convolutional networks for text classification (2018)

19. Yuan, C., Huang, H., Feng, C., Liu, X., Wei, X.: Distant supervision for relation extraction with linear attenuation simulation and non-IID relevance embedding. In: Proceedings of the AAAI Conference on Artificial Intelligence, vol. 33, pp. 7418–7425 (2019)

20. Yuan, Y., et al.: Cross-relation cross-bag attention for distantly-supervised relation extraction. In: Proceedings of the AAAI Conference on Artificial Intelligence, vol. 33, pp. 419–426 (2019)

21. Zeng, D., Liu, K., Chen, Y., Zhao, J.: Distant supervision for relation extraction via piecewise convolutional neural networks. In: EMNLP, pp. 1753–1762 (2015)

22. Zeng, D., Liu, K., Lai, S., Zhou, G., Zhao, J.: Relation classification via convolutional deep neural network. In: COLING, pp. 2335–2344 (2014)

23. Zeng, W., Lin, Y., Liu, Z., Sun, M.: Incorporating relation paths in neural relation extraction. In: EMNLP, pp. 1768–1777 (2017)

A Physical Embedding Model for Knowledge Graphs

Caglar Demir[✉] and Axel-Cyrille Ngonga Ngomo[✉]

DICE Research Group, Paderborn University, 33098 Paderborn, Germany
{caglar.demir,axel.ngonga}@upb.de

Abstract. Knowledge graph embedding methods learn continuous vector representations for entities in knowledge graphs and have been used successfully in a large number of applications. We present a novel and scalable paradigm for the computation of knowledge graph embeddings, which we dub PYKE. Our approach combines a physical model based on Hooke's law and its inverse with ideas from simulated annealing to compute embeddings for knowledge graphs efficiently. We prove that PYKE achieves a linear space complexity. While the time complexity for the initialization of our approach is quadratic, the time complexity of each of its iterations is linear in the size of the input knowledge graph. Hence, PYKE's overall runtime is close to linear. Consequently, our approach easily scales up to knowledge graphs containing millions of triples. We evaluate our approach against six state-of-the-art embedding approaches on the DrugBank and DBpedia datasets in two series of experiments. The first series shows that the cluster purity achieved by PYKE is up to 26% (absolute) better than that of the state of art. In addition, PYKE is more than 22 times faster than existing embedding solutions in the best case. The results of our second series of experiments show that PYKE is up to 23% (absolute) better than the state of art on the task of type prediction while maintaining its superior scalability. Our implementation and results are open-source and are available at http://github.com/dice-group/PYKE.

Keywords: Knowledge graph embedding · Hooke's law · Type prediction

1 Introduction

The number and size of knowledge graphs (KGs) available on the Web and in companies grows steadily.[1] For example, more than 150 billion facts describing more than 3 billion things are available in the more than 10,000 knowledge

---

[1] https://lod-cloud.net/.

This work was supported by the German Federal Ministry of Transport and Digital Infrastructure project OPAL (GA: 19F2028A) as well as the H2020 Marie Skłodowska-Curie project KnowGraphs (GA no. 860801).

© Springer Nature Switzerland AG 2020
X. Wang et al. (Eds.): JIST 2019, LNCS 12032, pp. 192–209, 2020.
https://doi.org/10.1007/978-3-030-41407-8_13

graphs published on the Web as Linked Data.[2] Knowledge graph embedding (KGE) approaches aim to map the entities contained in knowledge graphs to n-dimensional vectors [13,19,22]. Accordingly, they parallel word embeddings from the field of natural language processing [11,14] and the improvement they brought about in various tasks (e.g., word analogy, question answering, named entity recognition and relation extraction). Applications of KGEs include collective machine learning, type prediction, link prediction, entity resolution, knowledge graph completion and question answering [2,12,13,15,19,22]. In this work, we focus on type prediction.

We present a novel approach for KGE based on a physical model, which goes beyond the state of the art (see [19] for a survey) w.r.t. both efficiency and effectiveness. Our approach, dubbed PYKE, combines a *physical model* (based on Hooke's law) with an optimization technique inspired by *simulated annealing*. PYKE scales to large KGs by achieving a linear space complexity while being close to linear in its time complexity on large KGs. We compare the performance of PYKE with that of six state-of-the-art approaches—Word2Vec [11], ComplEx [18], RESCAL [13], TransE [2], DistMult [22] and Canonical Polyadic (CP) decomposition [6]—on two tasks, i.e., clustering and type prediction w.r.t. both runtime and prediction accuracy. Our results corroborate our formal analysis of PYKE and suggest that our approach scales close to linearly with the size of the input graph w.r.t. its runtime. In addition to outperforming the state of the art w.r.t. runtime, PYKE also achieves better cluster purity and type prediction scores.

The rest of this paper is structured as follows: after providing a brief overview of related work in Sect. 2, we present the mathematical framework underlying PYKE in Sect. 3. Thereafter, we present PYKE in Sect. 4. Section 5 presents the space and time complexity of PYKE. We report on the results of our experimental evaluation in Sect. 6. Finally, we conclude with a discussion and an outlook on future work in Sect. 7.

2 Related Work

A large number of KGE approaches have been developed to address tasks such as link prediction, graph completion and question answering [7,8,12,13,18] in the recent past. In the following, we give a brief overview of some of these approaches. More details can be found in the survey at [19]. RESCAL [13] is based on computing a three-way factorization of an adjacency tensor representing the input KG. The adjacency tensor is decomposed into a product of a core tensor and embedding matrices. RESCAL captures rich interactions in the input KG but is limited in its scalability. HolE [12] uses circular correlation as its compositional operator. Holographic embeddings of knowledge graphs yield state-of-the-art results on link prediction task while keeping the memory complexity lower than

---

[2] lodstats.aksw.org.

RESCAL and TransR [8]. ComplEx [18] is a KGE model based on latent factorization, wherein complex valued embeddings are utilized to handle a large variety of binary relations including symmetric and antisymmetric relations.

Energy-based KGE models [1–3] yield competitive performances on link prediction, graph completion and entity resolution. SE [3] proposes to learn one low-dimensional vector ($\mathbb{R}^k$) for each entity and two matrices ($R_1 \in \mathbb{R}^{k \times k}$, $R_2 \in \mathbb{R}^{k \times k}$) for each relation. Hence, for a given triple (h, r, t), SE aims to minimize the L_1 distance, i.e., $f_r(h, t) = ||R_1 h - R_2 t||$. The approach in [1] embeds entities and relations into the same embedding space and suggests to capture correlations between entities and relations by using multiple matrix products. TransE [2] is a scalable energy-based KGE model wherein a relation r between entities h and t corresponds to a translation of their embeddings, i.e., $h + r \approx t$ provided that (h, r, t) exists in the KG. TransE outperforms state-of-the-art models in the link prediction task on several benchmark KG datasets while being able to deal with KGs containing up to 17 million facts. DistMult [22] proposes to generalize neural-embedding models under an unified learning framework, wherein relations are bi-linear or linear mapping function between embeddings of entities.

With PYKE, we propose a different take to generating embeddings by combining a physical model with simulated annealing. Our evaluation suggests that this simulation-based approach to generating embeddings scales well (i.e., linearly in the size of the KG) while outperforming the state of the art in the type prediction and clustering quality tasks [20, 21].

3   Preliminaries and Notation

In this section, we present the core notation and terminology used throughout this paper. The symbols we use and their meaning are summarized in Table 1.

3.1   Knowledge Graph

In this work, we compute embeddings for RDF KGs. Let $\mathcal{R}$ be the set of all RDF resources, $\mathcal{B}$ be the set of all RDF blank nodes, $\mathcal{P} \subseteq \mathcal{R}$ be the set of all properties and $\mathcal{L}$ denote the set of all RDF literals. An RDF KG $\mathcal{G}$ is a set of RDF triples (s, p, o) where $s \in \mathcal{R} \cup \mathcal{B}$, $p \in \mathcal{P}$ and $o \in \mathcal{R} \cup \mathcal{B} \cup \mathcal{L}$. We aim to compute embeddings for resources and blank nodes. Hence, we define the *vocabulary* of an RDF knowledge graph $\mathcal{G}$ as $\mathcal{V} = \{x : x \in \mathcal{R} \cup \mathcal{P} \cup \mathcal{B} \wedge \exists (s, p, o) \in \mathcal{G} : x \in \{s, p, o\}\}$. Essentially, $\mathcal{V}$ stands for all the URIs and blank nodes found in $\mathcal{G}$. Finally, we define the *subjects with type information* of $\mathcal{G}$ as $\mathcal{S} = \{x : x \in \mathcal{R} \setminus \mathcal{P} \wedge (x, \texttt{rdf:type}, o) \in \mathcal{G}\}$, where $\texttt{rdf:type}$ stands for the instantiation relation in RDF.

3.2   Hooke's Law

Hooke's law describes the relation between a deforming force on a spring and the magnitude of the deformation within the elastic regime of said spring.

Table 1. Overview of our notation

Notation	Description
$\mathcal{G}$	An RDF knowledge graph
$\mathcal{R}, \mathcal{P}, \mathcal{B}, \mathcal{L}$	Set of all RDF resources, predicates, blank nodes and literals respectively
$\mathcal{S}$	Set of all RDF subjects with type information
$\mathcal{V}$	Vocabulary of $\mathcal{G}$
σ	Similarity function on $\mathcal{V}$
$\vec{x}_t$	Embedding of x at time t
F_a, F_r	Attractive and repulsive forces, respectively
K	Threshold for positive and negative examples
P	Function mapping each $x \in \mathcal{V}$ to a set of attracting elements of $\mathcal{V}$
N	Function mapping each $x \in \mathcal{V}$ to a set of repulsive elements of $\mathcal{V}$
$\mathbb{P}$	Probability
ω	Repulsive constant
$\mathcal{E}$	System energy
ϵ	Upper bound on alteration of locations of $x \in \mathcal{V}$ across two iterations
Δe	Energy release

The increase of a deforming force on the spring is linearly related to the increase of the magnitude of the corresponding deformation. In equation form, Hooke's law can be expressed as follows:

$$F = -k\,\Delta \tag{1}$$

where F is the deforming force, Δ is the magnitude of deformation and k is the spring constant. Let us assume two points of unit mass located at x and y respectively. We assume that the two points are connected by an ideal spring with a spring constant k, an infinite elastic regime and an initial length of 0. Then, the force they are subjected to has a magnitude of $k||x-y||$. Note that the magnitude of this force grows with the distance between the two mass points.

The inverse of Hooke's law, where

$$F = -\frac{k}{\Delta} \tag{2}$$

has the opposite behavior. It becomes weaker with the distance between the two mass points it connects.

3.3 Positive Pointwise Mutual Information

The Positive Pointwise Mutual Information (PPMI) is a means to capture the strength of the association between two events (e.g., appearing in a triple of a KG). Let a and b be two events. Let $\mathbb{P}(a, b)$ stand for the joint probability of a and b, $\mathbb{P}(a)$ for the probability of a and $\mathbb{P}(b)$ for the probability of b. Then,

$PPMI(a, b)$ is defined as

$$PPMI(a, b) = \max \left(0, \log \frac{\mathbb{P}(a, b)}{\mathbb{P}(a)\mathbb{P}(b)} \right), \tag{3}$$

The equation truncates all negative values to 0 as measuring the strength of dissociation between events accurately demands very large sample sizes, which are empirically seldom available.

4   PYKE

In this section, we introduce our novel KGE approach dubbed PYKE (a physical model for knowledge graph embeddings). Section 4.1 presents the intuition behind our model. In Sect. 4.2, we give an overview of the PYKE framework, starting from processing the input KG to learning embeddings for the input in a vector space with a predefined number of dimensions. The workflow of our model is further elucidated using the running example shown in Fig. 1.

4.1   Intuition

PYKE is an iterative approach that aims to represent each element x of the vocabulary $\mathcal{V}$ of an input KG $\mathcal{G}$ as an embedding (i.e., a vector) in the n-dimensional space $\mathbb{R}^n$. Our approach begins by assuming that each element of $\mathcal{V}$ is mapped to a single point (i.e., its *embedding*) of unit mass whose location can be expressed via an n-dimensional vector in $\mathbb{R}^n$ according to an initial (e.g., random) distribution at iteration $t = 0$. In the following, we will use $\vec{x}_t$ to denote the embedding of $x \in \mathcal{V}$ at iteration t. We also assume a similarity function $\sigma : \mathcal{V} \times \mathcal{V} \to [0, \infty)$ (e.g., a PPMI-based similarity) over $\mathcal{V}$ to be given. Simply put, our goal is to improve this initial distribution iteratively over a predefined maximal number of iterations (denoted T) by ensuring that

1. the embeddings of similar elements of $\mathcal{V}$ are close to each other while
2. the embeddings of dissimilar elements of $\mathcal{V}$ are distant from each other.

Let $d : \mathbb{R}^n \times \mathbb{R}^n \to \mathbb{R}^+$ be the distance (e.g., the Euclidean distance) between two embeddings in $\mathbb{R}^n$. According to our goal definition, a good iterative embedding approach should have the following characteristics:

C_1: If $\sigma(x, y) > 0$, then $d(\vec{x}_t, \vec{y}_t) \leq d(\vec{x}_{t-1}, \vec{y}_{t-1})$. This means that the embeddings of similar terms should become more similar with the number of iterations. The same holds the other way around:

C_2: If $\sigma(x, y) = 0$, then $d(\vec{x}_t, \vec{y}_t) \geq d(\vec{x}_{t-1}, \vec{y}_{t-1})$.

We translate C_1 into our model as follows: If x and y are similar (i.e., if $\sigma(x, y) > 0$), then a force $F_a(\vec{x}_t, \vec{y}_t)$ of attraction must exist between the masses which stand for x and y at any time t. $F_a(\vec{x}_t, \vec{y}_t)$ must be proportional to $d(\vec{x}_t, \vec{y}_t)$, i.e., the attraction between must grow with the distance between ($\vec{x}_t$ and $\vec{y}_t$).

These conditions are fulfilled by setting the following force of attraction between the two masses:

$$||F_a(\overrightarrow{x}_t, \overrightarrow{y}_t)|| = \sigma(x, y) \times d(\overrightarrow{x}_t, \overrightarrow{y}_t). \tag{4}$$

From the perspective of a physical model, this is equivalent to placing a spring with a spring constant of $\sigma(x, y)$ between the unit masses which stand for x and y. At time t, these masses are hence accelerated towards each other with a total acceleration proportional to $||F_a(\overrightarrow{x}_t, \overrightarrow{y}_t)||$.

The translation of C_2 into a physical model is as follows: If x and y are not similar (i.e., if $\sigma(x, y) = 0$), we assume that they are dissimilar. Correspondingly, their embeddings should diverge with time. The magnitude of the repulsive force between the two masses representing x and y should be strong if the masses are close to each other and should diminish with the distance between the two masses. We can fulfill this condition by setting the following repulsive force between the two masses:

$$||F_r(\overrightarrow{x}_t, \overrightarrow{y}_t)|| = -\frac{\omega}{d(\overrightarrow{x}_t, \overrightarrow{y}_t)}, \tag{5}$$

where $\omega > 0$ denotes a constant, which we dub the repulsive constant. At iteration t, the embeddings of dissimilar terms are hence accelerated away from each other with a total acceleration proportional to $||F_r(\overrightarrow{x}_t, \overrightarrow{y}_t)||$. This is the inverse of Hooke's law, where the magnitude of the repulsive force between the mass points which stand for two dissimilar terms decreases with the distance between the two mass points.

Based on these intuitions, we can now formulate the goal of PYKE formally: We aim to find embeddings for all elements of $\mathcal{V}$ which minimize the total distance between similar elements and maximize the total distance between dissimilar elements. Let $P : \mathcal{V} \rightarrow 2^{\mathcal{V}}$ be a function which maps each element of $\mathcal{V}$ to the subset of $\mathcal{V}$ it is similar to. Analogously, let $N : \mathcal{V} \rightarrow 2^{\mathcal{V}}$ map each element of $\mathcal{V}$ to the subset of $\mathcal{V}$ it is dissimilar to. PYKE aims to optimize the following objective function:

$$J(\mathcal{V}) = \left(\sum_{x \in \mathcal{V}} \sum_{y \in P(x)} d(\overrightarrow{x}, \overrightarrow{y}) \right) - \left(\sum_{x \in \mathcal{V}} \sum_{y \in N(x)} d(\overrightarrow{x}, \overrightarrow{y}) \right). \tag{6}$$

4.2   Approach

PYKE implements the intuition described above as follows: Given an input KG $\mathcal{G}$, PYKE first constructs a symmetric similarity matrix $\mathcal{A}$ of dimensions $|\mathcal{V}| \times |\mathcal{V}|$. We will use $a_{x,y}$ to denotes the similarity coefficient between $x \in V$ and $y \in V$ stored in $\mathcal{A}$. PYKE truncates this matrix to (1) reduce the effect of oversampling and (2) accelerate subsequent computations. The initial embeddings of all $x \in V$ in $\mathbb{R}^n$ are then determined. Subsequently, PYKE uses the physical model described above to improve the embeddings iteratively. The iteration is ran at most T times or until the objective function $J(\mathcal{V})$ stops decreasing. In the following, we

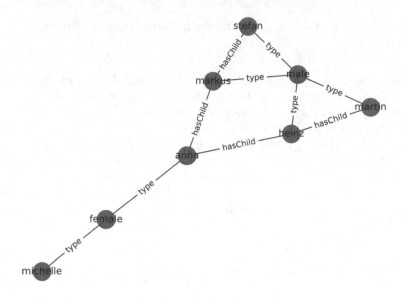

Fig. 1. Example RDF graph

explain each of the steps of the approach in detail. We use the RDF graph shown in Fig. 1 as a running example.[3]

Building the Similarity Matrix. For any two elements $x, y \in \mathcal{V}$, we set $a_{x,y} = \sigma(x,y) = PPMI(x,y)$ in our current implementation. We compute the probabilities $\mathbb{P}(x)$, $\mathbb{P}(y)$ and $\mathbb{P}(x,y)$ as follows:

$$\mathbb{P}(x) = \frac{|\{(s,p,o) \in \mathcal{G} : x \in \{s,p,o\}\}|}{|\{(s,p,o) \in \mathcal{G}\}|}. \tag{7}$$

Similarly,

$$\mathbb{P}(y) = \frac{|\{(s,p,o) \in \mathcal{G} : y \in \{s,p,o\}\}|}{|\{(s,p,o) \in \mathcal{G}\}|}. \tag{8}$$

Finally,

$$\mathbb{P}(x,y) = \frac{|\{(s,p,o) \in \mathcal{G} : \{x,y\} \subseteq \{s,p,o\}\}|}{|\{(s,p,o) \in \mathcal{G}\}|}. \tag{9}$$

For our running example (see Fig. 1), PYKE constructs the similarity matrix shown in Fig. 2. Note that our framework can be combined with any similarity function σ. Exploring other similarity function is out the scope of this paper but will be at the center of future works.

Computing P and N. To avoid oversampling positive or negative examples, we only use a portion of $\mathcal{A}$ for the subsequent optimization of our objective

---

[3] This example is provided as an example in the DL-Learner framework at http://dl-learner.org.

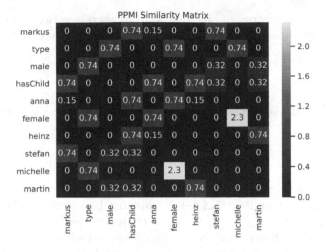

Fig. 2. PPMI similarity matrix of resources in the RDF graph shown in Fig. 1

function. For each $x \in \mathcal{V}$, we begin by computing $P(x)$ by selecting K resources which are most similar to x. Note that if less than K resources have a non-zero similarity to x, then $P(x)$ contains exactly the set of resources with a non-zero similarity to x. Thereafter, we sample K elements y of $\mathcal{V}$ with $a_{x,y} = 0$ randomly. We call this set $N(x)$. For all $y \in N(x)$, we set $a_{x,y}$ to $-\omega$, where ω is our repulsive constant. The values of $a_{x,y}$ for $y \in P(x)$ are preserved. All other values are set to 0. After carrying out this process for all $x \in \mathcal{V}$, each row of $\mathcal{A}$ now contains exactly $2K$ non-zero entries provided that each $x \in \mathcal{V}$ has at least K resources with non-zero similarity. Given that $K << |\mathcal{V}|$, $\mathcal{A}$ is now sparse and can be stored accordingly.[4] The PPMI similarity matrix for our example graph is shown in Fig. 2.

Initializing the Embeddings. Each $x \in \mathcal{V}$ is mapped to a single point $\overrightarrow{x}_t$ of unit mass in $\mathbb{R}^n$ at iteration $t = 0$. As exploring sophisticated initialization techniques is out of the scope of this paper, the initial vector is set randomly.[5] Figure 3 shows a 3D projection of the initial embeddings for our running example (with $n = 50$).

---

[4] We use $\mathcal{A}$ for the sake of explanation. For practical applications, this step can be implemented using priority queues, hence making quadratic space complexity for storing $\mathcal{A}$ unnecessary.

[5] Preliminary experiments suggest that applying a singular value decomposition on $\mathcal{A}$ and initializing the embeddings with the latent representation of the elements of the vocabulary along the n most salient eigenvectors has the potential of accelerating the convergence of our approach.

Iteration. This is the crux of our approach. In each iteration t, our approach assumes that the elements of $P(x)$ attract x with a total force

$$F_a(\overrightarrow{x}_t) = \sum_{y \in P(x)} \sigma(x,y) \times (\overrightarrow{y}_t - \overrightarrow{x}_t). \tag{10}$$

On the other hand, the elements of $N(x)$ repulse x with a total force

$$F_r(\overrightarrow{x}_t) = - \sum_{y \in N(x)} \frac{\omega}{(\overrightarrow{y}_t - \overrightarrow{x}_t)}. \tag{11}$$

We assume that exactly one unit of time elapses between two iterations. The embedding of x at iteration $t + 1$ can now be calculated by displacing $\overrightarrow{x}_t$ proportionally to $(F_a(\overrightarrow{x}_t) + F_r(\overrightarrow{x}_t))$. However, implementing this model directly leads to a chaotic (i.e., non-converging) behavior in most cases. We enforce the convergence using an approach borrowed from simulated annealing, i.e., we reduce the total energy of the system by a constant factor Δe after each iteration. By these means, we can ensure that our approach always terminates, i.e., we can iterate until $J(\mathcal{V})$ does not decrease significantly or until a maximal number of iterations T is reached.

Implementation. Algorithm 1 shows the pseudocode of our approach. PYKE updates the embeddings of vocabulary terms iteratively until one of the following two stopping criteria is satisfied: Either the upper bound on the iterations T is met or a lower bound ϵ on the total change in the embeddings (i.e., $\sum_{x \in V} ||\overrightarrow{x}_t - \overrightarrow{x}_{t-1}||$) is reached. A gradual reduction in the system energy $\mathcal{E}$ inherently guarantees the termination of the process of learning embeddings. A 3D projection of the resulting embedding for our running example is shown in Fig. 3.

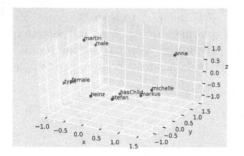 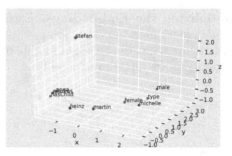

Fig. 3. PCA projection of 50-dimensional embeddings for our running example. Left are the randomly initialized embeddings. The figure on the right shows the 50-dimensional PYKE embedding vectors for our running example after convergence. PYKE was configured with $K = 3$, $\omega = -0.3$, $\Delta e = 0.06$ and $\epsilon = 10^{-3}$.

Algorithm 1. PYKE

Require: T, $\mathcal{V}$, K, ϵ, Δe, ω, n
    //initialize embeddings
    for each x in $\mathcal{V}$ **do**
        $\overrightarrow{x}_0$ = random vector in $\mathbb{R}^n$;
    end for
    //initialize similarity matrix
    $\mathcal{A}$ = new Matrix$[|\mathcal{V}|][|\mathcal{V}|]$;
    for each x in $\mathcal{V}$ **do**
        for each y in $\mathcal{V}$ **do**
            $\mathcal{A}_{xy} = PPMI(x, y)$;
        end for
    end for
    // perform positive and negative sampling
    for each x in $\mathcal{V}$ **do**
        $P(x)$ = getPositives$(\mathcal{A}, x, K)$;
        $N(x)$ = getNegatives$(\mathcal{A}, x, K)$;
    end for
    // iteration
    $t = 1$;
    $\mathcal{E} = 1$;
    while $t < T$ **do**
        for each x in $\mathcal{V}$ **do**
            $F_a = \sum\limits_{y \in P(x)} \sigma(x, y) \times (\overrightarrow{y}_{t-1} - \overrightarrow{x}_{t-1})$;
            $F_r = - \sum\limits_{y \in N(x)} \frac{\omega}{\overrightarrow{y}_{t-1} - \overrightarrow{x}_{t-1}}$;
            $\overrightarrow{x}_t = \overrightarrow{x}_{t-1} + \mathcal{E} \times (F_a + F_r)$;
        end for
        $\mathcal{E} = \mathcal{E} - \Delta e$;
        if $\sum\limits_{x \in \mathcal{V}} ||\overrightarrow{x}_t - \overrightarrow{x}_{t-1}|| < \epsilon$ **then**
            break
        end if
        $t = t + 1$;
    end while
    return Embeddings $\overrightarrow{x}_t$

---

5 Complexity Analysis

5.1 Space Complexity

Let $m = |\mathcal{V}|$. We would need at most $\frac{m(m-1)}{2}$ entries to store $\mathcal{A}$, as the matrix is symmetric and we do not need to store its diagonal. However, there is actually no need to store $\mathcal{A}$. We can implement $P(x)$ as a priority queue of size K in which the indexes of K elements of $\mathcal{V}$ most similar to x as well as their similarity to x

are stored. $N(x)$ can be implemented as a buffer of size K which contains only indexes. Once $N(x)$ reaches its maximal size K, then new entries (i.e., y with $PPMI(x, y)$) are added randomly. Hence, we need $O(Kn)$ space to store both P and N. Note that $K << m$. The embeddings require exactly $2mn$ space as we store $\overrightarrow{x}_t$ and $\overrightarrow{x}_{t-1}$ for each $x \in V$. The force vectors F_a and F_r each require a space of n. Hence, the space complexity of PYKE lies clearly in $O(mn + Kn)$ and is hence linear w.r.t. the size of the input knowledge graph G when the number n of dimensions of the embeddings and the number K of positive and negative examples are fixed.

5.2   Time Complexity

Initializing the embeddings requires mn operations. The initialization of P and N can also be carried out in linear time. Adding an element to P and N is carried out at most m times. For each x, the addition of an element to $P(x)$ has a runtime of at most K. Adding elements to $N(x)$ is carried out in constant time, given that the addition is random. Hence the computation of $P(x)$ and $N(x)$ can be carried out in linear time w.r.t. m. This computation is carried out m times, i.e., once for each x. Hence, the overall runtime of the initialization for PYKE is on $O(m^2)$.

Importantly, the update of the position of each x can be carried out in $O(K)$, leading to each iteration having a time complexity of $O(mK)$. The total runtime complexity for the iterations is hence $O(mKT)$, which is linear in m. This result is of central importance for our subsequent empirical results, as the iterations make up the bulk of PYKE's runtime. Hence, PYKE's runtime should be close to linear in real settings.

6   Evaluation

6.1   Experimental Setup

The goal of our evaluation was to compare the quality of the embeddings generated by PYKE with the state of the art. Given that there is no intrinsic measure for the quality of embeddings, we used two extrinsic evaluation scenarios. In the first scenario, we measured the type homogeneity of the embeddings generated by the KGE approaches we considered. We achieved this goal by using a scalable approximation of DBScan dubbed HDBSCAN [4]. In our second evaluation scenario, we compared the performance of PYKE on the type prediction task against that of 6 state-of-the-art algorithms. In both scenarios, we only considered embeddings of the subset S of V as done in previous works [10,17]. We set $K = 5$, $\Delta e = 0.0414$ and $\omega = 1.45557$ throughout our experiments. The values were computed using a Sobol Sequence optimizer [16]. All experiments were carried out on a single core of a server running Ubuntu 18.04 with 126 GB RAM with 16 Intel(R) Xeon(R) CPU E5-2620 v4 @ 2.10 GHz processors.

We used six datasets (2 real, 4 synthetic) throughout our experiments. An overview of the datasets used in our experiments is shown in Table 2. Drugbank[6] is a small-scale KG, whilst the DBpedia (version 2016-10) dataset is a large cross-domain dataset.[7] The *four synthetic datasets* were generated using the LUBM generator [5] with 100, 200, 500 and 1000 universities.

Table 2. Overview of RDF datasets used in our experiments

Dataset	$|\mathcal{G}|$	$|\mathcal{V}|$	$|\mathcal{S}|$	$|\mathcal{C}|$
Drugbank	3,146,309	521,428	421,121	102
DBpedia	27,744,412	7,631,777	6,401,519	423
LUBM100	9,425,190	2,179,793	2,179,766	14
LUBM200	18,770,356	4,341,336	4,341,309	14
LUBM500	46,922,188	10,847,210	10,847,183	14
LUBM1000	93,927,191	21,715,108	21,715,081	14

We evaluated the homogeneity of embeddings by measuring the purity [9] of the clusters generated by HDBSCAN [4]. The original cluster purity equation assumes that each element of a cluster is mapped to exactly one class [9]. Given that a single resource can have several types in a knowledge graph (e.g., BarackObama is a person, a politician, an author and a president in DBpedia), we extended the cluster purity equation as follows: Let $\mathcal{C} = \{c_1, c_2, \ldots\}$ be the set of all classes found in $\mathcal{G}$. Each $x \in \mathcal{S}$ was mapped to a binary type vector $type(x)$ of length $|\mathcal{C}|$. The ith entry of $type(x)$ was 1 iff x was of type c_i. In all other cases, c_i was set to 0. Based on these premises, we computed the purity of a clustering as follows:

$$\text{Purity} = \sum_{l=1}^{L} \frac{1}{|\zeta_l|^2} \sum_{x \in \zeta_l} \sum_{y \in \zeta_l} cos\Big(type(x), type(y)\Big), \tag{12}$$

where $\zeta_1 \ldots \zeta_L$ are the clusters computed by HDBSCAN. A high purity means that resources with similar type vectors (e.g., presidents who are also authors) are located close to each other in the embedding space, which is a wanted characteristic of a KGE.

In our second evaluation, we performed a type prediction experiment in a manner akin to [10,17]. For each resource $x \in \mathcal{S}$, we used the μ closest embeddings of x to predict x's type vector. We then compared the average of the types

---

[6] download.bio2rdf.org/#/release/4/drugbank.

[7] Note that we compile the DBpedia datasets by merging the dumps of mapping-based objects, skos categories and instance types provided in the DBpedia download folder for version 2016-10 at downloads.dbpedia.org/2016-10.

predicted with x's known type vector using the cosine similarity:

$$\text{prediction score} = \frac{1}{|\mathcal{S}|} \sum_{x \in \mathcal{S}} \cos\left(type(x), \sum_{y \in \mu nn(x)} type(y)\right), \qquad (13)$$

where $\mu nn(x)$ stands for the μ nearest neighbors of x. We employed $\mu \in \{1, 3, 5, 10, 15, 30, 50, 100\}$ in our experiments.

Preliminary experiments showed that performing the cluster purity and type prediction evaluations on embeddings of large knowledge graphs is prohibited by the long runtimes of the clustering algorithm. For instance, HDBSCAN did not terminate in 20 h of computation when $|\mathcal{S}| > 6 \times 10^6$. Consequently, we had to apply HDBSCAN on embeddings on the subset of $\mathcal{S}$ on DBpedia which contained resources of type `Person` or `Settlement`. The resulting subset of $\mathcal{S}$ on DBpedia consists of 428, 289 RDF resources. For the type prediction task, we sampled 10^5 resources from $\mathcal{S}$ according to a random distribution and fixed them across the type prediction experiments for all KGE models.

6.2   Results

Cluster Purity Results. Table 3 displays the cluster purity results for all competing approaches. PYKE achieves a cluster purity of 0.75 on Drugbank and clearly outperforms all other approaches. DBpedia turned out to be a more difficult dataset. Still, PYKE was able to outperform all state-of-the-art approaches by between 11% and 26% (absolute) on Drugbank and between 9% and 23% (absolute) on DBpedia. Note that in 3 cases, the implementations available were unable to complete the computation of embeddings within 24 h.

Table 3. Cluster purity results. The best results are marked in bold. Experiments marked with * did not terminate after 24 h of computation.

Approach	Drugbank	DBpedia
PYKE	**0.75**	**0.57**
Word2Vec	0.43	0.37
ComplEx	0.64	*
RESCAL	*	*
TransE	0.60	0.48
CP	0.49	0.41
DistMult	0.49	0.34

Type Prediction Results. Figures 4 and 5 show our type prediction results on the Drugbank and DBpedia datasets. PYKE outperforms all state-of-the-art approaches across all experiments. In particular, it achieves a margin of up to 22% (absolute) on Drugbank and 23% (absolute) on DBpedia. Like in the previous experiment, all KGE approaches perform worse on DBpedia, with prediction scores varying between <0.1 and 0.32.

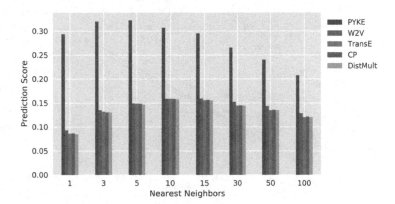

Fig. 4. Mean results on type prediction scores on 10^5 randomly sampled entities of DBpedia

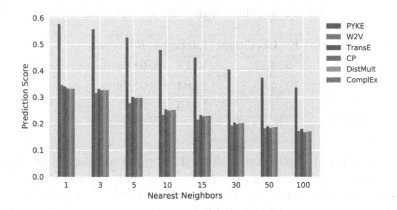

Fig. 5. Mean of type prediction scores on all entities of Drugbank

Runtime Results. Table 5 show runtime performances of all models on the two real benchmark datasets, while Fig. 6 display the runtime of PYKE on the synthetic LUBM datasets. Our results support our original hypothesis. The low space and time complexities of PYKE mean that it runs efficiently: Our approach achieves runtimes of only 25 min on Drugbank and 309 min on DBpedia, while outperforming all other approaches by up to 14 h in runtime.

In addition to evaluating the runtime of PYKE on synthetic data, we were interested in determining its behaviour on datasets of growing sizes. We used LUBM datasets and computed a linear regression of the runtime using ordinary least squares (OLS). The runtime results for this experiment are shown in Fig. 6. The linear fit shown in Table 4 achieves R^2 values beyond 0.99, which points to a clear linear fit between PYKE's runtime and the size of the input dataset.

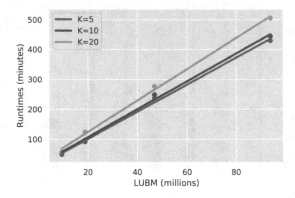

Fig. 6. Runtime performances of PYKE on synthetic KGs. Colored lines represent fitted linear regressions with fixed K values of PYKE. (Color figure online)

Table 4. Results of fitting OLS on runtimes.

K	Coefficient	Intercept	R^2
5	4.52	10.74	0.997
10	4.65	13.64	0.996
20	5.23	19.59	0.997

We believe that the good performance of PYKE stems from (1) its sampling procedure and (2) its being akin to a physical simulation. Employing PPMI to quantify the similarity between resources seems to yield better sampling results than generating negative examples using the *local closed word assumption* that underlies sampling procedures of all of competing state-of-the-art KG models. More importantly, positive and negative sampling occur in our approach per resource rather than per RDF triple. Therefore, PYKE is able to leverage more from negative and positive sampling. By virtue of being akin to a physical simulation, PYKE is able to run efficiently even when each resource x is mapped to 45 attractive and 45 repulsive resources (see Table 5) whilst all state-of-the-art KGE required more computation time.

Table 5. Runtime performances (in minutes) of all competing approaches. All approaches were executed three times on each dataset. The reported results are the mean and standard deviation of the last two runs. The best results are marked in bold. Experiments marked with * did not terminate after 24 h of computation.

Approach	Drugbank	DBpedia
PYKE	**25 ± 1**	**309 ± 1**
Word2Vec	41 ± 1	420 ± 1
ComplEx	705 ± 1	*
RESCAL	*	*
TransE	68 ± 1	685 ± 1
CP	230 ± 1	1154 ± 1
DistMult	210 ± 1	1030 ± 1

7   Conclusion

We presented PYKE, a novel approach for the computation of embeddings on knowledge graphs. By virtue of being akin to a physical simulation, PYKE retains a linear space complexity. This was proven through a complexity analysis of our approach. While the time complexity of the approach is quadratic due to the computation of P and N, all other steps are linear in their runtime complexity. Hence, we expected our approach to behave closes to linearly. Our evaluation on LUBM datasets suggests that this is indeed the case and the runtime of our approach grows close to linearly. This is an important result, as it means that our approach can be used on very large knowledge graphs and return results faster than popular algorithms such as Word2VEC and TransE. However, time efficiency is not all. Our results suggest that PYKE outperforms state-of-the-art approaches in the two tasks of type prediction and clustering. Still, there is clearly a lack of normalized evaluation scenarios for knowledge graph embedding approaches. We shall hence develop such benchmarks in future works. Our results open a plethora of other research avenues. First, the current approach to compute similarity between entities/relations on KGs is based on the local similarity. Exploring other similarity means will be at the center of future works. In addition, using a better initialization for the embeddings should lead to faster convergence. Finally, one could use a stochastic approach (in the same vein as stochastic gradient descent) to further improve the runtime of PYKE.

References

1. Bordes, A., Glorot, X., Weston, J., Bengio, Y.: A semantic matching energy function for learning with multi-relational data. Mach. Learn. **94**, 233–259 (2014)
2. Bordes, A., Usunier, N., Garcia-Duran, A., Weston, J., Yakhnenko, O.: Translating embeddings for modeling multi-relational data. Curran Associates, Inc. (2013)
3. Bordes, A., Weston, J., Collobert, R., Bengio, Y.: Learning structured embeddings of knowledge bases. In: Twenty-Fifth AAAI Conference on Artificial Intelligence (2011)
4. Campello, R.J.G.B., Moulavi, D., Sander, J.: Density-based clustering based on hierarchical density estimates. In: Pei, J., Tseng, V.S., Cao, L., Motoda, H., Xu, G. (eds.) PAKDD 2013. LNCS (LNAI), vol. 7819. Springer, Heidelberg (2013). https://doi.org/10.1007/978-3-642-37456-2_14
5. Guo, Y., Pan, Z., Heflin, J.: LUBM: a benchmark for owl knowledge base systems. Web Semant. Sci. Serv. Agents World Wide Web **3**(2–3), 158–182 (2005)
6. Hitchcock, F.L.: The expression of a tensor or a polyadic as a sum of products. J. Math. Phys. **6**(1–4), 164–189 (1927)
7. Huang, X., Zhang, J., Li, D., Li, P.: Knowledge graph embedding based question answering. In: Proceedings of the Twelfth ACM International Conference on Web Search and Data Mining. ACM (2019)
8. Lin, Y., Liu, Z., Sun, M., Liu, Y., Zhu, X.: Learning entity and relation embeddings for knowledge graph completion. In: Twenty-Ninth AAAI Conference on Artificial Intelligence (2015)
9. Manning, C., Raghavan, P., Schütze, H.: Introduction to information retrieval. Nat. Lang. Eng. (2010)
10. Melo, A., Paulheim, H., Völker, J.: Type prediction in RDF knowledge bases using hierarchical multilabel classification. In: Proceedings of the 6th International Conference on Web Intelligence, Mining and Semantics, p. 14. ACM (2016)
11. Mikolov, T., Sutskever, I., Chen, K., Corrado, G.S., Dean, J.: Distributed representations of words and phrases and their compositionality. In: Advances in Neural Information Processing Systems (2013)
12. Nickel, M., Rosasco, L., Poggio, T.: Holographic embeddings of knowledge graphs. In: Proceedings of the Thirtieth AAAI Conference on Artificial Intelligence, AAAI 2016 pp. 1955–1961 (2016)
13. Nickel, M., Tresp, V., Kriegel, H.P.: A three-way model for collective learning on multi-relational data. In: ICML, vol. 11 (2011)
14. Pennington, J., Socher, R., Manning, C.: GloVe: global vectors for word representation. In: Proceedings of the 2014 Conference on Empirical Methods in Natural Language Processing (EMNLP) (2014)
15. Ristoski, P., Paulheim, H.: RDF2Vec: RDF graph embeddings for data mining. In: International Semantic Web Conference (2016)
16. Saltelli, A., Annoni, P., Azzini, I., Campolongo, F., Ratto, M., Tarantola, S.: Variance based sensitivity analysis of model output. Design and estimator for the total sensitivity index. Comput. Phys. Commun. **181**(2), 259–270 (2010)
17. Thoma, S., Rettinger, A., Both, F.: Towards holistic concept representations: embedding relational knowledge, visual attributes, and distributional word semantics. In: d'Amato, C., et al. (eds.) ISWC 2017. LNCS, vol. 10587. Springer, Cham (2017). https://doi.org/10.1007/978-3-319-68288-4_41
18. Trouillon, T., Welbl, J., Riedel, S., Gaussier, É., Bouchard, G.: Complex embeddings for simple link prediction. In: International Conference on Machine Learning (2016)

19. Wang, Q., Mao, Z., Wang, B., Guo, L.: Knowledge graph embedding: a survey of approaches and applications. IEEE Trans. Knowl. Data Eng. **29**, 2724–2743 (2017)
20. Wang, X., Cui, P., Wang, J., Pei, J., Zhu, W., Yang, S.: Community preserving network embedding. In: AAAI (2017)
21. Xie, R., Liu, Z., Jia, J., Luan, H., Sun, M.: Representation learning of knowledge graphs with entity descriptions. In: Proceedings of the Thirtieth AAAI Conference on Artificial Intelligence, AAAI 2016, pp. 2659–2665. AAAI Press (2016)
22. Yang, B., Yih, W.t., He, X., Gao, J., Deng, L.: Embedding entities and relations for learning and inference in knowledge bases. arXiv preprint arXiv:1412.6575 (2014)

Iterative Visual Relationship Detection via Commonsense Knowledge Graph

Hai Wan[1] , Jialing Ou[1] , Baoyi Wang[1] , Jianfeng Du[2(✉)] , Jeff Z. Pan[3] ,
and Juan Zeng[4(✉)]

[1] School of Data and Computer Science, Sun Yat-sen University, Guangzhou, China
wanhai@mail.sysu.edu.cn, {oujl5,wangby9}@mail2.sysu.edu.cn
[2] School of Information Science and Technology/School of Cyber Security,
Guangdong University of Foreign Studies, Guangzhou, China
jfdu@gdufs.edu.cn
[3] Department of Computing Science, The University of Aberdeen, Aberdeen, UK
jeff.z.pan@abdn.ac.uk
[4] School of Geography and Planning, Sun Yat-sen University, Guangzhou, China
zengjuan@mail.sysu.edu.cn

Abstract. Visual relationship detection, *i.e.*, discovering the interaction between pairs of objects in an image, plays a significant role in image understanding. However, most of recent works only consider visual features, ignoring the implicit effect of common sense. Motivated by the iterative visual reasoning in image recognition, we propose a novel model to take the advantage of common sense in the form of the knowledge graph in visual relationship detection, named Iterative Visual Relationship Detection with Commonsense Knowledge Graph (IVRDC). Our model consists of two modules: a feature module that predicts predicates by visual features and semantic features with a bi-directional RNN; and a commonsense knowledge module that constructs a specific commonsense knowledge graph for predicate prediction. After iteratively combining prediction from both modules, IVRDC updates the memory and commonsense knowledge graph. The final predictions are made by taking the result of each iteration into account with an attention mechanism. Our experiments on the Visual Relationship Detection (VRD) dataset and the Visual Genome (VG) dataset demonstrate that our proposed model is competitive.

Keywords: Commonsense knowledge graph · Visual relationship detection · Visual Genome

1 Introduction

Visual relationship detection, introduced by [12], aims to capture a wide variety of interactions between pairs of objects in an image. Visual relation can be represented as a set of relation triples in the form of $(subject, predicate, object)$, *e.g.*, $(person, ride, horse)$. Visual relationship detection can be used for many high-level image understanding tasks such as image caption [1] and visual QA [6].

© Springer Nature Switzerland AG 2020
X. Wang et al. (Eds.): JIST 2019, LNCS 12032, pp. 210–225, 2020.
https://doi.org/10.1007/978-3-030-41407-8_14

Recently, visual relationship detection attracts more and more attention. Visual relationship detection methods can be categorized into two branches.

One branch includes those detection models that take into consideration not only the information from the dataset but also external knowledge. [18] proposed a teacher-student knowledge distillation framework making use of the internal and external knowledge for visual relationship detection. [10] constructed a directed semantic action graph and used deep variation-structured reinforcement to predict visual relationships.

Another branch includes those detection models that only consider prior images and their annotations. [12] not only proposed a typical model with language prior but also introduced the Visual Relationship Dataset (VRD) for visual relationship detection task. [19] applied a translation embedding model for visual relationship detection. [20] used a parallel FCN architecture and a position-role-sensitive score map to tackle the visual relationship detection. [5] exploited the statistical dependencies between objects and their relationships to detect visual relationships. [21] introduced deep structured learning for visual relationship detection. [9] proposed a deep neural network framework with the structural ranking loss to tackle the visual this task.

However, most of the recent works only consider the appearance or spatial features, while ignoring the implicit effect of common sense.

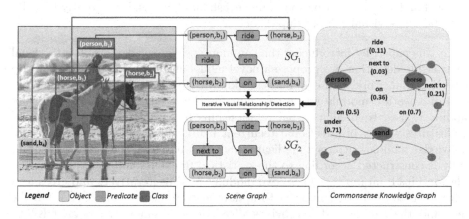

Fig. 1. An example image from VRD. The relation between $(person, b_1)$ and $(horse, b_2)$ is *ride*. Although $(horse, b_3)$ is similar with $(horse, b_2)$ in visual feature and positional feature, the relation between $(person, b_1)$ and $(horse, b_3)$ is *next to* but not *ride*.

Scene graph, introduced by [7], is a graph-based structural representation which describes the semantic contents of an image. Compared with scene graph, the well-known *knowledge graph* is represented as multi-relational data with enormous fact *triples* [2]. [17] further identified the *visual triples* of scene graph. A scene graph is a set of visual triples in the form of $(head\ entity, relation, tail\ entity)$ in which an *entity* is composed of its *entity type* with *attributes* and grounded with a bounding box in its corresponding image, and a *relation* is the edge from the *head entity* to the *tail entity*. An example in VRD is shown in Fig. 1. The relation between $(person, b_1)$ and $(horse, b_2)$ is *ride*. This visual triple is in the form of $((person, b_1), ride, (horse, b_2))$. The visual triple is shown in SG_1.

However, Fig. 1 also shows that, if only considering the appearance or spatial feature between $(person, b_1)$ and $(horse, b_3)$, it is more likely that the relationship between these two objects are incorrectly detected as *ride*, as shown in SG_1. To avoid that, we introduce the notion of the *commonsense knowledge graph (CKG)*, in which each triple is labeled with its conditional probability. For example, the conditional probability of *next to* with 0.21 between *horse* and *horse* in CKG is higher than *ride* with 0.11 between *person* and *horse*, so we can get the correct visual triple $((person, b_1), next to, (horse, b_3))$ after iteratively updating with commonsense knowledge graph, as shown in SG_2. This suggests that it is important to consider CKG in visual relationship detection. While the task is challenging and there are at least three challenges:

1. CKG is a global graph for the image set rather than a graph that aims at one image, while visual relationship detection focuses on a given image.
2. A pair of object classes may have different relations even in the same image (e.g. "person" and "horse" show in the CKG of Fig. 1), making it difficult to update CKG.
3. CKG and feature information of images should be considered jointly in order to facilitate visual relationship detection.

In this paper, by introducing the commonsense knowledge graph into visual relationship detection, we propose a novel model of iterative visual relationship detection framework with commonsense knowledge graph (IVRDC), which consists of a feature module and a commonsense knowledge module. The feature module is used to predict visual relationships by visual features and semantic features with a bi-directional recurrent neural network. The commonsense knowledge module outputs a predicate prediction based on the CKG, which initially is constructed according to the statistical frequency information of visual relationships from images. These two modules roll out iteratively and cross feed predictions to each other in order to update feature memory and CKG. On the one hand, the feature module provides a feedback to promote the global CKG to evolve towards the given image; on the other hand, the commonsense knowledge module offers commonsense to refine the estimates.

Finally, we evaluate our method by taking experiments on the VRD and Visual Genome (VG) datasets. Experiment results demonstrate that our proposed model outperforms the state-of-the-art methods.

The rest of this paper is organized as follows. We first introduce the preliminary in the next section. In the third section, we show our proposed model named iterative visual relationship detection with commonsense knowledge graph. Then we present the experiment results.

Due to space limit, omitted data, code, and supporting materials are provided in the online appendix (https://github.com/sysulic/IVRDC).

2 Preliminary

In this section, we first recall the definitions of scene graph and visual relationship detection. Then we give the definition of commonsense knowledge graph. We also recall the bi-directional recurrent neural network used in our model.

2.1 Commonsense Knowledge Graph

[17] identified the *visual triples* of *scene graph*. We only consider entities and relations without attributes in this paper and give the definition of scene graph as follows. *W.l.o.g.* we assume that all images are in a finite set $\mathcal{I}$. All *classes* in $\mathcal{I}$ are in a finite set $\mathcal{C}$. All *predicates*[1] in $\mathcal{I}$ are in a finite set $\mathcal{P}$.

Definition 1 (Scene Graph). Given an image $I \in \mathcal{I}$, its scene graph is a set of *visual triples* $\mathcal{T}_I \subseteq \mathcal{O}_I \times \mathcal{P}_I \times \mathcal{O}_I$, $\mathcal{O}_I$ is the object set and $\mathcal{P}_I$ is the predicate set. Each object $o_{c,I,k} = (c, b_{I,k}) \in \mathcal{O}_I$ is packed with a class $c \in \mathcal{C}$ and a bounding box $b_{I,k}$ in image I, where $k \in \{1, 2, ..., |\mathcal{O}_I|\}$. A visual triple is of the form $(o_{c,I,k}, p, o_{c',I,k'}) \in \mathcal{T}_I$, where the two objects $o_{c,I,k}, o_{c',I,k'} \in \mathcal{O}_I$ and the predicate $p \in \mathcal{P}_I$. In general, we name $o_{c,I,k}$ as *subject* and $o_{c',I,k'}$ as *object*.

There are 4 objects, 2 predicates, and 4 visual relation triples in the scene graph $\mathcal{T}_I$ of Fig. 1, *e.g.*, $((person, b_1), ride, (horse, b_2))$. For simplicity, we write it as $(person, ride, horse)$.

Definition 2 (Visual Relationship Detection). *Given an image $I \in \mathcal{I}$ and its object set $\mathcal{O}_I$, visual relationship detection is to detect the predicate p between two objects $o_{c,I,k}$ and $o_{c',I,k'}$, where $o_{c,I,k}, o_{c',I,k'} \in \mathcal{O}_I$ and $p \in \mathcal{P}_I$.*

As shown in Fig. 1, the predicate between *"person"* and *"sand"* is detected as *"on"* by the visual relationship detection. In other words, we construct a visual triple $(person, on, sand)$ for this image.

Definition 3 (Commonsense Knowledge Graph). Given an image set $\mathcal{I}$, the class set in $\mathcal{I}$ is $\mathcal{C}$, the predicate set in $\mathcal{I}$ is $\mathcal{P}$, the *commonsense knowledge graph* is a directed edge-labeled graph $\mathcal{G} = (\mathcal{C}, \mathcal{P}, \lambda)$, where each node $c \in \mathcal{C}$, each edge (c_s, p, c_o) represents a relationship between two nodes c_s and c_o ($c_s, c_o \in \mathcal{C}$, $p \in \mathcal{P}$), λ is the labeling function which means the confidence of (c_s, p, c_o), denoted by the conditional probability $P(p|c_s, c_o)$.

As shown in Fig. 1, $(person, on, sand)$ is an edge with its confidence $P(on|person, sand) = 0.5$. Intuitively, if two nodes are irrelevant, the confidence of the edge between them is zero. There may exist some edges that connect the same node, *e.g.*, $(horse, next\ to, horse)$.

---

[1] Throughout this paper, we identify that the *predicate* in visual relationship detection is the *relation* in scene graph.

2.2 Bi-directional Recurrent Neural Network

Bi-directional recurrent neural network (Bi-RNN), proposed by [15], is successfully applied in natural language processing. [11] improved the original Bi-RNN and applied it to detect visual relation.

Bi-RNN. In Bi-RNN, the vector x_i is the input of a sequence and y is the output, and h_i is a hidden layer. There are two hidden layers: a forward sequences $\overrightarrow{h}_i$ and a backward sequences $\overleftarrow{h}_i$.

$$\overrightarrow{h}_i = f(U_f x_i + W_f \overrightarrow{h}_{i-1} + b_f) \tag{1}$$

$$\overleftarrow{h}_i = f(U_b x_i + W_b \overleftarrow{h}_{i-1} + b_b) \tag{2}$$

$$y = \sum V_{f,i} \overrightarrow{h}_i + \sum V_{b,i} \overleftarrow{h}_i + b_y \tag{3}$$

where U_f and U_b denote the input-hidden weight matrixes. W_f and W_b denote the hidden-hidden weight matrixes. f is the activation function of the hidden layers (ReLU function). V_b and V_f denote the output-hidden weight matrixes. b_f, b_b and b_y denote the bias vectors.

While detecting visual relations between objects, the order of input sequences is of significance, because different orders can lead to distinct visual relationship detection results. For example, the visual relation between the object pair $(person, horse)$ can be totally different from that between the object pair $(horse, person)$. Bi-RNN can fit this character. To apply it to our model, we take the corresponding feature vectors of object pairs as inputs of Bi-RNN's and take the prediction vector as its output. The details will be shown in the next section.

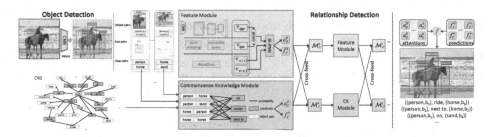

Fig. 2. The overview of our visual relation detection framework. Beside an object detector that gives a group of detected bounding boxes and their corresponding classification probability, the framework has two modules to perform detection: a feature module and a commonsense knowledge module. Both modules roll-out iteratively while cross-feeding beliefs. The final prediction f is produced by combining each prediction with attention mechanism.

3   Method

In this section, we propose a model named Iterative Visual Relationship Detection with Commonsense Knowledge Graph (IVRDC). The overall pipeline of IVRDC (Fig. 2) is divided into *object detection* and *relationship detection*. Relationship detection consists of two modules: *feature module* and *commonsense knowledge module*. Both modules roll-out iteratively while cross-feeding beliefs. The final prediction is obtained by combining predictions from each iteration with attention mechanism.

In object detection, for each image I, we use Faster R-CNN [14] to obtain a group of bounding boxes and their classes and pack each bounding box $b_{I,k}$ with its class c together to be an object $o_{c,I,k}$. So for each image, we obtain several objects labeled with classes and the corresponding boxes.

Visual relation prediction is to predict visual triples (*subject, predicate, object*). The feature module captures the interactions between objects by using feature vectors. And the commonsense module provides the conditional probability for reference. We construct a memory for iteration to store information. Then the model combines the outputs of the two modules, f_F and f_C, to update the two memories, $\mathcal{M}_F$ and $\mathcal{M}_C$. We will discuss the iteration and attention mechanism of each module in detail.

3.1   Feature Module

In the feature module, three features are taken into consideration: appearance feature, spatial feature and word vector. And the module employs Bi-RNN to learn those features to detect predicates [11].

We encode an image I of shape $H \times W \times C$, where H and W denote the height and the width, and C denotes the channels of the image. For our work, $C = 3$. For each image I, each candidate object $o_{c,I,k} = (c, b_{I,k}) \in \mathcal{O}_I$ has a bounding box $b_{I,k} = (x_{min}, y_{min}, x_{max}, y_{max})$ and its detected class c. Since visual information of an image can implicit interaction among objects and is particularly useful for visual relation detection, we construct an appearance feature v_{app} to encode visual information, which restores not only object features but also their context information. For preprocessing, we construct a new larger bounding box $b_{o,o'}$ to encompass the two boxes of an object pair (o, o'). We use VGG16 [16] to encode the region enclosed by $b_{o,o'}$, of shape $H' \times W' \times C$, where $H' = W' = 224$ and $C = 3$. The region through VGG16 net and we obtain the corresponding features. Then make it as inputs of a convolution net of two convolution layers and one 300-D fully-connected layer to get the appearance feature v_{app}.

Spatial information is also a key factor that influences our detection. The spatial feature is learned by a convolution neural network. In an image I, an object pair $(o_{c,I,k}, o_{c',I,k'})$ contains two bounding boxes $b_{o_{c,I,k}}$ and $b_{o_{c',I,k'}}$. First, we apply dual spatial masks for bounding boxes to get two binary masks, one for object $o_{c,I,k}$ and another for object $o_{c',I,k'}$. Then the masks are down-sampling to a predefined squaro (32×32) [5]. Finally, a convolution net of three convolution layers and a 300-D fully-connected layer take the masks as inputs to obtain the 300-D spatial feature v_{spa}.

Features mentioned above are visual features and express the relation between two objects. To consider the semantic feature and independence of objects, we represent an object class as a word vector. In this work, $Word2vec$ [13] is used to learn the word vectors. For an image I, each object $c_{c,I,k}$ has an object class c, then we can find the word vector corresponding to the name of c (e.g., $person$). The relation between two words is an inherent semantic relationship instead of the mathematics distance with one-hot vector. Obviously, similar object pairs may have similar relationships. For example, the relationship between "$person$" and "$sand$" is normally "on". "$horse$" and "$person$" are similar in semantic space. Then it can reason that $(horse, on, sand)$. Similarly, some infrequent relations can be learned by the normal relation. For a pair of object $(o_{c,I,k}, o_{c',I,k'})$ in the image I, we generate two feature vectors, $v_{w(o_{c,I,k})}$ and $v_{w(o_{c',I,k'})}$, for subject and object, simplify as $v_{w(s)}$ and $v_{w(o)}$.

Before feeding features into a Bi-RNN, we concatenate appearance feature v_{app} and spatial feature v_{spa} and make the concatenated vector through a fully-connected layer to obtain visual feature v_{vis}. Then we combine the visual feature and semantic feature. Applying Bi-RNN to predict relationships, we feed feature vector $v_{w(s)}$, v_{vis} and $v_{w(o)}$ to input x_1, x_2, and x_3 (shown in Eq. (1) and (2)), respectively. The Bi-RNN structure is shown in Figure 3.

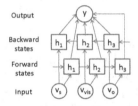

Fig. 3. Bi-RNN has three inputs in sequence ($v_{w(s)}$, v_{vis} and $v_{w(o)}$) and one output (predicate prediction y).

The output y is a $|\mathcal{C}|$-dimension vector. We use softmax function on y to compute the normalized probabilistic prediction to form the predicate f_F. The feature vector, including appearance feature, spatial feature and word vector, construct the memory $\mathcal{M}_F$ to store the visual and semantic information.

3.2   Commonsense Knowledge Module

In this part, we introduce how to construct the commonsense knowledge graph $\mathcal{G} = (\mathcal{C}, \mathcal{P}, \lambda)$ from a given image set $\mathcal{I}$ and how to use it in our framework. As defined before, the commonsense knowledge graph is a directed edge-labeled graph. First of all, we collect common sense from the training annotations and count the conditional probability that encodes the correlation between the pair of objects and the predicate. Each node $c \in \mathcal{C}$ represents an object class, e.g., "$person$" in Fig. 1. Each edge (c_s, p, c_o) represents a relationship between two node c_s and c_o, e.g.,$(sand, under, person)$ in Fig. 1. λ is the labeling function that shows the conditional probability of the relationship. The conditional probability can be formulated as:

$$P(p|c_s, c_o) = \frac{P(p, c_s, c_o)}{P(c_s, c_o)} \tag{4}$$

The commonsense knowledge graph is a universal graph, while visual relationship detection task is closely related to a particular image. To tackle this problem, we construct the subgraph of the commonsense knowledge graph $\mathcal{G}' = (\mathcal{C}', \mathcal{P}', \lambda)$. For each image, we use an pre-train object detector (Faster R-CNN) to detect objects, then according to the classes of those objects, we select all relative relationships from the global CKG. The nodes $\mathcal{C}'$ consist of the set of all the detected object classes and the edges $\mathcal{P}'$ are the corresponding relationships. This subgraph $\mathcal{G}'$ is only for the specific image with all the detected objects in the image and the connected edges. Then we set a threshold and distill the prediction f_C according to the subject node and the object node. When the prediction f_C updates, the subgraph will update the weights of the corresponding edges. Then we construct memory $\mathcal{M}_C$ to store the updated subgraph.

3.3 Iteration

The key component of the proposed model is to iteratively build up estimates. To deliver information from one iteration to another, we construct memories to store the information. The feature module uses feature memory $\mathcal{M}_F$ and the commonsense module use another memory $\mathcal{M}_C$.

At iteration i, the commonsense module distills the prediction $f_{C,i}$ and the feature module creates the prediction $f_{F,i}$ for a pair of candidate objects. Because $f_{C,i}$ ranges from 0 to 1, and the codomain of $f_{F,i}$ is uncertain, it is unreasonable to combine the two predictions directly. So the combination $f_{C,i+1}$ of the two predictions is given by

$$f_{C,i+1} = W_1 \circ f_{C,i} + W_2 \circ f_F \tag{5}$$

where W_1 and W_2 are weights, $f_{C,i+1}$ is the updated probability, $f_{C,i}$ denotes the result from the commonsense knowledge module, and f_F denotes the prediction from the feature module. Then $f_{C,i+1}$ can be used to get the updated memories, $\mathcal{M}_C^{i+1}$ and $\mathcal{M}_F^{i+1}$.

Then we update the feature memory $\mathcal{M}_F$ by a convolutional gate recurrent unit (GRU) [4]. F denotes a memory for a pair of candidate objects. F_{up} denotes a memory that we construct to update memory. We extract the appearance feature and the spatial feature from memory F. Then we combine $f_{C,i+1}$ with addition and convolution layers to form memory F_{up}. We update the feature memory as the following formula:

$$F_{i+1} = u \circ F_i + (1 - u) \circ \sigma(W_u F_{up} + W_F(r \circ F_i) + b) \tag{6}$$

where u denotes the update gate, r denotes the reset gate, F_{i+1} is the updated memory. W_f, W_F, and b are convolutional weights and bias, and $\circ$ is entry-wise product. $\sigma()$ is an activation function. After that, F_{i+1} is used to update memory $\mathcal{M}_F^{i+1}$.

The new memories, $\mathcal{M}_C^{i+1}$ and $\mathcal{M}_F^{i+1}$, will lead to another round of updated f_C and f_F and the iteration goes on. In this way, the feature memory can benefit from commonsense knowledge graph. At the same time, the subgraph of commonsense knowledge graph can get a better sense of the particular image.

3.4 Attention

To modify the model output, we generate the final prediction f by the combination of each iteration prediction instead of the last iteration prediction. To combine the predictions from each iteration, we introduce attention mechanism [3] to our framework. It means that the final output is a weighted version of all predictions using attentions. Mathematically, if the model iterate n times, then outputs $N = 2n$ (including n times feature module and n times commonsense module) prediction f_n by attention a_n, the final output f is represented as:

$$f = \sum_n^N w_n f_n \tag{7}$$

$$w_n = \frac{exp(a_n)}{\sum_{n'} exp(a_{n'})} \tag{8}$$

$$a_n = ReLU(W f_n + b) \tag{9}$$

where f_n is the logits before softmax w_n denotes the weight of each prediction, a_n is produced by f_n with an activation function $ReLU$. The introduction of attention mechanism enables the model to select feasible predictions from different modules and iterations.

3.5 Training

The total loss function consists of the feature module loss $\mathcal{L}_F$, the commonsense module loss $\mathcal{L}_C$ and the final prediction loss $\mathcal{L}_f$. To take more attention on the harder examples, we give different weights for the loss examples, based on the predictions from previous iterations. Then the cross-entropy loss is represented as:

$$w_{\mathcal{L}} = \frac{max(1.0 - p_{i-1}, 0.5)}{\sum max(1.0 - p_{i-1}, 0.5)} \tag{10}$$

$$\mathcal{L}_i = -w_{\mathcal{L}} log(p_i) \tag{11}$$

where p_i denotes the softmax output of the prediction for iteration i.

For model initialization, we use a pre-trained VGG-16 ImageNet model to initialize the CNN parameters of the appearance module and randomly initialize the spatial feature [5]. For word vectors for classes, we train our Word2vec model based on the class set and the triples in CKG. For Bi-RNN, it has two hidden layers and each layer has 128 hidden states. We roll out the feature module and the commonsense module three times and update the subgraph of commonsense knowledge graph at each iteration.

4 Experiments

We evaluate the proposed method on two recently released datasets. We first introduce datasets and experimental settings, and then analyze the experimental results in detail.

4.1 Datasets

We evaluate our proposed model on Visual Relationship Datasets (VRD) [12] and Visual Genome(VG) [8] shown in Table 1.

Table 1. Statistics of datasets

Dataset	$|\mathcal{I}|$	$|\mathcal{C}|$	$|\mathcal{P}|$	$|\mathcal{I}_{train}|$	$|\mathcal{I}_{test}|$
VRD	5,000	100	70	4,000	1,000
VG	99,659	200	100	73,801	25,857

VRD contains 5000 images with 100 object classes and 70 predicates. VRD contains 37,993 relation annotations with 6,672 type triples in total. Following the same train/test split as in [12], we split images into two sets, 4,000 images for training and 1,000 for testing.

VG contains 99,658 images with 200 object classes and 100 predicates. Totally, VG contains 1,174,692 relation annotations with 19,237 type triples. Following the experiments in [19], we split the data into 73,801 for training and 25,857 for testing.

4.2 Experimental Settings

According to [12], we use Recall@K as the major performance metric. Recall@K computes the fraction of times the correct relationships are predicted in the top K confident relationship predictions, as the following formula:

$$Recall@K = \frac{\sum_{i=1}^{\mathcal{I}} n}{\sum_{i=1}^{\mathcal{I}} m} \tag{12}$$

where n denotes the number of correct relationships in the top K confidence in i image, m denotes the number of the relationships labeled in ground truth in $i-th$ image. Following [12], we use Recall@50 (R@50) and Recall@100 (R@100) as evaluation metrics for our experiments. The reason using R@K is that the relationships in ground-truth are incomplete, in other words, some true relationships are missing.

Like [12], we evaluate our proposed method for the following tasks:

- **Predicate detection**: this task focuses on the accuracy of predicate prediction. The input includes the object classes and the bounding boxes of both the subject and object. In this condition, we can learn how difficult it is to predict relationships without the limitations of object detection.
- **Phrase/Union detection**: the task treats the whole triple $(sub, pred, obj)$ as a union bounding box which contains the subject and object. A prediction is considered correct if all the three elements in a triple are correct and the *Intersection over Union (IoU)* between the detected box and the ground truth bounding box is greater than 0.5.
- **Relationship detection**: this task treats a triple $(sub, pred, obj)$ as three components. A prediction is considered correct if three elements in a triple are correct and the IoU of subject and object are both above 0.5 with the ground-truth bounding box.

4.3   Comparative Results

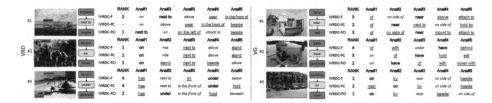

Fig. 4. Qualitative examples of relation prediction. We show the correct relation rankings and the top-5 answers from IVRDC-F, IVRDC-FC and IVRDC-FCI on VRD and VG. Relations in **bold**, *italic*, and <u>underline</u> fonts denote the correct, plausible, and wrong answers respectively.

Compare with Other Works. As mentioned above, visual relationship detection methods can be categorized into two branches: one takes external knowledge into consideration, such as LK [18] and VRL [10]; one only considers the internal knowledge of the dataset, which includes our model. So we do not compare our model with them and only compare with the state-of-the-art methods in the second branch. (1) **LP** [12] is a visual relationship detection model with appearance features and language prior. (2) **VTransE** [19] applies translation embedding to visual relationship detection and it is an end-to-end model with only visual features. (3) **PPR-FCN** [20] uses a parallel FCN architecture and a position-role-sensitive score map to tackle the task of "subject-predicate-object". (4) **DR-Net** [5] constructs appearance feature and spatial feature and makes full use of the statistical dependencies between objects and their relationships to predict visual relationships. (5) **DSL** [21] is a deep structured model that learns relationships by using the feature-level prediction and the label-level prediction. (6) **DSR** [9] is a newly designed model that can both facilitate the co-occurrence of relationships and mitigate the relation-incomplete problem.

Since the task of visual relationship detection is proposed, only VRD dataset is publicly released. All of proposed works conduct experiments in this dataset, and select data from the whole VG dataset [8] by themselves. Recently, VTransE has released their VG dataset. In VG dataset, we compare our proposed model with the model applying the same implement methods, which use the same dataset to train and test, *e.g.*, VTransE, PPR-FCN, DSL, and DSR.

Table 2. Performances of predicate detection, phrase detection and relationship detection on VRD, comparing with several state-of-the-art methods. We use "-" to indicate that the performance has not been reported in the original paper.

Model	Predicate Det.		Phrase Det.		Relation Det.	
	R@50	R@100	R@50	R@100	R@50	R@100
LP	47.87	47.87	10.11	12.64	0.08	0.14
VTransE	44.76	44.76	19.42	22.42	14.07	15.20
PPR-FCN	47.43	47.43	19.62	23.15	14.41	15.72
DR-Net	80.78	81.9	19.93	23.45	17.73	20.88
DSL	-	-	**22.61**	**23.92**	17.27	18.26
DSR	**86.01**	**93.18**	-	-	**19.03**	**23.29**
IVRDC-F	86.21	94.00	21.67	28.88	14.57	19.22
IVRDC-FC	87.71	94.61	**22.92**	**30.20**	**15.52**	**20.16**
IVRDC-FI	86.34	93.78	21.83	28.63	14.67	19.02
IVRDC-FCI	**88.34**	**94.69**	22.28	28.73	15.06	18.97

We used Recall@50 (R@50) and Recall@100 (R@100) as evaluation metrics for predicate detection, phrase detection and relation detection. From the result on VRD in Table 2, we can see that our proposed model outperforms others in predicate detection. Our proposed model works best on predicate detection, which improved 2.33 and 1.51 for R@50 and R@100 respectively by previous models. As for phrase detection, our method achieved 30.20 at R@100, which is over 25% relative improvement over the previous best result. At relation detection, our model achieved the average level of previous state-of-the-art models.

From the result on VG in Table 3, it is clear that our method surpasses all other methods at predicate detection, our best result achieved 85.40 and 85.26 for R@50 and R@100 respectively, which outperforms other methods by over 23.5% and 18.6%. As for phrase detection and relation detection, our model still outperforms most of other state-of-the-art models.

Due to the long tail distribution of relationships, it is hard to collect enough training images for all the relationships, especially for infrequent relationships. So it is crucial for a model to have the generalizability on detecting zero-shot relationships. The performances on zero-shot predicate, phrase and relationship detection are reported in Table 4. We only compare our proposed model with the models using the same input, *e.g.*, LP, VTransE, and DSR. From the result

Table 3. Performances of predicate detection, phrase detection and relationship detection using various methods on VG. We use "-" to indicate that the performance has not been reported in the original paper.

Model	Predicate Det.		Phrase Det.		Relation Det.	
	R@50	R@100	R@50	R@100	R@50	R@100
VTransE	62.63	62.87	9.46	10.45	5.52	6.04
PPR-FCN	64.17	64.86	10.62	11.08	6.02	6.91
DSL	-	-	**12.07**	**14.35**	**6.37**	**7.50**
DSR	**69.06**	**74.37**	-	-	-	-
IVRDC-F	80.71	82.29	10.90	13.46	6.02	7.31
IVRDC-FC	83.26	**88.44**	10.55	13.85	6.04	7.32
IVRDC-FI	72.76	74.40	9.57	11.98	5.34	6.54
IVRDC-FCI	**85.40**	88.26	**11.12**	14.00	**6.13**	**7.60**

Table 4. Performances of zero-shot predicate detection, phrase detection and relationship detection using various methods on VRD. The methods without reporting the performance on zero-shot setting are excluded from comparison.

Model	Predicate Det.		Phrase Det.		Relation Det.	
	R@50	R@100	R@50	R@100	R@50	R@100
LP	-	-	**3.36**	3.57	3.13	3.52
VTransE	-	-	2.65	**3.75**	1.71	2.14
DSR	60.90	79.81	-	-	**5.25**	**9.20**
IVRDC-F	53.81	74.94	2.30	2.74	1.54	1.79
IVRDC-FC	60.05	**78.69**	3.76	5.39	2.22	2.82
IVRDC-FI	56.54	75.79	3.00	5.13	1.53	2.48
IVRDC-FCI	**61.76**	78.52	**6.92**	**8.73**	**3.93**	**4.53**

on VRD in zero-shot learning demonstrated in Table 4, we can see that our proposed model works best on phrase detection. Our best result achieved 6.92 and 8.73 for R@50 and R@100 respectively. As for predicate detection, our method outperforms DSR for R@50. And our proposed model achieved the average level of the pervious models.

Compare Different Configs. We also compare different variants of the proposed model, in order to identify the contributions of individual components listed :

- IVRDC-F : Part of our model. We only use the feature module to predict the visual relationship without iteration.
- IVRDC-FI : Part of our model. We use the feature module and roll-out iteratively to obtain the predictions.

- IVRDC-FC : Part of our model. We combine the feature module and the commonsense knowledge module without an iteration.
- IVRDC-FCI : Our model introduced in Fig. 2.

From Tables 2 and 3, we observe that our best results outperform pervious best state-of-the-art results by up to 25%, and even our worst result achieved the average level. Moreover, our method with different components performs differently on the three detection tasks. IVRDC-FC is relatively strong in phrase detection and relation detection, while IVRDC-FCI performs better in predicate detection.

The results in Tables 2, 3 and 4 show: (1) The joint model IVRDC-FC significantly performs better in phrase detection and relation detection, which means that CKG is very useful in visual relation detection. The combination of feature module and commonsense knowledge module considerably outperforms the model IVRDC-F with only feature module. (2) The model IVRDC-FCI performs best in predicate detection. It indicates that iteratively using image features and CKG have benefit on enhancing predication detection by making use of image feature information and commonsense knowledge. (3) Relation detection has achieved the average level. Since the relation detection depends a lot on the accuracy of the object detector, our result is probably limited by the performance of the object detector. By using the same object detector of VTransE, our result outperforms VTransE by 32.6% in R@100.

Figure 4 further shows the predicted relationships on serval example images. As the example (*plate, have, sandwich*) in image VG#2 shown in Fig. 4, IVRDC-F with image features performs better in predict predicate according images, *e.g.*, *under*. IVRDC-FCI is able to learn the meaning of *have* from combining CKG and iterations, bringing it to a higher ranking. Since commonsense knowledge is a statistical result, the more a predicate occurs, the higher the probability of the predicate will be, *e.g.*, *on*.

5   Conclusion and Future Work

In this paper, we present a model of iterative visual relationship detection where commonsense captured in the form of commonsense knowledge graph. In our model, the feature memory and the commonsense knowledge graph facilitate each other iteratively. The experimental results show that our model surpasses the state-of-the-arts methods. It is illustrated that the commonsense knowledge graph is capable of enhancing the visual relationship detection task.

So in the future work, we will focus on the representation of common sense and consider completing the commonsense knowledge graph using knowledge graph completion technics.

Acknowledgment. This paper was supported by the National Natural Science Foundation of China (No. 61375056, 61876204, 61976232, and 51978675), Guangdong Province Natural Science Foundation (No. 2017A070706010 (soft science), 2018A030313086), All-China Federation of Returned Overseas Chinese Research

Project (17BZQK216), Science and Technology Program of Guangzhou (No. 201804010496, 201804010435).

References

1. Anderson, P., Fernando, B., Johnson, M., Gould, S.: SPICE: semantic propositional image caption evaluation. In: Leibe, B., Matas, J., Sebe, N., Welling, M. (eds.) ECCV 2016, Part V. LNCS, vol. 9909, pp. 382–398. Springer, Cham (2016). https://doi.org/10.1007/978-3-319-46454-1_24
2. Bordes, A., Usunier, N., García-Durán, A., Weston, J., Yakhnenko, O.: Translating embeddings for modeling multi-relational data. In: Proceedings of International Conference on Neural Information Processing Systems (NIPS2013), pp. 2787–2795 (2013)
3. Chen, L., Yang, Y., Wang, J., Xu, W., Yuille, A.L.: Attention to scale: scale-aware semantic image segmentation. In: Proceedings of CVPR, 2016, pp. 3640–3649 (2016). https://doi.org/10.1109/CVPR.2016.396
4. Chung, J., Gülçehre, Ç., Cho, K., Bengio, Y.: Empirical evaluation of gated recurrent neural networks on sequence modeling. CoRR abs/1412.3555 (2014). http://arxiv.org/abs/1412.3555
5. Dai, B., Zhang, Y., Lin, D.: Detecting visual relationships with deep relational networks. In: Proceedings of CVPR, 2017, pp. 3298–3308 (2017). https://doi.org/10.1109/CVPR.2017.352
6. Dong, L., Wei, F., Zhou, M., Xu, K.: Question answering over freebase with multi-column convolutional neural networks. In: Proceedings of ACL, 2015, pp. 260–269 (2015). http://aclweb.org/anthology/P/P15/P15-1026.pdf
7. Johnson, J., et al.: Image retrieval using scene graphs. In: Proceedings of CVPR, pp. 3668–3678 (2015). http://dx.doi.org/10.1109/CVPR.2015.7298990
8. Krishna, R., et al.: Visual genome: connecting language and vision using crowd-sourced dense image annotations. Int. J. Comput. Vis. **123**(1), 32–73 (2017). https://doi.org/10.1007/s11263-016-0981-7
9. Liang, K., Guo, Y., Chang, H., Chen, X.: Visual relationship detection with deep structural ranking. In: Proceedings of AAAI, 2018 (2018). https://www.aaai.org/ocs/index.php/AAAI/AAAI18/paper/view/16491
10. Liang, X., Lee, L., Xing, E.P.: Deep variation-structured reinforcement learning for visual relationship and attribute detection. In: Proceedings of CVPR, 2017, pp. 4408–4417 (2017). https://doi.org/10.1109/CVPR.2017.469
11. Liao, W., Lin, S., Rosenhahn, B., Yang, M.Y.: Natural language guided visual relationship detection. CoRR abs/1711.06032 (2017). http://arxiv.org/abs/1711.06032
12. Lu, C., Krishna, R., Bernstein, M., Fei-Fei, L.: Visual relationship detection with language priors. In: Leibe, B., Matas, J., Sebe, N., Welling, M. (eds.) ECCV 2016, Part I. LNCS, vol. 9905, pp. 852–869. Springer, Cham (2016). https://doi.org/10.1007/978-3-319-46448-0_51
13. Mikolov, T., Chen, K., Corrado, G., Dean, J.: Efficient estimation of word representations in vector space. CoRR abs/1301.3781 (2013). http://arxiv.org/abs/1301.3781
14. Ren, S., He, K., Girshick, R.B., Sun, J.: Faster R-CNN: towards real-time object detection with region proposal networks. In: Proceedings of NIPS, 2015, pp. 91–99 (2015). http://papers.nips.cc/paper/5638-faster-r-cnn-towards-real-time-object-detection-with-region-proposal-networks

15. Schuster, M., Paliwal, K.K.: Bidirectional recurrent neural networks. IEEE Trans. Signal Process. **45**(11), 2673–2681 (1997). https://doi.org/10.1109/78.650093
16. Simonyan, K., Zisserman, A.: Very deep convolutional networks for large-scale image recognition. CoRR abs/1409.1556 (2014). http://arxiv.org/abs/1409.1556
17. Wan, H., Luo, Y., Peng, B., Zheng, W.: Representation learning for scene graph completion via jointly structural and visual embedding. In: Proceedings of IJCAI, 2018, pp. 949–956 (2018). https://doi.org/10.24963/ijcai.2018/132
18. Yu, R., Li, A., Morariu, V.I., Davis, L.S.: Visual relationship detection with internal and external linguistic knowledge distillation. In: Proceedings of ICCV, 2017, pp. 1068–1076 (2017). https://doi.org/10.1109/ICCV.2017.121
19. Zhang, H., Kyaw, Z., Chang, S., Chua, T.: Visual translation embedding network for visual relation detection. In: Proceedings of CVPR, 2017, pp. 3107–3115 (2017). https://doi.org/10.1109/CVPR.2017.331
20. Zhang, H., Kyaw, Z., Yu, J., Chang, S.: PPR-FCN: weakly supervised visual relation detection via parallel pairwise R-FCN. In: Proceedings of IEEE, 2017, pp. 4243–4251 (2017). http://doi.ieeecomputersociety.org/10.1109/ICCV.2017.454
21. Zhu, Y., Jiang, S.: Deep structured learning for visual relationship detection. In: Proceedings of AAAI, 2018 (2018). https://www.aaai.org/ocs/index.php/AAAI/AAAI18/paper/view/16475

A Dynamic and Informative Intelligent Survey System Based on Knowledge Graph

Patrik Bansky[1], Elspeth Edelstein[2], Jeff Z. Pan[1(✉)], and Adam Wyner[3]

[1] Department of Computing Science, University of Aberdeen, Aberdeen, UK
`jeff.z.pan@abdn.ac.uk`
[2] School of Language, Literature, Music and Visual Culture,
University of Aberdeen, Aberdeen, UK
[3] School of Law and Department of Computer Science,
Swansea University, Swansea, UK

Abstract. In the paper we propose a dynamic and informative solution to an intelligent survey system that is based on knowledge graph. To illustrate our proposal, we focus on ordering the questions of the questionnaire component by their acceptance, along with conditional triggers that further customise participants' experience, making the system dynamic. Evaluation of the system shows that the dynamic component can be beneficial in terms of lowering the number of questions asked and improving the quality of data, allowing more informative data to be collected in a survey of equivalent length. Fine-grained analysis allows assessment of the interaction of specific variables, as well as of individual respondents rather than just global results. The paper explores and evaluates two algorithms for the presentation of survey questions, leading to additional insights about how to improve the system.

Keywords: Intelligent survey system · Dynamic and informative system · Linguistic grammaticality judgements

1 Introduction

This paper is about how to use knowledge graph to build an intelligent survey system. In fields such as Linguistics, Psychology, and Medicine, researchers rely on data from human participants, which are gathered either by verbal communication, written questionnaires, or Internet-based questionnaires. Online surveys are particularly popular in contemporary research due to their global reach, flexibility, ease of data analysis, and low administration cost, among other advantages [10]. However, research suggests that participant motivation in surveys decreases over time such that respondents are likely to engage in a sub-optimal way, lowering the overall quality of data collected [15]. Respondents may be reluctant to complete surveys due to low interest in participation, resulting in decreased response rates overall [18,28]. Internet-based questionnaires are also by nature less interactive than face-to-face data collection, limiting researchers' ability to

© Springer Nature Switzerland AG 2020
X. Wang et al. (Eds.): JIST 2019, LNCS 12032, pp. 226–241, 2020.
https://doi.org/10.1007/978-3-030-41407-8_15

follow up participants' answers in order to aid interpretation of results. In addition, while online questionnaires may be used to assess what populations find acceptable and the inferences made from global percentages, it would be informative to analyse of each respondent's answers to uncover fine-grained patterns and (in)consistencies. That is, it would be worthwhile to measure the judgements of individual participants rather than generalising over groups.

To overcome these restrictions on quality and quantity of information, it is widely believed [2,5,12,27] that a more dynamic approach to questionnaires would lead to a higher standard of data collected. One important factor in developing questionnaires is the *order of the questions*. *Research methods in psychology* [8] argues that the most interesting questions should be ranked at the beginning of the survey to catch a respondent's attention, while less important questions should be near the end.

Our previous work [31] proposes an architecture of knowledge driven intelligent survey system. The idea is to use Knowledge Graph as a semantic bridge between humans and computational systems, so as to facilitate customisability, transmission, re-usability, explainability and extensibility. The system provides three different components of exposure to relevant users: (1) the participants of the survey, (2) the domain experts, and (3) the knowledge engineers. The participants simply answer the questions: their role is to judge whether sentences are acceptable or unacceptable. The domain experts, such as Linguists, customise the knowledge structure to fit their needs, and knowledge engineers construct the basis of the semantic structure. For example, a knowledge driven intelligent survey system on linguistics provides information about syntactic relationships and features of each sentence. Upon participant submissions, researchers are able to see detailed information about these features and syntactic relationships. In addition, using the data collected, researchers are able to use the tool to organise and analyse data using pattern features and syntactic relationships to either confirm or refute their original hypotheses.

In this paper, we further develop the notion of knowledge graph based dynamic survey system that responsively selects questions from a larger pool provided by the researcher. Prioritisation of questions is based on interaction of researcher hypotheses and participant input, allowing optimisation of data quality and user responses. Although the proposed survey system is built for linguistic judgements, for the sake of evaluation, such an explainable architecture can in principle be applied to many other scenarios, such as one for monitoring a local community's opinion on whether an existing nuclear power plant should resume its operations or not. To enable such domain adaptation, per-subject optimisations or randomisation should be in place, in particular when the target issue is sensitive in having manipulations from the researcher, such as the case of nuclear power plant.

2   Background

2.1   Knowledge Graph

A knowledge graph $\mathcal{G} = (\mathcal{D}, \mathcal{S})$ consists of a data sub-graph $\mathcal{D}$ of interconnected typed entities and their attributes as well as a schema sub-graph $\mathcal{S}$ that defines the vocabulary used to annotate entities and their properties in $\mathcal{D}$. Facts in $\mathcal{D}$ are represented as triples of the following two forms:

- *property assertion* (h, r, t), where h is the head entity, and r the property and t the tail entity; e.g., (ACMilan, playInLeague, ItalianLeague) is a property assertion.
- *class assertion* (e, rdf:type, C), where e is an entity, rdf:type is the instance-of relation from the standard W3C RDF specification and C is a class; e.g., (ACMilan, rdf:type, FootballClub) is a class assertion.

A scheme sub-graph $\mathcal{S}$ includes Class Inclusion axioms $C \sqsubseteq D$, where C and D are class descriptions, such as the following ones: $\top \mid \bot \mid A \mid \neg C \mid C \sqcap D \mid \exists r.C \mid \leq n\, r \mid = n\, r \mid \geq n\, r$, where $\top$ is the top class (representing all entities), $\bot$ is the bottom class (representing an empty set), A is a named class r, r is a property and n is a positive integer. For example, the types of River and City being disjoint can be represented as $River \sqsubseteq \neg City$, or $River \sqcap City \sqsubseteq \bot$. We refer the reader to [25, 26] for a more detailed introduction of knowledge graphs.

2.2   Linguistic Background

Theoretical linguists working on morphosyntax, the structure of words and sentences, may use questionnaires to gather data needed to investigate grammatical structure within a given language or dialect. Surveys of this type seek *grammaticality judgements*, determinations of how *well-formed* sentences are, based on native speakers' knowledge of the language [30]. Input of this type is especially useful for investigating Non-Standard morphosyntactic forms which differ from more widely used Standard grammatical constructions. In addition, participants' judgements may cluster in particular patterns, but there may also be a level of individual variation that is obscured by global measurements of grammaticality. Moreover, 'naive' native speaker respondents make judgements based on *acceptability*, subject to the influence of factors such as pragmatic plausibility, rather than pure *grammaticality*, correctness of (morpho)syntactic structure [13]. To find such individual variation, researchers may wish to seek clarification through systematic follow-up questions, which can be complex to serve in current approaches to Internet-based data collection.

Our proposed system was evaluated in a use case on the grammaticality of the *Alternative Embedded Passive* (AEP) [7], which consists of a verb such as *need/want/like* followed directly by a passive participle, in contrast to *Standard Embedded Passives* (StEP), in which the passive participle is preceded by the non-finite passive auxiliary *to be*.

- *The dog needs walked* (AEP)
- *The dog needs to be walked* (StEP)

Linguistic acceptability was tested by giving respondents a binary choice over each question, where 0 stands for '*this sentence sounds strange to me*' and 1 stands for '*this sentence sounds good to me*'.

Previous linguistic studies on the AEP (without the presence of *to be*) point to *need* being the most commonly used main verb, followed by *want* and *like* [19]. Moreover, *Inanimate* subjects seem to be more acceptable with the use of *want* and *like* in the AEP than the StEP [7]. However, these findings are based on studies conducted only on the North American population using American English, and therefore may not apply to Scottish and Northern Irish speakers who use the AEP.

3 Requirements for an Informative and Dynamic System

Given the previous system, two main requirements emerged.

An Informative System. Respondents should be asked a sufficient and reasonable number of relevant questions about their grammars and few irrelevant or redundant questions. Sufficient means that we ask enough questions to address our hypotheses, and reasonable means we limit the number of questions we ask to about 30, consistent with other 'dialect' surveys [7,16]. Relevance here is:

- Testing the variables by using the researcher's annotations to ask questions including all linguistic features.
- Testing the hierarchy of acceptability of different linguistic features.
- Validation of grammatical points by checking responses about grammar rather than extraneous factors such as pragmatic plausibility.
- Filtering of questions to avoid those that are known, from prior questions, not to be appropriate to the speaker.

A Dynamic System. The dynamic system should serve the purposes of the informative system. In other words, the algorithms which deliver the questions to respondents ought to do so in such a way as to realise the requirements which make the system informative. This is in contrast to typical grammaticality judgement questionnaires, where the same questions are asked in every survey, not taking into account the participants' responses. In these traditional static surveys the order of the questions is predefined or entirely randomised in advance, and therefore cannot be changed as the survey is conducted. The fixed presentation of questions does not allow for a more tailored experience for the respondent and does not allow for user feedback in the form of comments to be taken into account. Additionally, the number of questions is limited, which means that a researcher may only be able to cover a select few variables of interest.

4 Knowledge Graph and Algorithms

In this section, we will present some knowledge graph based algorithms for informative and dynamic survey systems. Such survey systems are based on the notion of responsive sentence selection. In other words, the proposed survey system is able to dynamically select the next survey question, depending on the judgement of the previous question. We will first present the two ontologies as the schema of the knowledge graph of the survey system, which allows the kind of responsive sentence selection to be presented in the algorithms in Sub-sect. 4.2.

4.1   Knowledge Graph

Two key ontologies are designed for the proposed system: a general purpose Survey Ontology and a domain specific ontology, such as a Linguistic Feature Ontology.

The Survey Ontology contains classes such as SurveyQuestion, AnswerOption, SurveyAnswer and User, Participation, Hypothesis. It contains properties, such as hasSurveyUser, hasSurveyQuestion and hasSurveyAnswer. We refer the reader to [31] for more details of the Survey Ontology.

The Linguistic Feature Ontology has classes such as, Sentence, POS, Subject (Subject $\sqsubseteq$ POS), AnimateSubject (AnimateSubject $\sqsubseteq$ Subject), InanimateSubject (InanimateSubject $\sqsubseteq$ Subject), DefiniteSubject (DefiniteSubject $\sqsubseteq$ Subject), IndefiniteSubject (IndefiniteSubject $\sqsubseteq$ Subject), Verb (Verb $\sqsubseteq$ POS), MainVerb (with instances *need/want/like*, MainVerb $\sqsubseteq$ Verb), AEP (AEP $\sqsubseteq$ POS) and StEP (StEP $\sqsubseteq$ POS). The Linguistic Feature Ontology has properties, such as hasPOS and hasString.

When a linguistic researcher annotate survey questions (such as the one containing Sentence S1, *The dog needs walked*), a set of statements will be constructed in the knowledge graph:

- (theDog, rdf:type, DefiniteSubject), (S1, hasPOS, theDog),
- (theDog, rdf:type, AnimateSubject)
- (need, rdf:type, MainVerb), (S1, hasPOS, need),
- (walked, rdf:type, AEP), (S1, hasPOS, walked).

Based on the Linguistic Feature Ontology and the above statements, we can, e.g, classify the Sentence S1 as an instance of Sentence $\sqcap$ $\exists$hasPOS.DefiniteSubject $\sqcap$ $\exists$hasPOS.AnimateSubject $\sqcap$ $\exists$hasPOS.AEP (S1 is a Sentence that has a DefiniteSubject, an AnimateSubject and contains an AEP).

If a User U1 accepts S1, the survey system will have the following extra statements:

- (P1, rdf:type, Participation),
- (P1, hasSurveyUser, U1), (U1, rdf:type, User),
- (P1, hasSurveyQuestion, S1), (S1, rdf:type, Sentence),
- (P1, hasSurveyAnswer, *accepted*).

4.2   Algorithms

In this sub-section, we will present two algorithms that are able to responsively select sentence for the next question, with the help of sentence classification discussed in the previous sub-section (cf. the discussion of S1) .

Algorithm 1 considers the effects of linguistic features such as the choice of the main verb, namely *need, like, want*, as well as whether the subject is *Animate/Inanimate* or *Definite/Indefinite*. Along with these variables, the presence/absence of the non-finite passive auxiliary *to be* gives a total of $3*2*2*2 =$

24 possible combinations of relationships between features. These variables have been explored in previous work on this construction [7]. The linguistic researchers design 6 sentences for each of the above 24 combinations, resulting in 24 * 6 = 144 sentences, which are grouped into 12 family groups, each one of them has an AEP family of 6 sentences and a StEP family of 6 sentences.

Algorithm 1: Responsive Sentence Selection

Input:
g: current family group, which contains a set of ranked AEP sentences g.aep and a set of ranked StEP sentences g.step;
x: the top percentage of sentences to be considered in the first attempt;
Output:
$result$: the set of judgement results of selected questions from g

1 $result \leftarrow nil$;
2 $s_1 \leftarrow$ random-top(g.aep,x); //randomly select a sentence from the top $x\%$ of questions as the first question
3 $result \leftarrow result \cup (s_1, judgement(s_1))$;
4 **if** $judgement(s_1) = rejected$ **then**
5      $s_2 \leftarrow$ random-top(g.aep,x); //randomly select another sentence from the top $x\%$ of questions as the second question
6      $result \leftarrow result \cup (s_2, judgement(s_2))$;
7   **if** $judgement(s_2) = accepted$ **then**
8          $s_3 \leftarrow$ random-bottom(g.aep,x); //randomly select a sentence from the bottom $(100 - x)\%$ of questions as the third question
9          $result \leftarrow result \cup (s_3, judgement(s_3))$;
10   **end**
11 **else**
12     $s_2 \leftarrow$ random-bottom(g.aep,x); //randomly select a sentence from the bottom $(100 - x)\%$ of questions as the second question
13     $result \leftarrow result \cup (s_2, judgement(s_2))$;
14 **end**
15 $s \leftarrow$ random-top(g.step,x);//randomly select a sentence from the top $x\%$ of questions as the final question from the StEP family
16 $result \leftarrow result \cup (s, judgement(s))$;
17 **return** $result$;

The key challenge is how to select some of the 144 sentences into a survey, which typically includes about 30 questions. The main idea is to use results form some baseline studies of these 144 sentences to learning the acceptability ranking of these sentences and related families. Instead of covering every one of the 144 sentences, Algorithm 1 selects the next sentence based on user judgements of the current sentence (lines 4 and 7), resulting in having 2–4 sentences per family group.

Algorithm 2: Responsive Sentence Selection with Comment Understanding

---

Input:

g: current family group, which contains a set of ranked AEP sentences g.aep and a set of ranked StEP sentences g.step;

x: the top percentage of sentences to be considered in the first attempt;

SV: a queue of additional sentences with extra variables to be used;

SR: a queue of additional relaxed sentences to be used;

Output:

result: the set of judgement results of selected questions from g

1 $result \leftarrow nil$;

2 $s_1 \leftarrow$ random-top(g.aep,x); //randomly select a sentence from the top $x\%$ of questions as the first question

3 $result \leftarrow result \cup (s_1, judgement(s_1))$;

4 **if** $judgement(s_1) = rejected$ **then**

5      $s_2 \leftarrow$ random-top(g.aep,x); $result \leftarrow result \cup (s_2, judgement(s_2))$;

6   // If both s_1 and s_2 are rejected for the same reason, the next additional relaxed sentence

7   **if** $judgement(s_2) = rejected$ and $commenttype(s_1) = commenttype(s_2)$ **then**

8          $s_3 \leftarrow$ next(SR); $result \leftarrow result \cup (s_3, judgement(s_3))$;

9   **if** $commenttype(s_1) = \text{'to be'}$ **then**

10   **foreach** *sentence* s_i *in* g.step **do**

                $result \leftarrow result \cup (s_i, accepted)$;

11   **end**

12   **if** $commenttype(s_1) = other$ and $commentMain(s_1) \neq g.mainWord$ **then**

13   **foreach** *sentence* s_i *in* $similar(g, commentMain(s_1))$ **do**

                $result \leftarrow result \cup (s_i, accepted)$;

14   **end**

15   **else**

16          $s_3 \leftarrow$ random-top(g.aep,x);

         $result \leftarrow result \cup (s_3, judgement(s_3))$;

17   **end**

18 **else**

19      $s_2 \leftarrow$ next(SV); $s_3 \leftarrow$ next(SV); //Present the next 2 sentences with an additional variable

20      $result \leftarrow result \cup (s_2, judgement(s_2)) \cup (s_3, judgement(s_3))$;

21 **end**

22 $s \leftarrow$ random-top(g.step,x);//randomly select a sentence from the top $x\%$ of questions as the final question from the StEP family

23 $result \leftarrow result \cup (s, judgement(s))$;

24 **return** $result$;

In the setting of Algorithm 2, the linguistic researchers decide to drop the distinction of *Definite/Indefinite* Subjects, resulting in having 6 family groups, each of them has an AEP family of 12 sentences and a StEP family of 12 sentences. In order to consider even more candidate sentences (such as those in *SV* and *SR* of Algorithm 2) in surveys, Algorithm 2 allows the process of comments (lines 9 and 12) provided by users, so as to speed up the decision process: each family has 4 sentence slots; if some of these slots are not needed, additional sentences from *SV* and *SR* will be used. Consequently, Algorithm 2 allows the consideration of all the 144 sentences, as well as some additional sentences.

Note that some linguistic based optimisations and randomisation are used in the two algorithms. In order to adapt these algorithms to another domain or scenario, some per-subject optimisations and randomisation should be applied.

5   Case Studies and Evaluations

We present two case studies and associated evaluations of the algorithms.

5.1   Hypotheses

In order to address the requirements (informative and dynamic) and evaluate a tool that attempts to address them, two versions of the survey were implemented and conducted. The first version was found not to deliver sufficiently informative results, leading to development of a second version with adjustments to the algorithm employed; while the second version is an improvement over the first, we later discuss further refinements.

As described above, our case study examines the use of Alternative Embedded Passives, in which a verb such as *need*, *want* or *like* is followed directly by a passive participle, without the non-finite auxiliary *to be* found in Standard Embedded Passives.

- *The cat needs fed* (AEP)
- *The cat needs to be fed* (StEP)

The AEP has been claimed to be found among speakers in Scotland and Northern Ireland, but there has been little investigation of this feature for these populations. We therefore seek to investigate the following hypotheses:

- **Hypothesis 1**: Speakers who use AEP *like* will also use AEP *want*, and speakers who use AEP *want* will also use AEP *need*.
- **Hypothesis 2**: Some subset of speakers will allow inanimate subjects with AEP *want* and *like*, but not StEP *want* and *like*. Speakers who allow inanimate subjects with StEP *want* and *like* will also allow them with AEP *want* and *like*.

5.2   Case Study 1

Experiment Setup. Based on the results from [31], a pool of 144 sentences were divided into 24 families, paired into 12 groups comprising both AEP and StEP sentences. The sentences in each group shared the same set of linguistic features: main verb (*need, want, like*), subject (in)animacy, and subject (in)definiteness. For instance, the group for *need*, animate subject, and definite subject included the following sentences.[1]

– *The trees need pruned*
– *The house needs painted*
– *The windows need cleaned*
– *The plant needs to be watered*
– *The garden needs to be tended*
– *This room needs to be tidied*

The sentences were ranked according to their mean ratings in the baseline results from [31], which had 50 participants over six versions, each consisting of 24 sentences covering all combinations of the main verb, (in)definiteness, (in)animacy, and [$\pm to\ be$] variables. They were presented to participants according to Algorithm 1.

The family groups were ordered to present those with main verb *need*, followed by those with main verb *want*, followed by those with main verb *like*. For each rejected sentence participants were asked 'What would you say instead?'.

Forty-six participants, who were recruited through word of mouth and social media, completed the survey online. Each answered a minimum of 24 questions; those who chose to continue could answer up to 30 questions. At the end of the survey participants were provided with an individualised map comparing their answers on one of the AEP sentences (without *to be*) with other users who had made judgements on sentences with the same set of linguistic features. See Fig. 1.

Hypothesis Testing. The survey system has allowed examination of Hypothesis 1 in relation to individual speakers, rather than just over global percentages. Of 46 participants, 42 accepted AEP *need*. Thirty-eight of these participants accepted AEP *want*. Ten of these 38 participants accepted AEP *like*. There were no participants who accepted AEP *like* but not AEP *want*, or who accepted AEP *want* but not AEP *need*. These results therefore confirm the hypothesis that acceptance of *want* in this construction is a precondition for acceptance of *like*, and acceptance of *need* is a precondition for acceptance of *want*.

The system also allows testing of Hypothesis 2. Fifteen participants were asked to judge sentences with inanimate subjects for *want* and *like* in both the AEP and StEP constructions; a further four were asked to judge sentences with *want* in the AEP and StEP constructions, but not *like*.

---

[1] While the sentences may vary in singular/plural subject, this is not a relevant experimental variable, but provided only for variety.

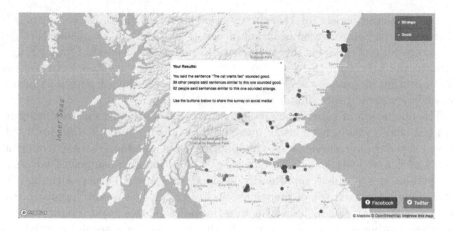

Fig. 1. Individualised map

Of these nineteen participants, four accepted an inanimate subject with AEP *want* but not StEP *want*, while one accepted an inanimate subject with StEP *want* but not AEP *want*, contrary to the expected pattern. The rest of the speakers either accepted or rejected all inanimate subjects in both constructions. For AEP *like* two speakers accepted StEP *like* with an inanimate subject, but rejected AEP *like* with an inanimate subject, also contrary to the expected pattern. Again, the rest either accepted or rejected inanimate subjects in both types of construction.

Dynamicity and Informativity. The dynamic approach used in this survey was effective in testing the *need > want > like* hierarchy of acceptance for the AEP (Hypothesis 1), in that it allowed all speakers to be asked questions for each of these main verbs, although the ordering of questions to prioritise *need* over *want* and *want* over *like* means that speakers may have been asked fewer questions overall about main verb *want* and especially *like*, as depending on their answers they may have been questioned about as few as eight family groups. For Hypothesis 1 we can therefore conclude that the survey was sufficiently informative.

At the same time, the algorithm used in this iteration of the survey, along with the limitation on the number of questions, meant that testing of Hypothesis 2 was limited. Several participants who did not use AEP *like* or *want* at all were asked to give judgements on this construction with an inanimate subject, resulting in the collection of data irrelevant to our hypothesis. Only 15 of the 31 participants who used AEP and StEP *want* were asked to give judgements on this verb with inanimate subjects; some of them also gave judgements on only a single sentence for the StEP or the AEP with an inanimate subject. The algorithm used in this iteration of the survey therefore failed to collect optimal data for testing Hypothesis 2, and was thus insufficiently informative.

The dynamic aspect of the survey was therefore partially successful. It allowed relatively strong confirmation of use of the AEP, as many speakers did not accept all sentences for this construction; had they been asked only a single sentence and rejected it the result would have been a false negative for use of the AEP. In other instances, though, the dynamic presentation of questions meant the survey collected superfluous or insufficient data.

The elicitation of superfluous judgements is a feature inherent to static surveys (i.e. those with a fixed set of questions for all respondents), and so in this respect the dynamic survey was still superior, as it eliminated these irrelevant questions for at least some participants. Unintentionally insufficient coverage of variables is a problem more easily avoided in a static survey, although by nature having a fixed set of questions circumscribes how many linguistic features a researcher can include in a questionnaire of this type. Below we will discuss amendments intended to remedy this problem in a second iteration of the dynamic survey.

5.3   Case Study 2

Experiment Setup. The same set of 144 sentences was used, divided into 12 families, paired into six groups, based on main verb and (in)animacy: (in)definiteness was not used as a variable, as it was deemed irrelevant to any hypotheses of interest.

A further 18 sentences were added to the set of possible questions in order to test a number of additional variables: use of adverbs with the AEP (e.g. *The books need sorted alphabetically)*; use of *by*-phrases (e.g. *My car needs checked by a mechanic*; use of purpose-clauses (e.g. *The screws need tightened to hold the shelf up*); questions (e.g. *Does the door need opened?*); negation (e.g. *Those carpets don't need cleaned*); and relative clauses (e.g. *Those are the shirts that need ironed*). These additional linguistic features were included to measure a number of other hypotheses examined in previous work, though which are tangential to the hypotheses we address in this paper.

In this iteration the system was coded to recognise comments in response to 'What would you say instead?', in particular, the use of *to be* or an alternative main verb *need*, *want* or *like*. The sentences were presented according to Algorithm 2, again using participants' judgements from the baseline survey for ranking of the 144 original sentences.

Fifty-three participants were recruited through paid social media advertising which targeted users in Scotland and Northern Ireland. Each participant gave judgements on 24 sentences and, as in Case Study 1, was presented with an individualised map upon completion of the questionnaire and encouraged to share the survey on social media.

Hypothesis Testing. Again, the system allowed testing of Hypothesis 1, that use of AEP *need* is a precondition for use of AEP *want*, and AEP *want* is a precondition for AEP *like*. Forty-six participants of 53 accepted AEP *need*, and

42 of these accepted AEP *want*. Of these 42, 17 accepted AEP *like*. A single participant appeared to accept AEP *want*, but not AEP *need*. However, closer inspection revealed that they did accept several of the sentences with additional variables (e.g. use of *by*-phrases), all of which had AEP *need*, and so did not contradict this hypothesis.

Of 35 participants who accepted both AEP and StEP *want*, 34 were asked about these with inanimate subjects. Five accepted an inanimate subject with AEP *want*, but not StEP *want*; two rejected an inanimate subject with AEP *want* but accepted one with StEP *want*. Of 15 participants who accepted both AEP and StEP *like*, 13 were asked about these with inanimate subjects. Two accepted an inanimate subject with AEP *like*, but not *StEP like*; one rejected an inanimate subject with AEP *like* but accepted one with StEP *like*. The rest of the speakers either accepted or rejected all inanimate subjects in both constructions for *want* and *like*. These results therefore weakly support Hypothesis 2, that inanimate subjects are more acceptable for *want* and *like* in AEP constructions than StEP constructions.

Dynamicity and Informativity. Because the sentences were divided into fewer families, and participants were not questioned about lower-ranked sentences, this survey was more effective in testing both hypotheses. The addition of comment understanding also meant that some questions could be eliminated, as participants' acceptance of StEP forms (with *to be*) and alternative main verbs could be confirmed by their responses to 'What would you say instead?'. As a result, it was possible to include additional sentences, testing more variables for many respondents.

While this iteration of the dynamic survey therefore addressed the problem of insufficient coverage of variables, thereby increasing informativity, presentation of superfluous questions to some participants still remained a problem. In particular, consistently 'Standard' speakers, i.e., those who do not use the AEP at all, were repeatedly presented with AEP sentences because their input of *to be* forms for 'What would you say instead?' meant that these StEP forms were marked as grammatical, triggering the algorithm to bypass [3]. These speakers were therefore never presented with StEP sentences. Instead, they were asked questions about the sentences with additional variables, all of which were AEP forms.

This issue was highlighted by a response left on social media by a participant that the questionnaire became 'boring' because all of the questions seemed to require 'the same grammatical addition'. Decreasing participant interest as the survey progresses therefore remains a problem, although it is notable that some 'Standard' speakers did complete the survey; this problem is potentially remedied by reducing the overall number of questions for participants whose answers indicate that they do not use the Non-Standard form, or introducing new variables and/or constructions for such users in order to increase participant engagement and level of informativity for researchers.

6   Related Work

6.1   Intelligent Surveys

One of the intelligent surveys systems already implemented is the *Dynamic Intelligent Survey Engine* DISE [29], which aims to have an as flexible as possible approach to creating a survey while avoiding being restricted. Similarly to our old system, it uses a wide variety of data methods and an advanced data collection approach with the intent to measure the consumer preferences. However, in contrast to our system, which uses a drag and drop interface for creating surveys, survey creating in their system is done by XML markup language, which may have a rather steep learning curve and thus cumbersome to learn. Furthermore, the system does not allow for conditional trigger for better user experience, nor does it use its knowledge to prioritise the most significant questions first.

6.2   Psycholinguistic Surveys

MiniJudge [22] is a tool specifically designed for theoretical syntacticians to help them design, run and analyse judgemental experiments in the minimum amount of time with maximised efficiency and without any prior training. This is achieved by 'minimalist' experimental syntax where experiments are conducted on a small participant group, sets of questions and quick a survey. Moreover, it offers automation of the statistical analysis of data, and thus is beginner friendly.

WebExp [17] is a software package to run psychological experiments over the internet and measure the respondents reaction time (latency). The system shows a nuance approach on collecting latency measurements and replicating lab-based conditions accurately across multiple platforms. Similarly *PsyToolkit*[2] has been specifically designed to setup, run and analyse questionnaires and reaction time experiments. Furthermore, the system links the experiments online, which can be easily embedded in social media networks and used for participant recruitment [33].

Other psycholinguistic tools include IBEX [6] *Internet Based EXperiments* which focuses on grammatical judgements. The questionnaire is presenting the sentences in a different variety of ways; *FlashSentence* method where sentences are 'flashed' to the participant for only a limited amount of time and *Dashed-Sentence* method where the sentences are presented either chunk-by-chunk or word-by-word. On the other hand, in order to make the research feasible across different groups with individual languages *Wordlikeness* allows to design questionnaires with text, audio, images and video files [4].

Lastly, many other popular survey system are used for information gathering in a field of linguists. One of which is *SurveyMonkey*[3] which allows people to develop surveys online, deploy it and test it to the community and then analyse collected data. Another one being *Amazon's Mechanical Turk (MTurk)*[4], where

---

[2] https://www.psytoolkit.org/.
[3] https://www.surveymonkey.com/.
[4] https://www.mturk.com/.

people complete surveys for money. Johnson suggests that using such a platform can provide a large participation-pool with necessary tools to build an experiment in quick and efficient manner [14]. *Turkolizer* [11] and *Turktools* [9] are two tools that run on this crowd sourcing platform. While this approach may potentially present benefits in large-scale experiments, this platform presents only a basic statistical analysis of the data. To do any form of knowledge powered services, for instance syntactic and semantic evaluation of the results, a knowledge structure would have to be implicitly hard-coded. As a result of this, the experiments data is hard to transmit, link or reuse.

6.3 Commercial Surveys

Whilst not as related to other intelligent/linguistic surveys, commercial surveys can provide a great insight on other aspects of surveys such as: *user interfaces, security* and *distribution* [3,32]. Many of which (aspects) are highly paramount as their primary goal is to attract as many customers as possible.

6.4 Adaptive Questionnaires

The use of adaptive questionnaires is a widely used concept in identifying learning styles of students. The most popular approach of learning style recognition is via the use of questionnaires. While they might be effective, they have disadvantages: (1) filling a questionnaire is time-consuming since questionnaires usually contain numerous questions; (2) learners may lack time and motivation to fill in long questionnaires; and (3) a specialist needs to analyse the answers [1].

Several questionnaire systems have been proposed to mitigate the above stated issues and automatically minimise the number of questions using various algorithms. *AH questionnaire* [24] used decision trees as the main algorithm and managed to reduce the number of questions by over 50% and achieved over 95% accuracy when predicting the students learning preference. A tool proposed by Noke-lainenet al. [23] uses Bayesian modelling as well as abductive reasoning and accomplished similar question reduction of 50% as in previous system. More relevant work to our system has been done with *Q-SELECT* [20] using neural network and decision trees to decrease the number of questions by trying to find the least influential question in the survey. Furthermore, it is capable of reordering the questions and thus provide a personalised questionnaire to the end-user. Recently, their system *T-PREDICT* has been further improved from 35% reduction of questions to over 85% reduction, while keeping the error rate comparable at only 12.1% [21]. However, none of these approaches address how to responsively select the next question given the judgement of the current question.

7   Conclusion

With the help of Knowledge Graph, we propose a dynamic approach to the questionnaire component of the survey, yielding more informative results. The questions are ordered by a model based on their importance. Once the questions are ordered, a set of conditional triggers are set to provide a more dynamic experience, which benefits the researcher in maximising the quality and quantity of data collected, and the user in creating a more varied survey. Follow-up questions are asked in a case of the user accepting or rejecting certain questions.

In the evaluation we have shown that the dynamic component can have a positive impact on the quality of the data as well as limiting the number of questions asked in the survey. The previous system performed 6 different surveys, each of which had 24 questions; a total of 50 people participated in those surveys. With our system we have managed to achieve the same results as the previous study in the one iteration of the survey, asking 28.2 questions on average with the same types of questions having only 25 participated in the survey. Such improvement is based on the semantic understanding of survey questions enabled by knowledge graphs.

References

1. Abernethy, J., Evgeniou, T., Vert, J.P.: An Optimization Framework for Adaptive Questionnaire Design. INSEAD, Fontainebleau (2004)
2. Callegaro, M., Wells, T., Kruse, Y.: Effects of precoding response options for five point satisfaction scales in web surveys. In: 2008 PAPOR Conference. Citeseer (2008)
3. Capterra: Survey software buyers' guide (2019). https://www.capterra.com/survey-software/#buyers-guide. Accessed 5 Mar 2019
4. Chen, T.Y., Myers, J.: Worldlikeness: a web-based tool for typological psycholinguistic research. Univ. Pennsylvania Working Pap. Linguist. **23**(1), 4 (2017)
5. Dolnicar, S., Grün, B., Yanamandram, V.: Dynamic, interactive survey questions can increase survey data quality. J. Travel Tour. Mark. **30**(7), 690–699 (2013)
6. Drummond, A.: Ibex 0.3. 7 manual (2013)
7. Edelstein, E.: This syntax needs studied. In: Micro-syntactic variation in North American English, pp. 242–268 (2014)
8. Elmes, D.G., Kantowitz, B.H., Roediger III, H.L.: Research Methods Inpsychology. Cengage Learning (2011)
9. Erlewine, M.Y., Kotek, H.: A streamlined approach to online linguistic surveys. Nat. Lang. Linguist. Theory **34**(2), 481–495 (2016)
10. Evans, J.R., Mathur, A.: The value of online surveys. Internet Res. **15**(2), 195–219 (2005)
11. Gibson, E., Piantadosi, S., Fedorenko, K.: Using mechanical turk to obtain and analyze english acceptability judgments. Lang. Linguist. Compass **5**(8), 509–524 (2011)
12. Guin, T.D.L., Baker, R., Mechling, J., Ruyle, E.: Myths and realities of respondent engagement in online surveys. Int. J. Mark. Res. **54**(5), 613–633 (2012)
13. Here, M., Now, P.: Bing, bang, bong. Blah
14. Johnson, D.R., Borden, L.A.: Participants at your fingertips: using amazons mechanical turk to increase student-faculty collaborative research. Teach. Psychol. **39**(4), 245–251 (2012)
15. Kaminska, O., McCutcheon, A.L., Billiet, J.: Satisficing among reluctant respondents in a cross-national context. Public Opin. Q. **74**(5), 956–984 (2010)

16. Katz, J.: The british-irish dialect quiz. New York Times, 15 February 2019
17. Keller, F., Gunasekharan, S., Mayo, N., Corley, M.: Timing accuracy of web experiments: a case study using the webexp software package. Behav. Res. Methods **41**(1), 1–12 (2009)
18. Kropf, M.E., Blair, J.: Eliciting survey cooperation: incentives, self-interest, and norms of cooperation. Eval. Rev. **29**(6), 559–575 (2005)
19. Murray, T.E., Simon, B.L.: At the intersection of regional and social dialects: the case of like+ past participle in american english. Am. Speech **77**(1), 32–69 (2002)
20. Mwamikazi, E., Fournier-Viger, P., Moghrabi, C., Barhoumi, A., Baudouin, R.: An adaptive questionnaire for automatic identification of learning styles. In: Ali, M., Pan, J.-S., Chen, S.-M., Horng, M.-F. (eds.) IEA/AIE 2014, Part I. LNCS (LNAI), vol. 8481, pp. 399–409. Springer, Cham (2014). https://doi.org/10.1007/978-3-319-07455-9_42
21. Mwamikazi, E., Fournier-Viger, P., Moghrabi, C., Baudouin, R.: A dynamic questionnaire to further reduce questions in learning style assessment. In: Iliadis, L., Maglogiannis, I., Papadopoulos, H. (eds.) AIAI 2014. IAICT, vol. 436, pp. 224–235. Springer, Heidelberg (2014). https://doi.org/10.1007/978-3-662-44654-6_22
22. Myers, J.: Minijudge: software for small-scale experimental syntax. Int. J. Comput. Linguist. Chin. Lang. Process. **12**(2), 175–194 (2007)
23. Nokelainen, P., Niemivirta, M., Kurhila, J., Miettinen, M., Silander, T., Tirri, H.: Implementation of an adaptive questionnaire. In: Proceedings of the ED-MEDIA Conference, pp. 1412–1413 (2001)
24. Ortigosa, A., Paredes, P., Rodriguez, P.: Ah-questionnaire: an adaptive hierarchical questionnaire for learning styles. Comput. Educ. **54**(4), 999–1005 (2010)
25. Pan, J., et al.: Reasoning Web: Logical Foundation of Knowledge Graph Construction and Querying Answering. Springer, Switzerland (2017). https://doi.org/10.1007/978-3-319-49493-7
26. Pan, J., Vetere, G., Gomez-Perez, J., Wu, H.: Exploiting Linked Data and Knowledge Graphs for Large Organisations. Springer, Switzerland (2016). https://doi.org/10.1007/978-3-319-45654-6
27. Puleston, J., Sleep, D.: The game experiments: researching how gaming techniques can be used to improve the quality of feedback from online research. In: Proceedings of ESOMAR Congress (2011)
28. Saleh, A., Bista, K.: Examining factors impacting online survey response rates in educational research: perceptions of graduate students. J. MultiDiscip. Eval. **13**(29), 63–74 (2017)
29. Schlereth, C., Skiera, B.: Dise: dynamic intelligent survey engine. In: Diamantopoulos, A., Fritz, W., Hildebrandt, L. (eds.) Quantitative Marketing and Marketing Management, pp. 225–243. Gabler Verlag, Wiesbaden (2012). https://doi.org/10.1007/978-3-8349-3722-3_11
30. Schütze, C.T.: The Empirical Base of Linguistics: Grammaticality Judgments and Linguistic Methodology. Language Science Press, Berlin (2016)
31. Soares, R., Edelstein, E., Pan, J.Z., Wyner, A.: Knowledge driven intelligent survey systems for linguists. In: Ichise, R., Lecue, F., Kawamura, T., Zhao, D., Muggleton, S., Kozaki, K. (eds.) JIST 2018. LNCS, vol. 11341, pp. 3–18. Springer, Cham (2018). https://doi.org/10.1007/978-3-030-04284-4_1
32. SoftwareAdvice: Buyer's guide, March 2019. https://www.softwareadvice.com/za/survey/#buyers-guide. Accessed 23 Apr 2019
33. Stoet, G.: Psytoolkit: a novel web-based method for running online questionnaires and reaction-time experiments. Teach. Psychol. **44**(1), 24–31 (2017)

CICO: Chemically Induced Carcinogenesis Ontology

Sungmin Yang, Hyunwhan Joe, Sungkwon Yang, and Hong-Gee Kim[⊠]

Biomedical Knowledge Engineering Laboratory, Seoul National University, Seoul, Korea
{syang90,hyunwhanjoe,sungkwon.yang,hgkim}@snu.ac.kr

Abstract. In vivo experiments have had a great impact on the development of biomedicine, and as a result, a variety of biomedical data is produced and provided to researchers. Standardization and ontology design were carried out for the systematic management and effective sharing of these data. As results of their efforts, useful ontologies such as the Experimental Factor Ontology (EFO), Disease Ontology (DO), Gene Ontology (GO), Chemical Entities of Biological Interest (ChEBI) were developed. However, these ontologies are not enough to provide knowledge about the experiments to researchers conducting in vivo studies. Specifically, in the experimental design process, the generation of cancer causes considerable time and research costs. Researchers conducting animal experiments need animals with signs of carcinogenesis that fits their research interests. Therefore, our study is intended to provide experimental data about inducing cancer in animals. In order to provide this data, we collect experimental data about chemical substances that cause cancer. After that, we design an ontology based on these data and link it with the Disease Ontology. Our research focuses largely on two aspects. The first is to create a knowledge graph that inter-links with other biomedical linked data. The second is to provide practical knowledge to researchers conducting in vivo experiments. In conclusion, our research is provided in the form of a web service, which makes it easy to use the SPARQL endpoint and search service.

Keywords: Biomedical ontology · Carcinogenesis · Biomedical linked data

Resource: http://bike.cico.snu.ac.kr/

1 Introduction

1.1 Background

Over the past few decades, research has been done to better understand and treat cancer. However, experiments on humans except for the purpose of treatment are impossible. Therefore, research using the model system, which is also known as a model organism, is actively conducted in biomedicine and biology, and as a result, vast amounts of disease-drug and gene-disease data is being produced. Following this, standardization and data structure design for effective data sharing and systematic management have emerged. The Experimental Factor Ontology (EFO) [1], Disease Ontology (DO) [2, 3], Gene Ontology (GO) [4], Chemical Entities of Biological Interest (ChEBI) [5] are examples

© Springer Nature Switzerland AG 2020
X. Wang et al. (Eds.): JIST 2019, LNCS 12032, pp. 242–254, 2020.
https://doi.org/10.1007/978-3-030-41407-8_16

of representative biomedical and biochemical ontologies. However, the above ontologies provide information for analyzing the results of experiments or represent the taxonomy of the domain. On the other hand, our study attempts to provide experimental data that will aid in the process or design of animal experiments. In particular, we attempt to support cancer research which is a major focus in academia and industry.

When designing cancer research, there are two main goals. It is to understand the mechanism of cancer and to devise new treatment methods. As a common process for studying these two goals, it is essential to have an experimental animal with a specific cancer type in the desired tissue. However, obtaining animal specimens with cancer is not as easy as it may seem, and is a costly process that requires a lot of effort and time. In vivo testing is often employed for observing the overall effects of an experiment on a living subject, usually animals, including plants. Many in vivo laboratories around the world are studying specific cancers with their own protocols. Researchers in other institutions or laboratories do a lot of work looking for protocols that meet experimental conditions.

There are three methods for obtaining animal specimens with cancer. The first is the most traditional way to produce the desired cancer by using chemicals to perform continuous treatment on animal subjects. The next is to use gene knock-out technology to totally inhibit the expression of a gene that is associated with the development of specific cancer [6]. Finally, the xenograft is a method of transplanting a portion of a human cancer tissue into a nude mouse so that the animal subject is cancerous [7]. The three ways have different economic costs and experimental procedures. It is difficult for the laboratories conducting animal experiments to obtain animal specimens having a disease in a manner suited to the research requirements. Here, we can help the economic and administrative aspects of animal experiment design. Our study aims to provide experimental data related to chemically induced cancers. This is the most economical, traditional method of experimental design. In addition, the chemicals used for cancer development, the duration of the treatment and the duration of the experiment are specified, which can greatly contribute to project time management. This knowledge can be used to save time and expenses.

We collect data and design ontology from experiments related to cancer induced by chemicals. Experimental data collected by us shows the TD50 as the amount of drug that can be used to induce cancer as a chemical. In toxicology, the median toxic dose (TD50) of a chemical substance or toxin is the dose at which toxicity occurs in 50% of cases.

The contributions of our research are as follow: 1. We integrated three independent databases about chemically induced cancer experiments into a knowledge graph. In addition, we made a knowledge graph from the Human-Mouse Disease Connection database that contains information about genes associated with specific cancer. 2. Cancers in the two knowledge graphs were then linked together using the Disease Ontology. After integrating these knowledge graphs together it is possible to search for the genes associated with the induced tumors. 3. We developed an application to share reusable resources and provide services.

1.2 Overview of Chemically Induced Carcinogenesis Ontology

Our study attempts to standardize and widely disseminate experimental data related to chemically induced cancers. Figure 1 describes the schematic process of our system. First, we collected experimental data from three source databases and disease-gene pairs from the Human-Mouse Disease Connection database [8]. We created a knowledge graph by integrating the two different datasets using the Disease Ontology. Finally, we developed the application and released the resource.

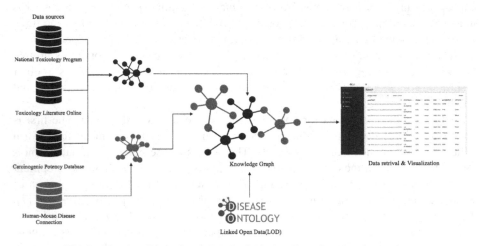

Fig. 1. The data lifecycle of chemically induced carcinogenesis ontology

The remainder of the paper is structured as follows. In the next section, we will discuss prior studies related to our research. In Sect. 3, we describe the dataset of the experiment and the chemical cause of carcinogenesis. Section 4 introduces our ontology and examines the results of our ontology based on real scenario. Next, Sect. 5 demonstrates an application that is reusable and allows users to easily access data. Finally, Sect. 6 describes conclusion and future work.

2 Related Work

Initial studies that collect and provide data related to animal experiments using chemicals include the Carcinogenic Potency Database (CPDB) [9], the National Toxicology Program, and Toxicology Literature Online (TOXLINE) [10]. The above three studies are provided in a structure designed by each person to experiment with chemically induced cancer. In addition, each database differs in the way it collects data and is provided as an independent system. First, TOXLINE features literature-based data collection and is up to date. Next, NTP is a program administered by the National Cancer Institute. NTP plays a critical role in generating, interpreting, and sharing toxicological information about potentially hazardous substances in our environment. Finally, the CPDB collects experimental data from the University of California, Berkeley and the Lawrence Berkeley National Laboratory. Unfortunately, these datasets existed separately even though they have the same purpose. In addition, the biggest problem is the simple search service that reflects only a part of the researchers' requirements and is difficult to access. For example, all three studies collected experimental data independently on the likelihood of developing cancer using chemicals and they are not integrated. All three systems are only able to perform searches with chemicals. This paper presents an knowledge graph called Chemically Induced Carcinogenesis Ontology (CICO). First, we integrate data from three sources into a knowledge graph. This improves data reusability for effective sharing and performs ontology modeling. In this paper we use knowledge graph to mean the total set of entities, their attributes and their relations with other entities [11]. DBpedia [12] is an example of a general-domain knowledge graph and KnowLife [13] is a knowledge graph for biomedicine. In addition, we use the Disease Ontology (DO) to map the experimental data to the Human-Mouse Disease Connection (HMDC) database to provide experimental data as well as a list of notable genes in the study.

3 Dataset of Chemically Induced Carcinogenesis Experiments

We acquired experiment data related to chemically induced carcinogenesis from the carcinogenic potency database (CPDB), published literature, the National Cancer Institute, and the National Toxicology Program. CPDB reports analysis of animal cancer tests used in support of cancer risk assessments for humans. It was developed by the Carcinogenic Potency Project at the University of California, Berkeley and the Lawrence Berkeley National Laboratory. It includes 6,540 chronic, long-term animal cancer tests from the published literature as well as from NCI-NTP. Our collected data consist of a total of 29,363 experiments. Some of the experimental data used a variety of chemical substances or single chemical substance in an experiment. At this time, all animal specimens are recognized as different individuals. Experimental data largely includes three important concepts: chemicals, model systems, and experiments.

First, we describe the chemicals used in the experiment. We have information on 1,817 chemicals and the capacity used in each experiment. The dosage of the chemical substance is adjusted according to the weight and dosing frequency of the test animal. Experiments that use chemicals to generate cancer are not 100% accurate. This is because all animals have a polymorphism in the gene and can induce different immune responses depending on sex and species. The most used chemical among various substances is 'Vinyl chloride' in Fig. 2a. It is a gas that has been used as an aerosol propellant and is the starting material for polyvinyl resins. Toxicity studies have shown various adverse effects, particularly the occurrence of liver neoplasms. The next most frequently used chemical is '1,3-butadiene', which is butadiene with unsaturation at positions 1 and 3. It has a role as a carcinogenic agent and a mutagen. As a final example of a chemical substance, 2-Acetylaminofluorene has induced hepatocyte nodules in comparison to normal liver. It is used to study the carcinogenicity and mutagenicity of aromatic amines [14]. These various chemicals can be administered to animal test groups in a number of routes. The way of routes is nine types such as diet, gavage, inhalation, intraperitoneal injection, intravenous injection, gelatin capsule and etc. in Fig. 2b. In the administration method, the experiments using diet and gavage accounted for half of the experiments.

Next, the model system refers to objects that are subject to experimental research in the field of biology. We collected about 49% of the mouse model, 48% of the rat data, 2% of the hamsters, most of which consisted of the rodent model and 1% of the primates model in Fig. 2c. These model systems have a strain name that corresponds to a unique subtype of species. Our system contains a total of 221 strains, of which the most commonly used strain is b6c for mouse models and the rat is used f34 strain for rat models which can be seen in Fig. 2d. However, some experimental data do not contain strain information. Nonetheless, depending on the strain of the mouse used, it is important information for researchers because the capacity of the chemical and tolerance of cancer may be different.

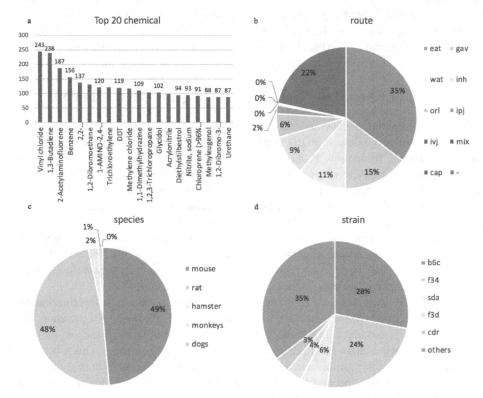

Fig. 2. Descriptive statistics. a, the distribution of 20 types of chemical substance and the number of experiments used in the experiment. b, various routes and distributions of chemical agents. c, distribution by various model systems. d, strain classification and distribution of model system.

Third, the concept of the experiment includes the above two factors together with the type of carcinogenesis and affected tissue. Our collected data includes tissue information from 193 cancers. The formation of tumors occurred most in liver tissue, followed by lung tissue, kidney, uterus, brain, and skin. We looked at the site and type of cancer in more detail. As a result, hepatocellular carcinoma, neoplastic nodule, and hepatoblastoma were found in the same liver tissue in Table 1. However, because the data is generated by various researchers, the names of the tumor types varied.

Table 1. Top 10 experiments related specific tumor type and tissue

Tissue	Tumor type	Number of experiments
Liver	Hepatocellular carcinoma	3,428
Liver	Hepatocellular adenoma	2,907
Liver	Neoplastic nodule	1,868
Lung	Alveolar/bronchiolar adenoma	1,321
Zymbal's gland	Adenoma	1,282
Lung	Alveolar/bronchiolar carcinoma	1,226
Liver	Hepatoma	808
Forestomach	Squamous-cell carcinoma	768
Rectum	Adenocarcinoma	590
Zymbal's gland	Carcinoma	549

4   Methodology for Ontology Development

We developed the ontology after analyzing the collected data. First, in the previous research, the information of three important objects was not structured and it was difficult to utilize them. We then subdivided one experimental data into eight classes and defined a new class (Human-Mouse Disease Connection) which has seen in Fig. 3. In this chapter, we will look at the meaning of each class, the properties it contains, and scenarios for our application.

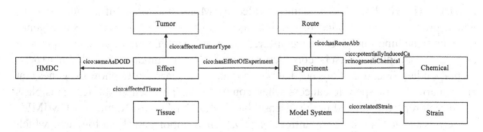

Fig. 3. Schema of chemically induced carcinogenesis ontology

4.1   Ontology Description

Experiment. Experiment class is the most important concept in the ontology we designed. :hasExperimentalModelSystem property has a link with the Model System class, and the :potentiallyInducedCarcinogenesisChemical property indicates the relationship with the chemical class. In addition, the Experiment class includes properties such as :dosingOfPossiblyInducedCarcinogenesis, :hasExperimentLowerConfidence, :hasExperimentUpperConfidence, :hasExperimentTime, :hasExposureTime, :hasReferenceOfExperiment, :hasRouteOfDose, :sourceOfExperiment, :xrefCPDBIdnum. The information that animal experimenters are curious about is the duration of the experiment, the dosage of the chemical, and the way the chemical is administered.

Model System. The Model System class contains information about the animal specimens used in the experiment. As described in Sect. 3, several species of animals are included, and the majority of animals are mice and rats. This class has three DataProperties and one ObjectProperty. First, DataProperty is :hasMutagencity, :hasSystemGender, :hasSystemSpecies, and ObjectProperty is :relatedStrain. Mutagencity expresses whether a chemical mutation occurred in a specific tissue or cell before conducting an experiment. The gender of the model system can vary depending on the purpose of each study. Therefore, the sex of the animal subjects used in the experiment can be important information. Finally, the species of the model system seems similar to each other but include genetic differences with different immune systems, which are considered essential for experimental research. Using information from the Model System, researchers can find specific experiments with species, race, and gender.

Chemical. The chemical class has the name of the chemical and the CAS number. For each piece of information, use the :hasChemicalsName property and the :hasCAS property. Researchers can use the chemical name or CAS number to find the carcinogenesis experiment.

Effect. There are four different tables associated to Effect class such as Tumor, Tissue, Experiment and HMDC. First, tissue table is sets of record including name and abbreviation of occurred tissue which has abnormal change. Next, tumor table incorporate the shape or the location of cancer at the tissue. Experiment table is described above and HMDC table explain below.

HMDC. The HMDC class is data provided by Mouse Genome Informatics (MGI), which provides genes related to specific diseases to human and mouse. Some genes have the same function but can have different names depending on the species. This is an important concept that must be considered when applied to humans using animal experimental studies. Because of this need, it is important for researchers to know the genes that are remarkable for specific cancers when conducting experimental studies. This class has three properties related to the disease :hasDOID, :hasDiseaseName, :hasOMIMIds properties and genes. There are EntrezGene ID, GeneSymbol, and HomologGene, which represent genetic information, and we provide genetic information by selecting a widely used GeneSymbol.

4.2 Scenario

The first scenario is to obtain relevant experiments using the chemical. The method of finding the experiments is possible with the chemical name or the CAS number. For example, a researcher uses a chemical called '1,3-BUTADIENE' in a laboratory and can use the following SPARQL query if you want to know the type and tissue of cancer that can be caused by this substance, along with references.

```
1.    SELECT ?experiment ?CAS ?TissueName ?TumorType ?reference
2.    WHERE {
3.              ?chemicalObj cico:hasChemicalsName "1,3-BUTADIENE".
4.              ?chemicalObj cico:hasCAS ?CAS.
5.              ?experiment cico:potentiallyInducedCarcinogenesisChemical ?chemicalObj.
6.              ?experiment cico:hasReferenceOfExperiment ?reference.
7.              ?effect cico:hasEffectOfExperiments ?experiment.
8.              ?effect cico:affectedTumorType ?tumor.
9.              ?effect cico:affectedTissue ?tissue.
10.             ?tissue cico:hasTissueName ?TissueName.
11.             ?tumor cico:hasTumorType ?TumorType.
12.   }
```

The chemical class of the ontology we have developed has the: hasChemicalsName and :hasCAS properties. If the researcher knows the name of the chemical or the CAS number, you can select the chemical used in the experiment. Next, the chemical class has a relationship with the experimental class as :potentiallyInducedCarcinogenesisChemical property. A reference to the experiment can be obtained with: hasReferenceOfExperiment. The experiment class also links to the Effect class with the :hasEffectOfExperiment property. As you can see in the scenario, you can use the :affectedTumorType property of the Effect class to find various types of tumors, and the :affectedTissue property to get associated with tissue. Through SPARQL results, researchers are provided with knowledge on various experiments using the desired chemical in Table 2. The results of the chemical-based search show five of the experiments for Scenario 1. All five experiments use the same chemical '1,3-BUTADIENE' and the CAS number for this substance is 106-99-0. The first experiment has acinar-cell carcinoma type of tumor in mammary gland tissue. This experiment is recorded in the NCI-NTP TR288 report. On the other hand, 217024 describes an experiment in which a follicular-cell adenoma tumor type of thyroid gland tissue was generated by the literature reference 'P E: Owen; amih, 48, 407-413; 1987'.

Table 2. An example response from a search with chemical name

Experiment	CAS	Tissue name	Tumor type	Reference
207573	106-99-0	Mammary gland	Acinar-cell carcinoma	TR288
207574	106-99-0	Subcutaneous tissue	Hemangiosarcoma	TR288
207606	106-99-0	Lung	Alveolar/bronchiolar carcinoma	TR288
207607	106-99-0	Ovary	Granulosa-cell tumor, malignant	TR434
217024	106-99-0	Thyroid gland	Follicular-cell adenoma	P E :Owen;amih,

In the second scenario, the purpose of the study is to focus on specific cancers. Firstly, the researcher finds the Disease Ontology (DO) ID or disease. Afterward, we provide experimental information that generates cancer in the mouse system and genes associated with specific cancers. In addition, the researchers attempt to know how much of the chemicals used in the experiment were used. For example, if the researcher is interested in a disease called 'hepatocellular carcinoma', the disease name can be used to search the list of experiments, or the DOID (DOID: 684) corresponding to 'hepatocellular carcinoma' can be used. In this study, genes related to mouse disease are provided by Human-Mouse Disease Connection (HMDC) class. This allows the researcher to give the insight to look at the relationship between the disease that interact with the notable genes when conducting experimental studies. Now, let's look at the SPARQL query in the second scenario.

```
1.    SELECT DISTINCT ?experiment ?chemName ?dosage ?species ?doid ?geneSymbol ?reference
2.    WHERE {
3.            ?do cico:hasDiseaseName "hepatocellular carcinoma".
4.            ?do cico:hasDOID ?doid.
5.            ?do cico:hasSpeciesOfrelatedGene "mouse, laboratory".
6.            ?do cico:hasGeneSymbol ?geneSymbol.
7.            ?effect cico:effect_sameAsDOID ?doid.
8.            ?effect cico:hasEffectOfExperiments ?experiment.
9.            ?experiment cico:dosageOfPossiblyInducedCarcinogenesis ?dosage.
10.           ?experiment cico:hasExperimentalModelSystem ?model.
11.           ?model cico:hasSystemSpecies ?species.
12.           ?experiment cico:potentiallyInducedCarcinogenesisChemical ?chemicalObj.
13.           ?chemicalObj cico:hasChemicalsName ?chemName.
14.           ?experiment cico:hasReferenceOfExperiment ?reference.
15.   }
```

Unlike the previous scenario, the second scenario includes disease-gene information other than experimental data. The researcher finds the data of the HMDC using the name of the target disease, and uses the: hasDOID property to obtain the DOID corresponding to the disease name and link it with the experimental data. We set the value of the has-SpeciesOfrelatedGene property to mouse to provide the disease-gene data related to the mouse model. Throughout the process, we know the genes and DOID values associated with the disease name. Next, you need to link with the effect class's effect_sameAsDOID property to find experiment data related to the disease. As a result, experimental data and disease-gene data can be integrated.

The next step is to get experiment information with the: hasEffectOfExperiments property. We obtained information about chemical dosage, model system information, and chemical information through :dosageOfPossibleInducinogenesChemical, :has-ExperimentalModelSystem, :potentiallyInducifiedCarcinogenesisChemical properties. The above query results can be seen in the Table 3 below. The results of the search using the disease name include the amount of chemicals and used substances, laboratory animals, Disease Ontology ID, disease related genes, and experimental references. All of the four results of the search were directed to the mouse system and experiments were conducted using different chemicals and dosage. The list of genes included in the result table is related to the mouse.

Table 3. An example response from a search with disease name

Experiment	Chemical	Dosage	Disease Ontology	Gene	Reference
222134	1'-HYDROXYESTRAGOLE	57.8	DOID:684	[IGF2R, CTNNB1,	E C :Miller;canr
206667	1,1,1,2-TETRACHLOROETHANE	124	DOID:684	MET, PDGFRL,	TR237
208304	(2-CHLOROETHYL)TRIMETHYLAMMONIUM CHLORIDE	599	DOID:684	PIK3CA, CASP8,	TR158
217922	(2-CHLOROETHYL)TRIMETHYLAMMONIUM CHLORIDE	11.4	DOID:684	TP53, AXIN1, APC, Nrlh4, Plau, Gnmt]	J R M :Innes;ntis

4.3 Mapping to Heterogeneous Classes

Our study involves two heterogeneous data sets. The first is experimental data using chemicals and the other is collection of disease-gene associations. The two datasets were generated independently so the disease names were annotated differently. Disease Ontology (DO) is one solution to solve this problem. The Human-Mouse Disease Connection (HMDC) has a unified name for each disease. On the other hand, integrated experiment knowledge graph has no standardized name for each disease. We need to generate a unified name for each disease in the experiment knowledge graph. First, we unified the names in the "affected tissue" and "type of tumor" properties. Each property can be obtained using the: affectedTissue and: affectedTumorType properties of the effect class. We manually identified 67 "affected tissues" and 388 "types of tumors". Table 4 shows some of the DOID results we created. The column "# of records" represent pairs of "affected tissue" and "type of tumor". We manually matched each pair of "affected tissue" and "type of tumor" with DOID. The reason for pairing is because it is difficult to determine the type of tumor without affected tissue. An example of this is when adenoma is the "type of tumor" as can be seen in Table 4. The tissue-tumor pair with the most records is a pair of "all tumor-bearing animals" and "more than one tumor type". Unfortunately, "all tumor bearing animals" cannot assign DOIDs. The reason is that there is no specific DOID that matches. The next largest set is hepatocellular carcinoma in liver tissue, which includes a total of 3,428 rows. We refer to the DO and assign DOID: 684 to this result. Tissue-tumor pairs having the same affected tissue and different types of cancer may be expressed with the same DOID since this is how Disease Ontology defines them. For instance, "type of tumor" hepatocellular carcinoma and hepatoma in Table 4. The next tissue with a lot of experimental records is lung. Experiments in lung tissue are performed by inhaling the injected drug into the respiratory tract. We store the generated DOID in the effect class as :sameAsDOID. We have seen how to utilize these heterogeneous classes in this section.

Table 4. The examples of curated Disease Ontology ID.

Affected tissue	Type of tumor	# of records	DOID
All tumor bearing animals	More than one tumor type; tumor types specified in paper	5,477	x
Liver	Hepatocellular carcinoma	3,428	DOID:684
Liver	Hepatocellular adenoma	2,907	DOID:0050868
Liver	Neoplastic nodule	1,868	DOID:1324
All tumor bearing animals	Tumor or more than one tumor type; Tumor types not specified in paper	1,645	x
Lung	Alveolar/bronchiolar adenoma	1,321	DOID:8003
Zymbal's gland	Adenoma	1,282	DOID:833
Lung	Alveolar/bronchiolar carcinoma	1,226	DOID:8003
Liver	Hepatoma	808	DOID:684
Forestomach	Squamous-cell carcinoma	768	DOID:5516

5   The CICO Resource in Use

We will discuss how to use resources through search and exploration. To demonstrate an integrated animal experiment knowledge graph, we have created a visualization tool that displays experimental data retrieved under various conditions. The visualization tool is based on the d2rq framework, available at http://bike.cico.snu.ac.kr/. The application of this study consists of 6 search categories (disease name, DOID, chemical name, CAS number, tissue, type of tumor). The following introduces the examples of a search term for each category: First, the disease name can be retrieved by the name of the cancer present in the Disease Ontology. For example, Breast Cancer, Lung Cancer, and hepatocellular carcinoma. Next, the search using the DOID is performed using the disease ID value of the Disease Ontology. For example, DOID: 3910, DOID: 4450, and DOID: 1324. The chemical name looks for various experiment data using the name of the chemical to be used. For example, 1,1,1-TRICHLOROETHANE, TECHNICAL GRADE, FUROSEMIDE, METHYLENE CHLORIDE, 1,2-DICHLOROBENZENE. The CAS number is another search method using a chemical. For example, 75-09-2, 106-99-0, and 95-50-1. Next, a tissue is a search method using the name of tissue in which cancer has occurred. For example, liver, lung, and kidney. Finally, a type of tumor can be detected by sarcoma, adenocarcinoma, adenocarcinoma, and adenoma. The search results include the name of the chemical that can cause carcinogenesis, the dose of use, mouse genes associated with cancer, and other additional information. Further information on the retrieved experiments can be viewed in detail through the URI. In the Resources tab, you can see instances of all classes. This application internally creates a SPARQL query when the user searches for a request and provides information to the user through the web UI. In addition, some users can retrieve information directly using SPARQL endpoints.

At the left of the UI, the menu bar allows the user to navigate search points and resources in Chemically Induced Carcinogenesis Ontology (CICO). Figure 4 represents an example of a search using a specific disease name which researches conducting in vivo experiments are interested. The amount of chemical used in each experiment, remarkable genes, and reference information are basically expressed.

Fig. 4. The detail of expression in CICO

6 Conclusion and Future Work

In this paper, we presented the Chemically Induced Carcinogenesis Ontology (CICO). It is useful knowledge for the biomedical and chemistry domain developed for researchers who conduct animal experiments, and semantic technician. Our research focuses largely on two aspects. The first is to create a new ontology that interlinks with other biomedical ontology. The second is to provide practical knowledge to researchers who conduct in vivo experiments. In conclusion, our research is provided as a web service that makes it easy to use SPARQL endpoints and resources.

The direction of our future research is divided into quantitative and qualitative extensions. First, quantitative expansion involves supplementing experimental data with chemicals and adding new experimental data using xenograft and gene knock-out techniques. It will also increase the number of genes associated with various diseases. Next, the need for qualitative expansion comes from researchers endeavoring to find objective and more reliable experiments. That is why we recommend an impersonal and more reliable experiment for researchers by introducing scoring techniques.

Acknowledgements. This research was supported by the MSIT (Ministry of Science and ICT), Korea, under the ITRC (Information Technology Research Center) support program, (IITP-2017-0-00398) supervised by the IITP (Institute for Information & communications Technology Promotion) and the Institute for Information & communications Technology Promotion (IITP) grant funded by the Korea government (MSIP) (No.2013-0-00109, WiseKB: Big data based self-evolving knowledge base and reasoning platform). Authors want to thank Junhyuk Shin for the discussions they had.

References

1. Malone, J., et al.: Modeling sample variables with an experimental factor ontology. Bioinformatics **26**(8), 1112–1118 (2010)
2. Bauer, S., Seelow, D., Horn, D., Robinson, P.N., Ko, S., Mundlos, S.: The human phenotype ontology : a tool for annotating and analyzing human hereditary disease. Am. J. Hum. Genet. **83**, 610–615 (2008)
3. Köhler, S., et al.: The human phenotype ontology in 2017. Nucleic Acids Res. **45**(D1), D865–D876 (2017)
4. G. O. Consortium: The gene ontology (GO) database and informatics resource. Nucleic Acids Res. **32**, 258–261 (2004)
5. Hastings, J., et al.: The ChEBI reference database and ontology for biologically relevant chemistry : enhancements for 2013. Nucleic Acids Res. **41**, 456–463 (2013)
6. Chen, S., et al.: Genome-wide CRISPR screen in a mouse model of tumor growth and metastasis resource genome-wide CRISPR screen in a mouse model of tumor growth and metastasis. Cell **160**(6), 1246–1260 (2015)
7. Morton, C.L., Houghton, P.J.: Establishment of human tumor xenografts in immunodeficient mice. Nat. Protoc. **2**(2), 247–250 (2007)
8. Blake, J.A., et al.: Mouse genome database (MGD) - 2017: community knowledge resource for the laboratory mouse. Nucleic Acids Res. **45**, 723–729 (2017)
9. Gold, L.S., Manley, N.B., Slone, T.H., Rohrbach, L., Garfinkel, G.B.: Supplement to the carcinogenic potency database (CPDB): results of animal bioassays published in the general literature through 1997 and by the national toxicology program in 1997–1998. Toxicol. Sci. **85**(2), 747–808 (2005)
10. Schultheisz, R.J.: TOXLINE: evolution of an online interactive bibliographic database. J. Am. Soc. Inf. Sci. **32**(6), 421–9 (1981)
11. Pan, J.Z., Gomez-Perez, J.M., Vetere, G., Wu, H., Zhao, Y., Monti, M.: Enterprise knowledge graph: looking into the future. In: Exploiting Linked Data and Knowledge Graphs in Large Organisations, pp. 237–249. Springer, Cham (2017). https://doi.org/10.1007/978-3-319-45654-6_9
12. Lehmann, J., et al.: DBpedia - a large-scale, multilingual knowledge base extracted from Wikipedia. Semant. Web **6**(2), 167–195 (2015)
13. Ernst, P., Siu, A., Weikum, G.: KnowLife: a versatile approach for constructing a large knowledge graph for biomedical sciences. BMC Bioinf. **16**(1), 1–13 (2015)
14. Rinaudo, J.A.S., Farber, E.: The pattern of metabolism of 2-acetylaminofluorene in carcinogen-induced hepatocyte nodules in comparison to normal liver. Carcinogenesis **7**(4), 523–528 (1986)

Retrofitting Soft Rules for Knowledge Representation Learning

Bo An$^{(\boxtimes)}$, Xianpei Han, and Le Sun

State Key Laboratory of Computer Science, Institute of Software,
Chinese Academy of Sciences, Beijing, China
{anbo,xianpei,sunle}@iscas.ac.cn

Abstract. Recently, a significant number of studies have focused on knowledge graph completion using rule-enhanced learning techniques, supported by the mined soft rules in addition to the hard logic rules. However, due to the difficulty in determining the confidences of the soft rules without the global semantics of knowledge graph such as the semantic relatedness between relations, the knowledge representation may not be optimal, leading to degraded effectiveness in its application to knowledge graph completion tasks. To address this challenge, this paper proposes a retrofit framework that iteratively enhances the knowledge representation and confidences of soft rules. Specifically, the soft rules guide the learning of knowledge representation, and the representation, in turn, provides global semantic of the knowledge graph to optimize the confidences of soft rules. Extensive evaluation shows that our method achieves new state-of-the-art results on link prediction and triple classification tasks, brought by the fine-tuned confidences of soft rules.

Keywords: Knowledge representation · Soft rules · Link prediction

1 Introduction

Knowledge graph (KG) resources such as Freebase [1] and YAGO [2] are widely used in many natural language processing (NLP) applications. Typically, a knowledge graph consists of a set of triples $\{(h, r, t)\}$, where h, r, and t stand for head entity, relation, and tail entity, respectively. Although with a very large scale, coverage or completeness of knowledge graph is a critical issue. For example, 75% persons in Freebase do not have their nationalities specified [3].

Recently, there has been increased interest in learning distributed representation of knowledge graph. By projecting all elements in a knowledge graph into a dense vector space, the semantic distance between all elements can be easily calculated, and thus enables many applications such as link prediction and triple classification [4].

Translation-based models, including TransE [5], TransH [6], TransD [7], and TransR [8], have obtained promising results in learning distributed representations of knowledge graph. Furthermore, ComplEx [9] achieves the state-of-the-art performances on KG completion tasks, such as triple classification and link prediction.

© Springer Nature Switzerland AG 2020
X. Wang et al. (Eds.): JIST 2019, LNCS 12032, pp. 255–270, 2020.
https://doi.org/10.1007/978-3-030-41407-8_17

Despite the success of the above methods in KG completion, they learn knowledge representation based on the triples in a given KG, which inevitably suffer from the incompleteness issue. The logic rules in the form of first order logic contain rich information, and useful for incomplete KG. For example, if the entity *'Kampala'* appears only once in a KG as <Kampala, capitalOf, Uganda>, we can inference the triple <Kampala, locatedIn, Uganda> based on the logic rule <*capitalOf* ⇒ *locatedIn*>. In addition, the logic rules are the structural constrains for the learning representations of relations. For the above reasons, there are a number of works encode the hard logic rules (defined by experts) into knowledge representation learning [10,11]. However, the hard logic rules are difficult to collect and domain specific. Therefore, RUGE [12] firstly employs soft logic rules which extracted automatically via modern rule mining systems [13] to enhanced the knowledge representation. The confidences of the soft logic rules are traditionally calculated based on the number of instances belonging or not belonging to the knowledge graph. However, the relatedness between relations and entities are ignored although they are critical to determining the confidences of extracted rules. For example, the greater similarity between *bornIn* and *nationality* is, the more likely the soft rule <*bornIn* ⇒ *nationalityOf*> is valid. Unfortunately, such inference is not considered in existing rule-enhanced methods for knowledge representation, which is the main difference with our method.

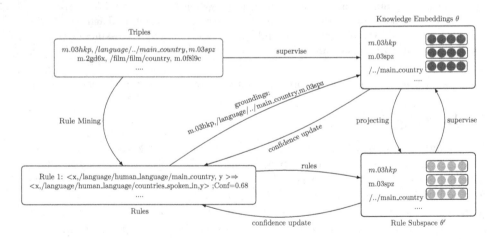

Fig. 1. Simple illustration of retrofitting soft rules for learning knowledge representation method.

To address the issue above, this paper proposes a retrofit model to enhance the knowledge representation, by simultaneously fine-tuning the confidences of soft rules. On the one hand, based on the intuition that the knowledge representation should be consistent with existing triples while be conform to the logic rules, the knowledge of soft rules is distilled into the distributed knowledge representation. More specifically, the learned knowledge representation is projected into a rule-regularized space, which is utilized as another supervisor to enhance the knowledge representation further. For example, as shown in Fig. 1, the vector of */language/human_language/main_country* is projected into the rule-regularized subspace θ' based on the rule of $< x, /language/human\_language/main\_country, y > \Rightarrow < x, /language/human\_language/countries\_spoken \_in, y>$, where x and y are variables that can be instantiated by entities. Note that the proposed method only optimizes the scores of rules instead of mining new rules. After that, the rule-regularized representation and the grounding of the rule *(m.03hkp, /language/../main_country, m.03spz)* is used as another supervisor for knowledge representation learning.

On the other hand, the soft rules are in turn enhanced by the knowledge representation based on the intuition that the confidences of soft rules should conform to the semantic relatedness of knowledge graph. Specifically, we update the confidences of the soft rules based on the semantic relatedness provided by the distributed knowledge representation. For example, given a soft rule $< x, /language/human\_language/main\_country, y > \Rightarrow < x, /language/ human\_language/countries \_spoken\_in, y}>$ and the existing triples set $\{ (x, /language/human\_language/main\_country, y)\}$, if the more validated triples $\{ (x, /language/human\_language/countries\_spoken\_in, y)\}$ are predicted based on knowledge representation, then the higher confidence the rule should have.

Extensive experimental results demonstrate that our model outperforms the state-of-the-art models, by fine-tuning the confidences of soft rules. The main contributions of this paper are trifold:

(1) To the best of our knowledge, this is the first work to utilize the knowledge representation to optimize the confidences of soft rules.
(2) The knowledge representation and soft rules are jointly optimized in our model, which is shown to achieve the new state-of-the-art performances on both the link prediction and triple classification tasks.
(3) Experimental results verify that the confidences of the soft rules are important for enhancing the knowledge representation, and it is critical to optimize the soft rules from current rule mining systems.

2 Related Work

Many structure-based knowledge representation learning methods have been introduced, such as Neural Tensor Network [4] and Single Layer Model [4]. Recently, various translation-based methods are introduced, including TransE and its extensions like TransH, TransD and TransR [5–8]. Trouillon [9] employed complex-valued embeddings to fit the structural information.

There are a number of methods which utilize text descriptions to enhance the knowledge representation, including entity names, wikipedia anchors, entity/triple descriptions and text mention of relations. The entity descriptions to enhance the knowledge representation [4]. [6] proposed a model which combines the entity embeddings with word embeddings by the entity names and Wikipedia anchors. Zhong [14] improved the model of [6] by aligning entity and text using entity descriptions. Zhang et al. (2015) proposed to model entities with word embeddings of entity names or entity descriptions. Xie [15] introduced a model to learn the embeddings of a knowledge graph by modelling both knowledge triples and entity descriptions. [16] generated different representations for entities based on the attention from the relation. [17] utilized relation mentions and entity mentions to enhance the knowledge representations.

The universal schema based models [18,19] enhance the knowledge representation by incorporating the textual triples, which assume that all the extracted triples express a relationship between the entity pair, and they treat each pattern as a separate relation. However, this line of research assumes that all the relation mentions express relationship between entity pairs, which inevitably introduces a lot of noisy information. For example, the sentence *'Miami Dolphins in 1966 and the Cincinnati Bengals in 1968'* does not express any relationship between *'miami_dolphins'* and *'cincinnati_bengals'*. Even worse, the diversity of language leads to the data sparsity problem. Xiao [20] proposed a generative model to handle the ambiguity of relations. Wang [21] extended the translation-based models by textual information, which assigns a relation with different representations for different entity pairs.

The path information has been proved to be beneficial for learning knowledge representation. PTransE [22] introduced path information between entities for enhancing knowledge representation. [23] encoded the relation path and text for learning knowledge representation. [24] first improved the knowledge embeddings based on reinforcement learning. [25] applied 2D convolution directly on embeddings to model knowledge graph.

Recently, injecting human knowledge into the neural network has become a new research hotspot, and the hard logic rules were exploited to enhance the knowledge representation. The hard logic rules and type constraints were introduced to enhance the knowledge embeddings [10,11,26,27]. [28] proposed to generate adversarial triples which conform to the logic rules based on adversarial neural network.

However, all of these models utilize hard logic rules, which are difficult to extract and usually are KG specific. [12] first enhanced the knowledge representation with soft rules extracted from the automatic rule mining system. But despite its apparent success, there remains a major drawback: the performance of this method is limited by the confidences of soft rules extracted by rule mining system, which usually ignores the semantic relatedness between the relations and entities. However, the semantic relatedness is critical to determine the logical relationship among relations. The main difference of our paper is that our model not only enhances the knowledge representation, but also optimizes the soft rules jointly.

3   Retrofitting Soft Rules for Learning Knowledge Representation

This section presents the basic concepts and our retrofit learning framework. We first introduce the resource for our model and present the base model for learning knowledge representation. Secondly, we introduce the method of enhancing knowledge representation with the soft rules based on the idea of knowledge distilling [29,30]. Finally, the approach of retrofitting the confidences of soft rules is presented.

3.1   Learning Resources

Triples. Given a knowledge graph with a set of observed triples $\mathbb{T} = \{(h_i, r_j, t_k)\}_1^N$, where $h_i, t_k \in \mathbb{E}$ and $r_j \in \mathbb{R}$. $\mathbb{E}$ and $\mathbb{R}$ are the sets of entities and relations respectively.

Soft Rules. Further considering a set of logic rules with confidences, denoted as $\mathbb{F} = (R_m, \lambda_m)_{m=1}^M$, where R_m is the m-th soft rule, and λ_m is the confidence of the rule. Specifically, a logic rule R consists of body and head expressions, which means that the head expression could be inferred by the body expression. For example, given a rule $(<x,bornIn,y> \Rightarrow < x,nationalityOf,y>)$, it indicates that $\forall(x, bornIn, y) \in \mathbb{T}$, the triple $(x, nationalityOf, y)$ could be inferred based on the rule. Note that the proposed model can utilize both the hard rules and soft rules.

Groundings. The groundings are the triples, which can be inferred based on the given knowledge graph and soft rules, and are not observed in the KG. Formally, given a rule $< x, r_1, y > \wedge < y, r_2, z > \Rightarrow < x, r_3, z >$, the (x, r_3, z) is a grounding only if $\exists y \in \mathbb{E} : (x, r_1, y) \in \mathbb{T} \wedge (y, r_2, z) \in \mathbb{T} \wedge (x, r_3, z) \notin \mathbb{T}$. In this paper, we encode the logic rules using t-norm fuzzy logics [31], and the groundings are applied softly in the optimization procedure. The truth scores of any logic rules are recursively calculated as:

$$
\begin{aligned}
[\neg A] &= 1 - [A] \\
[A \wedge B] &= [A][B] \\
[A \vee B] &= [A] + [B] - [A][B] \\
[A \Rightarrow B] &= [A][B] - [A] + 1
\end{aligned}
\tag{1}
$$

where A, B are logical expressions, which can either be a single triple or complex triples connected by logical conjunctions, such as $\neg, \wedge, \vee, \Rightarrow$; and $[A]$ is the truth score value of the expression A.

3.2   Triple Modeling

Intuitively, our proposed framework can employ any structure-based knowledge representation methods as the base model, such as TransE [5] and ComplEx [9]. In this paper, we follow ComplEx to model triples for its simplicity, efficiency, and state-of-the-art performances on knowledge graph completion tasks. Specifically, we represent each entity and relation with a complex-value vector. For a given triple (h, r, t), its score $[(h, r, t)]$ is calculated based on a multi-linear dot product:

$$score(h, r, t) = Re((\boldsymbol{h}, \boldsymbol{r}, \boldsymbol{t}))$$
$$= Re(\sum_d h_i r_i t_i) \tag{2}$$

where d is the dimension of the embedding space; $\boldsymbol{h}, \boldsymbol{r}, \boldsymbol{t} \in \mathbb{C}$ are the complex-valued representations for h, r and t respectively; $Re(\cdot)$ means keeping the real part of a complex value. A sigmoid function is introduced to map the score to the continuous truth value range (0, 1) as follows:

$$p_\theta(h, r, t) = \sigma(score(h, r, t))$$
$$= \sigma(Re((\boldsymbol{h}, \boldsymbol{r}, \boldsymbol{t}))) \tag{3}$$

where σ is the sigmoid function as $\sigma(x) = 1/(1 + exp(-x))$; θ is the knowledge representation which represents each relation and entity with a vector and $p_\theta(h, r, t)$ is the score function.

3.3 Distilling Soft Rules into Knowledge Representation

Our approach enables the knowledge representation to be learned from both the triples and general logic rules. To integrate the information of soft rules, we first construct a rule-regularized distribution $q_{\theta'}(h, r, t)$ by projecting $p_\theta(h, r, t)$ with the constraints from soft rules. The intuition behind $q_{\theta'}(h, r, t)$ is that the knowledge representation should not only satisfy with the observed triples, but also be consistent with the soft rules. Likewise in posterior regularization (PR) [32] and knowledge distillation [29], p_θ is projected into the regularized subspace as follows:

$$\min_{q, \xi > 0} KL(q_{\theta'}(h, r, t) || p_\theta(h, r, t)) + C \sum_{l, g_l} \xi_{l, g_l}$$
$$s.t. \quad \lambda_l (1 - \mathbb{V}_{q(h, r, t)}[r_{l, g_l}(h, r, t)]) \leq \xi_{l, g_l} \tag{4}$$
$$g_l = 1, ..., |G_l|, l = 1, ...|R|$$

where $KL(q||p)$ is the KL divergence of distribution q from p, which forces the $q_{\theta'}(h, r, t)$ to satisfy the observed triples; C is the regularization parameter; r_{l, g_l} is the groundings of rule l; G_l is all the groundings of l-th rule; and ξ_{l, g_l} is the slack variable for respective logic constraint, which induces $q_{\theta'}(h, r, t)$ to be consistent with the constraints of rules. For each grounding (h, r, t) of a soft rule l, the value of $\mathbb{V}_{q(h, r, t)}[r_{l, g_l}(h, r, t)]$ is expect to be 1 with confidence of λ_l. The problem has been proved to be convex by [30], such that it can be efficiently solved in its dual form with closed-form solutions. We directly present the solution here:

$$q(h, r, t) \propto p_\theta(h, r, t) exp^{-\sum_{l, g_l} C\lambda_l (1 - r_{l, g_l}(h, r, t))}$$

In this way, the $q_{\theta'}(h, r, t)$ is consistent with the existing triples while satisfies the soft rules.

Secondly, to encode the soft rules information into the knowledge representation θ, we update θ based on both the existing triples and $q_{\theta'}(h, r, t)$. The latter

---

Algorithm 1. Retrofit Framework

Input: Triples $\mathbb{T}$, Groundings $\mathbb{G}$, Soft Rules $\mathbb{F}$
Output: Knowledge Representation Embeddings θ, Confidences λ of the soft rules $\mathbb{F}$
1: Initialize Representation θ with base ComplEx model
2: Initialize Confidences λ from AMIE+
3: **while** not converged **do**
4:     Sample a minibatch $\{(h, r, t)\} \in \mathbb{S}$
5:     Projecting p_θ into rule-regularized subspace $q_{\theta'}$ with soft rules
6:     Update p_θ with $q_{\theta'}$ to distill rule information into knowledge representation
7:     Update λ with $q_{\theta'}$, p_θ and $\mathbb{T}$, which forces the soft rules to be in consistent with the semantic of KG
    end While
8: **return** Knowledge Representation θ, Confidences λ

---

explicitly includes soft rules information as regularization. The new objective is then formulated as a trade-off between imitating the rule-regularized function and existing triples as:

$$L = \frac{1}{|\mathbb{S}|} \sum_{\mathbb{S}} (1 - \pi) \ell(p_\theta(h, r, t), 1) \qquad (5)$$
$$+ \pi \ell(p_\theta(h, r, t), q(h, r, t))$$

where $\mathbb{S} = \mathbb{T} \cup \mathbb{G}$; $\mathbb{G}$ is the groudings; $|\mathbb{S}|$ is the number of triples in $\mathbb{S}$; π is the imitation parameter calibrating the relative importance of the two factors range $[0, 1]$; and ℓ is the cross entropy loss function, and our model aims to minimize L.

3.4   Retrofitting Soft Rules

This section presents the approach of retrofitting the soft rules based on the knowledge representation. We optimize the soft rules based on the intuition that the confidences of soft rules should reflect the global semantics of knowledge graph. Conventional rule mining systems generate the confidence of a rule based on the number of head triples belonging and not belonging to the given knowledge graph, which often suffer from the incompleteness of KG. Note that the knowledge representation is an effective supplement to this issue, which has achieved promising performances on the knowledge graph completion tasks. Therefore, we propose a method that utilizes the knowledge representation to retrofit the soft rules.

The soft rules are served as the constraints for generating $q_{\theta'}(h, r, t)$ (see Eq.(4)), intuitively, a rule with large confidence λ will induce a large truth scores for groundings of the rule. As a result, we update the confidences of soft rules by forcing the regularized model $q_{\theta'}(h, r, t)$ to be consistent with the given KG and the global semantics of knowledge graph from knowledge representation θ as follows:

$$\lambda^{t+1} = \underset{\lambda \geq 0}{argmin} \frac{1}{|\mathbb{S}|} \sum_{\mathbb{S}} \ell(q_{\lambda^t}(h, r, t), y)$$

where λ^t is the confidence of λ in the t-th iteration and y is calculated as:

$$y = \begin{cases} 1, \text{if}(h, r, t) \in \mathbb{T} \\ p_\theta(h, r, t), \text{otherwise}. \end{cases}$$

In this way, knowledge representation θ is optimized by the soft rules while the soft rules are retrofitted based on the representation iteratively.

3.5 Training Procedure

Similar to the Expectation-Maximization (EM) algorithm, in the proposed model, the knowledge representation learning and the soft rules optimization are performed alternatively through iterations. The whole training procedure of the our method is summarized in Algorithm 1. In this way, the logic information can be encoded into the knowledge representation, and the semantic relatedness information from knowledge representation can be transferred into soft rules.

4   Experiments

In this section, we describe the settings in our experiments and conduct extensive experiments on link prediction and triple classification tasks.

4.1   Experimental Settings

In this paper, our model is evaluated on three benchmark datasets: FB13, FB15K, and YAGO37 [4,8,12]. The statistics of the datasets are shown in Table 1. For fair comparison with RUGE, we employ AMIE++ [13] to automatically extract soft rules and their initial confidences from the data sets. In addition, to verify that our model has the ability to learn meaningful soft rules, we also conduct experiments using the same soft rules with all the confidences being uniformly initialized at 0.5.

Table 1. Statistics of data sets.

Dataset	FB13	FB15K	YAGO37
# Entities	75,043	14,951	123,189
# Relations	13	1,345	37
#Train	316,232	483,142	989,132
#Valid	5,908	50,000	50,000
#Test	23,733	59,071	50,000

Implementation. Note that our proposed framework is model-free, which could employ any structure-based knowledge representation learning method as the base model, such as TransE, TransH, and ComplEx. In this paper, we implement our framework based on ComplEx [9], which has achieved state-of-the-art performances on knowledge graph completion tasks [9] in Python3.6[1] with Pytorch[2]. To train the model, we generate negative triples using the local close word assumption [3]. Specifically, for a given triple (h, r, t), we generate the negative instances (h, r, t'), (h, r', t), and (h', r, t) by replacing the entity and relation with random entities and relations from $\mathbb{E}$ and $\mathbb{R}$.

Hyper-Parameter. To reduce training time, and to avoid overfitting, we pre-train the knowledge representation with ComplEx with the same parameters in each experiment. In our experiments, for both tasks the hyper-parameters are set by grid search as follows: the embedding dimension d in $\{50, 100, 150, 200, 300\}$, the learning rate η for SGD among $\{0.1, 0.001, 0.0001\}$, the margin λ among $\{0.5, 1.0, 2.0\}$, the number of negatives is in $\{2, 5, 10\}$ and the batch size among $\{100, 500, 2000\}$. The regularization parameter C in $\{0.1, 0.001, 0.0001\}$.

Note that the RUGE-uniform refers to RUGE [12] model implemented based on all the confidences of the soft rules are set at 0.5. The RUGE-AMIE refers to RUGE model implemented based on all the confidences of the soft rules are generated from AMIE++. The Our-uniform refers to our models implemented based on all the confidences of the soft rules are set at 0.5. And Our-AMIE refers to our model implemented based on the confidences of soft rules automatically generated from AMIE++.

4.2 Link Prediction

The task of link prediction aims to predict the missing head or tail entity for a triple, which is widely employed for evaluating the knowledge graph completion models [21,33]. Given a head entity h (or tail entity t) and a relation r, the system is asked to return a ranked list of candidate entities. Following [12], we conduct the link prediction task on FB15k and YAGO37 datasets.

In the testing phase, for each triple (h, r, t), we replace the head/tail entity by all entities to construct candidate triples, and calculate the scores of the candidate triples based on score function. We ranked all these entities in descending order of the scores. Based on the entity ranking list, the evaluation protocols include: (1) mean reciprocal rank of correct entities (MRR); (2) the median of the ranks (MED), and (3) the proportion of correct entities in top-N rank entities (Hit@N). A useful link predictor should achieve low MED, and high MRR or Hit@N. We tune the parameters on the validation sets. The best configurations obtained on the validation sets are: $d = 200$, $C = 0.01$, $\pi = 0.5$, $\eta = 0.01$ and margin $\lambda = 0.5$ on FB15K, and $d = 200$, $C = 0.015$, $\pi = 0.2$, $\eta = 0.01$ and margin $\lambda = 0.5$ on YAGO37. Our model is compared to the state-of-the-art base models, including TransE, DistMult, HolE, ComplEx, PTransE, KALE and RUGE, whose results were reported in their papers [5,9,11,12,22,34,35].

---

[1] https://www.python.org/.
[2] https://pytorch.org/.

Table 2. Evaluation results of link prediction.

| Method | FB15K | | | | | | YAGO37 | | | | | |
| | MRR | MED | Hit@N | | | | MRR | MED | Hit@N | | | |
			1	3	5	10			1	3	5	10
TransE	0.400	4.0	0.246	0.495	0.576	0.662	0.303	13.0	0.218	0.336	0.387	0.475
DistMult	0.644	1.0	0.532	0.730	0.769	0.812	0.365	6.0	0.262	0.411	0.493	0.575
HolE	0.600	2.0	0.485	0.673	0.722	0.779	0.380	7.0	0.288	0.420	0.479	0.551
ComplEx	0.690	1.0	0.598	0.756	0.793	0.837	0.417	4.0	0.320	0.471	0.533	0.603
PTransE	0.679	1.0	0.565	0.768	0.810	0.855	0.403	9.0	0.339	0.444	0.473	0.506
KALE	0.523	2.0	0.383	0.616	0.683	0.762	0.321	9.0	0.215	0.372	0.438	0.522
RUGE-Uniform	0.713	1.0	0.641	0.768	0.792	0.821	0.423	4.0	0.337	0.471	0.536	0.596
RUGE-AMIE	0.768	1.0	0.70	0.815	0.836	0.865	0.431	4.0	0.340	0.482	0.541	0.603
Our-Uniform	0.773	1.0	**0.717**	**0.823**	0.840	0.867	**0.435**	4.0	**0.353**	0.481	0.542	0.605
Our-AMIE	**0.774**	1.0	0.709	0.821	**0.842**	**0.871**	0.433	4.0	0.345	**0.483**	**0.545**	**0.606**

From Table 2, it can be seen that:

(1) Our proposed approach outperforms the base model (ComplEx). This finding supports our intuition that the soft rules are beneficial in the knowledge representation learning.
(2) Our model outperforms RUGE. A likely cause for the improvement is that the role of soft rules are further emphasized by the iterative optimization of their confidences.
(3) Our model achieved competitive performances with the uniform initialized confidences of soft rules, while the performances of RUGE had dropped significantly with the same setting. We believe this is because our model can optimize the confidences of soft rules to learn knowledge representation learning, rather than relying entirely on the rules from other models.
(4) A remarkable observation to emerge from the results is that our proposed model achieves state-of-the-art performance on the link prediction task, outperforming various strong baselines.

4.3   Triple Classification

In this section, we assess different models on the triple classification task. Triple classification, usually modeled as a binary classification task, aims to judge whether a given triple (h, r, t) is a true fact [4,5,21]. The negative triples are needed for evaluating various methods on this task. To fairly compared with other methods, we conduct the task on FB13 and FB15K data sets, both of which already have negative triples obtained by corrupting correct ones in test sets.

Given a triple (h, r, t), if the score obtained by function f is below the relation-specific threshold δ_r, then the triple will be classified as a true fact, otherwise, the triple is classified as a false fact. The δ_r is optimized by maximizing classification accuracy on validation dataset, and the values of δ_r of distinct relations are different. The model with the best classification accuracy on validation data is chosen, which ends up with the following parameter configuration: $d = 100$,

$C = 0.01$, $\pi = 0.2$, $\eta = 0.01$ and margin $\gamma = 0.5$ on FB13; and $d = 200$, $C = 0.01$, $\pi = 0.5$, $\eta = 0.01$ and margin $\gamma = 0.5$ on FB15K. Our model is compared to the state-of-the-art base models, including TransE, TranH, TransR, ComplEx and RUGE, whose results were reported in [5,6,8,9] and [12], respectively. The results of various models on triple classification are listed in Table 3.

From Table 3, it can be seen that:

(1) Our model improves the accuracies on triple classification task over the base models.
(2) Our method achieves better results than RUGE on both datasets. This finding suggests that it is important to retrofit the confidences of the soft rules to enhance knowledge representation.
(3) We find similar results as link prediction that our model achieves comparative performances with different confidences settings. However, the performances of RUGE dropped significantly with uniform initialized confidences. To make the matter worse, they have achieved worse results than ComplEx model, which means that the improper soft rules even weaken the performance.
(4) The improvement brought by our approach is slightly lower on FB13 than on FB15K (+4.9 vs +6.3 based on ComplEx). A likely cause for the less improvement on FB13 is that FB13 contains fewer number of relations than FB15K, which causes AMIE++ to extract fewer useful soft rules.

Table 3. Evaluation results of triple classification.

Model	FB13	FB15K
TransE	70.9 (+13.1)	79.6 (+15.1)
TransH	76.5 (+4.84)	80.2 (+14.2)
TransR	74.7 (+7.36)	81.7 (+12.1)
ComplEx	76.4 (+4.97)	86.2 (+6.26)
RUGE-Uniform	75.2 (+3.88)	87.5 (+4.68)
RUGE-AMIE	78.1 (+2.68)	90.2 (+1.55)
Our-Uniform	80.1	**91.7**
Our-AMIE	**80.2**	91.6

5 Detailed Analysis

To better understand the way the proposed method works, this section provides a detailed analysis of the quality of the confidences of the soft rules, and their influences on knowledge representation and link prediction tasks.

5.1 Confidences of Soft Rules

In this section, we further analyze how the quality of the soft rules evolves from the initial form, given by AMIE, to the final settings, updated by our proposed method. Several illustrative examples with different confidence levels from FB15K are listed in Table 4. The scores in the last column are learned by our proposed method.

Table 4. Rules with different confidence from FB15K.

No	Rule	AMIE	Our
1	/people/../marriage/type_of_union ⇒ /people/../marriage/spouse	0.97	1.0
2	/../location/.. ∧ /.../place_of_death ⇒ /../person/nationality	0.35	0.30
3	/language/../main_country ⇒ /location/../languages_spoken	0.69	0.77
4	/people/../people...profession ⇒. /people/person/profession	0.81	0.92
5	/people/../parents ∧ /../spouse ⇒ /people/person/children	0.80	0.91

From Table 4, it can be seen that the changes in confidences of the soft rules are in line with the intuition that they should be consistent with the semantic relatedness between entities. For example, the confidence of rule </people/../marriage/type_of_union⇒ /people/../marriage/spouse> is increased from 0.97 to 1.0, because they are indeed the same relation. By contrast, there are no direct semantic relatedness between /../location/.. ∧ /place_of_death and /../person/nationality, thus the confidence of the second rule in Table 4 is decreased from 0.35 to 0.30. In general, similar observation can be made on other mined soft rules, which explains why our proposed method is helpful in improving the quality of the knowledge representation.

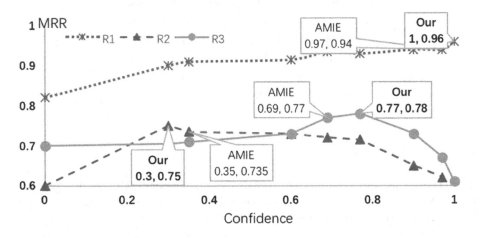

Fig. 2. The MRR of link prediction for each soft rules with different confidence settings on FB15K. (Color figure online)

Furthermore, we investigate the influence of the confidences of soft rules on the quality of the knowledge representation. To do so, we fix the confidences of several soft rules (as listed in Table 4) at different values without updating. From the test set, we collect the triples with the same head entities of those illustrative rules, and plot the MRR obtained by our model with different confidences for each rule, as presented in Fig. 2. In Fig. 2, lines 1–3 correspond to the first 3 rules in Table 4, respectively. It can be seen from Fig. 2 that the confidences of rules have a great impact on the learned knowledge representation. Confidences learned by our method have achieved the best result in all three cases. For example, for rule 2 (see the red line), the best result, namely MRR = 0.75, is obtained with our predicted confidence 0.3, whereas only obtain MRR = 0.735 with confidence 0.35 from AMIE. This finding suggests that our method can learn fine-grained confidences of soft rules, leading to effective link prediction.

5.2 Failure Analysis

In this section, we present a failure analysis to explore possible limitations and weaknesses of our model. In particular, several illustrative triples from the test set of FB15K are listed in Table 5. The tail entities of those examples are failed to be ranked in the top-5. In addition, we list the top-5 ranked tail candidates for each triple.

Table 5. The triples whose tail entities were failed to be ranked in top 5 candidates.

No	The triples in the test set	Top-5 candidates
1	Justin Timberlak, /people/people/profession, **Record producer**	Film actor
		Film
		PAS Giannina F.C.
		MTV movie award
		Musician
2	Victoria Beckham, /people/people/nationality, **England**	Celebrity
		Musical genre
		Oboe
		New York
		USA Neitsisaared
3	Apache License, /computer/software/license, **Gnu Public License**	Oxford School Atlas
		Thomas Mann
		Doc Waston
		American Idol
		Bsd Licenses

From Table 5, it can be seen that the first candidate entity predicted by our model for the first triple is *Film Actor*. However, it is interesting to find out that *Film Actor*, although not found in Freebase, is in fact a valid candidate according to the Wikipedia page[3]. This is also supported by additional evidences: the triple *(Film Actor,/people/person/profession, Justin Timberlak)* can be found in the training set, and according to the 4th rule in Table 4, *Film Actor* should receive a high score. Note that other top-ranked entities such as *Musician* are also valid candidates. Therefore, it is likely the case that our model has mined some new facts in addition to the ground-truth with high scores.

Indeed, the failures are mostly caused by the data sparsity problem, which results in relatively small coverage of rules. For example, we find out that there are no soft rule with */people/person/nationality* or */film/film/language* as the head relation, which may lead to false predictions for the second and third triples in Table 5. Furthermore, the entities in the triples only appear limited times in the training data (*Apache Licence* one time). All the above findings suggest that the data sparsity of relations may degrade the effectiveness of our method (and AMIE). This problem can be partially solved by adding a small number of manually defined hard logic rules, which can be easily incorporated into our model.

5.3   Learning Speed

To evaluate the efficiency of our proposed method, we compare our model with ComplEx and RUGE, and we conduct experiments on FB15k dataset on the same computer, with the configure as: CPU E5-2620, Memory 78G and GPU Tesla K40m. The training time consuming of all the models are listed in Table 6.

Table 6. The training time of different models.

Model	ComplEx	RUGE	Our	Our-uniform
Time	2922 s	3231 s	7519 s	9457s

From Table 6, it can be seen that our model is slower than ComplEx and RUGE model. But in most of the case, it is worthwhile to spend acceptable more time on learning better knowledge embeddings and soft rules in the training process. And in the test phase, all our models calculate the truth value of a candidate triple as formula (2). Therefore, the time consumption of the three models in the test phase should be basically the same.

6   Conclusions

In this paper, we have proposed a retrofit framework to enhance the knowledge representation and soft rules with each other in an iterative fashion. The soft rules are used as regularizations for learning knowledge representation, and the representation provides semantic relatedness for retrofitting soft rules. Our final results

---

[3] https://en.wikipedia.org/wiki/Justin_Timberlake.

have achieved new state-of-the-art performance on both link prediction and triple classification tasks. The additional analysis suggests that our model can effectively learn the appropriate confidences of the soft rules. Failure analysis shows that our method may suffer from the data sparsity issue, even though useful rules can still be extracted. In future work, we plan to extract soft rules in a uniform framework without depending on current rule mining systems.

Acknowledgments. This work is supported by the National Natural Science Foundation of China under Grants no. 61433015, 61572477 and 61772505.

References

1. Bollacker, K., Evans, C., Paritosh, P., Sturge, T., Taylor, J.: Freebase:a collaboratively created graph database for structuring human knowledge. In: ACM SIGMOD International Conference on Management of Data, SIGMOD 2008, Vancouver, Bc, Canada, June, pp. 1247–1250 (2008)
2. Suchanek, F.M., Kasneci, G., Weikum, G.: Yago: a core of semantic knowledge. In: International Conference on World Wide Web, WWW 2007, Banff, Alberta, Canada, May, pp. 697–706 (2007)
3. Dong, X., et al.: Knowledge vault: a web-scale approach to probabilistic knowledge fusion. In: ACM SIGKDD International Conference on Knowledge Discovery and Data Mining, pp. 601–610 (2014)
4. Socher, R., Chen, D., Manning, C.D., Ng, A.Y.: Reasoning with neural tensor networks for knowledge base completion. In: International Conference on Intelligent Control and Information Processing, pp. 464–469 (2013)
5. Bordes, A., Usunier, N., Garcia-Duran, A., Weston, J., Yakhnenko, O.: Translating embeddings for modeling multi-relational data. In: NIPS, pp. 2787–2795 (2013)
6. Wang, Z., Zhang, J., Feng, J., Chen, Z.: Knowledge graph embedding by translating on hyperplanes. In: AAAI, pp. 1112–1119 (2014)
7. Ji, G., He, S., Xu, L., Liu, K., Zhao, J.: Knowledge graph embedding via dynamic mapping matrix. In: Meeting of the Association for Computational Linguistics and the International Joint Conference on Natural Language Processing, pp. 687–696 (2015)
8. Lin, Y., Liu, Z., Sun, M., Liu, Y., Zhu, X.: Learning entity and relation embeddings for knowledge graph completion. In: AAAI, pp. 2181–2187 (2015)
9. Trouillon, T., Welbl, J., Riedel, S., Gaussier, É., Bouchard, G.: Complex embeddings for simple link prediction. In: International Conference on Machine Learning, pp. 2071–2080 (2016)
10. Rocktäschel, T., Singh, S., Riedel, S.: Injecting logical background knowledge into embeddings for relation extraction. In: HLT-NAACL, pp. 1119–1129 (2015)
11. Guo, S., Wang, Q., Wang, L., Wang, B., Guo, L.: Jointly embedding knowledge graphs and logical rules. In: EMNLP, pp. 192–202 (2016)
12. Guo, S., Wang, Q., Wang, L., Wang, B., Guo, L.: Knowledge graph embedding with iterative guidance from soft rules. In: Thirty-Second AAAI Conference on Artificial Intelligence (2018)
13. Galárraga, L., Teflioudi, C., Hose, K., Suchanek, F.M.: Fast rule mining in ontological knowledge bases with AMIE+. VLDB J. **24**(6), 707–730 (2015)
14. Zhong, H., Zhang, J., Wang, Z., Wan, H., Chen, Z.: Aligning knowledge and text embeddings by entity descriptions. In: EMNLP, pp. 267–272 (2015)

15. Xie, R., Liu, Z., Jia, J., Luan, H., Sun, M.: Representation learning of knowledge graphs with entity descriptions. In: AAAI, pp. 2659–2665 (2016)
16. Xu, J., Chen, K., Qiu, X., Huang, X.: Knowledge graph representation with jointly structural and textual encoding. arXiv preprint arXiv:1611.08661 (2016)
17. An, B., Chen, B., Han, X., Sun, L.: Accurate text-enhanced knowledge graph representation learning. In: Proceedings of the 2018 Conference of the North American Chapter of the Association for Computational Linguistics: Human Language Technologies, Volume 1 (Long Papers), pp. 745–755 (2018)
18. Riedel, S., Yao, L., McCallum, A., Marlin, B.M.: Relation extraction with matrix factorization and universal schemas. In: HLT-NAACL. pp. 74–84 (2013)
19. Toutanova, K., Chen, D., Pantel, P., Poon, H., Choudhury, P., Gamon, M.: Representing text for joint embedding of text and knowledge bases. EMNLP **15**, 1499–1509 (2015)
20. Xiao, H., Huang, M., Zhu, X.: Transg: a generative model for knowledge graph embedding. In: Proceedings of the 54th Annual Meeting of the Association for Computational Linguistics (Volume 1: Long Papers), vol. 1, pp. 2316–2325 (2016)
21. Wang, Z., Li, J., Liu, Z., Tang, J.: Text-enhanced representation learning for knowledge graph. In: To appear in IJCAI 2016, pp. 04–17 (2016)
22. Lin, Y., Liu, Z., Luan, H., Sun, M., Rao, S., Liu, S.: Modeling relation paths for representation learning of knowledge bases. arXiv preprint arXiv:1506.00379 (2015)
23. Toutanova, K., Lin, X.V., Yih, W.T., Poon, H., Quirk, C.: Compositional learning of embeddings for relation paths in knowledge bases and text. In: ACL2016, vol. 1, pp. 1434–1444 (2016)
24. Xiong, W., Hoang, T., Wang, W.Y.: Deeppath: a reinforcement learning method for knowledge graph reasoning. arXiv preprint arXiv:1707.0669 (2017)
25. Dettmers, T., Minervini, P., Stenetorp, P., Riedel, S.: Convolutional 2D knowledge graph embeddings. In: Thirty-Second AAAI Conference on Artificial Intelligence (2018)
26. Wang, Q., Wang, B., Guo, L.: Knowledge base completion using embeddings and rules. In: International Conference on Artificial Intelligence, pp. 1859–1865 (2015)
27. Guo, S., Ding, B., Wang, Q., Wang, L., Wang, B.: Knowledge base completion via rule-enhanced relational learning. In: Chen, H., Ji, H., Sun, L., Wang, H., Qian, T., Ruan, T. (eds.) CCKS 2016. CCIS, vol. 650, pp. 219–227. Springer, Singapore (2016). https://doi.org/10.1007/978-981-10-3168-7_22
28. Minervini, P.: Adversarial sets for regularising neural link predictors. In: Conference on Uncertainty in Artificial Intelligence (2017)
29. Hinton, G., Vinyals, O., Dean, J.: Distilling the knowledge in a neural network. arXiv preprint arXiv:1503.02531 (2015)
30. Hu, Z., Ma, X., Liu, Z., Hovy, E., Xing, E.: Harnessing deep neural networks with logic rules. arXiv preprint arXiv:1603.06318 (2016)
31. Hájek, P.: Metamathematics of Fuzzy Logic, vol. 4. Springer Science & Business Media, Dordrecht (1998)
32. Ganchev, K., Gillenwater, J., Taskar, B., et al.: Posterior regularization for structured latent variable models. J.f Mach. Learn. Res. **11**, 2001–2049 (2010)
33. Bordes, A., Weston, J., Collobert, R., Bengio, Y.: Learning structured embeddings of knowledge bases. In: AAAI Conference on Artificial Intelligence, AAAI 2011, San Francisco, California, USA, August (2011)
34. Yang, B., Yih, W.T., He, X., Gao, J., Deng, L.: Embedding entities and relations for learning and inference in knowledge bases. Eprint Arxiv (2014)
35. Nickel, M., Rosasco, L., Poggio, T.A., et al.: Holographic embeddings of knowledge graphs. In: AAAI, pp. 1955–1961 (2016)

Entity Synonym Discovery via Multiple Attentions

Jiale Yu, Weiming Lu$^{(\boxtimes)}$, Wei Xu, and Zeyun Tang

College of Computer Science, Zhejiang University, Hangzhou 310027, China
{27121115,luwm,21721155,21721114}@zju.edu.cn

Abstract. Entity synonym discovery is an important task, and it can benefit many downstream applications, such as web search, question answering and knowledge graph construction. Two types of approaches are widely exploited to discover synonyms from a raw text corpus, including the distributional based approaches and pattern based approaches. However, they suffered from either low precision or low recall. In this paper, we propose a novel framework SynMine to extract synonyms from massive raw text corpora. The framework can integrate corpus-level statistics and local contexts in a unified way via a multi-attention mechanism. Extensive experiments on a real-world dataset show the effectiveness of our approach.

Keywords: Synonym discovery · Distant supervision · Multi-attention

1 Introduction

People often describe a real-world entity in a variety of ways, which makes the text analysis and understanding more challenging. Thus, automatic entity synonym discovery has become a considerable task, and it can benefit many downstream applications, such as web search [7,8], question answering [35], knowledge graph construction [3], and social media analysis [1], etc.

One straightforward approach to obtain synonyms is from public knowledge bases, such as WordNet [10], ConceptNet [30] and DBpedia [15]. For example, WordBet groups terms into *synsets*, and DBpedia uses *Redirects to URIs* to indicate synonyms. However, these synonyms are constructed manually, which makes the coverage rather limited.

Many efforts have been made to discover synonyms automatically. Some approaches discover synonyms from query logs [5,25] and web tables [11]. However, these approaches are limited to structured or semi-structured data. In order to discover synonyms from massive raw text corpora, two types of approaches are widely exploited, including the distributional based approaches [31] and pattern based approaches [20].

The distributional based approaches assume that if two terms appear in similar contexts, they are likely to be synonyms. For example, "USA" and "the United States" are often mentioned in similar contexts, and they both refer

X. Wang et al. (Eds.): JIST 2019, LNCS 12032, pp. 271–286, 2020.
https://doi.org/10.1007/978-3-030-41407-8_18

to the same entity *country "USA"*. However, only using similar contexts may bring in noises into synonym discovery. For instance, "USA" and "Canada" are two countries but they have similar contexts in sentences. Different from the distributional based approaches, which consider the corpus-level statistics, pattern based approaches lay emphasis on the local contexts, which are the textual sequences from sentences. For example, we can find the pattern "commonly known as" from the sentence *"The United States of America, commonly known as the United States"*, since "The United States of America" and "the United States" are synonyms. With this pattern, we can find more synonyms from sentences in which two synonymous terms co-occur. However, the pattern based approaches are too strict, so they suffer from low recall.

In fact, in order to judge whether two terms are synonymous or not, there is always a bag of sentences mentioning these two terms. Therefore, the task of synonym discovery is mainly fed with a bag of sentences. However, there is a challenge since sentences in a bag inescapably have many noises, which does not reflect synonymous relations and would affect discovery performance. Thus, it is crucial to select valuable sentences in a bag for synonym discovery. But the approaches mentioned above only consider either corpus-level statistics or local contexts.

Therefore, in this work, we propose a novel framework, SynMine, which aims to extract synonyms from massive raw text corpora by leveraging existing synonyms from encyclopedias as *distant supervision*. The framework can integrate corpus-level statistics and local contexts in a unified way via a multi-attention mechanism. Extensive experiments on a real-world text corpus show the effectiveness of SynMine over many baseline approaches.

The rest of the paper is organized as follows. In Sect. 2, we review work related to our framework. In Sect. 3, we formally define the problem and describe the proposed framework in Sect. 4. In Sect. 5, we conduct experiments on a real-world dataset to illustrate the effectiveness of the proposed approach. Finally, we conclude our work with future directions in Sect. 6.

2   Related Work

Synonym discovery is a crucial task in NLP, and many efforts have been invested, especially focus on detecting synonyms from structured or semi-structured data such as query logs [5,6,25,33] and web table schemas [4,11]. While in this work, we aim to mine synonyms from a raw text corpus, which is more sophisticated and challenging.

There are various methods developed to deal with this kind of tasks. Textual pattern based methods aim at learning frequent textual patterns with seeds and then use these patterns to discover more target pairs, which is introduced to hypernym detection [29], relation extraction [24], and information extraction [16]. Distributional based methods attempt to detect synonyms [17,21] and hypernyms [27] by utilizing distributional features and training a classifier. Furthermore, Qu et al. [23] also proposed a combinational method for synonym discovery. Our approach integrates these two types of methods as well.

Our work is also related to the distant relation extraction task. Since most relation extraction works focus on supervised methods, which are time-consuming and need a great deal of manually annotated data. To address this issue, distant supervision approaches are proposed to align plain texts with a given KB and regard the alignment as supervision. Nevertheless, distant supervision suffers from the wrong label problem and may introduce lots of noises. Mintz et al. [19] neglected the data noises, while Riedel et al. [26] adopted the multi-instance method and at-least-one assumption. Zeng et al. [34] used piece-wise convolution neural networks to model sentence-level features and selected the most likely valid sentence to predict relations. Lin et al. [18] and Ji et al. [13] employed two different attention mechanisms into PCNNs to make better use of supervision information.

Inspired by these methods, our approach also adopts PCNNs with attention to capture the most related information. In addition, we integrate context features extracted by `SetExpan` model [28] as corpus-level supervision to improve the effect of attention.

3   Problem Formulation

Given an encyclopedia $\mathcal{E}$, we would like to build a synonym mining framework, and then discover all synonyms from a given text corpus $\mathcal{D}$.

For convenience, we list the main symbols used in this paper in Table 1.

Table 1. Meaning of symbols used.

Symbol	Meaning
T	A set of entity synonym pairs $T = \{\langle t_{i_1}, t_{i_2}\rangle | t_{i_1} \approx t_{i_2}\}_{i=1}^{|T|}$, where each entity synonym pair contains two terms (i.e. words or phrases) that refers to the same real-world entity. Here, $\approx$ means two terms are synonymous
S_i	A bag of sentences $\{s_1, s_2, ..., s_{|S_i|}\}$ for synonym pair $\langle t_{i_1}, t_{i_2}\rangle \in T$, where each sentence $s_k \in S_i$ contains two terms t_{i_1} and t_{i_2}
C	The context features $C = \{c_1, c_2, ..., c_{|F|}\}$, where each context feature $c_i \in C$ is a sequence of terms
w_{c_i}	The global attention weight for the context feature $c_i \in C$
w_{s_i}	The local attention weight for the sentence $s_i \in S$

Therefore, the problem could be formally defined as: Given an encyclopedia $\mathcal{E}$, we first extract a set of entity synonym pairs $T = \{p_i = \langle t_i, t_j\rangle\}$ from $\mathcal{E}$, and obtain a bag of sentences $S_i = \{s_1, s_2, ..., s_{|S_i|}\}$ for each entity synonym pair $p_i \in T$. The task of entity synonym mining aims to discover all synonyms from a given text corpus $\mathcal{D}$ by using T and $\{S_i | p_i \in T\}$.

4   The SynMine Framework

Our proposed **SynMine** integrates both local and global contexts to promote the synonym extraction. It consists of three main steps (Fig. 1): (1) a training set is constructed from encyclopedias as distant supervision, which includes a bag of sentences for each synonym pair. (2) the global attention for each context is calculated in the global attention module based on the above training set. (3) a piecewise convolutional neural network (PCNN) with a global-and-local attention is trained to predict whether a pair of terms refers to the same real-world entity.

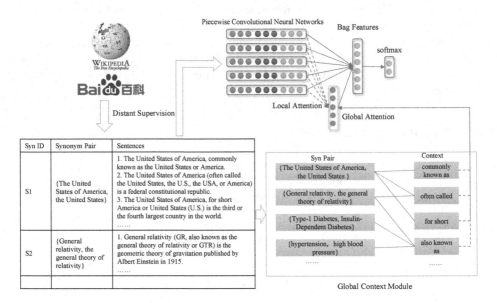

Fig. 1. Overview of the **SynMine** framework.

4.1   Distant Supervision Acquisition

In encyclopedias, we observed that *if two articles have redirect relations, then the titles of the two articles can be treated as synonyms.* In addition, *if an interlink links to an article, then the link's anchor text and the title of the article can also be treated as synonyms.*

Based on the assumptions, we obtain a set of synonym pairs, and then collect a bag of sentences for each pair. Finally, all the synonym pairs with their bags of sentences are collected as distant supervision. The table in the Fig. 1 shows an example of synonyms pairs with their bags of sentences. For example, a synonym pair ⟨*"United States"*, *"The United States of America"*⟩ ∈ T, and its corresponding bag of sentences includes "The United States of America, commonly known as the United States or America" and "The United States of America, for short America or United States (U.S.) is the third or the fourth largest country in the world".

4.2   Global Attention Module

We model the set of synonym pairs T and their corresponding bags of sentences $\{S_i | p_i \in T\}$ extracted from an encyclopedia $\mathcal{E}$ as a bipartite graph.

Given a sentence $s = \{t_1, t_2, ..., t_{|s|}\} \in S_i$, a context feature is extracted by matching term t_{i_1} and t_{i_2} in the sentence, which is the term sequence $t_{i_1+1}, t_{i_1+2}, ..., t_{i_2-1}$ between t_i and t_j. After extracting all context features from $\{S_i\}$, a bipartite graph is built, where the entity synonym pairs and the context features are two types of nodes in the graph. Figure 2 is an example of the bipartite graph.

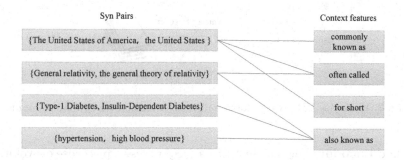

Fig. 2. Illustration of the bipartite graph.

After building the bipartite graph, we assign the weight for each pair of context features $c_k \in C$ and synonym pair $p_i = \langle t_{i_1}, t_{i_2} \rangle$ using the TF-IDF transformation as in [28], which is calculated as:

$$f_{c_k, p_i} = \log(1 + X_{c_k, p_i})[\log |T| - \log(\sum_{p_j \in T} X_{c_k, p_j})]$$

where X_{c_k, p_i} is the co-occurrence count between the context feature c and the synonym pair p_i. Similar to TF-IDF, each context feature and synonym pair can be considered as a "term" and "document" respectively.

Therefore, the global weight for context features c_k can be calculated as:

$$w_{c_k} = \tanh(\frac{\sum_{p_i \in T} f_{c_k, p_i}}{|T|}) \tag{1}$$

4.3   Piecewise CNN with Global and Local Attentions

When given a pair of terms t_{i_1} and t_{i_2}, we can retrieve a bag of sentences $S_i = \{s_1, s_2, ..., s_{|S_i|}\}$ from a text corpus through IR technologies, where each sentence $s_k \in S_i$ contains these two terms, Then, the bag of sentences can be encoded by the piecewise CNN with global and local attentions to form a *bag feature* $\boldsymbol{b}_i$ for the term pair $\langle t_{i_1}, t_{i_2} \rangle$. Finally, $\boldsymbol{b}_i$ is fed to a softmax classifier to predict whether term t_{i_1} and t_{i_2} are synonyms. The procedure is shown in Fig. 3.

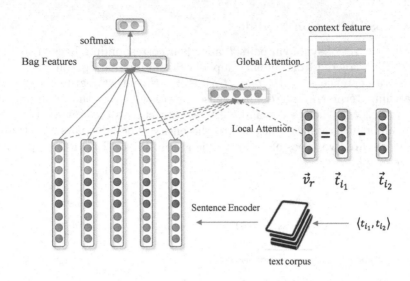

Fig. 3. Piecewise CNN with global-and-local attention for synonym mining.

Sentence Encoder. For each sentence $s \in S_i$, we use a piecewise convolutional neural network [34] to encode it at first.

Specifically, suppose $s = \{w_1, w_2, ..., w_{|s|}\}$, where w_i is i-th word in s, each word w_i is represented by the concatenation of its word embedding $\boldsymbol{w}_i$ and the position embeddings $[\boldsymbol{p}_i^1, \boldsymbol{p}_i^2]$, denoted as $\boldsymbol{v}_i = \boldsymbol{w}_i \oplus \boldsymbol{p}_i^1 \oplus \boldsymbol{p}_i^2$. $\boldsymbol{w}_i \in \mathbb{R}^{d_w}$ is pre-trained by the *word2vec*[1], and $\boldsymbol{p}_i^1 \in \mathbb{R}^{d_p}$ and $\boldsymbol{p}_i^2 \in \mathbb{R}^{d_p}$ encode the relative distances from word w_i to term t_{i_1} and t_{i_2} respectively.

As a result, the sentence s is represented by a matrix $\boldsymbol{s} = [\boldsymbol{v}_1, \boldsymbol{v}_2, ..., \boldsymbol{v}_{|s|}] \in \mathbb{R}^{|s| \times d}$, where $d = d_w + 2d_p$. Then, n filters $\boldsymbol{W}_f = \{\boldsymbol{W}_1, \boldsymbol{W}_2, ..., \boldsymbol{W}_n\}$ ($\boldsymbol{W}_i \in \mathbb{R}^{w \times d}$) are used for the convolution operation on the sentence s. For each filter W_i, the result of the convolution operation is $\boldsymbol{c}_i \in \mathbb{R}^{|s|-w+1}$, where the j-th element is $\boldsymbol{c}_{ij} = \boldsymbol{W}_i \otimes \boldsymbol{s}_{(j-w+1):j}$. When the sentence is divided into three segments according to the given term pair $\langle t_{i_1}, t_{i_2} \rangle$, $\boldsymbol{c}_i$ can also be divided into three parts $\{\boldsymbol{c}_{i,1}, \boldsymbol{c}_{i,2}, \boldsymbol{c}_{i,3}\}$ correspondingly. Then, a vector $\boldsymbol{p}_i = [p_{i,1}, p_{i,2}, p_{i,3}] \in \mathbb{R}^3$ is obtained by the piecewise max pooling $p_{i,j} = \max(\boldsymbol{c}_{i,j})$ $(j = 1, 2, 3)$. Finally, a vector $\boldsymbol{p} \in \mathbb{R}^{3n}$ is obtained by concatenating all $\boldsymbol{p}_i$s $(i = 1, 2, ..., n)$ to represent the sentence.

Local Attention Mechanism. Since the sentences in each bag are obtained through distant supervision, some sentences are invalid to prove the synonym relation between two terms. Therefore, we apply the attention model to reduce the impact of these invalid sentences.

Inspired by many knowledge graph embedding approaches, such as TransE [2], the relation can be represented by the difference vector between

---

[1] https://code.google.com/p/word2vec/.

two entities. Thus, the synonym relation could also be represented by the two synonym items $v_r = t_{i_1} - t_{i_2}$. Consequently, if a sentence s expresses the synonym relation, its embedding vector p should be similar to the vector v_r, and the sentence should have higher attention weight. We compute this intra-bag attention weight using the following formulas:

$$w_{s_i} = \frac{\exp(q_i)}{\sum_{j=1}^{|S|} \exp(q_j)} \tag{2}$$

$$q_i = W_a^T (\tanh[p_i; v_r]) + b_a$$

where p_i is the embedding vector of sentence $s_i \in S$, and $W_a \in \mathbb{R}^{1 \times (3n + d_w)}$ and b_a are parameters.

Training with Global and Local Attentions. Given a bag of sentences $S = \{s_1, s_2, ..., s_{|S|}\}$ for a term pair $\langle t_{i_1}, t_{i_2} \rangle$, we calculate the local attention weight $w_s = [w_{s_1}, w_{s_2}, ..., w_{s_{|S|}}]$ for S using Formulas 2. Then, if sentence $s_i \in S$ matches the global context feature $c(s_i) \in C$, then its global attention weight can be assigned as $w_{c(s_i)}$ using Formula 1. Therefore, the bag of sentences can be represented by integrating the local and global attentions as follows: $b = \sum_{i=1}^{|S|} (\alpha w_{s_i} + (1 - \alpha) w_{c(s_i)}) p_i$, where α is the trade-off parameter to tune the balance between local and global attentions.

In order to predict whether two terms t_{i_1} and t_{i_2} are synonymous, we feed the feature vector b into a softmax classifier. Thus, $p(t_{i_1} \approx t_{i_2} | S) = \frac{\exp o_1}{\exp o_1 + \exp o_2}$, and $o = W_s b + b_s$, where $o \in \mathbb{R}^2$ is the output, $W_s \in \mathbb{R}^{2 \times 3n}$ and b_s are parameters.

Finally, we define the cross-entropy loss as follows.

$$J(\theta) = \sum_{i=1}^{|T|} \log p(t_{i_1} \approx t_{i_2} | S_i; \theta)$$

where $\theta = \{p_i^1, p_i^2, W_f, W_a, b_a, W_s, b_s\}$. Then, we maximize $J(\theta)$ through stochastic gradient descent over shuffled mini-batches with the Adam [14] and the dropout strategy [12].

5   Experiments

5.1   Experimental Setup

Dataset. We evaluate SynMine and other baseline methods on a real-world dataset which is developed from Baidu Baike[2]. Baidu Baike is a Chinese encyclopedia and contains more than 15M articles with abundant synonyms.

We collect existing synonym pairs as positive examples and randomly sampled term pairs as negative examples. Then we align these pairs with articles in

---

[2] https://baike.baidu.com/.

Baidu Baike and obtain various bags of sentences. For evaluation, we randomly partition them into training, validation and testing dataset. The statistics are presented in Table 2.

Table 2. Dataset statistics

	Train	Validation	Test
#Synonym pair	41179	2170	2039
#Sentences	262159	14728	14932
#Avg Sentences per Syn pair	6.37	6.79	7.32

Compared Methods. We select the following baseline methods to compare with SynMine.

BMPM [32]: A matching-aggregation algorithm that applies a bilateral multi-perspective matching method for sentence matching. We treat entities and characters as "sentences" and "words" respectively and use a similar matching method to estimate the similarity of term pairs.

PCNN [34]: A piecewise convolutional neural network is used to represent a sentence, and then a bag is represented by the average of all sentence embeddings in the bag. In our task, we only need to judge the synonym relation.

PCNN+ONE [34]: The sentence is represented by PCNN, but the bag is represented by the most doubtless sentence.

PCNN+ATT [13]: PCNN is used as sentence encoder and an attention mechanism is employed to weight the sentences in the bag.

SetExpan [28]: An unsupervised approach for entity set expansion. In our approach, we treat each term pair as an "entity" in SetExpan.

We use *Precision*, *Recall* and *F1* as the evaluation metrics.

Implementation Details. In our experiments, we choose a Chinese NLP tool *HanLP*[3] for word segmentation, and pre-train the word embeddings on Baidu Baike articles. Here, we set $d_w = 100$ and $d_p = 5$.

For PCNNs, we set the size of filters as 3 and the number of feature maps as 230. We use Adam with an initial learning rate of 0.001 to do optimization. We also adopt the dropout strategy and set the dropout rate as 0.5. Parameter α is set as 0.5, since it can reach the best performance.

During training, we set the iteration number as 50 and use the validation set to select the best parameters.

5.2   Experimental Results

Effect of Global-and-Local Attention. Table 3 presents the performance of our SynMine compared with baselines.

---

[3] http://hanlp.com/.

Table 3. The performance of different methods.

Method	Precision	Recall	F1
BMPM	0.639	0.457	0.531
PCNN	0.901	0.654	0.758
PCNN+ONE	**0.924**	0.750	0.828
PCNN+ATT	0.872	0.786	0.826
SetExpand	0.868	0.753	0.806
SynMine	0.891	**0.810**	**0.849**

From Table 3, we have the following observations: (1) BMPM is inferior to other methods on all evaluation metrics. It indicates that context features of term pairs can provide a great deal of useful information for synonym predictions; (2) PCNN and PCNN+ONE achieve a higher precision but a lower recall which denotes that they tend to misclassify positive examples to negative. It shows that effective sentence selection can alleviate the wrong label problem but only selecting one sentence may lose lots of valuable information; (3) SynMine obtains the best performance on *Recall* and *F1* score, although it is a little inferior to PCNN+ONE in *Precision*. This is because it integrates corpus-level statistics and local contexts, and both of them are beneficial to sentence selection.

Figure 4 displays the aggregate precision/recall curves of all methods. We can see that SynMine achieves the best performance. It verifies the effectiveness of our proposed method and proves the reasonability of global-and-local attention.

We evaluate the precision of the top 100, top 200 and top 500 results in Table 4. The results show that: (1) All methods except BMPM achieve high precision. This indicates that the surface strings of terms cannot reflect the synonym relation well; (2) SynMine has a better ability to tolerate noises in sentences, so it performs best in the top 500 results, because more noises would occur in the latter results.

Influence of Hyper-parameters. The hyper-parameter α is the most important parameter in our experiments. We calculate all the *F1* scores with α from 0.0 to 1.0 to find the optimum value and the result is shown in Fig. 5. A smaller α emphasizes global attention while a larger α emphasizes local attention. We can clearly see from the curve that the *F1* score rises first with the increment of α, reaches a peak when α is 0.5, and then falls. It indicates that integrating both local and global attentions can tolerate more noises and achieve better performance.

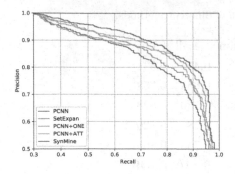

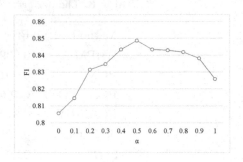

Fig. 4. Performance comparison of SynMine with baseline methods.

Fig. 5. Influence of the parameter α on the performance of synonym mining.

Table 4. The precision of the top 100, top 200, and top 500 extracted synonym pairs upon manual evaluation.

Method	Top 100	Top 200	Top 500	Average
BMPM	0.820	0.747	0.639	0.735
PCNN	1.000	0.980	0.904	0.961
PCNN+ONE	0.993	0.992	0.924	0.970
PCNN+ATT	0.997	0.987	0.909	0.964
SetExpan	0.987	0.972	0.890	0.949
SynMine	0.987	0.988	0.932	0.969

Influence of the Bag Size. To further analyze the impact of global-and-local attention, we also evaluate the prediction results with different bag sizes, as shown in Table 5. We can learn from the table: (1) All methods perform better in large bags than in small bags. The reason may be that large bags contain more sentences, which will bring more evidence for prediction, especially for the methods that use attentions to denoise the sentences. (2) PCNN does not use attention to denoise the sentences, so *Recall* decreases with larger bags, since larger bags have more noises, which would result in false negatives. (3) The *Recall* of SetExpan almost remains unchanged. This is because SetExpan uses global statistics to denoise the sentences, so it is less influenced by the noises. (4) PCNN+ONE, PCNN+ATT and SynMine all use attention to denoise the sentences, so they have better performance on *Recall*, and the *Recall* increases with the size of the bags. Because SynMine integrates both local and global attentions, it achieves the best performance on *F1*.

Table 5. The performance of different methods with different number of sentences in each bag (b_s).

Method	$b_s \in (0, 5]$			$b_s \in (5, 10]$			$b_s \in (10, 15]$			$b_s \in (15, \infty)$		
	P	R	F1	P	R	F1	P	R	F1	P	R	F1
PCNN	0.790	0.678	0.730	0.964	0.656	0.781	0.930	0.604	0.732	1.000	0.644	0.784
PCNN+ONE	0.874	0.653	0.747	0.906	0.726	0.806	0.937	0.800	0.863	0.986	0.867	0.923
PCNN+ATT	0.809	0.692	0.744	0.858	0.773	0.813	0.859	0.800	0.827	0.962	0.905	0.932
SetExpan	0.737	0.758	0.746	0.919	0.753	0.827	0.932	0.746	0.829	0.997	0.750	0.856
SynMine	0.809	0.755	**0.781**	0.886	0.785	**0.832**	0.933	0.808	**0.866**	0.978	0.903	**0.939**

5.3 Case Studies and Discussion

In this section, we provide some examples of synonym prediction with different methods in Table 6, and then discuss the false-positive and false-negative errors according to some examples shown in Tables 7 and 8.

Table 6 shows some examples of synonym prediction with SynExpan, PCNN+ATT and SynMine. In the first case, there are obvious patterns which indicate synonym relation in sentences, e.g. *also known as*. Thus, SynExpan and SynMine both have a correct prediction. However, PCNN+ATT has a low score for synonym relation prediction. While in the second case, because there is a pattern (又称, *known as*) between "文房用品 (stationery product)" and "镇纸 (paperweight)" in the Sentence 1 of Case 2 in Table 6, which makes SynExpan have a wrong prediction. Therefore, both the patterns and the context in the sentences should be considered for prediction.

In order to better study our model, we further randomly selected 30 false negatives and 30 false positives, and perform detailed error analysis.

The causes of false negatives can be summarized into four types as below, and we list the typical cases in Table 7.

1. 33.3% errors are caused by a large number of noisy sentences. Distant supervision may bring in lots of noise, and some entity pairs almost have no valid sentences. e.g., the semantics of "日本语 (Japanese)" and "日文 (Japanese)" in sentences are implicit.
2. 26.7% errors are caused by long-distance between two entities. CNN model can not capture long-distance semantics very well. Therefore, entity pairs with long-distance tend to be predicted as a negative example. For example, "馒头庵 (Mantou Temple)" has a distance more than ten words from "水月庵 (Shuiyue Temple)", which may dilute the semantics.
3. 23.3% errors are caused by the separation of coordinative synonym entities. It is difficult to identify the relation of two entities which have coordinative relation, since there are few context between these entities. For example, "地瓜 (Digua)" and "朱薯 (Zhushu)" are both the Chinese name of sweet potato as shown in the Case 3 in Table 7, but "葡萄 (grapes)" and

Table 6. Examples of synonym relation prediction with different methods, where "茴茴香 (foeniculum vulgare)" and "孜然粉 (cumin powder)" are synonyms, while "镇纸 (paperweight)" and "文房用品 (stationery product)" are not. † means correct prediction.

Cases	Prediction Score		
	SynMine	PCNN+ATT	SetExpan
Case 1: 安息茴香 & 孜然粉 **(foeniculum vulgare & cumin powder)** 1.孜然粉：孜然又名安息茴香。 (Cumin powder: Cumin is also known as foeniculum vulgare.) 2.孜然粉 主要由安息茴香 与八角、桂皮等一起调配而成。 (The cumin powder is mainly made up of foeniculum vulgare with star anise and cinnamon.) 3. 这道菜需要食盐 10g，胡椒粉和孜然粉（亦称安息茴香）适量。 (This dish requires 10g of salt and an appropriate amount of pepper and cumin powder (also known as foeniculum vulgare).	0.907†	0.493	0.998†
Case 2: 镇纸 & 文房用品 **(paperweight & stationery product)** 1. 镇尺是放在书桌案头上的文房用品，又叫镇纸 或纸镇。 (The town ruler is a kind of stationery products which is placed on the desk and known as paperweight or paper town. 2. 古代的文房用品 有很多，较常见的有笔筒、笔洗、墨床、镇纸 等。 (There are many ancient stationery products, such as pen holder, pen wash, ink bed and paperweight.) 3.文房用品 用来压纸的用品可分为压尺和镇纸 两类。 (Stationery product used for paper pressing can be divided into paper holder and paperweight.)	0.033†	0.052†	0.986

Table 7. Cases of false negatives, where two terms for synonym prediction are underlined. In Case 3, since "番薯", "地瓜", "甘薯", "山芋", "红苕", "线苕", "白薯", "甜薯" and "朱薯" are all the Chinese name of sweet potato, so we use Pinyin to distinguish them in sentences.

Case 1: 日本语 (Japanese) & 日文 (Japanese)   1. 他目前小隐于市，担任日本语 教师、日文 书籍与文件翻译。(He is currently hiding in the city, serving as a Japanese language teacher, Japanese book and document translation.)   2. 学校图书馆可以提供日本语 书籍、辞典、日语录音带、日文 书刊等。(The school library can provide Japanese books, dictionaries, Japanese audio tapes, and Japanese papers.)   3. 自 1997 年起，施旺红教授开始以森田疗法为主攻方向，并自学日本语，阅读了大量关于森田疗法的日文 原著。(Since 1997, Professor Shi began to focus on Morita therapy, and learned Japanese by himself, reading a lot of original Japanese works about Morita therapy.)
Case 2: 水月庵 (Shuiyue Temple) & 馒头庵 (Mantou Temple)   1.水月庵 因为馒头做得好，因此又有馒头庵 的诨号。(Because Shuiyue Temple made very delicious buns, so it obtained a nickname of Mantou Temple.)   2. 原来这水月庵 因它庙里做的馒头好，就起了这个诨号——馒头庵。(Because Shuiyue Temple made very delicious buns, people also call it Mantou Temple.)
Case 3: 地瓜 (Digua) & 朱薯 (Zhushu)   1. 番薯：俗称地瓜，又名甘薯、山芋、红苕、线苕、白薯、甜薯、朱薯 等。(Fanshu: commonly known as Digua, also known as Ganshu, Shanyu, Hongshao, Xianshao, Baishu, Tianshu, Zhushu and so on.)   2. 红薯又名白薯、地瓜、红苕、金薯、甘薯、朱薯，属旋花科植物。(Hongshu, also called Baishu, Digua, Hongshao, Jinshu, Ganshu, and Zhushu, is a kind of Convolvulaceae.)

"提子 (raisins)" are not synonyms as shown in the Case 2 in Table 8. However, they both have the coordinative relations.

4. 16.7% other errors.

Table 8. Cases of false positives, where two terms for synonym prediction are underlined.

Case 1: 食肉动物 (carnivore) & 白熊 (white bear)
1. 世界上最大的陆地食肉动物，又名<u>白熊</u>。(The world's largest land <u>carnivore</u> is also known as the <u>white bear</u>.)
2.<u>白熊</u> 又称北极熊，是世界上最大的陆地食肉动物，生活在北极圈。s(The <u>white bear</u>, also known as the polar bear, is the world's largest land <u>carnivore</u> and lives in the Arctic Circle.)
Case 2: 葡萄 (grapes) & 提子 (raisins)
1. 最喜欢的水果有：苹果、橙子、<u>提子</u>、<u>葡萄</u>。(My favorite fruits include apples, oranges, <u>raisins</u> and grapes.)
2. 韩娟还在丰收季节将绿色生产、口感良好的<u>葡萄</u>、<u>提子</u> 价格下调 40%。(Han Juan also reduces the price of green and good-growing grapes and <u>raisins</u> by 40% during the harvest season.)
3. 村干部先动员农民改种苹果树,后来又扩大种植梨树、<u>葡萄</u>、<u>提子</u> 等。(At first, the village cadres mobilized farmers to replant apple trees, and later to expand pear trees, grapes, <u>raisins</u>, and golden melons.)
Case 3: 胡颓子 (Hutuizi) & 本草拾遗 (Herbal Supplements)
1.<u>胡颓子</u> (本草拾遗)，别名蒲颓子、半含春、卢都子 (本草纲目)。(<u>Hutuizi</u>(<u>Herbal Supplements</u>) is also called Putuizi, Banhanchun and Luduzi (Compendium of Materia Medica).)
2.<u>胡颓子</u> (本草拾遗)：蒲颓子、雀儿酥、甜棒子 (湖北)，原产中国。(<u>Hutuizi</u>(<u>Herbal Supplements</u>), also known as Putuizi, Queersu and Tianbangzi (Hubei), is native to China.)
Case 4: 范德华力 (Van der Waals force) & 引力 (gravity)
1. 水分子之间的范氏<u>引力</u>，中国大陆的中学教科书称为"<u>范德华力</u>"。(Chinese middle school textbooks call Fan's gravity between water molecules as "<u>van der Waals force</u>.")
2.<u>范德华力</u> 包括<u>引力</u> 和斥力。(<u>Van der Waals forces</u> include <u>gravity</u> and repulsive force.)
3.<u>范德华力</u> 是一种电性<u>引力</u>，它比化学键弱得多。(<u>Van der Waals force</u> is an electrical <u>gravity</u> which is much weaker than chemical bonds.)

As for false positives, we categorize the causes into the following five types, and several examples are listed in Table 8.

1. 50.0% errors are caused by related entity pairs. Entity pairs with hypernym relation or causality relation are not distinguished well. e.g., "食肉动物 (carnivore)" is hypernym of "白熊 (white bear)", but our model mispredicts it.

2. 20.0% errors are caused by coordinative entities as discussed for the false negatives. This type of entity pairs often co-occurs with similar contexts, such as "葡萄 (grapes)" and "提子 (raisins)".

3. 16.7% errors are caused by a very short distance between two entities. For instance, "本草拾遗 (Herbal Supplements)" is the source of " 胡颓子 (Hutuizi or Elaeagnus pungens thunb)", so they are not synonymous. While, in the sentence "在成虫出孔盛期，喷菊酯类农药，2.5% 溴氰菊酯 (敌杀死)、2.5% 三氟氯氰菊酯 (功夫菊酯)、5% 高氰戊菊酯 (来福灵)、....", the entities in parentheses are synonymous with the entities in front of them. For example, "功夫菊酯" is the common name of "三氟氯氰菊酯 (cyhalothrin)", so they are synonyms. Thus, it is difficult to distinguish the relations only based on contexts and patterns.

4. 10.0% errors are caused by incomplete entity name. Wrong entity recognition in sentences will affect the results. For example, the first sentence of Case 2 in Table 8 shows that "范德华力 (Van der Waals force)" is synonymous with

"范氏引力 (Fan's gravity)" but not "引力 (gravity)". The error is caused by the wrong recognition of "引力 (gravity)".
5. 3.3% other errors.

In order to address the issues above, we can bring in entity types to avoid false predictions. Moreover, we will also attempt to introduce the transitive relation of the synonyms to improve the accuracy in our future work.

6   Conclusion

In this paper, we propose a novel framework SynMine to extract synonyms from massive raw text corpora. The framework can integrate corpus-level statistics and local contexts in a unified way via a multi-attention mechanism. Extensive experiments on a real-world dataset show the effectiveness of our approach.

In the future, we will explore reinforcement learning technologies [22] to further reduce the noises in sentences, and utilize advanced pre-trained models such as BERT [9] to improve the performance. In addition, entity type and transitive relation of the synonyms can also be utilized in the synonym prediction. Furthermore, polysemy of words should also be considered in the synonym prediction.

Acknowledgements. This work is supported by the Zhejiang Provincial Natural Science Foundation of China (No. LY17F020015), the Fundamental Research Funds for the Central Universities (No. 2019FZA5013), the Chinese Knowledge Center of Engineering Science and Technology (CKCEST) and MOE Engineering Research Center of Digital Library.

References

1. Antoniak, M., Bell, E., Xia, F.: Leveraging paraphrase labels to extract synonyms from twitter. In: FLAIRS Conference (2015)
2. Bordes, A., Usunier, N., García-Durán, A., Weston, J., Yakhnenko, O.: Translating embeddings for modeling multi-relational data. In: NIPS (2013)
3. Boteanu, A., Kiezun, A., Artzi, S.: Synonym expansion for large shopping taxonomies. In: AKBC (2019)
4. Cafarella, M.J., Halevy, A.Y., Wang, D.Z., Wu, E., Zhang, Y.: Webtables: exploring the power of tables on the web. Proc. VLDB Endow. **1**(1), 538–549 (2008)
5. Chakrabarti, K., Chaudhuri, S., Cheng, T., Xin, D.: A framework for robust discovery of entity synonyms. In: KDD (2012)
6. Chaudhuri, S., Ganti, V., Xin, D.: Exploiting web search to generate synonyms for entities. In: WWW (2009)
7. Cheng, T., Lauw, H.W., Paparizos, S.: Entity synonyms for structured web search. IEEE Trans. Knowl. Data Eng. **24**, 1862–1875 (2012)
8. Clements, M., de Vries, A.P., Reinders, M.J.T.: Detecting synonyms in social tagging systems to improve content retrieval. In: SIGIR (2008)
9. Devlin, J., Chang, M.W., Lee, K., Toutanova, K.: Bert: Pre-training of deep bidirectional transformers for language understanding. CoRR abs/1810.04805 (2018)
10. Fellbaum, C.: Wordnet: An Electronic Lexical Database (2000)

11. He, Y., Chakrabarti, K., Cheng, T., Tylenda, T.: Automatic discovery of attribute synonyms using query logs and table corpora. In: WWW (2016)
12. Hinton, G.E., Srivastava, N., Krizhevsky, A., Sutskever, I., Salakhutdinov, R.R.: Improving neural networks by preventing co-adaptation of feature detectors. CoRR abs/1207.0580 (2012)
13. Ji, G., Liu, K., He, S., Zhao, J.: Distant supervision for relation extraction with sentence-level attention and entity descriptions. In: AAAI (2017)
14. Kingma, D.P., Ba, J.: Adam: A method for stochastic optimization. In: ICLR (2015)
15. Lehmann, J., et al.: Dbpedia - a large-scale, multilingual knowledge base extracted from wikipedia. Semant. Web **6**, 167–195 (2015)
16. Li, Q., et al.: Truepie: discovering reliable patterns in pattern-based information extraction. In: KDD, pp. 1675–1684. ACM (2018)
17. Lin, D., Zhao, S., Qin, L., Zhou, M.: Identifying synonyms among distributionally similar words. In: IJCAI, vol. 3, pp. 1492–1493. Citeseer (2003)
18. Lin, Y., Shen, S., Liu, Z., Luan, H., Sun, M.: Neural relation extraction with selective attention over instances. In: ACL, vol. 1, pp. 2124–2133 (2016)
19. Mintz, M., Bills, S., Snow, R., Jurafsky, D.: Distant supervision for relation extraction without labeled data. In: ACL/IJCNLP, pp. 1003–1011. Association for Computational Linguistics (2009)
20. Nguyen, K.A., Schulte im Walde, S., Vu, N.T.: Distinguishing antonyms and synonyms in a pattern-based neural network. In: EACL, pp. 76–85 (2017)
21. Pantel, P., Crestan, E., Borkovsky, A., Popescu, A., Vyas, V.: Web-scale distributional similarity and entity set expansion. In: EMNLP, pp. 938–947. Association for Computational Linguistics (2009)
22. Qin, P., Xu, W., Wang, W.Y.: Robust distant supervision relation extraction via deep reinforcement learning. In: ACL (2018)
23. Qu, M., Ren, X., Han, J.: Automatic synonym discovery with knowledge bases. In: KDD, pp. 997–1005. ACM (2017)
24. Qu, M., Ren, X., Zhang, Y., Han, J.: Weakly-supervised relation extraction by pattern-enhanced embedding learning. In: WWW, pp. 1257–1266. International World Wide Web Conferences Steering Committee (2018)
25. Ren, X., Cheng, T.: Synonym discovery for structured entities on heterogeneous graphs. In: WWW (2015)
26. Riedel, S., Yao, L., McCallum, A.: Modeling relations and their mentions without labeled text. In: Balcázar, J.L., Bonchi, F., Gionis, A., Sebag, M. (eds.) ECML PKDD 2010, Part III. LNCS (LNAI), vol. 6323, pp. 148–163. Springer, Heidelberg (2010). https://doi.org/10.1007/978-3-642-15939-8_10
27. Roller, S., Erk, K., Boleda, G.: Inclusive yet selective: supervised distributional hypernymy detection. In: COLING, pp. 1025–1036 (2014)
28. Shen, J., Wu, Z., Lei, D., Shang, J., Ren, X., Han, J.: Setexpan: corpus-based set expansion via context feature selection and rank ensemble. In: ECML/PKDD (2017)
29. Snow, R., Jurafsky, D., Ng, A.Y.: Learning syntactic patterns for automatic hypernym discovery. In: NIPS, pp. 1297–1304 (2005)
30. Speer, R., Chin, J., Havasi, C.: Conceptnet 5.5: an open multilingual graph of general knowledge. In: AAAI (2017)
31. Wang, J., Lin, C., Li, M., Zaniolo, C.: An efficient sliding window approach for approximate entity extraction with synonyms. In: EDBT (2019)
32. Wang, Z., Hamza, W., Florian, R.: Bilateral multi-perspective matching for natural language sentences. In: IJCAI, pp. 4144–4150 (2017)

33. Wei, X., Peng, F., Tseng, H., Lu, Y., Dumoulin, B.: Context sensitive synonym discovery for web search queries. In: CIKM, pp. 1585–1588. ACM (2009)
34. Zeng, D., Liu, K., Chen, Y., Zhao, J.: Distant supervision for relation extraction via piecewise convolutional neural networks. In: EMNLP (2015)
35. Zhou, G., Liu, Y., Liu, F., Zeng, D., Zhao, J.: Improving question retrieval in community question answering using world knowledge. In: IJCAI (2013)

Towards Association Rule-Based Complex Ontology Alignment

Lu Zhou[1](✉), Michelle Cheatham[2](✉), and Pascal Hitzler[1](✉)

[1] DaSe Lab, Kansas State University, Manhattan, KS 66506, USA
{luzhou,hitzler}@ksu.edu
[2] Wright State University, Dayton, OH 45435, USA
michelle.cheatham@wright.edu

Abstract. Ontology alignment has been studied for over a decade, and over that time many alignment systems have been developed by researchers in order to find simple 1-to-1 equivalence alignments between ontologies. However, finding complex alignments, i.e., alignments that are not simple class or property equivalences, is a topic largely unexplored but with growing significance. Currently, establishing a complex alignment requires domain experts to work together to manually generate the alignment, which is extremely time-consuming and labor-intensive. In this paper, we propose an automated method based on association rule mining to detect not only simple alignments, but also more complex alignments between ontologies. Our algorithm can also be used in a semi-automated fashion to effectively assist users in finding potential complex alignments which they can then validate or edit. In addition, we evaluate the performance of our algorithm on the complex alignment benchmark of the Ontology Alignment Evaluation Initiative (OAEI).

1 Introduction

Ontology alignment is an important step in enabling computers to query and reason across the many linked datasets on the semantic web. This is a difficult challenge because the ontologies underlying different linked datasets can vary in terms of subject area coverage, level of abstraction, ontology modeling philosophy, and even language. Due to the importance and difficulty of the ontology alignment problem, it has been an active area of research for over a decade [21].

Ideally, alignment systems should be able to uncover any entity relationship across two ontologies that can exist within a single ontology. Such relationships have a wide range of complexity, from simple 1-to-1 equivalence, such as a Person in one ontology being equivalent to a Human in another ontology, to arbitrary m-to-n complex relationships, such as a Professor with a hasRank property value of "Assistant" in one ontology being a subclass of the union of the Faculty and TenureTrack classes in another. Unfortunately, the majority of the research activities in the field of ontology alignment remains focused on the simplest end of this scale – finding 1-to-1 equivalence alignments between ontologies. Indeed, identifying arbitrarily complex alignment is known to be significantly

© Springer Nature Switzerland AG 2020
X. Wang et al. (Eds.): JIST 2019, LNCS 12032, pp. 287–303, 2020.
https://doi.org/10.1007/978-3-030-41407-8_19

harder than finding 1-to-1 equivalences. In the latter case, a naive approach can compare every entity from the source ontology against every entity in the target ontology, which is feasible for small- and medium-sized ontologies. However, a complex alignment can potentially involve many entities from both ontologies, so pair-wise comparison is insufficient, and the search space become very large even for small ontologies. It is indeed very difficult for either a human expert or an automated system to evaluate all possible combinations [2,19].

In this paper, we propose a complex alignment algorithm based on association rule mining. Our algorithm automatically discovers potential complex correspondences which can then be presented to human experts in order to effectively generate complex alignment between two ontologies with populated common instance data. We evaluate the performance of our system on one of the benchmarks from the complex alignment track of the OAEI 2018,[1] the GeoLink benchmark, which contains around 74k instances from real-world datasets. Significant instance data, which is required for the association rule mining approach, is not available for the remaining benchmarks.[2] The main contributions of this paper are the following:

- The association rule-based algorithm automatically detects not only 1-to-1 equivalences, but also more complex alignment between two ontologies.
- A detailed analysis of the results provides a good understanding of the efficacy of this approach and identifies further directions for advancement.

There is a side contribution when we analyze the results, which is that our algorithm shows that shared instance data between two ontologies can be a good resource to improve the performance of ontology alignment.

The rest of the paper is organized as follows. Section 2 discusses related work in ontology alignment using association rule mining and instance data and complex ontology alignment, including existing alignment algorithms and relevant benchmarks. Section 3 gives background on the FP-growth association rule mining algorithm. Section 4 illustrates the association rule-based alignment algorithm in detail, along with the alignment patterns used to generate the alignment between ontologies. The analysis of the performance of the system is discussed in Sect. 5. Section 6 concludes with a discussion of potential future work in this area.

2   Related Work

Association rule mining has already been used for finding 1:1 simple alignments. AROMA [4] is a hybrid, extensional and asymmetric ontology alignment method that makes use of association rules and a statistical measure. It relies on the idea that "An entity A will be more specific than or equivalent to an entity B if the vocabulary used to describe A and its instances tends to be included in that of B

---

[1] http://oaei.ontologymatching.org/2018/complex/index.html.
[2] It might be available for OAEI 2019.

and its instances." In addition, association rule mining is also used in discovering rules in ontological knowledge bases [10] and logical linked data compression [15].

There are also some instance-based ontology alignment systems that utilize Abox information to generate 1:1 simple alignments between ontologies. GLUE [6] uses joint probability distributions to describe the similarity of concepts in two ontologies. For example, $p(A, B)$ is the probability that an instance in the domain belongs to both concept A and concept B. And then, if the instances of concept A and concept B are in isolation, GLUE uses the instances of A to learn a classifier for A, and then classifies instances of B according to that classifier, and vice-versa. FCA_MERGE also utilizes common instances between ontologies [22]. FCA_MERGE extracts instances from a given set of domain-specific text documents by applying nature language processing techniques. Based on the extracted instances, FCA_MERGE applies mathematical techniques to derive a lattice of concepts as a structural result of FCA_MERGE. More instance-based alignment systems have been discussed in the survey [26].

There are some related studies on creating algorithms to find complex alignment between ontologies. Early work on generating complex alignment is [19,20]. Therein, three complex alignment patterns were described, which are Class by Attribute Type (CAT), Class by Attribute Value (CAV), and Property Chain (PC). Based on these patterns, the authors generated complex alignments on the Conference and Benchmark datasets from the OAEI. [13] identified complex alignments by defining knowledge rules and using a probabilistic framework to integrate a knowledge-based strategy with standard terminology-based and structure-based strategies. More recent related work is currently being undertaken by Thieblin et al. [24]. They propose a complex alignment approach that relies on the notion of Competency Question for Alignment (CQA). The approach translates a CQA into a SPARQL query and extracts a set of instance data from the source ontology. Then the matching is performed by finding the lexically similar surroundings between the set of instance data and the instances in the target ontology. This approach resulted in the CANARD system [23]. However, the current version of the system is limited to finding complex correspondences that only involve classes. More complex correspondences containing properties are still not taken into account [23]. Another alignment system that works on the detection of the complex alignment is the complex version of AgreementMakerLight (AMLC) [9]. This system focuses on the complex Conference benchmark to find alignments that follow the CAT and CAV patterns.

In OAEI 2018, the first version of the complex alignment track [25] opened new perspectives in the field of ontology matching. It comprised four different benchmarks containing complex relations. However, the results from the first year were rather poor. Only 2 out of 15 systems, AMLC and CANARD, were able to generate any correct complex correspondences on the complex Conference and Taxon benchmarks, and the correct number of mappings found was quite limited. The very limited performance of the two systems of course shows avenues for improvement in the future. More details of evaluations and results can be accessed on the OAEI 2018 website.[3]

---

[3] http://oaei.ontologymatching.org/2018/complex/index.html.

Our algorithm differs from the above methods in several aspects. First, [9,13,19] focus on computing lexical or terminological similarity to decide on complex alignments, while our system takes advantage of instance data to generate association rules between ontologies. While the CANARD system also relies on the instance data, we use it in completely different ways. In addition, the current version of CANARD is limited to finding complex correspondences that involve only classes, while our algorithm does not have this limitation. Second, our evaluation of results is more detailed, in order to provide insight into how to improve the performance of complex alignment algorithms. Specifically, we break the evaluation process down into two subtasks: entity identification and relationship identification. We utilize a variation of traditional evaluation metrics called relaxed precision, recall, and f-measure [7] to present the final results of the full complex alignment.

3   Background

In order to help the reader understand how we apply association rule mining and the FP-growth algorithm on the ontology alignment task, we introduce here some concepts that we frequently mention in the rest of the paper.

Association Rule Mining. Our alignment system mainly depends on a data mining algorithm called association rule mining, which is a rule-based machine learning method for discovering interesting relations between variables in large databases [17]. Over the years, association rule mining has played an important role in many data mining tasks, such as market basket analysis, web usage mining, and bioinformatics. Many algorithms for generating association rules have been proposed, like Apriori [1] and FP-growth algorithm [11]. In this paper, we use FP-growth to generate association rules between ontologies, since the FP-growth algorithm has been proven superior to other algorithms [11] and will improve the algorithm in terms of run-time.

Transaction Database. Let $I = \{i_1, i_2, \ldots, i_n\}$ be a set of distinct attributes called items. Let $D = \{t_1, t_2, \ldots, t_m\}$ be a set of transactions where each transaction in D has a unique transaction ID and contains a subset of the items in I. Table 1 shows a list of transactions corresponding to a list of triples. The data in an ontology can be displayed as a set of triples, each consisting of subject, predicate, and object. Here, subjects represent the identifiers and the set of corresponding properties with the objects represent transactions, which are separated by the symbol "|". I.e., a transaction is a set $T = (s, Z)$ such that s is a subject, and each member of Z is a pair (p, o) of a property and an object such that (s, p, o) is a triple.

FP-growth. The FP stands for frequent pattern. The FP-growth algorithm is run on the transaction database in order to determine which combinations of items co-occur frequently. The algorithm first counts the number of occurrences of all individual items in the database. Next, it builds an FP-tree structure by inserting these instances. Items in each instance are sorted by descending order of their frequency in the dataset, so that the tree can be processed quickly. Items

Table 1. Triples and corresponding transactions

$s_1\ p_1\ o_1$
$s_1\ p_2\ o_2$
$s_1\ p_4\ o_4$
$s_2\ p_1\ o_1$
$s_2\ p_2\ o_2$
$s_2\ p_3\ o_3$
$s_2\ p_4\ o_4$
$s_3\ p_1\ o_1$
$s_3\ p_2\ o_2$

TID	Itemsets
s_1	$p_1|o_1,\ p_2|o_2,\ p_4|o_4$
s_2	$p_1|o_1,\ p_2|o_2,\ p_3|o_3,\ p_4|o_4$
s_3	$p_1|o_1,\ p_2|o_2$

Table 2. Examples of association rules

Antecedent	Consequent
$p_4|o_4,\ p_1|o_1$	$p_2|o_2$
$p_2|o_2$	$p_1|o_1$
$p_4|o_4$	$p_1|o_1$

in each instance that do not meet the predefined thresholds, such as minimum support and minimum confidence (see below for these terms), are discarded. Once all large itemsets have been found, the association rule creation begins.

Association Rule. Every association rule is composed of two sides. The left-hand-side is called the antecedent, and the right-hand-side is the consequent. These rules indicate that whenever the antecedent is present, the consequent is likely to be as well. Table 2 shows some examples of association rules generated from the transaction database in Table 1.

Support. Support indicates how frequently an itemset appears in the dataset. The FP-growth algorithm finds the frequent itemsets from the dataset based on the minimum support threshold. In our alignment system, the minimum support value is examined and set to 0.001 to guarantee the best performance.

Confidence. Confidence is an indication of how often an association rule has been found to be true, i.e. how often the presence of the antecedent is associated with the presence of the consequent. The minimum confidence can be tuned to find relatively accurate rules. In this paper, we use the minimum confidence of 0.3 as default value. And we tune the value to 1 when we mine the association rules that may contain complex relations, because our algorithm would focus on precision-oriented results.

Lift. Lift is the ratio of the observed support to that expected if the antecedent and consequent were independent. If the lift is greater than 1, it means that the two items are dependent on one another, which indicates that the association rule useful. In our approach, lift is used to choose between otherwise equal options when detecting simple mappings. When the confidence values of two association rules are the same, the one with higher lift value is selected as the basis for the mapping.

4   Association Rule-Based Alignment Algorithm

In this section, we introduce the proposed ontology alignment algorithm based on association rule mining in detail. Figure 1 illustrates the overview of our proposed algorithm.

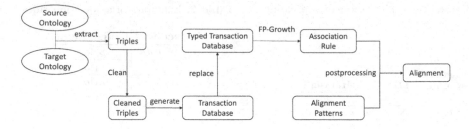

Fig. 1. Overview of the proposed alignment algorithm

4.1   Data Preparation

We first extract all triples ⟨Subject, Predicate, Object⟩ from the source and target ontologies. Each item in a triple is expressed as a web URI. After collecting all of the triples, we prepare the data as follows: we only keep the triples that contain at least one entity under the source or the target ontology namespace and also the triples that contain rdf:type information, since our algorithm relies on this information. After this, there are still some triples containing less useful information for association rule mining, which follow this format: x rdf:type owl:NamedIndividual. This triple is not very informative except stating the subject x is an individual. But, it frequently occurs in the dataset and may lead to noises when applying the FP-growth algorithm, since the frequency of occurrence impacts the results of FP-growth. So, we filter out such noise from the dataset as well.

After this filtering process, we generate the transaction database for the FP-growth algorithm based on all of the remaining triples. The subjects serve as the transaction IDs, and the predicates with the objects separated by the symbol "|" are the items for each transaction. Then we replace the object in the triples with its rdf:type,[4] because we focus on generating schema-level (rather than instance-level) mapping rules between two ontologies, and the type information of the object is more meaningful than the original URI. If an object in a triple has rdf:type of a class in the ontology, we replace the URI of the object with its class. If the object is a data value, the URI of the object is replaced with the datatype. If the object already is a class in the ontology, it remains unchanged. Tables 3 and 4 show some examples of the conversion.

4.2   Association Rule and Alignment Generation

We run the FP-growth algorithm on the transaction database and generate a set of association rules. Since we are trying to find the mappings *between* two ontologies, we focus on mining the rules whose antecedent only contains entities

---

[4] Our evaluation data has only single type. If there are multiple types of the object, it can also combine the subject and predicate as additional information to determine the correct type, or keep both types as two triples.

Table 3. Original transaction database

TID	Itemsets
x_1	gbo:hasAward|y_1, gmo:fundedBy|y_2
x_2	gbo:hasFullName|y_3, gmo:hasPersonName|y_4
x_3	rdf:type|gbo:Cruise, rdf:type|gmo:Cruise

Table 4. Typed transaction database

TID	Itemsets
x_1	gbo:hasAward|gbo:Award, gmo:fundedBy|gmo:FundingAward
x_2	gbo:hasFullName|xsd:string, gmo:hasPersonName|gmo:PersonName
x_3	rdf:type|gbo:Cruise, rdf:type|gmo:Cruise

from the source ontology and whose consequent only contains entities from the target ontology. The association rules tell us which source entities are related to which target entities, but they do not give us information on *how* those entities are related. In order to determine this, we analyze the output of the association rule mining step in light of the common alignment patterns introduced in [19, 27]. In the following, we introduce how we leverage these alignment patterns to filter the association rules and generate the corresponding alignment. The following examples that we use in this paper are from the GeoLink benchmark [27]. gbo: is the prefix of the namespace of the GeoLink Base Ontology (GBO), and gmo: is the prefix of the namespace of the GeoLink Modular Ontology (GMO). The alignment between the two ontologies contains both simple and complex correspondences. To deal with the redundancy of generated association rules, we always keep the simpler rule as the result. For example, there are two association rules generated by our system. Cruise in the GBO is equivalent to the domain of fundedBy with it range of FundingAward in the GMO. And Cruise in the GBO is also equivalent to Cruise in the GMO, which is the domain of fundedBy. Therefore, the two mapping rules are semantically equivalent. And we only keep the second rule which is the simpler one as our result.

Simple Alignment. Simple alignment is a set of simple correspondences that refer to basic 1-to-1 simple mappings between two ontologies, in which the entities involved may be either classes or properties.

1:1 Class Alignment. The first pattern is simple 1-to-1 class relationships. Classes C_1 and C_2 are from ontology O_1 and ontology O_2, respectively. So, we target the association rules with the following format:

Association Rule format: rdf:type\|C_1 → rdf:type\|C_2'
Example: rdf:type\|gbo:Award → rdf:type\|gmo:FundingAward
Generated Alignment: gbo:Award(x) → gmo:FundingAward(x)

The left and right hand side of the arrow represent the antecedent and consequent in the association rules, respectively. In the example, the association rule implies that if an individual x has rdf:type of gbo:Award, then x also has rdf:type of gmo:FundingAward. This means that gbo:Award is a subclass of gmo:FundingAward. If there is another association rule containing the reverse information, which means that gmo:FundingAward is also a subclass of gbo:Award then we can generate an alignment based on the two association rules stating that gbo:Award is equivalent to gmo:FundingAward. This method of choosing between subsumption and equivalence relationships is used for all of the following types of correspondences as well.

1:1 Property Alignment. This pattern captures simple 1-to-1 property mappings. The property can be either an object property or a data property.

(1) Object Property Alignment. Since we have the information of the type of the object in the association rule, we can use the type information to filter the mapping candidates. When we align two object properties, the range types of the properties are usually either equivalent to each other or compatible (because they are in a subclass or superclass relationship). In this paper, our algorithm is precision-oriented. Therefore, we require the object properties in the two ontologies to have equivalent (rather than compatible) ranges in order to be considered equivalent. Range equivalence is determined through the results of the simple class alignment introduced above. Object Property op_1 with its range type t_1 and object property op_2 with its range type t_2 are from ontology O_1 and ontology O_2, respectively. In order to find this alignment, we select the association rules with the following format:

> Association Rule format: $op_1|t_1 \rightarrow op_2|t_2$
> Example: gbo:hasAward|gbo:Award $\rightarrow$ gmo:fundedBy|gmo:FundingAward
> Generated Alignment: gbo:hasAward$(x, y) \rightarrow$ gmo:fundedBy(x, y)

We know from the results of the simple class alignment that gbo:Award is equivalent to gmo:FundingAward. This association rule says that gbo:hasAward is subsumed by gmo:fundedBy. If there is another association rule containing the reverse relationship, we can generate the mapping that gbo:hasAward is equivalent to gmo:fundedBy.

(2) Data Property Alignment. Similar to aligning object properties, when aligning two data properties, the range values of the two properties should be of a compatible datatype. In this paper, we only investigate equivalent datatypes. Data Property dp_1 with its range value t_1 and property dp_2 with its range value t_2 are from ontology O_1 and ontology O_2, respectively.

> Association Rule format: $dp_1|t_1 \rightarrow dp_2|t_2$
> Example:
>   gbo:hasIdentifierValue|xsd:string $\rightarrow$ gmo:hasIdentifierValue|xsd:string
> Generated Alignment:
>   gbo:hasIdentifierValue$(x, y) \rightarrow$ gmo:hasIdentifierValue(x, y)

(3) Data/Object to Object/Data Property Alignment. It is possible that two ontologists may model the same property differently – e.g., there is an example in the OAEI GeoLink complex alignment benchmark [27]. The entity hasIdentifierScheme is modeled as an object property in the GBO with a range of class IdentifierScheme. But, this entity is modeled as a data property in the GMO with a range of the string datatype. In this case, we calculate the Levenshtein string similarity between the labels of the two properties and keep the pairs within a predefined threshold (0.9 is examined to get the best performance). The association rule should have the following format:

> Association Rule format: $op_1/dp_1|t_1 \rightarrow dp_2/op_2|t_2$
> Example:
>> gbo:hasIdentifierScheme|gbo:IdentifierScheme $\rightarrow$
>>> gmo:hasIdentifierScheme|xsd:string
>
> Generated Alignment:
>> gbo:hasIdentifierScheme(x, y) $\rightarrow$ gmo:hasIdentifierScheme(x, y)

Complex Alignment. Complex alignment is a set of Complex correspondences that refer to more complex patterns, such as 1-to-n equivalence, 1-to-n subsumption, m-to-n equivalence, m-to-n subsumption, and m-to-n arbitrary relationship.

1:n Class Alignment. This type of pattern was first introduced in [19]. It contains two different patterns: the Class by Attribute Type pattern (CAT) and the Class by Attribute Value pattern (CAV). In addition, [27] introduced another pattern called Class Typecasting.

(4) Class by Attribute Type. This pattern states that a class in the source ontology is in some relationship to a complex construction in the target ontology. This complex construction may comprise an object property and its range type. Class C_1 is from ontology O_1, and object property op_1 and its range type t_1 are from ontology O_2.

> Association Rule format: rdf:type$|C_1 \rightarrow op_1|t_1$
> Example: rdf:type|gbo:PortCall $\rightarrow$ gmo:atPort|gmo:Place
> Generated Alignment: gbo:PortCall(x) $\rightarrow$ gmo:atPort(x, y) $\wedge$ gmo:Place(y)

In this example, this association rule implies that if the subject x is an individual of class gbo:PortCall, then x is subsumed by the domain of gmo:atPort with the range type of gmo:Place. The equivalence relationship can be generated by combining another association rule holding the reverse information.

(5) Class by Attribute Value. This pattern is similar to the previous one. It just replaces the object property with a data property. Class C_1 is from ontology O_1, and data property dp_1 and its datatype of the range value t_1 are from ontology O_2.

> Association Rule format: rdf:type$|C_1 \rightarrow dp_1|t_1$
> Example: rdf:type|gbo:Identifier $\rightarrow$ gmo:hasIdentifierScheme|xsd:string
> Generated Alignment: gbo:Identifier(x) $\rightarrow$ gmo:hasIdentifierScheme(x, y)

(6) Class Typecasting. This pattern indicates that an individual x of type C_1 in one ontology O_1 is cast into a subclass of C_2 in the other ontology O_2.

> Association Rule format: rdf:type$|C_1 \rightarrow$ rdfs:subClassOf$|C_2$
> Example: gbo:PlaceType $\rightarrow$ rdfs:subClassOf$|$gmo:Place
> Generated Alignment: gbo:PlaceType $\rightarrow$ rdfs:subClassOf(x, gmo:Place)

1:n Property Alignment. This pattern represents a Property Typecasting relationship that is defined in [27].

(7) 1:n Property Typecasting. This pattern is similar in spirit to the Class Typecasting patterns mentioned above. However, in this case, a property from one ontology is cast into a class assignment statement in the other ontology.

> Association Rule format: $p_1|t_1 \rightarrow$ rdf:type$|C_2$
> Example: gbo:hasPlaceType$|$gbo:PlaceType $\rightarrow$ rdf:type$|$gmo:Place
> Generated Alignment:
>   gbo:hasPlaceType(x, y) $\wedge$ gbo:PlaceType(y) $\rightarrow$ gmo:Place(x)

m:n Complex Alignment. This group contains the most complex correspondences.

(8) m:n Property Chain. This pattern applies, for example, when a property, together with type restrictions on one or both of its fillers, in one ontology, has been used to "flatten" the structure of the other ontology by short-cutting a property chain in that ontology. The pattern also ensures that the types of the property fillers involved in the property chain are typed appropriately in the other ontology. The class C_1 and property r_1 with its range restriction t_1 are from ontology O_1, and classes B_i and properties p_i with its range restriction d_i are from ontology O_2.

> Association Rule format:
>   rdf:type$|C_1, r_1|t_1 \rightarrow$ rdf:type$|B_1, p_1|d_1, \ldots,$ rdf:type$|B_i, p_i|d_i$
> Example:
>   gbo:Award, gbo:hasSponsor$|$gbo:Organization
> $\rightarrow$ rdf:type$|$gmo:FundingAward,
>   gmo:providesAgentRole$|$gmo:SponsorRole,
>   gmo:performedBy$|$gmo:Organization
> Generated Alignment:
>
>   gbo:Award(x) $\wedge$ gbo:hasSponsor(x, z) $\wedge$ gbo:Organization(z)
> $\rightarrow$ rdf:type$|$gmo:FundingAward(x)$\wedge$
>   gmo:providesAgentRole(x, y) $\wedge$ gmo:SponsorRole(y)$\wedge$
>   gmo:performedBy(y, z) $\wedge$ gmo:Organization(z)

In this example, the association rule implies that in the GBO, the property gbo:hasSponsor with the domain type of gbo:Award and the range type of gbo:Organization has been used to "flatten" the complex structure in the GMO by short-cutting a property chain. Note that in this pattern, C_1 and any of the B_i may be omitted (in which case they are essentially $\top$).

5   Evaluation

In this section, we show the experimental results of our proposed alignment algorithm on the OAEI GeoLink benchmark and analyze the results in detail. The GeoLink benchmark [27] is composed of two ontologies in the geosciences domain. These two ontologies are both populated with 100% shared instance data collected from the real-world GeoLink knowledge base [3], in order to help the evaluation of alignment algorithms depending on instance data.[5] The subset used for this study contains around 74k triples, which is suitable for applying association rule mining.

We originally planned to compare the performance of our system against pattern based system in [19], CANARD, and AMLC. However, the GeoLink benchmark is a property-oriented dataset which involves many object or data properties in the complex correspondences. As we discussed in Sect. 2, CANARD is currently limited to finding complex mappings that only involve classes. Even though pattern based system in [19] can generate property-based complex correspondences, like property chains, there are several rules that the system follows that largely limit its results, and it ends without finding any complex alignment on the GeoLink ontology pair. AMLC currently only works for the complex Conference benchmark [2,9]. Therefore, there are no complex alignment systems against which we could compare the performance of our system. So in this paper we are limited to reporting the performance of our system against the reference alignment when it comes to the identification of complex alignment. Performance on the identification of simple alignment is compared against that of systems that participated in the OAEI 2018.

Because the systems we compare against are only capable of identifying simple correspondences, we present the results on the simple and complex portions of the overall alignment separately.[6] For simple correspondences, we use the traditional precision, recall and F-measure metrics, in order to compare against other simple alignment systems. However, in order to provide more insight into the underlying nature of the performance on complex correspondences, we take a slightly different approach. Semantic precision and recall, which compare correspondences based on their semantic meaning rather than their syntactic representation [8]. This is done by applying a reasoner to determine when one mapping is logically equivalent to another. Even though the semantic approaches solve an important problem for evaluating alignments with complex correspondences, they still have several limitations. One is that the reasoning takes a significant amount of time, particularly for large ontologies. Furthermore, such reasoning is not possible if the merged ontology is not in OWL DL. The GeoLink benchmark is one example of this case, since there are many correspondences involving an object property on one side and a data property on another side, which is not

---

[5] https://doi.org/10.6084/m9.figshare.5907172.

[6] We are aware that this may not be the most general way to evaluate complex alignments, but the community does not yet have any guidelines or tangible results which could be used. And solving the evaluation problem is out of scope of this paper.

Table 5. The performance comparison of matchers on the simple alignment

Matcher	# of 1:1 Class Equiv.	# of 1:1 Class Subsum.	# of 1:1 Property Equiv.	Precision	Recall	F-measure
Reference alignment	10	2	7	-	-	-
Our results	10	0	5	**0.94**	**0.79**	**0.86**
CANARD [18]	9	0	3	0.67	0.63	0.64
DOME [12]	9	0	4	0.41	0.68	0.51
LogMap [14]	9	0	1	0.77	0.53	0.63
LogMapKG [14]	9	0	1	0.77	0.53	0.63
LogMapLt [14]	9	0	5	0.63	0.73	0.68
POMAP++ [16]	9	0	0	0.89	0.47	0.62
XMap [5]	9	0	0	0.39	0.47	0.43

permissible in OWL DL. Instead, we utilize relaxed precision and recall [7]. More specifically, a correspondence consists of two aspects: the entities involved, and the relationship between them (e.g. equivalence, subsumption, disjunction). In order to assess performance on both of these aspects, we evaluate them separately. This roughly corresponds to the first and second subtasks described for some of the test sets within the complex track of the OAEI.[7] However, the types of relationships we consider are limited to equivalence and subsumption rather than the arbitrary OWL constructs considered there.

5.1   Simple Alignment Evaluation

In the GeoLink benchmark, there are 19 simple mappings, including 10 class equivalences, 2 class subsumptions, and 7 property equivalences. Table 5 shows the simple mapping comparison between our algorithm and the matchers that participated in the OAEI 2018. We list the numbers of correctly identified mappings for each matcher and calculate the precision, recall, and f-measure. The confidence value for picking association rules is set to 0.3, since we find it generates the best performance for simple alignments.

Based on the results, our algorithm outperforms other systems on finding the simple mappings in this benchmark. We can argue that leveraging the instance data is a contributing factor, since our algorithm takes advantages of the instance data, while the other alignment systems do not use it. In addition, most traditional alignment systems focus on accurate detection only of 1:1 class equivalences, which limits their performance on this benchmark. The only 1:1 class equivalence that other alignment systems do not find, but our algorithm does, is gbo:Award(x) $\leftrightarrow$ gmo:FundingAward(x). This may also own to the populated instance data. The reason that our algorithm does not achieve 100% precision is that we mistakenly identify that gbo:PortCall is equivalent to gmo:Fix. The correct relationship should be subsumption. This relation can be easily refined by a semi-automated approach in the future.

---

[7] http://oaei.ontologymatching.org/2018/complex/index.html#hydrography.

Table 6. Similarity for relationship identification

Found relation	Correct relation	Similarity	Comment
=	=	1	Correct relation
⊂	⊂	1	Correct relation
⊃	⊃	1	Correct relation
⊂	=	0.8	Return less information, but correct
=	⊃	0.8	Return less information, but correct
⊃	=	0.6	Return more information, but incorrect
=	⊂	0.6	Return more information, but incorrect
⊂	⊃	0.3	Incorrect relation
⊃	⊂	0.3	Incorrect relation

5.2 Complex Alignment Evaluation

We set the confidence threshold to 1 when running the association rule mining algorithm in order to generate the results described in this section. This is a precision-oriented approach. However, these values can be tuned to fulfill various purposes of alignment systems.

As mentioned previously, in order to assess the quality of a mapping, there are two dimensions that we can look into. First, we can evaluate if the mapping contains the correct entities that should be involved based on the reference alignment. Another dimension is the relationship between the entities, like equivalence and subsumption. Based on this, we break the evaluation procedure down into two subtasks.

(1) Entity Identification: For each entity in the source ontology, the alignment systems will be asked to list all of the entities that are related in some way in the target ontology. For example, referring to the example we used above,

$$\mathsf{Award}(x) \wedge \mathsf{hasSponsor}(x, z) \leftrightarrow \mathsf{FundingAward}(x) \wedge \mathsf{providesAgentRole}(x, y)$$
$$\wedge \mathsf{SponsorRole}(y) \wedge \mathsf{performedBy}(y, z),$$

the expected output from an alignment system is that `hasSponsor` in the GBO is related to `FundingAward`, `providesAgentRole`, `SponsorRole` and `performedBy` in the GMO and `Award` in the GBO. Based on the two lists of entities from the reference alignment and the matcher, precision, recall, and f-measure can be calculated.

(2) Relationship Identification: In terms of the example above, an alignment system needs to eventually determine that the relationship between the two sides is equivalence. Based on our algorithm, if there is only one association rule holding the information, we consider the relationship to be subsumption. If there are two association rules containing the information for both directions, an equivalence relationship is generated. At this stage, we do not further assess

Table 7. Comparative performance of generating complex alignment

Matcher	1:n Property subsum.	m:n Complex equiv.	m:n Complex subsum.
Reference alignment	5	26	17
Our algorithm	3	15	7
Relaxed_Precision	0.60	0.90	0.53
Relaxed_Recall	0.36	0.36	0.16
Relaxed_F-measure	0.45	0.51	0.24

other complex relationships. Table 6 shows the different similarities for different situations. We slightly penalize differently for the situations in finding less information, but all the information returned is correct, and finding more information, but part of the information is incorrect. We do not penalize the incorrect relationship by giving a ZERO value because that would completely neglect the entity identification outputs without considering whether it is a reasonable result or a completely incorrect one. In order to generate the final results, we multiply the results from the entity identification by the penalty of the relations.[8] The formulas for computing the final results are as follows:

```
Relaxed_precision = Precision_entity × Relation_similarity
Relaxed_recall = Recall_entity × Relation_similarity
Relaxed_f-measure = F-measure_entity × Relation_similarity
```

Table 7 shows the results of our algorithm. In total there are 48 complex mappings in the reference alignment. For 1:n property subsumption, our algorithm finds 3 mappings that fall into this category. For example, we find that the domain of gbo:hasSampleType is equivalent to gmo:PhysicalSample. However, the correct relationship should be subsumption. So, the final result should be penalized based on Table 6. For m:n complex equivalence, since our default confidence value for complex alignment is 1, the alignment that we found may miss some entities that should exist in the alignment. For example, referring to the example we use in the entity identification, the expected output from the alignment system is that the property hasSponsor in the GBO is related to FundingAward, providesAgentRole, SponsorRole, performedBy in the GMO and Award in the GBO. However, our algorithm misses one entity which is performedBy in the GMO. Errors such as this may of course be easily corrected by human interaction. For m:n complex subsumption, our algorithm does not generate the correct relationships for all the mappings we found. However, overall, our association rule-based algorithm can effectively come up with rather high quality simple and complex alignment automatically.[9]

---

[8] To be accurate, it could also have been better aggregated with other aggregation functions rather than multiplication [7]. But we would not focus on this question in this paper.

[9] All the data and alignment that we use and generate can be accessed via the link http://tiny.cc/rojy4y. We utilize the Apache Spark frequent pattern mining library to generate association rules.

6   Conclusion

Complex ontology alignment has been discussed for a long time, but relatively little work has been done to advance the state of the art in this field. In this paper, we proposed a complex ontology alignment algorithm based on association rule mining. Our algorithm takes advantage of instance data to mine frequent patterns, which show us which entities in one ontology are related to which entities in the other. Then we apply common simple and complex patterns to arrange these related entities into the formal alignment. We evaluated our system on the complex alignment benchmark from the OAEI and analyzed the results in detail to provide a better understanding of the challenges related to complex ontology alignment research.

There are still some limitations of our algorithm. First, our system relies on instance data for mining the association rules, which is not available for all ontology pairs. However, this could possibly be resolved with automated instance data generation to populate common instances into the ontologies or instance matching techniques. Second, we incorporate some common patterns that have been widely accepted in the ontology alignment community in this paper. This could be another limitation, since the set of mapping patterns in our system is likely not comprehensive. However, our algorithm is extensible, more patterns can be easily added in the future as the need arises. Third, it is possible that there are situations that the association rule would fail in term of finding simple property alignment. For example, if there are two properties *livesIn* and *bornIn* in source and target ontologies respectively, and the association rules would say if livesIn|Place, then bornIn|Place if they occur frequently. *livesIn* and *bornIn* would be considered as equivalent. In this case, there are many different methods that could be applied to improve the performance, like using lexical-based comparison or utilizing external knowledge base to annotate these entities. Fourth, we are collaborating with other benchmark and system developers to enable the comparison and prepare our alignment system to participate in the complex alignment track of the OAEI.

Acknowledgments. This material is based upon work supported by the National Science Foundation under Grant No. 1936677 (https://daselab.cs.ksu.edu/projects/spex).

References

1. Agrawal, R., Srikant, R.: Fast algorithms for mining association rules in large databases. In: VLDB 1994, Proceedings of 20th International Conference on Very Large Data Bases, 12–15 September 1994, Santiago de Chile, Chile, pp. 487–499 (1994)
2. Algergawy, A., et al.: Results of the ontology alignment evaluation initiative 2018. In: Proceedings of the 13th International Workshop on Ontology Matching, OM@ISWC 2018, Monterey, CA, USA, 8 October 2018, pp. 76–116 (2018)
3. Cheatham, M., et al.: The geolink knowledge graph. Big Earth Data **2**(2), 131–143 (2018)

4. David, J., et al.: Association rule ontology matching approach. Int. J. Semantic Web Inf. Syst. **3**(2), 27–49 (2007)
5. Djeddi, W.E., et al.: XMap: results for OAEI 2018. In: Proceedings of the 13th International Workshop on Ontology Matching, OM@ISWC 2018, Monterey, CA, USA, 8 October 2018, pp. 210–215 (2018)
6. Doan, A., et al.: Ontology matching: a machine learning approach. In: Staab, S., Studer, R. (eds.) Handbook on Ontologies, pp. 385–404. Springer, Heidelberg (2004). https://doi.org/10.1007/978-3-540-24750-0_19
7. Ehrig, M., Euzenat, J.: Relaxed precision and recall for ontology matching. In: Integrating Ontologies 2005, Proceedings of the K-CAP 2005 Workshop on Integrating Ontologies, Banff, Canada, 2 October 2005
8. Euzenat, J.: Semantic precision and recall for ontology alignment evaluation. In: IJCAI 2007, Proceedings of the 20th International Joint Conference on Artificial Intelligence, Hyderabad, India, 6–12 January 2007, pp. 348–353 (2007)
9. Faria, D., et al.: Results of AML participation in OAEI 2018. In: Proceedings of the 13th International Workshop on Ontology Matching, OM@ISWC 2018, Monterey, CA, USA, 8 October 2018, pp. 125–131 (2018)
10. Galárraga, L.A., et al.: AMIE: association rule mining under incomplete evidence in ontological knowledge bases. In: 22nd International World Wide Web Conference, WWW 2013, Rio de Janeiro, Brazil, 13–17 May 2013, pp. 413–422 (2013)
11. Han, J., et al.: Mining frequent patterns without candidate generation: a frequent-pattern tree approach. Data Min. Knowl. Discov. **8**(1), 53–87 (2004)
12. Hertling, S., Paulheim, H.: DOME results for OAEI 2018. In: Proceedings of the 13th International Workshop on Ontology Matching, OM@ISWC 2018, Monterey, CA, USA, 8 October 2018, pp. 144–151 (2018)
13. Jiang, S., et al.: Ontology matching with knowledge rules. T. Large-Scale Data Knowl.-Cent. Syst. **28**, 75–95 (2016)
14. Jiménez-Ruiz, E., Grau, B.C., Cross, V.: LogMap family participation in the OAEI 2018. In: Proceedings of the 13th International Workshop on Ontology Matching, OM@ISWC 2018, Monterey, CA, USA, 8 October 2018, pp. 187–191 (2018)
15. Joshi, A.K., Hitzler, P., Dong, G.: Logical linked data compression. In: Cimiano, P., Corcho, O., Presutti, V., Hollink, L., Rudolph, S. (eds.) ESWC 2013. LNCS, vol. 7882, pp. 170–184. Springer, Heidelberg (2013). https://doi.org/10.1007/978-3-642-38288-8_12
16. Laadhar, A., et al.: OAEI 2018 results of POMap++. In: Proceedings of the 13th International Workshop on Ontology Matching, OM@ISWC 2018, Monterey, CA, USA, 8 October 2018, pp. 192–196 (2018)
17. Piatetsky-Shapiro, G.: Discovery, analysis, and presentation of strong rules. In: Knowledge Discovery in Databases, pp. 229–248. AAAI/MIT Press (1991)
18. Portisch, J., Paulheim, H.: ALOD2Vec matcher. In: Proceedings of the 13th International Workshop on Ontology Matching, OM@ISWC 2018, Monterey, CA, USA, 8 October 2018, pp. 132–137 (2018)
19. Ritze, D., et al.: A pattern-based ontology matching approach for detecting complex correspondences. In: Proceedings of the 4th International Workshop on Ontology Matching (OM-2009), Chantilly, USA, 25 October 2009
20. Ritze, D., et al.: Linguistic analysis for complex ontology matching. In: Proceedings of the 5th International Workshop on Ontology Matching (OM-2010), Shanghai, China, 7 November 2010
21. Shvaiko, P., Euzenat, J.: Ontology matching: state of the art and future challenges. IEEE Trans. Knowl. Data Eng. **25**(1), 158–176 (2013)

22. Stumme, G., Maedche, A.: FCA-MERGE: bottom-up merging of ontologies. In: Proceedings of the Seventeenth International Joint Conference on Artificial Intelligence, IJCAI 2001, Seattle, Washington, USA, 4–10 August 2001, pp. 225–234 (2001)

23. Thiéblin, É., et al.: CANARD complex matching system: results of the 2018 OAEI evaluation campaign. In: Proceedings of the 13th International Workshop on Ontology Matching, OM@ISWC 2018, Monterey, CA, USA, 8 October 2018, pp. 138–143 (2018)

24. Thiéblin, É., et al.: Complex matching based on competency questions for alignment: a first sketch. In: Proceedings of the 13th International Workshop on Ontology Matching, OM@ISWC 2018, Monterey, CA, USA, 8 October 2018, pp. 66–70 (2018)

25. Thiéblin, É., et al.: The first version of the OAEI complex alignment benchmark. In: Proceedings of the ISWC 2018 Posters & Demonstrations, Industry and Blue Sky Ideas Tracks at (ISWC 2018), Monterey, USA, 8th October–12th 2018 (2018)

26. Thiéblin, É., et al.: Survey on complex ontology alignment. Semant. Web J. (2019, to appear)

27. Zhou, L., Cheatham, M., Krisnadhi, A., Hitzler, P.: A complex alignment benchmark: geolink dataset. In: Vrandečić, D., et al. (eds.) ISWC 2018. LNCS, vol. 11137, pp. 273–288. Springer, Cham (2018). https://doi.org/10.1007/978-3-030-00668-6_17

Autonomous RDF Stream Processing
for IoT Edge Devices

Manh Nguyen-Duc[1]($\boxtimes$), Anh Le-Tuan[1,3], Jean-Paul Calbimonte[4],
Manfred Hauswirth[1,2], and Danh Le-Phuoc[1]

[1] Open Distributed Systems, TU Berlin, Berlin, Germany
manh.nguyenduc@campus.tu-berlin.de
[2] Fraunhofer Institute for Open Communication Systems, Berlin, Germany
[3] Insight Centre for Data Analytics, NUI Galway, Galway, Ireland
[4] University of Applied Sciences and Arts Western Switzerland HES-SO,
Sierre, Switzerland

Abstract. The wide adoption of increasingly cheap and computationally powerful single-board computers, has triggered the emergence of new
paradigms for collaborative data processing among IoT devices. Motivated by the billions of ARM chips having been shipped as IoT gateways
so far, our paper proposes a novel continuous federation approach that
uses RDF Stream Processing (RSP) engines as autonomous processing
agents. These agents can coordinate their resources to distribute processing pipelines by delegating partial workloads to their peers via subscribing continuous queries. Our empirical study in "cooperative sensing" scenarios with resourceful experiments on a cluster of Raspberry Pi
nodes shows that the scalability can be significantly improved by adding
more autonomous agents to a network of edge devices on demand. The
findings open several new interesting follow-up research challenges in
enabling semantic interoperability for the edge computing paradigm.

Keywords: Autonomous systems · Stream processing · Cooperative
sensing · Query federation

1 Introduction

Over the last few years, Semantic Web technologies have provided promising
solutions for achieving semantic interoperability in the IoT (Internet of Things)
domain. Ranging from ontologies for describing streams and devices [10,11],
to continuous query processors and stream reasoning agents [8], these efforts
constitute important milestones towards the integration of heterogeneous IoT
platforms and applications. While these different technologies enable the publication of streams using semantic technologies (e.g., RDF streams), and the
querying of streaming data over ontological representations, most of them tend
to centralise the processing, relegating interactions among IoT devices simply
to data transmission. This approach may be convenient in certain scenarios

© Springer Nature Switzerland AG 2020
X. Wang et al. (Eds.): JIST 2019, LNCS 12032, pp. 304–319, 2020.
https://doi.org/10.1007/978-3-030-41407-8_20

where the streams, typically time-annotated RDF data, are integrated following a top-down approach, for instance using cloud-based solutions for RDF Stream Processing (RSP). However, in the context of IoT, decentralised integration paradigms fit better with the distributed nature of autonomous deployments of smart devices [22]. Moreover, moving the computation closer to the edge networks, such as sensor nodes or IoT gateways, will not only create more chances to improve performance and to reduce network overhead/bottlenecks, but also to enable flexible and continuous integration of new IoT devices/data sources [19].

Thanks to recent developments in the design of embedded devices, e.g., ARM boards [23], single board computers are getting cheaper and smaller while increasing their computational power. For example, a Raspberry computer costs less than 40 EUR and its size is just roughly as big as the size of a credit card. Despite the size, they are powerful enough to run a fully-functioning Linux distribution that provides both *operational* and *deployment* advantages. On the one hand, they are both power efficient and cost-effective, while computationally powerful. On the other hand, their small sizes make it easier to embed or bundle them with other IoT devices (e.g., sensors and actuators) as a processing gateway interfacing with outer networks, called *edge devices*.

RDF Stream Processing (RSP) [21] extends the RDF data model, enabling to capture and to process heterogeneous streaming sensor sources under a unified data model. An RSP engine usually supports a continuous query language based on SPARQL, e.g. C-SPARQL [3] and CQELS-QL [15]. Hence, an edge device equipped with an RSP engine could play the role of an autonomous data processing gateway. Such an autonomous gateway can coordinate the actions with other peers connected to it to execute a data processing pipe in a collaborative fashion. However, to the best of our knowledge, there has not been any in-depth study on how such a decentralised processing paradigm would work with edge devices. In particular, an edge device has 10–100 times less resources than those of a PC counter-part which is originally the expected execution setting for an RSP engine. Hence, this raises two main questions: how feasible would it be to enable such a paradigm for edge devices, and how it would affect the performance and scalability. Putting our motivation in the context of 100 billion ARM chips that have been shipped so far [4], enabling computational and processing autonomy along with semantic interoperability will have a huge impact even for a small fraction of this number of devices (e.g. 0.1% would account for 100s millions devices).

To this end, this paper investigates how to realise this edge computing paradigm by extending an RSP engine (i.e., CQELS) as a continuous query federation engine to enable a decentralised computation architecture for edge devices. A prototype engine was implemented to empirically study the performance and scalability aspects on "cooperative sensing" scenarios. Our experiment results on a realistic setup with the biggest network of its kind in Sect. 4 show that our federation engine can considerably scale the processing throughput of a network of edge devices by adding more nodes on demand. We believe this is the largest experiment setup of its kind so far. The main contributions of the paper are summarised below:

1. We propose a novel federation mechanism based on autonomous RSP Engines and distributed continuous queries.
2. We present technical details on how to realise such a federation mechanism by integrating an RSP engine and an RDF Store for edge devices.
3. We carry out an empirical study on performance and scalability on "cooperative sensing" that leads to various quantitative findings and then opens up several interesting follow-up research challenges.

The paper is outlined as follows. The next section presents our approach on continuous federation based on autonomous RSP. Section 3 describes the implementation details of our federated RSP engine for edge devices. The setup and results of the experiments is reported in Sect. 4. We summarise related work in Sects. 5 and 6 concludes the paper.

2   Continuous Federation with Autonomous RSP

2.1   Preliminaries: RDF Stream Processing with CQELS-QL

CQELS-QL is a continuous query language for RSP that extends SPARQL 1.1 with sliding windows [15]. As an example, the CQELS-QL query below continuously provides the "updates for the locations of 10 weather stations which have reported the highest temperatures in the last 5 min". This query then is also used as Query Q3 in the experiments of Sect. 4.

```
1   SELECT ?sensor ?maxTemp ?lat ?lon
2   SELECT {
3       {SELECT ?sensor (MAX(?temp) as ?maxTemp)
4         STREAM ?streamURI [RANGE 5m ON sosa:resultTime] {
5             ?observation sosa:hasSimpleResult ?temp.
6             ?sensor rdf:type <TempSensor>; made:Observation ?observation.}
7           GROUP BY ?sensor}
8       ?streamURI prov:wasGeneratedBy ?sensor. ?sensor sosa:isHostedBy ?station.
9       ?station wgs84:Point ?loc. ?loc wgs84:lat ?lat; wgs84:lon ?lon.}
10  ORDER BY ?maxTemp
11  LIMIT 10
```

Listing 1. Query Q3 in CQELS-QL (prefixes are omitted)

In the original centralised setting, the above query can be subscribed to a CQELS engine installed in one *processing node*. Stream data in RDF formats (e.g JSON-LD or Turtle) can be provided to it from data acquisition nodes, called *streaming nodes*. These streaming nodes collect data from sensors of weather stations that can be geographically distributed in different locations. In practice, an edge device can host both a CQELS node and a streaming node, but we can assume they communicate via an internal process. As soon as the data is collected, the sensor data is pushed to the CQELS engine via a streaming protocol such as Websocket or MQTT. The incoming data continuously triggers the processing pipeline compiled from Query Q3. Consequently, the computing node that hosts this CQELS engine needs to have enough resources (bandwidth, CPU and memory) to deal with the workload regardless of how many stream nodes exist in the network. Hence, if the CQELS engine is only hosted on an edge device, the physical limits of its hardware quickly becomes a bottleneck as shown in Sect. 4. To create a more scalable processing system, we need to decentralise the processing pipelines of similar queries to a network of edge devices connected to these stream nodes. The following two sections describe our approach to enable this type of network.

2.2 Dynamic Subscription and Discovery for Autonomous RSP Engines

To enable a CQELS engine to work in a decentralised fashion, it would require the capability to operate as an autonomous agent which can collaborate with other peers to execute a distributed processing pipeline specified in CQELS-QL. An autonomous CQELS node can dynamically join a network of existing peers by subscribing itself to an existing node in the network, called a parent node, and it then notifies the parent node about the query service and streaming service it can provide to the network. These services can be semantically described by using vocabularies provided by VoCaLS [27]. For instance, VoCaLS allows describing the URIs of the streams and their related metadata (e.g. sensors that generated the streams), which are used in the query patterns of the query Q3. Hence, a subscription can be done by sending a RDF-based message via a REST API or Websocket channel. Listing 2 illustrates a snippet of a subscription message in RDF Turtle that is used in our experiments in Sect. 4.

```
1  <> a vocals:StreamDescriptor, vsd:CatalogService; dcat:dataset :NOAAWeather.
2  :NOAAWeather a vocals:RDFStream; prov:wasGeneratedBy :TemperatureSensor;
3  vocals:hasEndpoint :NOAAWeatherEndpoint; dct:title "Weather stream From Berlin".
4  :NOAAWeatherEndpoint a vocals:StreamEndpoint; dct:format frmt:JSON-LD;
5  dcat:accessURL "ws://192.168.178.5/noaa/berlin".
```

Listing 2. Example of subscription message in RDF

Based on the semantic description provided by the subscribed nodes, the parent node can carry the stream discovery patterns which use a variable in the stream pattern, as shown in line 4 of the query Q3. The variable *?streamURI* then can be matched in other metadata as shown in line 8. In this example, it is used to link with the sensors that generated this stream. Recursively, the subscription process can propagate the stream information upstream hierarchically, and vice versa, the discovery process can be recursively delegated to downstream nodes via sub-queries in CQELS-QL.

To this end, when an autonomous CQELS joins a network, it makes itself and its connected nodes discoverable and queryable to other nodes of the network. Moreover, each node can share its processing resources by executing a CQELS query on it. This will help us treat the query similar to query Q3 as a query to a sensor network whereby sensor nodes and network gateways collaborate as a single system to answer the query of this kind. Next, we will discuss how to federate such queries in "cooperative sensing" scenarios whereby such a network of autonomous CQELS processing nodes will coordinate each other to answer a CQELS-QL request in a decentralised fashion.

2.3   Continuous Query Federation Mechanism

With the support of the above subscription and discovery operations, a stream processing pipeline written in CQELS-QL can be deployed across several sites distributed in different locations: e.g., weather stations provide environmental sensory streams in various locations on earth. Each autonomous CQELS node gives access to data streams fed from streaming nodes connecting to it. Such stream nodes can ingest a range of sensors, such as air temperature, humidity and carbon monoxide. When the stream data arrives, this CQELS node can partially process the data at its processing site, and then forward the results as mappings or RDF stream elements to its parent node.

In this context, when a query is subscribed to the top-most node, called root node, it will divide this query to sub-query fragments and deploy at one or more sites via its subscribed nodes. A query fragment consists of one or more operators, and each fragment of the same query can be deployed on different processing nodes. Recursively, a sub-query delegated to a node can be federated to its subscribed nodes. All participant nodes of a processing pipeline can synchronise their processing timeline via a timing stream that is propagated from the root node. The execution process of sub-query fragments can use resources, i.e. CPU, memory, disk space and network bandwidth of participant nodes to process incoming RDF graphs or sets of solution mappings and generate output RDF graphs/sets of solution mappings. Output streams may be further processed by fragments of the same query, until results are sent to the query issuer at the root node. For example, the sub-query of the query Q3 in below Listing 3 can be sent down to the nodes closer to the streaming nodes, then the results will be recursively sent to upper nodes to carry out the partial top-k queries in lines 10 and 11 until it reaches the root node to carry out final computation steps to return the expected results.

```
1   SELECT ?sensor (MAX(?temp) as ?maxTemp)
2   WHERE{
3       STREAM ?streamURI [RANGE 5m ON sosa:resultTime]
4       { ?observation sosa:hasSimpleResult ?temp.
5           ?sensor rdf:type <TempSensor>; made:Observation ?observation.}
6       ?streamURI prov:wasGeneratedBy ?sensor.}
7   GROUP BY ?sensor
```

Listing 3. An example of the subquery of Q3

This federation process can be carried out dynamically thanks to the dynamic subscription and discovery capability above. Moreover, the processing topology of such as processing pipelines in our experiment scenarios of Sect. 4 can be dynamically configured by changing where and how participant nodes subscribed themselves to the processing networks. For example, we carried out five different federation topologies in Sect. 4. The biggest advantage of this federation mechanism is the ability to dynamically push some processing operations closer to the streaming nodes to alleviate the network and processing bottlenecks which often happen at edge devices. Moreover, this mechanism can significantly improve the processing throughput by adding more processing nodes on demand as shown in the experiments in Sect. 4.

3   Design and Implementation

To enable the cooperative federation of RSP engines on edge devices, we built a decentralised version of the CQELS engine, called Fed4Edge. Fed4Edge was implemented by extending the algorithms and Java codebase of the original open sourced version of CQELS [15]. Thanks to the platform-agnostic design of its execution framework [14], the core components are abstract enough to be seamlessly integrated with different RDF libraries in order to port to different hardware platforms. To tailor the RDF-based data processing operations on edge devices (e.g ARM CPU, Flash-storage and the likes), we integrated the core components of CQELS with the counterparts of RDF4Led [17], a RISC style RDF engine for lightweight edge devices. The Fed4Edge system will be open-sourced at https://github.com/cqels/Fed4Edge.

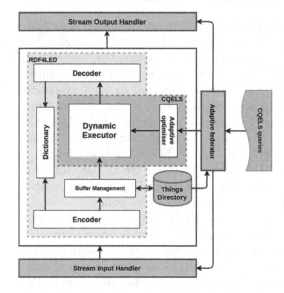

Fig. 1. Overview architecture of Fed4Edge

The architectural overview of the system is depicted in Fig. 1. The core components of CQELS and RDF4Led such as the *Dictionary, Encoder, Decoder, Dynamic Execution, Adaptive Query Optimiser, Buffer Manager* are reused in our Fed4Edge implementation. And the extension plugins of them such *Adaptive Federator, Thing Directory, Stream Input Handler* and *Stream Output Handler* are built to facilitate the federation mechanism proposed in Sect. 2. The technical details of these components are discussed next.

CQELS and RDF4Led share similar RDF data processing flows due to the fact that both systems apply the same RDF data encoding approach, which normalises RDF nodes into a fixed-size integer. By encoding the RDF nodes, most of the operators on RDF data can be executed on a smaller data structure rather than large variable-length strings. This approach is commonly used in many RDF data processors in order to reduce memory footprint, I/O time, and improve cache efficiency. The platform-agnostic design of CQELS allows the size of the encoded node to be tuned to adapt to a targeted platform without changing the implementation of other core components. Therefore, the Encoder, Decoder and Dictionary of RDF4Led can be easily integrated with CQELS for the RDF normalisation tasks. After receiving RDF data from RDF stream subscriptions via the Stream Input Handler, the data is encoded by the Encoder. The encoded RDF triples are then sent to the Buffer Manager for further processing. The Decoder waits for the output from the Dynamic Executor, transforms the encoded nodes back to a lexical representation before sending them to the Stream Output Handler. The Encoder and Decoder share the Dictionary for encoding and decoding. Instead of using a 64-bit integer for encoding node as in the original version of CQELS, the Dictionary of RDF4Led uses 32-bit integers, which entails less memory footprint for cached data. Therefore, backed by RDF4Led, Fed4Edge can process 30 million triples with only 80 MB of memory [17] on ARM computing architectures.

The Buffer Manager is responsible for managing the buffered data of windows and then feeding the data to the Dynamic Executor. Furthermore, the Buffer Manager also manages cached data for querying and writing the static data in the Thing Directory. Stream data is evicted from the buffer by the data invalidating policy defined by the window operators [12,15]. Meanwhile, the flash-aware updating algorithms of RDF4Led are reused in order to achieve fast updating for static data [17].

The Dynamic Executor employs a routing-based query execution algorithm that provides dynamic execution strategies in each node [12,13]. During the lifetime of a continuous query, the query plan can be changed by redirecting data flow on the routing network. The Adaptive Optimiser continuously adjusts the efficient query plan according to the data distribution in each execution step [15,17]. RDF4Led and CQELS employ a similar query execution paradigm. While CQELS uses routing-based query execution algorithms, RDF4Led executes SPARQL with a one-tuple-at-a-time policy. Therefore, the same cost model of the Adaptive Optimiser can be applied when calculating the best plan for a query that has static data patterns. The Buffer Manager treats the buffer for join results of the static patterns as a window, and depending on the available memory, it will apply the *fresh update* or *incremental update* policy.

The Adaptive Federator acts as the query rewriter, which adaptively divides the input query into subqueries. For the implementation used in our experiments in Sect. 4, the rewriter will push down operators as close to the streaming nodes as possible by following the predicate pushdown practice in common logical optimisation algorithms. The Thing Directory stores the metadata subscribed by the other Fed4Edge engines (cf. Section 2) in the default graph. Similar to [7], such metadata allows endpoint services of the Fed4Edge engines to be discovered via the Adaptive Federator. When the Adaptive Federator sends out a subquery, it notifies the Stream Input Handler to subscribe and listens to the results returning from the subquery. On the other hand, the Stream Output Handler sends out the subqueries to other nodes or sends back the results to the requester.

4   Evaluation and Analyses

4.1   Evaluation Setup

Datasets and Queries: To prepare the RDF Stream dataset for the evaluation, we used the SSN/SOSA ontology [10] to map sensor readings of the NCDC Integrated Surface Database (ISD) dataset[1] to RDF. The ISD dataset is one of

---

[1] https://www.ncdc.noaa.gov/.

the most prominent weather datasets, which contains weather observation data from 1901 to present, from nearly 20 K stations over the world. A weather reading of a station produces an observation that covers measurements for temperature, wind speed, wind gust, etc. depending on the types of sensors equipped for that station. Each observation needs approximately 87 RDF triples to map its values and attributes to the schema illustrated in Fig. 2. The data from different weather stations was split to multiple devices which acted as streaming nodes (i.e., the white nodes in Fig. 4). Each streaming node hosts a Websocket server which manages WebSocket stream endpoints. The data is read from CSV files in local storage, then mapped to the RDF data schema in Fig. 2 before streaming out.

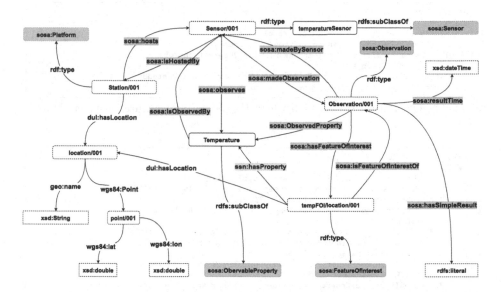

Fig. 2. RDF stream schema for NCDC weather data

We designed the following queries in order to show the advantages of cooperative federation for querying streaming data over a network of edge devices. Listings 4 and 5 respectively present the queries Q1 and Q2 that are used for measuring the improvement of the streaming throughput in simple federation cases. Q1 will return the updated temperature and the corresponding location and Q2 will answer the location where the latest temperature is higher than 30°. The subquery of Q1 and Q2 contains only triple patterns for querying streaming data. With these simple join patterns, the behaviour of the system is mostly influenced by the behaviour of the network. The filter at line 7 of Q2 will reduce the number of intermediate results sent from the lower node, and therefore, it can highlight the benefit of pushing down processing operators closer to the data sources.

For the queries that can show the collaborative behaviour of the participant edge nodes, we used the queries Q3 (as described in the example of Sect. 2) and query Q4 in Listing 6. The query Q3 has aggregation and top-k operators and the Q4 includes a complex join across windows.

```
1  SELECT ?temp ?lat ?lon ?resultTime
2  WHERE {
3      STREAM ?streamURI [LATEST ON ssn:resultTime] {
4          ?obs sosa:hasSimpleResult ?temp; sosa:resultTime ?resultTime.
5          ?sensor rdf:type iot:TempSensor; made:Observation ?obs.}
6      ?streamURI prov:wasGeneratedBy ?sensor. ?sensor sosa:isHostedBy ?station.
7      ?station wgs84:Point ?loc. ?loc wgs84:lat ?lat; wgs84:lon ?lon.}
```

Listing 4. Q1: Return updated temperature and the corresponding location.

```
1  SELECT ?lat ?lon
2  WHERE {
3      STREAM ?streamURI [LATEST ON ssn:resultTime]  {
4          ?obs sosa:hasSimpleResult ?temp; sosa:resultTime ?resultTime.
5          ?sensor rdf:type iot:TempSensor; made:Observation ?obs.
6          FILTER (?temp > 30) }
7      ?streamURI prov:wasGeneratedBy ?sensor. ?sensor sosa:isHostedBy ?station.
8      ?station wgs84:Point ?loc. ?loc wgs84:lat ?lat; wgs84:lon ?lon.}
```

Listing 5. Q2: Return the location where the latest temperature is higher than 30 degree.

```
1   SELECT ?city ?temp ?windspeed
2   WHERE{
3       STREAM ?streamURI [RANGE 5m ON ssn:resultTime] {
4           ?obs1 sosa:hasSimpleResult ?temp; sosa:resultTime ?resultTime.
5           ?obs1 sosa:hasFeatureOfInterest ?foi1.
6           ?foi1 ssn:hasProperty iot:Temperature. ?foi1 :hasLocation ?loc.
7           FILTER (?temp > 30) }
8       STREAM \textcolor{v}{?streamURI} [RANGE 5m ON ssn:resultTime] {
9           ?obs2 sosa:hasSimpleResult ?windspeed; sosa:resultTime ?resultTime.
10          ?obs2 sosa:hasFeatureOfInterest ?foi2.
11          ?foi2 ssn:hasProperty iot:WindSpeed. ?foi2 :hasLocation ?loc.
12          FILTER (?windspeed > 15) }
13      ?streamURI prov:wasGeneratedBy ?sensor. ?sensor sosa:isHostedBy ?station.
14      ?station wgs84:Point ?loc. ?loc geo:city ?city.}
```

Listing 6. Q4: Return the city where the temperature is higher than 30° and the wind speed is higher than 15 km in the last 5 min.

Hardware and Software: The hardware for the experiment is a cluster of 85 Raspberry Pi model B nodes, each one is equipped with: Quad Core 1.2 GHz Broadcom BCM2837 64bit CPU, 1 GB RAM and 100 Mbps Ethernet. All nodes are connected to five TP-LINK JetStream T2500-28TC switches. Each has 24 100 Mbps Ethernet ports 4 1000 Mbps uplinks shown in Fig. 3. As to the switching capacity, T2500-28TC has a non-blocking aggregated bandwidth of 12.8 Gbps. Four switches for connecting streaming nodes will be connected to the fifth one via the 1000 Mps links. This fifth switch is used to connected CQELS processing nodes. Every node uses Raspbian Jessie as the operating system and OpenJDK 1.7 for ARM as the JVM. We set 512 MB as the maximum heap size for the Fed4Edge engine.

4.2   Experiments

Fig. 3. The evaluation cluster of 85 Raspberry PI nodes

Baseline Calibration (Exp1): In this experiment, we calibrated the maximum processing capability of a processing node as the baseline for the following federation experiment. We increased the number of stream nodes to observe the bottleneck phenomena whereby increasing more streaming nodes decreases the processing throughput of the network. Each streaming node will stream out recorded data as its maximum capacity. We will use Query 1 and its two variants as the testing queries. These two variants are made by reducing four triple patterns into 1 and 2 patterns respectively. The throughput is measured by using a timing stream whereby each streaming nodes will send timing triples indicating when each of them starts and finishes sending their data. In each test we will equally split 500 k–1 M observations among streaming nodes and record how much time to process these observations to calculate the average throughput. Note that we separated the streaming and processing processes in different physical devices to avoid performance and bandwidth interference which might have an impact on our measurements.

Fan-out Federation (Exp2): To test the possibility of increasing the processing throughput by increasing more edge nodes as autonomous agents to the network, we carried out the tests on five topologies as shown in Fig. 4. The first topology (1-hop) in Fig. 4a was the configuration that gave the peak throughput in Exp1. Let k be the number of hops the data has travel to reach to the final destination, we will increase k to add more intermediate nodes to this topology to create new topologies. As a result, we can recursively add n nodes to the root node ($k = 2$, namely 2-hop) and then n nodes to the root node's children nodes ($k = 3$, namely 3-hop) whereby n is called the fanout factor (denoted as n-fanout). Then, we have $\sum_{i=0}^{k-1} n^i$ as the number of nodes of a topology with k hops and fanout factor n. We choose $n = 2$ and $n = 4$ (corresponding to the number of streaming nodes at the maximum throughput reported in *Exp1* below), thus, we have four new topologies with 3, 5, 7 and 21 processing nodes in Figs. 4b, c, d, and e. In each processing topology, the lowest processing nodes are connected with 4 streaming nodes. We will record the throughput and delay for processing three queries (Q1, Q2, Q3 and Q4) on these five topologies in a similar fashion to Exp1.

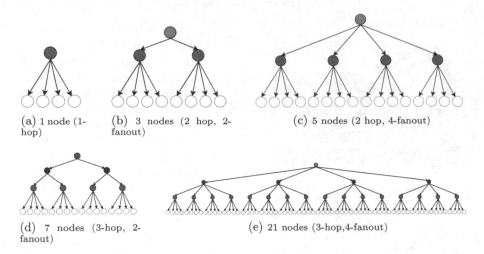

(a) 1 node (1-hop)

(b) 3 nodes (2 hop, 2-fanout)

(c) 5 nodes (2 hop, 4-fanout)

(d) 7 nodes (3-hop, 2-fanout)

(e) 21 nodes (3-hop, 4-fanout)

Fig. 4. Federation topologies

4.3   Results and Discussions

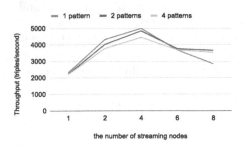

Fig. 5. Baseline calibration (Color figure online)

Figure 5 reports the results of the experiment Exp1. The maximum processing throughput for three variants of Query 1 on one single edge device is from 4200–5000 triples corresponding to 4 streaming nodes. It is interesting that increasing the number of streaming nodes more than 4 will gradually decrease the overall processing throughput. The results are consistent with different complexities of the variants of Query 1. We observed that the CPU usages were around 60–70% and the memory consumption is around 270–300 MB in all tests. Therefore, we can conclude that the bottleneck was caused by the bandwidth limitations. We also carried out a similar test with Q1 on a PC (Intel Core i7 i7-7700 K, 4 GHz, 1 GBb Ethernet and 16 GB RAM) as the root node which has more than 10 times of processing power, memory and network bandwidth than those of a Raspberry Pi model B. As we expected, the PC's maximum throughput is approximately 36k triples/second, around 8–10 times the one with a Raspberry Pi. Note that this PC costs more than the price of 40 Raspberry Pi nodes.

Figure 6a shows the results of throughput improvements via federating the processing workload on other intermediate nodes in four proposed topologies. The results show that adding more nodes will increase the processing throughput in general. Most queries have their processing throughput consistently boosted up as a considerable amount of processing load were done at the intermediate nodes. However, the increase is not consistently correlated with the total number of processing nodes. In fact, the topology with 5 nodes in Fig. 4d gives a slightly higher throughput than those of the topology with 7 nodes in Fig. 4c. This can be explained by the fact that both topologies have 4 processing nodes at the lowest levels (called leaf processing nodes, i.e, connecting to streaming nodes) but the data in the latter topology has to travel 1 more hop in comparison with the former. Due to our pushing down rewriting strategy presented in Sect. 3, these two upper blue nodes in Fig. 4c did not significantly contribute to the overall throughput but on the other hand cause more communication overhead.

Look closer to the reported figures, we see a high correlation between the number of leaf processing nodes, i.e. n^{k-1}, and the processing throughput in all topologies. This shows that our proposed approach is able to linearly scale a network of IoT devices by adding the more devices on demand. In particular, a network of 21 Raspberry Pi nodes can collaboratively process up to 74 k triples/seconds or equivalent to roughly 8500 sensor observations/second that are streamed from other 64 streaming nodes. Hence, the above 20 K weather stations across the globe of NCDC can be queried via such a network with the update rate 20–30 observations per minute which are much faster than the highest update rate currently supported by NCDC[2], i.e. ASOS 1-min data. Moreover, the processing capacity of this network is twice more than that of the above PC but it only costs roughly a half of the PC. Regarding the energy consumption, each Raspberry Pi only consumes around 2 W in comparison of 240 W of the above PC.

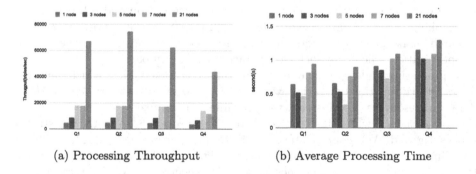

(a) Processing Throughput   (b) Average Processing Time

Fig. 6. Federation topologies

Figure 6b reports the average time for each observation to travel through a processing pipeline specified by each query on different topologies, i.e., average processing time. It shows that adding more intermediate nodes for query Q1 and Q2 can lower the average processing time as it can reduce queuing time at some nodes. That means communication time might be a dominant factor for the delay in these processing pipelines. In queries Q3 and Q4, we witness the

---

2 https://www.ncdc.noaa.gov/data-access/land-based-station-data.

consistent increase in processing time wrt. the number of hops which explains the nature of query Q3 and Q4 that needs more coordination among nodes. However, it is interesting that increasing 1 hop in organising a network topology just adds 10–15% delay while the maximum throughput gain is linear to n^{k-1}.

4.4 Follow-Up Challenges

We observed the CPU, memory consumption and bandwidth in our experiments. It is interesting that all tests used 60–70% of CPU (across 4 cores), 25–30% of physical memory and 20–40% of Ethernet bandwidth (i.e., 100 Mbps). Our reported performance figures show that edge devices have enough resources to enable semantic interoperability for the edge computing paradigm. From our analyses of hardware and software libraries, the most potential suspects for the processing bottleneck are related to the communication among the nodes. Hence, there is a lot of room to make our approach much more efficient and scalable. In this context, to help 100 billions and more edge devices to reach their full potential, we outline some interesting research challenges below.

The first challenge is how to address the multiple optimisation problems that such a federated processing pipeline entails. The first one is how to optimise an RSP engine for edge devices which have distinctive processing and I/O behaviours from those of PC/workstations due to their own design philosophies. The second challenge is about how to find optimal operator placements on very dynamic execution settings. The subsequent challenge is how to define cost models which are no longer limited to processing time/throughput, but need to cover several cost metrics such as bandwidth, power consumption and robustness.

Looking beyond database-oriented optimisation goals, another relevant research challenge would be how to model socioeconomic aspects as the control or optimisation scheme for such a cooperative system. In particular, autonomous RSP processing nodes can be operated by different stakeholders which have different utility functions dictating when and how to join a network and to share data and resources. To this end, the coordination strategies become related to the game theory which inspired some relevant proposals in both the stream processing and Web communities. For instance, [1] proposed a contract-based coordination scheme based on mechanism design, a field in economics and game theory that designs economic mechanisms or incentives toward desired objectives. Similarly, [9] also proposed to use mechanism design for establishing an incentive-driven coordination strategy among SPARQL endpoints. Inspired by this line of work, we also proposed an architecture for in-cooperating blockchain with RDF4Led [18] to pave the way to in-cooperate with such incentive and contract-based coordination strategies.

Regarding cooperation and negotiation among RSP autonomous agents, a potential research challenge is the study and exploration of protocols and strategies that follow the multi-agent system paradigm. Although early works on the topic [26] point at potential opportunities in this area, several aspects have not been studied yet. These include the usage of individual contextual knowledge for local decision making (potentially through reasoning) and for a resource-optimised distribution of tasks among a set of competing/associated nodes. The dynamics of these federated processing networks would need to adapt to changing conditions of load, membership, throughput, and other criteria, with emerging behaviour patterns on the sensing and processing nodes.

5   Related Work

Semantic interoperability in the IoT domain has gained considerable attention both in the academic and industrial spheres. Beyond syntactic standards such as SensorML, semantically rich ontologies such as SSN-O/SOSA [10] have shown a significant impact in different IoT projects and solutions, such as OpenIoT [24], SymbIoTe [25], or BigIoT [5]. Other related vocabularies, such as the Things-Description ontology, have also recently gained support from different IoT vendors, aiming at consolidating it as a backbone representation model for generic IoT devices and services. Regarding the representation of data streams themselves, the VoCaLS vocabulary [27] has been designed as a means for the publication, consumption, and shared processing of streams. Although these ontology resources provide different and complementary ways to represent IoT and streaming data, they require the necessary infrastructure and software components (or agents) able to *interpret* the stream metadata, and apply coordination/cooperation mechanisms for federated/decentralised processing, as shown in this paper.

The processing of continuous streaming data, structured according to Semantic Web standards has been studied in the last decade, generally within the fields of RDF Stream processing (RSP) and Stream Reasoning [8]. A number of RSP engines have been developed in this period, focusing on different aspects including incremental reasoning, continuous querying, complex event processing, among others [3,6,15,20]. However, most of these RDF stream processors lack the capability of interconnecting with each other, or to establish cooperation patterns among them. The coordination among RDF stream processing nodes is sometimes delegated to a generic cloud-based stream processing platform such as Apache Storm (e.g [16]) or Apache Spark (e.g [20]). In contrast, in this paper, we investigate a more decentralised environment whereby participant nodes can be distributed across different organisations. Moreover, the hardware capabilities of such processing nodes are different from the cloud-based setting, i.e. resource-constraint edge devices.

Regarding the distributed processing and integration of RSP engines on a truly decentralised architecture, different aspects and building blocks have surfaced in the latest years. Initial attempts to provide HTTP-based service interfaces for streaming data were explored in [3]. Other contributions in this line are the RSP Service Interface[3], and the SLD Revolution framework [2]. These propose the establishment of distributed workflows of RSP engines, using lazy-transformation techniques for optimised interactions among the engines. Further

---

[3] http://streamreasoning.org/resources/rsp-services.

conceptualisations of RDF stream processing over decentralised entities have been presented in works such as WeSP [7][4], which advocates for a community-driven definition of stream vocabularies and interoperable interfaces. Cooperation strategies among RDF stream processors, or *stream reasoning agents* is discussed in [26], introducing potential challenges and opportunities for federated processing through negotiation established across multi-agent systems.

6   Conclusion

This paper presented a continuous query federation approach that uses RSP engines as autonomous processing agents. The approach enables the coordination of edge devices' resources to process query processing pipelines by cooperatively delegating partial workload to their peer agents. We implemented our approach as an open source engine, Fed4Edge, to conduct an empirical study in "cooperative sensing" scenarios. The resourceful experiments of the study show that the scalablity can be significantly improved by adding more edge devices to a network of processing nodes on demand. This opens several interesting follow-up research challenges in enabling semantic interoperability for the edge computing paradigm. Our next step will be investigating on how to adaptively optimise the distributed processing pipeline of Fed4Edge. Another interesting step is studying how the communication will effect its performance and scalability on an Internet-scale setting whereby the processing nodes are distributed across different networks and countries.

Acknowledgements. This work was funded in part by the German Ministry for Education and Research as BBDC 2 - Berlin Big Data Center Phase 2 (ref. 01IS18025A), Irish Research Council under Grant Number GOIPG/2014/917, HES-SO RCSO ISNet grant 87057 (PROFILES), and Marie Skodowska-Curie Programme H2020-MSCA-IF-2014 (SMARTER project) under Grant No. 661180.

References

1. Balazinska, M., Balakrishnan, H., Stonebraker, M.: Contract-based load management in federated distributed systems. In: NSDI 2004 (2004)
2. Balduini, M., Della Valle, E., Tommasini, R.: SLD revolution: a cheaper, faster yet more accurate streaming linked data framework. In: ESWC (2017)
3. Barbieri, D.F., Braga, D., Ceri, S., Grossniklaus, M.: An execution environment for C-SPARQL queries. In: EDBT 2010 (2010)
4. Enabling mass iot connectivity as arm partners ship 100 billion chips. http://tiny.cc/uiefcz
5. Bröring, S., et al.: The big iot api-semantically enabling iot interoperability. IEEE Pervasive Comput. **17**(4), 41–51 (2018)
6. Calbimonte, J.-P., Corcho, O., Gray, A.J.G.: Enabling ontology-based access to streaming data sources. In: Patel-Schneider, P.F., et al. (eds.) ISWC 2010. LNCS, vol. 6496, pp. 96–111. Springer, Heidelberg (2010). https://doi.org/10.1007/978-3-642-17746-0_7

---

[4] http://w3id.org/wesp/web-data-streams.

7. Dell'Aglio, D., Della Valle, E., van Harmelen, F., Bernstein, A.: Stream reasoning: a survey and outlook. Data Sci. **1**(1), 59–83 (2017)
8. Dell'Aglio, D., Phuoc, D.L., Le-Tuan, A., Ali, M.I., Calbimonte, J.-P.: On a web of data streams. In: DeSemWeb@ISWC (2017)
9. Grubenmann, T., Bernstein, A., Moor, D., Seuken, S.: Financing the web of data with delayed-answer auctions. In: WWW 2018 (2018)
10. Haller, A., et al.: The modular SSN ontology: a joint W3C and OGC standard specifying the semantics of sensors, observations, sampling, and actuation. Semant. Web **10**(1), 9–32 (2019)
11. Kaebisch, S., Kamiya, T., McCool, M., Charpenay, V.: Web of things (wot) thing description. W3C, W3C Candidate Recommendation (2019)
12. Le-Phuoc, D.: Operator-aware approach for boosting performance in RDF stream processing. J. Web Semant. **42**, 38–54 (2017)
13. Le-Phuoc, D.: Adaptive optimisation for continuous multi-way joins over rdf streams. In: Companion Proceedings of the the Web Conference 2018, WWW 2018, pp. 1857–1865 (2018)
14. Le-Phuoc, D., Dao-Tran, M., Le Van, C., Le Tuan, A., Manh Nguyen Duc, T.T.N., Hauswirth, M.: Platform-agnostic execution framework towards rdf stream processing. In: RDF Stream Processing Workshop at ESWC2015 (2015)
15. Le-Phuoc, D., Dao-Tran, M., Parreira, J.X., Hauswirth, M.: A native and adaptive approach for unified processing of linked streams and linked data. In: ISWC 2011, pp. 370–388 (2011)
16. Le-Phuoc, D., Quoc, H.N.M., Van, C.L., Hauswirth, M.: Elastic and scalable processing of linked stream data in the cloud. In: ISWC, pp. 280–297 (2013)
17. Le-Tuan, A., Hayes, C., Wylot, M., Le-Phuoc, D.: Rdf4led: An rdf engine for lightweight edge devices. In: IOT 2018 (2018)
18. Le-Tuan, A., Hingu, D., Hauswirth, M., Le-Phuoc, D.: Incorporating blockchain into rdf store at the lightweight edge devices. In: Semantic 2019 (2019)
19. Munir, A., Kansakar, P., Khan, S.U.: IFCIoT: integrated fog cloud iot a novel architectural paradigm for the future internet of things. IEEE Consum. Electron. Mag. **6**(3), 74–82 (2017)
20. Ren, X., Curé, O.: Strider: a hybrid adaptive distributed RDF stream processing engine. In: d'Amato, C., et al. (eds.) ISWC 2017. LNCS, vol. 10587, pp. 559–576. Springer, Cham (2017). https://doi.org/10.1007/978-3-319-68288-4_33
21. Sakr, S., Wylot, M., Mutharaju, R., Le Phuoc, D., Fundulaki, I.: Processing of RDF Stream Data. Springer, Cham (2018)
22. Satyanarayanan, M.: The emergence of edge computing. Computer **50**(1), 30–39 (2017)
23. Smith, B.: Arm and intel battle over the mobile chip's future. Computer **41**(5), 15–18 (2008)
24. Soldatos, J., et al.: Openiot: open source internet-of-things in the cloud. In: Interoperability and open-source solutions for the internet of things. Springer (2015)
25. Soursos, S., Žarko, I.P., Zwickl, P., Gojmerac, I., Bianchi, G., Carrozzo, G.: Towards the cross-domain interoperability of iot platforms. In: 2016 European Conference on Networks and Communications (EuCNC), pp. 398–402. IEEE (2016)
26. Tommasini, R., Calvaresi, D., Calbimonte, J.-P.: Stream reasoning agents: blue sky ideas track. In: AAMAS, pp. 1664–1680 (2019)
27. Tommasini, R., et al.: Vocals: vocabulary and catalog of linked streams. In: International Semantic Web Conference (2018)

Certain Answers to a SPARQL Query
over a Knowledge Base

Julien Corman and Guohui Xiao[(⊠)]

Free University of Bozen-Bolzano, Bolzano, Italy
xiao@inf.unibz.it

Abstract. Ontology-Mediated Query Answering (OMQA) is a well-established framework to answer queries over an RDFS or OWL Knowledge Base (KB). OMQA was originally designed for unions of conjunctive queries (UCQs), and based on *certain answers*. More recently, OMQA has been extended to SPARQL queries, but to our knowledge, none of the efforts made in this direction (either in the literature, or the so-called SPARQL *entailment regimes*) is able to capture both certain answers for UCQs and the standard interpretation of SPARQL over a plain graph. We formalize these as requirements to be met by any semantics aiming at conciliating certain answers and SPARQL answers, and define three additional requirements, which generalize to KBs some basic properties of SPARQL answers. Then we show that a semantics can be defined that satisfies all requirements for SPARQL queries with **SELECT**, **UNION**, and **OPTIONAL**, and for DLs with the canonical model property. We also investigate combined complexity for query answering under such a semantics over *DL-Lite$_\mathcal{R}$* KBs. In particular, we show for different fragments of SPARQL that known upper-bounds for query answering over a plain graph are matched.

1 Introduction

SPARQL is an expressive SQL-like query language designed for Semantic Web data, exposed as RDF graphs. Recently, SPARQL has been extended with so-called *entailment regimes*, which specify different semantics to query an RDFS or OWL *Knowledge Base* (KB), i.e. data enriched with a background theory. This allows retrieving answers to a query not only over the facts explicitly stated in the KB, but more generally over what can be inferred from the KB.

The SPARQL entailment regimes are in turn largely influenced by theoretical work on *Ontology Mediated Query Answering* (OMQA), notably in the field of *Description Logics* (DLs). However, OMQA was initially developed for *unions of conjunctive queries* (UCQs), which have a limited expressivity when compared to SPARQL. It turns out that conciliating the standard (compositional) semantics of SPARQL on the one hand, and the semantics used for OMQA on the other hand, called *certain answers*, is non-trivial.

As an illustration, Example 1 provides a simple KB and SPARQL query. The dataset (a.k.a *ABox*) $\mathcal{A}$ states that `Alice` is a driver, whereas the background theory

© Springer Nature Switzerland AG 2020
X. Wang et al. (Eds.): JIST 2019, LNCS 12032, pp. 320–335, 2020.
https://doi.org/10.1007/978-3-030-41407-8_21

(a.k.a. *TBox*) $\mathcal{T}$ states that a driver must have a license (for conciseness, we use DLs for the TBox, rather than some concrete syntax of OWL). Finally, the SPARQL query q retrieves all individuals that have a license.

Example 1

$\mathcal{A} = \{\texttt{Driver(Alice)}\}$
$\mathcal{T} = \{\texttt{Driver} \sqsubseteq \exists\texttt{hasLicense}\}$
$q = \texttt{SELECT ?x WHERE \{ ?x hasLicense ?y \}}$

Intuitively, one expects `Alice` to be retrieved as an answer to q. And it would indeed be the case under certain answer semantics, if one considers the natural translation of this query into a UCQ. On the other hand, under the standard semantics of SPARQL 1.1 [8], this query has no answer. This is expected, since the fact that `Alice` has a driving license is not present in the ABox. More surprisingly though, under all SPARQL entailment regimes [6], this query also has no answer.

This mismatch between certain answers and entailment regimes has already been discussed in depth in [1], where the interpretation of the OPTIONAL operator of SPARQL is identified as a challenge, when trying to define a suitable semantics for SPARQL that complies with certain answers for UCQs. A concrete proposal is also made in [1] in this direction. Unfortunately, this semantics does not comply with the standard semantics of SPARQL when the TBox is empty. This means that a same query over a plain RDF graph may yield different answers, depending on whether it is evaluated under this semantics, or under the one defined in the SPARQL 1.1 specification [8].

We propose in this article to investigate whether and how this dilemma can be solved, for the so-called *set semantics* of SPARQL and certain answers. To this end, we first formulate in Sect. 4 some *requirements* to be met by any reasonable semantics meant to conciliate certain answers and standard SPARQL answers. Then in Sect. 5, we use these requirements to review different semantics. We also show that all requirements can be satisfied, for the fragment of SPARQL with SELECT, UNION and OPTIONAL, and for KBs that admit a unique *canonical model*. Finally, in Sect. 6, we provide combined complexity results for query answering under this semantics, over KBs in *DL-Lite$_\mathcal{R}$*, one of the most popular DLs tailored for query answering, which correspond to the OWL 2 QL standard. We show in particular that upper bounds for this problem match results already known to hold for SPARQL over plain graphs, which means that under this semantics, and as far as worst-case complexity is concerned, the presence of a TBox does not introduce a computational overhead. Before this, Sect. 2 introduces preliminary notions, and Sect. 3 reviews existing semantics for SPARQL over a KB. Proofs can be found in the extended version of this paper (https://arxiv.org/abs/1911.02668).

2   Preliminaries

We assume countably infinite and mutually disjoint sets N_I, N_C, N_R, and N_V of *individuals* (constants), *concept names* (unary predicates), *role names* (binary predicates), and variables respectively. We also assume a countably infinite universe U, such that $N_I \subseteq U$. For clarity, we abstract away from concrete domains (as well as RDF term types), since these are irrelevant to the content of this paper. We also assume that N_I, N_C and N_R do not contain any reserved term from the RDF/RDFS/OWL vocabularies (such as `rdfs:subClassOf`, `owl:disjointWith`, etc.)

2.1 RDF and SPARQL

An (RDF) *triple* is an element of $(N_I \times \{\texttt{rdf:type}\} \times N_C) \cup (N_I \times N_R \times N_I)$. An RDF graph $\mathcal{A}$ is a set of triples. For the concrete syntax of SPARQL, we refer to the specification [8]. Following [1], we focus on SPARQL queries whose triple patterns are either in $(N_V \cup N_I) \times \{\texttt{rdf:type}\} \times N_C$, or in $(N_V \cup N_I) \times N_R \times (N_V \cup N_I)$. For readability, we represent triples and triple patterns as atoms in prefix notation, i.e. we use $A(t)$ rather than $(t, \texttt{rdf:type}, A)$ and for $r \in N_R$, we use $r(t_1, t_2)$ rather than (t_1, r, t_2). If q is a SPARQL query, we use vars(q) to denote the set of variables projected by q.

We adopt (roughly) the abstract syntax provided in [14] for the fragment of SPARQL with the **SELECT**, **UNION** and **OPTIONAL** operators, using the following grammar, where t is a SPARQL triple pattern, and $X \subseteq N_V$:

$$q \quad ::= \quad t \mid \text{SELECT}_X q \mid q \text{ UNION } q \mid q \text{ JOIN } q \mid q \text{ OPT } q$$

In addition, if $q = \text{SELECT}_X q'$, then $X \subseteq \text{vars}(q')$ must hold. In order to refer to fragments of this language, we use the letters S, U, J and O (in this order), for SELECT, UNION, JOIN, and OPT respectively. E.g. "SUJO" stands for the full language, "UJ" for the fragment with UNION and JOIN only, etc.

If ω is a function, we use dom(ω) (resp. range(ω)) to designate its domain (resp. range). Two functions ω_1 and ω_2 are *compatible*, denoted with $\omega_1 \sim \omega_2$, iff $\omega_1(x) = \omega_2(x)$ for each $x \in \text{dom}(\omega_1) \cap \text{dom}(\omega_2)$. If ω_1 and ω_2 are compatible, then $\omega_1 \cup \omega_2$ is the only function with domain $\text{dom}(\omega_1) \cup \text{dom}(\omega_2)$ that is compatible with ω_1 and ω_2. We say that a function ω_2 *extends* a function ω_1, noted $\omega_1 \preceq \omega_2$, iff $\text{dom}(\omega_1) \subseteq \text{dom}(\omega_2)$ and $\omega_1 \sim \omega_2$. Finally, we use $\omega|_X$ (resp. $\omega\|_X$) to designate the restriction of function ω to domain (resp. co-domain) X, i.e. $\omega|_X$ is the only function compatible with ω that verifies $\text{dom}(\omega|_X) = \text{dom}(\omega) \cap X$, and $\omega\|_X$ is the only function compatible with ω that verifies $\text{dom}(\omega\|_X) = \{v \in \text{dom}(\omega) \mid \omega(v) \in X\}$.

A *solution mapping* is a function from a finite subset of N_V to U. If Ω_1 and Ω_2 are sets of solutions mappings and $X \subseteq V$, then:

$$\Omega_1 \bowtie \Omega_2 = \{\omega_1 \cup \omega_2 \mid (\omega_1, \omega_2) \in \Omega_1 \times \Omega_2 \text{ and } \omega_1 \sim \omega_2\}$$
$$\Omega_1 \setminus \Omega_2 = \{\omega_1 \mid \omega_1 \in \Omega_1 \text{ and } \omega_1 \not\sim \omega_2 \text{ for all } \omega_2 \in \Omega_2\}$$
$$\pi_X \Omega = \{\omega|_X \mid \omega \in \Omega\}$$

If q is a SPARQL query and ω a solution mapping s.t. $\text{vars}(q) \subseteq \text{dom}(\omega)$, we use $\omega(q)$ to designate the query identical to q, but where each occurrence of variable x in a triple pattern is replaced by $\omega(x)$.

We now reproduce the inductive definition of answers to a SPARQL query q over a graph $\mathcal{A}$, denoted sparqlAns($q, \mathcal{A}$), provided in [14] for the SUJO fragment (and for set semantics).

Definition 1 (SPARQL answers over a plain graph [14])

If q is a triple pattern, then $\text{sparqlAns}(q, \mathcal{A}) = \{\omega \mid \text{dom}(\omega) = \text{vars}(q) \text{ and } \omega(q) \in \mathcal{A}\}$
$\text{sparqlAns}(q_1 \text{ UNION } q_2, \mathcal{A}) = \text{sparqlAns}(q_1, \mathcal{A}) \cup \text{sparqlAns}(q_2, \mathcal{A})$
$\text{sparqlAns}(q_1 \text{ JOIN } q_2, \mathcal{A}) \quad = \text{sparqlAns}(q_1, \mathcal{A}) \bowtie \text{sparqlAns}(q_2, \mathcal{A})$
$\text{sparqlAns}(q_1 \text{ OPT } q_2, \mathcal{A}) \quad = (\text{sparqlAns}(q_1, \mathcal{A}) \bowtie \text{sparqlAns}(q_2, \mathcal{A})) \cup$
$\qquad\qquad\qquad\qquad\qquad (\text{sparqlAns}(q_1, \mathcal{A}) \setminus \text{sparqlAns}(q_2, \mathcal{A}))$
$\text{sparqlAns}(\text{SELECT}_X q, \mathcal{A}) = \pi_X \text{sparqlAns}(q, \mathcal{A})$

2.2   Description Logic KB, UCQs and Certain Answers

As is conventional in the Description Logics (DL) literature, we represent a KB $\mathcal{K}$ as a pair $\mathcal{K} = \langle \mathcal{T}, \mathcal{A} \rangle$, where $\mathcal{A}$ is called the *ABox* of $\mathcal{K}$, which contains assertions about individuals, and $\mathcal{T}$ is called the *TBox* of $\mathcal{K}$, which contains more abstract knowledge. An ABox is a finite set of atoms of the form $A(c)$ or $r(c_1, c_2)$, where $A \in \mathsf{N_C}$, $r \in \mathsf{N_R}$ and $c, c_1, c_2 \in \mathsf{N_I}$. A TBox is a finite set of logical *axioms*, whose form depends on the particular DL. For a KB $\mathcal{K} = \langle \mathcal{T}, \mathcal{A} \rangle$, the *active domain* of $\mathcal{K}$, denoted with $\mathsf{aDom}(\mathcal{K})$, is the set of elements of $\mathsf{N_I}$ that appear (syntactically) in $\mathcal{T}$ or $\mathcal{A}$.

The semantics of DL KBs is defined in terms of (first-order) *interpretations*. We adopt in this article the *standard name assumption*: an interpretation is a structure $\mathcal{I} = \langle \Delta^{\mathcal{I}}, \cdot^{\mathcal{I}} \rangle$, where the *domain* $\Delta^{\mathcal{I}}$ of $\mathcal{I}$ is a non-empty subset of U, and the *interpretation function* $\cdot^{\mathcal{I}}$ of $\mathcal{I}$ maps each $c \in \mathsf{N_I}$ to itself, and each $A \in \mathsf{N_C}$ (resp. $r \in \mathsf{N_R}$) to a unary (resp. binary) relation $A^{\mathcal{I}}$ (resp. $r^{\mathcal{I}}$) over $\Delta^{\mathcal{I}}$. An interpretation $\mathcal{I}$ is a *model* of a KB $\mathcal{K} = \langle \mathcal{T}, \mathcal{A} \rangle$ if it satisfies every assertion in $\mathcal{A}$ and axiom in $\mathcal{T}$. For the formal definition of "satisfies", we refer to [4].

If $\mathcal{K}$ is a KB, we use $\mathsf{mod}(\mathcal{K})$ to denote the set of models of $\mathcal{K}$. We focus on *satisfiable* KBs only, i.e. KBs that admit at least one model, since any formula can be trivially derived from an unsatisfiable KB. We also omit this precision for readability. So "any KB" below is a shortcut for "any satisfiable KB".

For a DL KB $\mathcal{K}$, an interpretation $\mathcal{I}_c \in \mathsf{mod}(\mathcal{K})$ is a *canonical model* of $\mathcal{K}$ if $\mathcal{I}_c$ can be homomorphically mapped to any $\mathcal{I} \in \mathsf{mod}(\mathcal{K})$. We say that a DL $\mathcal{L}$ has the *canonical model property* if every KB in $\mathcal{L}$ has a *unique* canonical model up to isomorphism. This is a key property of DLs tailored for query answering, and many DLs, e.g. *DL-Lite$_{\mathcal{R}}$*, $\mathcal{EL}$ or Horn-$\mathcal{SHIQ}$, have this property.

An interpretation (or an ABox) can also be viewed as a (possibly infinite) RDF graph, with triples $\{A(d) \mid d \in A^{\mathcal{I}}, A \in \mathsf{N_C}\} \cup \{r(d_1, d_2) \mid (d_1, d_2) \in r^{\mathcal{I}}, r \in \mathsf{N_R}\}$. This is a slight abuse (the RDF standard does not admit infinite graphs), but we will nonetheless use this convention throughout the article, in order to simplify notation.

A *conjunctive query* (CQ) h is an expression of the form:

$$h(\mathbf{x}) \leftarrow p_1(\mathbf{x}_1), \ldots, p_m(\mathbf{x}_m)$$

where h, p_i are predicates and $\mathbf{x}, \mathbf{x}_i$ are tuple over $\mathsf{N_V}$. Abusing notation, we may use $\mathbf{x}$ (resp. $\mathbf{x}_i$) below to designate the elements of $\mathbf{x}$ (resp. $\mathbf{x}_i$) viewed as a set. An additional syntactic requirement on a CQ is that $\mathbf{x} \subseteq \mathbf{x}_1 \cup .. \cup \mathbf{x}_m$. The variables in $\mathbf{x}$ are called *distinguished*, and we use $\mathsf{vars}(h)$ to designate the distinguished variables of CQ h. We focus in this article on CQs where each p_i is unary or binary, i.e. $p_i \in \mathsf{N_C} \cup \mathsf{N_R}$. A *match* for h in an interpretation $\mathcal{I}$ is a total function ρ from $\mathbf{x}_1 \cup \ldots \cup \mathbf{x}_m$ to $\Delta^{\mathcal{I}}$ such that $\rho(\mathbf{x}_i) \in (p_i)^{\mathcal{I}}$ for $i \in \{1..m\}$. A mapping ω is an *answer* to h over $\mathcal{I}$ iff there is a match ρ for h in $\mathcal{I}$ s.t. $\omega = \rho|_{\mathsf{vars}(h)}$.

A *union of conjunctive queries* (UCQ) is a set $q = \{h_1, \ldots, h_n\}$ of CQs sharing the same distinguished variables, and ω is an *answer* to q over $\mathcal{I}$ iff ω is an answer to some h_i over $\mathcal{I}$. Finally, ω is a *certain answer* to q over a KB $\mathcal{K}$ iff $\mathsf{range}(\omega) \subseteq \mathsf{aDom}(\mathcal{K})$ and ω is an answer to q over each $\mathcal{I} \in \mathsf{mod}(\mathcal{K})$. We use $\mathsf{certAns}(q, \mathcal{K})$ to designate the set of certain answers to q over $\mathcal{K}$.

CQs and UCQs have a straightforward representation as SPARQL queries. The CQ $h(\mathbf{x}) \leftarrow p_1(\mathbf{x}_1), \ldots, p_m(\mathbf{x}_m)$ in SPARQL syntax is written:

$$\mathrm{SELECT}_{\mathbf{x}} \ (p_1(\mathbf{x}_1) \ \mathrm{JOIN} \ .. \ \mathrm{JOIN} \ p_m(\mathbf{x}_m))$$

And a UCQ in SPARQL syntax is of the form:

$$h_1 \text{ UNION } .. \text{ UNION } h_n$$

where each h_i is a CQ in SPARQL syntax, and $\text{vars}(h_i) = \text{vars}(h_j)$ for $i, j \in \{1..n\}$.

3   Querying a DL KB with SPARQL: Existing Semantics

In this section, we review existing semantics for SPARQL over a DL KB. We start by briefly recalling some features of the W3C specification for the SPARQL 1.1 entailment regimes [6]. This specification defines different ways to take into account the semantics of RDF, RDFS or OWL, in order to infer additional answers to a SPARQL query. We ignore the aspects pertaining to querying blank nodes and concept/role names, which fall out of the scope of this paper, and focus on the entailment regimes parameterized by an OWL profile, i.e. a DL $\mathcal{L}$. In short, the $\mathcal{L}$-entailment regime modifies the evaluation of a SPARQL query q over an $\mathcal{L}$-KB $\mathcal{K} = \langle \mathcal{T}, \mathcal{A} \rangle$ as follows:

1. Triple patterns are not evaluated over the ABox $\mathcal{A}$, but instead over the so-called *entailed graph*, which consists of all ABox assertions entailed by $\mathcal{K}$. This includes assertions of the form $C(a)$, where C is a complex concept expression allowed in $\mathcal{L}$. The semantics of other SPARQL operators is preserved.
2. The SPARQL query can use $\mathcal{L}$-concepts in triple pattern, e.g. ∃hasLicense(x).

Consider again Example 1 under the OWL 2 QL entailment regime for instance, which corresponds (roughly) to the DL *DL-Lite$_\mathcal{R}$*. In this example, the query $\exists\text{hasLicense}(x)$ has $\{x \mapsto \text{Alice}\}$ as unique answer: since the entailed graph contains all ABox assertions entailed by $\mathcal{K}$, it contains the assertion $\exists\text{hasLicense(Alice)}$ (again, we use the DL syntax rather than OWL, for readability).

So the expressivity of the $\mathcal{L}$-entailment regime is limited by the concepts that can be expressed in $\mathcal{L}$. This is why [10] proposed to extend the semantics of the OWL 2 QL profile, retrieving instances of concepts that cannot be expressed in *DL-Lite$_\mathcal{R}$* (e.g. concepts of the form $\exists r_1.\exists r_2$). Still, under this semantics as well as all entailment regimes defined in the specification, the query $\text{SELECT}_{\{x\}}\text{hasLicense}(x, y)$ has no answer over the KB of Example 1, because the entailed graph does not contain any assertion of the form $\text{hasLicense(Alice}, e)$.

This point was discussed in depth in [1], for the SUJO fragment, and based on remarks made earlier in [2]. The current paper essentially builds upon this discussion, which is why we reproduce it below. A first remark made in [2] and [1] is that the OPT operator of SPARQL prevents the usage of certain answers, even when querying a plain graph (or equivalently, a KB with empty TBox). This can be seen with Example 2.

Example 2
$\mathcal{A} = \{\text{Person(Alice)}\}$
$q = \text{Person}(x) \text{ OPT hasLicense}(x, y)$

In this example, according to the SPARQL specification, the mapping $\omega = \{x \mapsto \text{Alice}\}$ is the only answer to q over $\mathcal{A}$, i.e. $\text{sparqlAns}(q, \mathcal{A}) = \{\omega\}$. But ω is not a certain answer to q over the KB $\langle \emptyset, \mathcal{A} \rangle$. Consider for instance the interpretation $\mathcal{I}$ defined by $\mathcal{I} = \mathcal{A} \cup \{\text{hasLicense(Alice}, 12345)\}$. Then $\text{sparqlAns}(q, \mathcal{I}) = \{\{x \mapsto \text{Alice}, y \mapsto 12345\}\}$. So $\omega \notin \text{certAns}(q, \langle \emptyset, \mathcal{A} \rangle)$.

Then in [2] and [1] still, the authors remark that in this example, ω can nonetheless be *extended* to an answer in every model of $\langle \emptyset, \mathcal{A} \rangle$. This is the main intuition used in [1] to adapt the definition of certain answers to SPARQL queries with OPT. If q is a query and $\mathcal{I}$ an interpretation, let $\mathsf{eAns}(q, \mathcal{I})$ designate all mappings that can be extended to an answer to q in $\mathcal{I}$, i.e.:

$$\mathsf{eAns}(q, \mathcal{I}) = \{\omega \mid \omega \preceq \omega' \text{ for some } \omega' \in \mathsf{sparqlAns}(q, \mathcal{I})\}$$

Then if $\mathcal{K}$ is a KB, the set $\mathsf{eCertAns}(q, \mathcal{K})$ of mappings that can be extended to an answer in every model of $\mathcal{K}$ is defined as:

$$\mathsf{eCertAns}(q, \mathcal{K}) = \bigcap_{\mathcal{I} \in \mathsf{mod}(\mathcal{K})} \mathsf{eAns}(q, \mathcal{I})$$

But as pointed out in [1], $\mathsf{eCertAns}(q, \mathcal{I})$ does not comply with SPARQL answers over a plain graph (i.e. when the TBox is empty). Indeed, if some ω can be extended to an answer in every model of the KB, then this is also the case of any mapping that ω extends (e.g. trivially the empty mapping). So in Example 2, $\mathsf{eCertAns}(q, \langle \emptyset, \mathcal{A} \rangle) = \{\{\}, \{x \mapsto \mathtt{Alice}\}\}$, whereas $\mathsf{sparqlAns}(q, \mathcal{A}) = \{\{x \mapsto \mathtt{Alice}\}\}$.

The semantics proposed in [1] is designed to solve this issue. The precise scope of the proposal is so-called *well-designed* SUJO queries (see [14] for a definition), in some normal form (no UNION in the scope of SELECT, JOIN or OPT, no SELECT in the scope of JOIN or OPT, and no OPT in the scope of JOIN).[1] Given a KB $\mathcal{K}$, the solution consists in retaining, for each maximal SJO subquery q', the *maximal* elements of $\mathsf{eCertAns}(q', \mathcal{K})$ w.r.t $\preceq$. An additional restriction is put on the domain of such solution mappings, based on the so-called *pattern-tree* representation (defined in [12]) of well-designed SJO queries. The UNION operator on the other hand is evaluated compositionally, as in Definition 1.

But as illustrated by the authors, this proposal does not comply with the standard semantics for SPARQL over plain graphs. Example 3 below reproduces the one given in [1, Example 4]:

Example 3
$\mathcal{A} = \{\mathtt{teachesTo(Alice, Bob)}, \mathtt{knows(Bob, Carol)}, \mathtt{teachesTo(Alice, Dan)}\}$
$q = \mathrm{SELECT}_{\{x,z\}}(\mathtt{teachesTo}(x, y) \text{ OPT } \mathtt{knows}(y, z))$

In this example, $\mathsf{sparqlAns}(q, \mathcal{A}) = \{\{x \mapsto \mathtt{Alice}, z \mapsto \mathtt{Carol}\}, \{x \mapsto \mathtt{Alice}\}\}$. Instead, the semantics proposed in [1] yields $\{\{x \mapsto \mathtt{Alice}, z \mapsto \mathtt{Carol}\}\}$.

Section 5.3 below defines a different semantics for evaluating a SPARQL query over a KB, which coincides not only with certain answers for UCQs (as opposed to the SPARQL entailment regimes and [10]), but also with the SPARQL specification in the case where the TBox is empty (as opposed to the proposal made in [1]).

Before continuing, other works need to be mentioned, even though they are not immediately related to the problem addressed in this paper. First, a modification of the entailment regimes' semantics was proposed in [11] for the SJO fragment extended with the SPARQL FILTER operator. For DLs with negation, it consists in ruling out a partial solution mappings if it cannot be extended to an answer in any model of the KB. Finally, another topic of interest when it comes to SPARQL and certain answers, but which falls out of the scope of this paper, is the treatment of *blank nodes*, discussed in the specification of SPARQL entailment regimes [6], and more recently in [7] and [9].

---

[1] This is without loss of expressivity, but normalization may cause an exponential blowup.

4   Requirements

As seen in the previous section, existing semantics for SPARQL answers over a KB fail to comply either with certain answers (for the fragment of SPARQL that corresponds to UCQs), or with SPARQL answers over a plain graph when the TBox is empty.

We will show in Sect. 5 that these two requirements are compatible for some DLs and fragments of SPARQL. But first, in this section, we formalize these two requirements, as properties to met by any semantics whose purpose is to conciliate certain answers and SPARQL answers. We also define three additional requirements (called OPT *extension*, *variable binding* and *binding provenance*), which generalizes to KBs some basic properties of SPARQL answers over plain graphs. We note that these requirements apply to arbitrary DLs, whereas Sect. 5 focuses instead on specific families of DLs.

If q is a SPARQL query and $\mathcal{K}$ a KB, we use $\mathsf{ans}(q, \mathcal{K})$ below to denote the answers to q over $\mathcal{K}$ under some (underspecified) semantics. This allows us to define properties to be met by such a semantics.

Requirement 1 states that $\mathsf{ans}(q, \mathcal{K})$ should coincide with certain answers for UCQs.

Requirement 1 (Certain answer compliance). *For any UCQ q and KB $\mathcal{K}$,*

$$\mathsf{ans}(q, \mathcal{K}) = \mathsf{certAns}(q, \mathcal{K})$$

Requirement 2 corresponds to the limitation of [1] identified in Sect. 3. It requires that $\mathsf{ans}(q, \langle \emptyset, \mathcal{A} \rangle)$ coincide with answers over $\mathcal{A}$, as defined in the SPARQL specification.

Requirement 2 (SPARQL answer compliance). *For any query q and ABox $\mathcal{A}$,*

$$\mathsf{ans}(q, \langle \emptyset, \mathcal{A} \rangle) = \mathsf{sparqlAns}(q, \mathcal{A})$$

As will be seen in the next section, it is possible to define semantics that verify Requirements 1 and 2, but fail to comply with basic properties of SPARQL answers over a plain graph. This is why we define additional requirements.

First, as observed in [11] for instance, the OPT operator of SPARQL was introduced to "not reject the solutions because some part of the query pattern does not match" [8]. Or in other words, for each answer ω to the left operand of an OPT, either ω or some extension of ω is expected be present in the answers to the whole expression. Let $\preceq_g$ be the partial order over sets of solution mappings defined by $\Omega_1 \preceq_g \Omega_2$ iff, for each $\omega_1 \in \Omega_1$, there is a $\omega_2 \in \Omega_2$ s.t. $\omega_1 \preceq \omega_2$. Then this property is expressed with Requirement 3.

Requirement 3 (OPT extension). *For any queries q_1, q_2 and KB $\mathcal{K}$:*

$$\mathsf{ans}(q_1, \mathcal{K}) \preceq_g \mathsf{ans}(q_1 \text{ OPT } q_2, \mathcal{K})$$

Another important property of SPARQL answers over plain graphs pertains to bound variables. Indeed, a SPARQL query q (with UNION and/or OPT) may allow *partial* solution mappings, i.e. whose domain does not cover all variables projected by q. For instance, in Example 2, $\omega = \{x \mapsto \texttt{Alice}\} \in \mathsf{sparqlAns}(q, \mathcal{A})$, even though the variables projected by q are x and y. In such a case, we say that variable x is *bound* by ω, whereas variable y is not. Then a SPARQL query may only admit answers that bind certain sets of variables. For instance the query $A(x)$ OPT $(R(x,y)$ JOIN $R(y,z))$ admits answers that bind either $\{x\}$ or $\{x, y, z\}$. But it does not admit answers that bind another set of variables ($\{y\}, \{x, y\}$, etc.). So a natural requirement when generalizing SPARQL answers to KBs is to respect such constraints. We say that a set X of variables is *admissible* for a query q iff there exists a graph $\mathcal{A}$ and solution mapping ω s.t. $\omega \in$ sparqlAns($q, \mathcal{A}$) and dom(ω) = X. Unfortunately, for queries with OPTIONAL, whether a given set of variables is admissible for a given query is undecidable. So we adopt instead a relaxed notion of admissible bindings. For a SUJO query q, we use adm(q) to denote the family of sets of variables defined inductively as follows:

Definition 2 (Definition of adm(q) for the SUJO fragment)

> *If q is a triple pattern, then* adm(q) = $\{$vars(q)$\}$
> adm(SELECT_X q) $= \{ \ X' \cap X \ \ | \ X' \in$ adm(q) $\}$
> adm(q_1 JOIN q_2) $= \{ \ X_1 \cup X_2 \ | \ (X_1, X_2) \in$ adm(q_1) $\times$ adm(q_2) $\}$
> adm(q_1 OPT q_2) $=$ adm(q_1) $\cup$ adm(q_1 JOIN q_2)
> adm(q_1 UNION q_2) $=$ adm(q_1) $\cup$ adm(q_2)

We can now formulate the corresponding requirement:

Requirement 4 (Variable binding). *For any SUJO query q, KB $\mathcal{K}$ and $\omega \in$ ans($q, \mathcal{K}$):*

$$\text{dom}(\omega) \in \text{adm}(q)$$

This constraint on variable bindings is still arguably weak though, if one consider queries with UNION. Take for instance the query $q = A(x)$ UNION $R(x, y)$. Then adm(q) = $\{\{x\}, \{x, y\}\}$. But the semantics of SPARQL over plain graphs puts a stronger requirement on variable bindings. If ω is a solution to q, then ω may bind $\{x\}$ only if ω is an answer to the left operand $A(x)$, and ω may bind $\{x, y\}$ only if ω is an answer to the right operand $R(x, y)$. It is immediate to see that Requirement 4 on variable bindings does not enforce this property. So we add as a simple fifth requirement:

Requirement 5 (Binding provenance). *For any SUJO queries q_1, q_2, KB $\mathcal{K}$ and solution mapping ω:*

> *if $\omega \in$ ans(q_1 UNION q_2) and $\omega \notin$ ans(q_2), then* dom(ω) $\in$ adm(q_1)
> *if $\omega \in$ ans(q_1 UNION q_2) and $\omega \notin$ ans(q_1), then* dom(ω) $\in$ adm(q_2)

5 Semantics

We now investigate different semantics for answering SPARQL queries over a KB, in view of the requirements expressed in the previous section. We note that each semantics is defined for a specific fragment of SPARQL only, and that this is also the case of Requirements 1, 4 and 5 (the other two requirements are defined for arbitrary SPARQL queries). So when we say below that a semantics defined for fragment L_1 *satisfies* a requirement defined for fragment L_2, this means that the requirement holds for the fragment $L_1 \cap L_2$.

Section 5.1 shows that adopting a compositional interpretation or certain answers, analogous to SPARQL entailment regimes (restricted to SUJO queries), is sufficient to satisfy Requirement 2, but fails to satisfy Requirement 1 for the SJ and U fragments already. Section 5.2 focuses on DLs with the canonical model property. For these, we consider generalizing a well-known property of certain answers to UCQs: they are equivalent to answers over the canonical model, but restricted to those that range over the active domain of the KB. We show that this solution satisfies Requirements 1 and 2 for the SUJO fragment, but fails to satisfy Requirement 3 for the O fragment already. Finally, Sect. 5.3 builds upon this last observation, and shows that it is possible to define a semantics that satisfies all requirements for the SUJO fragment.

Table 1 summarizes our observations (for KBs with the canonical model property only), together with observations about the proposal made in [1] (discussed in Sect. 3).

Table 1. Requirements met by alternative semantics for SPARQL over a DL KB (with the canonical model property). "A/B" stands for all fragments between A and B.

Semantics	Fragment	REQ1	REQ2	REQ3	REQ4	REQ5
Ahmetaj et al. [1]	pwdPT ($\subseteq$ SJO)	✓	x	?	✓	✓
Entailment regime (Definition 3)	UJO	✓	✓	✓	✓	✓
	SJ/SUJO	x	✓	✓	✓	✓
Canonical (Definition 4)	O/SUJO	✓	✓	x	✓	✓
Restricted (Definition 5)	SUJO	✓	✓	✓	x	x
Max. adm. can. (Definition 8)	SUJO	✓	✓	✓	✓	✓

5.1 SPARQL Entailment Regimes

Example 2 above showed that certain answer to a query with OPT may fail to comply with the standard compositional semantics of SPARQL (Definition 1) over a plain graph (i.e. when the TBox is empty). Then a natural attempt to conciliate the two is to proceed "the other way around": stick to the compositional semantics of SPARQL, and use certain answers for the base case only. This is in essence what the SPARQL entailment regimes propose for queries that correspond to the SUJO fragment (recall the restrictions on reserved RDF/RDFS/OWL keywords in triple patterns expressed in Sect. 2).

Because the specification of SPARQL entailment regimes [6] is too low-level for the scope of this paper, we provide a more abstract characterization of this approach for the SUJO fragment. If q is a query and $\mathcal{K}$ a KB, we call the resulting set of solution mapping the *entailment regime answers* to q over $\mathcal{K}$, denoted with $\mathsf{eRAns}(q, \mathcal{K})$, defined as follows:

Definition 3 (Entailment Regime Answers)

$$
\begin{aligned}
&\textit{If } q \textit{ is a triple pattern, then } \mathsf{eRAns}(q, \mathcal{K}) = \mathsf{certAns}(q, \mathcal{K})\\
&\mathsf{eRAns}(q_1 \text{ UNION } q_2, \mathcal{K}) = \mathsf{eRAns}(q_1, \mathcal{K}) \cup \mathsf{eRAns}(q_2, \mathcal{K})\\
&\mathsf{eRAns}(q_1 \text{ JOIN } q_2, \mathcal{K}) \quad = \mathsf{eRAns}(q_1, \mathcal{K}) \bowtie \mathsf{eRAns}(q_2, \mathcal{K})\\
&\mathsf{eRAns}(q_1 \text{ OPT } q_2, \mathcal{K}) \quad = (\mathsf{eRAns}(q_1, \mathcal{K}) \bowtie \mathsf{eRAns}(q_2, \mathcal{K})) \cup\\
&\qquad\qquad\qquad\qquad\qquad\quad (\mathsf{eRAns}(q_1, \mathcal{K}) \setminus \mathsf{eRAns}(q_2, \mathcal{K}))\\
&\mathsf{eRAns}(\text{SELECT}_X \ q, \mathcal{K}) \ = \pi_X \mathsf{eRAns}(q, \mathcal{K})
\end{aligned}
$$

It is immediate to see that entailment regime answers and SPARQL answers coincide over a plain graph. Indeed, in the base case (i.e. when q is a triple pattern), for any graph $\mathcal{A}$, $\mathsf{sparqlAns}(q, \mathcal{A}) = \mathsf{certAns}(q, \langle \emptyset, \mathcal{A} \rangle)$. Then the inductive definitions of sparqlAns$(q, \mathcal{A})$ (Definition 1) and eRAns$(q, \mathcal{K})$ (Definition 3) coincide. So entailment regime answers satisfy Requirement 2.

But they fail to comply with certain answers for UCQs (Requirement 1), for two reasons. First, the UNION operator is not compositional for certain answers in some DLs. Consider for instance Example 4 below:

Example 4
$\mathcal{A} = \{\texttt{Driver(Alice)}\}$
$\mathcal{T} = \{\texttt{Driver} \sqsubseteq \texttt{CarDriver} \sqcup \texttt{TruckDriver}\}$
$q = \texttt{CarDriver}(x)$ UNION $\texttt{TruckDriver}(x)$
Then certAns$(q, \langle \mathcal{T}, \mathcal{A} \rangle) = \{\{x \mapsto \texttt{Alice}\}\}$, but eRAns$(q, \langle \mathcal{T}, \mathcal{A} \rangle) = \emptyset$.

Second, the SELECT operator is not compositional for certain answers, even for some DLs that have the canonical model property. Consider for instance Example 5 below:

Example 5
$\mathcal{A} = \{\texttt{Driver(Alice)}\}$
$\mathcal{T} = \{\texttt{Driver} \sqsubseteq \exists \texttt{hasLicense}\}$
$q = \text{SELECT}_{\{x\}} (\texttt{Driver}(x) \text{ JOIN } \texttt{hasLicense}(x, y))$
Then certAns$(q, \langle \mathcal{T}, \mathcal{A} \rangle) = \{\{x \mapsto \texttt{Alice}\}\}$, but eRAns$(q, \langle \mathcal{T}, \mathcal{A} \rangle) = \emptyset$.

So entailment regime answers fail to satisfy Requirement 1 for the U and SJ fragments already.

5.2   Canonical Answers

We now focus on DLs with the canonical model property. We assume some underspecified DL $\mathcal{L}_{\text{can}}$ with the canonical model property, and use "an $\mathcal{L}_{\text{can}}$ KB" to refer to a KB in such DL. Then if $\mathcal{K}$ is an $\mathcal{L}_{\text{can}}$ KB, we use can$(\mathcal{K})$ to designate its canonical model (up to isomorphism).

An equivalent definition of certain answers for DLs with the canonical model property is the following: certain answers to a UCQ q over a KB $\mathcal{K}$ coincide with answers to q over can$(\mathcal{K})$, restricted to those that range over aDom$(\mathcal{K})$. We show that extending this definition to queries with OPT is sufficient to satisfy Requirements 2 (in addition to Requirement 1), but fails to satisfy Requirement 3.

If Ω is a set of solution mappings and $B \subseteq \mathsf{N}_\mathsf{I}$, let $\Omega \rhd B = \{\omega \in \Omega \mid \text{range}(\omega) \subseteq B\}$. Then we define the *canonical answers* to a query q over an $\mathcal{L}_{\text{can}}$ KB $\mathcal{K}$, denoted with canAns$(q, \mathcal{K})$, as follows:

Definition 4 (Canonical Answers). *For any SUJO query q and $\mathcal{L}_{\text{can}}$ KB $\mathcal{K}$:*

$$\text{canAns}(q, \mathcal{K}) = \text{sparqlAns}(q, \text{can}(\mathcal{K})) \rhd \text{aDom}(\mathcal{K})$$

Proposition 1 states that canonical answers comply with SPARQL answers over a plain graph (Requirement 2).

Proposition 1. *For any SUJO query q and $\mathcal{L}_{\text{can}}$ KB $\mathcal{K}$, canAns$(q, \mathcal{K})$ satisfies Requirement 2.*

From the observation made above, canonical answers also comply with certain answers for UCQs (Requirement 1). But they fail to satisfy OPT extension (Requirement 3), as illustrated with Example 6.

Example 6
$\mathcal{A} = \{\text{Driver(Alice)}\}$
$\mathcal{T} = \{\text{Driver} \sqsubseteq \exists\text{hasLicense}\}$
$q = \text{Driver}(x) \text{ OPT hasLicense}(x, y)$

In this example, Let $\mathcal{K} = \langle \mathcal{T}, \mathcal{A} \rangle$. Then $\text{canAns}(\text{Driver}(x), \mathcal{K}) = \{\{x \mapsto \text{Alice}\}\}$. However, $\text{sparqlAns}(q, \text{can}(\mathcal{K})) = \{\{x \mapsto \text{Alice}, y \mapsto e\}\}$, for some $e \notin \text{aDom}(\mathcal{K})$. Therefore $\text{canAns}(q, \mathcal{K}) = \text{sparqlAns}(q, \text{can}(\mathcal{K})) \triangleright \text{aDom}(\mathcal{K}) = \emptyset$. So $\text{canAns}(\text{Driver}(x), \mathcal{K}) \npreceq_g \text{canAns}(q, \mathcal{K})$, which immediately violates Requirement 3.

5.3 Maximal Admissible Canonical Answers

The canonical answers defined in the previous section fail to satisfy Requirement 3. We show how this definition can be adapted to satisfy all requirements, for the whole SUJO fragment.

Intuitively, in Definition 4, the restriction of $\text{sparqlAns}(q, \text{can}(\mathcal{K}))$ to solution mappings that range over $\text{can}(\mathcal{K})$ is too strong. Consider again Example 6, where $\text{sparqlAns}(q, \text{can}(\mathcal{K})) = \{\{x \mapsto \text{Alice}, y \mapsto e\}\}$. In this example, rather than filtering out this solution mapping (because it does not range over $\text{aDom}(\mathcal{K})$), one would want instead to *restrict* it to the active domain, which yields the desired mapping $\{x \mapsto \text{Alice}\}$.

To formalize this intuition, if Ω is a set of solution mappings and $B \subseteq \mathsf{N_I}$, let $\Omega \blacktriangleright B = \{\omega\|_B \mid \omega \in \Omega\}$. We can now define the *restricted canonical answers* $\text{restCanAns}(q, \mathcal{K})$ to a query q over an $\mathcal{L}_{\text{can}}$ KB $\mathcal{K}$, as follows:

Definition 5 (Restricted Canonical Answers). *For any SUJO query q and $\mathcal{L}_{\text{can}}$ KB $\mathcal{K}$:*

$$\text{restCanAns}(q, \mathcal{K}) = \text{sparqlAns}(q, \text{can}(\mathcal{K})) \blacktriangleright \text{aDom}(\mathcal{K})$$

However, restricted canonical answers still fail to satisfy the above requirement on admissible variable bindings (Requirement 4), as illustrated with Example 7 below:

Example 7
$\mathcal{A} = \{\text{Teacher(Alice)}\}$
$\mathcal{T} = \{\text{Teacher} \sqsubseteq \exists\text{teachesTo}, \text{teachesTo} \sqsubseteq \text{hasTeacher}^-\}$
$q = \text{Teacher}(x) \text{ OPT } (\text{teachesTo}(x, y) \text{ JOIN hasTeacher}(y, z))$

In this example, $\text{sparqlAns}(q, \text{can}(\mathcal{K})) = \{\{x \mapsto \text{Alice}, y \mapsto e, z \mapsto \text{Alice}\}\}$, for some $e \notin \text{aDom}(\mathcal{K})$. So restricting this solution mapping to $\text{aDom}(\mathcal{K})$ would yield the mapping $\{x \mapsto \text{Alice}, z \mapsto \text{Alice}\}$. However, $\{x, z\}$ is not an admissible set of variables for q, because q requires that whenever variable z is bound, variable y must be bound as well.

We now propose to further constrain restricted canonical answers in order to satisfy Requirements 4 and 5. We call the resulting solution mappings *maximal admissible canonical answers*, noted $\text{mCanAns}(q, \mathcal{K})$.

We start with the PJO fragment (i.e. queries without UNION) for simplicity, since for this fragment, Requirement 5 is trivially satisfied. If $\mathcal{S}$ is a family of sets, let $\max_{\subseteq}(\mathcal{S})$ designate the set of maximal elements of $\mathcal{S}$ w.r.t. set inclusion. And if Ω is a set of solution mappings and $\mathcal{X}$ a family of sets of variables, let:

$$\Omega \otimes \mathcal{X} = \{\omega|_X \mid \omega \in \Omega, X \in \max_{\subseteq}(\mathcal{X} \cap 2^{\text{dom}(\omega)})\}$$

We can now define maximal admissible canonical answers for the SJO fragment, as follows:

Definition 6 (Maximal Admissible Canonical Answers (SJO))

$$\mathsf{mCanAns}(q, \mathcal{K}) = \mathsf{restCanAns}(q, \mathcal{K}) \otimes \mathsf{adm}(q)$$

In order to generalize this definition to queries with UNION, we need to enforce Requirement 5. To this end, the provenance of each solution mapping needs to be taken into account. We define the set of *branches* of a SUJO query q, denoted with $\mathsf{branch}(q)$, as the set of SJO queries that may produce a solution to q, by intuitively "choosing" one operand of each UNION. For instance, if $q = A(x)$ OPT $(R_1(x, y)$ UNION $R_2(x, z))$, then $\mathsf{branch}(q) = \{A(x)$ OPT $R_1(x, y), A(x)$ OPT $R_2(x, z)\}$. The function $\mathsf{branch}(q)$ is defined inductively over q as expected:

Definition 7 (Branches of a SUJO query q)

If q is a triple pattern, then $\mathsf{branch}(q) = \{q\}$
$\mathsf{branch}(\text{SELECT}_X \ q) = \{ \ \text{SELECT}_X \ q' \mid q' \in \mathsf{branch}(q) \ \}$
$\mathsf{branch}(q_1 \ \text{JOIN} \ q_2) = \{ \ q_1' \ \text{JOIN} \ q_2' \mid (q_1', q_2') \in \mathsf{branch}(q_1) \times \mathsf{branch}(q_2) \ \}$
$\mathsf{branch}(q_1 \ \text{OPT} \ q_2) = \{ \ q_1' \ \text{OPT} \ q_2' \mid (q_1', q_2') \in \mathsf{branch}(q_1) \times \mathsf{branch}(q_2) \ \}$
$\mathsf{branch}(q_1 \ \text{UNION} \ q_2) = \mathsf{branch}(q_1) \cup \mathsf{branch}(q_2)$

According to the semantics of SPARQL over plain graphs, an answer to a SUJO query q must be an answer to some branch of q (the converse does not hold though; see e.g. [15, Example 1]). Or formally, for any SUJO query q and graph $\mathcal{A}$:

$$\mathsf{sparqlAns}(q, \mathcal{A}) \subseteq \bigcup_{q' \ \in \mathsf{branch}(q)} \mathsf{sparqlAns}(q', \mathcal{A})$$

So if $q' \in \mathsf{branch}(q)$, we use $\mathsf{sparqlAns}(q, \mathcal{A}, q')$ to denote the answers to q over $\mathcal{A}$ that may be obtained by evaluating branch q', i.e.:

$$\mathsf{sparqlAns}(q, \mathcal{A}, q') = \mathsf{sparqlAns}(q, \mathcal{A}) \cap \mathsf{sparqlAns}(q', \mathcal{A})$$

Similarly, we adapt Definition 6 to a branch q' of q:

$$\mathsf{mCanAns}(q, \mathcal{K}, q') = (\mathsf{sparqlAns}(q, \mathsf{can}(\mathcal{K}), q') \blacktriangleright \mathsf{aDom}(\mathcal{K})) \otimes \mathsf{adm}(q')$$

We can now generalize maximal admissible canonical answers to the SUJO fragment:

Definition 8 (Maximal Admissible Canonical Answers (SUJO))

$$\mathsf{mCanAns}(q, \mathcal{K}) = \bigcup_{q' \in \mathsf{branch}(q)} \mathsf{mCanAns}(q, \mathcal{K}, q')$$

It can be easily verified that Definitions 6 and 8 coincide for SJO queries, since in this case $\mathsf{branch}(q) = \{q\}$. Proposition 2 shows that maximal admissible canonical answers satisfy all requirements expressed in the previous section.

Proposition 2. *For any SUJO query q and $\mathcal{L}_{\mathsf{can}}$ KB $\mathcal{K}$, $\mathsf{mCanAns}(q, \mathcal{K})$ satisfies Requirements 1, 2, 3, 4 and 5.*

Table 2. Combined complexity of EVAL$_{sparqlAns}$ and EVAL$_{mCanAns}$. "-c" stands for complete, and "A/B" for all fragments between A and B.

Fragment	EVAL$_{sparqlAns}$	EVAL$_{mCanAns}$
UJ/SUJ	NP-c	NP-c
Well-designed JO	coNP-c	coNP-c
Well-designed SJO*	Σ_2^P-c	Σ_2^P-c
OJ/SUJO	PSPACE-c	PSPACE-c

6   Complexity

We now provide complexity results for query answering under the semantics defined in Sect. 5.3, for different sub-fragments of the SUJO fragment, and focusing on KBs in $DL\text{-}Lite_\mathcal{R}$ [3], a DL tailored for query answering, which corresponds to the OWL 2 QL profile. As is conventional, we focus on the *decision problem* for query answering, i.e. the problem EVAL$_{mCanAns}$ below. We also focus on *combined* complexity, i.e. measured in the size of the whole input (KB and query), and leave *data* complexity (parameterized either by the size of the query, or of the query and TBox) as future work.

> EVAL$_{mCanAns}$
> **Input:** $DL\text{-}Lite_\mathcal{R}$ KB $\mathcal{K}$, query q, mapping ω
> **Decide:** $\omega \in \mathsf{mCanAns}(q, \mathcal{K})$

Complexity of SPARQL query evaluation over plain graphs has been extensively studied (see [13] for a recent overview). When these results are tight, they provide us immediate lower bounds. Indeed, from Proposition 1, certain canonical answers satisfy Requirement 2, so EVAL$_{mCanAns}$ is at least as hard as the problem EVAL$_{sparqlAns}$ below.

> EVAL$_{sparqlAns}$
> **Input:**   graph $\mathcal{A}$, query q, mapping ω
> **Decide:** $\omega \in \mathsf{sparqlAns}(q, \mathcal{A})$

Table 2 reproduces results for EVAL$_{sparqlAns}$ in several commonly studied fragments that fall within the SUJO fragment. The OPT operator has been the focus of a large part of the literature, as EVAL$_{sparqlAns}$ has been shown to be PSPACE-complete for the OJ fragment already, in [15]. Particular attention has also been paid to so-called *well-designed* SJO and JO queries (see [14] for a definition), which have a natural representation as *pattern trees* [12], with a significant reduction from PSPACE to Σ_2^P and coNP-completeness respectively. For SJO, we follow [12] and focus on queries where the SELECT operator is terminal, i.e. where it does not appear in the scope of JOIN or OPT. The corresponding fragment is called SJO*. Finally, another fragment of interest is UJ, for which query answering is already intractable [15], thus contrasting with projection-free UCQs.

So for each fragment, we investigate whether EVAL$_{mCanAns}$ matches the upper bounds for EVAL$_{sparqlAns}$. The results are summarized in Table 2. Interestingly, all upper bounds are matched. This means that for these fragments, the presence of a TBox does not induce an extra computational cost (as far as worst-case complexity is concerned) when compared to SPARQL answers over a plain graph. This observation is analogous to well-known results for answering UCQs under certain-answer semantics over a *DL-Lite*$_\mathcal{R}$ KB [5], which matches the (NP) upper bound for UCQs over a plain graph.

Before explaining these results, we isolate a key observation:

Proposition 3. *If q is a JO query and $X_1, X_2 \subseteq$ vars(q), then it can be decided in $O(|q|^2)$ whether $X_1 \in \max_\subseteq(\text{adm}(q) \cap 2^{X_2})$.*

Proof. (Sketch.) If q is a JO query, we compute a family base(q) of sets of variables s.t. $|\text{base}(q)| = O(|q|)$, and s.t. each $V \in \text{adm}(q)$ is the union of some elements of base(q) and conversely, i.e. $\text{adm}(q) = \{\bigcup \mathcal{B} \mid \mathcal{B} \in 2^{\text{base}(q)}\}$. The family base$(q)$ can be computed inductively as follows:

- if q is a triple pattern, then base$(q) = \{\text{vars}(q)\}$.
- if $q = q_1$ JOIN q_2, then base$(q) = \{B_1 \cup B_2 \mid B_1 \in \min_\subseteq(\text{base}(q_1)), B_2 \in \text{base}(q_2)\} \cup \{B_1 \cup B_2 \mid B_1 \in \text{base}(q_1), B_2 \in \min_\subseteq(\text{base}(q_2))\}$
- if $q = q_1$ OPT q_2, then base$(q) = \text{base}(q_1) \cup \text{base}(q_1 \text{ JOIN } q_2)$

The induction guarantees that $|\min_\subseteq(\text{base}(q))| = 1$, so that $|\text{base}(q))| = O(|q|)$ must hold. Then in order to decide $X_1 \in \max_\subseteq(\text{adm}(q) \cap 2^{X_2})$, it is sufficient to: *(i)* check whether $X_1 \in \text{adm}(q)$, i.e. check whether $X_1 \subseteq \bigcup\{B \in \text{base}(q) \mid B \subseteq X_1\}$, and *(ii)* check whether there is an $X' \in \text{adm}(q) \cap 2^{X_2}$ s.t. $X \subsetneq X'$. This is the case iff there is a $B \in \text{base}(q)$ s.t. $X_1 \subsetneq X_1 \cup B \subsetneq X_2$. $\qquad\square$

We note that from the definition of adm(q), this property is independent from the semantics under investigation, so it holds for SPARQL over a plain graph. It also follows that deciding whether $X \in \text{adm}(q)$ for an arbitrary X and JO query q is tractable (consider the case where $X_1 = X_2$). Interestingly, this does not hold for the UJ fragment already. Indeed, immediately from the reduction used in [15] for hardness of EVAL$_{\text{sparqlAns}}$ in this fragment, deciding $X \in \text{adm}(q)$ for any X and UJ query q is NP-hard (we refer to the the extended version of this paper for details).

We now sketch the argument used to derive upper bounds for the SUJO, well-designed SJO* and UJ fragments (proofs can be found in the extended version). For simplicity, we focus on the well-designed SJO* fragment. The argument for queries with UNION is similar, but with additional technicalities, because the definition of certain canonical answers in this case is more involved (compare Definitions 6 and 8 above). We also simplify the explanation by assuming that the Gaifman graph of the query is connected. If $\mathcal{G}$ is a graph, we will use $V(\mathcal{G})$ below to designate its vertices.

From the definition of EVAL$_{\text{mCanAns}}$, $\langle \mathcal{K}, q, \omega \rangle$ is a positive instance iff $\omega \in$ mCanAns$(q, \mathcal{K})$, i.e. iff there is an ω' s.t. *(i)* $\omega = \omega'|_X$ for some $X \in \max_\subseteq(\text{adm}(q) \cap 2^{\text{dom}(\omega' \| \text{aDom}(\mathcal{K})))}\}$ and *(ii)* $\omega' \in \text{sparqlAns}(q, \mathcal{K})$.

So a (non-deterministic) procedure to decide whether $\omega \in \text{mCanAns}(q, \mathcal{K})$ consists in guessing an extension ω' or ω, then verify *(i)*, and then verify *(ii)*. From Proposition 3 above, *(i)* can be verified in $O(|q|^2)$. For *(ii)*, if $\omega' \in \text{sparqlAns}(q, \text{can}(\mathcal{K}))$, from well-known properties of can$(\mathcal{K})$ for *DL-Lite*$_\mathcal{R}$, it can be shown that:

- there must exist a subgraph $\mathcal{G}$ of can$(\mathcal{K})$ s.t. $V(\mathcal{G}) \cap V(\mathcal{A}) \neq \emptyset$, and the size of the subgraph of $\mathcal{G}$ induced by $V(\mathcal{G}) \setminus V(\mathcal{A})$ is linearly bounded by max$(|q|, |\mathcal{T}|)$.
- for each maximal connected subgraph $\mathcal{G}'$ of $\mathcal{G}$ s.t. $V(\mathcal{G}') \cap V(\mathcal{A}) = \emptyset$, it can be verified in $O((|\mathcal{G}'| + |\mathcal{T}|) \cdot |\mathcal{T}|)$ whether $\mathcal{G}'$ is a subgraph of can$(\mathcal{K})$.

So in order to decide *(ii)*, it is sufficient to guess $\mathcal{G}$, then verify that $\mathcal{G}$ is a subgraph of $\mathsf{can}(\mathcal{K})$, and then decide whether $\omega' \in \mathsf{sparqlAns}(q, \mathcal{G})$. Since $\mathrm{EVAL}_{\mathsf{sparqlAns}}$ is in Σ_2^P, whether $\omega' \in \mathsf{sparqlAns}(q, \mathcal{G})$ can be nondeterministically decided in time in $O(|q| + |\mathcal{G}| + |\omega'|) = O(|q| + |\mathcal{K}| + \omega)$ by some algorithm with an oracle for CONP problems. And a witness for this algorithm can be guessed together with $\mathcal{G}$ and ω' (without gaining a level in the polynomial hierarchy). We note that this last remark does not apply to the well-designed JO fragment: since $\mathrm{EVAL}_{\mathsf{sparqlAns}}$ is CONP-hard, such a procedure would instead imply a quantifier alternation.

The proof of CONP-membership for the well-designed JO fragment is significantly simpler. First, because the fragment does not allow projection, for any JO query q, $\mathsf{mCanAns}(q, \mathcal{K}) = \mathsf{canAns}(q, \mathcal{K})$ must hold. Then we consider the ABox $\mathcal{A}'$ that contains all atoms over the active domain that are entailed by $\mathcal{K}$, i.e. $\mathcal{A}' = \{A(c) \in \mathsf{can}(\mathcal{K}) \mid c \in \mathsf{aDom}(\mathcal{K})\} \cup \{r(c_1, c_2) \in \mathsf{can}(\mathcal{K}) \mid c_1, c_2 \in \mathsf{aDom}(\mathcal{K})\}$. $\mathcal{A}'$ can be computed in time polynomial in $\mathcal{K}$ and, by immediate induction on q, it can be shown that $\mathsf{canAns}(q, \mathcal{K}) = \mathsf{sparqlAns}(q, \mathcal{A}')$. Finally, from [14], deciding $\omega \in \mathsf{sparqlAns}(q, \mathcal{A}')$ is in CONP.

7   Conclusion and Perspectives

We identified in this article simple properties to be met by a semantics meant to conciliate certain answers to UCQs over a KB on the one hand, and SPARQL answers over a plain graph on the other hand. We formalized these properties as requirements, and evaluated different proposals (some of which were taken from the literature) against these requirements.

We also showed that these requirements can be all satisfied for the fragment of SPARQL with **SELECT**, **UNION** and **OPTIONAL** and DLs with the canonical model property. More precisely, we defined a semantics that matches all requirements. We also provided combined complexity results for query answering over a *DL-Lite$_\mathcal{R}$* KB under this semantics.

This work is still at an early stage, for multiple reasons. First, the semantics we defined is arguably ad-hoc, with a procedural flavor, and it would be interesting to investigate whether it can be characterized in a more declarative fashion. It must also be emphasized that if query answers defined by this semantics comply with all requirements, whether the converse holds (i.e. whether there may be answers that comply with all requirements, but are not returned under this semantics) is still an open question.

Data complexity may also be investigated, as well as algorithmic aspects, in particular *FO-rewritability*, i.e. the possibility to rewrite a query over a KB into a query over its ABox only, which is a key property for OMQA/OBDA [16]. Other DLs and/or fragments of SPARQL may also be considered.

Finally, and more importantly, additional requirements may be identified, possibly violated by the semantics we defined. If so, a key question is whether such an extended set of requirements can still be matched, for reasonably expressive DLs and fragments of SPARQL. A negative answer would constitute an argument for the SPARQL entailment regimes (or the extension of the OWL 2 QL regime proposed in [10]) as a default solution.

Acknowledgments. This research has been partially supported by the EU H2020 project INODE, by the Italian PRIN project HOPE, and by the Free University of Bozen-Bolzano through the projects QUADRO, KGID and GeoVKG.

References

1. Ahmetaj, S., Fischl, W., Pichler, R., Šimkus, M., Skritek, S.: Towards reconciling SPARQL and certain answers. In: Proceedings of the 24th International Conference on World Wide Web, pp. 23–33. ACM (2015)
2. Arenas, M., Pérez, J.: Querying semantic web data with SPARQL. In: Proceedings of the Thirtieth ACM SIGMOD-SIGACT-SIGART Symposium on Principles of Database Systems, pp. 305–316. ACM (2011)
3. Artale, A., Calvanese, D., Kontchakov, R., Zakharyaschev, M.: The DL-Lite family and relations. J. Artif. Intell. Res. **36**, 1–69 (2009)
4. Baader, F., Calvanese, D., McGuinness, D., Nardi, D., Patel-Schneider, P. (eds.): The Description Logic Handbook: Theory, Implementation, and Applications. Cambridge University Press, Cambridge (2003)
5. Calvanese, D., De Giacomo, G., Lembo, D., Lenzerini, M., Rosati, R.: Tractable reasoning and efficient query answering in description logics: the DL-Lite family. J. Autom. Reason. **39**(3), 385–429 (2007)
6. Glimm, B., Ogbuji, C.: SPARQL 1.1 entailment regimes. Technical report, W3C, March 2013
7. Gutierrez, C., Hernández, D., Hogan, A., Polleres, A.: Certain answers for SPARQL? In: AMW (2016)
8. Harris, S., Seaborne, A., Prud'hommeaux, E.: SPARQL 1.1 query language. W3C recommendation, W3C (2013)
9. Hernández, D., Gutierrez, C., Hogan, A.: Certain answers for SPARQL with blank nodes. In: Vrandečić, D., et al. (eds.) ISWC 2018. LNCS, vol. 11136, pp. 337–353. Springer, Cham (2018). https://doi.org/10.1007/978-3-030-00671-6_20
10. Kontchakov, R., Rezk, M., Rodríguez-Muro, M., Xiao, G., Zakharyaschev, M.: Answering SPARQL queries over databases under OWL 2 QL entailment regime. In: Mika, P., et al. (eds.) ISWC 2014. LNCS, vol. 8796, pp. 552–567. Springer, Cham (2014). https://doi.org/10.1007/978-3-319-11964-9_35
11. Kostylev, E.V., Cuenca Grau, B.: On the semantics of SPARQL queries with optional matching under entailment regimes. In: Mika, P., et al. (eds.) ISWC 2014. LNCS, vol. 8797, pp. 374–389. Springer, Cham (2014). https://doi.org/10.1007/978-3-319-11915-1_24
12. Letelier, A., Pérez, J., Pichler, R., Skritek, S.: Static analysis and optimization of semantic web queries. ACM Trans. Database Syst. (TODS) **38**(4), 25 (2013)
13. Mengel, S., Skritek, S.: On tractable query evaluation for SPARQL. arXiv preprint arXiv:1712.08939 (2017)
14. Pérez, J., Arenas, M., Gutierrez, C.: Semantics and complexity of SPARQL. ACM Trans. Database Syst. (TODS) **34**(3), 16 (2009)
15. Schmidt, M., Meier, M., Lausen, G.: Foundations of SPARQL query optimization. In: Proceedings of the 13th International Conference on Database Theory, pp. 4–33. ACM (2010)
16. Xiao, G., et al.: Ontology-based data access: a survey. In: Proceedings of the Twenty-Sixth International Joint Conference on Artificial Intelligence, IJCAI-18, International Joint Conferences on Artificial Intelligence Organization, pp. 5511–5519, July 2018

External Knowledge-Based Weakly Supervised Learning Approach on Chinese Clinical Named Entity Recognition

Yeheng Duan[1,2], Long-Long Ma[1(✉)], Xianpei Han[1], Le Sun[1], Bin Dong[3], and Shanshan Jiang[3]

[1] Chinese Information Processing Laboratory, Institute of Software, Chinese Academy of Sciences, Beijing, China
{yeheng2018,longlong,xianpei,sunle}@iscas.ac.cn
[2] University of Chinese Academy of Sciences, Beijing, China
[3] Ricoh Software Research Center (Beijing) Co., Ltd., Beijing, China
{bin.dong,shanshan.jiang}@srcb.ricoh.com

Abstract. Automatic extraction of clinical named entities, such as body parts, drugs and surgeries, has been of great significance to understand clinical texts. Deep neural networks approaches have achieved remarkable success in named entity recognition task recently. However, most of these approaches train models from large, high-quality and labor-consuming labeled data. In order to reduce the labeling costs, we propose a weakly supervised learning method for clinical named entity recognition (CNER) tasks. We use a small amount of labeled data as seed corpus, and propose a bootstrapping method integrating external knowledge to iteratively generate the labels for unlabeled data. The external knowledge consists of domain specific dictionaries as well as a bunch of handcraft rules. We conduct experiments on CCKS-2018 CNER task dataset and our approach achieves competitive results comparing to the supervised approach with fully labeled data.

Keywords: Named entity recognition · Weakly supervised learning · External knowledge

1 Introduction

Building named entity recognition system for clinical text could not only do great benefit to medical workers in their daily work, but also help to construct the large scale medical knowledge graph and perform other downstream tasks such as relation extraction, knowledge graph reasoning. Since electronic health record is a kind of text with very strong domain features, the entity recognition task in clinical texts faces even more challenge than that in other domains [1]. Firstly, rich labeled clinical corpus is relatively difficult to obtain due to the lack of uniform standards on labeling Chinese clinical health records [2] and medical data labeling costs vast human labor [3]. Secondly, clinical text contains abundant medical professional knowledge, such as rules, dictionaries and so on. Using external knowledge to guide the entity extraction has been proved an effective

© Springer Nature Switzerland AG 2020
X. Wang et al. (Eds.): JIST 2019, LNCS 12032, pp. 336–352, 2020.
https://doi.org/10.1007/978-3-030-41407-8_22

way to pursuit higher performance especially when the supervision signal is weak, and many works [4–6] have carried out successful approaches.

Traditional named entity recognition (NER) approaches can be categorized as rule based [7, 8], dictionary based [9, 10] and machine learning based [11–13] methods. With the rapid progress on deep learning technology, NER systems based on deep neural networks (DNNs) achieved remarkable success. Some recurrent neural networks (RNNs) based end-to-end models, especially bi-directional long short term memory-conditional random fields (Bi-LSTM-CRF) models gained the state-of-the-art results [14, 15]. To adapt these methods into a certain domain such as medical and health, effective ways are domain specific feature engineering [16, 17], multi-model ensemble [18] and incorporating external knowledge [19].

Most successful techniques, such as deep learning [20], require large scale ground-truth labeled training data, however it can be difficult to obtain strong supervision in many tasks due to the high cost of data labeling process. Thus, it is desired to enable machine learning techniques to work with weak supervision. Typically, weak supervision could be classified into three types, incomplete supervision, inexact supervision and inaccurate supervision [21]. However, it is difficult for a deep learning NER model to reach an ideal performance with only weak supervision because of the lack of semantic knowledge and insufficient domain information. At the same time, the lack of training data can easily lead to over-fitting of the model, which leads to low generalization ability. For example, a sentence "患者出现恶心、呕吐、腹痛、腹泻, 间断服用奥美拉唑等药物。", which means "The patient had symptoms such as nausea, vomiting, abdominal pain, diarrhea, and intermittently used omeprazole." We use only a small amount of training data to train a model, the corresponding entity recognition results are shown in Table 1.

Table 1. Recognition results of NER model with small amount training data.

患	者	出	现	恶	心	、	呕	吐	、
			symptom						
腹	痛	、	腹	泻	,	间	断	服	用
body	description		body	description					
奥	美	拉	唑	等	药	物	。		

From Table 1 we can see "腹\body 痛\description" and "腹\body 泻\description" are correctly predicted, "现恶心、\symptom" is wrongly predicted. And we can find that "奥美拉唑" is a drug entity but the model failed to recognize it. In fact, the drug entity "奥美拉唑" can be identified by domain dictionary, and the NER model can be enhanced by external knowledge to recognize "恶心" as a symptom entity. In such way, external knowledge is incorporated to enhance unlabeled data and consequently saves labeling costs. This brings out the main idea of our work, using bootstrapping method and the external knowledge to generate labels to reduce the labeling cost.

In this paper, we propose a weakly supervised learning approach for Chinese clinical named entity recognition task. We start from a weakly supervised learning model and propose an external knowledge-based method to enhance training data. Our approach save labeling cost by generating labels for unlabeled data automatically, and we eliminate noise using specific rules, supplement the labels with dictionaries. Our approach sharply reduces the need for labeled corpus size, and effectively avoids the over-fitting problem of weakly supervision trained model.

We conduct experiments on CCKS-2018 (China Conference on Knowledge Graph and Semantic Computing 2018) CNER task dataset and our approach performs closely to the trained model with fully labeled data.

The main contributions of our work are:

1. We propose an iterative weakly supervised learning architecture on Chinese clinical named entity recognition task, and experimental results demonstrate the effectiveness of our method.
2. We propose a method to automatically enhance training corpus utilizing the boot-strapping method with external knowledge, and it solves the problem of difficult acquisition of large-scale labeled training corpus.

2   Base Model

Named entity recognition can be regarded as a sequence labeling task. Different from English texts, Chinese texts don't have clear word boundary, and according to our statistic on CCKS-2018 CNER dataset, the entity mismatch caused by word segmentation take up more than 25% of all the labeled entities. So we perform the sequence labeling task on character level to alleviate such mismatch errors.

We use BIO (Begin, Inside, Outside) tagging scheme to tag the data into sequences. Our goal is to predict labels for a given sentence $s = \{w_1, w_2, \cdots w_n\}$ on each character with the same BIO tagging scheme that indicates the entity type and its boundary. The tagging scheme is shown in Table 2.

Table 2. Tagging Scheme.

Text	上	腹	部	疼	痛	。
Label	B-body	I-body	I-body	B-description	I-description	O

The NER model consists of three key components: embedding layer, Bi-LSTM layer and CRF layer. For embedding layer, we encode every Chinese character into a tensor representation which is concatenated by a 768 length pre-training embedding denoted as e_{bert}, and a 100 length word2vec [22] embedding denoted as e_{w2v}. In order to get a better context model of texts, we use BERT [23] as pre-training embedding. Then the sequence of tensors is fed into a Bi-LSTM neural network in order to capture the contextual features. Finally, a conditional random field (CRF) layer is used to capture the dependencies in tagging and determine the best tagging sequence for the sentence.

Embedding layer turns each character into tensor e_t.

$$e_t = [e_{bert}, e_{w2v}] \tag{1}$$

Since the powerful effect of Bert pre-training has already been proved, we use Bert pre-training as part of the character embedding of the input tensor in our base model. Besides, to make the performance better, we concatenate the 100 length word2vec tensor to Bert pre-training. Such representation form is inspired by recently successful works [24]. From our observation in experiments, we found this hybrid embedding carries out better presentation performance than both the single pre-train embedding of Bert and word2vec.

The Bi-LSTM network incorporates a gated memory-cell to capture long-range dependencies within the input tensors along both forward and backward directions. For each position t, LSTM computes h_t with input e_t and previous state h_{t-1}:

$$i_t = \sigma(W_i e_t + U_i h_{t-1} + b_i) \tag{2}$$

$$f_t = \sigma(W_f e_t + U_f h_{t-1} + b_f) \tag{3}$$

$$\tilde{c}_t = \tanh(W_c e_t + U_c h_{t-1} + b_c) \tag{4}$$

$$c_t = f_t \odot c_{t-1} + i_t \odot \tilde{c}_t \tag{5}$$

$$o_t = \sigma(W_o e_t + U_o h_{t-1} + b_o) \tag{6}$$

$$h_t = o_t \odot \tanh(c_t) \tag{7}$$

Where $h, i, f, o \in \mathbb{R}^{d_h}$ are d_h-dimensional hidden state, input gate, forget gate and output gate. The trainable parameters of LSTM are $W_i, W_f, W_c, W_o \in \mathbb{R}^{4d_h \times d_e}$, $U_i, U_f, U_c, U_o \in \mathbb{R}^{4d_h \times d_h}$ and $b_i, b_f, b_c, b_o \in \mathbb{R}^{4d_h}$. σ is the sigmoid function, and $\odot$ denotes elementwise production. Bi-LSTM computes both directions, left $\vec{h}_t$ and right $\overleftarrow{h}_t$, the final output is:

$$h_t = \vec{h}_t \oplus \overleftarrow{h}_t \tag{8}$$

The $\oplus$ symbol is the tensor concatenation operator.

The CRF layer connects with former output layers, parameters are presented as a transition matrix. For the output of the Bi-LSTM, the matrix of scores denotes as $f_\theta([x]_1^T)$, the element $[f_\theta]_{i,t}$ of the matrix is the score output by the network with parameters θ, for the sentence $[x]_1^T$ and for the i-th tag, at the t-th character. Transition score $[A]_{i,j}$ models the transition from i-th state to j-th for a pair of consecutive time steps. This transition matrix is position independent. Now denote the new parameters of the whole network as $\tilde{\theta} = \theta \cup \{[A]_{i,j} \forall i, j\}$. The score of $[x]_1^T$ along with a path of tags $[i]_1^T$ is then given by the sum of transition scores and Bi-LSTM network scores:

$$S\left([x]_1^T, [i]_1^T, \tilde{\theta}\right) = \sum_{t=1}^{T} \left([A]_{[i]_{t-1}, [i]_t} + [f_\theta]_{[i]_t, t}\right) \tag{9}$$

Then a softmax function calculates the conditional probability:

$$p\left([y]_1^T|[x]_1^T,\tilde{\theta}\right) = e^{S\left([x]_1^T,[y]_1^T,\tilde{\theta}\right)}/\sum_j e^{S\left([x]_1^T,[j]_1^T,\tilde{\theta}\right)} \tag{10}$$

Where $[y]_1^T$ is the true tag sequence and $[j]_1^T$ is the set of all possible output sequences. Then we use the maximum conditional likelihood estimation to train the model:

$$\log p\left([y]_1^T|[x]_1^T,\tilde{\theta}\right) = S\left([x]_1^T,[y]_1^T,\tilde{\theta}\right) - \log\sum_{\forall[j]_1^T} e^{S\left([x]_1^T,[j]_1^T,\tilde{\theta}\right)} \tag{11}$$

Here Viterbi algorithm [25] is used to compute $[A]_{i,j}$ and optimal tag sequences for inference.

3   External Knowledge-Based Weakly Supervised Learning CNER

Figure 1 is the architecture of our approach. We start from a labeled seed corpus and a weak supervision trained model. Because the supervision is rather weak at the initial stage, the model can only partially predict the right entities from unlabeled data. Our approach automatically and iteratively enhances the labels of unlabeled data with the help of external knowledge, and the enhanced data is used to train a more generalized model at the next iteration. At each iteration, we enhance a set of unlabeled data, update the external knowledge and train a more generalized model.

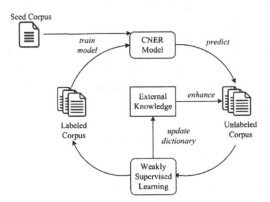

Fig. 1. Architecture of our approach

In this section we will discuss our approach in details, it is organized as follows. In Sect. 3.1 we introduce the acquisition of our external knowledge. In Sect. 3.2 we present the details of weakly supervised learning data enhancement process. In Sect. 3.3 we describe the training architecture of our CNER model.

3.1 External Knowledge Acquisition

External knowledge can be a powerful complement to training data when the quality of supervision is insufficient for the model to achieve a satisfactory performance. We collect extensive clinical domain knowledge from multiple sources and organize it into unified structure in our approach. The external knowledge consists of two main parts, clinical noise-eliminating rules and clinical entity dictionaries. The two parts are separately introduced as following.

1. Rule Construction:

Based on the observation on clinical entity domain features and medical literatures we design several kinds of rules to remove the noise from the weakly supervised model output. Some of the example rules are presented in Table 3.

2. Dictionary mining:

To generate the clinical entity dictionaries we collect named entities from various sources. Besides the seed corpus annotations, we also collect entity names from medical

Table 3. Rule examples

Rules		
Name	Explanation	Examples
Minimum length	Any one character entity to be a surgery or a drug	length(drug) > 1; length(surgery) > 1;
Parentheses and quotation marks mismatch	Entity with only one part of parentheses or quotation marks	"(" + . * + ")"; "(" + . * + ")"; " + .* + "; ' + .* + '
Comma ending	Entity should not end with comma	ent[length(ent)-1] not in (",", ";");
Part-of-speech rule filter	If the word part-of-speech conflicts the entity type we regard it as a noise word, for example, drug type entity should not be a verb or adjective	POS(drug) ! = verb.; POS(drug) ! = adj.; POS(surgery) ! = adj.; POS(body) ! = verb.; ...
Special context	Some special cases are determined by the context	Type("手") ! = body when in "手术"; Type("口") ! = body when in "切口"; Type("心") ! = body when in "心律";
...	...	...

domain literatures such as《人体解剖学名词》(Chinese Terms in Human Anatomy), open network resources such as "xywy.com", and other medical texts crawled from the internet. In order to make our dictionary as effective as possible, we generated the dictionaries comparing to the scale of experiment dataset. The statistics of our dictionaries is shown in Table 4.

Table 4. The statistics of five entity types

	body	symptom	description	drug	surgery
Dictionary Size	1637	9713	76	38828	19186

3.2 Weakly Supervised Learning Data Enhancement

At each iteration of our weakly supervised learning approach, we apply the data enhancement to training data. We pick a small set from unlabeled corpus as an unlabeled subset, and output the labels, therefore update the labeled corpus and the dictionaries. For every unlabeled subset, we generate the labels from two sources:

1. The output from the current CNER model, noise eliminated by rules. And the newly learned entity words are added to the external dictionary;
2. For those entities that the current model didn't recognize, we use external dictionary to complete the labels;

The overview of data enhancement process is presented in Fig. 2.

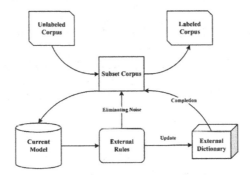

Fig. 2. Data enhancement process

When conducting external dictionary label completion, we use a string maximum matching algorithm [26, 27], which is a greedy search routine that walks through a sentence and find the longest string that matches the word in dictionary. The algorithm is summarized in Algorithm 1.

Algorithm 1 Dictionary Label Completion

1:**Input**: named entity dictionary D with corresponding entity types, a sentence $s = \{w_1, w_2, \cdots, w_n\}$, the longest word length l, shortest word length s, $l \geq s$
2:**Result**: labeled sentence
3:**Initialize**: $i \leftarrow 1$
4:**while** $i \leq n$ **do**
5: **for** $j \in [l, s]$ **do**
6:    **if** $\{w_i, \cdots, w_{max(i+j,n)}\} \in D$ **then**
7:      label $\{w_i, \cdots w_{max(i+j,n)}\}$ with the corresponding type.
8:      $i \leftarrow i + j + 1$
9:      **break**
10:   **if** $j == 0$ **then**
11:     $i \leftarrow i + i$

If the model prediction conflicts with the dictionary complement results, we firstly consider predictions of the current model output. And if dictionary labels one character as multiple entity parts, we use the prior strategy to decide which label should be chosen.

In this label completion process, the shortest word length s is an important parameter that should be properly adjusted. We initialize this parameter as 0, as the experiment goes further, short entities appear to bring more and more wrong cases, and the performance climbs slower. We gradually increased the shortest word length to 4, and this kind of wrong cases get effectively removed.

Thus we finish unlabeled data enhancement at each iteration. As the iterative process continues, the scale of the labeled corpus is enlarged and the performance of the CNER model is improved.

3.3 CNER Model Training Architecture

Current deep neural network based approaches are mostly end-to-end, we propose an iterative training method, and train a more generalized model by several iterations. The outline of our CNER approach is described in Algorithm 2.

Algorithm 2 Our CNER Approach

Require:

S: Seed corpus; *I*: Increment corpus; *U*: Unlabeled corpus;

External Knowledge: { *R*: Rules, *D*: Dictionaries};

Sub_i: the *i*-th subset of *U*;

M_i: CNER Model trained at *i*-th iteration

1: **Input**: *S*, *U*, *External Knowledge*

2: **Initialize**: $i \leftarrow 1$; $M_0 \leftarrow$ train with *S*; $I \leftarrow \emptyset$

3: **while** *U* is **not** $\emptyset$:

4:    $I \leftarrow I + Sub_i$

5:    $U \leftarrow U - Sub_i$

6:    M_i predicts $(S + G)$

7:    $I \leftarrow I$ filtered by *R*

8:    $I \leftarrow I$ supplemented by *D*, $D \leftarrow D +$ new entities in *I*

8:    $i \leftarrow i + 1$

10:    $M_i \leftarrow$ Train with $(S + I)$

11: **return** M_i

Our approach starts from a seed corpus and a weakly supervised model. We denote the dataset enhanced by our method as an increment corpus at each iteration, and we append a subset from the unlabeled corpus into the increment corpus. With the model trained at previous iteration, we enhance the increment corpus entirely, and obtain a new model by training with the seed corpus along with the increment corpus. This process ends till we make use of all the data in unlabeled corpus, and we get the final CNER model.

4 Experiments

4.1 Dataset

We conducted experiments on CCKS-2018 (China Conference on Knowledge Graph and Semantic Computing 2018) CNER task dataset.

CCKS-2018 CNER task dataset provides electronic health records data for clinical named entity recognition. It contains 600 documents in training set and 400 documents in testing set, labeled out 5 types of clinical named entities, body, symptom, description, drug and surgery. The statistics of entity on different categories are listed in Table 5.

Table 5. Statistics of different entity types.

Dataset	body	symptom	description	drug	surgery
Training	7048	2719	1866	913	1004
Validating	790	336	200	92	112
Testing	6339	1327	918	813	735

From the 600 documents of training set, we randomly picked 60 documents as a validating set. And we evenly separated the rest 540 documents into 10 subsets. We reserved the labels of one subset and take it as the seed corpus, and remove the labels of the left 9 subsets as the unlabeled corpus.

4.2 Experimental Settings

We implement all the evaluations on the 400 documents test dataset. We evaluate all the model performance with a strict evaluating standard, which defines a correct prediction as that the ground truth and extraction result share the same mention, the same boundaries and the same entity type. We use precisions (P), recalls (R) and F1-scores (F1) to evaluate the performance of every experimental model. True Positive, False Positive and False Negative predictions are denoted as TP, FP, FN, and the P, R, F1 are calculated as below.

$$P = \frac{TP}{(TP + FP)} \tag{12}$$

$$R = \frac{TP}{(TP + FN)} \tag{13}$$

$$F1 = \frac{2 * P * R}{(P + R)} \tag{14}$$

Parameter configurations may influence the performance of the models. We depict the parameter configurations in Table 6.

Table 6. Parameter configurations

Parameter	Value
Size of Bert embedding	768
Size of word embedding	100
Drop-out	0.2
Loss function	Cross Entropy
Adam learning rate	0.001
Early stopping patience	5 epochs
Shortest match length	Initialize: 0; Final: 4

4.3 Overall Experimental Results

We denote the approach using all the labeled training data as Fully Supervised approach. With the 10% labeled seed corpus we trained a baseline model and denote it as Seed Corpus Supervised approach. In order to depict the effect of the dictionary, we also did experiment without dictionary in our external knowledge, this is denoted as Our

Table 7. Overall experiment results

Approaches	P	R	F1
Fully Supervised	87.42	86.72	87.07
Seed Corpus Supervised	76.98	77.94	77.46
Our Approach (without dictionary)	87.13	78.89	82.80
Our Approach	85.34	86.15	85.74

Approach (without dictionary). Table 7 presents the comparisons of our approach to other approaches.

The overall experimental results show that our approach outperforms the seed corpus supervised model, and achieved 98% of the fully supervised model F1-score. We can see that the dictionary brings benefit to recall (78.89 → 86.15) and F1-score (82.80 → 85.74) of the model comparing to the seed corpus supervised model, but decreases the precision (87.13 → 85.34).

To illustrate the details of performance during the experiment, we also record the model performances at each iteration. The F1-scores are depicted in Fig. 3. The x axis depicts the proportion of enhanced data in unlabeled corpus, the y-axis denotes the F1 score of the corresponding model.

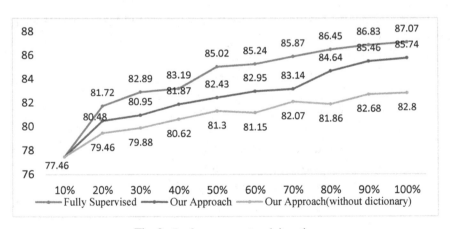

Fig. 3. Performances at each iteration

From Fig. 3 we can see that comparing to the fully labeled data trained model, our approach has shown the trend of pursuit from the early stage. Although in mid-term the improvement of performance slows down, benefiting from the reasonable control of noise, we finally achieve a satisfactory result. Comparing to the without dictionary approach, the role of dictionary is not obvious at early stage, but with the increase of the corpus, our approach gradually widens the gap.

4.4 Experiment Analysis

The overall experimental results show that our approach is an effective way to do the CNER task with weak supervision, under the guide of external-knowledge, we achieved over 98% of the fully labeled data trained model performance with only 10% of labeled training data.

The detailed recognition performance of different methods is presented in Table 8. By the analysis on performance statistics, we can see that the model without dictionary returns a good precision but the recall is relatively low. After incorporating the external dictionary, we get an obvious improvement on recall, but a little decline of the precision as sacrifice.

Table 8. Performances for each entity type.

Fully Supervised	body	symptom	description	drug	surgery
P	86.75	89.66	90.54	88.77	84.09
R	87.20	90.87	89.65	73.92	85.58
F1	86.98	90.26	90.09	80.67	84.83
Weakly Supervised					
P	77.32	79.82	78.27	78.27	66.80
R	80.66	73.93	84.75	62.48	70.34
F1	78.95	76.76	81.38	69.49	68.52
Without Dictionary					
P	86.17	92.65	89.04	89.38	82.12
R	80.53	78.82	84.97	60.02	78.10
F1	83.26	85.18	86.96	71.82	80.06
Our Approach					
P	85.57	88.70	78.24	88.26	84.35
R	86.56	88.77	88.89	78.60	82.86
F1	86.06	88.74	83.22	83.15	83.60

Based on the observation of experimental results we find that drug and surgery entities gain most obvious improvements on F1-score by our approach comparing to the weakly supervised method (drug: from 69.49 to 83.15, surgery: from 68.52 to 83.60), because these entity types get more benefits from the external knowledge. Our approach even outperforms the fully labeled model on drug type (our approach: 83.15, fully labeled model: 80.67). Because drug names often contain transliterated words from English, for example "吉西他滨" means "Gemcitabine" and "伊利替康" means "Irinotecan", such kind of entity is very hard to model only by word-embedding features, dictionary completion is rather powerful on drug entity. Meanwhile, surgery entities often appear in the form of long phrases, for example "腹腔镜下乙状结肠根治性切除术"

means "laparoscopic radical resection of the sigmoid colon", and the advantage of our dictionary completion algorithm is revealed dealing with such long phrases since we use the maximum matching algorithm. Description type, on the contrary, only gain a slightly improvement by external knowledge comparing to the weakly supervised model (weakly supervised: 81.38, our approach: 83.22), it even get a lower F1-score than the without dictionary method (without dictionary method: 86.96, our approach: 83.22). That's because description entities are not easy to be defined by external knowledge. For example, description entities "胀" means "inflation" and "痛" means "ache" can be wrongly recognized as symptom. The meaning of these words is likely to be confused with other kinds of entities and the none-entity phrases.

Dictionary completed data faces another problem. The external dictionary indicates an entity as soon as the word appears and don't take the context in consideration, which introduces a lot of wrong cases especially when the entity word is very short. Our solution is to adjust the shortest word length at the later iterations when conducting dictionary completion, because the model has already learned these short entities well, and we use dictionary mainly to label longer words, rather than introducing more noise.

5 Related Work

5.1 Clinical Named Entity Recognition

As the key area of artificial intelligence application, named entity recognition from clinical text has attracted considerable and extensive attention. Researchers in this field have proposed many effective solution approaches. These existing methods could be categorized as rule-based approaches, dictionary-based approaches, machine learning approaches and deep learning approaches.

In early time CNER research, rule based approaches used to take the dominant place. Friedman [7], Zeng [28] and Savova [29] made some successful systems for named entity recognition on medical texts. However rules are impossible to be enumerated, and the making of the rules always takes vast engineering cost.

Dictionary based CNER systems could effectively locate the entities that appeared in the dictionaries [30]. However the performance of this kind of method highly depend on the quality of the dictionaries, they can't handle entities that don't appear in the dictionaries. Meanwhile, in Chinese there are many characters or words have multiple meanings, these entities should be determined by the context, which dictionary based approaches could not solve and leads to a low precision result.

Machine learning based approaches usually consider CNER as a sequence labeling problem. Classical methods are hidden Markov models [12, 30], maximum entropy Markov models [11], conditional random fields [13, 31] and supported vector machine [32]. This kind of approach requires heavy work on feature engineering process, and it's rather difficult to find the best set of features combination.

The use of deep neural network for NER was pioneered by Collobert [33] in 2011, who proposed convolutional neural networks (CNNs) over the sequence of words. Huang et al. [34] proposed bidirectional LSTM encoder to replace CNN encoder. Lample et al. [35] introduced hierarchy in the architecture by replacing hand-engineered character-level features in prior works with additional bidirectional LSTM. The sequential CRF on top of the recurrent layers ensures that the optimal sequence of tags over the entire sentence is obtained.

5.2 Weakly Supervised Learning

Supervised learning techniques construct predictive models by learning from large scale training examples. In many tasks it is difficult to get strong supervision information such as fully ground-truth labels due to the high cost of data labeling. Weakly supervised learning technology has gradually grabbed attention.

One of the earliest papers on bootstrapping for NLP problems is made by Yarowsky [36], he presented an unsupervised learning algorithm for word sense disambiguation. Blum and Mitchell [37] used different types of features and introduced co-training for the problem of classifying Web pages.

Collins and Singer [38] used only 7 manually labeled "seed" examples to classify entities into three classes plus "other", they discussed the problem of using unlabeled examples in named entity classification.

Kozareva [39] proposed the method to automatically generate gazetteer lists from unlabeled data, and applied on Named Entity Recognition task using labeled and unlabeled data, it extracted from unlabeled data rely on n-gram and could be adapted to multi-languages. Teixeira [40] introduced a conditional random fields-based bootstrapping approach for NER.

Shen [41] carried out an active learning model for NER, and they achieved nearly state-of-the-art performance with just 25% of the original training data. Active learning method assumes that the ground-truth labels of unlabeled instances can be queried from an oracle. Kim [42] used LSTM and CRFs architecture and proposed method to use machine-labeled data to improve performance in clinical NER task. Their model obtains higher performance in 23.69% than the model that trained only a small amount of manually annotated corpus in F1-score.

6 Conclusion

In this work, we introduce an iterative weakly supervised learning architecture to perform the CNER task. We propose a bootstrapping CNER method integrating external knowledge acquired from rule construction and dictionary mining, and achieve a close performance comparing to the fully labeled data trained model. Our approach effectively reduces the need for the size of labeled training data, and properly takes the advantage of external knowledge in performing CNER task.

In the future our work will focus on more effective methods on acquiring useful external knowledge automatically, and make the iteratively bootstrapping process more efficient.

Acknowledgments. We sincerely thank the reviewers for their insightful comments and valuable suggestions. Moreover, this work is supported by the National Nature Science Foundation of China under Grants no. 61772505; the National Key R&D Program of China under Grant 2018YFB1005100.

References

1. Kundeti, S.R., Vijayananda, J., Mujjiga, S., Kalyan, M.: Clinical named entity recognition: challenges and opportunities. In: 2016 IEEE International Conference on Big Data (Big Data), pp. 1937–1945. Washington, DC (2016)
2. Jiang, Z., Zhao, F., Guan, Y., Yang, J.: Research on Chinese electronic medical record oriented lexical corpus annotation. Chin. High Technol. Lett. **24**(6), 609–615 (2014)
3. Deleger, L., et al.: Overview of the bacteria biotope task at bionlp shared task 2016. In Proceedings of the 4th BioNLP Shared Task Workshop, pp. 12–22 (2016)
4. Alfonseca, E, Manandhar, S.: An unsupervised method for general named entity recognition and automated concept discovery. In: Proceedings of the 1st international conference on general WordNet, Mysore, India, pp. 34–43 (2002)
5. Nadeau, D., Turney, P.D., Matwin, S.: Unsupervised named-entity recognition: generating gazetteers and resolving ambiguity. In: Lamontagne, L., Marchand, M. (eds.) AI 2006. LNCS (LNAI), vol. 4013, pp. 266–277. Springer, Heidelberg (2006). https://doi.org/10.1007/11766247_23
6. Sekine, S., Nobata, C.: Definition, dictionaries and tagger for extended named entity hierarchy. In: Proceedings of the language resources and evaluation conference (LREC), pp. 1977–1980 (2004)
7. Friedman, C., Alderson, P.O., Austin, J.H.M., Cimino, J.J., Johnson, S.B.: A general natural-language text processor for clinical radiology. J. Am. Med. Inform. Assoc. **1**(2), 161–174 (1994)
8. Fukuda, K., Tamura, A., Tsunoda, T., Takagi, T.: Toward information extraction: identifying protein names from biological papers. In: Pacific Symposium on Biocomputing, pp. 707–718 (1998)
9. Rindflesch, T.C., Tanabe, L., Weinstein, J.N., Hunter, L.: Edgar, extraction of drugs, genes and relations from the biomedical literature. In: Biocomputing 2000, pp. 517–528. World Scientific (1999)
10. Gaizauskas, R., Demetriou, G., Humphreys, K.: Term recognition and classification in biological science journal articles. In: Computional Terminology for Medical & Biological Applications Workshop of the 2nd International Conference on NLP, pp. 37–44 (2000)
11. Mccallum, A., Freitag, D., Pereira, F.: Maximum entropy markov models for information extraction and segmentation. In: Proceedings of the 17th International Conference on Machine Learning, pp. 591–598 (2000)
12. Zhou, G.D., Su, J.: Named entity recognition using an HMM-based chunk tagger. In: Meeting on Association for Computational Linguistics, pp. 473–480 (2002)
13. Mccallum, A., Li, W.: Early results for named entity recognition with conditional random fields, feature induction and web-enhanced lexicons. In: Conference on Natural Language Learning at Hlt-Naacl, pp. 188–191 (2003)
14. Gridach, M.: Character-level neural network for biomedical named entity recognition. J. Biomed. Inform. **70**, 85–91 (2017)
15. Habibi, M., Webber, L., Neves, M., Wiegandt, D.L., Leser, U.: Deep learning with word embeddings improves biomedical named entity recognition. Bioinformatics **33**(14), i37–i48 (2017)
16. Wang, Y., Ananiadou, S., Tsujii, J.: Improve Chinese clinical named entity recognition performance by using the graphical and phonetic feature. In: IEEE International Conference on Bioinformatics and Biomedicine (BIBM), pp. 5386–5488 (2018)
17. Yang, X., Huang, W.: A conditional random fields approach to clinical name entity recognition. In: 2018 CEUR Workshop Proceedings, vol. 2242, pp. 1–6 (2018)

18. Luo, L., Li, N.: DUTIR at the CCKS-2018 Task1: A neural network ensemble approach for Chinese clinical named entity recognition. http://CEUR-WS.org/Vol-2242/paper02.pdf (2018)
19. Zhang, S., Elhadad, N.: Unsupervised biomedical named entity recognition: experiments with clinical and biological texts. J. Biomed. Inform. **46**(6), 1088–1098 (2013)
20. Goodfellow, I., Bengio, Y., Courville, A.: Deep Learning. MIT Press, Cambridge (2016)
21. Zhou, Z.-H.: A brief introduction to weakly supervised learning. Natl. Sci. Rev. **5**(1), 44–53 (2018)
22. Mikolov, T., Chen, K., Corrado, G., Dean, J.: Efficient estimation of word representations in vector space. In: Proceedings of Workshop at ICLR (2013)
23. Devlin, J., Chang, M., Lee, K., Toutanova, K.: BERT: pretraining of deep bidirectional transformers for language understanding. arXiv preprint arXiv:1810.04805 (2018)
24. Zhang, J., Qin, Y., Zhang, Y., Liu, M., Ji, D.: Extracting entities and events as a single task using a transition-based neural model. In: Proceedings of the Twenty-Eighth International Joint Conference on Artificial Intelligence Main track, pp. 5422–5428
25. Rabiner, L.R.: A tutorial on hidden markov models and selected applications in speech recognition. Readings Speech Recogn. **77**(2), 267–296 (1990)
26. Liu, Y., Tan, Q., Shen, K.X.: The word segmentation rules and automatic word segmentation methods for Chinese information processing. Tsinghua University Press and Guang Xi, p. 36 (1994)
27. Xue, N.: Chinese word segmentation as character tagging. Int. J. Comput. Linguist. Chin. Lang. Process. **8**(1), 29–48 (2003). February 2003: Special Issue on Word Formation and Chinese Language Processing
28. Zeng, Q.T., Goryachev, S., Weiss, S., Sordo, M., Murphy, S.N., Lazarus, R.: Extracting principle diagnosis, co-morbidity and smoking status for asthma research: evaluation of a natural language processing system. BMC Med. Inform. Decis. Mak. **6**(1), 1–9 (2006)
29. Savova, G.K., et al.: Mayo clinical text analysis and knowledge extraction system (ctakes): architecture, component evaluation and applications. J. Am. Med. Inform. Assoc. JAMIA **17**(5), 507–513 (2010)
30. Song, M., Yu, H., Han, W.: Developing a hybrid dictionary-based bio-entity recognition technique. BMC Med. Inform. Decis. Mak. **15**(S-1), S9 (2015)
31. Skeppstedt, M., Kvist, M., Nilsson, G.H., Dalianis, H.: Automatic recognition of disorders, findings, pharmaceuticals and body structures from clinical text. J. Biomed. Inform. **49**(20140), 148–158 (2014)
32. Ju, Z., Wang, J., Zhu, F.: Named entity recognition from biomedical text using SVM. In: International Conference on Bioinformatics and Biomedical Engineering, pp. 1–4 (2011)
33. Collobert, R., Weston, J., Bottou, L., Karlen, M., Kavukcuoglu, K., Kuksa, P.: Natural language processing (almost) from scratch. J. Mach. Learn. Res. **12**(Aug), 2493–2537 (2011)
34. Huang, Z., Xu, W., Yu, K.: Bidirectional lstm-crf models for sequence tagging. arXiv preprint arXiv:1508.01991 (2015)
35. Lample, G., Ballesteros, M., Subramanian, S., Kawakami, K., Dyer, C.: Neural architectures for named entity recognition. In: Proceedings of NAACL-HLT, pp. 260–270 (2016)
36. Yarowsky, D.: Unsupervised word sense disambiguation rivaling supervised methods. In: Meeting of the Association for Computational Linguistics, pp. 189–196 (1995)
37. Blum, A., Mitchell, T.: Combining labeled and unlabeled data with co-training. In: COLT: Proceedings of the Workshop on Computational Learning Theory. Morgan Kaufmann Publishers (1998)
38. Collins, M., Singer, Y.: Unsupervised models for named entity classification. In EMNLP/VLC-99 (1999)
39. Kozareva, Z.: Bootstrapping named entity recognition with automatically generated gazetteer lists. In: EACL The Association for Computer Linguistics, (2006)

40. Teixeira, J., Sarmento, L., Oliveira, E.: A bootstrapping approach for training a ner with conditional random fields. In: Antunes, L., Pinto, H.S. (eds.) EPIA 2011. LNCS (LNAI), vol. 7026, pp. 664–678. Springer, Heidelberg (2011). https://doi.org/10.1007/978-3-642-24769-9_48

41. Shen, Y.: Deep active learning for named entity recognition. In: ICLR (2018)

42. Kim, J., Ko, Y., Seo, J.: A bootstrapping approach with CRF and deep learning models for improving the biomedical named entity recognition in multi-domains. IEEE Access 7, 70308–70318 (2019)

Metadata Application Profile Provenance with Extensible Authoring Format and PAV Ontology

Nishad Thalhath[1]([✉])(iD), Mitsuharu Nagamori[2](iD), Tetsuo Sakaguchi[2](iD), and Shigeo Sugimoto[2](iD)

[1] Graduate School of Library, Information and Media Studies, University of Tsukuba, Tsukuba, Japan
nishad@slis.tsukuba.ac.jp
[2] Faculty of Library, Information and Media Studies, University of Tsukuba, Tsukuba, Japan
{nagamori,saka,sugimoto}@slis.tsukuba.ac.jp,
https://www.slis.tsukuba.ac.jp

Abstract. Metadata application profiles (MAP) serve a critical role in the of metadata interoperability. Singapore framework recommends publishing the application profiles as documentation, with detailed usage guidelines aimed to maximize reusability and interoperability. Authoring, maintenance, versioning, and ensuring the availability of previous versions along with changelogs are vital steps involved in MAP publishing. The longevity of the schema is a critical part of metadata longevity. MAP should provide sufficient administrative information and versioning to ensure the provenance and longevity as a record of changes of the metadata instance. The authors propose to include actionable changelogs and provenance information within an extensible MAP authoring format. The proposal also includes a recommendation on MAP versioning and publishing with PAV, a lightweight ontology for Provenance, Authoring, and Versioning.

Keywords: Metadata · Metadata schema · Application profiles · Schema versioning · Semantic web · Linked data · PAV Ontology

1 Introduction

Metadata application profiles (MAP) are data element schemas from various namespaces mixed and customized for a specific application [9]. MAPs are the best mechanism to express consensus of any metadata instance by documenting the elements, policies, guidelines, and vocabularies for that particular implementation along with the schemas, and applicable constraints. Application profiles also provide the term usage specifications and support interoperability by representing domain consensus, alignment, and the structure of the data [1,10].

© Springer Nature Switzerland AG 2020
X. Wang et al. (Eds.): JIST 2019, LNCS 12032, pp. 353–368, 2020.
https://doi.org/10.1007/978-3-030-41407-8_23

Provenance information is vital for application profiles. Changelogs of application profile versions help to ensure the metadata instance's longevity. The longevity of the schema is essential for metadata longevity. Metadata schema provenance should be documented and maintained for the preservation of metadata [13]. Application profile should provide sufficient administrative information, such as creator, date of release, version, and usage rights. Versioning of the application profile is crucial as it is a record of the application profile as well as metadata changes. Keeping changelogs might help to migrate data-sets to new profiles or create crosswalks to upgrade the instances. For Linked Open Data (LOD), changelogs help to update linked datasets as well.

Through this paper, the authors are attempting to:

1. Extend and clarify a previously proposed [25] extensible authoring format [24] to include structured and actionable changeset with a notion that the source of the MAP can include an actionable timeline of its development.
2. Use a lightweight ontology to distinguish and point the source of the MAP as well as the published MAP resources [4].
3. Use the same ontology to notate the provenance information with identifiable roles on authoring, publishing, and contributing for collaborative MAP development.

The anticipated outcomes of these proposals are:

1. Distinguish the source of the application profile from the published versions to baseline the concepts of authoring formats and expression formats for application profiles.
2. Identifying and retrieving application profiles and its versions, including changelogs, can be automated with the help of semantic linking of MAP resources.
3. A source of MAP with an interoperable authoring format consists of an actionable timeline can help to maintain the longevity of the schema. Declared roles of contribution can act as a means of provenance for MAP resources.

1.1   Application Profile Expression Formats

Dublin Core Metadata Initiative (DCMI) defines one of the earliest guidelines to express application profiles, which can be in various formats, as Description Set Profiles (DSP). DSP is a constraint language for Dublin Core Application Profiles (DCAP) based on the Singapore framework for application profiles [18]. XML or RDF can be used as an expression format for DSP.

Singapore framework recommends publishing the application profiles in human- readable expression formats as a documentation, with detailed usage guidelines aimed to maximize reusability and interoperability. Expressing application profile in human readable formats require much more components than textual descriptions of first-order elements such as properties and classes. As a result, the expression of an application profile in human readable formats is expected to have schematic representation, changelogs as well as detailed administrative information.

For the machine-actionable expressions, other than the XML and RDF, new standards are emerging and being widely accepted. Evolution of Linked Data encourages to express the application profiles in semantic web friendly formats like JSON-LD and OWL. Considering the developments in data linking and reuse, compelling use cases for expressing application profiles in promising data validation formats like ShEx or SHACL is increasing. Including these futuristic expression formats in application profile publishing will expand the scope of its usage as well as assures long-term usability.

1.2   Current Status and Availability of Application Profiles

Application profiles are not standardized in terms of availability, maintenance, and distribution. It requires human involvement to identify MAPs [15]. Because of this manual effort, curating and archiving MAPs is difficult and costly. In addition to automated methods, numerous registry initiatives also rely on manual contributions. Most of the application profiles are available only in human-friendly formats, and to distinguish them from other types of documents; this requires human involvement in the identification process. It is challenging to extract structured application profile data from spreadsheets or PDF documents. Lack of versioning, changes logs, and access to previous versions have a substantial impact on metadata information's longevity and provenance. The absence of unified publication formats limits the automated processing of application profiles, thereby limiting the number of application profiles accessible in various attempts to register and curate them. The limited number of application profiles also restricts the primary purpose of metadata registries in using application profiles to promote interoperability and reuse [17]. There is also a lack of a standardized way to link data to the MAP it is based on [21,22].

1.3   Challenges in Application Profile Development

To develop and manage application profiles, there are recommendations such as Me4DCAP which provides a set of guidelines to define, construct, and validate MAPs [14]. However, authoring tools and formats which are dedicated to MAP is less in number. Usually, application profile maintainers have to use different tools to create different expression formats, and this makes the whole process tedious for most of the domain experts. As a result, a large number of application profiles were authored and published only in the human-readable document formats. Availability of previous versions is not ensured and most of the MAPs doesn't maintain older versions in a publicly accessible format.

Different communities have different levels of experience in the technical aspects of application profile expression formats. There is a severe lack of guidance for developing and publishing metadata application profiles. The barrier is the limited number of well-defined samples and initiatives for archiving and curating application profiles. For creating application profiles, there are not many well-accepted authoring formats or pre-processors.

1.4   Yet Another Metadata Application Profile (YAMA) as an Application Profile Authoring Format

Source formats used for application profile publication can be considered as an authoring format. This source formats can be processed with the help of processing tools such as a format converter or a parsing system to generate different expression formats of that application profile. A format to author the application profile cannot be considered as an expression of the application profile in all situations if the format is not a standard expression. The expression capabilities of such formats are dependable to its processors or conversion tools. This clear separation between authoring and expression formats is illustrated in Fig. 1.

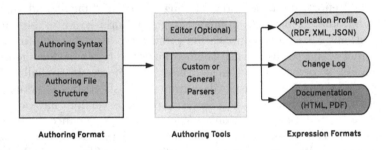

Fig. 1. Authoring formats and expression formats for application profiles

For application profile, authors proposes Yet Another Metadata Application Profile (YAMA) as an extensible authoring format to address shortcomings of previous proposals [23]. Despite extensive knowledge of MAP, YAMA is meant to be simple enough that domain experts can use it. YAMA uses YAML Ain't Markup Language (YAML), a robust human-friendly data serialization format with various implementations in most popular programming languages and considered to be JSON's superset [2]. Basic structure of YAMA MAP section is explained in Fig. 2.

YAMA is also an attempt to resolve the lack of a workflow in authoring metadata application profiles. Given the increasing popularity of workflows based on GitHub, different output formats, and extensibility to various proposals such as ShEx, DCAT, PROV removes the need for repetitive tasks in the maintenance of metadata application profiles. YAMA is an intermediate MAP format to produce or convert different standard application profile expression formats.

YAMA is extensible with custom elements and structure. For example, custom elements can be added to the document tree, as per the demand of the use case. The only restriction is that custom elements cannot be from reserved element sets. Capabilities of YAMA could be extended without any large-scale

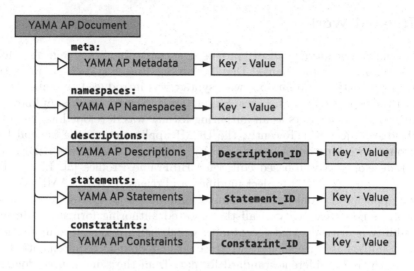

Fig. 2. Structure of YAMA MAP

implementation changes within the scope of YAML specification. YAMA is based on DC-DSP, and a minimal DC-DSP is mandatory to express a MAP in YAMA. YAMA also includes a structured syntax to record modifications of a YAMA document named as change-sets, in addition to extensible key-values and structure. YAMA change-sets can be used to record changes of a MAP over any other versions. Change-sets are adapted from RFC 6902 JavaScript Object Notation (JSON) Patch [19], with the changes marked as an action to a path. Every change use 'status' as a reserved value to indicate status changes like 'deprecation.' This extensible nature of YAMA documents is explained in Fig. 3.

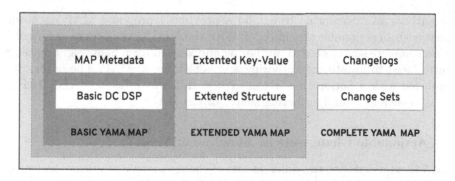

Fig. 3. Extensibility of a YAMA application profile

2   Related Work

As an application format, DCMI proposed a constrained language for Dublin Core Application Profiles named Description Set Profile (DSP). As an authoring format for DSP, a MoinMoin wiki syntax was introduced to embed Application Profiles in web pages. Later, Simple DSP (SDSP) [7]. A simplified form of DSP using spreadsheets as an authoring format was developed as part of the Metabridge project [17]. Recently, the DCMI application profile Special Interest Group is working on improving DSP [6]. Library of Congress BIBFRAME project developed a web-based editor for BibFrame Profiles [5]. Linked Data for Production 2 (LD4P2) project modified and released BIBFRAME editor for general application profile creation named Sinopia Profile Editor [11].

There is no extensibility of all these stated authoring formats. A format's extensibility is critical to its acceptance, which helps different communities to adopt a simple base format and introduce specific domain requirements. It will also help to create different standard formats from the same source document without relying on the common elements. The authors previously proposed an extensible authoring format named Yet Another Metadata Application Profile (YAMA) [25] using YAML[1] syntax and validated its extensibility over existing similar proposals [24].

Li and Sugimoto proposed a provenance model named DSP-PROV [13] to keep track of structural changes of metadata schemas. The DSP-PROV model applies PROV to the Dublin Core Application Profile. Different from the above proposal, this paper is treating application profile documents as a digital resource and attempting to use a lightweight ontology to map different versions of the published MAP and its provenance.

3   Methodology

The authors are attempting to extend a previously proposed MAP authoring format with an actionable timeline [23]. With the consideration that the format is to be a complete source of MAP authoring and versioning, a lightweight ontology is introduced to notate the authoring and versioning of MAP. The ontology is introduced with a notion that it can express different versions of the MAP as well as stakeholders and authoring source of the MAP.

3.1   Actionable Changesets as Timeline of MAP

YAMA is extended with two different sets of change mapping options. An actionable change record named 'changesets' - a collection of changes declared using a custom adaptation of JSON-PATCH - along with minimal metadata for the set of changes. Changesets are declared within the 'changes' path of the YAMA document. JSON patch is originally intended to use as HTTP-PATCH method for

---

[1] https://yaml.org.

JavaScript Object Notation (JSON) [RFC4627][2] - a standard format for storing and exchanging structured data. HTTP PATCH [RFC5789][3] method extends the Hypertext Transfer Protocol (HTTP) [RFC2616][4] as a method to perform partial modifications to resources. A simple JSON patch is shown in Fig. 4.

Adaption of JSON-Patch as a possible means of recording changes within the application profile authoring environment helps to makes the changes actionable without any lock-in as JSON-Patch is widely adapted and there are plenty of implementations in every popular programming languages. This acceptance helps the implementors to keep the format open for independent development and tooling within the workflow of MAP development.

A JSON Patch consists of sequential operations applied to a JSON object with one operation (op) element. As per RFC6902, valid operations are - add, remove, replace, move, copy, and test. Each operation must declare one path element which is a JSON Pointer - defined as per RFC6901 - points to a location to modify within the given JSON document. A JSON Pointer composed of a string of tokens separated by '/' characters. These tokens can be a specific key in objects or indexes of arrays.

The remaining part of a JSON Patch operation consists of more elements depends on the specific type of operation.

```
1  {
2      "op": "remove",
3      "path": "/statements/statement_id/"
4  }
```

Fig. 4. A basic JSON-Patch object indicating a removal operation

In theory, a YAMA document is a constrained YAML expression of a MAP which can be abstracted or converted into a valid JSON structure. The JSON patch is applied to this JSON structure instead of the YAML document. In order to make the JSON patch actionable for generating the pre or post-change versions of a MAP, authors extended the JSON patch by including a new optional elements **previous_value** which is applicable only for remove and replace operations. Another proposed additional element in the context of an application profile is **status** - which can notate the changes in status, such as deprecation, proposed, reserved, and obsolete. An example changeset expressed within YAMA is shows in Fig. 5. Minimal mandatory metadata elemets for YAMA changeset is given in Table 1.

Along with changesets, YAMA is extended with an optional changelog section, which is a human-readable list of changes with minimal metadata.

[2] https://tools.ietf.org/html/rfc6902.
[3] https://tools.ietf.org/html/rfc5789.
[4] https://tools.ietf.org/html/rfc2616.

```
1  # YAMA
2  changes:
3    cs_20181108_01:
4      version: 1.2
5      previous_version: 1.1
6      date: 2018-11-08
7      changeset:
8        ch_20181108_01:
9          op: replace # remove, add, replace, copy, test
10         path: /statements/pr_type/max
11         value: n
12         previous_value: 0
```

Fig. 5. Example of YAMA ChangeSet

Table 1. Metadata for the changeset

Element	Usage
version	Version of the MAP after the change
previous_version	Version of the MAP, to which the change is applied
date	Date of change in ISO 8601 (not the date of release)

Changelogs are not meant to be actionable but act as a structured collection of human-readable descriptions of changes, which can be changes intended to be documented but does not have any impact on the structure of the MAP document. Also, this section can serve as an alternate but meaningful textual representation of changes instead of utilizing the changeset. This changelog section is proposed for authors prefer to utilize another means of change management, such as a version control systems, or authors with minimal technical expertise on creating an actionable JSON-patch. A schematic representation of YAMA's provenance components and their outcome is expressed in Fig. 6.

3.2   PAV Ontology as a Means of MAP Provenance

Provenance, Authoring and Versioning ontology (PAV)[5] [4] is developed as a lightweight ontology for notating minimal information which is essential for documenting the provenance, authoring, and versioning of resources published in the web. PAV clearly distinguishes between contributors, authors and publishes of digital resources. PAV is capable of representing the provenance of originating resources that have been accessed, transformed, and consumed.

PAV utilizes the W3C provenance ontology PROV-O, in order to describe authoring, publishing, and digital maintenance of online resources. PAV does not define any explicit classes, domain, or ranges; instead, every property is meant to be directly used in describing an online resource. This direct usage minimalizes

---

[5] http://purl.org/pav.

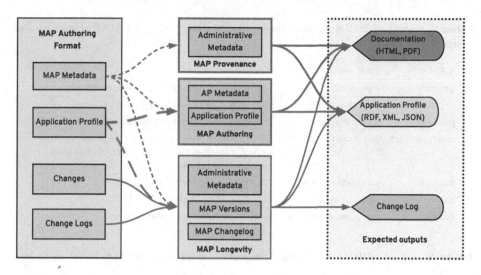

Fig. 6. YAMA with actionable changesets and changelogs mapped to their expected outputs

the efforts required for expressing resources using an ontology. Being lightweight over PROV-O is the main reason for considering PAV to be a means of expressing MAP resources [4].

There are vocabularies similar to PAV such as Dublin Core Terms (DC Terms) [3], PROV-O [12], OPM [16], and Provenance Vocabulary [8]. Among that PROV-O is the most suitable and previously considered in many other studies to express MAP provenance. PROV-O is similar to a generic framework for describing provenance in a different range of applications. However, using PROV-O alone may not be suitable in expressing necessary details for the specific provenance involving authoring and versioning. PAV can be considered as a specialization of PROV-O by facilitating more straightforward relationships for expressing common provenance for digital resources in the web [4]. PROV-O implements terms useful in tracing the origin of a resource, its derivations, and the relationship between these different resources. PROV-O is also capable of expressing the different entities contributed to the resource. In short, PROV-O can be considered as a general provenance data model extendable for domain-specific provenance information. For example, PROV-O does not distinguish between authors, editors, and contributors - which is a noticeable distinction in use-cases like collaborative MAP authoring and publishing based on public repositories such as GitHub.

PAV based framework is proposed in the context of MAP authoring and publishing with these intentions.

1. Identify the persons and organizations or agents involved in the application profile development. Also, distinguish their roles as contributor or creator of the published MAP.

Table 2. Subset of PAV authoring properties mapped to YAMA MAP metadata elements

YAMA	PAV element	Description
creator	pav:authoredBy	The author of the MAP (person or agent)
creator	pav:createdBy	The author of the MAP (person or agent)
publisher	pav:curatedBy	The Publisher, generally the organisation
contributors	pav:contributedBy	The collaborative agents, such as people who are not a part of the authors but contributed through GitHub etc
date	pav:authoredOn	The date of authoring the MAP
date	pav:curatedOn	The date of publishing the MAP
date	pav:contributedOn	Same as the date of publishing

Table 3. Subset of PAV provenance properties mapped to YAMA MAP metadata elements

YAMA metadata	PAV element	Description
creator	pav:createdBy	The author of the MAP (person or agent)
publisher	pav:createdWith	The tool, software or authoring format of the MAP. eg YAMA, Sinopia
date	pav:createdOn	The date of authoring the MAP
URL	pav:retrievedFrom	The published URL of the MAP
source	pav:importedFrom	The source of the MAP, eg: GitHub repository URL, Google Docs URL etc

Table 4. Subset of PAV versioning properties mapped to YAMA MAP metadata elements

YAMA metadata	PAV element	Description
version	pav:version	The version identifier of the MAP. A semantic version (SemVer) is recommended
previous_version	pav:previousVersion	Previous version identifier of the MAP. Current version is assumed to be a derived from this version
based_on	pav:derivedFrom	The base schema that the application profile is derived from. Example, DCAP, BibFrame, SDSP etc.
date	pav:lastUpdatedOn	The last updated date is expected, but this update is meant for changes that doesn't break the MAP structure, such as fixing a spelling
version	pav:hasVersion	MAP has accessible versions
version	pav:hasCurrentVersion	Current version of the MAP
version	pav:hasEarlierVersion	Earlier versions of the MAP

2. Mapping of MAP versions, release, and updates by distinguishes between published and last modified dates.
3. Track and distinguish the versions and source of the MAP, such as differentiating the provenance for the published versions of the application profiles and source repositories, the version control systems or authoring environment.

A detailed schematic explanation MAP versioning expression with PAV is narrated in Fig. 7. Tables 2, 3 and 4 shows the possible mapping of YAMA metadata elements a subset of PAV ontology.

4   Validation

To validate the proposal, a popular public application profile, The DCAT Application profile for data portals in Europe (DCAT-AP) can be used. DCAT-AP an application profile based on W3C's Data Catalogue vocabulary (DCAT). DCAT is implemented for describing public sector datasets in Europe to enable a cross-data portal search for open data sets and make them searchable. DCAT-AP is published in Joinup portal[6], but the sources are maintained in a GitHub repository[7]. DCAT-AP repository does not use any authoring format or preprocessors but maintains and releases the MAP in individual expression formats.

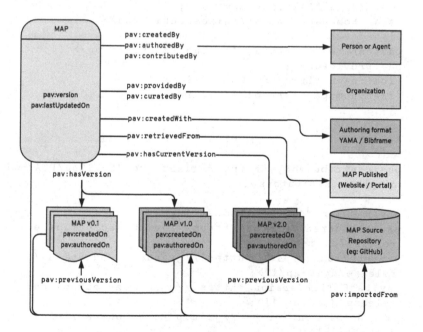

Fig. 7. MAP publication is expressed in PAV ontology

---

[6] https://joinup.ec.europa.eu/solution/dcat-application-profile-data-portals-europe.
[7] https://github.com/SEMICeu/DCAT-AP.

As a well-maintained MAP, the repository holds three different versions - v1.1, v1.2, and v1.2.1. RDF expression of the MAP points to the previous version, but the whole versioning is not mapped within the RDF [20]. A minimal expression of DCAT-AP provenance with PAV in RDF is demonstrated below.

```
1  @prefix xsd: <http://www.w3.org/2001/XMLSchema#> .
2  @prefix pav: <http://purl.org/pav/> .
3  @prefix foaf: <http://xmlns.com/foaf/0.1/> .
4
5  <https://joinup.ec.europa.eu/solution/dcat-application-
       profile-data-portals-europe>
6    pav:createdBy  [
7     foaf:name "DCAT-AP Working Group" ;
8     foaf:homepage <https://joinup.ec.europa.eu/node/64331>
9     ] ;
10   pav:authoredBy [
11    foaf:name "Makx Dekkers" ;
12    foaf:homepage <http://makxdekkers.com/>
13    ], [
14    foaf:name "Vassilios Peristeras" ;
15    foaf:homepage <http://www.deri.ie/users/vassilios-
       peristeras/>
16    ], [
17    foaf:Name "Nikolaos Loutas" ;
18    foaf:homepage <http://nikosloutas.com/>
19    ];
20   pav:curatedBy <https://joinup.ec.europa.eu/> ;
21   pav:providedBy [
22    foaf:name "European Commission" ;
23    foaf:homepage <http://ec.europa.eu/>
24    ] ;
25
26   # GitHub contributors, need not to be authors or
       editors
27   pav:contributedBy <https://github.com/SEMICeu/DCAT-AP/
       graphs/contributors>;
28
29   pav:version "1.2.1"^^xsd:string;
30   pav:hasCurrentVersion <https://joinup.ec.europa.eu/
       release/dcat-ap/121>;
31   pav:previousVersion <https://joinup.ec.europa.eu/
       release/dcat-ap/12>;
32   pav:hasErlierVersion <https://joinup.ec.europa.eu/
       release/dcat-ap/11>;
33   pav:hasVersion <https://joinup.ec.europa.eu/release/
       dcat-ap/121>;
34   pav:hasVersion <https://joinup.ec.europa.eu/release/
       dcat-ap/12>;
35   pav:hasVersion <https://joinup.ec.europa.eu/release/
       dcat-ap/11>;
```

```
36    pav:hasVersion <https://joinup.ec.europa.eu/node
      /69559>;
37    pav:wasDerivedFrom <https://www.w3.org/TR/vocab-dcat
      -2/>;
38    # GitHub main repository
39    pav:importedFrom <https://github.com/SEMICeu/DCAT-AP>.
40
41 <https://joinup.ec.europa.eu/release/dcat-ap/121>
42    pav:version "1.2.1"^^xsd:string;
43    pav:createdOn "2019-05-28"^^xsd:date;
44    pav:authoredOn "2019-05-28"^^xsd:date;
45    pav:importedOn "2019-05-28"^^xsd:date;
46    # GitHub repository versioned branch
47    pav:wasDerivedFrom <https://github.com/SEMICeu/DCAT-AP
      /tree/1.2.1>;
48    # GitHub repository draft version branch
49    pav:sourceAccessedAt <https://github.com/SEMICeu/DCAT-
      AP/tree/1.2.1-draft>;
50    pav:previousVersion <https://joinup.ec.europa.eu/
      release/dcat-ap/12>;
51    pav:hasErlierVersion <https://joinup.ec.europa.eu/
      release/dcat-ap/11>.
52
53 <https://joinup.ec.europa.eu/release/dcat-ap/12>
54    pav:version "1.2"^^xsd:string;
55    pav:authoredOn "2018-11-08"^^xsd:date;
56    pav:wasDerivedFrom <https://github.com/SEMICeu/DCAT-AP
      /tree/1.2>;
57    pav:importedFrom <https://github.com/SEMICeu/DCAT-AP/
      tree/1.2-draft>;
58    pav:previousVersion <https://joinup.ec.europa.eu/
      release/dcat-ap/11>;
59    pav:hasErlierVersion <https://joinup.ec.europa.eu/node
      /69559>.
60
61 <https://joinup.ec.europa.eu/release/dcat-ap/11>
62    pav:version "1.1"^^xsd:string;
63    pav:authoredOn "2016-06-08"^^xsd:date;
64    pav:wasDerivedFrom <https://github.com/SEMICeu/DCAT-AP
      /tree/1.1>;
65    pav:previousVersion <https://joinup.ec.europa.eu/node
      /69559>.
66
67 <https://joinup.ec.europa.eu/node/69559>
68    pav:version "1"^^xsd:string.
```

5   Limitations and Future Work

As an authoring format, YAMA can be extended to include the actionable changesets and parsable changelog. And PAV ontology can be used to point the source of the MAP, in which the YAMA changeset can be exposed as the timeline of the application profile. The main limitation of this approach is its inability in pointing to a standard format of the actionable changeset. A processor or system capable of understanding YAMA's YAML format as well as JSON-Patch is required to parse the changeset and develop the timeline of the application profile from it. So it is recommended that the authors or publishes tender required efforts to properly expose the changesets in other standard actionable formats as well. Even though YAML and JSON-Patch are comparatively more uncomplicated concepts for structured data, they demand the authors to have the skill sets and capabilities to deal with these formats. Mainly these formats need to be generated or modified using a 'real text editor' as there is not yet any known dedicated graphical editor implementation for YAMA.

PAV ontology is capable enough to point to versions and sources of the application profiles. The authors made this recommendation purely on the notion that MAPs are published as a package of expression formats and documentation. PAV is not directly usable in differentiating these formats within the application profile package or even pointing to individual format. For example, PAV may not be sufficient enough in distinguishing and pointing to the individual files representing the human-readable documentation or machine-actionable expressions like RDF and ShEx. Also, PAV mapping needs to implemented in templates or generators, used in producing expression formats from YAMA. Webpages liked to the application profiles requires to use RDFa or JSON-LD to include the ontology in expressing the versions and source with PAV.

The future work is to adopt ontologies to cover YAMA changesets with the capability of mentioning changes within an actionable and semantic approach. Notating the relation between individual expressions formats inside the publishable application profile package is also being investigated.

6   Conclusion

Providing a simplified authoring format can substantially promote the application profile creation efforts. Utilizing extensibility of this authoring format to include actionable changelog as the timeline of MAP creation can help in ensuring longevity. The authors are attempted to explain the possibility of a previously proposed extensible authoring format for application profiles with an advanced changeset. This paper also demonstrates adopting a lightweight ontology to notate the versioning of this application profiles with distinguishing its source from the published expressions. Any attempts to ensure the provenance and longevity of the metadata application profile will also help to ensure the provenance of the schema. Schema maintenance will help to achieve better goals in data interoperability and seamless linking of data with automated techniques.

Acknowledgement. This work was supported by JSPS KAKENHI Grant Number JP18K11984.

References

1. Baca, M.: Introduction to Metadata, July 2016. http://www.getty.edu/publications/intrometadata
2. Ben-Kiki, O., Evans, C., döt Net, I.: YAML Ain't Markup Language (YAML™) Version 1.2, October 2009. https://yaml.org/spec/1.2/spec.html
3. Board, D.U.: DCMI: DCMI Metadata Terms. https://www.dublincore.org/specifications/dublin-core/dcmi-terms/2012-06-14/
4. Ciccarese, P., Soiland-Reyes, S., Belhajjame, K., Gray, A.J., Goble, C., Clark, T.: PAV ontology: provenance, authoring and versioning. J. Biomed. Semant. **4**(1), 37 (2013). https://doi.org/10.1186/2041-1480-4-37
5. Library of Congress, L.: BIBFRAME Profile Editor (2018). http://bibframe.org/profile-edit/
6. Coyle, K.: RDF-AP, January 2017. https://github.com/kcoyle/RDF-AP, original-date: 2017–01-12T15:38:41Z
7. Enoksson, F.: DCMI: A MoinMoin Wiki Syntax for Description Set Profiles, October 2008. http://www.dublincore.org/specifications/dublin-core/dsp-wiki-syntax/
8. Hartig, O., Zhao, J.: Publishing and consuming provenance metadata on the web of linked data. In: McGuinness, D.L., Michaelis, J.R., Moreau, L. (eds.) IPAW 2010. LNCS, vol. 6378, pp. 78–90. Springer, Heidelberg (2010). https://doi.org/10.1007/978-3-642-17819-1_10
9. Heery, R., Patel, M.: Application profiles: mixing and matching metadata schemas. Ariadne (25) (2000). http://www.ariadne.ac.uk/issue/25/app-profiles/
10. Hillmann, D.: Metadata standards and applications (2006). http://managemetadata.com/, publisher: Metadata Management Associates LLC
11. LD4P2: Sinopia Profile Editor (2019). https://profile-editor.sinopia.io/
12. Lebo, T., et al.: Prov-o: The prov ontology. W3C recommendation 30 (2013)
13. Li, C., Sugimoto, S.: Provenance description of metadata application profiles for long-term maintenance of metadata schemas. J. Documentation **74**(1), 36–61 (2018). https://doi.org/10.1108/JD-03-2017-0042
14. Malta, M.C., Baptista, A.A.: A method for the development of Dublin core application profiles (Me4dcap V0.2): detailed description. In: Proceedings of the International Conference on Dublin Core and Metadata Applications, p. 14 (2013)
15. Malta, M.C., Baptista, A.A.: A panoramic view on metadata application profiles of the last decade. Int. J. Metadata Semant. Ontol. **9**(1), 58 (2014). https://doi.org/10.1504/IJMSO.2014.059124
16. Moreau, L., et al.: The open provenance model core specification (v1.1). Futur. Gener. Comput. Syst. **27**(6), 743–756 (2011). https://doi.org/10.1016/j.future.2010.07.005
17. Nagamori, M., Kanzaki, M., Torigoshi, N., Sugimoto, S.: Meta-bridge: a development of metadata information infrastructure in Japan. In: Proceedings International Conference on Dublin Core and Metadata Applications, p. 6 (2011)
18. Nilsson, M., Baker, T., Johnston, P.: DCMI: The Singapore Framework for Dublin Core Application Profiles, January 2008. http://dublincore.org/specifications/dublin-core/singapore-framework/
19. Nottingham, M., Bryan, P.: JavaScript Object Notation (JSON) Patch, April 2013. https://tools.ietf.org/html/rfc6902

20. The DCAT Application profile for data portals in Europe (DCAT-AP), April 2019. https://github.com/SEMICeu/DCAT-AP, original-date: 2017–09-13T07:53:27Z
21. Svensson, L.A.R.V.: Negotiating Profiles in HTTP, March 2017. https://profilenegotiation.github.io/I-D-Accept-Schema/I-D-accept-schema
22. Svensson, L.G., Atkinson, R., Car, N.J.: Content Negotiation by Profile, April 2019. https://www.w3.org/TR/dx-prof-conneg/
23. Thalhath, N., Nagamori, M., Sakaguchi, T.: YAMA: Yet Another Metadata Application Profile (2019). https://purl.org/yama/spec/latest
24. Thalhath, N., Nagamori, M., Sakaguchi, T., Sugimoto, S.: Authoring formats and their extensibility for application profiles. In: Jatowt, A., Maeda, A., Syn, S.Y. (eds.) ICADL 2019. LNCS, vol. 11853, pp. 116–122. Springer, Cham (2019). https://doi.org/10.1007/978-3-030-34058-2_12
25. Thalhath, N., Nagamori, M., Sakaguchi, T., Sugimoto, S.: Yet another metadata application profile (YAMA): authoring, versioning and publishing of application profiles. In: International Conference on Dublin Core and Metadata Applications, pp. 114–125 (2019). https://dcpapers.dublincore.org/pubs/article/view/4055. ISSN 1939-1366

An Ontology-Based Development of Activity Knowledge and System Design

Nami Iino[1,2,3](✉) ⓘ, Hideaki Takeda[2,4](✉) ⓘ, and Takuichi Nishimura[1](✉) ⓘ

[1] National Institute of Advanced Industrial Science and Technology, Tokyo, Japan
{nami-iino,takuichi.nishimura}@aist.go.jp
[2] The Graduate University for Advanced Studies, SOKENDAI, Kanagawa, Japan
[3] RIKEN Center for Advanced Intelligence Project, Tokyo, Japan
[4] National Institute of Informatics, Tokyo, Japan
takeda@nii.ac.jp

Abstract. This paper describes an ontology-based development of activity knowledge on a domain and the system we developed to support it. To understand human activities, it is important to explicitly describe the knowledge of each domain. However, there are some issues of knowledge development: the establishment of the efficient method and process, the improvement of the readability for humans and machines, and the regular improvement of knowledge after development. We thus introduced a process of knowledge development, which uses two different types of knowledge representation (activity knowledge and domain ontology) on a domain that requires technical skills. In this study, we practiced the process in the music field to investigate the effects of developing activity knowledge based on a domain ontology. The results showed that it enables deep understanding and extension of knowledge. Furthermore, we designed a system to help the ontology-based development of activity knowledge. We rewrote the activity knowledge using the system and received preliminary results on term control.

Keywords: Activity knowledge · Domain ontology · Knowledge representation · kNeXaR

1 Introduction

Human activities are diversifying in ways that require appropriate knowledge processing in accordance with the domain of each activity. In order to support human activities using information technologies, it is necessary to come up with a description form of knowledge that can be processed and with knowledge representations that make understanding and reasoning easier. In the knowledge engineering field, many domain ontologies have been developed to resolve these issues. Domain ontology here is defined as the knowledge conceptualized and hierarchized from a specific viewpoint in a specific domain. It enables not only deeper understanding of domain knowledge but also the collection and utilization of adequate information through multiple data integrations.

© Springer Nature Switzerland AG 2020
X. Wang et al. (Eds.): JIST 2019, LNCS 12032, pp. 369–384, 2020.
https://doi.org/10.1007/978-3-030-41407-8_24

The most pressing issue with domain ontologies is that it is difficult to (i) verify the validity by domain experts [1] and (ii) regularly improve the ontology on pace with developments in the field. Collaboration between computer engineers and domain experts is thus extremely important to build domain knowledge. Previous works in the field of knowledge representation have pursued mainly machine readability. We feel that workflow design to connect both experts and a method for easily extracting and organizing knowledge is important. In particular, knowledge representation that is easy to understand for domain experts and integration with a domain ontology would be helpful for our activities.

1.1 Motivations and Requirements

Our goal is to develop domain knowledge by collaboration with computer engineers (ontology experts) and domain experts and to use it on-site. Therefore, we recommend a process for knowledge development using two types of knowledge representation, activity knowledge and the domain ontology. Activity knowledge here means a knowledge representation of "how" to process the actionable events like procedural knowledge. The reason we treat two types of knowledge representation is that the activity knowledge expressing "how" and the ontology specifying "what" complement each other. For instance, ontology helps maintain consistency among the terms of activity knowledge and also helps deepen the understanding of domain experts while allowing processing by machines.

Figure 1 shows a process of developing domain knowledge. First, both ontology experts and domain experts collect knowledge from existing materials. Next, domain experts structure knowledge using a description form suitable for the domain and ontology experts develop and visualize a domain ontology. In the case of dealing with a domain involving technical skill, such as musical instrument performance, here we name the structured knowledge as activity knowledge. After developing the two types of knowledge representation, both experts improve knowledge representations repeatedly. Finally, domain experts acquire implicit knowledge through improving the activity knowledge or computer engineers utilize knowledge in various ways.

The features of this process are as below. This cycling process leads to extend and improve knowledge appropriately by sharing the various contents of the knowledge among both experts. The developed domain ontology provides principles such as the structure of the knowledge and terms to activity knowledge. Activity knowledge provides specific knowledge, which are described in each domain only, to domain ontology.

1. Domain experts develop activity knowledge to facilitate knowledge expansion and understanding.
2. Ontology experts develop a domain ontology with the same viewpoint as activity knowledge for knowledge processing.
3. Both knowledge are repeatedly improved by a cycle that enables them to expanded and for implicit knowledge to be acquired.

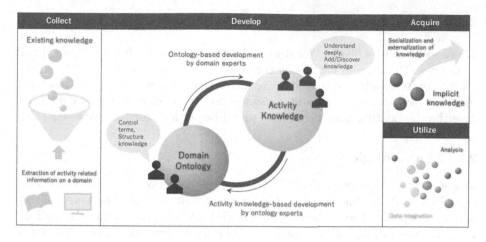

Fig. 1. A process of developing domain knowledge using activity knowledge and a domain ontology.

1.2   Contributions

In this study, we selected musical performance as a domain and implemented the ontology-based development of activity knowledge by following process. First, we introduced two types of knowledge representation we developed focusing on classical guitar rendition. Then, we improved the activity knowledge based on the domain ontology printed on paper and determined its effects. As a result, we found that enables (1) the discovery of specific items, (2) the improvement of knowledge and (3) deep understanding on the part of domain experts.

In order to enhance efficiency in ontology-based development of activity knowledge, we have developed a system, named kNeXaR, that helps describe activity knowledge by selecting the term of the ontology. In a preliminary investigation on the effect of this system, we compared the change before and after the terminologies of activity knowledge. The results demonstrated that kNeXaR can support the process and control the terms.

In summary, the main contributions of this paper are:

- A detailed practice of an ontology-based development of activity knowledge and demonstration of its effects.
- A system to support the ontology-based development of activity knowledge, and a simple demonstration about term control.

In Sect. 2 of this paper, we describe related works on the methodologies and knowledge representations of knowledge development. In Section 3, we describe the two types of knowledge representation we developed in the music field and report the results of the ontology-based development of activity knowledge. Then, we describe the system we developed and its effect in Sect. 4. We conclude with a brief summary and mention of future work in Sect. 5.

2   Related Work

There seems to be a demand for studies that provide knowledge development and guidelines. This section focuses on the relevance of representing domain knowledge in ontologies in a way that is easier for the domain experts and machines (collaborative development and consumption) with regard to readability. We describe the existing approaches that would be suitable for this purpose.

2.1   Methodologies

In ontology development, SWEET Ontologies[1] contains about 6,000 concepts organized in 200 ontologies describing earth system science that were built by ontology experts. The problem with SWEET Ontologies is that it is difficult to verify the validity of the ontologies by domain experts. In contrast, Gene Ontology is developed focusing on the is–a or part–of relationship by mainly domain experts to provide common vocabularies [2]. In the field of agriculture, Agriculture Activity Ontology[2] (AAO) was built for data integration by ontology experts and domain experts [7]. Such collaboration between experts is very significant when is comes to treating domain knowledge, it can not only cultivate collaboration among each experts but also achieve the development of reliable knowledge.

The modeling of development processes has been attempting. In the field of business, Uschold et al. generalized the process by which they developed the Enterprise Ontology [20]. Their process is as follows: (1) identification of purpose and scope, (2) Ontology building, (3) Evaluation, and (4) Documentation. This methodology is an informal ontology development, and they defined concepts using natural language in (2). In addition, there is a lot of discussion now about development processes in the knowledge graph field [8].

In music field, there are several approaches to using the knowledge: organizing the knowledge related to musical instruments [12], creating a semantic web of data on music-related information [21], linking music-specific vocabularies [13], and conceptualizing about musical notation [17]. Our approach focuses on to systematizing and representing the movements (actions) of a musical performance.

2.2   Knowledge Representations

Ontology can comprehensively and systematically represent objects and their relationships that are related to "what" in order to share and reuse knowledge. On the other hand, domains that require skill consist of various types of knowledge, and information related to "how" is especially important. Procedural knowledge can represent how to perform a process in a certain scenario. However, this knowledge requires (1) a machine-readable description in order to properly

---

[1] https://github.com/ESIPFed/sweet.
[2] http://cavoc.org/aao/ns/2/.

perform the process, (2) another knowledge that describes "what" like ontology does to ensure the consistency of the terms. To develop activity knowledge, a process that enables domain experts and ontology experts to represent domain knowledge including "what" and "how" from the same perspective is necessary.

Many visualization tools have been developed to promote understanding of ontologies. Visual Notation for OWL Ontologies (VOWL) can be customized to preference [14]. The OntoGraph was developed to provide documentation on existing OWL ontologies. It can create separate graphs for the classes, object and data properties, and individuals of an ontology [1]. Another approach to representing ontologies is Spreadsheets, which are used in a lot of domains. Populous has been used for ontology development such as Kidney and Urinary Pathway Ontology (KUPO)[9]. These tools cannot visualize complex structures that have blank nodes, however, some works have addressed to solve it by skolemization which the existing provides reliable tools support for customization [4,15]. For that reason, we feel it is necessary to use another description form or tools. Activity knowledge that provides high readability might help solve this problem.

The workflow proposed in some tools [3,18,19] allows domain experts to easily modify and scale ontologies as per the rapid need of the application. Furthermore, they also provide other features such as version control and visualization.

As a framework of knowledge representation in the product design field, the Functional Ontology was developed [11]. This ontology deals with knowledge about design rationale and can provide generality with high reusability by separating function (what to achieve) from the way of function achievement (how to achieve). In this study, we mitigate the notion and use it when developing the activity knowledge.

3   Development of Domain Knowledge

In this section, we present the practice of the ontology-based development of activity knowledge in a musical performance. We chose the classical guitar, as it has more techniques than other instruments.

3.1   Activity Knowledge

The problem with classical guitar is that there are no general textbooks, which tends to result in a lack of knowledge sharing among players or teachers and hinders the understanding and progress of students. Therefore, our previous work involved the collection and organization of knowledge related to classical guitar techniques [5]. In this study, we revised that knowledge by utilizing the Convincing Human Action Rationalized Model (CHARM)[16].

The basic components of CHARM are the action, which implies the change of states, the instance of action, the doer, additional information, and the manner. This model presents the action as a purpose and more detailed partial actions, but we distinguished between them to deal with the abstract purpose. In addition, there is an "achievement method" between the action layers that

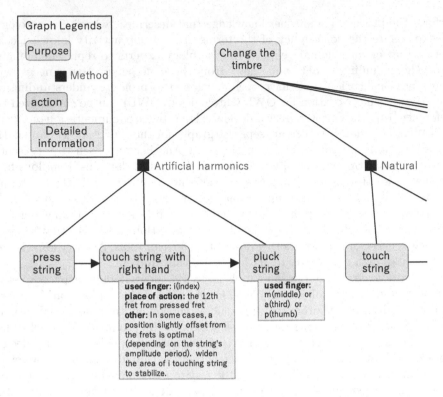

Fig. 2. An example of activity knowledge (Color figure online)

indicate the conceptualized principles of the physical law in state change [11]. We eased the idea of the achievement method (hereinafter called the "method") and defined it as "the technique for achieving the purpose."

There are three main contents of our activity knowledge: purpose, action, and method. In addition, we created items of detailed information as needed. Figure 2 shows an example of the activity knowledge developed on the basis of the above ideas. We adopted classical guitar renditions as the method. The green rectangle indicates the purpose, the black squares and blue letters present the method (guitar rendition), the blue rectangles indicate actions, and the orange rectangles describe the detailed information. In this example, the "Artificial harmonics" method is defined to achieve the purpose of "changing the timbre" and is performed in the order of the following three actions: "press string," "touch string with right hand," and "pluck sting." When performing "touch string with right hand," the index finger would be used. We can clearly distinguish the content of the knowledge in this way. However, in order to process this knowledge, we have to control the terminologies. Ontology helps achieve this by drawing from common concepts and conventions.

3.2 Domain Ontology: GRO

We developed a domain ontology, which is named Guitar Rendition Ontology[3](GRO), that conceptualizes the methods (guitar renditions) of activity knowledge and classifies them with an is–a relationship [6] (Fig. 3). This ontology consists of 96 primary concepts and 18 properties. The top concepts are as follows: *Percussive rendition* imitating percussion instruments; *Chord rendition* related to chord playing methods; *Ornament rendition* adding notes to decorate sounds; *Note value rendition*, which changes the length of the note value; *Articulation rendition*, which switches up the way of connecting between notes; *Timbre rendition*, which changes the timbre using strings; *Harmony rendition*, which changes the sounds; and *Fingering rendition*, which indicates the placement of fingers, the form of figures, and the manner of plucking.

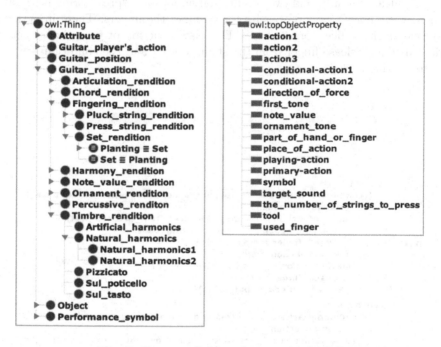

Fig. 3. Concepts (left) and properties (right)

To explain guitar renditions, we defined the following main properties: "target sound," which presents the kind of sound that is intended and/or imitated, such as a percussion sound, gliding sound, or overtone; "symbol," which indicates the kinds of symbols written in the musical score, such as articulation symbol, ornament symbol, or specific symbol; and action-related properties, as expressing the processes of actions is essential in GRO. We also added various properties

---

[3] We used the English version 2.3. https://github.com/guitar-san/Guitar-Rendition-Ontology.

as needed; for instance, "ornament tone" indicates added notes for decoration in the *Ornament rendition* (Fig. 3).

The description rules of actions are as follows: describe the order of action by "action+number," express the simultaneity and continuity of an action such as 'perform action A being performed during action B' by "primary-action" and "conditional-action," and explain the details of actions by several properties such as "used finger" and "place of action."

Figure 4 shows the description of *Artificial harmonics*. This rendition is described as a sequence of two actions (action1 and action2). In action1, players pluck a string with a finger on the body side of a guitar while pressing the same string with a finger on the neck side and touching a string with the indice (index finger) on the body side. The playing-action of the primary-action is "pluck string body" with one of three fingers; anular (third finger), medio (middle finger), or pulgar (thumb), and two conditional-actions are "press string neck" and "touch string body" with properties for usage of the fingers. Then, in action2, they release the indice from a string. The playing-action of the primary-action is described as "release finger from the string body," and the conditional-action is "press string neck."

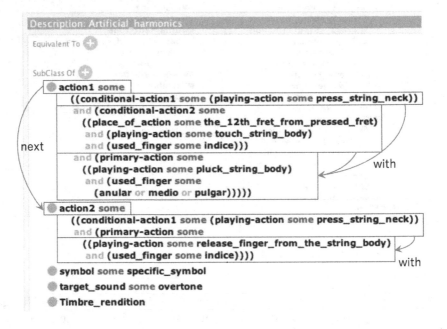

Fig. 4. An example of description of action

3.3 Ontology-Based Development of Activity Knowledge

In order to determine the effects of the process in the field of musical performance, we separately asked three domain experts (professional guitarists cum
instructors) to improve the activity knowledge. First, we visualized the Guitar
Rendition Ontology by using OWLAx [10] and presented the ontology and activity knowledge printed on paper. Then, the domain experts corrected or added to
the activity knowledge in handwriting. The renditions we selected were regarding
Timbre rendition and *Percussion rendition* of GRO.

Change in Knowledge. Table 1 shows the variation in knowledge for each
domain expert. For detailed information, we counted the number of items like
"used finger" and "place of action." As the results show, all of them on average
were increased. The items of the detailed information were added to the knowledge referring to the properties of GRO such as "part of hand or finger" and
"target sound." Furthermore, domain experts modified the description form to
express the sustained actions referring to the GRO's structures.

Table 1. Variations in knowledge. (a) and (b) are the name of purposes that correspond
to *Timbre rendition* and *Percussion rendition* of GRO.

	Before	Expert A	Expert B	Expert C	Average
(a) Change the timbre					
Method	5	+1	+1	+1	**+1.00**
Action	15	+3	+2	+0	**+1.67**
Details	28	+8	+9	+5	**+7.33**
(b) Make percussion sound					
Method	11	+2	+3	+0	**+1.67**
Action	25	+3	+6	+0	**+3.00**
Details	24	+1	+9	+3	**+4.33**

Subjective Evaluation. We also asked the domain experts about their opinions regarding the activity knowledge and GRO to examine the effects of the
ontology-based development of activity knowledge. Table 2 lists our questions
about readability (Q.1), appropriateness (Q.2), and usefulness (Q.3). Experts
gave scores on five-point scales, ranging from 1 (strongly disagree) to 5 (strongly
agree).

As shown in Table 3, all evaluations were positive. With regard to readability,
the score of activity knowledge was better than that of GRO, which means the
description form was easy for the domain experts to understand. On the other
hand, its adequacy scores were lower than GRO's because the structures of
the ontology are clear. According to the evaluation of the usefulness and the

Table 2. Questions.

	(a) Activity knowledge
1.1	Do you understand about the activity knowledge?
1.2	Do you understand the differences between actions and methods?
1.3	Do you understand the purpose of *Artificial harmonics*?
1.4	Do you understand the process of *Artificial harmonics*?
2.1	Are the purposes appropriate?
2.2	Are the classification of methods appropriate?
2.3	Are the descriptions of the action processes appropriate?
2.4	Are the items of detailed information appropriate?
3.1	Are activity knowledge useful for knowledge sharing among players?
3.2	Are activity knowledge useful when you teach the guitar?
3.3	Are activity knowledge useful for deep understanding of actions and processes?
3.4	Is it possible to add specific actions or information to activity knowledge?
	(b) Guitar Rendition Ontology (GRO)
1.1	Do you understand about the GRO?
1.2	Do you understand classes and properties?
1.3	Do you understand the classification of *Artificial harmonics*?
1.4	Do you understand the action process of *Artificial harmonics*?
2.1	Are the top concepts appropriate?
2.2	Are the classification of guitar renditions appropriate?
2.3	Are the descriptions of the action processes appropriate?
2.4	Are the properties other than the action appropriate?
3.1	Is GRO useful to understand activity knowledge?
3.2	Are the terms of GRO useful to improve the activity knowledge?
3.3	Are the methods of the activity knowledge properly classified in GRO?
3.4	Is GRO useful for deep understanding of actions and their processes?

Table 3. Scores.

	(a) Activity knowledge			(b) Guitar Rendition Ontology		
	Expert A	Expert B	Expert C	Expert A	Expert B	Expert C
1.1	5	4	4	5	5	4
1.2	5	5	5	5	4	5
1.3	5	5	5	5	5	5
1.4	5	5	5	5	4	5
2.1	3	5	4	5	5	4
2.2	4	4	4	5	5	4
2.3	5	4	4	4	5	4
2.4	4	4	3	4	5	5
3.1	4	5	4	4	4	5
3.2	5	5	5	4	4	5
3.3	4	5	5	4	5	4
3.4	5	5	3	4	4	5

experts' comments, we found that improving the activity knowledge with domain ontology promoted understanding on the part of the domain experts. These results demonstrate that the ontology-based development of activity knowledge enables (1) the discovery of items in a domain, (2) the improvement of knowledge representation, and (3) deep understanding on the part of domain experts.

4 System Design

This section describes the kNeXaR (kNowledge eXplication AugmenteR) system we designed and developed to support the ontology-based development of activity knowledge.

4.1 Architecture

kNeXaR was designed to describe activity knowledge based on the domain ontology. In the beginning, we dealt with nursing care-related knowledge, but now we intend to widen the domain to include instrument performance, education, and the manufacturing industry. The system's architecture, shown in Fig. 5, has following components: Ontology, Declarative Knowledge, and Procedural knowledge. Ontology is managed in OWL (Web Ontology Language) and all activity knowledge are managed in XML. However, we must extend data availability for RDF and SPARQL in order to process and reason knowledge. Declarative knowledge here is an extension of ontology that is a platform for adding or linking all kinds of informations (expertise, individual know-how, videos, etc.). Note that we do not use declarative knowledge in this study. Here, procedural knowledge indicates the activity knowledge and can be developed by various domain experts in accordance with domains, facilities, communities and so on.

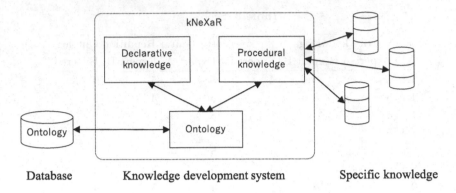

Fig. 5. System general architecture.

4.2   Functions

Figure 6 shows the activity knowledge-related windows: the right one presents the list of the ontology terms, the middle is the edit window for describing activity knowledge, and the left one presents the described knowledge. The description items of activity knowledge are based on the CHARM: *Action*, the *Case* for designating a case when an action performed, the *Subject* who performs an action, the *Object* of an action, the *Noun* of an action, the *Verb* of an action, the *Details of verb* to more fully explain the action, any *Risk* that is expected, the *Instance*

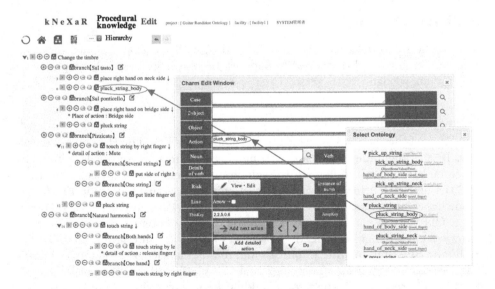

Fig. 6. Active windows used to describe the activity knowledge. The terms of the ontology to be selected are on the right, the items to describe or edit knowledge are in the middle, and lists of described knowledge are on the left.

of noun, a *Line*, which is the option to change from a simple line to an arrow, and *ThisKey* and *JumpKey* to link between actions. The *Risk* and *Instance of noun*, allow for the description of long sentences forming paragraphs. Data such as PDF and JPEG files can be attached to the *Risk* description item.

To ensure the terminology of activity knowledge, we recommend the ontology-based development as follows: First, the user imports or describes an ontology. Then, the user selects any concepts or properties of the ontology by clicking on the magnifying glass icon to the right of each item on the edit window. In the case shown in Fig. 6, the "select ontology" window of the *Action* item presents the registered action-related concepts of the Guitar Rendition Ontology. "Pluck string body" is selected and transcribed to the item in the edit window. And then, it listed the activity knowledge.

We described the activity knowledge, that we improved in Sect. 3.3, by using kNeXaR (Fig. 7). The top of the white rectangle presents the purpose of the knowledge, the red letters indicate methods (guitar rendition), the white rectangles (except the purpose) present actions, and the orange rectangles present the detailed information described in *Instance of noun*. The usability of the information system depends not only on the functions but also on a design that is attractive to users. We need to modify the design according to each user's or facility's preference.

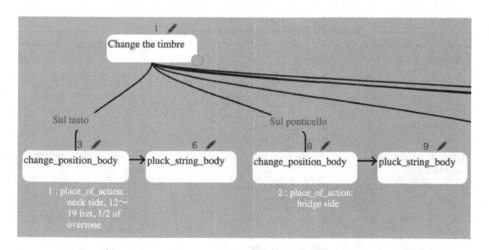

Fig. 7. A part of activity knowledge expressed by kNeXaR (Color figure online)

4.3   Term Control

We performed a simple investigation into the effect of terminology using kNeXaR. We used the Guitar Rendition Ontology and rewrote the improved activity knowledge (Sect. 3.3) using the function for ontology selection. We focused on the action-related terminology and checked changes before and after (1) the matching rate with the ontology and (2) the number of kinds of action.

Results showed that all terms were covered with the ontology's one, so the matching rate became 100% (Table 4). Also, the kinds of action were decreased, which means it controlled by using limited ontological terminologies effectively. Table 5 shows the details of the term changes. For example, "press string" was modified to "press string body" and "press string neck" (the latter two are subclasses of the former. "Place the right hand on the fingerboard side," that contained multiple information, was divided into two: the action was changed to "move to position body" and the detailed information, "place of action: fingerboard side," was added. "Place of action" is the ontological term. We also controlled the verbal representation, for instance, from "put a finger" to "touch a string," which express the same states.

Table 4. Changes of action in the activity knowledge for "Change the timbre": These are compared with the results of domain experts' improvement (Before) and of one that was rewrote by using the ontology selection function (After).

	Before	After
Number of action	19	
Matching rate	52.6%	100.0%
Kinds of action	10	8

Table 5. Results of terminological change

Before	After	
Action	Action	Detailed information
place the right hand on neck side	change position body	place of action: neck side
pluck string	pluck string body, pluck string neck	
place the right hand on bridge side	change position body	place of action: bridge side
touch string	touch string body, touch string neck	
put the palm of right hand	touch string body	part of hand or hinger: palm
put the little finger of right hand	touch string body	used finger: little finger
press string	press string body, press string neck	
touch string with left hand	touch string neck	
touch string with right hand	touch string body	
release the touched finger	release finger from the string, release finger from the string body	

These ambiguities of terminologies we found would be a significant issue for knowledge processing and reasoning. Ontology-based development helps improve the activity knowledge, and also the ontology. As such, we found that describing activity knowledge using kNeXaR provides the following benefits: (1) support of the ontology-based development of activity knowledge and (2) control of the terms.

5 Conclusion

In this study, we have presented the process to develop a domain knowledge using two type of knowledge representation: activity knowledge and a domain ontology. We practiced an ontology-based development of activity knowledge in detail on a musical instrument performance. Trough improving the activity knowledge based on the Guitar Rendition Ontology by domain experts, we determined the following observations: (1) the discovery of items in a domain, (2) the improvement of knowledge representation, and (3) deep understanding on the part of domain experts. Furthermore, we developed a system named kNeXaR (kNowledge eXplication AugmenteR) to help describe activity knowledge based on ontological terms, and demonstrated that kNeXaR can control the terms. In future works, we will test the process in different domains using kNeXaR.

References

1. Andrea, W., Rebecca, T.: Ontology development by domain experts (without using the "O" word). Appl. Ontol. **12**, 299–311 (2017)
2. Bada, M., et al.: A short study on the success of the gene ontology. Web Semant. Sci. Serv. Agents World Wide Web **1**(2), 235–240 (2014)
3. Halilaj, L., et al.: VoCol: an integrated environment to support version-controlled vocabulary development. In: Blomqvist, E., Ciancarini, P., Poggi, F., Vitali, F. (eds.) EKAW 2016. LNCS (LNAI), vol. 10024, pp. 303–319. Springer, Cham (2016). https://doi.org/10.1007/978-3-319-49004-5_20
4. Hogan, A.: Skolemising blank nodes while preserving isomorphism. In: Proceedings of the 24th International Conference on World Wide Web, International World Wide Web Conferences Steering Committee, pp. 430–440 (2015)
5. Iino, N., Nishimura, S., Fukuda, K., Watanabe, K., Jokinen K., Nishimura, T.: Development and use of an activity model based on structured knowledge - a music teaching support system. In: IEEE International Conference on Data Mining, The 5th International Workshop on the Market of Data (2017)
6. Iino, N., Nishimura, S., Nishimura, T., Fukuda, K., Takeda, H.: The guitar rendition ontology for teaching and learning support. In: IEEE 13th International Conference on Semantic Computing (2019). DOI: https://doi.org/10.1109/icosc.2019.8665532
7. Joo, S., Koide, S., Takeda, H., Horyu, D., Takezaki, A., Yoshida T.: Agriculture activity ontology : an ontology for core vocabulary of agriculture activity. In: The 15th International Semantic Web Conference (2016)
8. Joo, S., Koide, S., Takeda, H., Horyu, D., Takezaki, A., Yoshida T.: A building model for domain knowledge graph based on agricultural knowledge graph, SIG-SWO-047-10 (2019)

9. Jupp, S., et al.: Populous: a tool for building OWL ontologies from templates. BMC Bioinform. **13**(Supplement 1) (2012)
10. Kamruzzaman, S.Md., Krisnadhi, A., Hitzler, P.: OWLAx: a protégé plugin to support ontology axiomatization through diagramming. In: 15th International Semantic Web Conference (2016)
11. Kitamura, Y., Koji, Y., Mizoguchi, R.: An ontological model of device function: industrial deployment and lessons learned. Appl. Ontol. **1**(3–4), 237–262 (2006)
12. Kolozali, S., Barthet, M., Fazekas, G., Sandler, M.: Knowledge representation issues in musical instrument ontology design. In: 12th International Society for Music Information Retrieval Conference, pp. 465–470 (2011)
13. Lisena, P., et al.: Controlled Vocabularies for Music Metadata. In: Proceedings of the 19th ISMIR Conference, 424–430 (2018)
14. Lohmann, S., Negru, S., Haag, F., Ertl, T.: Visualizing ontologies with VOWL. Semant. Web **7**(4), 399–419 (2016)
15. Mallea, A., Arenas, M., Hogan, A., Polleres, A.: On blank nodes. In: Aroyo, L., et al. (eds.) ISWC 2011. LNCS, vol. 7031, pp. 421–437. Springer, Heidelberg (2011). https://doi.org/10.1007/978-3-642-25073-6_27
16. Nishimura, S., et al.: CHARM as activity model to share knowledge and transmit activity knowledge and its application to nursing guidelines integration. J. Adv. Comput. Intell. Intell. Inform. **17**(2), 208–220 (2013)
17. Rashid, S.M., McGuinness, D.L., Roure, D.D.: A music theory ontology. In: International Workshop on Semantic Applications for Audio and Music (2018)
18. Stellato, A., et al.: VocBench: a web application for collaborative development of multilingual thesauri. In: Gandon, F., Sabou, M., Sack, H., d'Amato, C., Cudré-Mauroux, P., Zimmermann, A. (eds.) ESWC 2015. LNCS, vol. 9088, pp. 38–53. Springer, Cham (2015). https://doi.org/10.1007/978-3-319-18818-8_3
19. Tudorache, T., Nyulas, C., Noy, M.F., Musen, M.A.: WebProtégé: a collaborative ontology editor and knowledge acquisition tool for the web. Semant. Web **4**(1), 89–99 (2013). https://doi.org/10.3233/SW-2012-0057
20. Uschold, R., Gruninger, M.: Ontologies: principles, methods and applications. Knowl. Eng. Rev. **11**(2), 93–136 (1996)
21. Raimond, Y., Abdallah, S., Sandler, M., Giasson, F.: The music ontology. In: Proceedings of the International Conference on Music Information Retrieval, pp. 417–422 (2007)

Author Index

Printed in the United States
By Bookmasters